CONFLICT
OF LOYALTY

GEOFFREY HOWE

CONFLICT OF
LOYALTY

POLITICO'S

First published by Macmillan London 1994

This edition published 2008
by Politico's Publishing, an imprint of
Methuen Publishing Ltd
8 Artillery Row
London
SW1P 1RZ

A CIP catalogue record of this book is available from the British Library.

ISBN 978 1 84275 196 1

Printed and bound in Great Britain by Biddles Ltd, King's Lynn, Norfolk

10 9 8 7 6 5 4 3 2 1

TO OUR CHILDREN,

CARY, AMANDA AND ALEC,

AND OUR GRANDSONS,

CHRISTOPHER AND JAMIE

CONTENTS

CONTENTS

CONTENTS

PREFACE

To govern is to choose. That is no less true of writing a memoir. This book is not so much about my *life* as about my *life* in politics. My childhood, family, education and practice at the Bar all feature, but for the most part simply to help make sense of what comes later. Even then the account is mercifully incomplete. The technicalities – of money supply or arms control, of tax reform or EC law – I have tried to eschew or at least keep under control. I have stayed instead with the main themes, where policies and personalities have come together in the shaping of events.

For one set of choices I hope I may be forgiven. There are many countries, many colleagues around the world, about whom I have written very little, or not at all. Britain's relations with great nations, continents even – such as China, Japan, Latin America or the Middle East – filled six years of my life with detail and drama, dialogue and sometimes delight. I shared much talk and travel, many transactions, with friends in the Commonwealth – peopled as it is, in the words of one of them, by 'the noble ghosts of Britain's past': from Canada and the Caribbean to Australia and New Zealand, from India and the sub-continent to Africa and the Pacific. To deal cursorily with all these would be diplomatic tourism at its most discourteous. To do them justice would lengthen this book unduly. That pleasure must wait for other opportunities.

And now, my thanks. I owe gratitude first to political colleagues and friends, who helped make so much possible – and often fun. A sample of their names appears in Appendix III; of my parliamentary private secretaries, Richard Ryder and David Harris bore the heaviest load. Each one of us owed our political existence to the dedicated support of party workers, officers and agents (in my case in four successive constituencies) and of meticulously hard-working constituency secretaries at Westminster: to all those who worked with and for me I am deeply grateful.

And then thanks are due to public servants of every grade, in both Houses of Parliament and throughout Whitehall, especially in Treasury and Foreign Office and probably most of all in private offices. The unsung work of all these people constantly eased my path; and many – too many to name – have been willing, indeed eager, to prompt, correct and amplify my memory. Librarians and archivists in Parliament and government alike have willingly helped trace and marshal documents, working in harness with members of the Institute of Contemporary British History, notably Peter Catterall and Matthew Elliott. The Founding Director of the Institute, Anthony Seldon, has been my chief mentor and inspiration. Not least am I grateful to him for the organization of two assiduous research assistants, William Evans and Oisin Commane. To David Harrison, as well as to Anthony Seldon himself, I am grateful for editorial advice on the Foreign Office chapters. To the Nuffield Foundation I owe thanks for financing most of the classification and indexation of my own papers.

For practical support over many years and subsequent critical scrutiny, I am indebted to a notable sequence of special advisers, especially Adam Ridley, Peter Cropper, John Houston and Adam Fergusson. Two people, in particular, deserve very special thanks for devotion beyond any reasonable call of duty, both in the management of my political life and in the subsequent chronicling of events: my last special adviser, Anthony Teasdale, and my last parliamentary personal assistant, Arabella Warburton.

The preparation of the final text and photographs would not have been possible without the huge expertise and patience of Peter James as editor, and the care and attention of both Lizzie Lawrence in my own office and Tanya Stobbs at my publishers.

To my own family I owe a unique debt of gratitude for their patience and support: Amanda, my younger daughter, has word-processed the entire text and offered shrewd editorial advice; and Elspeth, my wife, has been a constant source of wisdom and encouragement.

Geoffrey Howe
June 1994

PART ONE

THE ROAD TO
WESTMINSTER
1926–1970

CHAPTER ONE

FROM ABERAVON

═══

My Family

Aberavon was until 1921 the name of the Welsh borough of Port Talbot, where I was born. Aberavon is the name of the constituency where I contested my first two parliamentary elections, in 1955 and 1959. And Aberavon is the name of the Rugby Football Club, whose ground still lies below the grey stone semi, Glasfryn, Penycae Road, in which I drew my first breath on 20 December 1926.

Why should this English-speaking, London-living, Winchester- and Cambridge-educated and apparently uncymric Conservative trouble to trace his roots back to a grimy Welsh township, widely known only as the home of Britain's most modern steelworks? Even my wife Elspeth sometimes complains that the 'fiery Welshman', whom she recalls first won her heart, seems almost to have disappeared. But not all Welshmen are always fiery. And this particular Welshman is only half Welsh – though all Celtic. My mother Lili was born in 1896 at West Derby, Liverpool, the daughter of a Scottish father and a Cornish mother. Her father, Richard Thomson, was born the son of a crofter at Newcastleton, near Hawick and her mother, Annie Tadd, the daughter of a sea-captain, near Fowey. The young Thomson family joined the coal-rush migration to Cardiff. Grandfather Richard, a strict Presbyterian, was there able to establish a grocery chain, the Direct Trading Company. Its three dozen branches were spread throughout the coalfield. My mother was an identical twin and one of three equally attractive sisters. Half my life I seemed to be meeting elderly gentlemen who claimed to be one of their old flames. They were always remembered as the first girls to be seen driving cars in Cardiff during the First World War.

The Howes were Welsh-speakers and had lived in Glamorgan since at least the seventeenth century. My great-great-grandfather, John, born and buried at St Brides Major, had been a thatcher by trade. My father's father, Edward, had worked at Taibach Tinplate Works, Port Talbot. He was a founder-member of the Tinplaters' Union. The first lawyer in the family was my great-uncle, Edward T. Evans; his sister Hannah married my grandfather. E.T., as he was universally known, was something of an intellectual folk-hero. Self-taught, he won a first-class honours degree in law at London University and founded the solicitors' firm which my father later joined. He was said to be at ease with French, German, Latin, Greek, Hebrew – and classical Welsh. He conducted the Avon Valley Male Voice Choir at Eisteddfod level. Together with his brother-in-law, my grandfather, he founded two Calvinistic Methodist chapels, Carmel and Bethany: one Welsh, the other English. Years later, my parents divided their loyalties – and our attendances – between the two. I still have the card given to me at Sunday School on the occasion of King George V's Silver Jubilee in 1935. 'I ask you to remember', said his Majesty, 'that in days to come you will be the citizens of a great Empire.'

I regret not having learned Welsh: even my father's gradually became rusty, in a home with a monoglot mother. Politics came into the family when Great-Uncle E.T. and Grandfather Edward were both elected to the District Council, and E.T. to the Glamorgan County Council. In those days Wales was almost entirely a Liberal one-party state. So their party chose itself. My father, born in 1890, another Edward, took articles in his uncle E.T.'s law office. He served as a lieutenant in the Welch Regiment with General Allenby in Egypt and Palestine in 1917, and enjoyed reminiscing about his days with pyramids and camels. Quite soon after the war he was appointed Coroner for West Glamorgan and later Clerk to the Aberavon County Justices. For the rest of his life he took a lively, but strictly apolitical interest in local and national affairs.

My parents met, I believe, at Llandrindod Wells, one of the golf and boating spas at which South Wales professional families used to weekend in those days. They married at Cardiff in 1923. Their first child, Barbara, died of meningitis, not long before I was born. Years later my mother told me that she would not have had the courage to have another child had she not already been carrying me at the time of Barbara's death. Happily, just over two years later, I was joined by my brother Colin. A central figure in our childhood was my father's elder sister, Lillie. She worked almost all her life as Headmistress of Trefelin Infants' School in Port Talbot: I was to go on meeting her ex-pupils for the rest of my life. On holidays, at weekends or if my parents had gone away – quite often to watch Wales play at Murrayfield or Twickenham – Auntie Lil was always on hand. Her own house, near the centre of Port Talbot, was a home-from-home. It was not far from the Labour Exchange. The dole queue was a very real feature of my young life, but mercifully in the background rather than in the fabric of my existence. Colin and I learned to cycle in the back-lanes near by and to cook chocolate cake in her kitchen. Auntie Lil was plump and spinsterly – always, it seemed, the same middle-age. She spoiled us both no doubt, but, painlessly, she taught Colin and me to read at the age of four.

Partly perhaps because of my sister's early death, I was regarded as delicate. So I was quite often confined to bed with ailments like acidosis or tonsillitis, though I was far from disabled. This meant a lot of reading, of everything from *Just William* to the *Children's Encyclopaedia*. Colin and I worked our way through almost all of *Things to Make and Do*, from steam-propelled boats to telephones made with pigs' stomachs. The family had moved in 1932 from Glasfryn to Rockleigh, Pentyla, a larger, three-storey semi, set back from the main road to Swansea. The long garden sloped steeply up the mountain on the west side of the Avon valley. Mynydd Dinas, almost 1000 feet high, was splendid terrain over which to roam with our small gang of neighbourhood friends. But often Colin and I just played together in our attic playroom, with Hornby train or Quaker Oats model village. The small garden fishpond was converted to sand after Colin had fallen in when we were both reaching out for a floating snail-shell. 'Geoffrey pushed me' was ever thereafter an ineradicable – and unjust – piece of family folklore.

Rockleigh was a typically comfortable professional home of its day: no central heating but – until the war – a living-in maid at 12s 6d a week; four bedrooms, one bath and a baby grand piano in the 'lounge'. My parents drove a Standard drop-head coupé and a Morris 10, with a chauffeur on hand when necessary. The golf club on Saturdays was our main excursion and often a bone of contention, for my father would want to stay later than he should – and longer than the bored boys thought tolerable. Father and mother used to row, sometimes noisily, over this. Colin and I were always on our mother's side. It was only much later that bridge, for all the family, provided a sure-fire common link. At home, as at school, I never had any ability for ball games. Colin was only a little better.

Despite the golf-club visits, my father generally tried to be thoughtful and concerned for his family, in very practical ways. He kept large scrapbooks of school reports, press cuttings, photographs and letters of interest about every member of the family – my mother as much as

Colin and myself. He loved driving, showing us round South Wales, introducing us to places and friends. With strangers outside the family he was always friendly and forthcoming, and he was well respected. The coroner's role was one that suited him, in terms of presence and kindness and wisdom. But, to his sons at least, he was always a little reserved and unrevealing, and we responded in kind, trying dutifully to bridge the communication gap between generations, but never fully succeeding.

With my mother, it was always easier. Her personality was more sparkling and spontaneous, though more swiftly teased into short-lived flashes of anger. She and Colin or I would enjoy playing piano duets together, generally the Barcarolle from Offenbach's *Tales of Hoffmann*. She was never more than eight stone in weight, raven-haired and attractive almost all her life. When a stroke deprived her of speech at the age of eighty-one, her flashing smile remained, so that, as her grand-daughter Amanda said, 'You could still see the real Nana inside, trying to get out.'

Father didn't often talk politics, at least not in party terms, until I had become engaged in them. But, like most Welsh people, he was happy to discuss personalities, generally from the point of view of a friendly critic. I fancy he regarded this as most compatible with the quasi-judicial nature of his various offices. My brother Colin over the years developed something of the same habit, but with rather more sardonic overtones. Whenever he heard me quoting my paternal grandfather's trade union background, Colin would aver that my other grandfather, Thomson, had once had Manny Shinwell horse-whipped from Cardiff docks for trying to initiate a strike against master grocers. I was never quite sure that he had made it up. My mother's political approach was much more straightforward: she was, always had been, Conservative and didn't mind avowing her faith, though she never did so intolerantly. She was always ready to enlist under my banner.

My father died in 1958, after many months in hospital with progressive arterio-sclerosis of the brain. For only a very few years were we able to share together a common experience of legal practice, and by the time of my first election campaign he was already too ill to enjoy it as he would have wished to do. My mother, by contrast, was able vicariously to enjoy some of my success in politics as well as in law. She was door-to-door canvassing with me in Bebington in 1966 and was a keen witness of my swearing-in as Solicitor General in 1970. It was not until 1976, at the age of eighty-two, that she finally succumbed to the effects of her strokes.

To School

My first school was the one at which my aunt was headmistress. I then went to a little private school in Port Talbot before going, with Colin, as a day boy to a good local prep school, Bryntirion, where I stayed until 1938. We were of a different generation, or on a different school track, from four other Port Talbot boys: George Thomas (later Lord Tonypandy), Richard Burton, Clive Jenkins and Anthony Hopkins. Our father, with our mother's support, was determined to see us into a really first-class education (he had left school at sixteen) and had set his sights, and ours, on Winchester. To have a chance of winning a scholarship there, we needed to go to one of the few schools that aimed sufficiently high, Abberley Hall near Worcester. The two Howe boys first realized that they spoke with a Welsh accent only when the all-English teases got to work. In a few short weeks the Welshness had been all but washed away (though even today it occasionally creeps back if I am really roused – at least with a Welsh audience). Boy scouting in the school's ample wooded grounds, and on Abberley Hill near by, map-reading, cooking and modest play-acting added new dimensions to my life. So too did the beating I received from the Headmaster, Gilbert Ashton,* when the whole dormitory was discovered paired off in each other's beds. The 'filthy habit' for which we were punished escaped my understanding for a number of years. We were only keeping each other awake until the staff were abed, so that we could raid the kitchens in safety!

But I enjoyed Abberley, as indeed I did the whole of my education. That sounds smug, I know. But I consciously challenged the day-counting habit ('nine more days in this mouldy old school!') – and still do. I consider myself very lucky that I never fell into the rut of always wanting to be round the *next* corner, instead of making the most of where I was. The other would-be Winchester scholar, Michael Higgs, and I were in a class of two within the top class of nine. Michael came top of the 1940 College Scholarship Roll at Winchester. My sixteenth place gained me an exhibition rather than a scholarship, so I went not into the hot-house atmosphere of College but into an ordinary house of forty boys, Morsheads.

* One of the four cricketing Ashton brothers, all from my house at Winchester. A most sensitive and detailed account of life at Abberley may be found in Anthony Quayle's book, *A Time to Speak* (Barrie & Jenkins, 1990). He was ten years my senior, but not a detail had changed.

In 1939 the Howe family enjoyed the last of the five pre-war continental holidays we had together: always starting on the Belgian coast at Le Coq-sur-Mer (De Haan), but often touring as well, as far afield as Paris and the Alps. That year my father saw the Molotov–Ribbentrop pact as a signal to return home early. And my mother was briefly detained at Dover as a 'possible spy'; her striking, almost Iberian, good looks having aroused suspicion that she was a 'foreigner'. Her detention lasted long enough to excite but not to alarm us. Nine months later, as Hitler's forces reached the Channel coast, Colin and I took the first serious decision of our lives, at the ages of eleven and thirteen. Should we accept the invitation from our cousins in St Louis to spend the war on the other side of the Atlantic? We had no doubt that we should stay in Britain. I was deeply surprised, but very grateful, that our parents had left such a choice to us.

From Munich onwards the prospect of war had cast its shadow before it, and had heavily increased my mother's involvement in the community. Already a magistrate and NSPCC activist, she was now appointed Centre Organizer for the Women's Voluntary Services. Both our parents were now constantly active on public and charitable work. Colin and I were often out with Mother, selling Alexandra roses or collecting aluminium saucepans (for 'making Spitfires'). That was fun. Less often, we went with Father in his car to attend, as silent witnesses, at inquests that he was conducting: these offered frequent reminders of the hazards of life in a mining and industrial community. Over the years we became a family of well-intentioned busybodies, for whom 'good works' – politics of a kind – became almost instinctive. My father remained apolitical in practice, teasingly Lib–Lab in instinct, to offset my mother's Conservatism. But they were both happy to take advantage of the photo-opportunity when they met Lloyd George on a pre-war holiday. In a Labour-dominated township in a Labour-controlled county, we all of us learned the good sense of maintaining civilized relations with the local establishment.

A Wykehamist

And so to Winchester, its fourteenth-century, cloistered college buildings, Victorian brick-built boarding-houses and well-rolled cricket meadows. All this provided a haven, astonishingly, of relative peace for those whose time there largely coincided, as mine did, with the Second

World War. There was some turbulence, certainly. Air-raids on nearby Southampton had us sleeping on bunks in the house cellar, often for weeks at a time. Fire-watching – mainly reading mountaineering books in the house library – first got me into the pattern of managing on only four hours' sleep a night. Rationing was made tolerable by the careful management of dozens of individual pots and saucers of jam and butter, chocolate spread and peanut-butter. Home Guard duties came closer to the real thing. Termly briefings of the school by General Montgomery (his son David was under the 'Bobber' – Willie Whitelaw's old house-master) kept us in arm's-length contact with the war. It was he, Montgomery, who had directed every one of the battles personally. 'Make the enemy dance to *your* tune!' he would stress. 'Your tune!' Not I think for this reason, brother Colin and I promoted to pin-up status in our Rockleigh playroom Monty's rival and opponent respectively General Alexander and Field Marshal Rommel.

There were portents of peace as well: Field Marshal Lord Wavell was honoured in the school's Ad Portas ceremony,* on his way to govern India, and the art master, Professor R. M. Y. Gleadowe, designed the Stalingrad Sword – Britain's tribute to Russian courage. It was displayed in the nave of Winchester Cathedral, and I recalled it as a symbol of our friendship when I spoke in Moscow forty years later. It was not possible for anyone in my generation at Winchester to forget Britain's commitment to the common cause of European freedom. The conflict taking place, sometimes literally in the sky above our heads, was adding its own toll to the War Memorial Cloister Roll of Honour, from Cambrai to Crimea, past which we walked 'up to books' each day.

I owe special gratitude to two classics teachers. Cyril Robinson (the 'Bin', who had been Hugh Gaitskell's housemaster) had a meticulous and inspirational enthusiasm for Periclean democracy, encouraging his class to form itself into a Boule, through which we virtually governed our own syllabus.† And Spencer Leeson, Headmaster, and later Bishop of Peterborough, expressed a passionate commendation of Chartres Cathedral (would Hitler ever let us see it again?) that left us in no doubt that William of Wykeham's church was Catholic before it was Anglican. At their feet it was not possible to avoid thinking, even in 1944, of the wider Europe that would surely open up for us again at the end of the conflict.

* See p. 619 below.
† Here perhaps was the origin of my often remarked collegiate style of ministerial leadership.

The diversity of fellow-pupils, as much as the dons, opened my eyes to the sciences, social as well as physical, to the cinema, radio and photography, as well as to archaeology, debate and music, to numeracy as well as literacy. Dons like Eric Lucas, Spencer Humby, C. V. Durell, James Mansel and Eric James encouraged me to become engaged in founding or running the film, the photographic and the archaeological societies, even in making radio sets. I persuaded the authorities to change the rules, to allow us to have radios – but only if we made them ourselves.

I was one of the group which founded a film society early in the war. We had only a silent projector, so we showed all the old classics, from Eisenstein to D. W. Griffiths. The films arrived on a Saturday morning and it was my agreeable job to choose a musical sound-melody from the house 78 r.p.m. record library in time to provide a background to the film on the Sunday afternoon. It was the best possible way of acquiring complete familiarity with every side of every record in the library. For some old news-reels and comedy films, I was able to persuade Sidney Watson, the school director of music, to provide a simultaneous piano accompaniment. He enjoyed that as much as we did.

I scored brownie points by winning the inter-house National Savings Competition: my first encounter with creative accounting. 'What a gift he has for boosting a cause, what an election agent he would make,' wrote my housemaster Colin Hunter in one report. In another, the Bin expressed surprise, disappointment even, on learning that I was destined for the law. 'Geoffrey', he said, 'is exactly the sort of businessman we shall need after the war.' I think he came to regard politics as a good second-best. But it was Eric James – scientist, socialist, atheist and, later, High Master of Manchester Grammar and Vice-Chancellor of York University – who was my real inspiration at the Debating Society (of which I became secretary) and in revealing to me the whole process of political rhetoric. Almost my earliest speech was against the public ownership of the coal industry, and one of my first forays into radicalism was when I proposed a motion in favour of equal pay and opportunity for women. My opponents, I warned, had all the jokes on their side and none of the arguments. We lost by 27 votes to 10 (it was the same, only worse, at the Garrick Club general meeting, half a century later).

My two closest partners in the exploration of ideas and opportunities at Winchester were Robert Sheaf and Michael Nightingale, still my friends today. Robert was the idealist son of an agnostic surgeon, from whose sway he eventually emerged as a convert to the Roman

Church. Michael and I – and virtually all the rest – became, and remained, Anglicans, of fluctuating commitment. Robert and I spent many days on holiday near his home in Guildford, at the beautiful Pilgrims' Way church of St Martha's, drafting a political credo – alas, now lost – which we labelled the St Martha's Charter. I still have boxes of his letters, written from all round the world, in which he elaborated his side of our political dreams. The idea was, from the outset, that I should become Prime Minister, while he would settle for First Sea Lord. Robert went off to the Royal Naval College at Dartmouth at the age of seventeen, but by 1948 he had left the navy and our paths had crossed again in London. Michael Nightingale was the son of a stockbroker father, a friend of Belloc and the Chestertons (Nightingale, Sheaf and I were together to retain a life-long affection for the distributist policies and prejudices of G. K. C.). At school, Michael and I conducted a good deal of archaeological exploration together. By finding some fourth-century coins (of Emperor Constantius II, who died 361 AD) at a place called Dirty Corner, near St Mary Bourne, we helped to date one of the last Roman sites in Hampshire.

Wales was never long out of my mind. All my friends came to spend long holidays *à deux* in Port Talbot. (It was only in each other's homes that we became known to each other by Christian rather than surnames.) My entry for the specialist essay prize in my last year at Winchester was a study of 'The Influence of Rome and the Romans on Wales and the Welsh Language'. My *nom de plume* was 'Cymru am Byth' (Wales for ever). One of my main sources was a small Welsh–English dictionary, which was in those days obtainable from Woolworths for sixpence. I read and marked it from cover to cover.

The one school activity that did not arouse my enthusiasm was organized games. Exercise was compulsory, to the extent of six 'hours' a week. Fortunately there was a variety of measured ways in which one could meet that target. I always looked for the least time-consuming. Setpiece runs were the best answer to this: a thirteen-minute run to and from Tonbridge, over the River Itchen, counted as 'half an hour'. Here too I got the rules changed, so that agricultural work or 'digging for victory' might qualify as exercise. In this way, and with a little rowing thrown in, I was able to avoid any activity that required an aptitude for striking a ball.

In every respect I felt that Winchester was a tremendously stimulating environment. It was a great privilege to be there: ever implicit in that privilege was the moral duty to help those who were less fortunate than oneself. This, we were always told, was the true meaning of the College motto, 'Manners makyth man'. One other piece of Wiccamical advice was contained in a mural in Wren's beautiful School Hall: 'Disce aut discede. Manet sors tertia: caedi.' Unusually, it is even crisper in English: 'Learn, leave or be licked.' It was a useful encouragement to self-discipline.

Conscription

Arranging a planned exit from Winchester – to university and to army at the same time – while war was still being waged required some thought. The key was not to await conscription but to volunteer. This enabled one to have some influence over not only choice of regiment but also date of departure. I was able to enter the Royal Signals: my passion for radio had been amplified by my discovery that the heavily encumbered signal platoon were transported to school field days by taxi, while the rest marched out. And I was able to gain a university place through an open scholarship in classics. But it was a close-run thing. In those days, Oxbridge scholarship exams, organized in groups of colleges, were spaced throughout the year. Oxford's were mainly at Christmas. That cleared away most of the *really* bright Wykehamists, who had been ahead of me. Even so, in my two Oxford attempts I had seemed some way off scholarship level. The advice of my classics tutor, J. B. Poynton, had been not to offer any paper on the composition of Greek verse: my versification was so bad that it was seen as a positive handicap. Even so, for my Cambridge attempt at Easter, I decided to disregard the advice – and I was right, for the twenty-eight marks out of a hundred that I secured for Greek verse were just enough.

So I was able to slip through, in housemaster Colin Hunter's words, to 'the right college at the right university'. Just as Winchester had been better for me than Eton – less conceited and more collegiate – so Cambridge was better than Oxford. And Trinity Hall, with almost 600 years' reputation as the leading law college, was ideal for my chosen profession. The assumption that I should be going into the law was well established by the time I left Winchester. I had been kibitzing in my father's (and mother's) court-rooms for years, and very much savouring the taste of the law. Even the Bin's disappointment – I took his opinion seriously – had not dissuaded me. The Bar, moreover, seemed a natural progression from my father's office, where I had done holiday work for a year or two. There is a kind of hierarchical succession in the profession: barrister's clerks like their sons to become solicitors; solicitors think of their sons as going to the Bar. So why not me? My father had researched the answer well. During the war Bar students who were in the forces were allowed to 'eat their dinners' *in absentia*. An old friend of his, Judge Kirkhouse Jenkins, was a bencher of the Middle Temple. So, almost as soon as I had left Winchester, I enrolled as a student at that inn. As a result, my terms were fully kept by the time I left the army to go up to Cambridge.

For Cambridge was not to happen for three years. Recruitment to the Signals, with the chance of getting a commission, took me first to a six-month 'short course' in physics and advanced mathematics at the University College of the South West (now Exeter University, but then a part of London). Even in those days Winchester timetabling had been flexible enough for a classicist to achieve reasonable competence in those subjects. So the work was interesting but not oppressive. Another cathedral city, halfway between Dartmoor and the sea, was a splendid place to spend my first summer out of school. (We wore our uniform less often than I had at Winchester: the Home Guard had by now been disbanded.)

My two dozen colleagues were a congenial cross-section, a Geordie, a Paddy, a Jock, a Wolf, a Taffy and so on: there was even an Etonian. Inevitably 'Geoff' ended up sharing a room with 'Taffy', Percy John, an earnest and most engaging medical student from Cardiff. (He was to join me for breakfast in 1993 at the Park Hotel, Cardiff – the setting, exactly seventy years earlier, for my parents' wedding reception.) A lot happened during our six months at Exeter: VE-Day on 8 May, the first general election for ten years on 5 July and the first ever nuclear explosion at Hiroshima on 6 August. So the war we were being trained to fight was over before our formal military training had begun.

For VE-Day I travelled overnight to London with the only Cornishman on the course, a sparkling pianist and later the author of outstanding geographic textbooks, Jackie Lowry. Our Devon Regiment uniforms – which were our proper kit, even though we wore them normally only once a week – ensured us a bogus heroes' welcome, with free food from Paddington to Parliament Square. We were in the crowd to hear Winston Churchill speak from the Treasury buildings, and were within ten yards of his car as he drove into New Palace Yard.

Jackie's letter to his parents in Falmouth implied real surprise at finding that his new companion, 'a public schoolboy', was a 'very decent fellow!': the concept of 'one nation' was still a little way off. But that didn't prevent us becoming involved in the subsequent general election campaign. For some reason that I can't now recall, most of our group had been persuaded to enlist in support of Exeter's Liberal candidate, Mrs F. E. G. Morgan. I fancy that we chose her as a result of some encouragement from a friend at the Baptist chapel, which we patronized most Sunday evenings because of the quality of coffee and cakes on offer. Certainly I can still remember the packed public meeting, addressed by the Liberal Party leader, Sir Archibald Sinclair, which cheered to the echo his parting cry: 'Best of luck on the fifth of July!' It proved to be a forlorn hope. At Exeter, Mrs Morgan did indeed save her deposit, with 6220 votes. But nationally only twelve Liberal members made their way to Westminster. The result was not calculated to boost a young man's confidence in the future of the party.

CHAPTER TWO

SOLDIER AND STUDENT

Military Life

So austerity with Attlee took the place of war with Winston. Three years
in the army introduced me to my first fan letter: I was deputed by my
barrack room at our Primary Training Unit to write to the dazzling
young girl who sang 'Let him go, let him tarry' in *Way to the Stars*. Her
name was Jean Simmons, but we never did get a reply. Then, at the
Mons OCTU (Officer Cadet Training Unit) in Aldershot, I enjoyed the
parade-ground magnificence of Regimental Sergeant Major Britton.
Years later, I was able to call on him, a newly discovered pensioner
constituent, widowed, at Caterham. It was just before Christmas, and as
he offered me first 'A whisky, Saaah?' and then, 'One of my mincepies,
Saaah?' his undiminished voice shook the block of tiny flats almost to
their foundations. It had been no part of his job, I gathered, to read the
single-page essays each cadet had had to write on 'my aims in life'. I
suspect I was unique in restating my schoolboy ambition to become
Prime Minister. That would scarcely have seemed consistent with my
rating in a unit boxing contest I had done my best to avoid: 'runner-up
for best loser'.

Next came six months at the Royal Signals OCTU, Catterick.
Weekends cycling from the gentleness of nearby Wensleydale and
Swaledale on to the surrounding fells sparked my lifelong enthusiasm
for hill-walking. The officer in charge of my course, John Osborn, one
of the Sheffield steelmakers, was years later a colleague as Conservative
MP for the Hallam division of his native city. And Ronald Needs, old
enough to have seen active service in the Battle of Ardennes, just beat
me to the 'best cadet' ranking and was subsequently a partner as secretary
of the Bow Group. Second Lieutenant Howe was posted for almost two
years to Nanyuki, at the foot of Mount Kenya. Exactly on the equator,

Nanyuki provided a happy escape from snow-bound Britain during the 'Shinwell winter' of 1946/7.

It was the job of East African Signals to provide radio links between the seven King's Africa Rifles and Northern Rhodesian Regiment battalions which provided internal security from Kampala to Dar-es-Salaam, from Lusaka to Nairobi. I was second in command of the Signals unit which served Northern Kenya and Uganda. Twenty British and a hundred African signallers were commanded, with my assistance, by Captain David Legge DCM. He had joined the army from the dole queue in Darlington in 1932 and had risen through the ranks. Probably the only Labour voter in the Nanyuki HQ officers' mess, he was predictably nicknamed 'Clem'. Kenya in the late 1940s was still a white settlers' paradise, temperate and orderly. On the Kikuyu reserve during my time a handful of fanatics calling themselves Watu Wa Dinyo Christo ('Men of Christ', because like Mau Mau they claimed perverted Christian roots), staged a fierce outburst of savagery. This brief portent of the later Mau Mau years was soon quashed: our radio trucks were briefly mobilized throughout the reserve. Uganda too was green and fertile, awash with bananas and cotton, and still safe for Asian traders. Makerere College was a nascent African university.

Most of my black signallers had seen service in the Burma campaign with the 11th East African Division. Sergeant Mbela Kasema BEM was one who had come to represent them in London on the Victory Parade. The concept of a single Empire, with a common citizenship, was very real. Mbela still corresponded with a girlfriend in Chalk Farm. Black, brown and white had been equally ready to die in a common cause. It was part of my job to explain, in weekly current-affairs classes for my signallers, why 'Bwana Kingy George' was a more just ruler than 'Bwana Joe Stalin'. Within a recklessly short time I chose to regard my Swahili as equal to the task. I took comfort from the fact that for all of us Swahili was a language that came second to our tribal tongue. Quite soon too I was happy to join Clem in a quietly successful campaign to secure the election to the all-white Sports Club of Nanyuki's first black police inspector. Were we not all grown-up children of the same 'great empire' that King George had commended in his Sunday-school message of 1935?

But politics scarcely featured in my real enjoyment of peacetime soldiering – before peacetime accounting had caught up with it. We young officers enjoyed such powers as no twenty-year-old should be entitled to exercise. A clutch of jeeps and motorbikes was always to hand. We camped and safaried in Kenya's Northern Frontier deserts, where the sun always shone. We fished for Nile perch at Jinja on Lake Victoria and for trout in Mount Kenya's well-stocked streams, the monkeys chattering alongside us as we tried to keep our hooks out of the low-slung tropical rainforest. My hill-walking matured into mountaineering on Kenya and Kilimanjaro. Mount Kenya's rocky twin peaks of Nelion and Batian (17,000 feet) were too severe for an amateur. But the gently sloping glacier up to Point Lenana (16,800 feet) was a manageable excuse for camping safaris among the giant groundsel of the Mackinder Valley. A five-day expedition on Kilimanjaro took me to the breathtaking rim of the volcano, which is Africa's highest mountain (19,000 feet). I was looked after by four porters and a gentle Mchagga guide. As I struggled up the last 3000 feet of snow-covered scree before dawn on the last morning, the guide was ever ready with his bottle of sweet, cold tea. 'Nataka chai kidogo, Bwana?' he asked, as attentively as any airline stewardess. The whole expedition, all found and including his services and those of the porters, cost only 160 East African shillings – not quite half my pay for the month. It would be many years before I should again be able to live so well. The friendly loyalty of those with whom I served in Kenya and Uganda left me with a lasting affection for Africa and its peoples – and mercifully free from the delusions of Empire.

Before leaving Nanyuki in June 1948, I was offered promotion to captain, but only if I was willing to extend my service by three months and go to Mogadishu to command the Somali Signal Troop. For that I should have to go straight from Somalia to Cambridge. I took the easy option, for the sake of a 'demob' holiday already arranged: climbing in Scotland, followed by a week that my brother Colin had arranged at the second Edinburgh Festival. The long walk through the Lairig Ghru from Aviemore to Braemar seemed positively fertile after the rigours of Cuillin and Loch Coruisk on Skye. And then to my first experience of the Glyndebourne company and *Don Giovanni*, with a dozen other concerts and the tattoo. I loved it, of course, though I still wondered if I was right to have avoided that struggle with the Somali Youth League.

Trinity Hall

No such doubts assailed me about my three years at Cambridge. I shared rooms there successively with two other law students (both of Gray's

Inn), who became life-long friends, Gordon Adam and Richard Stone. Gordon, a serious-minded Ulsterman schooled in Canada who went on to become a director and general manager of Barclays Bank, much enhanced the austerity of our set of rooms with a regular supply of Irish peat. He also exposed me to a flow of stimulating friends from Queen's, Belfast, and to a taste of the Anglo-Irish problem, which was to haunt me years later. Dick Stone, like Adam an only son, was a more gregarious character, and one of the tiny number to own a car: a 1936 Standard 10, called Blossom. He was for years a close partner in Tory politics as chairman first of CUCA (the university Conservative Association), then of the Bow Group; he was later a leader of the Admiralty Bar. Trinity Hall provided exactly the right opportunity to take legal studies seriously but not obsessively. First-class honours in the first part of the Tripos were followed by a 2(1) in Part II and in the following LL B. I became chairman and vice-chairman respectively of the college and university law societies. Intra-university moots introduced me to my Oxford opposite number, whose signature was already twice as large as life, Jeremy Thorpe; and to Mr Justice (Sir Frederick) Sellers, later to be one of my sponsors when I applied for Silk.

During my first year I followed the other half of the Hall tradition and resumed a brief and undistinguished rowing career (Trinity Hall Fourth Boat). This quickly gave way to politics. The tiny Liberal Party had by now in my mind been squeezed into irrelevance. Three years of increasing austerity and apparent incompetence from the Attlee government had left me in no doubt that the post-war Conservative Party should inherit the Liberal mantle: humane social policy and free-market economics. So I enlisted in CUCA. Although the Hall was a small college it had a great sense of mutual solidarity: the lawyers and politicians supported the oarsmen on the towpath; and the rowers and the rugger club provided a formidable block vote when the politicians needed it. Dick Stone and I were only two of the five Hall men who chaired the university Tories in my time; Greville Janner and Edward Greenfield were similarly propelled into the chair of the Labour Club.

Participation in Union debates was a natural corollary. Even then that was not my strongest suit. I was elected to the committee but not to office. The great debating stars of my era included Percy Cradock and Norman St John Stevas. Years later Percy Cradock, then our ambassador in Peking, was to be my highly skilled collaborator in the Hong Kong negotiations:* by then my five years' experience as a senior Cabinet minister gave me (I like to think) the confidence to match his far from diffident intellect. Dick Stone and I had no difficulty in choosing a twenty-first-birthday present for Norman, already a peacock: a champagne swizzle-stick. In his thank-you letter he commended our services on the CUCA Committee in terms that would have served as well for a Prime Minister extending thanks to departing colleagues.

One of my closest political friendships from Cambridge days was one of the strangest. Jack Ashley and I took opposite sides in a huge procedural row when he was president of the Union. I was leader of the group that compelled him to call a special general meeting. As I handed him the petition, he reacted with the utmost ferocity: 'I'm never going to speak to another bloody Tory again – never as long as I live.' His side won the ensuing debate. He went on to marry one of our best Conservative college representatives, Pauline Crispin. Bygones swiftly became bygones. He honoured me with an invitation to speak against him (and Hugh Dalton) in his presidential debate. I had not met his like before: four or five years older than the rest of us, he had already seen service as a Widnes borough councillor and on the executive of the Chemical Workers' Union. He was a revisionist before the term had been invented. Yet his roots in the Labour movement were deep enough to give him enduring authority. I remain convinced that the Labour Party lost a potentially great leader when deafness so tragically inhibited his career. I have rejoiced at the courage of each of his subsequent achievements. Four decades later we were in the same intake to the House of Lords.

My own failure to get a first in my final year was excused in my eyes – if not my father's – by the diversity of my Cambridge life. I was out of college as much as I was in: mountaineering in Snowdonia and the Alps, yachting on the Broads; editing, as much as writing, a weekly column for Oxford's *Isis* magazine; and experiencing my first real love. My Cambridge fiancée, Liz Jones, was eventually carried away by Oliver Pemberton – the Simon opposite her Sorrel in the CU Mummers production of *Hay Fever*. After their marriage, they owned and managed a Cheshire prep school, until she was tragically killed in a head-on collision on the old A1. Cambridge theatre was especially proud at the time of Julian Slade. We had already acclaimed two of his May-week

* See Chapter 25 below.

productions, *The Lady May* and *Bang Goes the Meringue*, so for all of us his *Salad Days* became a life-long reminder of the times on which 'we said we'd never look back'.

My Eye on Parliament

But politics was still my main pursuit: our Cambridge mafia included Denzil Freeth, Tony Buck, Douglas Hurd and Patrick Jenkin. Denzil's career was the most meteoric: a junior minister within ten years, he *left* the House of Commons in the year of my arrival there. Tony's too was sadly incomplete: a successful Navy minister with Ted Heath, one of my backers for the leadership in 1975, he never hit it off with Margaret Thatcher. Patrick and Douglas were both more obviously long-distance runners, with Douglas already a speaker of measured fluency. Tony Lloyd – who could as easily have been a Law Officer as a Law Lord – was another.

This was a time when inter-university politics were starting to come to life. On the Tory side the main melting-pot was at the half-yearly meetings of the FUCUA (Federation of University Conservative and Unionist Associations). It was here that the idea of the Bow Group was first conceived. A number of us had identified the need for an intellectual centre 'to combat the influence of the Fabian Society'. Those very words eventually found their way into the first Bow Group constitution. Our early leaders included Peter Emery, in those days an elegantly energetic bridge-player (from Oxford), Bruce Griffiths (London), another product of a South Wales (Aberdare) grocery family and later my junior at the Aberfan Tribunal and a Crown Court judge, and Denzil Freeth.

We had different anxieties in different universities. At Cambridge we were worried by the tendency of most non-white undergraduates to join the socialist side of the House in Union debates. Dick Stone and I (we were always arguing about the pace of withdrawal from Empire: Dick's father had been the last British Chief Justice of Bombay) organized a special group for colonial students. Julian Amery (already MP for Preston North, and as dynamic as his wartime record with Balkan resistance fighters suggested) came to address a joint meeting, under my chairmanship, of CUCA and the African Students Club. At about the same time I was one of the leaders of an all-party protest group against the deposition by Labour Commonwealth Secretary Patrick Gordon Walker of the Bechuanaland chief Seretse Khama. The cause of com-

plaint, unbelievable though it seems today, was Khama's marriage to
'former London typist, Ruth Williams', as the *Telegraph* always labelled
her.

An active member of this group was Hall man Radclyffe Cadman. A
fellow oarsman from a Natal sugar farm, Radclyffe also planned the
Broads holiday that Dick Stone and I shared with him and a group of
energetic South African girls in 1951. He went back to practise at the
Natal Bar and enter South African politics. He was the last leader of Jan
Smuts' United Party and was later in partnership with Chief Buthelezi,
as Administrator General of Natal. This preoccupation with a liberal
view of our imperial responsibilities was to prove a strong strand in
Bow Group thinking for several decades. The 'wind of change' was
stirring, in our minds at least, ahead of its time.

I was exercised by similar stirrings on another topic – Britain's
relations with Europe. I do not recall that it was much troubling us at
Cambridge, nor indeed in wider FUCUA circles. But during the summer
of 1950, when Parliament had been required to consider Britain's
attitude to the then emerging Schuman plan for European partnership,
I was deep into the argument with my Wykehamist friend Robert Sheaf.
He had by now left the navy for a job in London theatre-land and was
active in Hampstead's then very lively mock Parliament. (This was a
special kind of debating society – Robert's scene, and not mine.) He
had written to ask me whether I thought he should there echo the Attlee
government's deliberate refusal to participate in the Schuman plan.

In a long letter (written from Port Talbot on 7 July 1950), I urged
him to take the opposite view. 'Why', I asked him, 'should "foreign" be
a word of disapproval unless designed to rouse the most insular
prejudices?' Why should the 'surrender of British sovereignty' be 'unjustified' simply because it was 'unprecedented'? To say that 'we can
perfectly well stand on our own feet as we have done in the past' struck
me, I said, as 'unduly optimistic, and quite out of touch with the realities
of our day and age'. I went on to argue, specifically, that 'active British
leadership in some more positive form of European union is essential
politically'. This would, I added, have 'the subsidiary advantage of
ensuring that any such body that is set up without our help will not be
German-dominated'. I concluded, specifically on the Schuman plan:

> Taking the narrowest technical view, the government were quite right to
> decline to commit themselves in advance to this indefinite body. But to
> have allowed negotiations to reach such a state that the French felt

themselves forced to force the pace with increasingly unrealistic ideas; and
to have ultimately allowed the talks to proceed without there being a
British representative at the conference table – that was the folly.

The sentiment that I was expressing so clearly, more than four decades
ago, rings just as true today. How I wish I could have done more to
persuade my countrymen (and women) to accept it!

For my last Cambridge birthday, 20 December 1950, my father gave
me a copy of Sir Gilbert Campion's book on *Procedure of the House of
Commons*. I had never shared with my parents the idea (on which Robert
Sheaf and I had agreed at Winchester) that I should one day be Prime
Minister. It would have been even more vainglorious in 1950 than no
doubt it was in my schooldays; for already our 'First Sea Lord' had
actually left the navy. But the family were by now well aware of my
parliamentary ambitions. Exactly six months later, on 19 June 1951,
Father and Mother were both present for my graduation as Bachelor of
Arts and Bachelor of Laws. Thanks to their unflagging confidence and
support, I was almost ready for the double life of law and politics.

CHAPTER THREE

BARRISTER BOWMAN

Temple and Poplar

The transition from Cambridge to Bar student was almost immediate. The Bar final examinations were held in December 1951. My companion throughout my first year in London was that other Cambridge Conservative, Patrick Jenkin. We had already made one constituency speaking tour together, in support of the Tory challenger in Aneurin Bevan's Ebbw Vale constituency, Graeme Finlay. Patrick – despite his names – was Scottish. His Cambridge interests had extended beyond politics to the presidency of the Strathspey and Reel Club. Already he had found Monica, his wife-to-be. The flat that he and I found to share was in Denning Road, Hampstead – two very basic rooms for three guineas a week. Equipped with a recipe book (lots of powdered eggs) 'For Brides, Bachelors and Beginners', Patrick did most of the cooking and I did the washing up. One of his uncles sent us a haggis once a month. These seemed to fare well enough in the pressure cooker – until one exploded and fired the cooker's safety valve into the ceiling. For the thought-free Bar exams of that era, we both rehearsed the same crude mnemonics, and passed with very similar results. On the evening of 6 February 1952 the Master Treasurer of Middle Temple, former Labour Lord Chancellor Lord Jowitt, called us to the Bar, along with fellow students Norman St John Stevas and Robin Day. In the course of that very night King George VI died. The young Queen Elizabeth and the Duke of Edinburgh flew back to London from Kenya – and it was in the Queen's and not the King's Bench Division of the High Court that I was to practise at the Bar.

It was not an easy time to be starting in the profession. Less than 2000 barristers were in practice (compared with almost 8000 today). Two-thirds of those who actually started were destined to drop out within a couple of years. I served my pupillage, and then stayed on, in the London chambers of a well-established Wales and Chester Circuit practitioner, Norman Richards. Slightly gruff on first acquaintance and seemingly casual with paperwork, he was a shrewd judge of material, human as well as written – and a master of court-craft. He went on to become the Senior Official Referee. My first brief, to advise on an arcane point of company law, came from my father: he was determined to be the first! I continued for many years to handle a varied, if modest, flow of work from the family firm. Ours was a common-law, largely circuit, set of chambers. Ewen Montagu, Judge Advocate of the Fleet, inventor (and author) of *The Man Who Never Was*, led a large group of Western circuiteers. Rose Heilbron, just in Silk, was our only Northerner (and only woman); Norman Richards and I were the only Welshmen. It was from Norman that I inherited most of my best clients: the Medical Protection Society, the Police Federation and, most important of all, the Iron and Steel Trades Confederation. The largest union in the steel industry, the ISTC was the direct descendant of the Tinplaters' Union, which my grandfather had helped to found almost a hundred years before. Most of this was personal-injury and professional-negligence work. But a clientele of that calibre took time to build up. For my first three years in practice (including my pupillage year) my annual gross earnings were no more than £100, £200 and £400 respectively. Only in the third year did I make a modest net profit. So the £1200 with which my father had launched me was crucial to my survival.

The days on which there was nothing to do gave plenty of time for me to devote to the new-born Bow Group. We owe the name Bow to the shrewd intervention of Colonel Cecil Joel. He was political secretary of the Constitutional Club (then still alive in Northumberland Avenue) and also chairman of the Poplar Conservatives. He saw a chance of attracting some youthful talent to that fragile Association by offering the emerging group facilities at the Bow and Bromley Constitutional Club, alongside Poplar Town Hall in the Bow Road. It was there that the founding officers held their first meeting in February 1951. A number of us, including Elspeth and myself, were thus drawn into social and political work in that part of London for years to come. Membership of this new think-tank, as we should now call it, was restricted to university graduates under the age of thirty-six. It was deliberately non-sectarian and open to all *bona fide* Conservatives. The group has never taken a vote on any policy issue, a principle that was severely tested under the pressure of the Suez affair. Pamphlets have been published from all (Tory) points of view, solely on the strength of their quality and not of doctrine. If there was any guiding intellectual principle of the Bow Group, it was perhaps contained in one of my favourite phrases – that we were seeking to make the Tory Party fit for *Observer* and *Guardian* readers to live in.

Our first pamphlet, produced in 1952 by Anthony McCowan of Oxford University (later a Lord Justice of Appeal), was on the then novel theme of *Coloured People in Britain*. The choice was a direct consequence of our concern about the political orientation of so many of the future colonial leaders then studying in Britain. In 1952 the total of 'coloured people' in the country was no more than 35,000, half of whom were seamen and the other half students. It was the next decade that saw the explosive growth of immigration – getting on for a million people, first from the Caribbbean and then from India and the sub-continent. The Bow Group got full marks for having started work on an important topic, which was then no bigger than a man's hand.

Elspeth

It was in these early days of Bar and Bow Group that I met Elspeth, at a party given at the Wimbledon home of Guy's Hospital 'blue-baby surgeon' Russell Brock, a future president of the Royal College and member of the House of Lords. My brother Colin was engaged to Brock's eldest daughter Angela, and Elspeth had been at school at Wycombe Abbey with one of her two younger sisters, Mary. I had arrived late, after a Bow Group committee meeting just off Trafalgar Square. I had telephoned Mary Brock to ask, 'Is it still worth my coming?' It was. I was on to Mary the next morning to discover the phone number of the shy and attractive blonde I had just been in time to meet.

Elspeth was the younger daughter of the fourth marriage of author, architectural critic and *bon viveur* P. Morton Shand, of Eton and King's, Cambridge, whose family home was in Lonmay near Fraserburgh. He died in his beloved France, near Lyons, in 1960. Elspeth's mother Sybil was a woman of great patience and charm; like my mother she survived her husband for a number of years – so our children had the huge benefit of two lively and attentive grandmothers. In those days the Shands lived in Norland Square, off Holland Park Avenue. Patrick Jenkin's wife Monica had moved into Denning Road, and I had found single-room digs close to Elspeth off Kensington Church Street.

Elspeth's father had told her that she could marry anyone she liked 'so long as he isn't a lawyer, a politician or a Welshman'. But it was not long before she asserted her independence.

After a visit to Wales for mutual reconnaissance, and at the age of twenty, Elspeth accepted my proposal on Indian Independence Day, 15 August 1952. I attended upon her father, for a very nervous dinner. Exceptionally, he set his prejudices to one side and accepted my formal bid for his daughter's hand. We announced our engagement on Armistice Day, 11 November 1952. Nineteen-fifty-three was the *annus mirabilis* during which, on 2 June, news of the Hunt–Hillary expedition's first ascent of Everest coincided with the Coronation of Her Majesty Queen Elizabeth II. Elspeth and I, with a dozen other friends, were in our places on the Hyde Park side of Park Lane – rainsodden but cheerful – well before dawn. Hours later, after the Coronation procession had passed, we watched the rest of the event at the Notting Hill home of family friends on one of the country's few television sets. It was an exciting time to be young.

We were married later that year, on 29 August, by John Stott at St Peter's, Vere Street. Dick Stone was my best man and Gordon Adam one of the groomsmen. I later acted as best men at each of their weddings. Mary Brock was one of our bridesmaids. There was a last-moment hitch in the ceremony. It was only when actually seated in the church that I remembered Elspeth's insistence that she would not accept the duty to 'obey' her husband. But John Stott told Dick Stone and me that he could not drop the word: the routine in his church was invariable. So it was left to Dick, as best man, to give Elspeth this harsh news on the steps of the church. To our surprise – and relief – she accepted this ruling. But, she says, she kept her fingers crossed.

We set up our first home in a basement flat in Wimpole Street. Elspeth continued working as a secretary, to the principal of the Architectural Association's school of architecture, until shortly before the birth in August 1955 of our eldest daughter Cary. In each of those first two years of our marriage Elspeth's salary – at £9 per week significantly more than my earnings at the Bar – was crucial to our modest prosperity. It was only in 1958 that we bought our first car, a second-hand Morris 1000. And it was on our first continental motoring holiday that our twins were conceived. In June 1959 Amanda and Alec were born – like Cary – at my brother's first teaching hospital, the Middlesex. I received the news on Crewe station, on the way back from Chester Assizes, and we soon moved into a maisonette in Upper

Wimpole Street, one block closer to the zoo. All three children were christened at St Peter's, Vere Street, and we all remained a part of the family service there for the eleven years that we remained in the area. It was not until 1970 that we moved out of W1 to a house in Lambeth's up-and-coming Fentiman Road.

The first twenty years or so of our marriage, and most of my life at the Bar, were shaped by a strong Welsh dimension. Much of my practice was on the Wales and Chester Circuit. Circuit leaders of the day, from whom I learned a lot, included the future Labour Lord Chancellor Elwyn Jones and the future Law Lord Edmund Davies. My work for the steelworkers' union arose from industrial accidents in most parts of Wales. As well as the large new strip mills at Margam, Trostre, Velindre and Shotton, there were still a number of smaller works, as far afield as Llanelli and Gorseinon, Birkenhead and Brymbo. The manhandling of red-hot packs of steel was giving way to the console control of white-hot strip, but the sense of craft and camaraderie remained. It was a good industry to work with. Its wide spread enabled me to travel throughout the Principality and so to pick up a steadily growing flow of criminal (and other civil) work. My first appearance in the Court of Appeal was before Lord Denning and Lords Justices Birkett and Morris (later of Borth-y-Gest). 'We're all waiting, Mr Howe,' said Denning, 'to hear if you can pronounce the name of your clients. 'My lords, the Llantrisant and Llantwit Fardre Rural District Council' were my first confident words. Characteristically, Denning had taken the trouble to confirm that I was Welsh and so, very kindly, put me at ease.

The Parliamentary Candidate

This work pattern made it relatively easy to contemplate standing for the two general elections of 1955 and 1959 in my home constituency of Aberavon. There was no contest for the nomination. The local Conservatives were delighted to find themselves with a 'Port Talbot boy' with the beginnings of a plausible future in national politics. And I was equally pleased to be able to cut my teeth in congenial circumstances: I had no wish to enter the Commons until I had established my professional and financial independence – after, say, ten years in practice.

Our two Aberavon campaigns were great fun. Porthcawl was the only Tory foothold in the constituency. Yet even in the mining villages of Blaengwynfi, Glyncorrwg and the rest of the Avon valley (no less than seven collieries were still working in 1955), we received a friendly welcome from most Labour activists: many of them had worked with my father, mother or aunt in some context or other. 'Pity you're on the wrong side, boyo' was their most frequent greeting. My small band of supporters, including old friends like Dick Stone, Patrick Jenkin and Robert Sheaf, were surprised by the absence of bitterness. Elspeth – six months pregnant with Cary in May 1955 – used to pat her tummy and make much of her growing interest in family allowances. She campaigned with equal gusto in both elections.

In 1959 Ian Gow, still training to be a solicitor, joined our team. We had come across him at a Bow Group meeting, where his enthusiasm had been instantly infectious. It was a huge bonus to discover that he was another Freddyite, from my old house at Winchester. So far as I know, he had never been to Wales before, and he was undisguisably English. But his spontaneity enabled him to make friends quickly, everywhere. In Aberavon, even on our loudspeaker, he surprised as the acceptable voice of English Conservatism.

But the most that could be said for the outcome of our energetic campaigns – fought largely on Labour's threat to renationalize the Abbey Steelworks – was that I polled more votes than any other Conservative candidate before or since. In 1955 I cut the majority of Labour's veteran Member, Rhondda-born ex-NUT president Bill Cove, by 2320.* My father was fit and well enough to take real pleasure in that, my debut on the national stage. He died three years later, after quite a long spell in hospital. For the 1959 contest, Labour had a new candidate, barrister and future Secretary of State for Wales John Morris. He clawed back almost half of that.† On that occasion one aged Aberavon elector was deeply shocked by the immaturity of the three candidates from which he had to choose: I was the eldest at thirty-two, the Welsh Nationalist was a few months younger and Morris was only twenty-seven. So one spoilt ballot paper had no cross upon it – just the disenchanted sentence 'May the best *child* win!' Meanwhile, the national results moved steadily our way: Eden's overall majority in May 1955 was fifty-eight and MacMillan's in October 1959 a round hundred.

The longer-run importance of the Aberavon contests was in their impact on my campaigning style. As the 1950s evolved, so my thinking

---

* Cove, W. G. (Lab) 29,003; Howe, R. E. G. (Con) 12,706; Labour majority 16,297.
† Morris, J. (Lab) 30,397; Howe, R. E. G. (Con) 12,759; Lewis, I. M. (Plaid Cymru) 3066; Labour majority 17,638.

– and that of Bow Group colleagues – moved increasingly towards free-market liberalism. Even the One Nation group (later regarded, even if mistakenly, as synonymous with 'wetness') was pressing the case for rigorous economic change. Iain Macleod, later seen as a champion of the Tory left, was just as convinced as Enoch Powell that 'Change is Our Ally' (the title of the One Nation group's second publication). I was more than willing to press that case. But I had to learn how to do so to an audience which had long believed Conservatives to be born complete with horns and cloven hooves. In an Aberavon setting, Toryism with a human face was *de rigueur*, and that often required plain-speaking of a kind which might offend more traditional Conservatives.

It was probably this which prompted the most personal section of my election 'newspaper' ('Aberavon Express') in the 1959 campaign. 'Too many politicians', I proclaimed, 'have adopted an attitude of resigned helplessness in face of a party policy which they dislike.' Too many have 'never tried to comprehend the widespread feeling of cynicism and despair at the whole business of party politics'. I contrasted this with my own 'reluctance to accept ready-made answers to political questions' and my willingness to 'depart from the party line – when the merits of the case require it'. My party's overriding aim, I concluded, was 'to reconcile prosperity with social justice'. Even today that doesn't seem a bad balance between pragmatism and principle.

Pamphleteering

These general election campaigns were short-lived. Aberavon was not the kind of seat that expected constant nursing for years in advance, and my legal work took me there quite often enough to maintain effective contacts. So most of my mainstream politics was done in London or at conferences elsewhere. From 1953 onwards Elspeth was as involved as I was in the social as well as the political life of the Bow Group, to the extent that she became known as the Bow Group Wife. One visiting speaker, Sir John Foster QC, expressed admiration for the Group's practice of polyandry. I became chairman in 1955. Throughout the 1950s and 1960s the Bow Group was producing a steady flow of pamphlets and books. Although there was no conscious policy line to these, we tried to fit them into a broad framework of economic rigour and social awareness.

My first two pamphlets roughly balanced in this way. The first (*The*

Lifeblood of Liberty, 1954) contained proposals for local government reform, a well-researched attempt at consensus; unsurprisingly, we did not tackle the rating system. (I am conceited enough to think that our proposals would have been entirely apt four decades later – avoiding the upheavals of 1972 and 1992). The second (*Houses to Let*, written with Colin Jones in 1956) was a radical free-market prescription for the removal of rent control, but carefully tempered to mitigate the problems of sudden change. It was favourably noticed by leading articles in *The Times, Manchester Guardian* and *Economist*: 'a bold proposal', said the last-named. Three decades later it was still too bold for some, but I like to think we helped set the tone for Duncan Sandys' Rent Act of 1957: for a Tory reformer of some courage, his was a surprisingly modest step along this difficult road.

Interestingly enough, this was only the first of many topics which we found ourselves tackling at the same time and in the same mode as authors from the Institute of Economic Affairs. This was founded in the same year as *Crossbow* (1957) and we quite quickly gravitated into contact with each other. The IEA was avowedly and successfully non-political, with regular support from MPs of independent mind of all parties, such as the unstuffy Labour Party chairman Douglas Houghton and the quango-bashing Liberal Leader Joseph Grimond. Economic liberalism was – and is – its core commitment. The three men who share the principal credit for this long-running dynamo of economic radicalism are Anthony Fisher, who provided the money and much of the inspiration, Ralph Harris, challenging and tenacious general director for thirty years (later Lord Harris of High Cross), and Arthur Seldon, scholarly and sensitive editorial director over the same period. Both Harris and Seldon were regular contributors to *Crossbow* from the earliest years. Keith Joseph, then a junior minister in the Macmillan government, and I were among the first Tory politicians to establish regular contact with the Institute. In 1969 I was asked by Arthur Seldon to offer my view of Margaret Thatcher as a possible target for the Institute. My response was cautiously encouraging:

> I am not at all sure about Margaret. Many of her economic prejudices are certainly sound. But she is inclined to be rather too dogmatic for my liking on sensitive issues like education and might actually retard the cause by over-simplification. We should certainly be able to hope for something better from her – but I suspect that she will need to be exposed to the humanizing side of your character as much as to the pure welfare-market-

monger. There is much scope for her to be influenced between triumph and disaster.

In 1968 Ralph Harris enlisted me as a member of the IEA's international equivalent, the Mont Pelerin Society, founded by Nobel-prize-winning economist Friedrich Hayek and, from Britain, John Jewkes and Lionel Robbins in April 1947. I have been a member ever since.*

This was the background to a continuing flow of Bow Group publications, many of which I helped to edit. They had a similar collective balance. One series addressed socially conscious topics like patronage and the arts, the future of public schools, mental-health law and urban renewal. The other series tackled more natural targets for market economics: state-owned industry, competition law, wider ownership and tax reform. The launch of *Crossbow*, by Harold Macmillan, as early as October 1957 was a very significant move: in welcoming the Prime Minister, I expressed the hope that 'our elders in politics had the courage of our convictions'. He replied with the exhortation that we should not 'suffer from an excess of orthodoxy'. *Crossbow* was designed as a quarterly vehicle to get our ideas across to a wider audience: it is one of the few political wholesale markets founded in the years following the Second World War that is still going strong. For the sake of clarity we adopted four editorial principles: democratization of the Conservative Party; liberalization of the economy; a multiracial Commonwealth; and a realistic appreciation of Britain's role in the world. The last of these was intended to leave open the question of our attitude towards Europe; and the first two to combine One Nation social policies with economic liberalism. Nobody ever chafed at that balance.

Our editors over the first twenty years included talented journalists like Colin Jones, who went on to edit the *Banker* for many years, and Michael Wolff, who later – as Ted Heath's right-hand man – impressed Jim Prior as 'one of the most outstanding men of his generation'.[1] Our first woman editor, Patricia Hodgson, was later head of policy and planning at the BBC. Then there were future ministers like David Howell, Leon Brittan and Tim Raison. Together with Christopher Chataway and Trevor Philpott, Tim conceived in 1957 the notion of a World Refugee Year. Within less than twelve months we had persuaded the United Nations to adopt this proposal. Judy Hillman,

---

* Only four other UK politicians have ever belonged: Enoch Powell, John Biffen, Rhodes Boyson and Joseph Grimond.

later planning correspondent of the *Evening Standard*, *Guardian* and *Observer*, was a long-serving member of our editorial board, who went on to co-author a pre-emptive biography of me.[2] I like to think that one of my own editorials, for spring 1961, was not untypical of our approach:

> Are we perhaps becoming too reluctant to take really basic decisions for change, too anxious to let sleeping dogs lie, too concerned to see that no vested interest is disturbed? Need we be so concerned to preserve every law, every tax, every institution, every social service we have inherited from the past?

It was a strikingly radical brand of Conservatism.

I had one last venture on the Welsh political scene, one of several in partnership with Tom Hooson, a Tory cousin of the QC (and Liberal life peer) Emlyn. Tom, a bachelor, had a successful career in the advertising industry. After being a chairman of the Group in 1959, he became a surprisingly committed MP for the Brecon and Radnor constituency. He was always determined that the Bow Group should be more than a one-generation phenomenon. His success can be judged from the fact that he died – tragically early from cancer in 1985 – as one of the ninety-six Bow Group Members of Parliament. Our joint product, in 1959, was a policy document on the Welsh economy entitled *Work for Wales*. I said on his death (he was the first of our friends for whom I had to deliver the memorial address), 'I shall never forget the enthusiasm that he brought to that task – and the eye for detail, often transmitted to me on scruffy, energetic scraps of paper.'

The document's first chapter, 'A Call for Courage', was an uncannily specific trailer for the changes that finally came to the Principality – indeed to the whole Kingdom – under Margaret Thatcher's Premiership. 'Britain's economic problem', we said, 'is how to remain competitive in a fast-changing world.' To achieve this we should have to seize every opportunity for dynamic change: 'The longer we avoid facing reality the greater will be the hardship when we are eventually obliged to do so.' For that reason we should oppose subsidies that are other than transitional for inefficient farms, marginal mines and declining industries. We should work instead for a virile, flexible and thoroughly competitive Welsh economy. There followed a 100-page programme for doing just that. The sadness is that it had to wait for the two Conservative Secretaries of State of the 1980s, Nicholas Edwards and

Peter Walker, to carry it into effect. The hardship was indeed the harder for having been put off for so long. But there was no alternative.

Party Conferences

Aberavon provided me for many years with the base for my attendance as a representative at party conferences. My first was from Cambridge in 1950; I have attended, with Elspeth, virtually every year since 1953, and in my conference life played many parts. First I was an awe-struck spectator, then a leaflet-disher-out for *Crossbow*; soon I was a seat-hunter, looking for opportunities to impress, hoping to be called in one of the top debates. The saddest change has been in the tightening of security. Time was when you could find yourself walking beside senior ministers, the Prime Minister even, along Blackpool prom.

One of my earliest big opportunities was in the annual law-and-order debate at Brighton in 1961. I had submitted, from Aberavon, a 'liberal' motion, calling not for hanging and flogging but for a prison-building programme, strengthened probation services, longer sentences and – crucially – the establishment of a scheme to compensate the victims of violent crime. Some weeks later we were on family holiday near Coutances in Normandy, renting a farmhouse in a tiny hamlet called Boisroger. It was a shock to receive a telegram (there was no phone in those days): 'Please ring Sir Toby Aldington at Conservative Central Office.' What on earth, I wondered, can the party's deputy chairman (and MP for Blackpool North) want with me? 'Would you be willing', asked the great man, when finally I had got through to him, 'to move your motion as an amendment to the usual hanging and flogging motion?' Flattered to be involved in such high-level scheming, I agreed. 'But', he added (there's always a 'but'), 'the people here would be much happier if you dropped the last bit, about compensation for violence.' Treasury worried about the cost, Home Office about the principle and so on. 'You know the kind of thing.' It was a tough choice to throw at a candidate, who obviously relished the opportunity for 'star-billing'. Happily my fledgling political instinct prompted me in the right direction. 'Certainly not,' I said. 'If I'm going to have to take this on, you mustn't take the sugar off my pill.' Aldington agreed to consider my point. A few days later came the reply. Reluctantly, he said, the 'authorities' had agreed to give me a chance.

The debate, when it came, was one of the high points of the

conference. Tempers ran high. Our reforming amendment was carried by a large majority. A few months later, I was invited by Henry Brooke, by then Home Secretary, to join a committee which he set up to consider detailed proposals for compensation. I served also on a Justice study group for the same purpose. Within two years a suitable scheme was established, as we advised, without having to resort to legislation. It was one of the first in the world and served well for many years. It was an early lesson in the importance of sticking to one's guns.

We stuck too to the same holiday house in Boisroger for the next ten years or more, always taking both grandmothers. It was an idyllic compromise. When the sun shone, only a couple of miles away at Gouville-sur-Mer there were huge west-facing beaches, never crowded. When the weather was less kind, the 75-hectare farm furnished endless diversions for the children and the surrounding countryside provided excursions galore, from Mont St Michel to Bayeux and the invasion beaches. The children's pleasure in Boisroger increased as the years went by, for we had decided to save them from our own sense of linguistic imperfection by sending them, for the first eight years of their schooling (four for Alec), to the Lycée Français de Londres. I don't think any of us ever had cause to regret the decision. Boisroger came to a tragic end in 1972 when our hosts, the Michels, were both drowned at sea. The boat in which they had been collecting lichene (a pharmaceutical seaweed) was overloaded and capsized: neither of them could swim.

Member of Parliament

Bow Group work was now facing competition not just from the growth of my legal practice but from the decision that it was now time for me to look for a winnable constituency. Like many before me, I did not find that easy. I must have applied for a dozen or more – and was fortunate to miss selection for the Orpington by-election. Held in March 1962, it was the first to record a mega-swing against the Conservative government of the kind which in later decades became almost habitual. A 14,760 Tory majority gave way to one of 7855 for the Liberal, Eric Lubbock, and the excellent Tory candidate, Peter Goldman, was swept away, never again to appear on the parliamentary stage. Eventually, in 1963, I was selected for Bebington, in the Wirral corner of the Wales and Chester Circuit: it combined Port Sunlight and part of Birkenhead (almost to the gates of Cammell Laird's shipyard) with Liverpool commuter territory and a dash of Cheshire squirearchy. We rented, jointly with another Cambridge Bow Grouper, John Biffen, a cottage at Malpas in South Cheshire, conveniently between my Bebington and his Oswestry constituency. John, then still a bachelor, had been elected for Oswestry – in the last pre-Orpington by-election – in October 1961. His defeated Labour opponent, Brian Walden, entered the House when I did. Brian and John were quickly recognized as perhaps the most sparkling debaters of our generation. John was soon perceived as 'sound' as well. He made a most compatible and entertaining member of our weekend family.

The majority of 9861 which I had inherited at Bebington from Sir Hendrie Oakeshott – a modestly patrician man, as was appropriate for Alec Douglas-Home's PPS* – seemed likely to provide a perch that would sustain me for a secure parliamentary career. But I had reckoned without a surprise factor that was special to Merseyside. A significant part of the vote in that part of the world had for years rested upon the success of the Conservative Protestant Working Men's Clubs, which had been founded by Sir Archibald Salvidge near the start of the century, when Irish arguments had had a special force. But people – even Irish people, on Merseyside at least – were now more inclined to vote with their class than with their Church. So the Protestant Working Men's votes were melting before our eyes. On 15 October 1964, in a three-cornered fight with the Liberals, I was elected to the House of Commons safely enough, but with a majority that had shrunk to 2209.† The five (out of nine) Liverpool seats which the Tories had previously held had been cut to two. And Harold Wilson had moved into 10 Downing Street, albeit only with a tiny overall majority of four. A second general election within months seemed probable. So my parliamentary career was off to a distinctly shaky start. But having the letters 'MP' after my name was too much of a thrill for me to realize just how insecure that base had already become.

---

* Parliamentary private secretary. Confusingly, the same abbreviation applies to a principal private secretary (an official not a political appointment).
† Howe, R. E. G. (Con) 26,943; Brooks, E. (Lab) 24,734; Tompkins, M. J. G. (Lib) 7765; Conservative majority 2209.

CHAPTER FOUR

IN AND OUT OF PARLIAMENT

Conservative Government

My first day in Parliament, 27 October 1964, was a day of great excitement for me, but it was a day of truth for the Conservative Party. For here I was, here we were, taking our places on the Opposition side of the chamber. For most of my colleagues it was the first time they had been there for thirteen years. For me, and for some sixty-five other new boys and five new girls, it was where parliamentary life started. For all of us it was the signal that the post-war Butskellite settlement, the portmanteau ideology which symbolized the consensualist instincts of the Tory Rab Butler and Labour's Hugh Gaitskell, and which had sustained the Tory Party so well, was at an end.

The smallness of Labour's majority was no cause for comfort. It only underlined the imminence of a second round, for Labour were bound to seek an early chance to enlarge their bridgehead. And so it proved. In March 1966, less than eighteen months later, Wilson called the expected election. Labour in government had established sufficient credibility – or issued enough promises – to persuade the British people to extend their mandate. They were returned to power with an overall majority of ninety-six seats. The forty-seven Labour gains included Bebington. Labour's Edwin Brooks, a gentle, intelligent geographer from Liverpool University, took my place with a comparable majority of 2337.* Brooks was generous enough, and unusual enough, to express the hope that his opponent would be back in Parliament as soon as possible, though not of course as the Member for Bebington.

I was deeply downcast. For they had been good days on Merseyside, even if sadly short-lived. The motor industry – Vauxhall and Ford, newly arrived at Ellesmere Port and Halewood – seemed to be going

---

* Brooks, E. (Lab) 30,545; Howe, R. E. G. (Con) 28,208; Labour majority 2337.

from strength to strength. The Beatles were in the first flush of youth. Scouse morale was high. Shadows over the shipyards at Cammell Laird were almost the only portent of the depression that was soon to blight the region. And our Bebington constituents had treated this South Walian and his London Scottish wife with great kindness. The constituency was soon redistributed to the party's disadvantage, and I had to seek a less arduous return route to Westminster. But three years in the north-west had helped to strengthen my sense of the importance of non-metropolitan politics. My parliamentary career had been rudely interrupted. As Elspeth and I returned at 3 a.m. on 1 April to Hollybank Cottage in Malpas (to which the whole family had become very attached) I sent a disconsolate telegram to Charles Humphreys, my long-suffering clerk in the Temple: 'Brother, can you spare a dime?' His political prodigal had come home to roost, even if only for a time.

So the years of Labour government between 1964 and 1970 were divided for me into two distinct halves. Eighteen months in the House of Commons, then four years back at the Bar – though still heavily engaged in politics. The parliamentary year and a half saw me, and the party, through a great deal of change. Like most of my contemporaries, I made my maiden speech early: I should have felt foolish to face the electorate again without having made one. I tried to make the case for integrating tax and benefit systems – RAYN (Receive As You Need) as well as PAYE – a trail-blazer for what eventually (and abortively) became the tax credit scheme.

Meanwhile, Alec Douglas-Home, now Leader of the Opposition after just twelve months at Number 10, set in hand an immediate review of party policy. He put Ted Heath in charge of this. Ted, with characteristic zeal, launched some thirty study groups. I became involved in two of these, both initially under Keith Joseph's leadership: health and social security was the first; trade union reform the second. I qualified for the first by my previous writings in this field, and by election as secretary to the back-bench party committee on that topic; and for the second by my experience of trade union law and my membership of a Justice research group on this topic under the chairmanship of Professor Otto Kahn-Freund. It took many years for the first topic to achieve front-line attention. The second was to dominate British politics for the next twenty years, and it became one of the three key topics for Ted Heath's early policy work. The other two were tax reform and machinery of government. Ted's approach was one with which I could easily identify. The gusto of his earlier assault on Retail Price Maintenance was soon matched by zeal for this workmanlike agenda. And on Europe I was genuinely attracted by the sincerity and passion of Ted's commitment. I did not find it easy to warm to him personally, but I liked what he stood for.

The first, short Wilson government was dedicated to the broader issues, largely of economic management. This too became the responsibility of Ted Heath, as Home's Shadow Chancellor. He sparkled as an energetic critic of Callaghan's first Budget. Reginald Maudling, the former Chancellor, began to fade into the background as Shadow Foreign Secretary, as Home was himself able to dominate that field. The other two personalities who continued to attract the admiration of new members like myself were Iain Macleod and Enoch Powell. So when, in July 1965, Alec Douglas-Home announced his retirement, the choice of successor lay between these four – Heath, Macleod, Maudling and Powell. For reasons which never impressed me as entirely sufficient, Macleod ruled himself out. Maudling had always struck me as much too languid for the role. But still I was left with a difficult choice.

Enoch Powell had long been a charismatic figure to those Tories of my generation who had been seeking a more principled, market-based approach. He had for years been a guru to whom Bow Group pamphleteers went for advice. Tom Hooson and I had done so on *Work for Wales*. In formulating the case against incomes policy or rent control, the forceful logic of his thinking appealed to us. He had had that pulling power even in the days when he had sounded, as he had once done, more like a university lecturer than a politician. It was only his so-called 'rivers of blood' speech in April 1968 which set us apart. In Ted Heath's words, I 'could not accept the inflammatory nature of his approach to the very difficult problem of race relations'. Only six months before, as Shadow Defence Secretary at the Brighton party conference, he had stirred me, and many others, by commending withdrawal from East of Suez to a more European base. Some months after Ted Heath had sacked him from the Shadow Cabinet for his race-relations outburst, I told *Daily Telegraph* readers of my suspicion that 'most Conservatives would agree that if Mr Powell did not exist then it would be necessary to invent him'.[1] How else, I asked, would the argument for 'denationalizing' ('privatization' had yet to be invented) the telephones secure a hearing, let alone the docks, road haulage or the mines? (There was no doubting my proto-Thatcherite credentials.)

Ted Heath Becomes Leader

So for me the choice that had to be made, on 27 July 1965, between Edward Heath and Enoch Powell was far from easy. Three or four days before, I had had a strenuous argument in the tea-room with another new member, Michael Alison. Our approach to economic policy was very similar. He had worked with Enoch Powell for some years at the London Municipal Society, an outpost of Central Office. So he surprised me by discarding his boss and pressing instead the case for Ted Heath ('Better judgement,' he said). I urged him to back Enoch, on grounds of 'principle before everything else'. When we met again just after the result had been announced, we found that our mutual advocacy had been so successful that we had both changed sides. So mine was one of the votes that gave Ted Heath his overall majority, with 150 votes to Maudling's 133 and Powell's 15. Over the next thirty years the gap between me and my former idol was to be driven even wider – first by race, then by Europe and, finally, by Ireland.

By October 1965, I had become part of Ted's official team. My first front-bench appointment was as one of several junior spokesmen under Keith Joseph's Shadow Cabinet leadership, with the combined portfolio of labour and social services. This left me still in the same two policy groups. Keith was a fascinating man to work with: hugely intelligent (a fellow of All Souls) yet immensely unsure of himself; eager to question everything, including not least his own premises; always thinking aloud, even the unthinkable. To make a long journey with him was like travelling with a foraging squirrel: he was constantly tearing articles out of newspapers, writing notes to himself and stowing them about his person. Problems sometimes arose for him from the need to make order from this whirlwind of ideas, and so to arrive at sustainable executive decisions.

The work we were doing on health and social security was not destined to lead to early policy commitments, but it was to shape many of the struggles of the next twenty years. And it gave me the chance to develop and publish in April 1965 some ideas of my own in a pamphlet entitled *In Place of Beveridge* for the Conservative Political Centre. 'Do we wait', I asked, for the foreseeable future and however affluent we may become, to 'perpetuate a huge machinery whereby the State re-distributes such a large proportion of the national income?' I launched one of many attacks on the notion that we should regard inflation as indefinitely tolerable. A universal and universally indexed state-run pension scheme, I argued, could all too easily entrench such inflationary expectations. I pressed the case for private-sector pensions and transfer-ability and emphasized the overriding need for more competition and greatly reduced levels of inflation. A society, I concluded, in which more people were able to choose 'the time at which they could retire . . . the way in which their retirement would be financed' would certainly be 'a freer one than that to which we were accustomed'.[2]

This did not prevent Richard Crossman, in the second Wilson government, enacting a universal earnings-related state pensions scheme. One of the ways in which we mobilized opposition to this was through an all-party movement that I had suggested, STOP (Save The Occupational Pension). Lord Shawcross was our chairman and Arthur Seldon of the IEA our intellectual dynamo. Ted Heath's 1970 election victory came just in time for Keith Joseph, as Social Services Secretary, to replace Crossman's scheme with a more modest two-tier system. But that too was largely scrapped by Barbara Castle in 1974, to make way for her own state earnings-related pensions scheme (SERPS). I was then her shadow. Labour's majority was only four, and Barbara Castle was commendably ready to accept the moderating advice of her number two, Brian O'Malley. We were able to hammer out a more or less agreed scheme, so that pensions ceased – for a decade anyway – to be a political football. Ten years later (in 1985) Margaret Thatcher pressed Norman Fowler towards virtual privatization of SERPS. But she too was obliged to compromise, and the modifications that Norman was eventually able to make have brought the resultant structure pretty well into line with the arrangements that I had suggested exactly twenty years before.

The other task, on which Keith Joseph led us skilfully through the important work ahead of the 1966 general election, was the reform of trade union law (or industrial relations law, as it more appropriately became known). The proposals contained in our 1966 election mani-festo were not massive: we were calling then for legally enforceable agreements, registration of trade unions and a system of industrial courts to 'enforce' a code of good industrial relations practice. Keith Joseph was then asked by Ted Heath to confine his attention to the wide Social Services portfolio. The work of Shadow Employment Secretary was taken over by Robert Carr. It was with him that I worked intensively in the two years before the 1970 election on the proposals which we later unveiled.

Queen's Counsel

During the four years that I was once again out of Parliament (1966–70), the centre of gravity of my life shifted back to the Temple. In 1965, while still in the House, I had taken Silk – that is to say I had been appointed Queen's Counsel, at the relatively early age of thirty-eight. This sometimes hazardous career move requires a barrister to give up the voluminous paperwork of a junior practice and enables him to specialize in advocacy of a more difficult (and better-paid) class. Just occasionally the move is disastrous – if, for example, the new Silk turns out to have overestimated his own marketability. Generally it works out well, but there tends to be a hiatus during the change. In my case that could have been serious, since the switch was uncomfortably close to the time when I lost my place in the House. The transition was eased by my appointment in 1966 as deputy chairman of Glamorgan Quarter Sessions. This part-time judicial appointment (it no longer exists in that form) offered valuable experience and a useful 'shop window'. I was quite quickly getting more diverse legal work. It was at the same time more stimulating (and more rewarding) than would have been long days and nights of opposition in the House. Without such direct political experience, my chances of office in a future Conservative government were bound to be adversely affected. Happily a good deal of the legal work that came my way offered strong political insights, and I made the most of other opportunities to remain on the political scene.

Two major public inquiries, very different from each other, formed an important part of my legal diet. First, in 1966, came the inquiry by Lord Justice Edmund Davies into the Aberfan disaster. I was instructed as counsel for about one dozen Coal Board officials. The question was how far any of them might be to blame for the catastrophic black avalanche of coal slurry that had swept away a village school, killing 144 people, including 116 children. I was deeply moved by the whole sombre experience. I was fulfilling the most fundamental role of an advocate, acting as an insulator between those accused and the avenging fury of the public. As a politician, I was appalled by the insensitivity of a state-owned industrial monolith in a small community, whose livelihood depended upon it. The Coal Board had paid scant attention to Merthyr Borough Council. I learned too the capacity of even a conscientiously conducted public inquiry to inflict injustice on those whose conduct it has to examine. Colliery managers' conduct was all too easily criticized with the wisdom of hindsight.

Very soon, in 1969, I was obliged myself to understand this lesson. For the second inquiry was one that I had been asked to chair. With the help of three expert colleagues, I had to probe allegations of cruelty and other misconduct at Ely Hospital, Cardiff. Even with the lessons of Aberfan in mind, I doubt if we entirely avoided inflicting injustice on some members of the hospital staff. It can happen so easily with a tribunal whose chairman was obliged, as I had been, to combine the role of judge and prosecutor. I learned too from this case of the tenacity with which officialdom can resist the sanction of publicity for manifest mismanagement. Anthony Howard describes Richard Crossman's decision to publish in full the report which my colleagues and I had prepared as 'perhaps the bravest action of his career'.[3] But he would never have had that opportunity had we not insisted upon our right (and duty) to submit our full report. The Welsh Board of Health initially tried to compel us to prune and edit it. We did not do so. We submitted instead a further version in which we protested at 'the editorial pressure to which we have been subjected'. The Board was thus obliged to accept our full report. Even then, it was only with the help of Crossman's special adviser, Brian Abel-Smith – another Cambridge contemporary – that we had actually been able to get the document on to his desk.

I enjoyed three other opportunities of studying the way in which the law could shape social attitudes – for better or for worse. The first was through service from 1965 to 1967 as a member of the committee under Mr Justice Latey, which was appointed by Wilson's first Lord Chancellor, Gerald Gardiner, to consider the age of majority: was twenty-one too high an age for legal maturity, in the emancipated age in which we lived? On the whole we thought yes. A sparkling report in favour of eighteen was largely penned by one of our number, the Sunday newspaper columnist Katherine Whitehorn. On one issue, John Stebbings, future president of the Law Society, and I prepared a minority report: the age of responsibility for marriage without parental consent. Divorce was three times more likely for couples who married when both were below the age of twenty-one than when both were above. A majority of people under the age of twenty-four were opposed to any change in the law. 'It's hard', we said, 'to see any reason why teenagers should be dragged kicking and screaming into the permissive atmosphere of the twenty-first century, if they have no burning desire to come along.' But, in a Parliament with a large Labour majority, it was the view of the majority that later prevailed.

The second such task was in the more sensitive field of race relations. PEP (Political and Economic Planning, forerunner of today's Policy Studies Institute) invited me in 1967 to join in a study of the effectiveness of anti-discrimination legislation in the United States and Canada. This was to be undertaken with Geoffrey Bindman, a London solicitor, and under the chairmanship of Professor Harry Street of Manchester University. It gave me the opportunity to visit several of the more informative race-relations scenes on the other side of the Atlantic – from Ontario, with an established set of human-rights commissions, to Los Angeles, recently racked by race rioting and arson in Watts County. Our report, broadly in favour of sensitive and well-constructed legislation, was published at the right time, for the Home Secretary Roy Jenkins had found it necessary to consider wholesale amendment of the Race Relations Bill which he had introduced. Once again I dissented from my colleagues on some points – on this occasion because I thought they expected the law to do too much, to intrude too deeply into personal relationships. But the broad thrust of our recommendations, for the establishment of a Race Relations Board with effective powers of conciliation and enforcement, helped the government to reshape the legislation in a way that was acceptable to most parliamentary opinion.

The third 'disadvantaged' group which I had the chance to consider was (much too coyly) identified in the title of our report, *Fair Share for the Fair Sex*. This was the product of a committee set up by Ted Heath under the chairmanship of Sir Anthony Cripps QC, to make recommendations to the Conservative Party about legal discrimination against women. Probably our most important recommendations when we reported in 1969 were for the use of the electoral roll (instead of property qualification) as the basis of jury service; and for changes in the discriminatory tax treatment of married women. This last proposal had to wait eleven years before I was able, in my 1980 Budget, to take the first steps towards implementing the change. Eight years later the job was completed by Nigel Lawson.

The Politics of Education

Probably the most politically productive of all my out-of-House experience was in education. Elspeth and I were already doing some practical work in this field in London's East End. Ever since the Bow Group introduced us to Poplar, we had remained involved there. Elspeth did Care Committee work (school-based support for parents who had problems coping with their children) and became engaged in the management of several local schools. When she was appointed a Juvenile Court Justice of the Peace for Inner London, she sat often in the Bow Road court. I was persuaded to stand in Poplar as a Conservative candidate for the London County Council in 1958. There was no risk of being elected! For several years in the early 1960s, I was actually chairman of the Poplar Conservative Association. Not least because of the Bow Group link, we had a distinguished sequence of future ministers as parliamentary candidates: Peter Emery, Gerry Vaughan and Kenneth Baker.

I became very familiar with the mounting problems of dereliction in London docklands. Even in those days, the Isle of Dogs had its own Residents' Association, which was winning by-elections in that ward. Elspeth's experience first inspired her interest in the Pre-school Playgroup movement. In 1966 she wrote a CPC pamphlet about it entitled *Under Five.* She was becoming an increasingly well-qualified political figure in her own right. She had been on the Heath Policy Group on education and was co-opted to membership of the Inner London Education Authority when the Tories were in control in 1968. At the same time I was appointed chairman of the governing body of a 'developing comprehensive' (a euphemism for two recently merged secondary moderns) at Langdon Park in Poplar. Elspeth had been a governor of one of the schools for many years before that, but she went on to the chair of a different girls' school. We had both seen something of the hardship that could be inflicted by authoritarian and insensitive management of resources that were often already overstretched.

That was the background against which I was instructed in 1967 on behalf of a group of parents and ratepayers in the other London borough of Enfield: they included Ross McWhirter,* one of the twin

* Following several legal actions relating to the freedom of the individual, Ross was killed by IRA assassins in 1975.

editors of the *Guinness Book of Records*, and Ralph Harris, then chairman of the IEA. Enfield had violated the law in several respects in the way they had set about closing or amalgamating some eight schools (including Enfield Grammar School), with a view to creating new comprehensive schools in their place. The council sought to invoke the authority of the Secretary of State for Education, Patrick Gordon Walker, for their irregular way of proceeding. My clients challenged this. In the lower court the judge thought that, on a balance of convenience, the plan should be allowed to proceed, even though the law had been broken. But in the Court of Appeal Lord Denning, Master of the Rolls, took a different view. 'The Department of Education and the Council', he said, 'are subject to the rule of law and must comply with it, just like everybody else.'[4] Council and Secretary of State, in scheming partnership with each other, tried to circumvent the court order, but without success. Three times within sixteen days the socialist government was declared to be acting unlawfully.

This case, and others of the same kind, reinforced my political interest in education. Elspeth and I became involved, with Tyrell Burgess (a don at the London School of Economics) and Anne Corbett (education correspondent of *New Society*), in the formation of another all-party pressure group (which flourishes today), the National Association of Governors and Managers (NAGM). And in speeches at Reigate and Penarth in 1968 and 1969 I proposed, for the first time anywhere, a parents' charter: parents should be given rights to consultation, to representation on school governing bodies and of appeal against decisions of local education authorities allocating children to particular schools. 'In an age when consumer protection is rightly required in so many fields,' I said, 'parents should be given enough detailed and accurate information to enable them to choose between different schools that aspire to excel in different specialities.' I pressed too for more private spending on schools, to raise standards and widen choice, and for the introduction of loans to help finance the expansion of higher education. Two decades were to pass before most of this thinking came to bear fruit. Eventually it did, in legislation introduced by Secretaries of State in the second half of Mrs Thatcher's decade at Number 10.

Industrial Relations

Finally it was industrial relations law that came to dominate my life in the years before and after the 1970 general election. Curiously, I had not been drawn into this topic when the opportunity first presented itself. That was in 1958, when the Society of Conservative Lawyers* worked to produce almost the first set of proposals for reform, entitled *A Giant's Strength. Crossbow* gradually paid increasing attention to the subject. But it was my role as legal correspondent to the *Sunday Telegraph* since its foundation in 1961 that drew me in decisively. The paper's first editor, Donald McLachlan,† became intensely interested in the case of a trade unionist called Douglas Rookes who had been cruelly victimized in a 'closed shop' at Heathrow. I helped to publish his story. His case was an important factor in persuading Justice, the all-party group of lawyers, to set up the Kahn-Freund research group which I have already mentioned. As yet, however, this activity had not produced any major shift in political attitudes to trade union law. Neither party raised it as an issue in the 1964 election. But it was at almost that moment, as Harold Wilson moved into Number 10, that the House of Lords gave judgement in the *Rookes* case.[5]

This forced the whole topic on to the political agenda. In April 1965 Wilson appointed a Royal Commission, under the chairmanship of Lord Donovan (a former Labour MP, by then a law lord) to consider the whole question of 'trade union law'. For the next three years Labour were thus able to sidestep the question. Donovan was not expected to report until 1968. For the Tories, however, an important issue had been opened up. The policy group on which I sat, first under Keith Joseph's, then under Robert Carr's chairmanship, produced a series of proposals. The first, in 1965, were in time to find a place in our 1966 election manifesto, *Action Not Words*. The second – a separate policy document entitled *Fair Deal at Work* – appeared in April 1968. We had beaten the Donovan Commission by just one month.

Meanwhile the industrial relations scene had been going from bad to worse. The mines, the docks and the motor industry were increasingly at the mercy of wild cat strikes. In face of this, Labour's Employment

* In those days known as the Inns of Court Conservative and Unionist Society.
† Briefly before the war, he had taught at Winchester; he was tragically killed in a motor accident in 1971.

Secretary, Barbara Castle, in January 1969 produced far-reaching proposals in a White Paper entitled *In Place of Strife*. But the Wilson government proved unable, in face of internal opposition led by Jim Callaghan, to enact this package. From the Opposition benches, we did nothing to help it on to the statute book. We were probably reluctant to see Labour steal our electorally attractive 'anti-union' clothing. Jim Prior has subsequently argued that we should have done better, for our party as well as for the country, to help Barbara Castle overcome the resistance of her own dissenters.[6] But that would have required this strange coalition to defeat not just her back-benchers but most of her Cabinet colleagues as well. Such a contortion would, I think, have defied even Harold Wilson's special skills. Either way, it was clear that an incoming Tory government would need to have ready a workable package of measures. It was on this that we concentrated from 1968 on.

My own involvement in this field (in due course as Solicitor General), coupled with the pioneering work of the Conservative Lawyers' Society, led our critics to argue – indeed to believe – that we were hopelessly lawyer-dominated in our thinking. But I was the only lawyer in the three-man team that masterminded our final approach. Robert Carr was the Shadow Employment Secretary. His own industrial experience and powerful sense of justice made him determined to secure a balanced and practical approach. He left much of the detailed work to a working partnership between myself and an unusually gifted Conservative Party official, Stephen Abbott. Stephen had spent much of his working life with the large engineering group, Metal Box, for most of the 1950s managing their West Indies subsidiary. As a young officer, he had been taken prisoner by the Japanese and had played in real life almost exactly the role created by Alec Guinness in *The Bridge on the River Kwai*. Abbott had learned man-management and human relations the hard way. He came to the Conservative Research Department in 1960 specifically because he saw the need for fundamental reform of our entire system of industrial relations. He was profoundly right – and particularly well qualified for the task.

All the proposals put forward in the second half of the 1960s – Donovan's and Castle's no less than our own – had one thing in common. They all required substantial intervention by the law and the courts – which was, for Britain, a revolutionary concept. This is no place to discuss the details of competing proposals, but Stephen Abbott, Rober Carr and I were totally persuaded that it was a revolution whose time had come. That was why the unions fought so fiercely over two decades to resist every proposal of this kind. And it is why the Labour Party was twice fatally divided by their attempts to tackle the problem: once in 1969, over *In Place of Strife*, and again in 1979, during the so-called Winter of Discontent.

My own final analysis started from the Report of the 1906 Royal Commission on Trade Disputes and Trade Combinations*

The Socialist pioneer, Sidney Webb, was one of its five members. The Commission rejected the notion that trade unions should enjoy immunity from liability for damage which they might, by strike action or otherwise, inflict upon outsiders. 'What was denied to religion', said Webb and his colleagues, 'ought not . . . to be conceded to Trade Unionism' (paragraph 34). In a personal Addendum to the Report, Webb commended some Australian proposals which came close to foreshadowing our own approach in 1971. 'I cannot believe', said Webb, 'that a civilized community will permanently . . . abandon the adjustment of industrial disputes – and incidentally the regulation of the condition of the life of the mass of its people – to . . . the arbitrament of private war.' The Commission's advice was largely disregarded by Campbell-Bannerman's Liberal government. Their 1906 Trade Disputes Act laid the foundations of the system – unique to this country – from which eventually developed the disorderly chaos of our own time. It took sixty years for the unions fully to realize the 'giant's strength' with which Parliament had then endowed even the most unofficial form of industrial action. Ironically, the particular provision (section 3 of the Act) that granted such wide immunity had been added to the Bill in an amendment suggested by a young Liberal researcher, one William Beveridge. It was actually tabled and moved by another much older Liberal, Sir Charles Dilke. It was essential, we believed, to tackle historically fundamental problems of this kind. But, if that was the case, it was important to ensure that our alternative could be seen as fair and balanced.

This led us to look, as we refined our basic thinking (much of which had already been disclosed), at precedents outside this country. Abbott's Caribbean and American experience drew him in that direction. So too did my own earlier studies in the field of anti-discrimination legislation. If a sensitively crafted law could be used – as Labour already argued and as we had accepted – to deal with race relations, why should we not study the other half of American experience, 'labor relations' legislation?

* Under the Chairmanship of Andrew Graham Murray, QC, (Lord Dunedin), HMSO, Cd. 2825

So Abbott and I, with Robert Carr's blessing, undertook an extensive visit to North America in the spring of 1970. We compared notes with practitioners, industrial relations experts as much as lawyers, in both capital cities, and also in Toronto. The Ontario Labor Relations Board, then under the chairmanship of a remarkably sensitive labour lawyer, Jacob Finkelman QC, was, if anything, the model for our own National Industrial Relations Court: a balanced board of up to four lay members drawn from 'both sides of industry', sitting under the chairmanship of a High Court judge. The substance of this idea we had already put forward, in 1968, in *Fair Deal at Work*. But on matters of style we were learning a lot across the Atlantic. Most important, we thought, was the Labor Relations Board's ability to combine authority with informality ('Justice in a lounge suit' was the phrase I later used to commend the approach to Sir John Donaldson, the first judge of our new court). We were impressed too by the balanced and comprehensive quality of each of the North American legal systems. Like Barbara Castle's proposals, they were concerned not just with the imposition of cooling-off periods or pre-strike ballots but also with the need to provide proper procedures for union recognition and for the rights of union members – against unions as well as against bosses.

By the time the 1970 general election was upon us – unexpectedly early, after less than four years – our plans were virtually complete. Ted Heath and Robert Carr, above all, were satisfied with them because of their balance and fairness. Every obligation upon unions or workers was matched by an enforceable right or benefit. One later critic of our entire approach had the grace to comment that our proposals arose 'from a quite subtle understanding of the problems of industrial relations and a keen awareness of the difficulties of enforcement'.[7] He rightly attributes much of this to Stephen Abbott's energy and commitment. It was argued afterwards that we were committed to doing too much. Even now I do not accept that charge. But at least we were ready – and modestly convinced of the wisdom of our approach.

The 1970 General Election

All this input to the policymaking process I had been able to make from outside Parliament. My freedom from the Whips had left me available not just for my legal practice but usefully to roam the world on policy work as well. Yet it had left me short of the Commons' knockabout experience that could have given me more confidence at the despatch-box in the years ahead. And, just now, I still had to find myself a new constituency. It was dispiriting to be on the trail for the second time in five years. There was a limit to the number of publicized 'rejections' one could take without becoming unsaleable. I lost out to Patrick McNair-Wilson in the New Forest, Dudley Smith at Warwick and Leamington and Sir Brandon Rhys-Williams in Kensington. My chance finally came with the retirement of Sir John Vaughan-Morgan, a founder member of the One Nation Group, from what was then the Reigate constituency: its 7514 majority (in a bad year) seemed safe enough for all seasons. The 267 applicants were finally thinned down to two of us, Chris Chataway and myself, to appear in what was dubbed the 'Reigate primary'. For the first time the television cameras and other media were admitted to see the final contest, before some 600 members of the Association.

Chataway – Olympic athlete (and former world record-holder), television newscaster and former junior minister – was the favourite. I was intensely nervous. So were both our wives. Anna (Chataway's first wife) and Elspeth were each required to make short speeches on the duties of a Member's wife: 'an unnecessary impertinence', commented Julian Critchley, who was there as a journalist, having failed himself to make the short-list. Elspeth said not a word about her own ability or interests. Most important, she said, was to realize that an MP's wife is 'just an ordinary wife' and that MPs 'need slightly more love and attention than most other breeds of husbands'. It was not the kind of speech to expect from a future deputy chairman of the Equal Opportunities Commission. But it was, said Critchley, 'the best speech of the evening'. So we won by a majority of about two to one. And Chataway was free, as it happened, to return to Parliament ahead of me. He was elected in 1969 at a by-election in Chichester caused by the death of the sitting member, Bill Loveys. I had to bide my time. John Vaughan-Morgan, when I next saw him, felt he had to apologize for still being alive.

The general election in fact came on 18 June 1970. It had been called by Harold Wilson almost on impulse – or so it seemed – at a moment when Labour had recovered a brief, but substantial, lead in the opinion polls. The swift summer campaign offered little chance for me to get the feel of a new constituency. News reached us on the last Friday evening of the campaign at the Haycutters Arms, Broadham Green, of the opinion poll lead for Labour of 12.4 per cent. We had certainly detected no sign of this. But in those distant days the Reigate count did not take place until 'the morning after'. So at the end of polling day Elspeth and I drove up to town (for the traditional *Telegraph*–Savoy election-night party) with some anxiety. As we crossed Mitcham Common, the first result came through for Guildford. David Howell had secured a swing in his favour of 6 per cent. So it continued for the next half-dozen results. It was clear that we had won. The polls had been decisively trounced. Our sense of relief was immense. My own count the next day became in effect a victory celebration. Reigate gave me a majority of 13,029 in a three-cornered fight with a swing in our favour of 4.8 per cent.* There were seventy-seven Conservative net gains. Ted Heath, in a victory as decisive as it was unexpected, had secured an overall majority of thirty.

The Cabinet was announced on the Saturday. The following week I was back again on circuit, to lead Bruce Griffiths in an industrial-injury case at Newport Assizes. In the middle of Tuesday afternoon, I was called out of court to the telephone: Ted Heath asked me to join the Government as Solicitor General, with special responsibility for our long-planned Industrial Relations Bill. I was, of course, delighted to accept – and then asked, rather foolishly, 'Where do I go next?' 'Run like hell', said Ted, 'for the Solicitor General's office before anyone else gets there.' So I left Bruce Griffiths to finish our case, which he did with complete success. By the time I was back in Fentiman Road the evening bulletins were carrying the news that the new Solicitor General would be known as Sir Geoffrey Howe. Eleven-year-old Amanda piped up from her bath, 'Well done, Daddy! Does that mean I'll be Lady Amanda?' At the next day's celebration party at Number 10, Ted greeted me with 'Congratulations on the K, Geoffrey.' 'You didn't tell me about that,' I replied. 'They didn't tell me either,' said Ted. I began to see the meaning of 'honours arriving with the rations'. But I was glad to be back in Parliament, excited to be there in support of our new Conservative Prime Minister and delighted almost beyond belief at my appointment to the highest job for which I could possibly have hoped. The tasks ahead were precisely those for which I had been preparing myself.

* Howe, R. E. G. (Con) 28,462; Farley, M. P. (Lab) 15,433; Vaus, K. J. (Lib) 8952; Conservative majority 13,029.

PART TWO

====

THE HEATH
GOVERNMENT
1970–1974

CHAPTER FIVE

SOLICITOR GENERAL

A Law Officer

The Attorney General throughout Ted Heath's government was Peter Rawlinson. Roman Catholic, with distinguished war service in the Irish Guards, Peter already had almost twenty-five years' experience at the Bar. He had been Solicitor General in the Macmillan government for the two years following the ruthless 1962 reshuffle on the Night of Long Knives. Our paths had crossed occasionally. We were now set to get much closer. Few partnerships are so close as that between Attorney General and Solicitor General.

The two Law Officers are *the* source of considered legal opinions for the Cabinet. They are always jealous of their independence of other lawyers, not excluding the Lord Chancellor. My own experience reminds me that any lawyer–minister is constantly tempted to offer legal advice, upon the basis of half-forgotten and outdated recollection. But at the start of my career as Solicitor General I manifestly deferred to the Lord Chancellor, Quintin Hailsham. For I had to receive my seals of office from him and at the same time to take an oath of loyalty to Her Majesty. All this solemn ritual, in the Lord Chancellor's office, was to be witnessed by my wife, children, mother, mother-in-law and other fond admirers. As it happened, the Lord Chancellor and I had been engaged – until the eve of the election – on opposite sides of a case about petfood. My clients, Spillers Ltd, were makers of the dogfood Kenno-meat. Quintin's had been Quaker Oats Ltd, who were seeking to market a competitor catfood, to be called Ken-L-Meat. Not surprisingly, we had sued for infringement of the copyright in our tradename. I had won the case before the trial judge. Quintin had succeeded in the Court of Appeal. We were on the way to the House of Lords when the election intervened.

As I stood now before the Lord Chancellor, wearing my court dress and full-bottomed wig, I had forgotten all about the case. When I had finished stumbling through my medieval oath of office, the Lord Chancellor – silent behind his desk until then – rose to his feet and stumped towards me. He thrust into my hands the impressive red-leather casket containing my scroll and seals of office. 'Guaranteed, my dear boy,' he said, 'to contain absolutely nothing but Kennomeat.' In the eyes of my family at least, the honourable office of Solicitor General never recovered the dignity that it lost on that happy occasion.

The Law Officers' Department is one of the oldest, certainly the smallest and often the least popular of all departments. One of my predecessors, whose picture adorned our 'chambers' corridor in the Royal Courts of Justice, was Sir Richard Rich. He had prosecuted the former Lord Chancellor Thomas More in 1534. One of the first jobs Peter Rawlinson and I had to do together was to advise Heath (and Foreign Secretary Alec Home) that they were indeed entitled, under the Simonstown Agreement, to resume arms sales to South Africa. Almost the entire department – less than twenty people, including secretaries, drivers and messengers – worked through a weekend to produce our Joint Opinion. Within three days it appeared as a White Paper. Difficult and important legal problems of this kind followed one another in quick succession. But I was unable to give Peter the continuous legal back-up that I should have liked, for the production of the Industrial Relations Bill required me to spend many days away from the department – first in the Department of Employment, later in the House of Commons. During my second year as Solicitor, the European Communities Bill had the same effect. This increased the burden on the Attorney himself and also upon our legal secretary, Tony Hetherington. A constituent of mine from Lingfield, Hetherington seven years later moved on to become Director of Public Prosecutions.

But some at least of the forensic burden I was able to share with the Attorney. Were we entitled to terminate our joint venture with France on the production of Concorde? Not for the first time the Treasury were pressing for cancellation. I had to attend at Number 10 to give Ted Heath the same advice that our predecessors (Elwyn Jones and Frank Soskice) had given Wilson in 1964. The contract was unbreakable. Julian Amery, who was at my meeting with the Prime Minister, confirmed with a smile that that had indeed been his intention when he struck the deal as Minister of Aviation in 1962. 'We wanted', he said 'to be sure – with the French.'

Were we to prosecute the 'shocking' new Ken Tynan revue *Oh!*

Calcutta! under the Obscene Publications Act? Rather than trying ourselves to pre-guess a jury's verdict, I had a novel idea. We sent most of my former colleagues on the Latey Committee (on the age of majority) – Anglican cleric, professor of consumer law, comprehensive school headmistress, Sunday newspaper columnist – to view the show and give us their individual verdicts. Not a single sketch secured a majority for conviction. So the courts were not troubled. And the Attorney (and the government) avoided embarrassment.

Would we agree with the editor of the *Sunday Times*, Harold Evans, to mount – as his lawyers suggested – a 'friendly' action, so that the courts could decide whether a proposed feature about thalidomide would amount to contempt of court? Yes, we gladly agreed. But that didn't prevent Evans later claiming that the Attorney had threatened him with imprisonment – and quite unjustly casting poor Rawlinson as the villainous scourge of a free press and of suffering children. Even in those days the *Sunday Times* was single-minded in the promotion of its own interests.

At least twice I was able to help the Education Secretary, Margaret Thatcher. She was in one of the jobs traditionally regarded as suitable for the Cabinet's 'statutory woman'. The *Little Red School Book* was an allegedly obscene Maoist text that had been troubling her (and many others). This time we were able to secure a conviction. I also helped her to strike down some unduly restrictive school catchment areas, which inhibited parental choice in our own county of Surrey (Peter Rawlinson was Member for Epsom). Then in her first Cabinet job, still young and bubbly, Margaret waxed very enthusiastic about whatever she had in hand. Yet she remained very heedful of her own department's advice. In each of these cases she had come to me specifically for support against her 'own people' (I had, after all, triumphed over them in the Enfield schools case); and I had not disappointed her.

The most internationally sensitive problem followed the arrest of an attractive Palestinian terrorist, Leila Khaled. She had tried to hijack an El Al airliner when it was reported to be 'south of Clacton' *en route* from Amsterdam to New York. Khaled's male partner was killed. The plane diverted to Heathrow, and she was handed over to the British authorities. Within the next four days no less than three airliners, including a BOAC VC-10, were hijacked and landed at Dawsons Field in Jordan. Hundreds of passengers were there held hostage, including sixty-five Britons. Among the demands made by the hijackers was the release of Leila Khaled. That could happen only if the Attorney General decided –

and it was for him alone to do so – that a prosecution would not be justified under English law. It was only after he had requested advice from the Foreign Secretary and then considered, independently, the whole of the evidence that Peter decided that a prosecution was by no means sure to succeed. 'South of Clacton' left open the chance that, at the moment when the offence was committed, the plane was over the North Sea and so outside the jurisdiction. That risk of failure, in a case of such potentially wide importance, persuaded the Attorney to let Khaled go free.

Far more difficult problems awaited us in Northern Ireland. On 30 January 1972 thirteen civilians were shot dead by British Army units on the streets of Londonderry. For the Nationalists that day became 'Bloody Sunday'. Within two months the Westminster government was obliged to assume responsibility for direct rule of the Province of Ulster. Peter Rawlinson became its Attorney General. I never had time, from my other commitments, in the National Industrial Relations Court as well as in the House, to play a matching role as Solicitor General. So, with the assistance of a newly established – and very brave – Director of Public Prosecutions for the Province, Barry Shaw, Peter Rawlinson had to bear a hugely increased burden of responsibility. He was close to being single-handed in the Law Officers' Department until I was replaced, in November 1972, by Michael Havers QC, Member for Wimbledon. During my partnership with Peter, I developed an immense respect for his integrity, his judgment and his courage. After leaving office in 1975, he returned to eleven years' private practice at the Bar and served for a time as chairman and president of the profession. Sadly, Margaret could never bring herself to recognize how well qualified he was to serve as Britain's first Roman Catholic Lord Chancellor. Even today there is no one to whom I should more confidently turn for wise counsel than Peter Rawlinson.

Drafting the Industrial Relations Bill

But I was to spend almost more of my first two years in the company of Robert Carr, Secretary of State for Employment, than with Peter Rawlinson. Robert was a gentle, thoughtful man, who had spent his first five years in the Commons as Anthony Eden's PPS. A scientist by training, his experience in industry fitted him well for this job. I enjoyed working with him, and was given an office in his department at St

James's Square. Stephen Abbott was there too, as a special adviser. Our senior civil servant partner, the under secretary in charge of the 'Bill team', was John Burgh. He had held much the same post during Barbara Castle's preparation and introduction of her own proposals, *In Place of Strife*, and had previously been her principal private secretary.* Contrary to subsequent mythology, there was no huge or lasting gulf between incoming doctrinaire Tory 'hawks' and resident Ministry of Labour 'doves'. Robert Carr, when he first embarked upon this topic, had been, if anything, a super-dove. Officials had probably started from that premise as well. But most had by now been ranged alongside Harold Wilson and Barbara Castle through the long 'Battle of Downing Street'; this was Peter Jenkins' title for his book[1] about Wilson's long struggle to 'get your tanks off my lawn, Hughie' (Hugh Scanlon, then general secretary of the powerful Engineering Union, AUEW). Once, quite early in our work together, Robert Carr asked his permanent secretary, Sir Denis Barnes, 'Are you a hawk or a dove on this one, Denis?' The reply was memorable: 'I'm not a hawk, I'm an eagle, Secretary of State.' So we were all in this together – two teams of experts (of different kinds), who had spent some years studying the subject and had come to similar strategic conclusions. I suspect that Bernard Ingham, whom I met then for the first time in the Department of Employment's Press Office, had been on much the same learning curve. He was well focused, forthright – and unobtrusive. Even the tactical and technical problems that remained were largely common ground, though often very difficult.

Many commentators, looking back years later, wonder why and how we made the choice between a softly-softly, step-by-step approach and the comprehensive package with which we actually went ahead. There were, I think, three reasons. First, we had a great sense of urgency: a key problem on our predecessors' agenda could not be allowed to wait. Second, if even Labour had failed, by sweet reason between comrades, to achieve a compromise or phased approach, how could we hope to do better? But what we could do – and this was our third answer – was to ensure a firm and balanced approach. This was the essential, upon which Robert Carr insisted. We had to have a case that could be seen as

---

* On one occasion during our work on the Bill, John excused himself because he had an important lunch date with a lady guest. A day or two later, I realized that it had been Barbara Castle's birthday. For a moment or two at least, I felt as though Burgh was behaving like a wayward paramour, returning to a former love. I soon got over the shock.

reasonable by any fair-minded observer on the other side. We were aiming not to 'outlaw' the unions, still less to 'clobber' them, but to offer them a responsible role in a modern system of industrial relations.

So we produced a consultative document on 5 October 1970, just ahead of our party conference. It was based on eight principles, which were, said Robert Carr, 'non-negotiable'. In our view, they really did offer a balanced package. Details we were certainly prepared to discuss. The trade union movement, led by Victor Feather, argued that they had to reject such an 'uncompromising' approach. The reason for the mindless opposition that followed was simpler than that. Ted Heath's biographer puts it very clearly: 'Jones and Scanlon, leaders respectively of the TGWU and AUEW, were determined to exert again the political muscle that had humbled Wilson and Barbara Castle, to inflict a similar defeat on Heath and Carr.'[2] From then on, it is clear in retrospect, the battle lines were drawn – at least for the rest of that Parliament.

There was, even so, another card that we had hoped to play: simplicity. People must, we had said, be able to understand our new law. To that end I had scoured the world for attractively simple precedents in plain English. I had, with expert help, produced a complete redraft of an illustrative part of Barbara Castle's Bill. It was our hope, I said, in a note prepared for that very special priesthood, the parliamentary draughtsmen, that 'everyone concerned with the Bill will share our desire to make "law with a human face"'. So, proudly, Robert Carr and I presented our 'plain English' drafts to the then senior parliamentary counsel, Sir John Fiennes. But they never got beyond him. The idea of accepting some external input was too revolutionary to be tolerable. There was only one man in the office who could tackle our problem – and he had provided all the earlier material on the same topic. If we wanted our Bill quickly – and we did – then we had to have it his way, or not at all. Robert Carr and I were furious, but in truth unreasonable. We had a case, of course, but not one that could be achieved on such a timescale – least of all by an office that was grossly understaffed and overworked. It still is. Even as Leader of the House, almost twenty years later, I failed to make any serious impact on this problem. Only the most determined government will be able to secure change in this most conservative, conscientious and neglected Whitehall cranny.

Enactment

So the Bill, as published on 3 December 1970, was for me a particular disappointment. It was a most complex piece of legislation. It was going to be hard to sell, in Parliament as well as to the trade union movement. Its value as a foundation for the 'law with a human face', for which we yearned, was sharply reduced. We settled down for the long parliamentary battle ahead. Second reading was on 14 and 15 December.* Robert Carr and Ted Heath made the two opening speeches. I had the doubtful privilege of winding up on the second day. It was the first of many tumultuous occasions to come on this Bill, and the most daunting. It was only the third speech I had made since my return to the House in June. Between 18 January and 24 February 1971, Robert Carr and I spent over a hundred hours on the front bench alone together. No other post-war programme Bill had taken so long.

During those long hours the House of Commons took many different forms. At one moment it was like a salon or a seminar, with a dozen or so real experts earnestly engaged in a common search for the right answer. Minutes later, both sides of the House had filled with partisans who knew nothing of the arguments and were waiting only to vote. The salon had been turned into a noisy arena. The speech I was making had to transform itself in mid-flight. At the end of the report stage, MPs had to vote in sixty-three consecutive divisions, over more than eleven hours. Our parliamentary colleagues were much more tolerant than we deserved. For it would have been possible – as I later discovered – to draft the so-called guillotine motion so as to dispose of all the outstanding amendments in one or two compound votes. But we weren't then as skilled in confrontational politics as we were later obliged to become. One aspect of this particular confrontation had struck me as particularly sad. That was the uncompromising bitterness with which Barbara Castle opposed every aspect of our Bill. The problems we were facing were exactly the same as those that she had tried to tackle. So too were many of the solutions. How I wished then that she could have seen her way to joining us in the task of shaping

* The second reading is a general debate on the merits of the Bill (the first reading is a formality). The Bill then goes either to a standing committee or to a committee of the whole House for detailed scrutiny. There follows the report stage, a less detailed examination taken on the floor of the House. After a third reading, the Bill goes to the House of Lords, where the same procedure is followed.

them! But our reaction to her own earlier efforts might be seen as equally unconstructive.*

It was at about that time that we had a particularly disagreeable foretaste of the worst kind of violence, from a self-styled anarchist group calling itself the Angry Brigade. They bombed the home of the Employment Secretary, Robert Carr, and my name was found to be on their hit list. We received a number of telephone threats, and a twenty-four-hour police guard was mounted on our home. It is surprising how quickly such things become part of the routine. When I arrived home early one evening, Amanda spoke up brightly, 'Oh, by the way, Daddy, I took another threatening phone call for you this afternoon.' It was a strange world in which our children were having to grow up. The hazards have not grown any less since then.

The Industrial Relations Act, as it finally became, received the royal assent on 5 August 1971. The National Industrial Relations Court and the (wholly benign) unfair dismissals provisions of the Act came into force on 1 January 1972, and most of the rest within the next two or three months. During the first half of that year there were two major, well-publicized flurries of litigation. Then, according to much subsequent political folklore, the Act became a dead letter – never to be resurrected. Worse than that, the Act was seen by many as the cause of the deadlock with the miners which provoked the general election of 28 February 1974 and our consequent defeat. This last was certainly not the case. The miners' strike was about incomes policy and nothing else. It was a situation for which the Act was not designed and in which it was never invoked.

Beyond doubt, however, the two major tests of the legislation did the Act's reputation great harm. The first arose in face of a threatened national railway work-to-rule, in April 1972. Maurice Macmillan had just taken over from Robert Carr as Employment Secretary. The reshuffle had been made necessary by Willie Whitelaw's departure to become the first Secretary of State for Northern Ireland. Macmillan (intelligent, engaging and hesitant, he had never really escaped from his father's shadow) decided, after taking my advice, to seek a cooling-off order from the NIRC. I appeared on his behalf in the first major case before the Court. After a couple of days' argument we secured our order, for a fourteen-day period. Rather than risk the large fines that could be imposed, the rail unions, after some havering, complied with

* See p. 47 above.

that ruling. So far, so good. But at the end of the fourteen days there was still no sign of a settlement. So we resorted – mistakenly, as should have been clear at the time – to the second measure provided for under this part of the Act. We applied for and obtained an order for a compulsory union members' ballot on the offer that was already on the table. The result was a decisive three-to-one vote in favour of resumed industrial action. The strike was eventually settled at a modestly higher figure. But the damage was done. The unions were seen, so it was thought, to have 'made a mockery of the Act'.

The two remedies which we had sought consecutively were not in fact examples of unique Conservative folly. Barbara Castle, following American precedent, had provided for very similar remedies. Our mistake had been not in our design but in our use of them. We were wrong to believe that we had to use them both, in quick-fire succession in the same dispute. I believe that, if Robert Carr had still been at St James's Square, his temperament and experience would have equipped him better than either Macmillan or me to appreciate that point.

The second mishap arose from a long-festering dispute between dockers and road hauliers about containerization in the port industry. Dockers at several ports had started blacking the container lorries. On 23 March 1972 the NIRC, under its first chairman, Sir John Donaldson, declared this to be an 'unfair industrial practice'. The Court ordered a group of Liverpool dockers to desist. The dockers' union, the TGWU, following TUC policy, at first refused to recognize, still less to obey, the Court. But when it was fined £55,000 and faced the sequestration of all its assets, the TGWU obtained TUC permission to change tack. The fine was paid. The new Court was recognized. And the union appealed to the Court of Appeal. To our astonishment (and dismay) Lord Denning, Master of the Rolls, sitting with two colleagues, quashed the NIRC order. The TGWU, they ruled, was not responsible for the actions of its officials who were organizing the blacking.

This ruling undermined the whole rationale of the Act. For Robert Carr and I had gone as far as we could to ensure that in such situations it was the Union and not the individual member who should be penalized. The case proceeded speedily to the House of Lords. Within six weeks the Court of Appeal's ruling was reversed. Our own intended view of the law was restored. But by then much more serious damage had been done. For, during the interval while Denning's mistaken view of the law prevailed, the NIRC in similar cases (which were continuing to come before it) had no option but to impose penalties on individual trade unionists. Within a few days three London dockers were for this reason sent to prison by the NIRC.

They had thus achieved the martyrdom that they so keenly desired. Sympathy action and supportive demonstrations multiplied. The Act was, understandably, blamed. The crisis was abated by unconventional action. A little-known governmental agency, the Official Solicitor, applied to the Court of Appeal on the dockers' behalf. Lord Denning and his colleagues ordered the men's release. The theoretical justification was that the NIRC had acted upon insufficient evidence. So the Act was sidestepped, set aside even, as a result of Lord Denning's latest intervention. Theoretically, this arose only from an application by counsel for the TGWU, Peter Pain QC (later Mr Justice Pain). The union's advisers and Lord Denning had no doubt about the intended purpose of the intervention. But, as became apparent afterwards, this application was made only after Lord Denning had himself suggested it.

Whatever the precise sequence of events, it is clear that Lord Denning and his colleagues had realized the consequences of their original error. Parliament, at our bidding, had intended liability for unfair industrial action to fall not upon the individual trade unionists but upon the funds of these giant organizations, which had since 1906 been immune from liability. That was the central mischief at which the Act was directed. And the Court of Appeal, by setting that aside, for six fatal weeks until the Lords restored the position, had torpedoed the fragile vessel, which Robert Carr, Stephen Abbott and I had so carefully designed. It was a remarkable twist of history. Lord Denning had, for many years, been giving judgments that were skilfully designed – so far as judge-made law could achieve it – to curb the excessive power of trade unions. Why then this tragic aberration? I suspect that he and his Appeal Court colleagues were, unconsciously perhaps, as wary as trade unionists of the novelty that was the National Industrial Relations Court. They felt the need to demonstrate in some way that, no less than the rest of the High Court, it was subject to their surveillance. There may even have been a touch of jealousy at the attention that was being paid to the crisp clarity of Mr Justice Donaldson's written judgments. Judicial prose of a quality to command the front page of the tabloid press had previously been Lord Denning's virtual monopoly.

However that may be, the credibility of the Act had been gravely damaged. Much has since been written about how all the difference would have been made by this or that change in our approach. A different approach to registration, for example? But, unlike the Castle proposals, our scheme did not depend on this. It was only the unions that suffered from non-registration. Using the ordinary courts instead of the NIRC? But the unions could have objected as much to a judge 'in wig and red dressing-gown' (as they had often put it) as in a lounge suit. And so on. Whichever way we had designed our system, some element of struggle or confrontation was inescapable. We had always expected that. And we expected the passage of time to be our best ally. A second Conservative election victory would have enabled us to make some adjustments, perhaps largely symbolic, and the system would have grown into place. Even as it was, much of our structure did survive Michael Foot's flamboyant 'repeal' of 'the Act' after Labour's 1974 election victory. The Employment Appeal Tribunal – in place of our NIRC – and the whole fabric of unfair-dismissal law, which it still oversees, survived unchanged. For much of our Bill was indeed re-enacted verbatim, at Michael Foot's bidding, albeit under a different name. We had fought the first battle – the battle which Jim Callaghan had twice caused Labour to dodge. We had opened the way for the step-by-step approach of Jim Prior and Norman Tebbit. 'The earlier Act', says John Campbell, expressing one view, 'can be seen as a necessary precursor of the later ones.'[3] For Robert Carr and myself the repeal of our Act was indeed a traumatic experience. Years of work, it seemed, were being cast away – and work that would have succeeded in its aim had it been allowed to survive. Today, I find it easier to take a more philosophic view. We *had* helped to fashion a stepping stone for history.

European Communities Bill

There was one other great enterprise that I, as Solicitor, helped to launch. One morning in April 1971 I was sitting alone in my huge room in the Royal Courts of Justice. The Industrial Relations Bill had just about cleared the House of Commons. Peter Rawlinson was preparing himself for total immersion in Ulster's affairs. And in walked Jake Davies, one of our senior legal assistants. He and I had for years eaten at the same Middle Temple lunch table,* together with other contemporaries like Paddy Mayhew and Stephen Tumim. He was carrying a huge pile of papers. 'Good God, Jake,' I exclaimed, 'what on

* Davies was tragically killed three years later in a Turkish airliner that crashed *en route* from Paris to London.

earth is that?' 'Solicitor,' he said (Jake was always emphatic about formality), 'they are the papers for the most important Opinion you'll ever have to give in your life: how to provide for our entry into the Common Market.'

This was to be my principal task for the next twelve months. It was another commitment for which I had been preparing myself, half consciously, for many years. My initially pro-European instinct had been consolidated by the impact of the 1956 Suez débâcle. If Britain was ever, in Dean Acheson's cruel phrase, to find a role for herself (Britain, Acheson had said in 1956, had lost an empire but still not found a role), I became convinced that would have to be in Europe. So when Harold Macmillan in 1961 proclaimed his government's intention to apply for membership of the Community, I was strongly in support. The far-sighted arguments set out in the frankly political pamphlet that Macmillan himself produced, just ahead of the Llandudno party conference in 1962, went to the heart of the matter: 'One thing is certain. As a member of the Community, Britain would have a strong voice in deciding the nature and the timing of political unity. By remaining outside, we would be faced with a political solution in Europe which ran counter to our views and interests, but which we would do nothing to influence.'[4]

We supported this decision in *Crossbow*. I had arranged to publicize there in July 1962 one of the earliest plain-language texts on the legal consequences of this move. This was a supplement by Dennis Thompson entitled *The Rome Treaty and the Law*. It was significantly more explicit than some official publications about the 'new and revolutionary' legal implications of the change. 'The Community', said Thompson, 'has power to make laws which are binding on the citizens of the member states.' So I was more than half able to understand the papers that Jake Davies placed in front of me.

I had plenty of time to consider them. The entry negotiations had still not been concluded. On 23 June 1971, however, Geoffrey Rippon, who had been conducting these, returned in triumph from Luxembourg. His style had struck exactly the right balance between lawyerly small print and politically broad brush. A White Paper outlining the terms was rushed out on 7 July. A week later Heath received a tumultuously favourable reception when he spoke at a special meeting on Europe of the Conservative Central Council. There followed a five-day Commons debate, to 'take note' of the White Paper. At the Brighton party conference, on 13 October 1971, Enoch Powell made one of his many impassioned pleas against accession. But Ted Heath and the Foreign

Secretary Alec Home carried the day by the huge majority of 2474 to 324 (most unusually for a Tory conference, Ted Heath had insisted on a full card vote). There remained the crucial parliamentary vote on the principle of the White Paper. Only at the last moment did Heath accept the advice of his Chief Whip, Francis Pym, in favour of a free vote on the Conservative side. This was the key to success. It made it much easier for Labour pro-marketeers to defy their own Whips and vote in support of entry. On 28 October the six-day debate was wound up by Jim Callaghan and by the Prime Minister himself. Heath was able to announce that the House of Lords had just voted in favour of entry by 451 votes to 58. And the Commons delivered a majority of 112: Ayes 356, Noes 244. Thirty-nine Tories had voted against and sixty-nine Labour pro-marketeers in favour, with twenty more abstaining.

Thus far I had taken virtually no public part in the proceedings. My work on the European Communities Bill had all been off-stage. I was now based in a new 'second home' in the Cabinet Office in Whitehall. Geoffrey Rippon was the Cabinet Minister with overall responsibility for the accession arrangements. But he was still engaged on many loose negotiating ends. So I was effectively in charge of work on the Bill, in very close partnership with senior parliamentary counsel, Sir John Fiennes. The constitutional issues with which we were grappling were frighteningly fundamental. Some of the effects had been described in our *Crossbow* supplement of nine years before – in particular, the concept of directly applicable Community law. This was the power of Community institutions 'to give decisions in the future which are immediately binding on all persons who are within the jurisdiction of the member states'. One September weekend I re-read all Enoch Powell's arguments against the legitimacy of the entire exercise. Did we, I asked myself, really have the authority of the British people to effect such a change? Had we been sufficiently candid about the implications? In the end I concluded that the technical aspects had indeed been explained, in documents beginning with those published by the Wilson government in 1967. The electorate *had* endorsed the principle of membership. The final crucial stage could properly be entrusted to Parliament itself. For the very sovereignty of Parliament entitled that body to manage or deploy that sovereignty, on behalf of the British people, in partnership with other nations on such terms as Parliament itself might decide.

The question still remained how exactly that was to be done. This is no place to discuss the fascinating technicalities. Speculation ranged between the possible need for a Bill of a thousand clauses and the chance that we should achieve all that was necessary in a one-clause conjuring trick. In the end, John Fiennes and I achieved something of a *coup de théâtre*, by producing a Bill of just twelve clauses and four schedules, all in a mere thirty-seven pages. In retrospect, that was the easy part. It was the parliamentary handling that was to test us more severely. Labour were (officially) determined to fight the Bill line by line. And we still had up to three dozen dissidents on our own side. Led by men of tenacious integrity, like Enoch Powell, Neil Marten, Derek Walker-Smith and John Biffen, they were never to let us off the hook. But they always played within the rules. Unlike their heirs of the 1990s, the Maastricht rebels, they never voted against their own government on procedural questions. Honourable friends were not transformed into personal enemies.

The second-reading debate (16–19 February) was the first hurdle. This brought me to the heart of the parliamentary battle, for I had to open the second day's debate, speaking immediately after Harold Wilson himself. He purported to denounce the way in which I had achieved by legal guile 'the imposition – literally at a stroke – of an alien system of law', the whole of the Code Napoléon. I retorted that he had been ready, if only his own accession negotiations had succeeded, to proceed in exactly the same way. And so he would be on some future occasion if ever – God forbid! – it fell to him to resume the case in our place. It was only in the present context, at the bidding of a Tory Prime Minister, that he was unprepared to do so. 'The Right Hon. gentleman himself', I said, 'acts on a classic Bonapartean text: "Not tonight, Josephine."'

When Ted Heath wound up for the government on the third evening, he made it clear that the vote was a matter of confidence. It was the first really important parliamentary occasion in which I had been directly engaged. The Industrial Relations Bill had often been tough but never nailbiting. The Strangers' and Peers' Galleries were packed as I had never seen them before. I sat on the front bench, awaiting the return of the Tellers: 'Ayes, 309. Noes, 301.' A majority of just eight votes. It was enough. Fifteen Tories had voted against us, five more had abstained. That night, and on many others, we had reason to be grateful for the support of five Liberals and for the regular abstention of at least as many Labour Members.

For a second parliamentary year, I was committed to a long war of attrition. Geoffrey Rippon and I were on parade in the Commons for debates on the Treaty and the Bill for a total of 325 hours, spread over fifty-three days. I had to make no fewer than ninety-one speeches. There were 104 divisions, and we won every one of them. Our majority once fell as low as four, when several on our own side were late getting back from a party at Duncan Sandys' house. Several times I had to speak at inordinate length, in order to spin out the debate long enough for our modest majority to return to the House. In all these tribulations I was cheerfully and efficiently sustained by two successive parliamentary private secretaries, first Kenneth Clarke and then Peter Rees: Peter, a contemporary of mine who had taken Silk in 1969, was a tax expert and Treasury minister in the making. He took over from Kenneth when he went to the Whips Office in 1972: this appointment, only two years after his arrival in Parliament, was an early recognition of Kenneth's already relaxed but energetic political potential.

Our success in getting the Bill through the Commons committee stage without defeat or amendment meant that there was no report stage.* By now we had spotted a number of points on which – so our experts advised – the Bill needed to be tidied up by amendment. We knew that the coming debates in the Lords would be relaxed. So it would normally have been a straightforward matter to achieve such changes in the Upper House. But this time there was a real problem. For every amendment carried in the Lords would later require fresh and separate consideration in the Commons. That opened up grave new risks of government defeat. Could we not, asked Ted, manage without the amendments? I was invited to attend Cabinet to support Geoffrey Rippon. If we were to avoid the risk of later problems in the courts, we argued, we had to have the amendments. Ted Heath and the rest of the Cabinet slapped us down. So the Bill went through as it was. And not one of the threatened legal disasters has ever happened. It was a useful lesson. One should not allow the best to be the enemy of the good. Sir John Fiennes deserves the lion's share of the credit for the Bill. He was as pleased as I was with the final verdict of one august critic. J. D. B. Mitchell, Professor of Community Law at Edinburgh University, described the Bill as 'an artistic piece of legislation, which ingeniously achieves the desired results and avoids betraying any of the essential characteristics of Community law'.[5] The lawyer's reassuring verdict marked the end of a fascinating chapter. But for the politician and constitutionalist it was indeed the start of a brand-new volume of British history.

* See footnote on p. 61 above.

CHAPTER SIX

INTO THE CABINET

Minister for Trade and Consumer Affairs

On Guy Fawkes' Day 1972, my life in the Heath government underwent dramatic change. I had been speaking at the now defunct Conservative College, at Swinton in Yorkshire. Ted rang me there and invited me to join his Cabinet. He wanted me to become Minister for Trade and Consumer Affairs, a second Cabinet minister in the Department of Trade and Industry. The Secretary of State, Peter Walker, had been offered by Ted a choice between myself and Margaret Thatcher. History might in several ways have been different if Peter's choice had gone the other way – and if Margaret had been ready to accept the assignment.

At the time I knew nothing of this – nor anything about the job I was being asked to do. But that hardly mattered, given the prospect of actually entering the Cabinet. Astonishingly, I was moving ahead of many contemporaries, who had sweated through the years of parliamentary opposition while I was still outside. The final irony was that it was Peter Walker under whom I was to serve. For years past we had been undeclared rivals. If I was the archetypal Bow Grouper, Peter was my Young Conservative opposite number. He was destined to remain a most effective ministerial partner for years to come.

My first job with him, as it transpired, was to assume almost dictatorial control over prices throughout the nation's economy. For on the following day, Monday 6 November, Ted Heath announced to Parliament the commencement of a ninety-day 'freeze' on pay and prices, rents and dividends. The Minister of Consumer Affairs was also to be known – to Ted Heath at least – as the 'Minister for keeping down prices'.

That was to be the more far-reaching and more thankless part of my new job. The more entertaining and approachable assignment was as

Britain's first Minister of Consumer Affairs. I was to derive much pleasure and job-satisfaction from that role. I had been a member of the Consumers' Association since its inception in 1957. A Bow Group pamphlet[1] of the same date had given strong backing – on the strength of my legal advice – to the right of such an organization to offer critical public comment on the quality of goods and services. My economic instincts were not offended by the idea of sensible intervention on behalf of the consumer.

Competitive markets, access to information and freedom from mal-practice were all important features of a properly functioning market economy. And there were many parts of the state sector where the need for consumer protection was even more acute than it was in the market place. The definition of a 'customer', I told the National Council of Social Service in December 1972, should be quite simply 'a citizen who requires goods or services'. Our 'clients, patients, cases', I said, are 'essentially no different in their needs and desires, in terms of service, from the customers of shops and garages'. I was in effect advocating an early version of the Citizen's Charter. And through the passage of the Fair Trading Bill – a measure that had been under preparation for some months – we increased the scope and effectiveness of our competition law. The Office of Fair Trading (as well as the abortive Consumer Protection Advisory Committee) was set up under this Act. We were lucky to secure the services of John Methven as the first director general. Gordon Borrie was a worthy successor. The Stock Exchange and the legal and accountancy professions were for the first time opened up to scrutiny by the competition authorities. We began making our way towards the Big Bang and the opening up of London's financial markets.

One of the responsibilities which I took on as Minister for Consumer Affairs was the metrication programme, launched some years before by our Labour predecessors. I was glad to have Cabinet backing, including that of the Secretary of State of Education, Margaret Thatcher, for the view that our schools should henceforward teach our children in metric rather than imperial measures. It is a tragedy that decades later we were the only Commonwealth country not to have completed the change-over many years before.

As Britain's first Minister for Consumer Affairs, I became, on 6 July 1973, the first ever Cabinet Minister to take part in that great British institution, the Jimmy Young programme. Jimmy was then, as for years to come, one of the most professional of British broadcasters. In later years, as Chancellor of the Exchequer, I regarded my post-Budget appearance on his programme as one of the most important. It was as champion of the consumer of broadcasting services that I witnessed a revealing cameo of life in Ted Heath's Number 10. In November 1972 the Prime Minister had called together a small group of Ministers to consider who should be the next chairman of the BBC. Others present included Tony Barber, Willie Whitelaw and Margaret Thatcher – educationalists as well as consumers had an interest in broadcasting policy. I put forward the name of Andrew Shonfield, independent-minded economics editor of the *Observer* and author of a powerful dissent from the report of the Donovan Commission (on trade unions). 'I think not,' said Ted, 'he's got much too high an opinion of himself.' 'But most men *do*, Prime Minister!' said Margaret, to general mirth and my surprise. The exchange of glances between Margaret and Ted did not suggest the blossoming of a beautiful friendship.

But the relaxed informality of the occasion was not untypical of the atmosphere in the Heath government. The Prime Minister was always the dominant figure, but the Cabinet remained essentially a group of friends as well as colleagues. Most of us felt free from day to day and week to week to get on with our own job. It is remarkable in retrospect how much independence I enjoyed – as a non-Cabinet minister – to handle such central issues as the industrial relations and European Community legislation. Very seldom did I need to go beyond my immediate ministerial leader, Robert Carr or Geoffrey Rippon, for the clearance of any decision. Really important issues went to Downing Street. Only very occasionally did the unimportant ones reach the Cabinet room. I remember one such case. No less than three times, we discussed the new site for an artillery range that had to be moved if London's third airport was to go to Maplin on the Essex marshes. The Scottish and Welsh Secretaries of State rejected the range. So did the Environment Secretary on behalf of Dorset, the English alternative. The Chancellor of the Exchequer never, that I can recall, protested at the cost of keeping three alternative sites available, apparently in perpetuity. The issue never was decided. And Maplin never did get built. So perhaps all was for the best. I daresay the Ministry of Defence are still hanging on to the sites – all four of them. But this was not a typical case!

Our discussions rarely, if ever, leaked. This was another contrast with life in the 1980s. Leaks from the Heath government were so exceptional that I can think of no example. This was, I think, as much a cause as a consequence of confidence between colleagues. We were thus working in an atmosphere in which a body like the Think-Tank could operate successfully. This Central Policy Review Staff (to give it its proper name) was one of Ted Heath's most successful innovations. Lord (Victor) Rothschild, wealthy, independent-minded and intellectual, was its first head. His colleagues included people like the young William Waldegrave, Peter Carey, later to become permanent secretary at the Department of Trade and Industry (DTI), and Adam Ridley, later one of my most trusted special advisers at the Treasury.

I recall only one instance of trouble between the Tank and the Heath government. The cause wasn't a leak but an accidental public row. Heath was due (on 24 September 1973) to make a bullish speech about the British economy. On that same day, by chance, Victor Rothschild told a gathering of research scientists in Wiltshire that, if Britain did not improve her economic performance, she would soon become a minor rather than a major country. The two points of view were by no means incompatible. But Rothschild's speech stole all the headlines, and Heath was furious. The occasion sticks in my mind because, just one day before, I had made Rothschild's very point to a Rotarian conference in Scarborough. On our present rate of growth, I said, by the 1990s 'we shall have less wealth per head of the population, not merely than other members of the European Community, but than the Spaniards or the Portugese'. The Solicitor General's speech was less prominently reported than Lord Rothschild's. And I survived to make a very similar diagnosis in the opening paragraphs of my first Budget speech in June 1979.

As it was, the Heath Cabinet was able, for example, to spend a full day at Chequers, considering a CPRS presentation of alternative econ-omic scenarios – some deeply gloomy – without seeing them later splashed all over the newspapers. Margaret Thatcher and her colleagues were never able to do the same. Only ten short years later, we had come to feel that we were living in a different, leak-driven world. And the process of open thinking – even within government, let alone between government and people – had been enormously, and damagingly, retarded. If the cause of open government is to prosper, then the cause of secure confidentiality within government has to prosper as well. A truly plural democratic society cannot hope to survive without a renewal of confidence and trust between government and media.

There were at least two areas of policy where some of Ted Heath's colleagues may have felt they were less in his confidence than they ought to have been. Industrial policy came first. I was only on the fringes of this debate. It led to the production, in April 1971, of the Industry Bill, with its substantial provisions for government support to ailing businesses and depressed regions. The Bill itself was never directly within my ken, but I can recall the atmosphere in which its last stages were finally carried through the Commons. A handful of our own back-benchers, led by John Biffen and Jock Bruce-Gardyne, had been opposing the Bill. In order to outflank them the report stage (on the floor of the House) had been fixed for a Friday when they were expected to be away. They were not. And the 'payroll vote' (ministers and PPSs) were whipped to see the Bill through. I remember three very truculent ministers – all out of sympathy with the Bill – consoling each other over a picnic supper in John Peyton's room at the House. Peyton was then Minister of Transport. His two colleagues were John Eden, Minister of Posts – and the Solicitor General.

I was more directly, though only intermittently, involved in this unhappy field of industrial policy when as Solicitor I advised the DTI and Number 10 – sometimes even the House of Commons – on the legal handling of the many 'lame ducks' that characterized the period. On one occasion I found myself suddenly summoned to the Commons at about 8.30 one evening in February 1971 to make a statement about the legal implications of the impending 'rescue' of Rolls-Royce. This case was being handled in Washington by the Attorney General, Peter Rawlinson. Peter's absence made it necessary for the Solicitor to face the Commons – in all my ignorance. It is remarkable that the essentially political step of taking control of the bankrupt Rolls-Royce company was being handled not by any departmental minister as an act of policy but by the Law Officers as a purely legal consequence of misfortune.

It was in much the same way that I became more directly involved with Upper Clyde Shipbuilders. I was in the office of John Davies, then Secretary of State for Trade and Industry, when he first accepted, by telephone, a government commitment to pay one week's wages for that bankrupt company's workforce. It is hard now to recall the almost panic-driven atmosphere in which this kind of liability was being incurred, in the vain struggle to keep unemployment below the menacing total of one million. That figure was reached on 20 January 1972. Those of us who later became critics of Heath government policies, but who went along with them at the time, do well to remember the climate of those days. We were living then in an era whose fears, hopes and prejudices had been shaped in an earlier generation. We were all of us on the same learning curve, and we were not all learning at the same speed.

Price Controller

For how else did I find myself, on 6 November 1972, assuming responsibility as the nation's comprehensive price controller? Inflation in the third quarter of that year had fallen to 6.5 per cent, compared with 10 per cent a year earlier. But the government's informal pay policy, known as 'N−1' (N minus one: each pay settlement to be 1 per cent lower than the preceding one), had that spring been savaged by miners and railworkers alike, who won 27 and 16 per cent respectively. Ted Heath had not been able, even after months of effort, to secure agreement with the TUC on any kind of voluntary approach. There was mounting public and press clamour for a statutory pay and prices policy. At the 1972 party conference in Blackpool, the main economic motion pressed the case for success against inflation. It was proposed, on behalf of his pensioner-constituents, by Eastbourne's recently adopted Tory candidate, Ian Gow. In the course of the debate Angus Maude, the influential right-wing Member for Stratford-upon-Avon, was surprised to hear himself saying that we needed to introduce a prices and incomes policy. And when Ted Heath announced just that in the Commons on 6 November it received an almost universal welcome.

I don't think it was just the prospect of Cabinet membership, beginning that very day, that dulled my reaction to the scattered voices of dissent: in the Commons Enoch Powell and a few of my other old friends, in the public prints a Professor Alan Walters (whom I did not know) and finally a small but growing chorus from the Institute of Economic Affairs. For the die was now cast, with support from the parliamentary party and the entire Cabinet. Keith Joseph, still at Social Services, and Margaret Thatcher, still at Education, did not dissent. But neither of them ever became as directly concerned as I was to be with the economic policy of the Heath government. (I used to wonder afterwards what Iain Macleod would have said to all this. Either way, we greatly missed the sound of his voice on our side.)

Enoch Powell alone voted against the Counter-Inflation (Temporary Provisions) Bill that had then to be introduced. John Biffen, Jock Bruce-Gardyne and Neil Marten abstained. Two statutory agencies were established to impose and manage the necessary controls: the Price Commission and the Pay Board. I was mainly concerned with the first. Some idea of the climate of opinion can be divined from the fact that Sir Arthur Cockfield was happy to accept the chairmanship of the Price

Commission. He was as single-minded there as he had been, twenty-one years before, as a Commissioner for Inland Revenue. Thirteen years later, he was likewise the driving force behind Jacques Delors' Single Market programme. I was glad to be relieved of direct ministerial responsibility for enforcing a freeze on all prices. My office had been much dismayed, during the ninety-day freeze, by news that the Vicar of Trumpington had doubled the charge for brass-rubbing in his church. Was I really to secure, and to deliver by special despatch-rider, an order-in-council requiring the Vicar to restore his original prices? I had a better idea. Tony Nieduszynski, my private secretary, was a former theological student. I asked him to phone the priest: could he perhaps give as much heed to the wishes of the Lords Temporal as he would ordinarily to those of the Lord Spiritual? The Vicar was happy to oblige. On that occasion at least the will of Parliament prevailed. But even in Arthur Cockfield's capable hands the regime's credibility and effectiveness gradually ebbed away.

Ted Heath presided over endlessly patient Chequers meetings to plan our moves from Stage One to Stage Two to Stage Three of our counter-inflation policy. I remember one long afternoon session in the Long Gallery of the great house. Growing bold, I started to argue in favour of a much less regulated approach. Was it not, I asked, 'more consistent with our original market-based philosophy'? When Ted Heath came, some time later, to reply, he pragmatically (and sharply) brushed aside 'the philosophic anxieties' of the 'Minister for keeping down prices'.

But it was over pay that our real problems arose. Even the Pay Code, which we had to produce, was the subject of 'philosophic consideration' on my part. For in 1955 the Bow Group had produced a pamphlet, *National Wages Policy*, which had envisaged the use of some kind of agency in the arbitrament of contentious pay claims. The feudal barons of the labour market, the pamphlet's author James Driscoll argued, could and should be persuaded to prefer some form of 'alternative dispute resolution' to crude industrial conflict. (Driscoll was wise enough too to argue the need for this to take place in a climate of firm monetary restraint.) It was this kind of discretionary system that I hoped we might be able to design. But it was not to be. The lawyers insisted that a pay board administering a pay code could be allowed no discretion whatsoever. It was the small print, and only that, which had to prevail. This unflinchingly rigid approach led us in the end to the 1973–4 miners' strike, the three-day week and the general election débâcle of February 1974.

'Who Rules Britain?'

The process was made the more inevitable by other decisions, which seemed sensible enough at the time. The small group of ministers concerned with the counter-inflation policy – Prime Minister, Chancellor of the Exchequer, Employment Secretary (still then Maurice Macmillan) and myself – were engaged in an endless series of tripartite talks with the TUC and the CBI. This meant that I quite often attended at National Economic Development Council (NEDC) meetings in place of my Secretary of State, Peter Walker. There was plenty for him to do elsewhere. I learned from my exposure on these occasions just how easy it was for government, almost inadvertently, to surrender control of policy to such non-elected bodies. But I learned too the positive value – provided government kept the initiative – of being able to exchange views about policy with some of the main actors in the economy. 'Democracy', A. J. Balfour used to say, 'is government by explanation.' This is why I later cherished a good deal more patience for NEDC than some of my more theoretically purist colleagues. For Margaret Thatcher, NEDC always remained a 'talking-shop', a place for more of what she called 'ram-shammy'. Our problem in those early days was not so much the talk itself as the extent to which we allowed ourselves to make damaging policy concessions.

In order, for example, to obtain the TUC's nominal 'assent' to our pay policy we accepted a number of other constraints. We maintained our commitment to a high-growth policy, despite the soaring dollar price of oil and other inflationary risks. 'This time,' Ted Heath declared to the September 1973 meeting of NEDC, 'we are determined to sail through the whirlpool.' Money-supply figures – previously little heeded – were increasingly being pressed upon us by worried critics. The growth rate of M3, said the critics, had risen from 10.4 per cent in 1970–1 to 28.1 per cent in 1972–3. Don't worry, I was instructed to say in the House (by a Treasury brief that I had far from properly mastered), the corresponding figures for an alternative measure, M1, have *fallen* from 16.5 to 7.8 per cent. (During my time as Chancellor, ten years later, the monetary roles were ironically reversed: in the early 1980s we in the Treasury were praying in aid the broader aggregates, notably sterling M3, and our critics were citing the narrower bases, M0 or M1.)*

---

* Gordon Pepper has attempted to reconcile all this in a later booklet, *Money, Credit and Inflation* (IEA, 1990). Even with the benefit of hindsight he does not find it easy.

The overriding political realities were unaffected. In October 1973 the Yom Kippur War renewed the conflict between Israel and her Arab neighbours. The price of oil to Britain had more than doubled (from $2.50 to $5 per barrel) since the beginning of the year. By January 1974 it had topped $11. And the confrontation with the miners, which had begun as a work-to-rule, was moving towards a complete stoppage. The 'three-day week' (with all its signals of economic stringency) was adding to the gloom, without enhancing the prospects of settlement. Yet the Coal Board, and so the government, had no room left for effective manoeuvre. For as virtually their opening offer the NCB had offered the absolute maximum allowed by the pay code. This 'limit bid' had failed to take the trick. We were all now left groping for an alternative way around our own government-imposed limit which did not allow our opponents to proclaim that Stage Three of our pay policy had been overthrown.

Inside government, and more widely in the party as a whole, the mood was growing in favour of an early election. 'Who rules Britain?' would be our rallying cry – though nobody was very clear just how the position would be changed, even by a decisive government victory. Peter Carrington and Jim Prior, party chairman and deputy chairman respectively, were the leading protagonists of an early election. They had support from the Chancellor, Tony Barber, who was now in no doubt about the need to rein back the boom which will always be linked with his name. He had been in many ways an imaginative and tax-reforming Chancellor; but it was as their manager and not their originator that he was responsible for the central economic policies of the Heath government. By now he well knew what stringent measures lay ahead. Willie Whitelaw and Francis Pym, former and present Northern Ireland Secretaries, led the argument on the other side, with support from Robert Carr. Timing was by now critical. A new electoral register was due to come into force on 15 February 1974. Conservative chances were thought to be much better ahead of that date. We were more efficient, it was said, at dealing with postal voters, whose importance increased with the age of the register. The last polling day that gave us that advantage was Thursday, 14 February. To achieve that date, a decision to dissolve Parliament would have to be taken not later than Thursday, 17 January.

A growing number of us in Cabinet, where I was still the most junior, began adding our weight to those in favour of an early poll. Ted Heath, very much contrary to most people's expectations, set in motion an elaborate procedure for consulting Cabinet colleagues about this question. 'This is not a question for Cabinet,' he said, 'but for me as Prime

Minister. But I am anxious to have your advice.' There was no great meeting. We went instead to see him in twos and threes in his study. I went with David Windlesham, another ex-chairman of the Bow Group, then Leader of the House of Lords and from 1989 Principal of Brasenose College, Oxford. We were both in favour of an early appeal to the country.

I was present at one other crucial moment in this indecisive saga, the NEDC meeting of 9 January 1974, with Tony Barber as usual in the chair. Sidney Greene, sincere and serious-minded leader of the National Union of Railwaymen, started to make an obviously considered statement to the meeting. Clearly he was doing so with the support of his four or five trade union colleagues. The TUC, he said, were prepared to regard the mining dispute as a special and distinctive case. If the government was willing to facilitate a settlement between the miners and the National Coal Board, other unions would refrain from using such a settlement as an argument in their own negotiations. We had received no advance warning of this *démarche*. But Greene took such care in the making of it that I had no doubt of its importance in their eyes. I scribbled a note to Tony Barber, sitting beside me, to the effect that we should take care to look as though we were at least ready to give some consideration to what the TUC had just suggested. His response was in the event rather less forthcoming than that. I do not recall it as an outright rejection, but certainly he wanted to avoid giving the impression that we were ready to be pushed. He talked to Ted Heath by telephone at the end of the meeting. Ted did not demur. I felt that the TUC had made a move which added to rather than diminished our difficulties. For whatever the precise terms of Tony's response, their offer was one that either side could still take up. It had served to buy them a little more time. And Ted Heath allowed it to do so. A week later, on 16 January, a special gathering of union general secretaries endorsed Greene's 'special case' offer. And a day later the early-election opportunity had vanished.

We did not realize then the significance of the missed opportunity – missed certainly from the point of view of the hawks, who wanted an early appeal to the country, but missed too, it could be argued, from the point of view of the doves as well. For suppose we had taken the TUC at their word, would not that have allowed us to test their good faith as it were to destruction? Possibly. I doubt if the situation would have been allowed to develop with that much clarity. But the moment passed. Barely three weeks later we were off to the electorate nonetheless, for a poll to be held on 28 February. All the last-minute manoeuvring had done nothing to avoid, but had managed only briefly to postpone, that contest.

Electoral Defeat

All elections leave behind them a taste that is flavoured by the result. I thought that February 1974 was a miserable contest. This was not just because of the unavoidable disasters: the Pay Board calculation that made it look as though the government had its miners' pay arithmetic all wrong; the bald statement by the CBI chief, Campbell Adamson, that the Industrial Relations Act should be repealed; Enoch Powell's stark advice to Tory voters that they should vote Labour – against the Common Market. Not one of these was decisive. The struggle was dispiriting not least because of the wind and rain and cold in which it was fought, the first February election for twenty-four years. Above all it was miserable, in retrospect, because we lost.

I was very conscious throughout – not least because of its impact in my own constituency* – of the upsurge in the Liberal vote, which in the event was some 19 per cent of the total votes cast. There were 4.5 million more Liberal voters than there had been in 1970, a good many no doubt drawn from the ranks of previous abstainers. But at least a million, it has been estimated, came from each of the two main parties. I was (and remain today) convinced that we could have done more to prevent that haemorrhage of our own support. At first, the party bosses at Central Office could not be persuaded to take the threat seriously. And then, when it was almost too late, they could not be convinced of any single message that would meet my purpose. I was not often in Smith Square during this campaign. But, when I was, my message to Central Office was always the same: we must address the Liberals more directly. 'The trouble is', Willie Whitelaw was prone to say, 'they're different in different parts of the country. Your Liberals are quite different from mine.' He was at least half right. But I still believe that 'Liberals' are the kind of people who can be persuaded to respond to a thoughtful message of the right kind.

I was in no danger in my own constituency. My majority over the

---

* Many boundaries had been redrawn since 1970. The enlarged half of my old Reigate constituency with which I had stayed was henceforward known as East Surrey.

Liberal in second place was still over 8000.* But nationwide the electorate had given us a hung Parliament. Labour (301) had four seats more than the Conservatives (297). There were a dozen Ulster Unionists, on whose votes we could no longer rely, and nine other Nationalists. Even with the support of the fourteen Liberals we could not hope to command a majority. After two days' rather unseemly bargaining, it was clear that the Liberal Leader, Jeremy Thorpe, was unwilling to deliver their support. The Cabinet met twice on Monday 4 March, and Ted Heath went to the Palace that evening to tender his resignation, on behalf of us all.

It was a bitter disappointment. For me – and how much more so for Ted Heath – this first instalment of government represented a tragically unfinished piece of business. At least we were into Europe – but we were very far from being under way: Labour were committed, heaven help us, to 'renegotiating the terms'. And the central battle to transform our economy, above all to correct the imbalance between union power and the rest of society, was being abandoned at the worst possible time and in the worst possible circumstances. My dismay at our government's loss of office in 1974 far exceeded my personal sense of grief at losing my own seat in 1966.

But I had, I think, begun to learn a little about the economic management of a democratic society. How to defeat inflation without destroying economic dynamic? I addressed a *Financial Times* conference on 'Pay, Prices and the Economy' on 31 January 1974, just four weeks before polling day. I was beginning to outline a fresh approach to the future. Every previous shot at incomes policy, I said, had been followed by a bout of free collective bargaining. But just as surely each round of free collective bargaining had itself been followed, just as inevitably, by another round of control. Was it not sensible, I asked, to try to find, for incomes as well as prices, some more lasting alternative to this round-about? The underlying flexibility of the market was just as essential for the measurement of relationships between incomes as it was for the measurement of relationships between prices. It was hard to believe that all these problems could be solved by reliance on fiscal and monetary mechanisms alone. Government was inevitably involved in deciding, from case to case, just how much cash was available on the taxpayer's side

* Howe, R. E. G. (Con) 23,563; Vaus, K. S. (Lib) 15,544; Allonby, D. L. (Lab) 6946; Conservative majority 8019.

of every public sector bargaining table. In such circumstances government must find it equally necessary to accept at least some responsibility for evolving institutions that may help resolve similar conflicts and tensions in the private sector.

The shock of losing office had been very great. Regrouping for the future was to prove very difficult. For Ted Heath the struggle was to be his last. Yet at least some outlines of our approach to victory in 1979 were beginning to emerge. We were all at the start of a long slow march.

PART THREE

===

OPPOSITION
1974–1979

CHAPTER SEVEN

THATCHER COUP

A Second Defeat

The Conservative Party, in February 1974, was back where it had been in October 1964. The one initiative that mattered was the calling of the next election. Once again it was Harold Wilson who would decide. He had survived for eighteen months in 1964 on a majority of four. As a minority government, even Wilson could not last that long. This time the second round would come more quickly.

All the questions we had to decide followed from that. What position to adopt for the election that was already imminent? Too little change, and we risked a more decisive rejection. Too much change, and we risked huge loss of credibility. But we could be certain of one thing: this was no time – indeed, there *was* no time – to change our leader. Yesterday's champion could not overnight become today's discard. Happily that thought, at least, was in nobody's mind. Ted Heath himself was clear about our purpose. We had been trying to shape policies that were also in the national interest. We had deserved to succeed, so it was important for us to regain the opportunity to do so. Others were less convinced that that was a realistic view, but it was at the very least important to keep to the minimum Labour's hold upon the future. Damage limitation was a vital objective.

This was the prospect that faced Ted Heath's Shadow Cabinet. He made some changes in his team. Whitelaw became effectively his deputy (while also overseeing Employment). Tony Barber would retire at the next election, so Robert Carr took over the Treasury and Jim Prior replaced him on Home Affairs. Margaret Thatcher moved from Education to Environment: Heath had already decided that housing was to be an important issue, and may well have taken the view (rightly, as his biographer points out)[1] that Margaret would be both zealous and amenable in that position. I took on the Social Services.

Our agenda began to choose itself. Already there were Labour proposals to deal with. Capital transfer tax had been unveiled in Denis Healey's first Budget – introduced, remarkably enough, within four weeks of the election. Labour was committed to 'devolve' power to new assemblies in Edinburgh and Cardiff. And the Crossman–Joseph pension *mélange* came on to my desk, with Barbara Castle back as my opposite number. Economic policy problems were once again to dominate. The new Employment Secretary, Michael Foot, was already busy 'repealing' the Industrial Relations Act – actually, as I have said, leaving quite a lot of it in place. The key question remained: were we going to re-enact the 'offending' statute? The Act was widely – though wrongly – seen, even by some colleagues, as one of the main causes of our defeat. That was certainly the popular view. Robert Carr and I had had clear ideas about changes that could have followed a Tory victory in February. For the present, at least, they had to take a back seat. And so did we, on this issue. On 26 June Ted Heath announced that we did not intend to reintroduce the Industrial Relations Act. But the problems it had addressed had certainly not disappeared.

Incomes policy, the real cause of our electoral débâcle, was a different question. Keith Joseph, still a senior member of the Shadow Cabinet, had been allowed by Ted Heath to take on a 'roving assignment', seeking out the reasons for Britain's economic failure. A little later Ted blessed the notion that Keith should set up a new Tory think-tank, the independent Centre for Policy Studies. Very soon this began leading Keith along paths of his own. He was quickly back in partnership with our old friends at the IEA. Foremost among his other mentors were Alan Walters and Alfred Sherman. I knew the second better than the first, whose path had crossed mine only recently. I had come across Sherman at the *Telegraph* and the IEA. A former communist, he was by now a zealot of the right, and good ideas all too often lost their charm in the light of the zeal with which he espoused them.

Keith Joseph certainly did not need Sherman's help to start moving away from incomes policy and towards the philosophy that had, however briefly, inspired our 1970 manifesto. He reopened the question at an early meeting of Shadow Cabinet, in May 1974. For most of the colleagues it was too soon to start discarding the policies of government, and too close to the next election. Margaret was willing to give Keith some less than full-blooded support. I too backed Keith's argument that we needed to re-examine the principles of our policy. But, I said, we should find common ground between the two schools of thought. Little did I know for just how long I was going to find myself embroiled in that task.

Keith Joseph had given active help to the Bow Group in its early days and had been my mentor in my first Shadow job (in 1965–6). We had each stuck to our own last as members of Ted's Cabinet, but back in Opposition our practical friendship was renewed. Keith was more impatient than any of the rest of us for a fresh start. With the help of Afred Sherman, by now installed as first director general of the Centre for Policy Studies, Keith embarked upon a series of fundamentalist speeches. With that engaging blend of naivety and intelligence which endeared him to his friends (and infuriated his critics) he launched a candid critique of most of the premises of recent Conservative policy. This first took serious form in a speech he planned to make at Preston on Thursday, 5 September. This was only days before the start of the second election campaign of 1974. News of Keith's planned speech reached Heath's office on the Monday and caused immediate alarm. Messages were sent to the two colleagues thought to be closest to Keith, Margaret and myself. Could we possibly have a word, to persuade him to make his speech less damaging, to tone down at least some of the self-criticism?

So the three of us met, Margaret, Keith and I, on the morning of Tuesday, 3 September, at the newly established CPS office in Wilfred Street, Victoria. By the time we got there, we had all heard the overnight news. Ted Heath's boat, *Morning Cloud III*, had foundered in a force-nine gale off the Sussex coast. Two of the seven crew members, including one of Ted's godchildren, had perished at sea. It was a tragic background to the meeting of three kindred spirits in a rather dingy, paper-strewn upper room. Margaret and I were both genuinely anxious to secure some changes in Keith's text, for neither of us was as electorally innocent as he was. But the structure of the speech was all of a piece. Unemployment mattered less than inflation. Government policy had been, and was, almost the only cause of both. We had to abandon the false Keynesian gods of the last twenty years and return to true Conservatism. Keith did in fact agree to some changes, but they could not affect the central message.

When the speech came, later in the week (5 September), it was hailed by press and opponents alike as evidence of a gaping Tory split. But the damage was frankly less serious than I had feared. More important in the long run perhaps was the impact of the brief, unplanned conclave at

Wilfred Street. Consciously or unconsciously, it seemed somehow to
consolidate a nascent sense of partnership between the three of us:
Joseph, Thatcher and Howe.

But neither Margaret nor I hesitated to throw ourselves wholeheartedly into the campaign that was now upon us. My role was a modest
one, for social policy played no significant part in this election. Margaret,
on the other hand, was in the front line throughout. Three of our most
important policy promises were on her front. Each one had started as
somebody else's idea. The most straightforward was for the sale of
council houses to their tenants, at heavily discounted prices. This was
Peter Walker's brainchild, a form of privatization which Margaret was
persuaded to take on board for the years ahead. The second policy was
a pledge to cap residential mortgage interest rates at a maximum rate of
9.5 per cent. The idea was as politically reckless as it was economically
feckless. Margaret, of course, knew that, and for a time she resisted the
proposal. But Ted prevailed upon her and she then championed it with
gusto. Fortunately, that policy did not last beyond the end of the
campaign. (Only later was Margaret herself to learn the hypersensitivity
to high interest rates which overcomes successive occupants of Number
10.) Her third pledge – like the others, adopted only with reluctance –
was to have a more lasting impact. For Margaret promised, again with
firm encouragement from Ted, that we would, if elected, abolish the
domestic rating system. This was coupled with a commitment to replace
the rates 'by taxes more broadly based and related to people's ability to
pay'. Fifteen years later, this pledge returned to haunt us in the ill-
translated guise of the poll-tax.

But Margaret's pledges were not at the heart of Ted Heath's October
campaign. The party's central effort was in stark contrast to the 'Who
governs Britain?' challenge of the spring. Chastened by that result, we
were now presenting ourselves as champions of a government of national
unity. For Ted Heath himself this was a more agreeable role. It was
designed – again in contrast to our spring song – to appeal to Liberal
floaters. The matching fear was that it would demotivate our own
loyalists. In the result, the October 1974 election never really took light
on either side. Wilson and Heath were by now equally battle-soiled. It
was the fourth time the two leaders had fought each other in eight years.
The electorate displayed their boredom by staying at home, registering
two million fewer votes than had been cast on 28 February. In my own
constituency, the Liberal tide had receded, but Labour had gained very

little ground.* The result was much less of a disaster for the Tories than it might have been. We lost twenty seats overall. This gave Labour 319 seats to our 217; but, with thirteen or fourteen seats each to the Liberals, the Nationalists and the Ulstermen, Labour's overall majority was no more than three. We had lost, certainly. But disaster had been averted.

A Change of Leader

Once again at Westminster there was only one topic of conversation. The question was not 'Should Heath go?' but 'When?' Members just back from three weeks 'on the doorstep' all echoed the same tale. It was Heath's personality above all that had turned the electorate away from us. Hatred – yes, that was the word used – for 'that man' was no less than it later became for 'that woman'. He was regarded as stubborn and insensitive: the verdict was all too simple and less than just, but that was the perception. He was thus seen by his parliamentary colleagues as a loser. It was inconceivable that they would let him lead them into a fifth campaign.

Most of Ted's friends and advisers could see this clearly. They urged him to stand down swiftly. I was not close enough to be in this group, but I took the same view. If Ted did wish to make a fight of it, he would have been best advised to submit himself forthwith for re-election. Instead he waited to be pushed. Within days of the general election, the executive of the 1922 Committee unanimously called for a leadership election to be held 'not necessarily at once, but in the foreseeable future'. It was for the Leader to trigger this process. But for the moment the rules were being reviewed by Alec Home. While he was doing so, I myself teamed up with Ian Gow to tell Keith Joseph that he would have our support if he chose to stand, and no doubt others were doing the same. Keith seemed willing to accept the challenge. But not for long. For on 19 October 1974, at Edgbaston, he made an insensitive speech about 'the high and rising proportion of children . . . being born to mothers least fitted to bring children into the world'. His remarks were instantly denounced, much as Powell's 'rivers of blood' speech had been.

---

* Howe, R. E. G. (Con) 22,227; Vaus, K. S. (Lib) 12,382; Allonby, D. L. (Lab) 7797; Conservative majority 9845.

Keith, naive rather than deliberately provocative, was genuinely surprised by the fuss. Given time, it would certainly have died down. But that would not have erased the impression. Sadly, I concluded that Keith's judgment was too erratic for him to be entrusted with leadership of the party. By the middle of November he had withdrawn his name from the list of possible contenders.

Ted Heath made some changes in the Shadow Cabinet for the new session of Parliament. Alec Home retired after almost two unbroken decades of sure-footedness at Number 10 and in foreign or commonwealth affairs; he was replaced at Foreign Affairs by Geoffrey Rippon. And Margaret Thatcher was moved to a new role, as Robert Carr's number two on Treasury affairs. She was to lead the opposition team against Denis Healey's second Finance Bill. It was to be an unexpectedly starring role. For by Christmas three things had happened. First, Alec Home completed his task of revising the party leadership election rules. The most important change was the requirement that the winner should secure a 15 per cent majority over the nearest contender. (It was this which was to prove fatal to Margaret Thatcher's survival in 1990.) Second, Edward du Cann, chairman of the 1922 Committee, wisely ruled himself out as a candidate; and third, Margaret Thatcher transformed herself into a entirely credible challenger. Her leading role in the battle against capital transfer tax had given her the chance to display her combative qualities at their best.

Shortly before Christmas Margaret invited me to her home in Flood Street for a talk. Gordon Reece, whom I knew slightly from the world of television, was the only other person present. Margaret's purpose was not to recruit me as a campaigner on her behalf. She wished only to be sure that I was not myself intending to stand. I was happy to give her that assurance, for my candidature had not then struck me as remotely credible. So I wished her well in her own campaign. Reece was clearly in place already as one of her most creative minders. The decisive lift to her credibility came when Airey Neave, Member for Abingdon since 1953, decided to put his weight behind her. Neave was a dour, determined man, whom I never came to know well. Renowned for his escape from Colditz, rejected throughout the Heath era, his single purpose was to secure Heath's departure. Once du Cann had withdrawn from the race, Margaret became Neave's only choice.

The contest itself started on 23 January 1975 and was over within three weeks. For the first ballot, Margaret Thatcher was Ted Heath's only effective rival. Although I had been eager to support Keith Joseph as an alternative to Ted, I had not yet been persuaded of Margaret's fitness for that role. The third name on the ballot paper was that of Hugh Fraser. He was, like Neave, an individualistic war veteran. (We were colleagues on the board of Sun Alliance.) The only probable effect of Fraser's intervention was to provide an alternative to abstention, for those who wanted Heath out but didn't want a woman in his place. I had by now given more thought to the idea that I should put my own hat in the ring. A few contemporaries had started pressing me to do so. One reason for my reluctance was that I was addressing a series of legal conferences in Canada during the second half of January. So it was in British Columbia that I took a phone call from Antony Buck, MP for Colchester, Navy Minister in the Heath government and an old Cambridge friend, who reported that my name was now being seriously canvassed in at least some press speculation.

I was back in Britain to give my first-round vote to Ted. At 4 p.m. on Tuesday, 4 February I heard Edward du Cann announce the astonishing result:

Margaret Thatcher	130
Edward Heath	119
Hugh Fraser	16

One thing was clear immediately. For Ted Heath it was the end, and within hours he had resigned. But one thing, strange as it may now seem, seemed less clear. Despite Margaret Thatcher's stunning success in ousting Heath, no one then concluded that she was already bound to be his successor. The first round had been seen by many, from the outset, as no more than a semi-final. A whole group of others, including myself, now felt free to let our names go forward for what was still seen as the 'real thing'.

So that night a group of would-be supporters gathered at our home in Fentiman Road. Tony Buck had taken the lead in getting them together. Elspeth was still in North America, enjoying the New England winter holiday with my cousin Sheila Burton from which I had had to return early. Elspeth's absence was a measure of just how lightly we had been taking my own possible part in the contest. The gathering was made up mainly of Bow Group members and fellow lawyers: Leon Brittan, Norman Fowler, Elaine Kellett-Bowman, Ken Clarke, Peter Temple-Morris, Ian Gow, David Walder and two or three others. David was a talented author with a most irreverent sense of humour, who died tragically young only four years later. The most enthusiastic of all those present – on this, as on so many other occasions – was Ian Gow. The case which they put to me was not that I had a chance of winning. Rather they urged me to stake a claim to front- rather than middle-rank rating in the next stage of Conservative politics. My concern was to assess the risk that I might end up with a derisory vote, and so set back that very cause. It took them several hours to persuade me to run. I still needed assurance that I had Elspeth's support for this venture. Over the line from snow-clad Connecticut, she echoed precisely my own anxieties. 'But', she concluded, 'if you think it's right, then go ahead.' And I did.

I took the opportunity presented by my mini-manifesto to explain my position:

> A number of parliamentary colleagues have urged me to put my name forward in the second ballot for the leadership of the Conservative Party. I am grateful for their support and advice. It is clear that the party must now unite under a new leader in presenting the country with the case for the free society. That surely must be founded upon realistic economic policies. And it must be one that cares about every citizen.
>
> The case for that kind of Conservatism needs to be argued forthrightly – and with understanding, compassion and candour. Plainly I wish to play a leading part in that campaign. Whatever may be the shortcomings of the present electoral procedure, it is clearly intended, on the second ballot, to provide for a range of choice between possible alternatives. It can also serve to indicate the degree of support within the parliamentary party for different styles of leadership.
>
> With all these arguments in mind, I have agreed to let my name go forward as a candidate in the second ballot for the leadership of the Conservative Party.

Two features strike me now as interesting about that text: first, the almost explicit reflection of the principles we had prescribed for *Crossbow*, fifteen years before; and second, the foretaste of argument over 'different styles of leadership' that was destined fifteen years later to signal conflict with the leader whom we were about to elect.

Three others allowed their names to go forward in this second round. The serious contender was Willie Whitelaw, seeking, as Ted Heath's natural heir, to reclaim the party from Margaret's threatened 'right-wing takeover'. Jim Prior was there with almost exactly the same motives as mine: to strengthen his claim to a share of the future. It was said afterwards that Humphrey Atkins had encouraged us both to stand. If so, his motives would have been hard to divine. He told me no more than that I was perfectly entitled to stand if I wanted to. A Chief Whip could hardly have said less. The fourth late entrant was John Peyton, another former prisoner-of-war and long-serving Member for Yeovil. I had come to enjoy his friendship as a prickly, forthright, fellow participant in some of the hairier corners of the Heath government's industrial policy. Coping with the collapse of the Mersey Docks and Harbour Board had been our first joint battle honour.

Tony Buck's weekend assessment of my likely support suggested that I might get twenty-five votes. The margin of error was no greater than usual, for my actual tally was nineteen. Margaret Thatcher's victory was decisive:

Margaret Thatcher	146
William Whitelaw	79
Geoffrey Howe	19
Jim Prior	19
John Peyton	11

I had hoped to do better. But I had fared as well as Jim, and I had avoided ignominy. Margaret had won above all because, like all the others, she wasn't Ted – and, like none of the others, she had had the guts to offer her colleagues the choice. I had no great expectations of the future, as Margaret came to select her Shadow Cabinet. One piece was already in place. For Willie Whitelaw, with characteristic loyalty and sense, had immediately expressed willingness to serve Margaret in whatever capacity she chose. Peter Walker and Geoffrey Rippon, on the other hand, had decided not to join her team. Her former boss, Robert Carr, had also left. Reggie Maudling was back as Shadow Foreign Secretary. (He had had to leave the Heath Cabinet three years before because his name had been linked with that of a corrupt architect, John Poulson.) Keith Joseph was widely, and rightly, seen as the man who had blazed the trail for Margaret's victory. Certainly I expected him to take the vital post of Shadow Chancellor.

So my first talk with Margaret, newly installed in the Leader's rather sombre panelled room at the Palace of Westminster, took me completely by surprise. 'I've decided,' she said, 'to leave Keith in overall charge of policy. So I'd like you, Geoffrey, to be my Shadow Chancellor.' The three of us, she explained, would be able to work together on our economic policies. 'For we're the ones who have the same idea of where we need to go.' I agreed with that, certainly on economic policy, and that was to be the heart of the matter for years to come. I was left to guess just why Margaret had chosen me, rather than Keith, for the Shadow Chancellorship. I had little doubt that Keith's Edgbaston speech – and his own reaction to that – had played a large part. Advice from Willie Whitelaw, I also suspected, had weighed in her mind as well. Margaret was much more disposed to accept wisdom from that quarter than her critics, and even her fans, have ever been prepared to acknowledge.

Two days after her triumph, Margaret Thatcher came to Committee Room 14 at the House of Commons to address the regular 6 p.m. Thursday meeting of the 1922 Committee. The room was packed. Unusually, Shadow Cabinet members were present as well. The new leader, escorted by the chairman Edward du Cann, entered the room through a door opening on to the platform. She was flanked only by the all-male officers of the Committee. Suddenly she looked very beautiful – and very frail, as the half-dozen knights of the shires towered over her. It was a moving, almost feudal, occasion. Tears came to my eyes. The Conservative Party had elected its first woman Leader. And this over-whelmingly male gathering dedicated themselves enthusiastically to the service of this remarkable woman. By her almost reckless courage she had won their support, if not yet their hearts. A new bond of loyalty had been forged.

CHAPTER EIGHT

THE RIGHT APPROACH

A New Style

Margaret's stint as Opposition Leader, the hardest job in British politics, was to last longer than any of us had expected. It seemed at first unlikely that the Labour government could survive even as long as four years, to October 1978, on a majority of only three. In the event we were obliged to maintain the weary routines of opposition well into a fifth year.

The first six months were a period of peace within the party. They were overshadowed by the European referendum campaign. The pro-EC coalition was led by a grand alliance of the great and the good, with Roy Jenkins and Willie Whitelaw at their head. In my own constituency I had two noble champions with whom to link hands, Lord Houghton and Lord Byers, former chairmen of respectively the Labour and Liberal parties. The meetings at which I spoke, up and down the country, were crowded, good-humoured and confident. Far and away the dominant figure was the man whom we had just cast aside, Ted Heath. He enjoyed a combination of resurrection and Indian summer. Margaret, so far from being jealous, seemed almost glad to be playing a secondary role in a cause that was not very close to her heart. The outcome – two to one in favour, on a 64.6 per cent poll – appeared to lay the European question finally to rest.

The real years of opposition divided themselves, in retrospect, into three phases. The first lasted until not long after Harold Wilson's surprise resignation on 15 March 1976. It was a period of hyperactivity in Parliament and of soaring inflation and unemployment in the real economy. The second phase came with Jim Callaghan's emergence as Harold Wilson's successor at Number 10. He skilfully formed a strikingly one-sided pact with the Liberal Party. This gave Labour near-assurance of Liberal support in exchange for a moderation that Callaghan would always have been glad to make his own. Only a few months later, in September 1976, Callaghan was obliged to constrain his options still further, by accepting conditions imposed by the International Monetary Fund. This was certainly a devastating national humilation. We did not find it difficult to lay much of the blame for this on Labour's Chancellor, Denis Healey. But Callaghan was again able almost to make a virtue of necessity. And we were able to make a necessity out of his virtue, when he confessed to his 1976 party conference:

> We used to think that you could just spend your way out of a recession and increase employment by cutting taxes and boosting government spending. I tell you, in all candour, that that option no longer exists and that in so far as it ever did exist, it only worked on each occasion since the war by injecting bigger doses of inflation into the economy, followed by higher levels of unemployment as the next step.

Economic policy dictated by the IMF started to seem a good deal more convincing than anything Labour had intended for itself. By the summer of 1978, many of the economic indicators were beginning to look quite good for Callaghan. His avuncular claim to have established Labour as the natural party of government was developing at least some plausibility. So an election that autumn – always the most likely date – looked more and more probable. This was to be my first election campaign without the active involvement of my mother. She had survived for less than a year after the stroke that destroyed her speech; she died in a Porthcawl nursing home in August 1976. So ended, for Colin and myself, our last family connection with South Wales – though we both remained frequent visitors to the Principality.

By the summer of 1978 Elspeth and I (with Leon Brittan, still a bachelor, and as lively a travel-companion as he was a political partner), were on our first-ever visit, as guests of the People's Republic of China, to Peking, Xinjiang and Shanghai. The New China News Agency published a confused report of a call on Vice-Premier Gu Mu in Peking by 'Conservative MP Sir Geoffrey Howe and his wife Leon Brittan'. To set the record straight, Elspeth and I celebrated our silver wedding on 29 August 1978, at a banquet given by the Mayor of Shanghai. We then hastened home, for the election that almost everyone expected Callaghan to call, just as soon as he had addressed the TUC conference at Brighton on 5 September. To our astonishment, he let the opportunity pass. So began the third and final phase of our years in opposition.

The 'natural party of government' started six months of transformation into the party that gave us the Winter of Discontent. This last catastrophic phase of Labour rule was to prove decisive in paving the way for Conservative government under Margaret Thatcher's leadership.

The four intervening years were made no easier by the sense of deprivation we all felt in the early stages. No private office, no department, no press officer, no car, no driver. My only 'staff' was my excellent commons secretary, Pippa Norcliffe-Roberts. Her work load increased enormously. My own work had to diversify as well. I judged it impossible to combine a major Shadow portfolio with effective practice at the Bar. So I had to find other ways of earning a living, if only to make up for the loss of a ministerial salary. I was fortunate to serve as a non-executive director of three very dissimilar companies: EMI, the electronic–entertainment group, Sun Alliance insurance and AGB Research, Europe's largest market-research group, fast-growing under the chairmanship of its founder, Bernard Audley. Very different from life at the Bar, this was all invaluable experience of the commercial world for a trainee Chancellor of the Exchequer. I was able gradually to enlarge my office, taking on a second secretary, Amanda Colvin, who went on to work for Margaret Thatcher when we moved back into government, and a research assistant, Douglas French, later himself Member for Gloucester.

All this revolved around the tiny Westminster room which was all that Shadow ministers had for an office. So it was a great blessing to have found a constituency house, which was just as rural as our former Cheshire cottage. Henhaw, on the edge of Nutfield, one of many hospitable villages in East Surrey, was to be our country home for a decade before we moved to the splendour of Chevening. A well-established and agreeable base was as important to Elspeth as it was for me. She now had full-time – and controversial – work, as the first deputy chairman of the Equal Opportunities Commission. This took her to Manchester for three days each week. Her working contacts, with industrial, academic and trade union leaders, strengthened the independence of her thinking. At the same time it broadened the political base of my own approach. She accompanied me to Nairobi for an international fiscal conference in 1975 and was herself invited by President Kenyatta's wife to address an audience of Kenyan women. The *East African Standard* headline on the report of her speech was much more striking than anything I might have said: 'British sex act explained'.

There was change too in working with a new party leader – and a

very different style of leadership. Margaret was changing some of the
people as well. Among the first to go was Ted Heath's longest-serving
and most effective adviser, Michael Wolff, an early editor of *Crossbow*
and a close personal friend. He had had a successful career with the
Beaverbrook press before becoming Ted's main speechwriter and (with
Douglas Hurd) one of his closest confidants. Ted had recently given
him a new position as director general of the party. It was perhaps too
much to expect a new leader to leave him in this key post. But the move
was a particular blow for his wife Rosemary and their two daughters,
for Michael died suddenly, and tragically young, while still *en route* to a
fresh job and a pension. By contrast, Margaret left in place as head of
Conservative Research Department the young Christopher Patten. He
was to prove one of the central figures in the fairly haphazard process of
Opposition policymaking.

Even less than Ted, it seemed, was Margaret a methodical organizer
of her political life and of the people who helped her manage it. One of
the prime tasks of a competent civil service is to make order of the
inevitably jumbled helter-skelter of a busy politician's work. And a
competent civil service is just what no Opposition can afford. By
comparison with any department of state, the Opposition Leader's office
was always hopelessly understaffed for the many jobs that came its way.
Like every Leader, Margaret developed a coterie of her own – with men,
and one or two women, outside as well as inside Parliament. Many of
these came to her through networking with Keith Joseph. His wide
policy-search role was serviced by the Centre for Policy Studies. It is
difficult to exaggerate the importance of the continuing intellectual
stimulus which Keith provided over many years, not just for Margaret
but for all his colleagues. Many of the brighter intellects on the right of
the spectrum had an individualism about their approach which made
their ideas difficult of access and hard to mobilize. Keith's blend of
courtesy and tenacity enabled him generally to get the best out of such
people. His willingness to share his thinking with us, often out of sheer
excitement, kept us fresh in the face of many challenges. And he was
always a loyal friend.

Counter-Inflation Policies

From all this I set up, with Margaret's support and authority when I
really needed it, an effective structure for evolving the party's economic

policy. The main component was what we called the Economic Recon-struction Group, with me in the chair and Adam Ridley as secretary and organizer. All those with economic responsibilities in Shadow Cabinet, as well as members of my Treasury Shadow team, were members, including Keith Joseph, Jim Prior, John Nott, Ian Gilmour, Patrick Jenkin, John Biffen, Nicholas Ridley, David Howell, Peter Rees, Nigel Lawson and Arthur Cockfield. With outside experts and other parlia-mentary colleagues we tackled the policy work under three general headings: public expenditure, tax reform and economic strategy. Public expenditure we reviewed in partnership with each of the Shadow spending ministers, under the direction of one of our three Research Department workers, George Cardona. Well before the end of our time in opposition, we had completed a Shadow public expenditure review. Much of this we were able to implement soon after arrival in office. Some of the most difficult decisions owed a good deal to the courage with which Patrick Jenkin had managed his Shadow responsibility for the social services. On tax policy, we had formidable expertise at our command, from a willing corps of volunteer professional advisers. Peter Cropper, with substantial City experience, had returned to the Research Department specifically for this work. From a ceaseless flow of ideas we were able to distil a formidable array of proposals, which found their way into Nigel Lawson's early Budgets as well as my own. Central to our tax strategy was my determination to switch the tax burden from taxes on income, investment and enterprise to taxes on consumption and expenditure. I had devised many different ways of getting this message across – from time to time even in song. To the Welsh party conference in 1978 I performed a new version of 'We'll Keep a Welcome':

> They'll keep a taxman on the hillsides,
> They'll put up rates in all the vales,
> If you come home to Labour Wales.
> We'll make a tax cut on the hillsides,
> We'll pay a bonus in the dales,
> When you come home to Tory Wales.

There were two issues of such central importance that they extended far beyond my Treasury remit: our policies for counter-inflation and for industrial relations. Jim Prior was determined, as Shadow Employment Secretary, to keep the latter under his control. His political strength was probably at its height at this time, so he was able very largely to maintain that position. Keith Joseph and I, on the other hand, remained convinced that the imbalance of power in Britain's labour market could not remain off our agenda. Margaret, I knew, shared the same view. But none of us felt confident that the time had yet come to reopen the question. Supposedly it was confrontation with the unions that had provoked Ted Heath's defeat in 1974. Just as Churchill had had to contend, in 1951, with the myth of being a warmonger, so Margaret had now to avoid the charge that she was thirsting for confrontation. For the moment at least, we had no difficulty in accepting Jim's advice that we should bide our time.

But on counter-inflation policy I was sure that we needed to readdress the issues – and to go on doing so. My Economic Reconstruction Group was designed for just this. All wings of the party were represented there. Our task was, if possible, to renounce political theology and to find a way of describing a practical approach that everyone could accept. Experience on the front line of Ted Heath's prices and incomes policy had convinced me that we had to break away from a rigid, institutionalized structure, but I was equally determined to fend off the heady, irresponsible rhetoric of 'free' collective bargaining. Even before becoming Shadow Chancellor, I had begun to focus on this argument. In a speech given to the Huddersfield Chamber of Commerce in January 1975 and written in collaboration with Professor Brian Griffiths, who was later to head Margaret Thatcher's Policy Unit, I stressed the duty of government to convince 'both sides' of the labour market of the 'consequences and realities of monetary and fiscal policy'. This was the way to escape, as we had to do, from formal incomes policy.

Almost eighteen months later, I returned to the theme in a talk to the Bow Group, with the increased authority of Shadow Chancellor. My collaborator for this was another ex-chairman of the Group, Peter Lilley – not yet a Member of Parliament. 'I do not believe,' I said, 'that this problem will most easily be solved by those of us who are tempted to see the answer in theological absolutes.' But, if we were to secure acceptance of the economic imperatives of a strict economic policy, consideration would have to be given to the way in which incomes are determined: 'If not an "incomes policy", then at least "a policy for incomes".' The speech was widely noticed, as a serious attempt to stake out fresh common ground – and not just for the Conservative Party.

All this was an echo of the passionate debate taking place within my Economic Reconstruction Group. Keith Joseph and Jim Prior were the most consistent protagonists there. Ian Gilmour, possibly the most committed champion of the incomes policy, yet always somehow semi-detached from the fray, was less regular in his attendance. The same debate was taking place in Parliament itself, for Labour were moving yet again towards an increasingly statutory framework for their own incomes policy. Eventually we *were* able to reach a practical compromise within our Group. It saw the light of day in October 1977 in *The Right Approach to the Economy*, which had been co-authored by Keith Joseph, Jim Prior, David Howell and myself – and edited by Angus Maude. Alongside firm monetary and fiscal policies, and steadily reducing targets for money supply and public borrowing, we stressed the need for 'realistic and responsible' collective bargaining. The government, we said, 'must come to *some* conclusions about the likely scope for pay increases, if excess public expenditure or large-scale unemployment is to be avoided. This view would have to be discussed by government with 'major participants in the economy' in some kind of forum. The National Economic Development Council (NEDC), we suggested, might well be the most appropriate setting. We made a number of connected pro-posals: a more independent role for the Bank of England, regular and public contact between the Bank and an appropriate parliamentary committee, and attendance by the Governor as a member of NEDC.*

Taken as a whole, the booklet was a true concordat of all our views. Originally we had intended it for publication as a party policy document. But when we brought it to Shadow Cabinet for approval, Margaret was unwilling to commit herself – not least to the elements of tripartism that we suggested. So the caution of the booklet's subtitle was inescapable: 'Outline of an Economic Strategy for the Next Conservative Govern-ment'. The indefinite 'an' was a deliberate disclaimer. The document was in fact well received, by both press and party conference. This had an interesting effect. Within three weeks, Margaret was ready to adopt our text as her own. '*We* have spelt out our proposals in some detail,' she said to the House of Commons 'in *our* recent pamphlet, *The Right Approach to the Economy*.' Nothing, I thought, succeeds like success.

Yet the success was still far from complete. One problem was recurrent uncertainty about the long-run credibility of my position as Shadow Chancellor. My parliamentary performance, against the ever ebullient Denis Healey, was too often seen as lack-lustre: 'Like being savaged by a dead sheep' was the indelible mark that Denis made upon my

* All of this we were able to achieve during my time as Chancellor.

reputation with one of his ripostes.* This critique tended to prompt me still further into over-preparation. I was often said to be noticeably better when obliged to perform extempore. But it was hard to take the risk of that approach, at least on major occasions. Other more impressive debaters – John Nott, for example – were obvious alternatives for my job. A not unsympathetic voice from Merseyside put the point starkly: 'Sir Geoffrey badly needs to do something about his performance if he wants to be sure of Mrs Thatcher's vote when the time comes for her to choose her Chancellor of the Exchequer.'[1] This lack of long-term authority made it harder for me to curb the recidivist tendencies on both sides of the incomes-policy debate. They surfaced again in the autumn of 1978. Labour were running into difficulty with their imprudently tough pay guideline of 5 per cent, and Margaret had once again been unable to resist the temptation to commend the alternative of 'free' collective bargaining.

The issue arose within days for discussion at the party conference, in a debate in which Ted Heath was expected to speak, and to which I should have to reply. This was always one of the most important conference occasions. Each year my team of helpers and I put more work into this performance than into most of the rest put together. For there were at least three targets that had to be hit. First, I had to convince the party that we had a detailed and workable response to their central anxieties, most notably on taxation. Gradually, we had persuaded the party that I should be able to lighten the tax burden on enterprise, investment and success. But this would be possible only if we were ready to raise substantially the taxes on expenditure. 'Pay as you spend, not pay as you earn' became a sure-fire applause line. Second, we had to make headway in bridging ideological divides within the party. Nowhere was this more important than on pay policy. And, last but not least, I had to bring the audience enthusiastically to its feet at the end of the speech. This kind of conference success could do a good deal to offset the effects of a shaky parliamentary reputation.

The challenge was particularly testing in 1978. For Ted Heath, in a powerful if graceless speech, had come close to denouncing Margaret for irresponsibility. In my reply, I set out once again to narrow the divide. 'We must return', I said, to realistic, responsible collective

---

* It mattered not that the remark had been recycled: Denis Healey thought he was echoing a Churchill jibe about Attlee; others recall Sir Roy Welensky's original use of the phrase at the expense of Iain Macleod.

bargaining, 'free from government interference'. Monetary policy was not an alternative to that conclusion, it was its essential complement. 'We have, as Ted Heath said, to use every means at our disposal. We shall discuss with union leaders and employers the implications of our economic and monetary policies.' I closed by putting our policies in a broader context. 'No politician or political party alone', I said, 'can transform the prospects of our country.' We had to achieve not just an improvement in our economy but a transformation in national attitudes too. The next election would be only the starting point. 'It will be a hard struggle. There will be setbacks, there will be reverses.' But we could have confidence 'because our policies and our cause are right'.

The total political effect of the speech was gratifying. For John Cole in the *Observer* I was 'growing daily in stature and confidence' and from Elinor Goodman in the *Financial Times* I got 'the day's highest marks for improvement'. Most important, against the background of my low standing in the spring, was Patrick Sargent's comment that I really did look like the next Chancellor. 'MPs' verdict', he said in the *Daily Mail*, was that the speech, and the cheers it earned, 'clinched the job'.

But I still had not brought to an end the party's internal debate about incomes policy. The standing ovation that I received was misinterpreted by some (including Ted Heath and his biographer)[2] as an endorsement not of my carefully balanced compromise but of Margaret's earlier championship of 'free' collective bargaining. So two weeks later I renewed my exposition of the policy on which I thought we were agreed. In a speech to Wallsend Conservatives, I explained why I deliberately eschewed the term 'free' collective bargaining. 'That', I said, 'can imply a return to recklessness, where the sky becomes the limit.' The freedom that we stressed was freedom from government interference. But for the rest, I said, '"realism" and "responsibility" are the key words'. I had to return to the same theme times without number in the years ahead. Eternal vigilance is said to be the price of freedom. So too it is a vital buttress for responsibility. This was one issue on which Margaret's instinct remained always at odds with mine. She was ever in danger of slipping back on to the wrong side of the fence.

The fence was never a favourite perch for our new leader. All too many leaders are tempted to regard a balanced position as inconsistent with 'true leadership'. Margaret became increasingly adept at using an unheralded public utterance as the means of signalling a policy shift away from some previously agreed balance. Willie Whitelaw was greatly troubled by one early example of this. In January 1978, Margaret proclaimed her sympathy for inner-city dwellers who feared being 'swamped' by the tide of coloured immigration. This triggered a major debate. As a direct result, Willie was obliged to tighten our policy. Our manifesto thus included a pledge to establish a register of all New Commonwealth citizens entitled by family connection to settle in Britain. Willie in fact regarded this as quite unworkable in practice. Once he was installed in the Home Office, he succeeded in getting it dropped.

Stepping Stones

Jim Prior lived, I know, in fear of a similar lurch in the field of industrial relations policy. As the GCHQ story was years later to underline,* Margaret's gut instincts were never well disposed towards trade unions. Neither Keith Joseph nor I had abandoned our (I hope more balanced) view that, at the right time, reform in this field was essential. In *The Right Approach to the Economy* – the common-ground testament to which we had all assented – Keith and I had been willing to hold back on this front. But we were convinced that this gigantic economic millstone could not be for ever neglected. Keith was able to discover some helpers who were willing to carry the argument forward. The key figure was a Wykehamist businessman and one-time regular soldier, John Hoskyns.

Hoskyns had achieved great success as an entrepreneur in the field of computer electronics and was now restless to play a part in tackling Britain's economic problems. He had the resources (and the independence) that would allow him to do so. All the political parties, he thought – and he had tried most of them – were woefully bad in thinking out and planning a strategy that was half adequate for the nation's needs. Keith encouraged Hoskyns (and his colleague Norman Strauss, formerly one of Unilever's corporate planners) to produce just such an economic policy statement for us. This project was christened 'Stepping Stones'. Blessed by Margaret, its joint overseers were Keith and myself.

By mid-November 1977 the 'Stepping Stones' report was ready. It was apocalyptic in its diagnosis, but the picture it presented was very similar to that which the Heath Cabinet had received from Lord Rothschild and the CPRS. The task of an incoming Tory government,

* See Chapter 23 below.

we were warned, would require a sea-change in Britain's political economy. A Tory landslide would not by itself be enough. Our pre-election strategy had to include plans for the removal of political obstacles to its implementation. Greatest of these obstacles was the negative stance of the trade unions. Unless a satisfying and creative role for them could be developed, national recovery would be impossible. To compete with Labour in seeking coexistence with an *unchanged* union movement would ensure continued economic decline, masked initially by North Sea oil. There was nothing to gain (except just possibly office without authority) and everything to lose by such a 'low-risk' approach. Skilfully handled, however, the rising tide of public feeling could transform the unions from the Labour Party's secret weapon into its major liability. This way the fear of union–Tory conflict could be laid to rest. The last point was the absolutely essential 'Stepping Stones' insight. Equally crucial to the whole strategy was the perception that there were plenty of other things that needed to be put right, in management, in education, in government, across the board.

Margaret's initial reaction was enthusiastic. Hoskyns' analysis was in close accord with her own, as well as with Keith's and with mine. But it was a good deal more subtle, and likely to be more effective, than anything we had produced thus far. Remarkably the report never reached the public domain. So the debate could be conducted in unusually rational and effective circumstances. How, above all, was Jim Prior to be persuaded? John Hoskyns and I first saw him to discuss the report in December 1977. His immediate fear was that the strategy could, if clumsily handled, simply unite a union movement that was already showing cracks under its own internal stresses. Hoskyns entirely understood that risk. But, he argued, we could not 'shed that risk by simply shedding the strategy', because that would 'carry a bigger risk of complete failure in office'. Of course, 'Stepping Stones' should not be seen as 'a pretext for a general letting off of steam about union stupidity or abuses'. But carefully handled it could help us chart the way ahead.

This was not the only general policy thinking going on within the party. Conservative Research Department had been producing its own strategy papers. It was now possible to place Chris Patten's latest – more cautious and pragmatic – paper on 'Implementing Our Strategy' along-side 'Stepping Stones'. Shadow Cabinet met to discuss them both on 30 January 1978. Those present included party chairman Peter Thorney-croft, Francis Pym, Ian Gilmour, John Peyton, John Davies and Angus Maude. Our expectation then was of a general election before the end of the year. The mood at the meeting fortified Margaret's instinct for caution rather than her more fundamentalist feelings. The long-term 'Stepping Stones' proposals were remitted for further consideration by a group under the restraining chairmanship of Willie Whitelaw. Meanwhile it was important that we should campaign to win the support of union members. We should criticize 'in an appropriate tone', the actions, speeches and policies of trade union leaders. But 'this should not be the centrepiece of our election strategy'. Jim Prior was to take the lead in any such campaign. 'Only he should deliver major speeches on the trade unions.' I felt that we had missed an opportunity. The declared objective was 'to win the support of union members'. The significance of the long-term strategy had not been taken on board.

We had still to study, rather than to propound, Hoskyns' quartet of policies: 'good housekeeping', which, if adopted long before, would have stopped us getting into such a mess; 'turn-around', which would have to get us out of it; 'outflanking', which would make it difficult, probably impossible, for union leaders to do anything but help the turn-around; and 'symbolic', which would prove that the other measures were not prompted by anti-union prejudice.

For a long time there was little practical action on this front. Hoskyns reported in July that Jim had only just made his first speech along the lines suggested. In the hope of encouraging more, he circulated to the rest of us the abundant material he had prepared. I managed to secure agreement from Margaret – and thus from Jim – that some of the rest of us might now break the silence on this subject which we had observed for so long.

In two lengthy speeches I began to tackle our central themes. In the first, at Conservative Central Office in August 1978, I questioned the right of union leaders to speak, still less to electioneer, on behalf of their members. One out of every three miners, three out of every five ASTMS members, three out of every four shop-workers, I pointed out, had contracted out of their union's Labour Party membership. So the union block vote should have no place in our constitution. Labour leaders, union leaders, should not be allowed to impose a closed shop on electoral choice. And in the second speech, given to Kirklees Chamber of Commerce the following month, I spelt out the 'Stepping Stones' case explicitly. 'Let me make it clear,' I said, 'I am not arguing that the unions bear the sole responsibility, or anything like it, for Britain's economic decline.' Weak management, extravagant governments – we had all played our part. But a trade union movement whose most contentious policies are not supported by a majority of its members and whose leaders are wedded to an economic system which has failed in practice – 'such a movement remains a major obstacle to the economic recovery that could be within our power'.

Already the argument was moving on, despite ourselves. 'The union question', wrote Peter Jenkins in the *Guardian*, 'is now at the heart of British politics.' The taboo had been broken. 'Media treatment of Geoffrey Howe's recent speeches', reported John Hoskyns on 2 November 1978, 'has been very different from their familiar response, at the beginning of this year, of "union-bashing".' Meanwhile Labour had seriously overrated the success of their incomes policy. They had compounded their mistake by seeking to establish a 5 per cent norm for the winter ahead, 1978–9, and Prime Minister Jim Callaghan, to our astonishment, frustration and delight, had told the TUC annual conference that the election (which they had all expected that month) had been adjourned, indefinitely. Callaghan – driven, we thought, by cowardice rather than cunning – had decided to gamble the future of his government on the good behaviour of his union cronies (and paymasters) through the winter ahead. He had done so in the context of an increasingly tight and rigid pay policy.

So began Labour's last fatal season of power, the 'Winter of Discontent'. The critical breakdown occurred when Ford Motors conceded a 15 per cent pay increase. The government's attempt to apply sanctions, rather ludicrously, against the offending employers was rejected by the House of Commons. Four Labour MPs had declined to support Callaghan. So there followed an endless rash of strikes, directed at members of the public at their most vulnerable. Hospital wards were closed, graves were not dug, rubbish piled up in the streets. Suddenly the argument that Hoskyns had been urging us to make was being made for us. Jim Prior himself was obliged to concede the case for changes in the law. Margaret, for her part, was persuaded to limit the list of measures for which we should press. On 15 January she devoted a well-judged party political broadcast to the issue. The measures which she then put forward found their way into our manifesto a few months later: specifically she proposed reforms of the law on picketing and on the closed shop, and measures that would oblige unions to pay more of the costs of strikes. The 'Stepping Stones' prescription for developing the public argument had not been followed. For Margaret, on this as on other occasions, had proved reluctant to commit herself and her team to a measured strategy. But events had happily conspired to enable heart and head to come together, in response to the great crisis of the moment. The 'Stepping Stones' analysis remained available to offer guidance through the years ahead.

CHAPTER NINE

LAST LAP

═══

Drawing the Threads Together

Not all policy-making in opposition was committee-dominated. One freelance foray landed me in a friendly joust with my prospective working partner, the permanent secretary to the Treasury, Sir Douglas Wass. We had met but did not know each other well. Giving the Johnian Lecture early in 1978, Wass had, unusually, joined the Chancellor of the Exchequer and the Governor of the Bank of England in a running public debate about monetary policy. I saw no reason why the Shadow Chancellor should not join in. Speaking at the Dyers' Hall on 9 March, I teased Wass about the obvious scepticism of his attitude to monetary policy (which was already at the heart of Labour's economic policy). It '*may* be seen', he had said, 'to have an impact' on the exchange rate; it is '*thought* to have a bearing on' the price level; it is '*believed to influence*' the rate of inflation – and so on. He could hardly have been less committal. I went on, by contrast, to argue the case for 'a precise commitment to a long-term de-escalation in the rate of growth of money supply, in line with firm monetary targets'. This was one of the first public airings of what was to become, in my 1980 Budget, the Medium-Term Financial Strategy. Following this exchange, Douglas Wass and I arranged to meet each other once or twice over lunch. We turned a friendly truce into a potential for working rapport.

I derived rather more fun from an idea that emerged from discussion with Nicholas Ridley. Artistic and aristocratic, irreverent and witty, intelligent and original, Nick was occasionally erratic – but never boring. He started this time from Tony Wedgwood Benn's notion of 'planning agreements' between government and major businesses. Why not, thought Nick, stand the idea on its head? '*Non*-planning agreements' could be designed to set certain businesses free from many statutory and other restraints. It was a form of selective deregulation. By strange chance virtually the same idea had occurred at almost the same time to the Fabian geography professor and maverick town-planner Peter Hall. We took the non-plan concept that was at the heart of his idea and before long emerged with the idea of Enterprise Zones. My enthusiasm for this sprang from my own experience of urban dereliction and devastation in at least three places: the Upper Swansea valley, Merseyside and – above all – London dockland, where the Bow Group had been born. Why not, I argued, aim to create 'the Hong Kong of the 1950s' inside inner Liverpool or inner Glasgow? Small selected areas of inner cities could be simply thrown open to all kinds of initiatives with minimal, if any, planning controls and extensive freedom from taxation (local as well as national).

We developed the idea in detail. Then we tried to sell it to Margaret, for inclusion in the manifesto. We did not succeed. For her it smacked too much of 'regional policy' by another name. Such Heathian overtones masked the merits of its very dry authorship. But I was determined that the idea should survive, so I transformed it into a major speech. The Bow Group staged a special dinner at the Waterman's Arms on the Isle of Dogs. There, in the midst of dockland dereliction at its most depressing, I launched the idea of Enterprise Zones. I proposed too the enforced sale of publicly owned land and the establishment of urban development corporations. 'I hope', I said, 'we shall find communities queuing up to apply for Enterprise Zone status. . . . If the Tribune Group or the Socialist Workers' Party wanted to be a part of an Enterprise Zone to themselves – well, why not?' Two years were to elapse before Margaret Thatcher finally bought the idea. It featured in my 1980 Budget speech and was the trail-blazer for several other policies of the 1980s.

The European Monetary System came into existence during our last year in opposition. I had to present our view of this development in the first-ever Commons debate about it on 29 November 1978. No one could then have had any notion of the explosive impact of this mechanism on Conservative politics over the next fifteen years. Certainly there was no suspicion of this potential in the meeting that I called on 25 October. The wisely experienced European Christopher Soames, two hard-headed economists John Nott and Nigel Lawson, the former Chief Whip Francis Pym, and Adam Ridley made a well-balanced team. We were not unanimous on every point, but we agreed on the essentials. This was not a pro- or anti-European issue, nor was it a question of choosing between the philosophies of fixed or floating exchange rates. We agreed that 'We should pronounce in favour of the EMS.' This was the right course politically and in terms of economic advantage. There were risks in entering the system in our present condition after four years of Labour rule. But given a Conservative government, committed to tighter monetary and expenditure discipline and liberalized exchange controls, we should be well placed to join the system. 'Fundamentally,' I concluded in reporting all this to Margaret Thatcher, 'we *do* believe in German principles of economic management.' We should be able to get ourselves alongside them. Meanwhile, we needed 'an exercise in damage limitation and not in recrimination'. That would have been wise advice for many years to come.

The position had not changed by the time we had to prepare our manifesto for the 1979 European elections, due on 8 June. The text on which our Euro-candidates then stood – which was agreed with Margaret Thatcher before her arrival at 10 Downing Street – was very clear:

> We regret the Labour government's decision – alone amongst the Nine – not to become a full member of the new European Monetary System. We support the objectives of the new system, which are currency stability in Europe and closer co-ordination of national economic policies, and we shall look for ways in which Britain can take her rightful place within it.

This was exactly the basis on which I had commended the system to the House on 29 November 1978. 'A set of rules applying nationally and internationally', I said, 'should be respected, and would show a desire to eliminate inflation within the national boundaries and to secure as far as possible stability between currency units.' That view owed a good deal to a talk that Adam Ridley and I had had, a year before, with the then Governor of the United States Federal Reserve Bank, Arthur Burns. 'Monetarist' though he was (Milton Friedman had been one of his pupils), he had already concluded in favour of an attempt to reconstruct something like the Bretton Woods international exchange rate structure. That had been torn apart by the collapse of the dollar in 1971. Within six years of that, Burns was renewing his call for a 'broadly shared agreement that international financial affairs require a "Rule of Law"'. Margaret Thatcher did not, I think, appreciate that this had been my own starting position in 1979. Some months at the Treasury persuaded me that the oil-induced volatility of the pound sterling created difficulties for our immediate membership of the Exchange Rate Mechanism of the EMS. But that problem was not destined to last indefinitely.

In 1984–5 I was persuaded once again in favour of ERM membership. That was not, as Margaret Thatcher later asserted,[1] because I had been seduced by craven Foreign Office thinking to defect from earlier, immovable Treasury hostility. Times had changed – and so had the balance of the arguments. By 1984–5 Foreign Office and Treasury, Foreign Secretary and Chancellor, had all been persuaded that, on the merits, the time *was* right for accession to the mechanism. Oil-induced volatility of the pound sterling had paled into insignificance. This view was in line with the balanced position on which we had all been agreed in 1978–9.

For the twelve-month run-up to the 1979 election – we had been ready since the summer of 1978 – I kept our economic plans up to date with the help of a very compact group. We normally met at my home in Fentiman Road: Keith Joseph, Arthur Cockfield and Peter Rees, our two tax experts, and Adam Ridley and his helpers. A fourth parliamentarian had by now become indispensable: Nigel Lawson. Nigel had graduated from journalism into politics: 'teenage scribbler' to City editorship of the *Sunday Telegraph*, to speech-writing for Alec Home to manifesto-writing for Ted Heath. He entered the Commons, as Member for Blaby, in 1974. His economic thinking was as stimulating as it was (often) dogmatic, his output of typewritten wisdom as fluent as his speech could (sometimes) be irritatingly halting. Once in the House he swiftly became a scourge of Wilson, Callaghan, Healey and the rest of Labour's economic team. His evident ambition was matched by his massive ability. The limits to that ambition (Number 11 rather than Number 10) were set by an all-too-manifest reluctance to tolerate fools even badly, let alone gladly. We became – and remain – firm friends, if never soulmates. The partnership between his strategic thinking and that of Peter Walker laid the foundations for Margaret Thatcher's most important victory, over Arthur Scargill. Much later, her growing determination to disregard his advice, and so discard his loyalty, was equally certainly a major cause of her final demise.

These Fentiman Road meetings were the setting in which our Research Department advisers played a central part in drawing all the threads together. The Conservative Party – and I daresay the other parties as well – owes a special debt of gratitude to the people who fulfil this self-effacing but vital role. For some, it is a useful apprenticeship for a fully fledged political career. But for others, often the more important, it requires dedication and discretion to match that of senior civil servants, without any certainty of matching rewards. Peter Cropper was throughout my time a meticulously conscientious co-ordinator of taxation policy; his highly principled career was less well recognized than it should have been. Adam Ridley's input across the whole field of economic policy was even more important – and was eventually recognized as such. His career, which stretched from a stint in Lord Rothschild's CPRS to Research Department in the Heath era and to shared responsibility for all our manifestos and policy documents between 1975 and 1983, ran remarkably parellel to my own. Perhaps his most important achievement was to function as a bridge between different economic ideologies, outside as well as within the Tory Party. It was almost as important to build understanding with economic commentators like Sam Brittan, Tim Congdon, Gordon Pepper and Peter Jenkins as to reconcile thinking within the Shadow Cabinet. Equally important were our links with academic thinkers, from the London Business School to the IEA (and even the NIESR),* from Walter Eltis to Alan Walters. Adam Ridley and Nigel Lawson played often contrasting but always constructive roles on all these fronts.

Heading for Victory

All this preparation was brought to an end at the end of March 1979. The cause of the Callaghan government's downfall was not one that I had foreseen. It had no direct link with economic policy. The occasion was straightforward enough: a motion of no confidence that we had tabled for debate on 28 March. The difference arose from the fact that this motion was, unusually, supported by the Scottish Nationalists. Margaret's opening speech concentrated on the consequences of Labour policy: high taxation, over-government and above all destruction of the rule of law by the gross excesses of trade union power. The Winter of Discontent had become the most strategically placed Stepping Stone we could have wished for. Willie Whitelaw made the most of it in his closing speech. As so often, the purely debating honours went to Callaghan (skilful condescension was his technique) and Michael Foot (in those days still at his brilliant best). I awaited the result of the division with more interest than hope. Then we saw Spencer Le Marchant, the Conservative Whip, step up to the Clerks' table, to read out from the tellers' slip, 'Ayes, 311. Noes, 310.' The unbelievable had

* National Institute of Economic and Social Research.

happened. For the first time since Ramsay MacDonald had been defeated in 1924, a government had been brought down by a no-confidence vote of the House of Commons. Callaghan behaved with dignity. He would recommend to the Queen, he told the House, that Parliament should be dissolved. 'We shall take our case to the country.' So began the general election campaign that ended on Thursday, 3 May.

The opening was one of tragedy. Two days after the no-confidence debate, on Friday, 30 March, I was in my room on the Shadow Cabinet corridor when there was a loud, unfamiliar thumping noise, which felt almost as though it was within the building. The small number of people still there on a Friday stepped into the corridor. 'What on earth is that?' we asked each other. Soon the answer came, on the House bush telegraph: a car bomb. In the exit from the underground car-park, Airey Neave, Margaret Thatcher's right-hand man, destined to be her first Secretary of State for Northern Ireland, had been mortally wounded. It was a fearful foretaste of the years ahead, in which the thump of bombs, the news of death, was to become all too familiar.

The Election itself was long overdue. Our manifesto had been all but ready for a September campaign. Chris Patten, Adam Ridley and Angus Maude had been keeping it up to date. The only major change had been the addition of the proposals affecting trade unions that Margaret had foreshadowed in January.The rest was cautiously in line with the 1977 text of *The Right Approach to the Economy*. The National Freight Corporation was almost the only identified target for privatization. Our tax and economic management proposals were all clearly spelt out. In the economic team we had one profoundly worrying problem: the Clegg Commission. One of the by-products of the winter's industrial strife had been the appointment, only weeks before the final Commons vote, of a Commission on Pay Comparability, under the chairmanship of Professor Hugh Clegg of Warwick University. His task was to investigate relative rates of pay in the public and private sectors, and to make recommendations. Labour had already undertaken to honour the Clegg recommendations. They had, in our words, already signed a blank cheque. What were we to do?

Our declared policy was to contain public sector pay increases within increasingly strict cash limits on public spending. Yet already the Scottish teachers were pressing Teddy Taylor, our Shadow Scottish Secretary, to disclose our response to this central question. They were only the first of many to join the queue. Nigel Lawson and I, with robust help on the detail from Adam Ridley, endeavoured to hold the line. But such discipline is more than flesh and blood can stand throughout a general election campaign. The party chairman, Peter Thorneycroft, erstwhile super-dry, aligned himself with Teddy Taylor, Jim Prior and soon a host of others. Margaret Thatcher has been denounced for her 'rashness' in conceding the open-ended Clegg commitment. I can think of no other democratic leader who would have resisted for as long as she did. But she did at least maintain our opposition to Teddy Taylor's other would-be bid for Scottish votes – the abolition of tolls on all the Scottish road-bridges.

We had only one other thing to attend to before the campaign got under way. Denis Healey had been due to introduce a full Budget on Tuesday, 3 April 1979. This was now clearly out of the question. But some provision had to be made, in order to keep in being those taxes – notably the income tax – which each year have to be reimposed afresh by Parliament. So Parliament had to agree to the high-speed enactment, before dissolution, of what was christened a 'stand still Budget'. Nigel Lawson and I had to confer with Denis Healey (and his Chief Secretary, Joel Barnett) to agree the contents of the 'holding' Finance Bill that would be necessary. So we met the two of them in the Chancellor's room at the House of Commons. It was a pre-emptively incestuous occasion. For Denis was flanked by his principal private secretary, Tony Battishill, poised until that moment to help with his imminent – but now half-aborted – Budget speech. Within weeks he was to be helping me with mine. Meanwhile, we had to agree a shape for the neutral Budget that Parliament would pass in the next few days. Personal income tax allowances, we agreed, should be uplifted in line with inflation. This was obligatory, as a result of the Rooker–Wise–Lawson amendments that we had earlier imposed upon the government. There was now the risk that it would look like a tax relief, for which the government might claim the credit. So we imposed a condition, scarcely necessary in practice, that the reliefs should not take effect until after the election was over.

And so to the campaign itself. It was the first that I had had to fight as a senior party figure at the heart of the battle. Press conferences at Central Office, nationwide broadcasts on all the standard programmes – *Question Time*, *Election Call*, *Any Questions* and the rest – were part of the routine. Only one issue developed enough flurry to require close attention. Labour sought to publicize a series of half-truths about our programme – privatize the health service, freeze pensions and the like. One affected me most closely: the suggestion that we were going to 'double VAT'. We had no difficulty in denying it. For there was no prospect, on even the most gloomy of expectations, of our having to go beyond a rate of 15 per cent. Some critics afterwards thought it pedantically misleading to rest our case on the fact that twice 8 per cent (the then basic rate) was 16 and not 15 per cent. They also overlooked the fact that some goods (about 6 per cent of the basket) were already taxed at 12.5 per cent: the weighted average impact of the existing dual rate was 8.5 per cent. So our denial was more than technically correct.

But all that was part of the small change of election campaigning. Elspeth had the burden of 'nursing' East Surrey on all but two days of each week. My party workers gave her energetic support. I recall, by contrast, long, sometimes wearying, journeys from end to end of the kingdom, often in support of candidates doomed to defeat as well as of those destined for higher things. It was always interesting, often exhilarating and sometimes great fun. I recall particularly two days in southern Scotland with the then area chairman, Russell Sanderson (later Lord Sanderson and Minister of State). Our last meeting one day was at Newton Stewart, Galloway, in support of Ian Lang, not then a Member of Parliament, but from 1990 the Secretary of State for Scotland. As I rose to speak, I scanned my memory for some local connection that I could claim, some story that I could tell. Suddenly my mind flashed back to my demobilization leave in 1948. I had stayed with my parents and family friends in that very county, at a small resort town called Portpatrick. It was there, I recalled, that I had first dared to embrace, on a cliff-top bench, my long-cherished childhood love. She was now happily married to another, who had become a tax-exile in the Channel Islands. A Conservative victory at this election, I proclaimed, would give me the chance to cut taxes, and above all to make it worthwhile for real entrepreneurs to return to Britain. Who knows, I might be able to tempt 'the girl from Portpatrick' back to our shores. Russell Sanderson made a careful note of my closing question.

Soon it was all over. The majority in my own constituency was sharply increased, to more than 19,000 over my Liberal challenger.* Nationwide, with 339 Conservatives to 269 Labour seats, our majority of forty-four was solid enough. In retrospect, as so often, our victory looked inevitable – flowing with the tide of history. Callaghan forecast

---

* Howe, R.E.G. (Con) 28,266; Liddell, Mrs S.M.(Lib) 8866; Harries, W.G. (Lab) 7398; Smith, D.W. (NP) 452; Conservative majority 19,400.

as much to his special adviser, Bernard Donoughue: 'There are times, perhaps once every thirty years, when there is a change in politics. . . . There is a shift in what the public wants. . . . I suspect there is now such a sea-change – and it is for Mrs Thatcher.'[2] Callaghan had been more confident than I was about the result. But he was right. Our moment had come.

PART FOUR

=====

CHANCELLOR OF
THE EXCHEQUER
1979–1983

CHAPTER TEN

MY FIRST BUDGET

Number 11

Our election victory came almost as a surprise. Yet we had been preparing for it for so long, expecting it even, that the next few days seem in retrospect to have run almost on autopilot. Margaret called me to her study at Number 10. 'As you know, Geoffrey,' she said, 'I want you at the Treasury.' Anything else would have been a shock, but it was good to hear the actual words. Margaret was confident and radiant, very collected and calm. Ian Gow was ecstatically on hand.

Margaret told me of her wish to put John Nott in the Department of Trade and to give me John Biffen as my Chief Secretary: he would have responsibility for control of public spending. Biffen had not been as closely involved in the detail of policy as the other John, but he was an immensely shrewd and effective parliamentarian. We had done enough work on public expenditure to ensure that he would be well briefed. There were few surprises in the rest of the list. Margaret had left most of her Shadows with the same portfolios: Whitelaw at the Home Office, Prior at Labour, Hailsham for the Woolsack. Peter Carrington's move to the Foreign Office made obvious sense, and Christopher Soames was a 'big' man, who would make a natural Leader for the Lords.

Most of the new Cabinet came together for the first time in Buckingham Palace, at 6 p.m. on the Saturday evening. Almost like new boys at school, we struggled to cope with the modest, but complex, rituals of taking the oath and kissing hands. We were all much more excited and nervous than we tried to appear. The Queen herself was reassuringly matter-of-fact.

For me there was the particular thrill of being presented, for the first time, with a splendidly solid silver seal of office. To my astonishment, I was allowed to take it home for the weekend. So the Sunday-morning victory party we laid on at Henhaw for our key constituency workers acquired, as its dramatic centrepiece, the Chancellor of the Exchequer's huge seal gleaming in the spring sunshine on a table placed on our Surrey lawn.

But the *first* telephone call after the announcement of my appointment had come not from a constituent, but from Denis Healey. 'Geoffrey,' he said, 'I want to wish you the best of luck on the bed of nails. And Edna has some advice for Elspeth too.' The kitchen at Number 11, Edna Healey wanted to warn, was positively antediluvian – iron gas-rings, antique sinks and sombre décor. She urged Elspeth to insist, as a condition of our occupancy, that these features be put right. This was our introduction to the handsome house that was to be our London home and my working office for the next four years. We took advantage of the Bank Holiday Monday that followed the election to explore this inheritance, already evacuated by the Healeys.

Eleven Downing Street is one of the last three houses surviving from the substantial terrace erected by the spec builder Sir George Downing in 1686. (The third is Number 12, the ground floor of which serves as office for the government Chief Whip and his staff.) Number 10 became the official residence of the Prime Minister in 1732, and Chancellors have made their base at Number 11, with occasional intervals, since 1806. The latter's accommodation is strictly divided between the magnificent public rooms – study and adjacent sitting room, truly grand State Drawing Room and an oak-panelled dining room by Sir John Soane – and the scarcely less spacious private apartment, which embraces the upper floors of Number 12. In our day this included a largely self-contained top-floor flat, ideal for our student twins. Happily the neighbours never complained of Alec's noisy rehearsals on his drum kit, which at the time played a central part in his life at York University.

There were some striking contrasts within the house. The public rooms, for example, were fully serviced by Her Majesty's Government. Every morning a small army of green-coated cleaning ladies would be on parade, reinforced weekly by the Whitehall clock-winder. And throughout each working day – until the close of play, whenever that might be – the front door was manned by Dennis Davey ('Dennis the Door'), who had proved himself a splendidly efficient factotum to the Barbers and Healeys. He became almost a member of our family as well.

But all these cleaning, not to mention clock-winding, activities stopped short of the extensive private part of the house, which was entirely for us to staff and service. This was no less true of the corresponding private flat in Number 10. British Prime Ministers must be unique among heads of government around the world, I should judge, in having to provide and pay for their own cleaner, cook and so on. We were lucky to be able to take to Number 11 the housekeeper who had been with us already for more than ten years, Mrs Megan King. Her home was Blaengwynfi, in the Aberavon constituency. The quality of the furnishings and décor, in private and public rooms in Numbers 10 and 11, reflected the courage and the taste of the last occupants who had dared to commit public funds to 'refurbishment'.

Edna Healey was certainly right about the kitchen. It had an antiquated institutional-sized gas cooker and surely the first dishwashing machine ever made, which persistently leaked. Throughout the eleven years of living in a government-provided house, we were always trying to strike the right balance: maintaining a historic house, without incurring odium for living it up at public expense. But we had no doubt about the need to modernize the kitchen. Elspeth's sister Mary, an interior designer, was able (unpaid) to organize an attractive, not too elaborate, kitchen/breakfast room, which looked straight down Downing Street. It became *the* family meeting place at Number 11. Our one other extravagance, a year or two later, was to arrange the production of an attractively illustrated history of the house.

My arrival in Downing Street produced one disagreeable side-effect. Elspeth felt obliged, and rightly so, to give up her position as deputy chairman of the Equal Opportunities Commission. She had been appointed to this full-time job when the EOC was first established by the Wilson government in 1975. She had much enjoyed the work. Under the chairmanship of former Labour Party national agent Betty Lockwood, the Commission – established in the context of all-party support for the legislation – had got off to a reasonably good start. It was financed by the taxpayer. It was bound by its nature to be controversial from time to time.

The Commission might even indeed have cause to bring enforcement proceedings against government itself. If that were to happen then, we both felt instinctively, the conflict of interests within the family would be publicly unacceptable. Years later, when government policy – for different pension ages for men and women, for example – was successfully challenged by the Commission, that point became very clear. But in 1979 Elspeth's decision was sharply criticized by some 'feminist' opinion. A few years later when she had become a student at the London School of Economics, this gave rise to a curious situation. For one writer in a book of essays edited by her then tutor, Howard Glenister, cited Elspeth's decision to resign from the EOC as proof of the 'insincerity' of her commitment to the cause of equal opportunities. There followed a flurry of activity by the libel lawyers – and, for Elspeth, an apology in open court. I fancy that if the same alleged conflict had arisen in today's changed circumstances neither Elspeth nor I would feel so anxious about it.

The Treasury Team

I was eager to get to work in the Treasury, of course. My ministerial team was complete by the time I arrived there early on the Tuesday morning. There had been a large number of possible players, including the many colleagues involved in the Economic Reconstruction Group. Some key figures went to other departments – Keith Joseph to Industry, David Howell to Energy, Patrick Jenkin to DHSS – but there were still plenty of stars left. My first Chief Secretary, John Biffen, was an old friend from Cambridge and the Bow Group; we had shared the cottage at Malpas, Cheshire, in my Bebington days, when he was already a Shropshire Member. He was an unusual colleague: reflective, notably self-sufficient and seldom roused, but a formidably attractive Parliamentarian. We had shared a youthful admiration for Enoch Powell. John had remained more single-minded than I, notably but not only on Europe. He had steered clear of 'Heathite corruption' by remaining (along with a handful of others, like Jock Bruce-Gardyne and Nicholas Ridley) resolutely opposed to prices and incomes policies of every kind. Like Michael Foot he was a very platonic person, in the sense that he lived exclusively in the realm of ideas. For him the word was all, action at best secondary and at worst extremely painful, to be avoided at all costs. This made him a naturally restraining influence on most policy questions – even, as it turned out, on the effective control of public expenditure. Yet, once won over to a policy, he proved a vital pillar of support, especially when talking to the Prime Minister.

The rest of my Treasury team chose itself, from the work that we had for years been doing together. Arthur Cockfield moved naturally into place as my Minister of State in the Lords. A truly formidable polymath, he had reported to me as a diligent and committed chairman of the Prices Commission when I was 'Minister for keeping down prices' in the Heath government, and had been the most important tax expert during my four years as Shadow Chancellor. I came to treat him throughout my first three years at the Treasury as a uniquely valuable, all-purpose 'mobile reserve'. He joined the Cabinet as Secretary of State for Trade in 1982.

Peter Rees became my Minister of State in the Commons. A tax Silk and veteran of many Finance Bill debates, he had represented Dover since 1970 and had been one of my PPSs during my time as Solicitor General. The most technical details of tax reform were always within his capable and experienced grasp. In 1981 he was appointed Minister of Trade, and he returned to the Treasury as Chief Secretary in 1983. He was less happy in the field of public expenditure than he had been with tax reform.

Last but far from least was the Financial Secretary, Nigel Lawson. Even in opposition he had established himself in a class of his own – bubbling with ideas, restlessly energetic in offering them for consideration and tenacious in pressing them if they were coolly received. Our partnership was to go through many adventures before the end.

The incoming team included the trio of special advisers who had been serving us from Conservative Research Department through the Opposition years: Peter Cropper (his main input was on taxation), George Cardona (public expenditure) and Adam Ridley (the whole field of economic advice). Adam had been, and was to remain, one of the most assiduous and committed intellects in our team. He never forgot the need to stay in touch with, and perhaps to influence, opinion leaders on the 'other' side.

I chose as my parliamentary private secretary at the Treasury Ian Stewart, Member for Hitchin. An experienced merchant banker and shrewd political judge, he filled the PPS slot admirably until his appointment as a junior Defence minister in January 1983. As an enthusiastically expert numismatist, he particularly relished supporting my role as Master of the Mint.

The Chancellor's office was on the second (ministerial) floor of the Treasury, signalled by the highly polished bright-red linoleum in all the corridors. It was a spacious panelled room and contained a plaque recording that 'in this room the Air Council held their meetings throughout the course of the Second World War'.

Among those waiting to receive me at the Treasury were the two officials who were to be my chief guides there. Douglas Wass, intellectual, austere but eager, had been the permanent secretary since 1974. We had come to know each other after the 'armistice' that had followed our public crossing of swords over monetary policy a year before. What

Wass did not know, although he might have guessed, was that he was one of those whom we had considered dislodging, or replacing, on our arrival in office. Margaret and Nigel, in particular, were disturbed that he was so obviously not 'one of us'. But although he was, in John Biffen's words, 'not sympathetic to the new policies, he carried out his duties with dignity'. Indeed I had the impression that he was sceptically eager, along with most of his colleagues, to join in a genuinely fresh and determined onslaught on the 'British disease' with which they had grappled in vain for so long. The other central Treasury figure was my principal private secretary, Tony Battishill. Our paths had already crossed, at the 'standstill Budget' meeting with Denis Healey. As PPS he was involved in four Budgets, two with Denis and two with me. He went on, deservedly, to become chairman of the Board of Inland Revenue.

Preparing the Budget

The new Cabinet met for the first time, informally, on Tuesday 8 May. The mood was not triumphant. We were rather like a family which had just moved into a new house, taking pleasure in fitting our furniture into the rooms. I explained how we had come to settle the date of my first Budget (conventionally on a Tuesday). The earlier the date, the sooner we should be able to count on the revenues that would flow from the higher indirect taxation we intended to impose. Our options were limited. The European election had already been fixed for Thursday 7 June, and the UK Parliament needed to be in recess for a week or two before that. Yet 29 May, only three weeks away, was clearly too soon. So 12 June it had to be. We had five weeks in which to complete our work. Cabinet's first formal meeting, two days later, concluded with a comment from the Prime Minister that was soon to have a hollow ring. 'There must', she said, 'be no leaking of confidential documents.'

Our first full Budget meeting, with the five ministers and about a dozen officials together, took place on 9 May. It was an alarming experience, though not for the reason I had feared. Sir Douglas Wass had fielded his full team of second permanent secretaries and heads of department: Sir Anthony Rawlinson, Sir Lawrence Airey, Kenneth Couzens, Sir Fred Atkinson (chief economic adviser), Sir William Pile (head of the Inland Revenue) and Douglas Lovelock (Customs and Excise). Adam Ridley and the private secretaries, together with another official who turned out to be a vital figure, Brian Unwin, the head of the Treasury's Central Unit, completed the cast.

My expectation had been that we should run into a barrage of expert and sceptical questioning and advice, even opposition to our more radical ideas. Denis Healey and, more pointedly, the IMF may have turned the Treasury into 'reluctant monetarists', but still I had expected an instinctively Keynesian reaction to our ideas. Was it not, in any case, part of the officials' job to test neophyte political thinking? Far from it. Expertise and advice, yes. Scepticism and opposition, no. It was like an extremely well-drilled wartime operations room. In less than two hours I had outlined, and the meeting had taken on board, our key proposals. I drew a clear distinction between those which were for this year and others which were for the longer-term context, in which my first Budget would take its place. Our plans were subjected to analysis and clarification. We had anticipated most of the queries, thanks not least to meticulous pre-planning by Arthur Cockfield and Peter Cropper. Our strategy had been well advertised. The central instruments of monetary policy were already in place, as a result of well-established IMF surveillance. In those days the simple yardstick of sterling M3 was still regarded with widespread respect.

So the principal components were agreed. By the time I left for Number 11 that evening, they had been laid out in a brilliantly comprehensive and crisp ten-page minute. The ability to produce such a working record is one of the main requirements for a good private secretary. Battishill would have consulted the experts before finalizing a text of this importance. It was to serve as our action plan for the next month. We carried the process forward in five full-dress meetings of this kind. In retrospect I am amazed at how few meetings were necessary.

And so began the evolution of the working method which I found both agreeable and effective during my time in the Treasury. It was essentially collegiate and progressive. I tried to draw from everyone present their best insight into each question and so to distil the right conclusion. Quite often the process needed more than one stage, while further expert analysis was obtained. At the end it was for me to decide. Some commentators have remarked on the 'indecisiveness' of this technique. I believe it has turned out to be no more than prudent. Many of our most critical decisions needed subsequently to be applied and defended with tenacity. Most of them withstood the test of time. It was as well they had been properly tested first.

Many of the decisions we implemented that summer seem in retrospect quite straightforward. A modest reduction in the target band for monetary growth was to be matched by a sharp reduction in the PSBR (public sector borrowing requirement). Our aim was to reduce the figure from £9.25 billion (5.25 per cent of gross domestic product) in Labour's last year, 1978–9, to £8.25 billion (4.25 per cent of GDP) in 1979–80. (In the result we badly overshot, at almost £10 billion.) This required us to rein back public expenditure substantially in the year which was already under way. This in turn gave an early and non-doctrinaire shove to the privatization process. Once again our opponents had blazed the trail with their earlier sale of some 17 per cent of HMG's holding in BP. We set out to sell another £500 million worth.

Some projects were much too complex for a first Budget – reform of the capital taxes (CTT and CGT) and taxation of short-term benefits, for example – but a number of important pledges were easy to deliver, such as ending the taxation of war widows' pensions; and along with the legislation for pay and price control, dividend control was simply allowed to lapse. No less easy to deliver was a package of measures for the encouragement of entrepreneurs, particularly small businesses: reductions in the burden of corporation tax on small companies and of development land tax. This fairly widespread distribution of small but significant reliefs was immensely helpful to the overall impact of a Budget – all the more so, as I was to discover on later occasions, when the overall message was forbiddingly severe.

At the heart of this first Budget, we had one overriding question to resolve: how and how far should we implement our central, well-trailed promise of significant improvements in incentives at all levels – by means, of course, of substantial cuts in the income taxes?

My Treasury team and I had never succumbed – never seriously anyway – to the mistaken interpretations of Lafferism, which have led some US policymakers so far astray. The theory, associated with Professor Art Laffer, is (expressed in simplistic form) that all taxes discourage economic activity, so cutting any tax will almost automatically deliver a higher total yield to the Revenue. Some tax cuts will deliver a bigger offsetting increase in yield than others. This was especially true on incomes and enterprise. We were ready to agree with this insight, at least when it was applied to the grotesquely high, almost confiscatory, rates of taxation – from 83 to 98 per cent on every pound above £25,000 a year – which were still being imposed in the UK in 1979. We scarcely needed Laffer to persuade us that these rates could and should be cut substantially, at the very least without loss of revenue.

But we had no such illusion about the likely effect of reductions in the basic rate of 33 per cent. Every penny I chose to knock off the rate payable by the 19 million taxpayers would cost the Revenue almost £500 million. Yet the level of income tax payable by the average taxpayer had to be reduced substantially. Not just because his or her income was more highly taxed than that of most of our overseas competitors. Not just because he or she felt demotivated. But, most important of all, because it would be politically impossible to make the large cuts in top rates that were necessary without achieving some comparable reduction in the direct tax burden of the average citizen.

The main problem arose from the long-standing (and, more important, long-growing) imbalance of the British tax system: income taxes too high, expenditure taxes too low. The only solution was to make what we had come to call a large 'tax switch' – from taxes on income to taxes on expenditure, mainly but not solely to VAT. 'Pay as you spend', we had argued for the previous years, 'makes far more sense than pay as you earn.' The argument had got through and had played an important part in winning the election.

Rising inflation over many years had eroded the yield from the specific excise duties, on things like tobacco, alcohol and petrol. Successive Chancellors had been reluctant to increase these sufficiently to make up for the fall in their real value. So they had allowed that self-same inflation to lower the real value of the tax threshold at which income taxes started to bite. We had to tackle both sides of the equation. There was a limit to what we could get out of VAT. We did not intend to raise the yield of VAT by extending its coverage. To impose it on previously exempt purchases such as food, children's clothes and shoes would have been politically disastrous. Clearly we needed to proceed by raising the rate. The question was by how much. That depended on how far we should sensibly go in cutting income taxes.

We were sure that we had to bring the top rates down at least to the European average, say to 60 per cent. The impact of the 15 per cent surcharge on so-called 'unearned' income had also to be lightened – and, in due time, abolished. For the basic rate, we had long felt that a reduction of anything less than 3 per cent – from 33 to 30 pence in the pound – would fall well short of expectations. These cuts in income tax, we were advised, would reduce the revenue by no less than £4250 million. It was these direct tax cuts that we were determined to achieve.

So this was the minimum amount that we had to raise by increasing indirect taxes. Every increase of that kind would, of course, come through as an increase in the retail price index. Yet that had to happen if the yield of the specific excise duties was not to fall still further. For those taxes simply to stand still in real terms, they needed to go up in line with inflation, by at least 10 per cent. This would itself add to the RPI. An increase in the VAT rate would have a similar effect, but only in the first year. Thereafter its yield would rise automatically as a percentage of any rise in prices. My fellow Treasury ministers and I were determined to make the most of the long-term revenue potential of a higher VAT rate. So we had planned a substantive hike from the existing double-rate structure of 8 per cent and 12.5 per cent to a single flat-rate figure. None of us was surprised by our final choice of 15 per cent. It had always looked the most plausible of the options set out in our pre-election planning documents: and it did *not* amount – if compared with the existing double-rate structure – to the 'doubling of VAT' of which we were to be accused. To combine that with a 10 per cent hike in excise duties would raise the retail price index by almost 4.5 per cent.

This was the point on which I needed prolonged discussion with the Prime Minister. She had long accepted our central tax theme: the switch from income to expenditure taxes. Indeed she had often proclaimed it. But now came the ambivalence which Margaret often showed when the time came to move from the level of high principle and evangelism to practical politics. And, once in Number 10, the practical politics were very important. The RPI figure was engraved on her heart – indeed re-engraved, from month to month. So now that we had come to the point of decision, she expressed herself anxious, understandably, about the possible RPI effects. At our first bilateral meeting, on 22 May, she was inclined to stick at a VAT flat rate of 12.5 per cent. I argued that our first Budget provided 'our only opportunity to make a radical switch from direct to indirect taxation and thus honour the commitment on which our credibility depends'. My Treasury colleagues, I told her, were unanimous that 'the higher rate was an essential foundation for future budgetary policy'.

For our second talk on this topic, on 24 May, John Biffen came with me to Number 10 to argue the case. The tax switch and 15 per cent rates were not ideas that had originally had his support, but he was now ready to back me strongly. He argued that the tax switch was essential; he believed the country would be facing industrial unrest in a couple of years, such as would make a later hike unthinkable. We needed to do it now if at all. Eventually we were able to find a compromise. If we refrained from any increase in excise duties on tobacco and alcohol, then even with a VAT rate of 15 per cent the RPI would rise by 'only' 3.6 per cent. And almost all that increase would drop out of the twelve-months RPI figures in a year's time, as the higher VAT rate was absorbed into the system. So that is what we agreed.

Critics have subsequently argued that we were reckless to contemplate any of these changes at a time when inflation was already accelerating as a result of earlier Labour policies. Interestingly enough, that case was never put to us by any of our official advisers. I have never been remotely persuaded that our ultimate success in the battle against inflation was severely affected by the scale of our VAT switch. In July the following year, 1980, when the VAT increase dropped out of the index, the annual inflation rate fell to 16.9 per cent. By April 1983 it was down to 4 per cent, the lowest figure since 1968. And we had secured a hugely important and lasting change in the tax structure.

The task of transforming Budget measures once agreed into something that will pass as a Budget speech is a truly daunting experience, especially the first time round. Chunks of the speech material arrive on the Chancellor's desk from all directions, drafted by a dozen different non-speech-writing) hands, from monetary economists to Customs officials. The challenge is to weld all this material into, say, 12,000 words of consistent prose style. When uttered they need simultaneously to convince at least three quite different audiences: one's parliamentary colleagues; a huge diversity of radio and television listeners; and the phalanx of financial analysts, overseas as well as in the City. On this first occasion, we were still working on an incomplete fifth or sixth draft as we ran into the last weekend before Budget Day. But I was able to capture almost the only suggestion that had been made by Sir Anthony Rawlinson, my second permanent secretary. A laconic but deeply thoughtful man – alas, killed in a climbing accident in 1986 – he offered the aphorism: 'Finance must determine expenditure, not expenditure finance.' My use of it in this speech earned me an (undeserved) place in the 'Sayings of the Week' columns. In later years I was able to break the back of the process by supervising a sub-editorial team armed with a number of drafts at Number 11 throughout the preceding weekend.

There was no knowing what kind of hazard might disturb the progress of a Budget from conception to delivery. During my first Budget preparation a note was brought in to one of our later meetings. It was left to Brian Unwin (later the head of Customs and Excise) to tell us the contents. The statisticians had just discovered an error of £0.25 billion in the calculation of the PSBR. The resulting consternation was happily short lived. For I learned that this particular statistic (the PSBR) had long been measured (who can wonder?) only to the nearest £0.25 billion. This meant that a shift of only a few million pounds – say from £123 million to £127 million – could have a much larger apparent effect. It didn't need a great deal of creative accountancy to remove this particular error. But it was a nasty moment.

There was one piece of poetic encouragement as I entered the last pre-Budget lap. From Russell Sanderson, who had heard my closing campaign speech at Castle Stewart in County Galloway, came the following reminder in verse:

> Remember the girl at Portpatrick,
> Acquainted to you, Sir, by name,
> Who abandoned the shores of this country
> To preserve her own capital gain.
>
> Well! Now her friend is the Chancellor,
> Who last month said again and again,
> 'We'll cut tax' and save you and your family
> From the tax man who drives us insane.
>
> So here's to your Budget on Tuesday,
> I'm sure you'll stand up to the strain,
> Just stick very close to that promise
> And you'll notch up another 'Blue' gain!
>
> For there's lots like the girl from Portpatrick,
> Who wait for a glimmer of hope,
> To prove you can stick to that promise
> And that you and the Tories can cope.

Stand and Deliver

Budget Day itself was a uniquely exciting experience. Douglas Wass compared it to Boat-race Day.[1] Elspeth declared that it was like having a baby. As a mere Shadow Chancellor, I had been very patronizing about the whole process. To the Addington Society, in 1977, I had described the 'archaic ritual' as about as appropriate to a modern democracy 'as tally sticks to the international money market'.[2] That may yet be the right view, as a matter of technical management of economic policymaking. But for the Chancellor at least it would be a pity to lose all the fun. The ritual involves a traditional weekend photo-opportunity: from Henhaw, over the years, we visited the Red Lion and the White Hart at Bletchingley, the Bell and the Dog and Duck at Outwood (and even once climbed the windmill there). These follow an audience with Her Majesty the Queen on the eve of Budget Day, the Budget Cabinet early on Budget Day itself, then the traditional walk in St James's Park, the appearance with Gladstone's battered box on the steps of Number 11, the speech itself before a packed House of Commons (unusually attentive, unless very specifically provoked), a presentation to the back-bench Finance Committee and, last but by no means least, the Budget Broadcast.

The audience with Her Majesty is an occasion which gives one a sense of perspective. The Chancellor goes to see the Queen in her private sitting room at Buckingham Palace. He arrives at what is known as the King's Door, one of the less obtrusive doors in the inner courtyard. On the Budget Eve which lives most clearly in my mind, I arrived just as the Prime Minister and Finance Minister of New Zealand, Robert Muldoon, was leaving after his audience with Her Majesty. Suddenly I was reminded of what small fry I was in the royal diary: only one of almost four dozen countries with whose affairs and statesmen she had to be familiar – and, still more to the point, the twelfth Chancellor of the Exchequer whom she had had to encourage while he described his first Budget. *My* first Budget was her twenty-eighth. Even so, her interest went far beyond the requirements of courtesy and was most supportive of her new Chancellor.

It must be acknowledged that, at least in the early years of the Thatcher era, the Budget Cabinet had almost joined the previous evening's Palace audience on the 'dignified' rather than the 'efficient' side of Bagehot's constitutional analysis. By then all the decisions had been taken and the speech written; Cabinet on that morning was little more than a chance for colleagues to wish the Chancellor well. This was particularly the case from 1979 to 1981, in which years there was no significant prior discussion of the Budget in Cabinet. Colleagues were, of course, always consulted about changes concerning their own departments, and, except in 1979 when we were in effect implementing the manifesto, I discussed my main themes with senior colleagues. I should have wished to do more than this to extend internal understanding of our plans. But Margaret was always, and with increasing reason, preoccupied by fear of leaks. So Budget secrecy had acquired a new dimension. Ian Gilmour was absent from Budget Cabinet on European business, and no other colleague expressed dissent. Most indeed were enthusiastic about the boldness of my approach and wished me well.

The one feature of the Budget Day ritual for which I had been undergoing dress rehearsals since 1975 was the Budget Broadcast, for the Shadow Chancellor has each year the task of delivering a Budget Reply Broadcast. I had established a team and a technique for that purpose. I had had the good fortune to enlist the sympathetic support and advice of Antony Jay (best known as one of the creators of *Yes, Minister* and a producer of great skill and experience). It was he who gave me confidence in the face-to-face informality which had become, I like to think, most characteristic of my broadcasting style. We had tried also to establish a reputation for consistency and integrity by making imaginative use of charts and mobiles in support of an objectively presented tele-prompted text.

One's first real Budget Broadcast is different, of course, from those given as Shadow Chancellor. It comes at the end of a long, testing day. However well prepared in advance, I was never able to finalize the text until I had been able to sense the parliamentary reaction to the Budget itself. So it was always a real scamper to get the text ready for recording at Number 11, by 8 p.m. at the latest (the first broadcast was just one hour later). In 1979 we ran into a novel hazard. I was presenting my Budget in mid-June – not, as was usual, in March or April – and nobody had remembered that at this time of year every house in Downing Street was filled (agreeably enough) with the sound of martial music emanating from Horseguards Parade. For this was the season for repeated performances of the colourful ceremony of Beating the Retreat. As I sat down to make my first recording, the air was suddenly filled with drum-beating and 'A Life on the Ocean Wave'. This background was overwhelming and irrepressible. Our first desperate thought was to write a new Richard Dimbleby-style intro to my text: 'As you can hear, I am speaking to you tonight from the heart of the Empire.' The alternative was simply to hope for an interval long enough to allow us to record. We decided to try that. In the end we got away with one clear take for the recording, just nine minutes long.

For the Budget speech itself of course there was no equivalent dress rehearsal. For this occasion only, the water in the decanter next to the government despatch-box is customarily replaced by a beverage of the Chancellor's choice. On the day, my diary clerk, John Nelson, whose job this was, came to take my order. 'Gin, I think', I replied, as

shorthand for gin and tonic. 'What, neat gin, Chancellor?' came his
shocked reply. I was so glad he had asked.

The speech went fairly smoothly. Hansard records only two moments
of real surprise (Hon. Members: 'Oh!') in the course of my seventy-
three minutes. One was prompted by my announcement that future
state pension increases would be based not on 'the movement of prices
or earnings, whichever is the greater', but solely on prices. This was a
significant shift, which has substantially benefited the Exchequer in the
years that have followed, while the great majority of pensioners have
meanwhile enjoyed large increases in that part of their income that
comes from private savings. (Those without savings – particularly the
older pensioners – have been able to benefit, at least to some extent,
from more selective improvements in their favour.) The other gasp of
surprise greeted my announcement of an increase of 2 per cent, to 14
per cent, in the Bank's minimum lending rate. But there was no instant
expression of surprise or dismay at my two major tax changes: threepence off the basic rate of income tax and the adoption of a uniform
VAT rate of 15 per cent. The tax switch had been well enough
foreshadowed, it seemed, by the consistency of our arguments over half
a decade.

I feel now that nothing like enough notice was taken of the diagnosis,
expressed at the start of my speech:

> France and Germany's combined share of world trade in manufactured
> goods, which in 1954 was almost the same as Britain's alone, is now more
> than three times as large as ours. The French people now produce half as
> much again as we do. The Germans produce more than twice as much,
> and they are moving further ahead all the time. . . .
>
> In the last few years the hard facts of our relative decline have become
> increasingly plain, and the threat of absolute decline has gradually become
> very real.

The late Peter Jenkins, however, focused on this in his most perceptive
book, *Mrs Thatcher's Revolution*: 'Whereas in 1970, decline was still the
unmentionable, now it was official.'[3] That was why our first Thatcher
Budget had to signal a sharply new beginning, with the prospect of a
long haul ahead. And so, I think, it did – most significantly with my
chilling figures based on the problems of manufacturing industry.

But it is, I think, worth comparing the subsequently recorded reaction
of at least one colleague, Employment Secretary Jim Prior, with that of

others at the time. Jim tells us in his memoirs that my 1979 Budget struck him as 'really an enormous shock', which he actually claims 'was to do so much harm'. It became clear, Jim writes, that Thatcher, Joseph and Howe 'really had got the bit between their teeth and were not going to pay attention to the rest of us at all'.[4] This sense of shocked outrage from someone who was meant to be at the core of the government came as a considerable surprise to me. For if the press were agreed upon one thing about the Budget, it was the view expressed on the *Economist*'s front cover: 'It's what you voted for', and even by the *Daily Mirror*: 'No one who voted Conservative can complain.' That this was so was strikingly confirmed for me by encounters with voters soon after the Budget. For example, when I drove to my constituency at the end of the week, I was flagged down by a gang of Surrey County Council workmen repairing the road. 'We just wanted to thank you very much,' they said. 'Those tax cuts are great.'

These were tiny pointers to the impact of my first Budget on my own political standing. 'Office' as the *Economist* pointed out, 'does wonders for politicians. . . . Nobody made the mistake of addressing Sir Geoffrey Howe as Shadow Chancellor. As the real thing, he looked and sounded twice the man he had been before.' There was quite a lot more of the same. I tried hard not to let it go to my head. But it was useful credit in the bank against the hard times that were to lie ahead.

More important by far was the extent to which the Budget had started to get across the government's central political case. Relief and opportunity were on the way for those who were ready to try to help themselves. Already the government was steering a course away from the troubled 1970s, with a clear idea of our policy objectives and methods – and a strong political will to succeed. Margaret Thatcher's tenacity was crucial here. But so too was the remarkable, long-run coherence of my Treasury ministerial team and its advisers. Officials were constantly, and quite properly, testing our credibility. On public spending, but only on that, our resolution faltered during the first year or so. But, for the rest, I was confident that every member of my team was consistently giving the same message. Ministers do indeed mean what they say. It was probably only in 1981 that the dragon of doubt was finally slain.

CHAPTER ELEVEN

MENACING AND MENACED

―――

Tokyo Economic Summit

Chancellor as Budget-maker is one of the highest-profile roles in British politics. The public have the impression – which seems to have survived the 1993 Budget reforms – that his sole job is the imposition and design of taxes. But that is only one of a number of tasks, which are all interconnected. Economic policy is a giant web, so that if you adjust any one financial factor, scores of others immediately react. This is in interesting contrast with foreign policy problems, many of which can be considered as free-standing conundra.

Even as Chancellor I was soon obliged to take in at least the main features of the overseas scene. The most novel experience for me was attending the Tokyo Economic Summit (28–29 June 1979), three weeks after the Budget. The seven top industrial economies – Canada, France, Germany, Italy, Japan, the UK and the United States – were represented at these annual gatherings by their heads of government and their Foreign and Finance Ministers.

Our flight out across the Soviet Union introduced me to the 'finest airline in the world' (as it was dubbed by John Dickie, the *Daily Mail*'s veteran diplomatic correspondent), the fleet of Royal Air Force VC-10s. For me in later years as Foreign Secretary, these ageing, fuel-hungry jetliners were to become almost a second home. Superbly staffed, professionally faultless and always on time, they were (and still are, the few that are left) an invaluable diplomatic tool. All this I still had to learn. More immediately I was impressed by the oddity of an aircraft with three neatly curtained beds, one for each of the ministers aboard. As Margaret's and Foreign Secretary Peter Carrington's pyjamaed figures emerged or disappeared, from time to time, on either side of the aisle, I was put in mind of Dorothy Lamour and Bob Hope.

Before traversing the tundra of Siberia, we had to refuel at Moscow.

This provided a chance for the Soviet Prime Minister, Alexei Kosygin, to meet the woman already dubbed by the Tass news agency (in 1976) the 'Iron Lady'. The ninety-minute meeting at the airport, over a caviar-and-champagne supper, was useful for each side to get something of a feel for the other. There was no agenda for such an informal occasion, but Margaret took the opportunity to reproach the Russians for the impact of Communism upon Vietnam. As a result, the British territory of Hong Kong was being overwhelmed by fleeing boat-people. Kosygin took no practical notice of that, but described the occasion as 'a very good meeting'. I was able to gain a first impression of the then-so-confident style of Soviet leadership – destined to move much higher on my agenda in a few years' time.

The Summit in Tokyo itself offered a splendid chance to study at close quarters an important cross-section of world leaders. Giscard d'Estaing (with François-Poncet), Helmut Schmidt and President Carter (with Cyrus Vance) were all still in harness. Two of the other Prime Ministers, Giulio Andreotti and Joe Clark (Canada), were later to serve with me as Foreign Ministers. Two other near-immortals of the West German Liberal Party were also there: Count Otto von Lambsdorff, Economics Minister, and Hans-Dietrich Genscher, already in the fifth of his seventeen years as Foreign Minister of the Federal Republic.

The plenary working sessions took place at Akasaka Palace, under the chairmanship of one of Japan's most respected Prime Ministers, Masayoshi Ohira. We had first met when he was Foreign Minister, during my first visit to Tokyo as Minister for Trade in 1972. He had a habit of closing his eyes, so that even his closest friends were frequently uncertain whether he was just thinking or actually asleep. When he was presiding over the Tokyo Summit he truly did doze off for several minutes. The meeting was reduced to embarrassed silence until a ministerial neighbour prodded him back to life.

That apart, the meeting was significantly more businesslike and effective than many of its successors. The OPEC Summit, which was meeting at the same time, had engineered a compromise which left oil prices 'only' 50 per cent higher than in 1978. Tokyo responded with a sensibly practical plan for curbing oil consumption, for boosting nuclear programmes and for 'stability in the foreign exchange market', with a pat on the back for the newly born European Monetary System.

The real star turn of the Summit was Margaret Thatcher, making her first appearance on the world stage as Prime Minister. In those days it was still the custom for each head of government to make a separate closing statement to the final press conference – a fearful recipe for competitive tedium. As the newest member, Margaret was the last head to perform. The 'press corps' assembled at the new Otani Hotel contained a startingly large clutch of Japanese women – some journalists, no doubt, but many more diplomatic and political wives, secretaries and the like, all fired with curiosity by this female phenomenon. Margaret did not disappoint them. Speaking without a note (but far from extempore) she sparkled alongside the soberly scripted statesmen who had gone before. Roy Jenkins, present as President of the European Commission, found himself uncomfortably cast as the epilogue. For the first time I realized just how powerful an international champion Britain now had.

More Summits

That first summer also marked my introduction to a number of other groups in which Finance Ministers played their part in international affairs. Top show was the annual meeting of the International Monetary Fund and World Bank, held that September in Belgrade. Marshal Tito, with less than eight months to live and sorely crippled, still radiated presidential authority. Even Yugoslavia itself seemed in working order. This was also the setting for my first G5 meeting – of the Finance Ministers and central bank governors of France, Germany, Japan, the UK and the US (the original core of the Summit Seven). Three or four times a year this exclusive conclave was still in those days able to meet virtually unobserved and unreported. The Bank of England's Gordon Richardson and the Bundesbank's Karl Otto Pöhl were the banking doyens. Richardson's impressively measured wisdom (on which I came to rely a great deal) was occasionally masked by almost too much discretion. Pöhl had the authority of success and was correspondingly more forthright. It took me a little time to appreciate the full value of G5, but the camaraderie of colleagues who shared the burden of having to say no more often than they could say yes became immensely important.

ECOFIN is the arcane name of another international group which I joined that summer. My first attendance at this Council of EC Finance Ministers was only ten days after the election, on Monday, 14 May. I began as I was destined to go on. I was glad to be back in Brussels, I said (I had attended Council meetings as Minister for Trade in 1973–4), but I was dismayed that Britain's budgetary burden was so grossly out of line with our resources. Unless this was tackled 'before the end of this year', I warned, with hopeless optimism, 'the Community will find itself in serious crisis'. What Roy Jenkins calls the BBQ (the Bloody British Question)[1] was firmly on my plate, destined to stay there for years, the more so after my move to the Foreign Office. Finance Ministers habitually played a secondary role in the handling of this particular topic, the key discussions culminating at European Council level, attended only by heads of government and Foreign Ministers. So I was not present, for example, at the famous Dublin Summit at the end of November 1979. But I totally endorsed the substance of our case. Indeed, as Chancellor, I was ready – if it ever came to that – to authorize tough action, conceivably the withholding of our contribution, in support of that case. But even in those early days my approach would have been more modulated than Margaret's. I saw reports of her bald statement at the post-Dublin press conference: 'I am only talking about our money, no one else's; there should be a cash refund of our money to bring our receipts up to the average level of receipts in the Community.' And I thought the point could have been more persuasively put.

Abolishing Exchange Control

It was not long before I was able to accomplish one ambition that a number of us had long cherished – the abolition of exchange control. Several court-room encounters in the late 1960s had convinced me of the totalitarian nature of this regime. The item had been kept off the agenda for too many years by the forces of ignorance, timidity and inertia. It is hard for people now to recall just how far Britain in 1979 was still locked into a statist mentality.

The controls had originally been imposed on the outbreak of war in 1939. Many other countries which had done the same had very largely removed the controls after the war – the US almost immediately and completely, and even Germany before too long. But in Britain our controls remained the most systematic in the industrialized world. Our original wartime emergency regulations had been deliberately re-enacted in statutory concrete by Hugh Dalton in the Exchange Control Act 1947.

They had cost us dear. Our overseas assets and investment income had fallen as a proportion of national capital and gross national product very sharply. Overseas investment income in the 1970s was down to under 1 per cent of GNP. The invisibles account looked like going into deficit. The financial markets were being stifled. Competition was stunted. Pension funds and institutions were being prevented from getting the best return on capital. Popular capitalism – and personal freedom for travellers as much as businessmen or investors – was fatally undermined. The spirit of enterprise was shackled, when it so obviously needed to be unleashed.

Voices like that of the Institute of Economic Affairs at that time stood out as brave exceptions to this long-running consensus in favour of control. It was a splendid IEA pamphlet from John Wood and Robert Miller calling for abolition in February 1979 that helped to break the intellectual ice-pack. But there were many sceptics in the City as well as in Whitehall who counselled caution. Only once had I raised it politically. In November 1978, significantly enough in the first commons debate on the European Monetary System, I had described the apparatus of exchange control as 'a bureaucratic hallmark of a society that has no confidence in itself and its own economic management'. As a result, I argued, 'we should move steadily towards more freedom and more relaxation of exchange controls'. Nigel Lawson, with my authority, reasserted the argument in course of the 1979 election campaign.[2] But we stopped short of a firm commitment. The question was in any case too sensitive to feature in our 1979 manifesto.

Within a few days of my arrival at Number 11, I had my first official encounter with the Governor of the Bank of England. The positive case for action quickly became clear. The pound was rising, and likely to go higher, he argued, because of 'favourable market sentiment, linked in particular to North Sea oil'. This created problems for the non-oil manufacturing sector. There was therefore a strong case for the relaxation of exchange control 'simply as a means of moderating upward pressures on the rate'.

This was the green light I had hoped for – and, incidentally, an early insight into the importance for manufacturing industry of exchange rate policy. Nigel Lawson eagerly accepted my invitation to chart the way ahead. We adopted the Deng Xiaoping principle: 'We must move forward boldly with careful steps.' Margaret Thatcher had no difficulty in accepting my initial proposal for a 'substantial first step'. John Biffen added a characteristic footnote. We should present it, he said, as 'a UK decision, with happy EC consequences', but certainly not one that was driven by any sense of obligation to the Community. I was able to announce this first substantial step in my Budget speech.

Once the first step had been taken, the argument for further progress made itself, a view strongly supported by John Nott at the Department of Trade, where the petrocurrency boost to sterling was having a discouraging affect on UK trade. I was able to make a fresh announcement within six weeks, on 19 July – this time in favour of capital movements within the European Community.

After our summer break, I began asking 'What's the next step?' By 19 September Nigel Lawson and Treasury officials responsible for international finance were advising me to scrap the remaining controls 'forthwith'. Fred Atkinson, our chief economic adviser, warned of the risks of this 'fairly momentous decision', as he quaintly described it. John Biffen and the Governor too had some cautionary words to offer. Within a week, Nigel, the Governor and I were round again at Number 10. The Prime Minister's initial reaction too was against any further action 'until the government's market philosophy was being seen to work'.

But the pound was still rising. So we looked for another 'gradualist step'. At a meeting with Nigel Lawson and Adam Ridley during the party conference at Blackpool on 10 October we concluded, however, that no further intermediate stage could be devised. It really was all or nothing. So I returned to the charge with the Prime Minister, presenting another minute for her to read on her return from the seaside. Still unconvinced, she called a further meeting, attended by Peter Carrington and John Nott as well as the Governor, Nigel Lawson and myself and some of the key officials. She explained why she remained apprehensive and reluctant to go all the way at this time. We pointed out that any further delay would have a knock-on effect on our imminent sale of BP shares. Eventually she was persuaded. 'On your own head be it, Geoffrey,' she joked at the end of the meeting, 'if anything goes wrong.'

So it was decided that we should walk over the edge of the cliff and see what happened. I made the historic announcement to the House of Commons on 23 October 1979, having told the Cabinet only a few hours before. Michael Heseltine alone had objected both on the merits and because Cabinet had not been consulted. Margaret and I explained – and he reluctantly accepted – that such an acutely market-sensitive matter simply had to be decided in that way. This was the only economic decision of my life that caused me to lose a night's sleep. But it was right.

Our initial concern had been triggered by the need to offset the previously harmful impact of our newfound oil wealth. But more positively it enabled us too to make the most of the benefits of North Sea oil, to help convert it into a permanent income for our economy. The pound rose by 25 per cent in the year after exchange controls came off. Predictions of doom and gloom – most notably that sterling would collapse – proved unfounded. The risk if anything was the reverse: if we had not abolished exchange controls, it is clear in retrospect that the recession would have been worse. Not everyone saw it in quite the same way. The *Guardian* reported that 'All evening, the Bank of England was bombarded with calls from people who simply could not believe what Sir Geoffrey had said.'[3] Denis Healey predictably called our decision 'reckless, precipitate and doctrinaire'. William Keegan was even rash enough to make a prediction: 'Unless economic miracles occur, we shall have controls reimposed in some form by 1985.'[4]

In the result, abolition improved the return on capital, and thus the efficiency of our economy. It forced the City to become more competitive, and helped consolidate it as a world financial centre. It enabled us to build up huge overseas assets and earn a substantial income from them. We sent out a message to the world about our commitment to liberal economics as the means of reviving Britain. The success of that approach helped fortify the commitment of other countries, not least those in the European Community, to the same course. It *was* an act of faith, but it worked. Most surprising of all perhaps, the consequent loss of jobs for 750 controllers at the Bank of England, so far from being a cause for concern, provoked the production of a celebratory tie, which I wear to this day.

I valued particularly the reaction in the House of my old mentor, Enoch Powell: 'Is the Right Hon. gentleman aware', he said, 'that I envy him the opportunity and the privilege of announcing a step that will strengthen the economy of this country, and help restore our national pride and confidence in our currency?' My brother Colin, taking a sardonic and broadly benevolent interest in my career, was prompted to draw my attention to Michael White's double-edged comment in the *Guardian* of 24 October: 'Sir Geoffrey had come of age. After years in the shadow of Ted and then Margaret he must now be considered a menace in his own right.' Praise indeed!

Public Spending Cuts

As Chancellor I felt much more menaced than menacing. It was in the struggle to gain – and keep – control of public spending that all the pressures piled upon each other. For Prime Minister, almost as much as for Chancellor, it was our least escapable item on the agenda. Throughout my time at the Exchequer, it was the issue which brought Margaret and me most closely together. She warmed instinctively and possessively to the Prime Minister's formal title, First Lord of the Treasury. It almost made up for never having been Chancellor herself.

No sooner was my first Budget out of the way with its own starter tranche (£3.5 billion) of public spending 'cuts' than we had to face our first July Cabinet. This was the occasion for Cabinet's first collective discussion of the following year's public spending programme. In later years this was to be one of our most testing annual hurdles. Margaret and I from the outset appreciated the need to concert a well-thought-out approach. For my part, I valued the chance to share with colleagues my assessment for the year ahead. But it was important to know first how we could arrive at a presentable conclusion, without too much overt strife. There was no point in alarming the markets if that could be avoided.

In July 1979 the picture was even more cheerless than we had expected. Our own policy measures were bound, for a year, to boost the high and rising inflation rate we had inherited. Few people then shared our expectation of a sharp fall over the second and third years. So too with economic growth. The official Treasury was then disposed to forecast a fall in GDP two or three times larger (up to 6.5 per cent) than actually occurred.

We were committed from the outset to find extra money for the police. On defence spending, my Treasury team and I fought hard to avoid a commitment to increase NATO expenditure annually by 3 per cent more than the rate of inflation. Before the election, Ian Gilmour had loyally declined to commit the party to this. But after the election it was Francis Pym who took over the Defence portfolio, and he was (wrongly) advised that the party was already committed to the NATO target. We challenged this at a meeting of the Cabinet Defence Committee, and we lost, with Margaret on the wrong side. She retained this ambivalent attitude towards defence spending for some years to come. On value for money she was generally supportive of my tough Treasury line. Together we cut back extravagant plans for the new Trident base and knocked out the fifth submarine. 'Gold-plating' contracts were always in our joint sights. But it was only when I left the Treasury, after a long series of battles with the defence establishment, that Margaret finally accepted the need to subject the defence budget to cash controls as tight as every other.

This meant that in 1979 we should have to find economies from other programmes for the year ahead of about £4000 million. The Cabinet, moreover, agreed in principle to seek similar savings in the following year and thus to limit the growth in spending for 1980–1 to £500–£1000 million. This was our first time round this particular rock, and it seemed easy enough at this stage for a new Cabinet to reach that general conclusion. It was not until September, when John Biffen got into the detail of sharing the sacrifices, that ministers with high-spending programmes were fully to realize what battles they had to face.

This ready acceptance of 'austerity' seems surprising today when it can be set alongside the picture later drawn by some former colleagues. Jim Prior, Ian Gilmour (Peter Carrington's number two in the Commons) and Francis Pym, for example, seem to look back upon a Cabinet that was from the outset riven by intellectual conflict between 'obsessive monetarists' and a generally pragmatic and resistant majority who were repeatedly overborne. It was not like that at the time. Nobody expressed doubt, for example, about the basic need to keep public borrowing under control – which meant bringing it down. So far from being a novel 'Thatcherite' idea, this was no more than a continuation of the 1976 IMF prescription which Labour had been obliged to take. We incoming Conservatives were different in that we intended voluntarily to avoid spending excesses of the kind that had obliged Labour to go to the Fund for help. We were committed as well to a range of supply-side reforms* that would promote overall economic growth. This would make the squeeze less tight. But the need for firm public spending control was, for all of us, a given. And, for all of us, it was difficult. But it was not seen – certainly not at that stage – as intellectually or politically perverse. More than once that summer I was publicly reported to have described the immediate outlook as 'almost frighteningly bad'. That was no exaggeration.

---

* Economists' jargon for measures that increased the efficiency of supply rather than demand, for example deregulation, privatization, competition policy and tax reform.

Working with Mrs Thatcher

During those early months, the working partnership between Downing Street neighbours was usefully enlarged. The connecting door between Number 10 and Number 11 made it easy to have informal contact at short notice. The near permanent presence in Number 10 of Margaret's first – and pre-eminently her best – parliamentary private secretary, Ian Gow, also helped enormously. By eight o'clock in the morning he was invariably at his desk in the small office to the left of the Cabinet Room. He came to express his devotion to Margaret in extravagant but entirely credible terms. 'I shall love her', he used to say, 'for the rest of my life.' And so it remained, through all the turmoil of conflicting views over Ireland, until the moment of his brutal murder by the IRA in July 1990. He was one of my oldest political friends and certainly my closest. A fellow Wykehamist, we had been at the same house, but he was ten years younger. We had several subsequent differences in political view – mainly over Ireland, though sometimes Europe too. But our pattern of friendship and partnership remained intense. He was one of the tiny band who had backed my leadership bid in 1975. His friendship with Margaret was different, but no less close. His departure from her side in 1983, after four years as her PPS, may be seen in retrospect as one of the prime causes of her slowly developing isolation – even from formerly close colleagues, like Nigel Lawson and myself. Ian Gow was possibly the only mediator who might have saved Margaret Thatcher from herself.

In those Treasury days, certainly, Ian was therefore a constant channel of communication between us, always able and willing to arrange for me to see Margaret at short notice. During my time at Number 11, her Treasury private secretaries – Tim Lankester and Michael Scholar – were, in their different role, almost equally ready to help, but not quite so continuously to hand. My regular pattern of contact with the Prime Minister comprised a weekly 'bilateral' (this was part of the bureaucratic routine for senior colleagues, with agenda items and sometimes papers flagged up in advance) and two or three brief informal chats a week, before or between other meetings. Every two or three weeks I used to go through for a Sunday-evening chat over a drink in the flat upstairs. There was nothing that struck me as particularly remarkable about this kind of relationship. It offered the chance of more or less random, but often useful, unrecorded chats. I remember on one occasion commending the news that Bernard Ingham was to be Margaret's new press officer; I had first got to know him as the competently gruff character whom Robert Carr had inherited from Barbara Castle. During the Falklands conflict, when I was not on the relevant Cabinet Committee, Margaret had shared with me some of her anxieties about the possible settlements that Francis Pym had been trying to broker.

It was only in later years, when our contacts were far less intimate, that I realized the value, in terms of unspoken influence, of this kind of relationship. It was reflected in one other, less usual arrangement, whose existence did not become publicly known for some years. This was the Thursday Breakfast Group. On the day of the weekly Cabinet meeting, we used to meet for breakfast in the flat at Number 10. Regular participants apart from Margaret (and Dennis when he was at home), Ian Gow and David Wolfson (the Prime Minister's chief of staff – always, in my experience, a rather guarded, silent character) were industry Secretary Keith Joseph, John Nott, John Biffen and myself. This pattern became established before the government was many months old. The presumed purpose of this gathering was to anticipate the day's Cabinet agenda, to identify hazards and opportunities so that we might collectively be better prepared for them. It was characteristic of Margaret's curious lack of organizational insight that these occasions were unprepared and seldom, if ever, exploited for any long-term purpose. Her success in office owed more than she ever acknowledged to the simple bureaucratic skills of people like Sir Robert Armstrong, secretary to the Cabinet. It was the same shortcoming that had prevented us making the most effective use of the powerful analysis contained in 'Stepping Stones' – and was in 1982 to lead to John Hoskyns' disenchanted departure from Number 10, where he had headed the Policy Unit (or think-tank).

The breakfasts had some value in maintaining the collective morale of those who participated. More important perhaps, they fortified the Prime Minister's self-confidence and helped, I think, to overcome her recurrent sense of isolation in her own Cabinet. By the same token, they fostered the sense of conspiratorial disunity within the government. The arrangement could not remain secret for ever. But there was no certainty even among close colleagues about who was 'in' and who was 'out'. (Jim Prior is one of those who have wrongly included Nigel Lawson, Norman Tebbit and others in the list.)[5] This increased the scope for mutual suspicion. One of us should have had the sense to question the arrangement for that very reason. But I am afraid I never did. The group's existence was first publicly disclosed by Hugo Young in the *Sunday Times* of 30 November 1980. At that time I was facing a parliamentary mini-tempest over my autumn statement* and Young was not alone in writing a critical piece. It was particularly galling that he chose to hang his story on my supposed non-membership of the group, describing me as 'a notable absentee . . . from this . . . inner circle of her most intimate counsellors'. It was difficult to deny one's non-membership of a group so powerful and so secret that its very existence might not be publicly admitted! I took comfort from Thiers' advice that 'for those who govern the first thing required is indifference to newspapers'.

I seldom myself felt anything like as isolated from the mainstream of the party as this cabalistic description of the government might imply. The course we were following was little different from what we had promised in the years of opposition. There were doubters, of course, even within the Cabinet, but there always had been. In the years of opposition I had tried hard with them to hammer out common positions, which both 'monetarists' and 'pragmatists' could share. That had been the purpose, and success, of *The Right Approach to the Economy*, itself the basis of our 1979 manifesto. Translating it all into practice in the real world was sometimes more difficult, occasionally much more difficult, than I had expected. But then life is like that.

So I find it surprising even today to discover the vehemence with which some colleagues claim to have been reacting at the time to policies and decisions which were within the limits – though occasionally close to the edges – of the consensus towards which we were all trying to work. Certainly I gained no impression at that time of the deep misgivings which people like Jim Prior and Ian Gilmour appear to have felt even over the 1979 Budget. Still less did I realize the depth of Jim's concealed contempt for the 'all-theorist' composition of my Treasury team – without, for shame, 'any experience of running a whelk-stall'. Hardly a whelk-stall manager himself, he apparently shared this view with those other experienced whelk-stall managers, Francis Pym and Norman St John Stevas. This belated regret does less than justice to the success of our work together between 1975 and 1978 in the Economic Reconstruction Group. The wide spectrum of party opinion from which this and other economic groups were drawn had enabled us to achieve before the election an extraordinarily close degree of robust consensus.

* See Chapter 13 below.

Sadly this was to be followed, when the going got rough, by an increasing propensity for some apparently to disclaim what had previously been agreed.

If this was the real extent of the Cabinet divisions from the very commencement of the Thatcher administration, then the Prime Minister may have felt justified in maintaining the kind of fine networking on which she came so much to rely. In the long run, however, it was this behaviour pattern that was to prove self-destructive. The effectiveness of the government would have been strengthened and not weakened had it been built upon wider debate within its ranks. Breakfasts would have been better used for building bridges between colleagues rather than barriers against them.

Two Speeches: Autumn 1979

None of this potential discord greatly disturbed my passage along the learning curve of my first autumn in the Treasury. One week after the September IMF meeting in Belgrade, I started on a diverse, sometimes testing, domestic routine.

The party conference provided only my second opportunity to speak as a minister from this daunting platform, and my first as Chancellor. There was always a warmth about these occasions, which offered the chance to meet a host of briefly known but genuine friends, accumulated over the years in hundreds of constituency visits and regional tours. And, as everyone affirms, Blackpool's splendidly Edwardian Winter Garden setting always makes the conference audience more responsive than anywhere else. This time I had only stark signals to convey. 'Be under no illusions', I said, 'about the difficulties that lie ahead. . . . Upheavals in the price of oil have created a harsh world in which Britain will have to find her own salvation. . . . Public spending and borrowing have to be firmly controlled.' I reminded them – although they hardly needed it – of the extent to which we had already set about fulfilling our programme of tax reform, and I warmly welcomed the austere motion under debate, which 'emphasized the importance of fighting inflation and called for strict monetary control'.

This severe message nevertheless provoked a warm standing ovation. They were no doubt glad once again to welcome a Conversative Chancellor. Throughout the next decade, in all my jobs, the conference never failed to give me solid support. I always tried to present them with the unvarnished truth. Unvarnished most certainly did not mean unprepared. Every year my small army of helpers and I took more trouble with this twenty-minute speech than with any other except the Budget itself. These two occasions could not be more different in setting and in objective, but in each case a truly effective impact depends upon the care with which the performance is prepared. At the party conference I generally worked late into the night, alone, on the finishing touches.

The Mansion House banquet – in 1979 just a week later – was more formal. Given annually by the Lord Mayor of London for the City banking fraternity, it is a white-tie affair surrounded with pomp and ceremony. To Elspeth's recurrent dismay, tradition decreed that it was a men-only occasion – with the notable exception of Mary Donaldson, already an elected member of the City Council and, in due course, the first female Lord Mayor. The handful of wives who were invited dined separately as guests of the Lady Mayoress and were later allowed into a lofty gallery so that they might listen discreetly to their husbands' wisdom. There is an insurmountable contrast between the massive setting of the Egyptian Hall – where I have seldom heard anyone succeed in raising as much as a giggle – and the monetary technicalities which are the expected rhetorical diet. It is not easy to construct a text which will withstand scrutiny by a thousand scribes and analysts and at the same time stimulate, entertain even, a well-fed City audience. To cap it all, if the Chancellor happens to utter a news-making observation, the television clips will show him dressed, most inappropriately, like Fred Astaire.

In the city as in Blackpool, I stuck to my tune. The abolition of exchange, as well as dividend, pay and price control – not to mention higher-rate tax cuts – guaranteed a receptive audience. 'Her Majesty's Government', I assured them, 'is resolved to carry through the painful measures necessary to cut inflation and inflationary expectations.' Nobody could say they hadn't been warned.

Spending Pressures

The stark Blackpool message was just as well, for the economic skies were destined to go on darkening for two years to come. The next step came on 1 November, when John Biffen unveiled our public spending plans for the year ahead, 1980–1. Our longer-term survey covering the next three years was a task that needed extra time. Described as 'the most fundamental and far-reaching public spending review since Plowden started',* it was to be ready only just in time for next year's Budget. For 1980–1, we planned to peg total spending at the same level as in the current year, 1979–80. That meant pruning £3500 million off the level of spending already planned – and that was £500 million short of the figure we had been aiming for as recently as July.

Margaret was moved to reproach John Biffen for this 'failure'. I tried to adopt a more usefully sympathetic approach. For it became clear, after a very few months, that John was not one of nature's fiscal Rottweilers. He had not, after all, been one of our pre-election scrutineers of public spending. I had asked Nigel Lawson to join the Chief Secretary's working group – Nigel was more than ready to add his weight to the axe. I was prepared at least to be grateful for John Biffen's parliamentary skill in presenting the reduction which together they had achieved. This was one of many days when back-benchers were cheered by John's skilful presentation of tough tidings. Our philosophy was clearly spelt out in the White Paper itself: 'Higher public expenditure cannot any longer be allowed to precede, and thus prevent, growth in the private sector.'

The impact of the announcement was summed up by Malcolm Rutherford in the *Financial Times*: 'There can be no doubt by now – as there was at the beginning in the higher reaches of the Treasury – that the Tories mean what they say. They have a philosophy and they are putting it into effect.'

Less than two weeks later the party's resolve was to be tested still more firmly. For we had run into our first funding crisis. The problem came to a head with publication of the money-supply figures for the month of October 1979: sterling M3 grew by 2 per cent in that banking month, equivalent to an annual rate (since June) of 14 per cent – well outside our target ranges of 7–11 per cent. More important than that bare figure was the consequential fact that the purchasers of government debt had in effect gone on strike. They were unwilling to finance our debt at the then minimum lending rate of 14 per cent.

This should not be seen as too astonishing. Nor was it by the commentators of the City and financial press. For inflation was by now running at an annual rate of 16 per cent. So it was in the United States, where interest rates had moved up 4 per cent since the summer, to 18

* Public expenditure control had for almost two decades followed the system suggested in the Plowden report of 1961.

per cent. So on Thursday, 15 November I had to present the Cabinet (in the morning) and the House of Commons (in the afternoon) with an emergency package of measures. At its core was an unprecedented increase of 3 per cent in MLR, to the equally unprecedented (and subsequently unmatched) level of 17 per cent. I also proposed legislation that would require the North Sea oil companies to advance by two months their payment of almost £750 million worth of petroleum revenue tax. In addition, I made two important technical announcements about monetary control: first, the so-called corset (the Supplementary Special Deposit Scheme) would be continued for only six months more; and second, I proposed a study of the alternative of monetary base control.

The corset placed penalties on banks if their deposits grew above certain levels. With the abolition of exchange controls, the corset became an anachronism in that banks were able to make use of their international branches when their deposits exceeded the corset controls in the UK. The Eurosterling market grew from £14 billion to £23 billion between the ending of exchange controls and June 1980, when the corset was finally abolished. With hindsight, we should have taken action with the corset earlier. Even so, such a move during 1979 – when attention was focused so much on the month-by-month money-supply figures – would have been politically very damaging, especially at a time of such high interest rates.

The study of monetary base control (MBC) surfaced in the following March (1980) in the form of a Green Paper. This option centred around the theory that the Bank of England could control the money supply directly by manipulating and targeting the small deposits held by the clearing banks at the Bank. These deposits were seen as the 'base' of the total deposits of the banks. This MBC option, while energetically advocated by some British individuals – notably Gordon Pepper of the stockbroking firm of W. Greenwell – was mainly pushed by American monetarists. The system did not, however, sit comfortably with British practice. In contrast to the United States, the UK institutional set-up made the monetary base an unreliable indicator of the monetary stock. In no way could it be established as the basis of a totally new policy, at a time of so much change and turbulence in other respects. It is worth remembering that the US Federal Reserve, at this time, had initiated under Paul Volcker an MBC system. This did reduce inflation but at the expense of fluctuating interest rates. Despite this, mainly thanks to Pepper's personal influence on her at this time, Margaret Thatcher was particularly keen on this idea. She was ever on the look-out for some more automatic method of monetary control that would – as she hoped – avoid or reduce the need to raise interest rates. Not surprisingly, this magic formula was never to be found.

The remarkable feature of this story, in retrospect, was the way in which this disagreeable mixture of very high interest rates and possibly complex technical changes was received. People, even Treasury ministers, let alone the rest, were shaken, of course, at the thought of what we were having to do. Yet in Cabinet there was no significant dissent. The packed afternoon meeting of the 1922 Committee, which I attended especially to explain the measures, was described afterwards as 'a reasonably cheerful affair'. I record this not to suggest any special presentational skill on my part. On the contrary. What it does show, however, is the extent to which the monetary framework of counter-inflationary discipline was then being taken for granted, accepted as decisive. It had after all been in place for three full years since its reintroduction,* at the behest of the IMF, by Denis Healey in September 1976. By 1977 he had been prepared to say that 'we cannot master inflation unless we have control of the money supply'. In the following year Jim Callaghan had used the same argument in support of their decision to 'publish quantified monetary targets'.

And by Conservatives at least, or most of them, monetarism was still being taken on trust. We were not reluctant converts after all, but people who had reflected long and hard about the problems and who could be thought to know what we were about. With not too much conceit, I hope, I liked to believe that I collected at least some personal credit for my earlier experience with Ted Heath's prices and incomes policy. I was manifestly not a fanatic. I believed in trying to explain how my approach had evolved and why I thought it made sense. There was a widespread conviction that it deserved to be given a chance. This was so even though we practitioners – if I may so describe myself – were already beginning to detect real difficulty in setting, sometimes even in reading, the monetary compasses by which we were aiming to steer.

So too with public spending, we found ourselves chasing a moving target. There were three principal reasons for this. The most repeatedly irritating was the hammer-blow impact of the series of public sector pay awards that were being made along lines endorsed by the Clegg

* I say reintroduction because the IMF had required my predecessor, Chancellor Roy Jenkins, to establish a similar regime in 1969–70.

Commission on pay comparability. This looked like, and indeed was, a series of own goals. But they had already been scored when we had, against my advice, committed ourselves during the election campaign to accepting in advance the outcome of Clegg's deliberations. Those colleagues[6] who were now inclining once again towards a pay policy, even a pay freeze, as a means of resisting these included some who had most strongly backed the original commitment to accept Clegg. In truth, there was probably no electorally manageable way in which we could have avoided the whole of this burden. A part – but not all – of it was an inescapable consequence of Labour's last pay policy, if the labour market was not for ever to be facing intolerable distortions.

Nationalized industries – and the impossible search for the right balance between higher subsidies and higher prices – were the second recurrent threat to our sanity. Subsidies could not grow for ever. Sooner or later – and it was always the wrong time – the distortions and deceptions would have to be unwound and squeezed out of the system. Meanwhile, we were getting the worst of all worlds. Rising prices for the consumer as well as rising subsidy bills for the Chancellor reduced market pressures for greater efficiency in the industries involved. This was, for me, a powerfully developing argument for privatization. We had to go on fighting off critics, within as well as without, who expected us to square the impossible circle.

The third contributor to our woe was the rising bill for social security, notably retirement pensions and unemployment benefit, both of which were pledged benefits – that is to say, their value had to be updated annually in line with the retail price index. Indeed, when we came into office, each of these was linked not only to prices but to earnings as well, whichever was the higher. This link had, of course, the effect of producing a large increase in the social security budget as a direct consequence of any price increase. This argument added to the temptation to 'keep prices low' by subsidies. Each distortion would compound the other.

All these problems added to the difficulty of getting on top of public spending, of the budget deficit and indeed of inflation itself. But they did not, as some colleagues were beginning to suggest, give any kind of support to a case for setting aside our strategy. On the contrary, they argued for setting it on firmer foundations, within more secure guidelines.

Origins of the Medium-Term Financial Strategy

It was this line of thinking that had long attracted me and my Shadow
Treasury team towards some kind of medium-term framework for
monetary and fiscal discipline. As far back as *The Right Approach to the
Economy* in 1977 we had commended such an approach: 'Monetary
targets openly proclaimed and explained can have a crucial effect in
reducing inflationary expectation.' In my March 1978 reply to Douglas
Wass' Johnian Lecture I had argued that a 'precise commitment to a
long-term de-escalation in the rate of growth of money supply' was 'the
only option for the longer term'. Nigel Lawson, Adam Ridley and I had
often discussed the idea. I remember being delighted when Nigel
encapsulated it in the phrase 'Rules rule, OK?'

As soon as my 1979 Budget was out of the way, Nigel was anxious
to get ahead with this notion. I was equally glad for him to do so – with
the ready help of Adam Ridley and Peter Middleton. Middleton was
one of the most stimulating of the Treasury's under secretaries and
throughout my time a key adviser on monetary policy. Upwardly mobile
and original, he was clearly destined for the top – and did indeed end
his Treasury career as permanent secretary. So it was that 'there
emerged', as I later told the Institute of Fiscal Studies, 'the rigorous
discipline of the Medium-Term Financial Strategy. For that we owe a
greal deal to the clear-sighted tenacity of its chief draughtsman, Nigel
Lawson.'[7] It was perhaps the most important innovation of my 1980
Budget, on which work was by now well advanced. Our own thinking
about the MTFS had been well supported, carried forward indeed, by
an important group of outside experts in a Treasury seminar which I
had convened on 5 November 1979. I was much in favour of this kind
of outside contribution.

The team with which we tackled this task was greatly strengthened
when I persuaded the Prime Minister on 8 October to agree to the
appointment, as chief economic adviser to the Treasury, of Terence
Burns of the London Business School. This followed from the retirement of his worthy but unexciting predecessor, Fred Atkinson. The in-
house advice was predictably in favour of a similarly safe appointment.
By contrast, Burns – although a member of the Treasury's academic
panel – came from outside the system. The son of a Durham miner, he
had made a great impression as head of Professor Jim Ball's forecasting
team at the London Business School. We had been drawing for several

years on the work of the LBS team. I liked Burns because his thinking was based upon a commonsense and unfanatical monetary approach, and I was happy to risk such a youthful, but stimulating appointment to the equivalent of permanent-secretary rank.

My experience as a barrister had made me, in any case, impatient of categorizing people by age or nominal rank. In the competitive world of the Bar you were either a QC or a junior and, more important, either good or bad at your job. To this day I can never recall the relative seniority of an under – or an assistant – secretary. (I am even less at ease with the Foreign Office elaborations on the same hierarchical nomenclature.) I was for this reason predisposed to choose people on the grounds of ability rather than age or gender. I was shortly to appoint the Treasury's first woman press officer, Rosalind Gilmore. So, when Terry Burns came to see me at Number 11 to receive my formal invitation, I felt entitled to flatter him by recording our courage in entrusting a mere thirty-eight-year-old with such formidable responsibility. He took the wind out of my sails with the news that he was still only thirty-five. But I never had cause to regret my invitation. Terry hit the ground running, as they say, and made an important contribution to the thinking behind my 1980 and three subsequent Budgets. Twelve years later, still only forty-eight years old, Sir Terence Burns succeeded Sir Peter Middleton as permanent secretary to the Treasury.

One of the jobs we had to complete before we could get on with the 1980 Budget was the preparation of the so-called Industry Act forecast. This obligation to produce a more or less comprehensive twice-yearly forecast of the future of the economy had been laid upon the Treasury at the instance of Jeremy Bray, the earnestly intellectual Labour mathematician, who had promoted an amendment to that effect to Anthony Wedgwood Benn's Industry Act of 1975. Some Conservatives – not least those who had opposed the idea in parliamentary debate, Nigel Lawson among them – regarded this provision with distaste, as unduly redolent of economic planning, intellectually and politically misleading. Nigel went as far as to suggest complete repeal of the Act.

I never developed quite his hostility towards the concept. I had for years been citing the A. J. Balfour dictum I have already quoted* (It was one of Alec Home's favourites as well), that 'Democracy is government by explanation'. But I was more than ready to agree with Nigel that the figures originally supplied by the Treasury were, as he put

* See p. 77 above.

it, 'unbelievably gloomy'. So in the Red Book (the Financial Statement and Budget Report) that was published as usual on Budget Day, we did substantially modify the prospect from which we had started. Instead of a 6.5 per cent fall in GDP during 1980 and inflation unchanged at 19 per cent through to June 1981, we actually predicted a GDP fall of only 2.5 per cent and inflation down to 13.5 per cent. In the result, we had not been optimistic enough in our management of the raw data: GDP actually fell less, by only 2 per cent, and inflation fell faster, to 11.5 per cent. This experience reinforced my lawyerly scepticism of economic theorists.

Even the more optimistic version of the forecast on which we were building the 1980 Budget underlined the long-term nature of our task. This had always been my central perception. The same message lay at the heart of the Cabinet's agenda at the turn of the year. A gloomy view of the future. And the gloom stretched into the middle distance. That had long been my understanding of the prospect that faced us. How then to shape a message of hope?

CHAPTER TWELVE

THE APEX OF MONETARISM

Planning the 1980 Budget

Our 1980 Budget-making process actually got off to an uncertain start
because of what the press dubbed an ecclesiastical banana skin. For there
emerged an awkward clash between my choice of Budget Day and the
date already fixed for the enthronement of the new Archbishop of
Canterbury – Elspeth's old friend Robert Runcie, then Bishop of St
Albans. Budget date seemed virtually to choose itself, or so we thought.
It had to be before 5 April – the start of the financial year – if we were
to get the maximum yield from any increase in indirect taxes (direct tax
changes normally operated automatically with effect retrospectively from
that date). The House would rise for the Easter recess on Maundy
Thursday, 3 April. So the latest Tuesday on which I could open my
Budget was 25 March. Within a few hours of our announcing that day,
all Heaven was let loose. Bob Runcie was understandably very distressed
that the historic Canterbury ceremony looked like being blotted off the
screens by a barrage of Budget news. I was able very quickly to reassure
him. Bishop came before Budget. We moved our event to the following
day, Wednesday, the 26th.

Meanwhile, my Treasury team and I were working flat out on the
agenda which we already had very clearly in mind. My 1979 Budget had
launched a first, bold onslaught on our priority targets: the public
spending and monetary explosions, and above all the need to switch the
tax burden from Pay As You Earn to Pay As You Spend. Now for the
all-important longer term.

The immediate outlook was far from easy. Even the 'optimistic'
version of our own Treasury forecast expected GDP to fall during 1980
by 2.5 per cent. There were three principal causes for this: the weakness
of world demand (severely affected by successive hikes in the oil price:
it had nearly quadrupled over the previous twelve months and risen

almost twenty-fold since 1973), our own inflation rate (at 16 per cent) and, perhaps most serious of all, the long-run relative decline of our own economy. As I was to stress to the House at the start of my 1980 Budget speech, 'it would take time to check, and then to reverse, Britain's long-run economic decline – time and resolute commitment to the right strategy for a period of years ahead'.

'A period of years ... the long run ... time and resolute commitment'. This was my insistent keynote: the need for commitment and success over a period of years. And this objective had to be pursued along three parallel tracks: public spending control, supply-side reform and counter-inflation policy.

It will be clear to the most casual student of contemporary government that public spending has an infinite capacity to expand, regardless of the resources available. The remorseless quality of this thrust is fully appreciated only by the tiny band of people who have had responsibility, as Finance Ministers or officials, for trying to control it. This virtuous club can boast some surprising members, abroad as well as at home. Jacques Delors, in his days at the Trésor (the French Finance Ministry), often re-echoed the sentence from my first Budget speech: 'Finance must determine expenditure, not expenditure finance.' Years before that, Chairman Mao himself used constantly to stress that 'thrift must be the guiding principle of government'. I always heard the same message in speeches at annual meetings of the International Monetary Fund from successive Finance Ministers of the People's Republic of China. And within recent British history the memoirs of Labour ex-Treasury ministers and their advisers tell the same tale: Roy Jenkins, Leo Pliatzky, Joel Barnett and Denis Healey.

Yet despite the best efforts of the two last-named – and Joel Barnett explains that his grip, such as it was, was fatally weakened during Labour's last pre-electoral year – the situation we inherited was almost as bad as if the IMF had never visited Denis Healey's Treasury. He and Joel had made the most of what Denis called 'sod-off year' – the year (1978) in which he got rid of the men from the IMF.

The spending plans that we inherited in 1979 were in fact too high and set to grow considerably faster than production. That was on top of the record of the two previous fifteen years, in which public spending had grown from 38 to 44 per cent as a proportion of GDP. The social security budget in particular had grown in the previous ten years by about 50 per cent, more than three times the 15 per cent increase in GDP over the same period. It was, as I said, in my Budget speech, 'a striking example of the nation's capacity for spending money before it has been earned'. It was by no means the only one, I might have added.

It was for these reasons that we had undertaken, as I told the House, 'the most far-reaching review of medium-term expenditure plans since they began twenty years ago' – a review which was crucial to our prospects of success in any other direction. John Biffen, it will be recalled, had informed the House of Commons on 1 November of our revised spending plans for 1980–1 only. So John had until Budget Day, 26 March 1980, to produce, with help from Nigel Lawson, Sir Anthony Rawlinson's well-tried Treasury team and our special advisers (George Cardona particularly), an even tougher prospectus for the balance of the period up to and including 1983–4. Wisely or not (but characteristically) John warned the nation, in a speech that he made on 19 January, to 'prepare itself for three years of unparalleled austerity'. This proved to be a suitable trailer for two hard-fought Cabinet meetings on the 24th and 31st. We then managed to win agreement to significant savings in the structure of short-term benefits, so as to mitigate the poverty trap.

In the end, John and his team squeezed almost £1 billion more out of the plans we had already announced for the year ahead – a total saving of £5 billion at current prices on the plans of our predecessors for 1980–1. Beyond that we were able to blueprint progressive reductions in total expenditure throughout the rest of the Parliament, so that spending in 1983–4 would be about 4 per cent lower, in real terms, than in 1979–80. As will be seen, this required me to announce in the Budget several so-called 'shock' changes in policy, which were in fact more easily accepted than Cabinet had feared.

While the Chief Secretary and his team were tackling the expenditure side of the equation, Arthur Cockfield and Peter Rees, with the enthusiastic help of Inland Revenue and Customs officials led by Sir William Pile and Douglas Lovelock respectively, were addressing themselves to our extensive and long-range agenda for tax reform. My first Budget, radical though it had been, had scarcely been able to touch most of the topics on which we had worked during the opposition years. Peter Cropper, our perceptive special adviser in this field, had brought with him to the Treasury the 'Dossier for Incoming Ministers', which analysed and summarized our detailed proposals for no less than 100 significant tax reforms.

The work that I had put in hand on these was driven primarily by supply-side considerations: we were seeking above all the reforms that would make the tax system less hostile to enterprise and wealth-creation, more hospitable to investment and economic growth. The objectives for fiscal reform were efficiency, equity, simplicity – and manpower savings in the Revenue Departments. Peter Rees and Arthur Cockfield between them mustered huge experience and authority on all these topics, Arthur not least from his fourteen years' experience with the Inland Revenue. We were less driven than might be thought by a passion for cutting the total tax burden. Indeed we had no option. Once reduction of the public sector borrowing requirement to a reasonable level had been (rightly) given priority, tax cuts had to take a back seat.

The Medium-Term Financial Strategy

The third component in our pre-Budget agenda was our most important innovation, the Medium-Term Financial Strategy. The notion, which I aired in the previous chapter, deserves further explanation.

The quarter of a century between 1945 and 1971 now looks like some kind of economic golden age. For it was the period in which the world economy – victor and vanquished, developed and developing – experienced the most sustained and widespread growth in living memory. And not just growth but stability as well. Price stability, or something like it, was the norm by which we then lived. Between October 1958 and May 1960, for example, the UK retail price index did not move by more than one point in either direction. There was exchange rate stability too: during the first twenty-five years of my political life the pound sterling/US dollar exchange rate changed on only two occasions.

This kind of analysis had led all Britain's political leaders – and most economic analysts – to conclude by the middle of the inflationary 1970s that success against inflation was a crucial component of a return to long-run economic growth and stability, particularly in the UK. Reconsidering this question some two decades later, I find it impossible to reach a different conclusion.

At the time of writing, such absolutism against inflation has once again gone out of fashion, at least in the United Kingdom, largely as a result of our humiliating withdrawal from our most recent counter-inflationary discipline, the Exchange Rate Mechanism of the EMS. Within two short decades between 1972 and 1992, the United Kingdom succeeded in testing to destruction no less than three alternative counter-inflationary structures: Ted Heath's prices and incomes policy, Callaghan–Thatcher monetary policy and Thatcher–Major exchange rate anchorage. In each case we have perhaps reposed too much of our faith in just one disciplinary mechanism and paid too little attention to the other factors which need to be kept in focus at the same time.

But that in no way impairs the legitimacy, indeed the necessity, of having some such framework in place. And there is no serious argument among economists that such a framework must provide for control of the supply of money and credit. (Nobody would dream of arguing the opposite in, for example, Switzerland or the Federal Republic of Germany.) I was to explain in my Budget speech:

> This is at the heart of what 'monetarism' means in practice. It is a great pity that its practical, commonsense importance has been so confused by arid, theoretical dispute. Certainly the word should never have become a term of political abuse – least of all for and by those who have in the past claimed to make a virtue of practising it.

There is, of course, more than enough room for argument about the comparative merit of the alternative bases for monetary policy. One option is an external standard – a fixed exchange rate or the gold standard, as was Britain's case for most of the nineteenth and twentieth centuries. The alternative depends upon the setting of explicit domestic monetary targets for the economy in question. The collapse of the dollar in 1971 forced the abandonment of the Bretton Woods fixed exchange rate system. This obliged the United Kingdom, like other countries, to switch to the only alternative, of compliance with domestic monetary targets. This became clear to the Labour government, but only after the sterling crisis of 1976.

Thus monetary policy, including the publication of and attempted compliance with monetary targets, was already an established part of Britain's economic policy and of those of several other countries at the moment when Margaret Thatcher and I moved into Downing Street. This cannot be stated too often, particularly to those critics in my party who love to portray our arrival in office as the start of an era of uncoupled dogma and unprecedented lunacy.

The important innovation that we proposed with the establishment of the Medium-Term Financial Strategy was to set out monetary targets for a period of years ahead. This I explained in my 1980 Budget speech:

Restraint of the growth of money and credit is, then, essential, and it needs to be maintained over a considerable period of time in order to defeat inflation. . . . Our strategy sets out a four-year path for monetary growth, public spending and tax policies. By 1983–4 (the last year covered by our plans) the target rate of growth of money supply will be reduced to around 6 per cent – just half the rate of growth in the present year.

The case for such an approach struck me at the time as commonsense rather than revolutionary. Not only was it a natural follow-through from the sensible lesson that the IMF had imposed upon our predecessors, it was also an evolution that we had been foreshadowing in our speeches and writing. Nigel Lawson cites an article which he had written in the early autumn of 1978;[1] and immediately after the MTFS had been formally unveiled in my Budget speech, Alan Budd (then at the London Business School, later the Treasury's chief economic adviser) reminded *Daily Telegraph* readers that the idea of a medium-term financial plan had been specifically canvassed by the Business School in their *Economic Outlook* for October 1977.

Even so the MTFS was not immediately welcomed within government. The Bank of England, for example, were never entirely persuaded, although obliged, to accept an arrangement which diminished their ultimate discretion over monetary policy. The official Treasury was divided: Douglas Wass was one of the sceptics; Peter Middleton and Terry Burns (of course) were on the right side. John Biffen was characteristically sceptical of anything so definite and 'inflexible'. Less predictably, having failed to carry the day in our collegiate discussions within the Treasury, he made his views known by writing directly to Margaret Thatcher. He was perfectly entitled to do this, as a fellow member of the Cabinet. Even so, I was disconcerted by such direct action by a colleague from my own team.

Margaret Thatcher needed no encouragement to resist the idea. I had to press it upon her at several meetings during the February run-up to the Budget. She reacted instinctively against what she called 'graph-paper economics' – I suspect because she too was reluctant to surrender a discretionary power (generally to bring or keep interest rates down). I was eventually able to persuade her with two arguments: the MTFS was likely to act, at any rate to some extent, as a straitjacket on the ambitions of spending ministers; and, more important I think, it was likely to offer us a more reliable path towards lower interest rates. This was the decisive argument at Number 10. (Ironically, the same argument was later to have the same effect in John Major's hands, in persuading Margaret Thatcher to agree to Britain's membership of the EMS Exchange Rate Mechanism.)

Union Reform: How Fast to Proceed?

The world outside the Treasury, while we were engaged in this abstruse but fundamental analysis, had not been getting more cheerful. Unemployment had continued to rise (to 1.4 million at the last count before the Budget). On New Year's Day 1980 the state-owned steel industry was plunged into its first ever national strike. This industrial action by the steel workers who had been my favourite, as well as my best, clients at the Bar was a great personal sadness for me. But there was no way in which the government could sensibly intervene (least of all with cash) to 'save' an industry which was losing £7 million a week before the strike and well over twice that during each of the thirteen weeks for which it lasted. My home town of Port Talbot suffered severely. But, happily, the Abbey Works (as it then was) survived to become one of Europe's most competitive plants. As I told a Cambridge audience in July 1982, 'It is only in the last three years that the people of Port Talbot have been obliged to discover that 5500 people can make as much steel as 12,000 people had previously been employed to do.'[2] This was only the first of the grim series of public sector strikes in which we learned to use the 'limitless' resources of the Exchequer to finance a struggle long enough to prevail over the militants. It was tragic that so many different groups of workers apparently needed to learn by first-hand experience that the government would not change its mind or course. Such experiences did much to strengthen the case for privatization, which later gained decisive authority.

The steel strike had another important side-effect at this time. For it served to reopen questions about the adequacy or pace of Jim Prior's Employment Bill. Did our plans to curb union immunities go far enough or should emergency measures be speedily introduced, to ease the plight of the private steel producers, who were being harassed by intensive secondary picketing and blacking of their goods? The question grew in urgency as a result of apparently conflicting decisions by the Court of Appeal and the House of Lords. In December the House of Lords redefined trade union immunities in the widest possible terms.

Six weeks later the Court of Appeal ruled that the union action being taken against the steel producers was unlawful.

Jim Prior had introduced our first Employment Bill for its second reading on 17 December 1979. This contained the first (relatively modest) tranche of measures with which we were readdressing the reform of industrial relations. Jim's Bill was limited to four principal topics. First, government cash was to be made available – if requested – for union elections, strike calls or rule changes when these were conducted by secret, postal ballots. Second, the right to picket was to be limited to a person's own place of work. Third, anyone who lost his job as the result of the operation of a closed shop was to be given the right to cash compensation; and the introduction of new closed shops was made much more difficult. Fourth, there was a rather specialized prohibition of coercive methods of union recruitment. Most important of all, in my view, any penalties imposed by the Bill – particularly for unlawful picketing – were imposed only upon the person who organized the picket and not upon the relevant union. Jim Prior regarded this as a positive virtue because the alternative, as he put it, 'would have risked taking us back to the 1971 Industrial Relations Act, in which unions were made liable for their members' actions'[3] and so consolidated union resistance. This was all of great interest to me, not least because of my earlier involvement with our 1971 Act. Jim's opinion was in fact wholly perverse, since the 1971 Act had faltered for exactly the opposite reason because, instead of the TGWU being fined, the Pentonville Five had been sent to prison.

The question came before E Committee (the Cabinet's Economic Strategy Committee) on Wednesday, 6 February 1980. I felt that it raised once again, in clear form, the case for exposing trade unions as such to liability for the consequences of damaging industrial action. We should be ready, I argued, to restrict, if not eliminate, their immunity from legal liability for such activity. This was one of the long-standing mischiefs that arose from the original Trades Disputes Act of 1906. Jim sought to rebut this as part of 'Geoffrey's usual approach of wholesale reform'.[4] My support came notably from Keith Joseph and the Prime Minister. Quintin Hailsham, the Lord Chancellor, was strongly opposed to me. So were the two Peters – Carrington and Walker (the latter held the Agriculture portfolio) – as well as Ian Gilmour and the Home Secretary, Willie Whitelaw. Jim had rallied enough of the traditionalist old guard to uphold his more cautious approach.

I had to accept that conclusion. But I was determined to keep up the longer-term pressure for changes on this front. I had already prepared, in consultation with John Hoskyns and the Number 10 Policy Unit, a further speech on this theme. I had been planning to deliver this in Taunton at the coming weekend (9 February). I knew that Margaret was not out of sympathy with my thinking. So I concluded that the speech would carry the case forward in moderate style. The government was looking at the present Bill, I explained, as a 'first step in this long process' of law reform, in order to see what further changes may be necessary. I assured my audience of the government's 'patient and reasonable determination, over the weeks and months and years that lie ahead, to perform our duty in this direction with all deliberate speed'.

The press hailed this measured statement of our long-term aims as evidence of a serious Cabinet split. If indeed there was a divide, it had been better defined in a lecture on Conservatism delivered in Cambridge two days earlier by Ian Gilmour. He had attacked one of Margaret's patron saints, Professor Hayek, and described the 'prevailing ideology' as a 'threat to social order'. Jim Prior was more upset by the timing of my speech than by its content. He mobilized colleagues on E Committee (13 February) and in Cabinet (14 February) with threats of his own resignation if his step-by-step line did not prevail. On the substance of the Bill then before the House, he was successful. But we did secure from him a commitment to produce a Green Paper on the crucial, wider issue of union immunity. My concern had been to keep up this pressure for further radical changes in the future. Margaret clearly took the same view, for she seized the opportunity at Prime Minister's Questions that same afternoon (14 February) to announce that plans were in hand to ensure that people on strike claiming social security benefits would in future be deemed to be receiving strike pay from their union. Their family's right to benefit would be correspondingly reduced. This was another example of the way in which Margaret was learning to make the most of the Prime Minister's authority. At this stage of our long partnership I was generally on the side that could count on her support.

Maintaining the Economic Consensus

That did not save me, however, from expressions of back-bench anxiety about our wider economic policy, which were becoming more frequent. The Chief Whip, Michael Jopling, ran an efficient system to alert us to such signals. One group which included three members of the Blue

Chips dining club, who were later in John Major's Cabinet – Chris and John Patten and William Waldegrave – wanted child benefit increased by at least £1. Geoffrey Rippon, now a senior back-bencher, was 'considering voting against the Budget unless UK interest rates came down to North American levels'. My Treasury colleague Peter Rees commented shrewdly on this that Paul Volcker – just appointed to chairmanship of the Federal Reserve – 'may well make his threat an idle one'. And so he did, by taking US interest rates over the next year up to a high of 21 per cent.

Several other back-bench groups were making comparable noises. The so-called Chelsea Five (Hugh Dykes, Charles Morrison, Bob Hicks and David Madel, under the leadership of Nick Scott, the Member for Chelsea) signed up, as 'very worried friends', to a letter which listed the customary worries – unemployment, interest rates, cash limits, high public sector pay, 'monetarism'. But, like everybody else, they were notably short of alternative prescriptions. I tried to ensure that each such group was treated sympathetically, not least because of complaints from some colleagues of 'difficulty of getting Treasury ministers engaged in serious discussion'. To the Chelsea Five, for example, I replied, 'No one is more aware than I of the fact that our economic problems are formidable and misunderstood and demand all the discussion and explanation that time permits.' And within two months they had had two meetings (described as 'good-natured and responsible'), one with my special advisers for over an hour and a shorter one with me at Number 11. A year later, before the 1981 Budget, they were back again for more.

Inevitably, it was not possible to give every group of would-be dissenters similar treatment. It was hard work and time-consuming. But it was essential to try. I have no doubt that 'approachability' was immensely desirable – and played a useful part in seeing my Treasury team through at least some of the worst patches.

None of this would have been possible, incidentally, had our special advisers not been men of great patience, who shared my respect for this kind of two-way consumer dialogue. Adam Ridley, Peter Cropper and George Cardona each filled several filing boxes a year with the records of correspondence and exchange of this sort. They played an equally important, though very different, role in maintaining smooth relations with and between members of my ministerial team. At almost exactly this date (4 March 1980) two of my advisers reported to me, 'with the utmost trepidation', rising tension and irritability in Peter Rees.

He's doing his best to go along loyally but . . . he is not always getting a fair hearing for his thoughts and views. This makes him express himself in a slightly abrupt and contrary way. That makes you cut him out of the discussion (understandably) but, more important, brings lengthy criticism on his head from Nigel and Arthur, to which he doesn't always have the opportunity to reply.

The other anxiety is simply that Nigel does talk non-stop at every meeting to the detriment, or at the cost of, interventions from everyone else. Since officials in particular feel they must defer to ministers, it can be very frustrating for them, particularly at larger meetings.

This offers, perhaps, an insight into my 'collegiate' style of management of the Treasury. It was useful to hear comments of this kind on the impact of some of the fellows upon each other. I found private, as well as practical, opportunities for trying to correct the balance of loquacity.

All this stands in contrast with the extent to which Margaret Thatcher's Cabinet ministers were, or were not, able to share their 'thoughts and views' with each other. One of the back-bench dissidents, Charles Morrison, had told us that he warmly endorsed Ian Gilmour's 'recent speech'. He was referring to Ian's Cambridge lecture on Conservatism in February. Nine months later in November 1980, Ian made what he describes as a 'second mutinous speech', again at Cambridge, since he regarded that as, he says, 'preferable to acquiescent silence'. The speech seems to have matched his aspirations. For Ian apparently argued that 'monetarism was a passing fad', that there were alternatives to the government's economic policy, which was creating 'alienation and misery'.[5] There is here a most regrettable curiosity. For Ian had scarcely ever broken his silence on any of these matters, either in Cabinet or in any other private dialogue or communication with me – before or after we had come into government. During our four years together in Shadow Cabinet, I had secured his membership of the Economic Reconstruction Group, over which I presided as Shadow Chancellor. Even there he had seldom offered an alternative view or input. Certainly he never sent me a copy of either of his Cambridge speeches. To this day I find it difficult to reconcile his six years of laconic comradeship with the immensely detailed (often retrospective) economic wisdom set out in his book, *Dancing with Dogma.**

---

* The 171 detailed footnotes to his two chapters (II and IV) on economic policy would fuel several years of full-time academic study.

Not that I imagined that he, or any of the other self-styled wets, was wildly enthused by the balance of our economic policy. For myself, I should have been happy to have this out with them, in open debate in Cabinet, as indeed I had been in opposition, as chairman of the Economic Reconstruction Group. But this was not Margaret's instinct – not unless she was herself the moving spirit who was anxious to question or challenge existing policy. Ian had, therefore, some justification for his subsequent charge that 'economic policy was not that of the Cabinet but of a secretive monetarist clique'. This is one reason why I was glad the Prime Minister accepted my advice, in a minute of 29 February 1980, that arrangements should be made to discuss the Medium-Term Financial Strategy at Cabinet on 13 March. 'I shall', I said, 'be preparing a short paper for that purpose following further discussion with the Governor early next week.' And so indeed I did. Some subsequent literature suggests that this 'momentous encounter' was cancelled because Margaret and I had 'lost our nerve'.[6]

Yet when Cabinet met on 13 March, we did indeed discuss the MTFS. I prescribed the idea as a logical development of the 'letters of intent' which our Labour predecessors had been obliged to send to the IMF. By contrast, we were setting out our own programme for medium-term self-discipline. I stressed, finally, the need to illustrate the 'modest realism of our goals and to marshal the wider support which will follow from so doing'. Some individual members questioned the prudence of such a plan, echoing arguments that I had heard from others (including Margaret herself) at earlier stages. I do not recall whether Ian Gilmour said anything. He was certainly present. In his book he says only that the reception was 'less than ecstatic'.[7] The Cabinet certainly endorsed my proposal, especially as it was seen as 'desirable in this way to offer the prospect of eventual economic growth with possible tax cuts by 1982–3'. Both these expectations were fulfilled by that date and for six subsequent years. Too much for too many, no doubt; but that is for a later part of my story.

There is an unresolved mystery about the reluctance, the failure even, of the self-styled wets ever to react more sharply, more collectively or even more constructively against the policies we were following. Jim Prior offers one explanation. It would be 'dangerous', he felt, if the wets formed themselves into a cabal since that would run the risks of immediate castigation for 'conniving together against the leadership'.[8] I can understand that anxiety – up to a point. It was probably one reason, it may be thought, why Nigel Lawson and I did not attempt to broaden the base of our objections to Margaret's policy on the Exchange Rate Mechanism in 1989. But it is a less convincing reason for widespread, though far from unveiled, reluctance to raise these issues with me as Chancellor. It is hard to see any reason for that but the extreme difficulty, when it came to the point, of deploying any coherent alternatives.

The Indispensable Anchor: The 1980 Budget

My 1980 Budget finally came to birth in more or less conventional fashion. There was this year one new feature about my photo-call stroll among the crocuses of St James's Park – the first public appearance of our new Jack Russell terrier. Born a few months before at Woodbury, South Devon – the farmhouse home of Amanda's prospective in-laws, John and Dorothy Glanvill – he was christened, almost *ex officio*, Budget. It was actually Katherine Whitehorn who suggested the name. It was to be a passport to instant canine fame, on the front page of every newspaper. The cover of the *Economist* ran the headline: 'Dog Days Budget'. We shared a garden with Number 10, so within weeks the press was speculating about the risk of flying fur when Budget met Wilberforce, the enormous cat that had for years been resident next door.

The afternoon departure from Number 11 to the House of Commons this year came near to losing its most important prop, the venerable Budget box. Used by every Chancellor since Gladstone except Jim Callaghan (who happily failed to set a new fashion), the box had the previous year been bundled unceremoniously into a dusty cupboard and maltreated as a piece of discarded office furniture. Only just in time it was found by a heritage-minded Treasury official, Stanley Godfrey, who made it his business to Save the Box. Now it lives most of the year in a handsome felt-lined, solid oak case, made specially by the Department of the Environment and much grander than the box itself.

This year's speech (which is all that the box ever contains) was the longest of the five that I was to deliver, 120 minutes. For in 1980, uniquely at that date, I was presenting both sides of the Budget at the same time, the Public Expenditure White Paper as well as the customary tax-raising revenue proposals. This had come about by accident rather than design. We had needed extra time to draw up our long-term spending plans. But the change was hailed by many as a rational development; Parliament and ministers were thus obliged more closely than before to match their gross spending habits with their net income. This is the argument which had that year persuaded the Armstrong Committee (set up by the Institute of Fiscal Studies under the chairman-ship of Lord Armstrong of Sanderstead, former head of the Civil Service), to recommend this simultaneity as a general practice. The notion was later accepted by Norman Lamont, and Kenneth Clarke was the first to pioneer the process in 1993. As our experience in 1980 suggested, the Chancellor (and his Treasury team) were to find it a most exhausting procedure. Even from the point of view of the Opposition, as expressed by Jim Callaghan on this occasion, the volume of resultant printed material is far more than can sensibly be absorbed in a single day. I should not be surprised if the old timetable were to return.

The central, long-term message of my Budget was clear enough. 'Politics', I said, 'is not only the art of the possible; it is also the art of the necessary.' And necessity required 'courage over a period of years' to carry through strategy 'for the medium term . . . the defeat of inflation . . . and for the restoration of prosperity by the encouragement of enterprise'.

The crucial figures in support of this long-term view were set out in the Medium-Term Financial Strategy. That established a target range for the growth of sterling M3 of 7–11 per cent for 1980–1, and set out a path, declining by 1 per cent a year, to reach a range of 4–8 per cent by 1983–4. The document set out a similar track for reduction of the public sector borrowing requirement as a percentage of GDP from 4 per cent (£8.5 billion) in 1980–1 to 1.5 per cent in 1983–4. (In Denis Healey's worst year this figure had risen to 9 per cent.)

There was another important fortification for this prudence. We deliberately made extremely cautious assumptions about the future rate of economic growth. After the 1980 recession (which we forecast as a fall of 2.5 per cent GDP, and which turned out not quite so badly at minus 2 per cent of GDP), we assumed that the economy would grow by an average of only 1 per cent a year up to 1983–4. In the event, we achieved an average growth rate of 1.5 per cent.

A great deal has been written since about the 'naivety' with which I approached the settling of the MTFS, selected the monetary target range, accepted the linkage between monetary growth and scale of public borrowing, ignored the impact of cyclical fluctuations on both these things – oh and a good deal more besides. I may not have been an expert in any of these things but nor was I heedless of any of them. This should be quite apparent from a close study of my Budget speech and the accompanying Red Book. One of the greatest challenges of the Chancellor's job is the extent to which he has to make judgments and reach conclusions about a huge range of technical subtleties of this kind – in the last resort in the name of common sense. I like to think my training equipped me to do just that.

On many points the path had been worked out and followed during the previous four years by Denis Healey and the IMF (and had customarily been prescribed by that body in a hundred other cases). Nobody had urged me to depart from that in any significant respect, for example by choosing some monetary yardstick other than sterling M3. (I recalled at the time that this was the measure that had been specifically commended by Professor Alan Walters for the purpose of evaluating the Barber Boom some seven years before.)* It is true that over the next two years we ran into difficulties in managing the sterling M3 figures, but the wisdom of hindsight does not point, even now, to any clearly better course. The largest single cause of overshooting in the monetary figures was the consequence of our decision (which was not then and has not since been seriously questioned) to abolish the corset on the banks (the Supplementary Special Deposit Scheme). My Budget speech warned specifically that the effect on the monetary figures of removing this distortion could not be predicted in advance.

One further point deserves to be noted about this central feature of the 1980 Budget. The MTFS was the indispensable anchor for my much tougher (and vital) 1981 Budget. Taken together, the four Budgets that were designed within the MTFS framework (1980–3) succeeded in getting inflation down to 4 per cent by 1983, and in laying the foundations for nine uninterrupted years of economic growth.

But this was far from being the only ingredient in the Budget speech. There were no less than sixty detailed tax changes to announce, together with at least two dozen politically important changes in public spending plans. The changes affecting social security and the welfare state were carefully balanced. Most benefits – retirement pensions and supplementary benefit, for example – were to be fully protected against inflation. But short-term benefits (sickness and unemployment, for example) were for the first time to become liable to income tax. Beveridge himself had recommended this. For forty years 'administrative problems' had made it 'impossible'. Arthur Cockfield had, characteristically, found a way

---

* The Professor subsequently acknowledged this in *Britain's Economic Renaissance* (OUP, 1986).

through. Child benefit was to be increased, but only by 75 pence – less than many of my back-benchers had wanted. And prescription charges were to be raised to £1: this announcement provoked a brief but predictable hubbub from the Labour benches. All this 'harshness' was offset, however, by large increases in benefits for the disabled and one-parent families (each was already almost 50 per cent better off than they had been when we came into office).

Most controversial of all the benefit changes was the decision to reduce payments to the families of those who went on strike by £12 per week and to make such benefits liable to tax. I have already recounted how this proposal for which I had long campaigned had been 'disclosed' by Margaret Thatcher only a few weeks before, as a by-product of the Cabinet struggle which she and I had been waging with Jim Prior. I was not dismayed that it fell to me to make the announcement in my Budget speech.

I had some other interesting proposals to make. First came my promise to tackle the discrimination in the tax treatment of husband and wife; this was a vindication not only of Elspeth's work on the Equal Opportunities Commission but of my own campaigning on the Cripps Committee more than a decade before. My Green Paper on this topic reflected my own strong preference for consultation before any major tax reform. (So, incidentally, did my parallel promise of a Green Paper on the future structure of corporation tax.)

Next came a pair of proposals affecting income tax: first, the abolition of the lower-rate band of taxation levied at 25 per cent of the first £750 of taxable income. This complexity had been of little or no practical benefit; its abolition allowed us to achieve an Inland Revenue staff saving of 1300 (making a total of 3000 in my first two Budgets: over the previous decade the numbers had risen from 87,000 to 113,000). My second income tax proposal involved an increase of 20 per cent in the taxable value of a company car; this loophole had been growing hugely in value, and in all fairness, in my view, had to be stopped up. Margaret Thatcher challenged this fiercely when she (later) found out the details. It was wrong, she thought, to treat 'our own people' so harshly. Nevertheless, I carried the change forward gradually over the rest of my time at the Treasury. Nigel kept up the pressure when he took over.

Two other groups of proposals completed the balance of the 1980 Budget: first, a set designed to 'promote private endeavour' for private sector housing, for the National Heritage, for charitable work, and to encourage the spread of profit-sharing and wider share-ownership. Over the next four years I was able to extend all these proposals. The second group I had dubbed the 'enterprise package'. It was directed above all to the encouragement of small business and included well-focused reforms of capital transfer, capital gains and development land taxes, specific incentives for new small workshops and nursery factories and a trail-blazing new venture-capital scheme. This last was in face of opposition from the Inland Revenue, who were fearful that I was opening the way to some massive rip-off.

Finally there was my hobby-horse of Enterprise Zones. Margaret was not disposed to resist the idea, now that it came from a Chancellor in office – and when unemployment, above all in areas of urban dereliction, was a growing problem. The grey men of officialdom, of whom I had warned in my speech at the Waterman's Arms two years before, were understandably resistant, but they co-operated once it was clear that we meant business. So I was able to propose the establishment 'in the first instance' of about half-a-dozen zones, about 500 acres each, with the following benefits: 100 per cent capital allowances for industrial and commercial buildings, complete relief or exemption from development land tax, rating, industrial development certificates and industrial training levy and dramatically simplified planning and customs procedures.

Budget Reception

This description of my first full Budget, prepared in office and not in opposition, displays the immense personal authority and responsibility that this process lays upon the Chancellor. The detail is enormous and fascinating, and, at this early stage of a radical government, the canvas was immensely broad. The Chancellor's speech comes as near as anything in British politics can to approximating to a President's State of the Union address in Washington. And the Chancellor at the despatch-box has moments during a Budget speech when the scale of his authority comes home to him. I have in mind those points when he says quite baldly, 'The increased duties on whisky, wine and beer which I propose will take effect at midnight tonight. . . . I shall be increasing the duty on petrol, from 6 p.m. tonight, by the equivalent, including VAT, of 10 pence a gallon.' It is difficult not to savour the sense of power that these words imply.

This is one reason why I was glad to make it plain that the Enterprise Zone idea was anything but politically partisan, since my thinking had taken place, as I told the House, in parallel with that distinguished Fabian (and old friend) Professor Peter Hall. This touch, within a minute or two of the end of my two-hour speech, helped to secure a remarkably generous response to the Budget from Opposition as well as government benches.

The reception on my own side was certainly warm. At my late-afternoon meeting with the back-bench Finance Committee the desks were well and truly banged in welcome. The verdict that it was 'a good Tory Budget', with its particular blend of toughness and compassion, had the useful result, as Michael Jopling had predicted, of heading off objections from those who had looked for more generosity, for example on child benefit. I went on to the Budget Broadcast and our own post-Budget party at Number 11 in cheerful mood. This year we had opened the occasion to the youngest of our family friends, godchildren and the like. The children loved the chance to watch on a monitor my recording of the Budget Broadcast in the room next door – and shrieked with horror when I stumbled over a line and suddenly interrupted the first take with a loud oath. They thought we were already on air.

In the weeks that followed, the Budget played surprisingly well with both press and people. There were critics of course. But the *Sunday Times* snapshot poll recorded a 47–36 per cent majority who regarded the Budget as good for Britain. I was especially touched by a letter from the Rector of Northolt – '(i) a lifelong socialist, and (ii) not prone to flattery' – who described the Budget as 'socially just to an unusual degree. . . . I have here a huge working-class population, and I would like to thank you for your courage and fairness.' (I wonder if those who take the trouble to write such letters realize how tremendously they add to the confidence of the recipient?) And fainthearts on our own benches were urged by John Biffen, in his speech at the end of the debate, to remember that my strategy was for a full Parliament. 'Inflation', he said, 'would not be killed by a cavalry charge.'

It was this long-term, low-expectational note that I had been most anxious to stress and which came through most clearly. 'A responsible Budget for the long haul', said the *Daily Telegraph*. This confidence was increasingly reflected in foreign press comment. Philip Revzin in the *Wall Street Journal* noted that 'each new bad economic statistic seems only to reinforce the determination' of Margaret Thatcher and her Chancellor of the Exchequer. And so it did. Our first year in office was one in which our practical, if unromantic, partnership indeed continued to grow.

CHAPTER THIRTEEN

POST-CORSET DISTORTIONS

Diversions

By Easter 1980 I seriously craved a real holiday. And most happily our lifelong friends Ruth and John Button made a pre-emptive bid for us to join them at their home in Guernsey for the whole of Easter week. Ruth was the 'girl from Portpatrick' (and John her 'tax exile' husband), who had featured in my Scottish election campaign. This was our first visit to the island, which became an annual post-Budget retreat. It was an ideal contrast with the pressures of Westminster. Enjoying their own benevolent tax system, the inhabitants could take a detached view of this familiar face in their midst. He was no problem to them.

The post-Budget open season (I was normally able to leave the parliamentary handling of the Finance Bill to the Chief Secretary and other ministers) provided opportunities for some of the less humdrum aspects of the Chancellor's job. I was able, for instance, to enjoy the strangely named Trial of the Pyx. For this ritual the Chancellor was obliged to appear, as Master of the Royal Mint, before the Goldsmith's Company, empanelled as a jury, to hear their verdict on the quality of the coinage, for whose production he had been responsible during the year. The proceedings were customarily under the direction of the Queen's Remembrancer, a fancy title for the senior Queen's Bench Master – at that time my old friend Sir Jack Jacob.

This antique pattern of quality control, technically skilled and practically important, was very nearly 700 years old. Almost everyone else involved appeared by custom in robes or other finery. It was, I thought, an occasion that called for the Chancellor's only available regalia to be mobilized. This magnificent, heavily mothballed, black-and-gold Privy Councillor's robe had been, so it was said, the cause of fierce quarrels between Disraeli and Gladstone. Neither of them had been very anxious to acknowledge that it was departmental property, and each for a time claimed it as his own. I found that its appearance was greatly enhanced if I wore beneath it the court dress, breeches and silver-buckle shoes of my Queen's Counsel kit. The outfit clearly needed a hat of some kind. So I acquired a smart tricorne from Messrs Ede and Ravenscroft. Thus was born the 'Chancellor's uniform'. The Deputy Master, Jeremy Gerhard, spotted that at least one other participant in the ceremony – the chairman of Customs and Excise – arrived flying a flag on his car. Heraldic designers at the Mint were instantly set to work so that, for this occasion only in the Chancellor's year, the Master of the Mint's car is 'allowed' to sport a fluttering standard.

I am glad to say that 'my' coinage always passed the arduous assay tests to which it was subjected. In one of his years in the hot seat, Denis Healey was less fortunate, when some of his coinage was found to be short-weight. I understand that he escaped without any formal penalty. During my four-year reign as Master, we commenced the modernization of Britain's over-weight coinage. The 20p coin was first released in June 1982 and the £1 coin in April 1983. I fear that it was left for Nigel Lawson to bear the (short-lived) public wrath at the withdrawal (in 1984) of the £1 note.

This was also the season for doing the rounds of the specialist party conferences – the Conservative Women's Organization, the party in Scotland in May and in Wales in July. This year I was bidden to give the keynote speech of the CBI's annual dinner in May. On my Scottish journey I paid my first visit to Scotland's booming North Sea oil industry. BP gave us a thorough briefing at their shore HQ at Aberdeen and flew us out the next day to their Forties Field rig. On our return helicopter journey, the pilot circled over the Manse at Lonmay, where Elspeth's grandfather had been born over a century before.

The Wider World

This was the time of year too at which the Chancellor could turn to his overseas agenda. In those days the spring meetings of the International Monetary Fund and World Bank were customarily held at some overseas centre away from Washington. This exercise cost the organization – not to mention the host country – up to $1 million a year. I was able, before I left the Treasury, to secure the discontinuance of this extravagant perambulation. But in 1980 we did all go to Hamburg. Our first evening there was memorable for a moving performance by the Hamburg State

Opera of *Fidelio*. The prisoner's chorus was sung before the stark setting of a concentration camp. One of our most experienced fund-watchers, Mary Hedley-Miller, then a Treasury under-secretary, had wisely urged me to cut the Burgermeister's reception in favour of the Opera. Even she could not foresee the circumstances of the next day's start to our proceedings. We were held up for almost an hour by the delayed arrival of the US Treasury Secretary, Bill Miller. He had needed time with his team to absorb the news, which I had just heard on the BBC World Service, that the US attempt to rescue their hostages from Teheran had ended in humiliating failure in the desert. Many hearts went out to him, as he strove to make a confident entry – in the quietly jubilant presence of the Iranian Central Bank Governor, Ali Reza Norbari, and his aides.

This debacle did nothing to ease the problems we already faced as a result of the American attempt to freeze Iranian deposits with US banks overseas. This action had been taken, by presidential decree, after the Iranian seizure of American hostages in November 1979. But the cross-frontier legal problems had not been thought through. We were anxious to worst the hostage-takers, of course, but just as determined to maintain London's reputation as a centre where investment could not be interfered with on political grounds. Bill Miller came to breakfast with me at Number 11 soon after the desert fiasco. Our view was that matters had to be left for decision by the English courts, but we would certainly see if there were other ways in which we could help. A dramatic opportunity occurred on the last day of the month, 30 April. Terrorists had seized the Iranian embassy in London and were holding twenty hostages there – two BBC journalists, one policeman and seventeen Iranian diplomats. Our Special Air Services, in a daring attack, overcame the terrorists and freed the hostages. This action did nothing to ease the financial problems, but it added immensely to the reputation of Britain and of our government under Margaret Thatcher's leadership. We were able – through the skilful agency of the Bank of England (in partnership with the Algerian Central Bank) – to play a crucial role in the final cash–hostage settlement.

This year it was Italy's turn to host the G7 Economic Summit (22–23 June), in Venice, under the Presidency of Italy's new Prime Minister, Amintore Fanfani. The British were billeted in the luxurious and heavily guarded Danieli Hotel, on the Grand Canal. We were ferried noisily to and from the main meeting place in the Cini Foundation, the former Benedictine monastery on the island of San Georgio Maggiore. In terms of politically significant output, this Summit was notable as the birthplace of the European Community's crucial Venice Declaration on the Middle East peace process. In the preparation of this text, which was to serve as a sheet-anchor of sanity for many years to come, Britain's Foreign Secretary Peter Carrington played a leading part. For the Finance Ministers, and certainly for me, Venice was one of many staging posts in the process of shifting the balance of international economic opinion away from fine-tuning inflation-tolerant, pseudo-Keynesian consensus towards the more robust, monetarily based approach to which, for example, the Bundesbank and the IMF itself continue to adhere. This process was also accompanied – indeed still is, up to a point – by the search for a refurbished Bretton Woods-type arrangement for greater stability in international currency arrangements.

Margaret Thatcher and I were together on only two other continental missions that year: the bilateral Summits in Bonn and Paris. For these occasions the Prime Minister and four or five Cabinet colleagues would emplane at Northholt, generally on one of the slow-moving RAF Andovers of the Queen's Flight, and spend a whole day (including dinner) conferring with their opposite numbers in the French or German government. There would in due course be a return match, in the early days at Chequers but later more usually at Downing Street. Italy was also a partner, though slightly less frequent, in such exchanges, which served more often as occasions for getting to know one another, for demonstrating solidarity, than for the conduct of serious business. They became more important during my time as Foreign Secretary. Those during my Chancellorship retain a special interest because they occurred during the Schmidt and Giscard eras in Germany and France respectively. Margaret, in particular, found this easier than the Kohl–Mitterrand period that was to follow, quite simply because the two earlier heads both spoke exceptional English and were quite ready to do so during less formal proceedings. But there was always a tension between Margaret and Giscard, inspired perhaps by the difficulty (for each of them) in trying to remember that they were, politically at least, on the same side.

At the opening of such occasions in Bonn, the custom was for the ministers, led by Schmidt (later Kohl) and Thatcher, to stand in line outside the modern, not unattractive, Chancellery building. The morning sun shone on to the Henry Moore statuary, of which both Helmuts (in their turn) were very proud. And the discreetly uniformed German military band would play both national anthems. On this first occasion, our team included Peter Carrington MC and Francis Pym MC, both decorated for gallantry against the Germans. The German side included Count Otto von Lambsdorff, badly wounded in the same war. As I stood in this parade, listening to the tune which I had first heard forty years before as Lord Haw-Haw's signature tune, my spine tingled with excitement. Reconciliation was sometimes truly palpable in our new European rituals.

The other regular summer fiesta for economic ministers was the so-called OECD Ministerial in Paris. The Organization for Economic Co-operation and Development evolved from the OEEC (a product of the Marshall Plan era and intended to promote economic partnership in Europe alone). OECD membership now extended beyond 'free' Europe to include other capitalist countries – Japan, Canada, Australia, New Zealand, the USA. It served as a kind of multinational think-tank for this client group of governments. Once a year ministers assembled (a kaleidoscopic mixture of Finance and/or Foreign and/or Trade and/or Economic) to be briefed, to exchange views and to give the OECD officials a steer into the year ahead. Inevitably a heavily compromised communiqué – often a dry-run for the forthcoming Economic Summit – was the main product. I attended these functions, in one form or another, from 1973 to 1990, and I have to confess that I enjoyed them. They offered further opportunity to influence international economic thinking in a more market-orientated direction. The first Secretary General with whom I had to deal, an able Dutchman called Emil van Lennep, had old-fashioned views, as well as a certain opinion of himself, so that it was important (if all OECD Reports on our own economic policy were not to be unhelpful to HMG) to persuade him of the validity, the seriousness, the sincerity even, of our own approach. We made quite good headway before the time came for him to retire in 1984.

The topic on which OECD probably made the most important impact over the years – although still not sufficient to shift the great boulder very far – was agricultural policy, even including the European Community's Common Agricultural Policy. I tried to help this along with some 'typically British' sallies each year. 'When we have finished beating our swords into ploughshares,' I used to say, 'we must start beating our ploughshares into golf-clubs.' The Japanese were always amused by this, but never willing to do anything about it. So every grain of rice eaten in Japan remained home-grown, sold at five or six times world prices.

The OECD Secretariat was a job that I wanted to see filled by a

Briton when van Lennep left. We seldom succeded in filling as many international vacancies as we might reasonably expect. (Peter Carrington to NATO Secretary General in 1984 was an unusual break.) This was sometimes because we – more often than not Number 10 – did not think them important enough. But quite often it was because we concluded that we could not take the risk of putting forward the name of an existing parliamentarian for fear that we should lose the resultant by-election. I had my eye on Terence Higgins, the Tory Member for Worthing, for the van Lennep vacancy. He had been Treasury minister under Ted Heath and later a forthright chairman of the Treasury and Civil Service Committee. But the mention of his name to Margaret evoked the near-automatic reply: 'We daren't risk a by-election.'

It is easy to criticize the narrowly politicized view that was having this effect. But, as the years went by, it became increasingly hazardous, even in safe seats, to risk a by-election by appointing an incumbent to outside office. We just got away with it with the translation of Willie Whitelaw to lead the House of Lords after the 1983 election and of Leon Brittan to the Brussels Commission in 1989. In Penrith and Richmond (Yorks) our general election majorities of 15,421 and 19,526 respectively were almost overthrown. Even more significant in Margaret's mind, I think, had been the outcome of the Warrington by-election in 1981: this was caused by the appointment (without, so it is said, any consultation with Margaret or the Whips) of the sitting Labour Member, Sir Thomas Williams QC, to a seat on the Crown Court bench. The seat was narrowly held by the Labour candidate, Doug Hoyle. But Warrington acquired notoriety as the launch-pad for Roy Jenkins' successful return to Westminster politics and the blossoming of the SDP. Margaret never forgot the lesson: 'No avoidable by-elections.' So van Lennep was followed, as Secretary General of the OECD, by the archetypically excellent French *énarch*, Jean-Claude Paye.

The Community Budget Question

Certainly the most time-consuming of the overseas circuits for the Chancellor, even in those days, was that which sprang from our membership of the European Community. The formal commitments involoved a monthly Monday meeting in Brussels of the Finance Council (ECOFIN), which often involved a Sunday journey out, and an 'informal' working weekend, once in every Presidency. (The Presidency moved from country to country in a predetermined order on 1 January and 1 July of every year.) I quite soon added to this timetable the prospect of a weekend spent once or twice a year in managing a realignment of exchange rates in the European Monetary System: as the only Minister whose (non-belonging) currency was unaffected by the proceedings I was normally invited to take the chair.

Although ECOFIN meetings were frequent and lengthy, the agenda in those early years was not usually crowded. Before the Single European Act of 1986 speeded up the single-market agenda by allowing more majority voting, potentially useful proposals – such as an insurance services directive – would linger on the agenda literally for years. There were three main topics on which I made it my business, at meeting after meeting, to try reshaping colleagues' opinions as firmly as possible: the need to keep down the overall EC Budget, the need for fundamental reform of the CAP and the need to redress (on a durable basis) the huge injustice of Britain's budgetary contribution. In simple terms, the UK, one of the less prosperous member-states, was in 1980 paying into the EC Budget £1000 million more than she was receiving back in benefits. (By contrast, every other country except Germany was a net recipient.) Very seldom, if ever, did Finance Ministers have executive responsibility on these last two points: that usually rested with Agriculture or Foreign Ministers. But my intra-European John the Baptist role was far from tedious and far from useless. The main task of negotiating our case with the Community was undertaken at that time by the two Foreign Office Ministers, Peter Carrington and Ian Gilmour. Ian had at that time a special responsibility for European policy. At less frequent, but more crucial, occasions – generally the half-yearly European Council meetings – Margaret Thatcher (more or less literally) took up the cudgels. As Britain's Exchequer spokesman I took every opportunity to press the stark arithmetic of our case. And in the Treasury we made plans for the ultimate weapon in these negotiations: the actual witholding of Britain's contributions to the Community. Nonetheless, even in my Treasury days I suspect that I came to be seen as the soft cop in contrast to the hard-cop persona that enfolded Margaret Thatcher's fierce championship of our case.

It was during this summer of 1980 that we attended one of the more strenuous informal weekends, at Taormina, in the island of Sicily. Saturday evening's entertainment ended with a tantalizing midnight visit to the beautiful Graeco-Roman theatre. Sunday afternoon was devoted to a deafeningly long helicopter flight across the slopes of Mount Etna to Agrigento's Valley of Temples, radiant beneath a setting sun. We then flew in Italian military transport to the formal ECOFIN meeting in Luxembourg. One may wonder about the purpose of such exercises. This prolonged encounter – not least the long flight to Luxembourg – offered a uniquely useful opportunity for me to convey the balanced British Budget message to Francis-Xavier Ortoli, French Vice-President of the Commission, with responsibility for financial and budgetary matters. This shrewd Corsican, another superbly well-qualified French meritocrat, was later to play an important role in shaping the Commission's perception of our case.

My EC missionary role also required me to keep up a sequence of visits to the key European capitals, to present as persuasively as possible, both in speeches and in one-to-one meetings with other Financial Ministers, the inescapably reasonable arithmetic that lay at the heart of our budgetary case. Roy Jenkins has doubted the value of this exercise,[1] since I had no authority to indicate a negotiating figure. That was to misunderstand my role. I was on my rounds not as a negotiator but as an advocate. The negotiation was all being done either at European Council level or, as opportunity arose (and more fruitfully), between Foreign Ministers. So I was not myself engaged in the discussions in Brussels and Luxembourg at the end of May 1980. These enabled Peter Carrington and Ian Gilmour to present to Margaret at Chequers the important initial agreement which in the result provided for the rebate of two-thirds of our net contribution for each of the two years 1980 and 1981 – and for a comparable approach in the following year.

The deal was communicated to me by telephone while I was visiting a firm of building contractors in my constituency on Friday, 30 May. I discussed this outcome with my Treasury advisers. We had in any case kept in constant touch with our negotiators. I concluded that the deal was not merely the best that we were likely to get but intrinsically reasonable. I took care to see that this view was conveyed to Chequers. I was not able to join the prolonged wrangle between Margaret and Peter and Ian that followed. My view was very effectively represented at the meeting by Treasury Assistant Secretary Rachel Lomax. But, even when the Chequers meeting broke up, Margaret had not been persuaded to accept the proposed agreement.

The weekend press took a different view. At Ian Gilmour's suggestion, they had been briefed to regard the proposed settlement (rightly) as a considerable success for Britain and (with a little less accuracy) as a success for which all the credit should go to the Prime Minister. On the

Monday morning she presided over a special Cabinet to consider the offer. Hers was almost the only voice to be raised, even then, against it. I spoke firmly in support of the deal. And Margaret was persuaded, reluctantly, to accept this two-year ceasefire on the European front. But this particular battle remained a most provocative piece of unfinished business.

A Taxing Problem and Monetary Guidelines

The industrial natives at home were by now starting to become restless. And not without good reasons: falling production, fast-increasing unemployment, and high inflation. This peaked at 21.9 per cent in May 1980 and then fell back below 17 per cent as the previous year's VAT increase dropped out of the annual comparison. Business leaders were dismayed too by the state of the pound, up from $2.08 at the time of my first Budget to $2.28 a year later and still rising. (Few people realized how much this process owed not just to the soaring pound but also to the falling value of the dollar, as the Carter administration ebbed towards its close.) On 3 July 1980 the position eased a little, as we allowed MLR down one point to 16 per cent – still below the rate of inflation.

On the same date Cabinet was due for a general economic discussion ahead of our first consideration (on 10 July) of the public spending plans for 1981–2 and beyond. Public spending (and so the PSBR) was running well ahead of target. So too were the money-supply figures as measured by sterling M3. Some voices were raised in opposition to the tightness of our general policy. But the discussion never got out of hand and Margaret was able in her summing up to reaffirm our strategy. On 10 July, Cabinet endorsed the need for a substantial reduction of £2000 million in the public expenditure planning total for 1981–2. We were to face greater difficulty when the August and September money-supply figures came through.

But the worst and most persistent problem arose in the field of monetary policy. I had warned in my Budget speech that the removal of the corset (the scheme for limiting bank lending) in June was bound to produce some overshoot in the sterling M3 figures. When it happened the size of this phenomenon astonished us all. In July *and* August, sterling M3 grew by almost 5 per cent in each month – more than the equivalent of our central target for the entire year (9 per cent) in just eight weeks.

Margaret Thatcher and I reacted very differently to this news when the July figures were released on 9 August. We were both on holiday. Margaret was in Switzerland for a week. Elspeth and I were in Greece for three weeks with John and Susan Baring – first at the house which they had taken at Khalkis in Euboea and then, with Sue alone, at a house we had rented on Mykonos (from where we visited Delos). We got to all the remotest beaches on a pair of Lambrettas; and none of the visitors spotted the Chancellor, scooting to and fro, disguised in his Greek sea-captain's flat hat. I was intrigued to find still on sale in Athens a paperback edition of the Bin's *History of Greece*. Entranced by the mystic loveliness of Delos, and wishing to proclaim the success of his book, I sent him – we had taken tea with him in his home at Winchester only a few weeks before – a postcard of the Delos Lions. I was amazed to hear in reply that the classical hero of my youth, by then aged ninety-four, had never himself been able to visit Delos. The cheap and easy travel facilities of our age are all too often taken for granted.

Margaret's rather more formal 'holiday' arrangements enabled her to follow up her monetary dismay immediately – with Fritz Leutwiler, head of the Swiss Central Bank, and the late Karl Brunner, then of Rochester University, a monetary economist who was also on hand. In Greece, I was happily less encumbered by potential advisers. Those who were with the Prime Minister responded by laying the blame quite simply upon the Bank of England, for its refusal to adopt the monetary-base method of controlling the money supply. Margaret needed little encouragement to look askance in that direction. She returned to London determined to renew the search for the magic monetary-base box, which would achieve stricter control of the money supply without any risk of higher interest rates.

I was, of course, dismayed by the figures but much less inclined to believe that we were likely to find any instant solution. It was after all less than six months since we had committed our MTFS very firmly to the well-established sterling M3 targets. We had warned that the removal of the corset (as often happened with that garment) would reveal distortions of unknown size. And so it had.

As for monetary-base control, we had looked into that, as I had told the House in my Budget speech, in the previous autumn. And we had published an open-minded Green Paper about it in the spring. That was due for discussion at a seminar which Bank and Treasury officials were to hold (remarkably at Church House, Westminster) at the end of September with academics and City economists. So at least one inquest on the summer's surprise figures was already in hand.

Margaret was far from content with that prospect. She summoned the Governor and his deputy to Number 10. Each was, for good reason, at a meeting overseas. So Margaret was left to wax eloquently angry with their rather startled substitutes, John Fforde and Eddie George, the Bank's home executive director and deputy cashier respectively. (Eddie George, one of the real pros, for whose judgment I had considerable respect even then, was candid enough to tell the Prime Minister that, whatever the figures might be saying, we should be seeking a way to get interest rates down. He succeeded Robin Leigh-Pemberton as Governor of the bank in 1993.)

That meeting ended inconclusively. Margaret launched into a series of Number 10 seminars (which I attended together with other Treasury ministers and officials) on the whole range of monetary questions. Quite soon, Alan Walters, to be brought on board from the beginning of 1981 as Margaret's economic adviser, cast his shadow before him. In partnership with the Prime Minister's erstwhile mentor, Alfred Sherman (who had not yet been discarded), Walters commissioned yet another report on monetary policy, this time from Professor Niehans of Berne University. (Switzerland was the only country in which monetary-base control had ever been applied in practice for more than a short time.) After five weeks' work Niehans had reported in favour of using the monetary base, although warning that it was by no means a guarantee of lower interest rates. Peter Middleton advised me that the report 'was strong on views but not on analysis and evidence'. But this, he thought, was 'not surprising from someone unfamiliar with our institutions'.

Against this background of intellectual turmoil, which Margaret's interest was doing nothing to diminish, those of us with day-to-day responsibility to markets as well as to Parliament had to continue taking operational decisions. Nigel Lawson noticed that in the course of the seminars which Margaret had inspired she was sometimes less than courteous towards me – provoked, he thought, by my 'manner and mode of argument'.[2] I had much more cause to be angry with her often ceaseless and hectoring interruptions. But nothing, it seemed, would staunch them before they had run their course. I would then resume, at the point at which I had been interrupted. I was not to be put off. I kept returning to fundamentals, irritating as that might have been. Sterling M3 was our chosen, and well-publicized, target. It had served effectively in that role for at least four years. Moreover, it had been the aggregate which had enabled Alan Walters – almost alone – to warn against the inflationary consequences of the Barber Boom, at a time when ministers (including myself) were commending M1 to Parliament as the more reliable alternative.

The advocates of monetary-base control had not carried the day when we had examined their case a year before. Nor had they done so at the Church House conference of a few weeks before. Since Switzerland had been the only laboratory for MBC, we should be neither surprised nor over-impressed by Swiss academic testimony in its support. Paul Volcker had apparently had some short-lived success with it in America a year before, but only at the cost of high, volatile interest rates. Eventually, at the end of a series of gruelling meetings, we came back to our starting point. We had to make the best of the case to which we had committed ourselves, with sterling M3 as the important, if no longer the only, monetary lodestar of our policy.

As we returned to our working agenda, I took an important decision about making the best of Alan Walters' appearance on the scene. So far as possible, my Treasury advisers and I should keep alongside him and him alongside us. We should not challenge his independence nor interfere in any way with his direct line to the Prime Minister. But we should be sure to let him know how we were thinking, and do our best to stay aware of his state of mind. Peter Middleton volunteered himself for the role of link-man and proved very effective in the role, even if never absolutely so – that would have been to expect the impossible. Alan was never happier than when he was making some exclusive input into the Prime Minister's thinking, except when he was taking (or claiming) the credit for having done so.

Politics of Public Spending Control

By November 1980 two items dominated our practical agenda: the completion of the public expenditure review and the preparation of my Autumn Statement to Parliament. This had to deal with our (statutorily required) economic forecast and social security proposals for the following year, as well as with expenditure. Early in September, and again in

October, I minuted Margaret with warnings that the expenditure
overshoot was continuing to grow. Inevitably I should have to try to
place our monetary policy in perspective as well.

   All this had also to be set in the wider political context. The October
party conference at Brighton had attracted diverse notices from the
press. Some saw it as full of coded messages of dissent from Cabinet
wets, others as uneventful and flat. My economic debate foreshadowed
the Prime Minister's 'not for turning' phrase. I offered no prospect of
tax reductions but warned instead of continued pressure on public
spending. If there could be relief for anyone, then it would be for
business and industry. 'There is no alternative to the course on which
we are set. . . . Have no fears – we shall not falter. We shall not flinch.
We shall win through.' Later that evening, as Elspeth and I walked from
our hotel after dinner to the Young Conservative dance, we encountered
a number of 'Right to Work' demonstrators, including some from my
home town, Port Talbot, whose jobs had gone in the aftermath of the
steel strike. Suddenly a group of them surged across the pavement
towards us. One raised his hand and strode up to me. His challenge was
much less alarming than his approach: 'You know my Auntie Megan,
don't you?' he asked. And indeed we did: Megan King was still our
housekeeper in London. We were delighted by this chance meeting with
one of her nephews, who had sadly lost his job at the Abbey steelworks
only months before.

   More belligerent noises were coming from the leaders of British
business. Engineering industry output in the Midlands had slumped by
25 per cent in three months. Earnings were still rising fast, by 22 per
cent in the year to August. (Business leaders were as ever reluctant to
recognize their own responsibility for that.) Unemployment, the headline figure, leaped by 200,000 in the same month. And three out of
every five CBI members were expecting to lay off labour in the next four
months. The pound had risen by early September to $2.40 and interest
rates, after the one-point fall in July, were still stuck at 16 per cent. At
the CBI's autumn conference Michael Edwardes, chairman of what was
then British Leyland, declared that if the government couldn't 'find a
way of living with North Sea oil' we should do better to 'leave the
bloody stuff in the ground'. The CBI's new director general, Terence
Beckett, committed himself to his celebrated 'bare-knuckle fight' on
industry's behalf. The actual confrontation at Number 10 a week later
was less aggressive. But the case was sustained when the chairman of
ICI, Maurice Hodgson, came to Downing Street to warn the Prime

Minister that his company were about to report their first ever quarterly loss.

All this meant falling revenue and rising expenditure for the Treasury. We were well braced to accept some inescapable increase in government borrowing as this dismal half of the economic cycle worked itself through. Some of that was already provided for in my original Budget expectation of a PSBR (1980–1) of £8500 million. But already that looked like being overrun by some £3000 million, of which only about half was due to the unexpected depth of the recession.

So it was important to secure the extra £2000 million of savings on which the Cabinet had agreed in July. Important but in the end impossible, even after three exceptionally long Cabinet discussions (including one special meeting on 4 November). We had two prime targets for savings of more than £500 million each: defence procurement costs and welfare benefits. I saw the Ministry of Defence as recidivist over-spenders. Programme after programme exceeded budgeted cost by up to £1000 million; the Stingray torpedo and the Nimrod radar system programme were among the worst offenders. But Francis Pym was determined to keep up the pressure. He let it be known that he was prepared to resign if thwarted. As he was by convention entitled to do, he wheeled the Chiefs of Staff in to lobby the Prime Minister. This was not an occasion which the Chancellor was expected to attend, but Margaret was well briefed on my behalf. Indeed she scarcely needed briefing since we were both of the same mind on the strategy – or at least I thought we were. In fact she had two distinct minds of her own: and not for the first time the Iron Lady overruled the would-be Iron Chancellor that was within her. Margaret's heart had joined the argument on Francis' side – and overruled her head (which was on mine). But she did not forgive Francis for the advocacy which had caused her to submit: within two months he had been moved away from Defence to lead the House of Commons. His later post-Falklands spell as Foreign Secretary was seen as a necessity rather than an act of forgiveness.

Patrick Jenkin, my old flatmate, defended his social security budget with vigour and skill. In earlier discussion with the Chief Secretary, Patrick had accepted that John Biffen's proposals for pensions and other benefits to be increased by less than the rate of inflation (so as to yield savings of £600 million) should be on the agenda. But when this suggestion came up for Cabinet discussion Patrick made very plain that it was politically impossible. He read out the Prime Minister's own specific undertakings, given on television at the time of the election, to maintain the purchasing power of benefits. Prime Minister, Chancellor and Chief Secretary alike were obliged to retreat. We had to be content with our success the previous year – when Patrick had courageously supported us – in breaking the link between pensions and earnings (as opposed to prices).

Autumn Statement 1980

It was immediately clear to me that I should have to look for extra revenue. Some critics have tried to present this decision as evidence of my determination to 'wreak vengeance upon the high-spending wets'. But life was not so emotional or irrational. My reasoning was quite straightforward. Exchange rate and interest rates alike were, plainly and as a matter of common sense, too high for anything like comfort for industry. As a result of post-corset distortions, the sterling M3 figures had, for the moment at least, blown themselves right off the map. So they could not by themselves be allowed to stand in the way of lower interest rates. And cutting interest rates was the only thing the government could do to ease the upward pressure on the exchange rate. Two other possible causes of sterling buoyancy – the pound's petrocurrency status and the Prime Minister's reputation for financial probity – were beyond our control. There was, however, one possible obstacle to lower interest rates: the risk that we might not be able to sell enough government debt to meet our burgeoning borrowing requirement. This was far from a theoretical consideration. Less than twelve months before the very same risk had obliged us to *raise* interest rates by a record 3 per cent. If the monetary side of the MTFS was for the moment adrift – and it was – there was all the more reason for us to be seen to take the fiscal side seriously.

So my forthcoming Autumn Statement, despite all our protestations to the contrary, began to look very like a revenue-raising Healey-style mini-budget. We needed to lay a secure foundation for a cut in interest rates. It clearly made sense to avoid any measures that would disadvantage the hard-pressed manufacturing industry, which needed help. Two taxable targets did present themselves: the North Sea oil companies, whose buoyant revenues were one of the reasons for the strength of the pound; and those who were still employed, whose real incomes had continued to rise (partly because of the strength of the pound), despite the decline in the economy as a whole. So, on 24 November, I announced what were in effect two tax increases: National Insurance contributions, for employees only, were to go up by one percentage point, from 6.75 to 7.75 per cent, with effect from 1 April 1981. And North Sea oil producers were to pay, with effect from 1 January 1981, a new supplementary petroleum duty (SPD) of 20 per cent of the gross return on each field.

Each of these changes was expected to yield an extra £1 billion in 1981–2. In addition I was able to take credit for some £650 million, which was now to be refunded to us from the EC. We had already announced, with modest fanfare, the allocation of some extra £245 million to the Community Enterprise and other employment programmes. And we had been obliged, with much less enthusiasm, to concede substantial extra cash aid to British Leyland, British Steel and other nationalized industries. In addition, I announced three relatively modest changes in methods of monetary control, which had emerged from the many technical wrangles that had followed our Green Paper on the monetary base. These were intended to cool, even to conclude, the MBC argument; and, we hoped, to depoliticize changes in interest rates. Finally, I told the House that 'the Bank of England, with my approval, is this afternoon announcing a reduction in minimum lending rate of two percentage points' (down from 16 to 14 per cent, the level from which we had raised it just twelve months before). We had struggled mightily to achieve just this.

It was, of course, strange that I should myself be announcing a cut in the MLR at the same time as I was announcing changes that were intended to make its behaviour less political. Even so, we were able to persuade the markets, however reluctantly, that we still had some idea where we were going – and, more important, that we still had some of the courage that was necessary to take us there. The following day *The Times* greeted my 'package of measures as a brave attempt to put the government's economic strategy back on course'. But the *Financial Times* was less impressed: 'The Chancellor's Statement yesterday was better than it looked, though the country may still need some convincing.'

That was the problem. Presentationally, my Statement was a disaster. Sam Brittan, very often a firm supporter, writing under the headline 'The Tragedy of Sir Geoffrey', said that 'there are times when presentation can reach such a low level that it can have an adverse effect on policy'.[3] There is no doubt that my Statement was about as shapeless and lacking in explanatory or thematic structure as such a text could possibly be. The truth is that it was not the product of any initially coherent strategic inspiration but rather the result of what looks in retrospect like a long trudge through a seemingly endless series of multiple-choice examination questions. The search for the answers had itself been so wearing that we were glad simply to have got most of them right (as I think we had). By convention the Autumn Statement was extremely short. We did not want to admit, even to ourselves, that this one was different. So I failed to give the task even a fraction of the attention that I devoted to a proper Budget speech. Yet the occasion was scarcely any less important.

There is one other strangeness about this failure to give enough attention to presentation of the message in the House: at almost exactly the same time, I was presenting the same case much more effectively in speeches not to the House but in the outside world. Just ten days before I made my Autumn Statement I had, for example, been telling a Dorking audience that the most popular complaint from those who manage industry had been that governments do not have the wisdom and courage to draw up a strategy and stick to it. 'It makes a change', I remarked drily, 'to be criticized for too much constancy of purpose.' We had put off the necessary remedies for too long. 'The price we are now paying', I explained, in an almost verbatim echo of my twenty-year-old tract on the Welsh economy,* – declining output, low living standards – is the price of refusing, over many years, to face the facts and to take the tough decisions that were necessary.' So those who thought that somewhere out there were policies which, if only we would embrace them, would painlessly solve our problems were cherishing a dangerous illusion. 'I must tell you plainly', I concluded, 'that no such option exists.'

The manifest gap in style between that speech and my clearly less cogent parliamentary presentation reflects most of all, I think, a particular lack of confidence in face of the House of Commons. The more direct advocacy that came naturally to me on party platforms was always more difficult to combine with the more meticulous official drafting which came more usually to hand for a 'Statement by the Chancellor of the Exchequer'. And the non-parliamentary speeches were, of course, more open than statements to the House to the influence of political thinking by my special advisers. Their preparation was, quite simply, less rushed. I suspect that I am not the only minister to have felt inhibited in this way.

* See p. 32 above.

Flawed Statement

There was a particular flaw in this Autumn Statement – or there was perceived to be – which was thought seriously to aggravate my offence. We had decided, I told the House, to increase, by one full percentage point, the *rate* of National Insurance payable by employees, and to leave the employer's contributions unchanged. So my Statement referred to both those things. But I had not, however, referred to a series of changes which took place more or less automatically in such inflationary times: and that is that the bands of income, on which such contributions were levied and calculated, were also raised (at the starting and the finishing point) broadly in line with inflation. This meant, of course, that since price and wage levels had risen all round by about 20 per cent there would, as happened normally every year, be an increase in the cash payable by employers and by employees alike. But the real burdens and the relationship between those two burdens (after taking account of inflation) would not have changed at all. So I had said nothing in my Statement about any of these automatic changes. Neither Denis Healey nor anyone else in the House of Commons on 24 November had a single word of complaint about this.

Yet suddenly a huge storm broke about my head. The worst kind of parliamentary offence had been committed, it was said. I had concealed from the House, even if I had not intended to do so, the fact that employers would be paying a figure variously put at £386 million, £573 million or £900 million more than in the previous year. And so on and on. It would be tedious to rehearse the arguments again. I was convinced that I had done no wrong – substantially, presentationally, least of all morally – and continued so to argue up to and through the debate on the economy that was in any case due to take place three days later.

My task in that debate was not made any easier – nor was my temper improved – by the fact that John Biffen, in a series of media interviews in the intervening two days, expressed the view that 'it would have been better if the situation had been explained in the House'. News of my dismay at these remarks soon reached him, and he was quick to write me a note in which he expressed himself:

truly sorry that yesterday was deemed unhelpful – but in all conscience I thought the interviews had served a good purpose. . . . It saddens me that

some words of mine might be construed as having an almost Butlerian*
opaqueness bordering on double-entendre. I think your action has been
straightforward and beyond reproach.

With the wisdom of hindsight it is clear that I misjudged this whole
sequence of events. However innocent my original omission, I should
have been wiser (and John Biffen's view was confirmed in the Thursday
debate, in generous asides on this point, by Jim Callaghan and Ted
Heath) to express regret at my failure to give the whole picture and to
acknowledge that it would have been better had I done so.

For misfortunes never come singly. This was the very day on which
news of our twenty-one-year-old son Alec's involvement with the
Campaign for Nuclear Disarmament burst upon an unsuspecting world.
He was in his last year at York University and was press officer for the
local branch of CND. They had planned, for the Friday of that very
week (28 November), a march through York to protest at the forthcoming deployment of Cruise missiles. Alec was to have dressed up as US
President-elect Ronald Reagan and to have led through the streets of
York, by a noose tied around her neck, a female student dressed and
made up as Margaret Thatcher.

As soon as York journalists guessed that Alec might be a member of
the Chancellor's family, his house was under siege. Speaking from his
hiding-place in a broom cupboard, he had told his mother of his
predicament. He would be considering it with his student colleagues
later that day. Alec explained to the press: 'My father and I respect each
other's political differences. . . . The problem is that at the moment,
even though I'm exercising my rights as a citizen, it will be politically
reflected on him. . . .' In the end, Alec and his friends called off the
Reagan–Thatcher part of their demonstration and settled for a more
conventional protest march. I was due to speak to two university
audiences in Oxford during the course of that Friday. As I walked
through the snow from one to the other, I was beset by television and
other journalists wanting my comments on Alec's 'disgraceful' behaviour. I tried to emulate his self-restraint. Gradually the 'storm' began to
subside.

Hugo Young, however, kept the pot boiling by writing in the *Sunday
Times* about 'the Chancellor's fatal flaw' – apparently my lack of

* R. A. Butler had been notorious in his day for double-edged remarks of this kind,
known as 'Rabisms'.

compatibility with the Prime Minister. It was his insight that was fatally flawed, since it depended upon a mistaken belief that I was excluded from membership of the 'breakfast club' of Prime Ministerial intimates.* But my denial of that, a week later, was necessarily delphic. I described as 'without foundation the suggestion that the Prime Minister has a minor group of ministers, whether meeting at breakfast or any other time, from which the Chancellor is excluded'. This did not prevent a bout of speculation about my future. A week later, the *Economist* was in arbitral mood: 'undoubtedly some blame for the failures in government economic policy can be set at Sir Geoffrey's door', but some too at Mrs Thatcher's, most notably for her willingness to challenge her own strategy by pressing for particular expenditures or tax reliefs. 'For Mrs Thatcher to sack her Chancellor now would be an unmistakable sign of panic and unfair to a man who has been more ideologically loyal to her than many of her Cabinet.'4

Christmas Reprieve

Not for the first time, comfort in such circumstances came from my post bag. One new Member quoted the Prime Minister, who had been asked at a recent private dinner to comment on Cabinet meetings: 'Well, really it's very lonely. It's really Geoffrey and me against the rest of them.' It didn't always feel like that, I have to say. But at this stage, on all the big decisions, it still really was. And my long-retired prep-school head-master, Gilbert Ashton, wrote from Abberley: 'All strength to your elbow and the P.M.'s too in your efforts, which I believe are gradually succeeding in getting your message across to the country.'

And so indeed it began to seem. For the *Financial Times* of 2 December reported a speech in the City of London in which my colleague, Sir Ian Gilmour, 'defended the Chancellor of the Exchequer from what he claimed had been unfair attacks on the Government's economic policy'. It was regrettable and unfair, said Ian, 'that fire should be directed personally against the Chancellor. Newspapers and people who are attacking him now would be applauding him next spring when inflation is recognized to be declining steeply.' Praise from the ranks of Tuscany was praise indeed. So I felt moderately fortified for almost my last pre-Christmas engagement of 1980, lunch with the Council of the

* See pp. 147–8.

Stock Exchange, a traditional date in the Chancellor's calendar. This year I decided to build upon that tradition by casting the light-hearted speech that was expected of me in a form which would enable me to sing it to a familiar Sullivan melody. I began:

> When the pound stays high and hardly seems to falter
> When the CBI complains of MLR
> When the pressures mount for policies to alter
> And the world recession bites both near and far
>
> When the corset is so awkward to untangle
> And the money figures threaten to overrun
> It's no surprise your nerves get in a jangle
> – A Chancellor's lot is not a happy one. (REPEAT)

And I concluded:

> Our problems are not short-term but deep-seated
> The things we're doing really must be done
> I am quite determined not to be defeated
> – A Chancellor's lot is quite a happy one. (REPEAT)

CHAPTER FOURTEEN

'THE MOST UNPOPULAR BUDGET'

———

Changing Places: January 1981

And so to 1981, the year that witnessed the birth of my most controversial Budget. It is unnerving (as well as exhilarating, it must be said) to be so closely identified with an event which seems destined for ever to provoke the fiercest historical, academic and ideological conflict. The ferocity is all the more remarkable for being aroused not by personality but by questions of doctrine and judgment.

But the year started with a more personally agreeable event: the marriage of our good friend Leon Brittan. His bride was Diana Petersen, whom we had come to know well during their long courtship in his Cleveland and Whitby constituency. The civil ceremony, organized in London by his elder brother Samuel, was followed by a reception for a large cohort of well-wishers under our auspices in the main state room at 11 Downing Street.

On that very day, 5 January, Margaret carried through the first significant reshuffle of her administration. This saw the promotion of Leon to the Cabinet, as my number two – Chief Secretary to the Treasury. I couldn't resist the temptation to postpone my brief speech to the health of the bride and groom until the 'release time' for the news of the Cabinet changes, at seven o'clock. I was thus able to offer double-barrelled congratulations to Leon and at the same time to delight the rest of the company with news of his promotion.

My own role in connection with the reshuffle was, as almost always, fairly detached. I was not one of the small, slightly variable group whom Margaret consulted directly and regularly about these things. The Chief Whip, Michael Jopling, and Willie Whitelaw were the central figures, along with Ian Gow. Ian generally canvassed my views, so that the

Prime Minister and I had a good idea of each other's thinking, and Margaret would often take advantage of our Sunday-evening drink sessions to sound out my reaction to some of her ideas. I had sensed her mounting irritation with the engaging but self-indulgent indiscretions of Norman St John Stevas, Leader of the House and Minister for the Arts – who lost his place. I knew that Angus Maude, a shrewd and experienced voice in Cabinet as Paymaster General, was ready to go. Francis Pym's stubbornness on behalf of his defence budget had earned him Margaret's resentment, so he was moved over to lead the House. (When the time came, eight and a half years later, for me to be offered the same job, I had no illusions about Margaret's modest view of that post.) John Nott moved to Defence, and John Biffen took his place at Trade. Both Margaret and I saw Nott as a trustie, who could be relied upon to get on top of the brass-hats. Ironically, the Falklands conflict thrust him into a role which he could never have expected.

John Biffen had shown himself to be a reluctant axe-man. More than I had realized at the time, much of our difficulty on the public spending side had sprung from John's distaste for detail and instinct for compromise. His capacity for stylish comment, which could sometimes irritate as much as it entertained, made him later a very popular Leader of the House. '£M3', he commented in a generous farewell note, 'has improved dramatically on my departure from the Treasury.' But I was disappointed – like Margaret, I suspect – that our friendship never quite blossomed into the working partnership for which I had hoped. For the present, his free-trading instincts were regarded as apt for Trade.

Hence the vacancy in my team. Nigel, I know, had hoped for the job of Chief Secretary, not unreasonably. But he had yet to find his way on to Willie Whitelaw's preferred list. This, I think, is the reason why Leon's name came forward. He had already impressed Willie – and others – by his work as Minister of State at the Home Office. And Margaret knew that I had long had great confidence in his all-round ability, not least in his unique blend of disciplined toughness and personal charm, just what was needed in a good Chief Secretary. So I felt no need to press Nigel's claim, perhaps (and rather selfishly) because he was still to remain in my team, alongside Leon. (I have since reproached myself slightly for not having given Nigel any warning word of what was afoot. He heard the news only just ahead of the public announcement and was clearly dismayed – though characteristically not for long.) This cautious reshuffle modestly tilted the Cabinet balance – Brittan in place of Stevas – in support of our economic strategy. And

Leon's capacity for making almost weekly supportive speeches added a good deal to our public firepower.

Economic Background to the Budget

These changes took place at the start of the crucial planning period for the Budget, which I was to present on 10 March. We had two months to go. Already the likely setting, as I was later to explain it to the House, was becoming clearer. The world was in deep but still inflationary recession, largely the result of the huge oil-price increases of the two preceding years. Since 1978 the world price had more than trebled, from $12 to $40 per barrel. The oil-producing countries of OPEC collected in 1980 about 10 billion more in export receipts than they had in 1978. So the rest of the world had that much less to spend on other goods and services – and governments were obliged, at the same time, to cope with the huge inflationary spiral triggered by higher oil prices. Small wonder that during 1980 output had fallen sharply in all but one of the seven major economies: and that in the twenty-four OECD countries some three million people had lost their jobs, while average inflation rates remained in double figures.

As if that world perspective was not bad enough – it was all too easy to forget it – we still had our own uniquely British handicaps to cope with. *Some* businesses in Britain still led the world. But too many others – often whole industries, like steel – had lagged far behind, in the mistaken belief that change could be postponed indefinitely. Even during the previous three years British unit labour costs had risen three times as fast as those of our competitors.

There were moreover major imbalances within our economy to be taken into account. The first was between consumers and companies, between people and businesses. Individuals had benefited greatly from the strong pound and often from large pay increases as well. Between 1977 and 1980 the real after-tax income of people had risen by about one-sixth. During the same period the real disposable income of industrial and commercial companies had fallen by one-quarter. Within the business sector itself, there was a comparable contrast between the fortunes of the oil companies and the banks, on the one hand, and most manufacturers on the other, who were hard pressed.

The human consequences of all this were deeply disturbing. Put simply, people were becoming more expensive, yet producing no more.

Rising costs were pushing up prices, so that businesses were selling less, becoming poorer and cutting jobs. As a result, unemployment had risen fast as well – by almost a million in the last year.

Most of these tides of economic change were beyond any possible reach of government to control. But they had a profound effect on government finances. Recession had reduced tax revenues. Rising unemployment had pushed up benefit costs. Poor performances, often soaring losses, by nationalized industries were costing much more. And, as I have already recounted, colleagues had been unable, even if willing, to reduce or even control their spending programmes. Inevitably therefore, the amount we had to borrow – the public sector borrowing requirement – was moving way ahead of all our estimates. So too was the rate of growth of the money supply, at least as measured on the basis that had been accepted for the previous decade, sterling M3. Even so, the cut of 2 per cent in MLR (down to 14 per cent), which we had secured with my 1980 Autumn Statement, was still in place. And inflation had fallen from its peak of 21.9 per cent to 13.0 by the turn of the year.

Within the Treasury my ministerial colleagues, my advisers and I had been watching these matters developing week by week and had no doubt about the scale of the problems confronting us. An early opportunity for sharing these pre-Budget insights with the Prime Minister and some of her advisers came at a Saturday seminar at Chequers on 17 January. The cast included Keith Joseph, Terry Burns, Robin Ibbs, John Hoskyns and Alan Walters (the last-named had officially joined the Prime Minister's team shortly before on 1 January).

This meeting is one of several that features in the subsequent accounts of the evolution of the 1981 Budget. Most of the participants have been keen to take credit (sometimes to apportion blame) for what eventually emerged. So there has been no lack of over-simplification in these narratives. All this was being played out on at least three stages: within the Treasury, within Number 10 and in contacts between the two. Most of the subsequently alleged battle-lines were by no means so apparent (to me at least) at the time. 'The Treasury', 'officials', sometimes 'the Bank', are often cast in misleadingly monolithic mode. Surprisingly heroic roles are sometimes attributed to individual performers, occasionally by unexpected witnesses. Alan Walters, for example, secured this tribute from Anthony Harris of the *Financial Times*: 'He gave this advice and the policy was reversed fairly quickly and everything started coming all right.'[1]

Some of Walters' champions (not excluding the Professor himself) credit this returned traveller from North America with near-visionary insight. There was often a semi-messianic quality about his enthusiasm – about his silences even. Most of us were greatly interested by his input, which had nevertheless to be seen as coming from someone who had been out of the London scene for some years. This was one reason why I had established the Middleton–Walters dialogue and arranged for him to receive copies of the Treasury papers. We were seldom afforded the same insight into the – often assertive rather than analytical – papers which went to Margaret from Walters (or from the rest of the Policy Unit). This was, I suppose, understandable, for those working together at Number 10 (not excluding the Prime Minister herself) must from time to time have wanted to cherish a world of intimacy, which they could regard as their own.

It was for the same reason, I fancy, that Margaret would quite often – more frequently as the years went by – cite advice she had received from 'one of my people' or 'my people'. It seemed sometimes as though she was Joan of Arc invoking the authority of her 'voices'. The Prime Minister was understandably reluctant to reveal the balance of her telephonic kitchen cabinet. Quite often, I suspect, the voice was that of Woodrow Wyatt – which she may have thought sufficient reason for cloaking it in anonymity. Fortunately, John Hoskyns, then head of her Policy Unit, and I had worked together long enough and closely enough – particularly in the early days of 'Stepping Stones'* – to retain an easy familiarity and willingness to exchange ideas. This mutual confidence helped a good deal to pull the act together.

Destroying the Myth

So much then for the background to the Chequers seminar. Terry Burns and I arrived there with a clear view of the Treasury's expectations. The 1980–1 PSBR now looked as though it was going very substantially to overshoot my 1980 Budget forecast of £8.5 billion. The 1981–2 deficit would, of course, be higher. The gap was likely to be larger than the £1.5 billion we had expected after taking credit for the increases announced in my Autumn Statement. We should probably be looking for total tax increases of about £3 billion. The Budget, I explained,

* See pp. 104–8 above.

would have to be very tough. Margaret Thatcher was, as I told the Institute for Fiscal Studies in 1991,[2] 'not amused'. She was very concerned at the politics of that prospect, and I could hardly blame her. But I had no doubt, in those days, about my ability ultimately to obtain her support for policies as tough as might be necessary.

As the weeks went by, the forecast figures did not get any better. We had plenty of anguished debate within the Treasury about the right reaction. There was no argument about the objective. Whatever the answer to the theoretical differences about monetary aggregates (sterling M3, M1, M0 and all the rest), we all wanted to get interest rates down – for its own sake and because the pound was, by any practical standards, too high. If that was to happen, we had to borrow less. Whatever the background of my Treasury advisers – 'Keynesian', 'monetarist' or agnostic – nobody was arguing that we could let the PSBR go hang. The only question was by how much we should or could rein it back. Douglas Wass and Bill Ryrie, recently appointed second permanent secretary, later to take over at the Overseas Development Administration of the Foreign Office, were among those on the side of the doves. All my ministers and special advisers, backed by Terry Burns and Peter Middleton, were on the side of the hawks. In our earliest assessments, the 1981–2 PSBR was forecast at £11.5 billion. In order to get that below £10 billion, which I then thought desirable, we should need to raise taxes by some £1.5 billion. However, by 10 February 1981, when I was again discussing all this with the Prime Minister at Number 10, the forecast PSBR for 1981–2 had risen to £13 billion. On the basis that a PSBR of £10 billion was the maximum that would be wise – given market perceptions and the desirability of securing a further cut in interest rates – taxes would need to go up by £3 billion.

Subsequent news from the forecasters was not reassuring. By the time of our next meeting at Number 10, on 13 February, attended by Burns and Walters, the PSBR forecast had risen to £13.5–£13.75 billion. I said that the tax hike would have to go up to £3.5 billion. Walters took the view that the forecasters still probably understated the problem. He pressed for a figure of £4 billion. Margaret reacted angrily, exclaiming that she had not been elected to put up taxes. Quite right too – nor had I! So I was grateful for Alan Walters' support at that meeting for my side of the argument. But the problem still remained: how were we to raise such a large sum? We had accepted already the need to 'double-index' the excise duties – to raise them by twice the rate of inflation. And we were ready to raise income tax thresholds by only half the inflation rate. But Margaret and I were both very reluctant to bridge the remaining gap by putting the basic income tax rate up by the one penny that would be necessary.

Alan Walters and the rest of the Number 10 team submitted a later minute to the Prime Minister in which they called for tax increases of no less than £5 billion, including specifically an increase in the basic income tax rate. John Hoskyns supported this with a personal note to me (dated 10 February) in which he reaffirmed his 'desperate concern about the Budget strategy' and his real fear of a mid-year funding crisis. 'You should', he urged, 'give the country a *real shock*; which would be good for the authority and credibility of government, you and Margaret, and is the only chance of a "break-out".' My own thinking was by this time not very different. From Alan Walters, on 25 February, I received an even more pressing note: following a luncheon at the Union Discount Bank, he told me, he had concluded that 'a really satisfactory figure for the PSBR would be £7 billion'. This suggestion, which would have meant a tax hike of some £7.5 billion, came near to taking Alan off our charts altogether. It was best ignored.

By the time of my last meeting with Margaret before she took off to the United States on 26 February, for her first meeting with President Ronald Reagan, I had completed my final review of the prospect within the Treasury. By now, the forecast PSBR for 1981–2 had risen yet again. The figure we eventually published on Budget Day was no less than £14.5 billion. The case for increasing taxes had grown still stronger. I had remained resistant to the idea of any increase in the basic rate (whose reduction had been a hallmark of my first Budget). I eventually accepted Arthur Cockfield's alternative advice, in favour of freezing the personal allowances for a year. This 'extraordinarily bold move', as Margaret describes it,[3] enabled me to tell her that I had been able, without changing the basic income tax rate, to achieve a forecast PSBR of no more than £10.5 billion, with a net tax hike of £4 billion. This was reported to those concerned by her private secretary, Tim Lankester. Alan Walters recalls being informed, as he puts it, that 'the Prime Minister has told Geoffrey to put taxes up by £4 billion'.[4] More accurately, Margaret had endorsed my judgment of what was necessary – and Alan Walters had played a most useful role in persuading her in that direction.

Here perhaps is one source of the myth about the paternity of the difficult judgments at the heart of the 1981 Budget, the implication being that the Budget was somehow 'made in Number 10' against

'Treasury' advice. The key Budget judgments were, in fact, fashioned from the outset by the Chancellor of the Exchequer with the help of other Treasury ministers and special advisers, and on the strength of an understandable spread of opinion within the Treasury itself. They took full account of the advice that was forthcoming from Professor Walters and others at Number 10 and elsewhere. Only one source of official advice that was normally available never in fact reached me in 1981. In 1980, and in each subsequent year, there was available to the Chancellor a long, considered letter from the Governor of the Bank of England. Its central advice was always about what used to be called the 'Budget judgment'. In 1981 this never came. No explanation has ever reached me for the fact that on the fiscal equivalent of St Crispin's Day, the Governor of the Bank of England remained, apparently, 'still abed'.

The tax increases which I actually proposed in my Budget speech reduced the forecast PSBR in 1981–2 by £4 billion from £14.5 billion (6 per cent of GDP) to £10.5 billion (4.5 per cent of GDP). In the event, the out-turn was considerably better, at £8.5 billion. The final structure of the entire budgetary package was as harsh as it was comparatively straightforward. I had announced in November my plans to raise £1 billion extra from the North Sea oil industry (supplementary petroleum duty) and about the same amount from the proposed 1 per cent increase in employees' National Insurance contributions. Double-indexed indirect taxes – alcoholic drinks, tobacco, road fund duties, vehicle excise duty and car tax – raised almost £2.5 billion. (This put up the RPI by 2 per cent, rather than by the 1 that might have been expected.) Higher income tax, achieved by freezing the personal allowances, produced almost £2 billion.

There was one major additional item. The banks, whom I had identified as a possible target the previous year, had to pay some £400 million to the Exchequer in the form of a once-for-all 2.5 per cent levy on their non-interest-bearing deposits. This was the price of their 'undue' profitability in otherwise hard times. To my great sadness this induced the resignation of someone whom I regarded as one of our Treasury team, Tim Renton. Tim had been John Biffen's parliamentary private secretary since 1979, and had gone wth John to the Department of Trade. Nothing in politics is for ever, however. For Tim was able, less than two years later, to return as *my* PPS, first in the Treasury and then at the Foreign Office. In due course he served with me as an outstandingly wise Minister of State in that department – and as Margaret Thatcher's last Chief Whip.

The 1981 Budget was not solely concerned with increasing taxes. I included a package of tax reductions (worth some £600 million in total) and other measures, all of which were designed to 'help business': the most important new items were the Loan Guarantee Scheme, the Business Start-up Programme and the Business Opportunities Programme. I was able also to limit the adverse effect of the increase in income tax on the lower paid by announcing a fully indexed increase in child benefit and one-parent-family benefit. And in the name of fiscal justice I continued my modest onslaught on the taxation of fringe benefits – motor cars and petrol once again.

Almost the last matter for consideration was the relationship between our continuing monetary puzzle and the balance of our fiscal strategy. For I have to confess that the pursuit of a particular figure for any particular monetary aggregate had played a very modest role in our deliberations on the fiscal balance of this Budget. Yet, at the base of our more pragmatic judgments, that vital factor was always there. Our critical objective was to ensure that we were not setting out to borrow so much that interest rates were bound to rise if we were to succeed in raising the money. So I was in no doubt about the need to reaffirm our commitment to the MTFS. It had indeed been crucial in setting a ceiling to the size of our PSBR. I sought too to maintain continuity by keeping sterling M3 as the yardstick for medium-term policy, with a new target range of 6–10 per cent over the fourteen months to April 1982. This target was, however, based on the actual figure for sterling M3 in banking in February 1981. (In other words I made no attempt to claw back the 'base drift' that had already occurred). A short section of my speech was devoted to an explanation of our evident failure to hit our targets during the current year.

Two other changes of long-term importance deserve a mention. The first was my announcement that public spending would henceforth be planned and controlled in cash rather than in volume terms. I say more about the implementation of this in the following chapter.* The second was the introduction of an indexed gilt-edged security. This important innovation was effectively an extension of the principle of the National Savings so-called 'granny bond'. Nigel Lawson had worked hard to persuade the Bank of England, the Prime Minister – and indeed the Chancellor – of the worth of this innovation. All these changes were certainly to prove their worth.

---

* See p. 219 below.

So the 1981 Budget had finally taken shape in my mind and remained to be put into presentable form in the two weeks that remained, with the help of my well-integrated crew in the Treasury.

I was amused, at about this time, to derive some encouragement from a telegram from our Ambassador in Peking, my old Cambridge contemporary Percy Cradock. It was a routine report of a speech by the Chinese Vice-Premier Yao Yilin on China's economic performance: 'He admitted that the potential dangers caused by persistent financial deficits, price rises and the over-issuing of currency had made necessary further economic readjustment. Both revenue and expenditure would be reduced in 1981 to balance the budget at a lower level.' This document had been laid before me by a thoughtful Treasury official, with the comment: 'Your colleague hard at work!' And it did indeed offer some modest encouragement.

I was rather more reassured, I must say, to receive a note from Peter Thorneycroft, former Chancellor of the Exchequer and still chairman of the party. His reckoning was straightforward and supportive. The 'huge disbursements . . . now foreseen . . . must present you with funding problems for 1981–2 of great complexity'. If I had in mind (as he very much hoped) some easement in MLR then I 'must be looking for more revenue'. And so to his central point. I should not, he said, feel bound by past constraints. Personal incomes had not been suffering and 'a move on direct taxation might save you much difficulty later'. If I did decide to raise more in direct taxation, Peter urged me to do it 'as boldly and openly and as fairly as you can'. Clearly, Peter would have preferred me to proceed by raising the basic rate rather than by freezing thresholds. So there was an important tactical difference between us. But apart from that it was immensely encouraging to have his strategic support.

So it is perhaps a little strange in retrospect that Margaret and I were content, indeed determined, to proceed in the traditional way – to present the Budget next, in effect, to Parliament and the nation without any further (or effective) consideration by Cabinet as a whole. We had only, of course, to negotiate the pre-Budget Cabinet on the morning of Budget Day itself. For that we had developed a routine: I made a point of seeing, in course of the preceding Monday, the senior members of Cabinet, to obtain their endorsement of the general shape of the Budget. And so I did on this occasion. Willie Whitelaw, Peter Carrington, Francis Pym and Jim Prior were all kind enough to come and see me in my study at Number 11. None of them was over the moon at the prospect that I disclosed. But Jim was the only one to argue against my judgments almost in principle. In his own words, 'I couldn't say anything bad enough about it.'⁵

The Making of History

In Cabinet the following day, however (again in Jim's words), 'Geoffrey received overwhelming support.'⁶ The other three 'elder statesmen' all took the line that if the Chancellor thought we needed tough measures to stick to our policy, then so be it. Jim was openly critical. So too were Peter Walker and Ian Gilmour. But the Budget was generally accepted, albeit – it must be said – without a great deal of enthusiasm.

No one had any strategically different alternative to offer. Jim Prior was the most interestingly incoherent. He was never reluctant to express a view. That was part of his great strength as a colleague, even if his input did not always add up. Retrospectively, Jim has articulated his earlier criticism of the MTFS and the 1980 Budget on the basis that 'Geoffrey thought he could control three things – government spending, government borrowing and the money supply. But within a year all three were out of control.'⁷ As a statement of fact this was, alas, unexceptionable. But it was never clear what was meant to follow from this insight. Jim never argued that we should not be seeking to control any or all of those things. His only case, so it seemed, was that if it was likely to be impossible, or at least difficult, to achieve these objectives, then it was politically imprudent even to try. Or at any rate to try too hard.

This is, I know, no more than a parody of the wets' case, and it is unfair to lodge it so firmly in Jim's mouth, when he was, in so many other respects, a colleague of courage, conviction and charm. But it is difficult, as it was then, to translate his objections into any practical alternative policy. As I look back now upon this unresolved argument between dries and wets – unresolved because it was scarcely ever really joined – I am more and more convinced that it would have been possible, if the issue had been fully debated, to establish a much wider area of common ground. This would greatly have strengthened our common position – and so the credibility of the policies to which we were committed. But, if Margaret was temperamentally disinclined to seek wider consensus in support of our policy, it was at least a blessing that Jim, and his fellow dissidents Peter Walker and Ian Gilmour, were equally unwilling to follow through the logic of their own position. For we know now that they held a dissenting breakfast, on the morning of the Budget, and seriously considered together the possibility of resignation. They rejected it because of their fear of being identified, exposed and crushed as a hostile cabal.* This reluctance on their part enabled us at least to maintain the (less than wholehearted) partnership which sustained our economic policy through its most testing time.

So to my third Budget speech, ninety-two minutes long – and received by a surprisingly calm House. Perhaps the most startling feature of the afternoon was when the gaunt figure of the former Liberal Leader, the veteran Jo Grimond, rose to interrupt me – just when I was proposing a complex anti-tax-avoidance measure (to deal with the so-called Vestey case). 'Not even for the Right Honourable gentleman', I observed, 'do I wish to break the tradition of an uninterrupted Budget Statement.' I never did find out what Jo had been wanting to say. Deliberately, I exposed the forbidding arithmetic, with the prospect of large net tax increases, at an early stage in my speech. So the House had no unfounded expectations of blessings to come. Michael Foot, in his instant reply to the House, dubbed it a 'no hope' Budget.

The subdued reaction in the House was soon overshadowed by increasing hostility from some of our own back-benchers. When I went to the usual meeting of our back-bench Finance Committee, the atmosphere was very different from what I had experienced in the two previous years. There was still, fortunately, a hard core of loyalty, which got me through that meeting at least. Plenty more was going to be needed. For the most loudly reported Conservative reaction on the Wednesday morning came from Peter Tapsell, the Member for Horncastle. He was well known for his 'strong City connections' – which, he no doubt felt, had long qualified him for a place on the Treasury front bench. (Two years had elapsed since he had resigned from my shadow front-bench team, without any really convincing explanation, in December 1978.) He made his view of the Budget very clear in an instant press release: 'Economically illiterate . . . fundamentally wrong in concept and frequently maladroit in detail'. The Prime Minister, he thought, 'owes it to the country and to the Conservative Party to find a Chancellor of the Exchequer who will command confidence and hope.' The very intemperance of the sentiment demeaned the advocate as much as the argument.

This strident line was echoed, predictably, by the *Guardian*: 'A

See p. 473 below.

message of perverse destruction'. Even previously faithful commentators found it hard to give support. 'Time is running out for Sir Geoffrey,' said the *Sun*. Most of the broadsheets were a little more restrained in their judgment. For the *Financial Times* the Budget was 'an admission of defeat'. But 'the painful fiscal decisions' were 'necessary', because the government had 'lost control of public spending, to a combination of Cabinet revolts and failure to budget for the cost of Clegg'. Leon Brittan's brother Samuel had two bites at the cherry: on Wednesday he was, by his standards, almost lyrical: 'It is always a relief when a Chancellor sits down on Budget Day without having announced any major strategic blunders.' On Thursday, however, he was less charitable: 'undoubtedly a badly judged Budget'.

In truth, there was a straight choice of judgments – political and economic. On one side were those who regarded the Budget, quite literally, as mad. Some of their judgments and forecasts turned out so grotesquely unfulfilled that they should be for ever set alongside any later observations from the same commentators. Francis Cripps and Wynne Godley, for example, saw this as 'a severely disinflationary Budget that will cause a hyper-slump such as Britain has never see before'. They were, they said, 'amazed and aghast that the British Government should have taken such drastic action on [this] basis'.[8]

This was followed, three weeks after the Budget, by the famous letter to *The Times* from 364 economists (including seventy-six professors and five out of the six surviving ex-chief economic advisers to Britain's post war governments – among them Terry Burns' immediate predecessor, Fred Atkinson). 'There is no basis', they thundered, 'in economic theory or supporting evidence for the Government's ... present policies. [They] will deepen the depression, erode the industrial base of our economy and threaten its social and political stability. . . . The time has come to reject monetarist policies and consider urgently which alternative offers the best hope of sustained economic recovery.' Their timing could not have been more apt. The fall in national output came to an end in that very quarter. Over the next eight years real GDP grew by an average of 3.2 per cent per annum. And the 364 economists found themselves immortalized. For in my Mansion House speech that year I deployed for the first of many times the line (which John Kerr and I had devised from an Art Buchwald original) that an economist is a man who knows 364 ways of making love – but who doesn't know any women.

But we did have *some* robust support. 'The Chancellor must be congratulated on yesterday's Budget. It was bold, harsh and courageous: and these were just the qualities needed.' So declaimed the *Daily Telegraph*, endorsing my conclusion that 'to change course would be fatal'. Ronald Butt in *The Times* crisply summarized my case: 'Penal interest rates damaging industry have been the consequence of the failure with public spending; now, to allow interest rates to come down without throwing the financial strategy to the winds, Sir Geoffrey has produced quite the most unpopular Budget in my memory.'

The gulf between the two sides of the argument was enormous. It was hard to believe they came from within the same national audience. But it was immensely encouraging for a beleaguered Chancellor to have such unwavering advocates on his side. Above all it was good to be able to count on support of the kind that the Prime Minister herself proclaimed the day after the Budget at, of all places, a *Guardian* Young Businessman of the Year luncheon. 'This Budget', she said, 'is the only hope for Britain's sustained and genuine revival and I hope that many people will in fact see it in that light.' Support from parliamentary colleagues was intriguingly diverse, from my former PPS, still then 'left wing', Ken Clarke, telling Elspeth of his certainty that 'we will look back on Geoffrey's performance yesterday as a key point in his emergence from his most testing time', to the 'hard-line' though always maverick John Nott generously writing out in full Bunyan's 'Who would true valour see' right through to 'shall *life* inherit!' My ever watchful special adviser, Peter Cropper, reported his own modest piece of market research: 'Breakfast at the Reform Club is normally a sepulchral time. Each of the last two mornings members have broken the rules to come over and say what a splendid Budget it was. So be of good cheer!' Even urban motorists generated one light-hearted comment. Princess Margaret wrote, by chance two days after the Budget, accepting an invitation to dine at Number 11, and closed: 'Perhaps for the very long journey to your house you would be kind enough to send me a can of petrol.'

Not for the first time I was glad that I had accepted the invitation, which by now came regularly, to appear two days after the Budget on Robin Day's *Question Time*. I never enjoyed this programme as much as its radio forebear, *Any Questions?* That still had a courteous, Dorset village-hall quality, in which the benign ghost of Freddie Grisewood still seemed to be setting the tone. *Question Time*, by contrast, was strident, with the studio audience all too easily provoked to proffer simplistic prejudice. But the size of its regular audience made it an important platform, and Robin (occasionally as intolerable as he was intolerant) was a brilliantly diverting chairman. So I always took the occasion seriously. This time I enjoyed it. 'The support from the audience surprised me,' wrote one viewer. 'The country is full of people like me, who draw inspiration from people in the public eye who are prepared to stand firm on principles.' I was lucky, it must be said, in the BBC's choice of my sparring partner – 'the innumerate Stan Orme', as Ivan Fallon unkindly dubbed him, an immensely decent AEU official, who went on to chair the Parliamentary Labour Party and was well at home with the intricacies of social security, but not of taxation.

But if television was kind to me on this occasion, the writing press provided a shabby example of the kind of misbehaviour which makes them so hard to love. As I emerged from Number 11 on Budget Day, to confront the familiar battery of cameras and microphones, Elspeth was using her small camera to take some unusual shots of Downing Street from our side of the threshold. One of the pressmen got the same idea. 'May we develop your film, Lady Howe?' he cried. 'Yes,' she replied, 'so long as you don't print anything without letting me vet it first.' That was the last she thought about it until the next day. Imagine our shock at seeing a whole page of the *Daily Express* devoted to some of her (shaken, out-of-focus) pictures under the headline 'Howe not to' – complete with professional critique by David Bailey. When the film did come back it was accompanied by the gift of a camera – an extravagant token of repentance that Elspeth could not properly accept. Though not a serious incident, it was a depressing example of cavalier ill-manners from the fourth estate.

Alongside this sad little vignette, the concluding stages of my most controversial Budget seemed relatively straightforward. Conservative back-benchers' dismay focused in the end only on the large increase which I had imposed on the cost of rural transport. During the Finance Bill committee stage on the floor of the House, several dozen of our people threatened to support an Opposition amendment that would have halved my increase of twenty pence a gallon in the duty on petrol and diesel fuel oil. If carried, this would have cost the Treasury about £600 million in lost revenue. We were able to quell this revolt by conceding the case on diesel fuel alone. This would cost £85 million in 1981–2 and £135 million in a full year; and I stressed that I should have to find other ways of raising the same money. And so I did when two months later, on 3 July, I persuaded the House to add another threepence to the tax on a pack of cigarettes and to make comparable increases on the taxes on betting and bingo. So I was able to recoup exactly the £85 million that I had to concede by accepting a cut in diesel taxation. 'Sir Geoffrey seemed determined', said the *Financial Times*, 'to show that he was not prepared to have his Budget strategy undermined, and to teach his own back-benchers a lesson.'

I was not in the business of teaching anyone lessons. I just wanted to be sure that we kept in place the Budget arithmetic which I saw as the key to our economic recovery. And so we had. But we still had a hard year to come.

CHAPTER FIFTEEN

SUMMER RESHUFFLE

Relations with Number 10

Life in the Treasury must seem, on my account so far, to have been quite orderly and sequential. True there was an inevitable tidal pattern – from Budget to public spending review, to Washington for the IMF to Autumn Statement, to Christmas. But this gives much too predictable an impression. The reality was much more disorderly and episodic, with always a shoal of issues crying out for management at the same time and a parallel series of diary engagements, Cabinet meetings and committees and other irregular events within or around which one had to squeeze the continuous kaleidoscope of crisis.

Throughout this turmoil there was the one partnership that had to be kept as strong and effective as possible – the link between the First and Second Lords of the Treasury. Several factors worked in its favour. Most important was Margaret Thatcher's powerful, if sometimes erratic, 'Treasury instinct'. She was likely at least to start on my side. Even this could be a two-edged sword. For, if ever we were at odds, that was soon apparent to colleagues. It could quickly become a source of weakness, when there should be strength. And just because of her long-standing interest in Treasury affairs, she had a number of firmly fixed prejudices – against fixed exchange rates, for low interest rates, against the Treasury as an institution – which lurked like ill-concealed reefs below the surface of most discussions.

When it came to managing these hazards, the Whitehall system – not least the physical intimacy between the Downing Street houses – offered many advantages over the casual contacts that were characteristic of life between Opposition leader and Shadow Chancellor. The Cabinet Secretariat, and the constancy of almost instant contact between private secretaries at Number 10 and in the Treasury, avoided many possible misunderstandings.

The relationship between these different manifestations of the system changed substantially, often imperceptibly, as the years in government rolled by. Looking back today, I am struck by the disciplined pattern of business that seems to have prevailed – and I think did prevail – during our first years in office. Striking too is the frequent involvement of most ministerial colleagues in many of the difficult issues. Some of this was probably because we were still feeling our way, sometimes in personal relationships, as well as in the machinery of government. This early collectivism of the Thatcher Cabinet was not always apparent from the public rhetoric.

Take, for instance, pay policy – or 'policy for pay' as we preferred to describe it. Some commentators see this as an area where ministers were to perform one of their most important U-turns. Thus we are seen as arriving in office totally hostile towards *any* public discussion of wage bargaining, least of all of actual levels of pay. We were seen as ideologues who simply muttered monetary formulae, to which trade unionists and wage bargainers had to 'conform or else'. Jim Prior lends some substance to this picture. He rightly recalls the words on which we had all agreed in *The Right Approach to the Economy*, way back in 1977:

> In framing its monetary and other policies the government must come to some conclusions about the likely scope for pay increases if excess public expenditure or large-scale unemployment is to be avoided; and this estimate cannot be concealed from the representatives of employers and unions whom it is consulting.

'If only', bemoans Jim, 'we had stuck more firmly to those words . . . at least a part of our early difficulties might have been mitigated!'[1]

But that is exactly what we sought to do, from a very early stage. In July 1979, for example, E Committee (the Cabinet's Economic Strategy Committee, with the Prime Minister in the chair) agreed upon the need to improve awareness of 'the Government's Pay Policy' (*sic*) by means of a major publicity campaign. At two subsequent meetings in September, we were clear that this should not involve the setting of a *general* norm for the next pay round. But we did have to establish cash limits, ahead of public sector pay negotiations for 1980–1, so as to impose discipline on pay negotiators but in a flexible and realistic manner. Granted that this was to be our approach, 'it would be impossible', we agreed (almost echoing our 1977 words), 'to prevent the pay assumptions implicit in these figures becoming public knowledge'. So it was from the outset.

Certainly I cannot recall a moment when I was not banging on about unit labour costs and the need for 'responsibility' over pay. But one can understand why the opposite impression gained ground. For there were certainly some colleagues – most notably Keith Joseph, John Biffen (often echoing Enoch Powell) and sometimes Margaret herself – who could never quite shake off their old dismay at the very idea of 'preaching' to 'free' economic agents about the (surely inevitable, desirable) consequences of strict monetary policy. Occasionally they actually said as much, which certainly did not enhance our collective credibility. This generally subterranean difference of emphasis was an occasionally recurrent cause of tension between Margaret and myself.

This was no less true of our different attitudes towards the National Economic Development Committee (NEDC or Neddy), the tripartite body that had been set up by Harold Macmillan through the agency of Selwyn Lloyd in 1962, as a means of extending the common ground of understanding between government and 'both sides of industry'. For Margaret and Keith in particular this prospect of regular contact with trade union leaders came close to supping with the Devil. It was only a short step away, or so they feared, from 'beer and sandwiches at Number 10', incomes policy and the rest. They were fearful, as it seemed, of exposing themselves to demands by which they might be compromised. I was, curiously, more confident of being able to use such contacts for exposition, without fear of becoming tainted by 'heresy'.

By this time I had no more use for a formal incomes policy than they did. But I also believed, as I had made clear as long ago as January 1975, that 'Government has a plain responsibility to initiate and sustain a dialogue with both sides of the labour market'.[2] I had taken part in the work of NEDC during my time in the Heath government, and I had subsequently been impressed by the not dissimilar German institution of 'concerted action'. On this basis, I had secured in *The Right Approach to the Economy* a commitment to the value of NEDC in this role. This was not specifically reaffirmed in the much shorter text of our 1979 manifesto, but by September 1979 I was able to secure from E Committee a recommendation that NEDC should hold a special discussion at its December meeting of 'economic prospects generally with a view to influencing attitudes towards pay determination'. It was agreed too that the Governor of the Bank of England should become a member of NEDC and that he should appear regularly before the newly established Parliamentary Select Committee on Treasury Affairs. Gordon Richardson brought authority to both roles. I knew that the

most difficult NEDC discussions could almost always be steered towards
a rational conclusion by involving the wisdom of the Governor at the
right moment. I regarded my chairmanship of the monthly NEDC
meetings as an interesting and important obligation. Many of my
colleagues – notably Jim Prior, Michael Heseltine (when he was
Environment Secretary, 1979–83) and Patrick Jenkin – took the same
view of the value of this forum for the informal exchange of (generally)
sensible views. I was already on Christian-name terms with every
member of the Council – and I saw that business was conducted on that
basis. Usually, though not quite always, leadership of a restrained and
rational kind was forthcoming from Len Murray, general secretary of
the TUC, and Ray Pennock, former deputy chairman of ICI and then
president of the CBI.

Certainly the work of NEDC served to curb one fallacy that threatened at one time to grip my thinking – the belief that Britain (in short-
hand) need not be dismayed by the prospect of a declining manufacturing sector. This is not to be confused, of course, with the inevitable fall
in the percentage of people *employed* in manufacturing. What I have in
mind is the decline in the competitiveness, quality or technological value
of the country's economic base. The 'flow of funds' argument led some
economists to argue – or so it seemed – that we could manage just as
well in the course of an indefinite shrinkage of our industrial capability.
But NEDC studies pointed up very sharply the disappearance or decline
of activities which ought to be well within the capacity of a mature
economy – and a contribution to the diversity of its strength. One
report showed, for example, that we exported two-thirds of the office
equipment that we made (which seemed splendid) and imported two-
thirds of the office equipment that we used (which seemed odd). All
became clear, and alarming, when we were shown that our exports were
mainly low value-added goods (chairs and manually operated duplica-
tors) and the imports were much higher value-added word processors,
computers and the like.

I was anxious for Margaret to be exposed to debate of this kind, and
perhaps to lead some of it. But this kind of 'ram-shammy', as she called
it, was never her natural scene, save perhaps when she had organized it
for herself, at a Number 10 seminar. On the two or three occasions
when I was able to persuade her to take the chair of NEDC, I think she
enjoyed herself well enough. But the visits were always a little fraught,
not to say nerve-racking, for the organizers. Geoffrey Chandler, NEDC's
director general – an almost too dedicated servant of the organization

and its ideals – was particularly tense on such occasions. Margaret was generally good at leading discussions of a hard-nosed, practical subject – such as Information Technology Year, which offered Kenneth Baker his entrée to ministerial rank in 1981. But at other times we only just steered clear of what could have been damaging clashes with union leaders. I had no doubt about the value of NEDC as a generator of economic innovation and understanding. I was disappointed by Nigel's later reduction of its role – still more by Norman Lamont's decision to abolish it.

IMF in Gabon and the Ottawa Summit

The IMF's half-yearly meeting for 1981 – still on safari – was held at Libreville, capital of Gabon. This was my first visit to francophone Africa – and to the continent's third-richest country (expressed in terms of wealth per head: Gabon had useful reserves of oil). It was no surprise, therefore, that we met in a monumental conference centre (greatly underused, since characteristically it had been purpose-built for a one-off visit by the Organization of African Unity). We were entertained at a mass banquet given at one of his palaces by the country's ruler, President Bongo. I was later granted a personal audience at another, only slightly more modest, residence. The President wore a huge cloak, within which his hands intermittently disappeared, so that he could suddenly add a strange gesture to his speech by raising the whole thing like a tent. Our seance was, unusually in my experience with heads of state, interrupted by a long telephone call from his wife.

The conference involved one piece of important business which went disconcertingly awry. The previous chairman of the Interim Committee, Filippo Pandolfi, had resigned that office, following his transfer from the Italian Finance Ministry to the Agriculture Ministry. And the Americans had suggested that I was a suitable candidate for the vacancy. I was ready to let my name go forward but only if I was unopposed. In order to avoid any charge of self-promotion, we left it to the Americans to canvass the field. The only other possible candidate, it transpired, was Canada's Allan MacEachen, who was thought not to want the job. Even so, it was a mistake to leave it all to the Americans, not least since the newly elected Reagan Republican team were still inevitably inexperienced. In the result, the deal we thought had been done fell embarrassingly apart. When my name was proposed, the ensuing pause was ended by the Algerian Minister's nomination, to my great dismay, of Mac-Eachen as an alternative. The proceedings immediately took off, rather like an American Convention with country spokesmen rising in turn to declare their choice. It quickly began to look likely that I should lose this election in tropical Africa, for which I had never expected to run. So I hastened to withdraw my name and leave the field clear for the excellent Canadian.

Allan MacEachen and I thereafter worked together in close partnership for a number of years; he moved from Treasury to Foreign Ministry about a year before I did the same. Within a few weeks he was able to welcome me, as well as Margaret Thatcher and Peter Carrington, in Ottawa for our third G7 Economic Summit. Our host this year was the long-serving Pierre Trudeau. Trudeau's chosen venue was Canadian Pacific Railway's giant 'log cabin' hotel at Montebello, just outside Ottawa. It was our first chance to see Presidents Reagan and Mitterrand in action together on the international stage. Reagan was every bit as genial, as folksy and as apparently articulate as I had come to expect. He was marvellously at home in a golf buggy (an irresistible shared photo-call with Margaret Thatcher). His formal interventions were generally brief and often apparently dependent upon his famous clutch of anno-tated prompt cards. I came to know from earlier (and later) encounters that there was much more to the man than that. Mitterrand, by contrast, was much more sober and 'presidential'. His people generally ensured that he was the protocol superior to Reagan by being the last of the two heads of state to arrive. And Mitterrand managed to walk in such a way that he almost added a cubit to his modest stature.

But Trudeau was undoubtedly the star of this occasion. His seductive and tenacious bilingualism – as apt for handling monoglot heads of state as for the self-confident Canadian media – added authority to his enthusiastic charm. As for the substance of the occasion, I was greatly disappointed by the way in which real issues were often unduly masked by courtesy or deference. I had, for example, been led to expect my European colleagues to join me in pressing the Japanese for effective action on their notorious trade restrictions. But punches were disappointingly pulled. I was to learn over the years that this was indeed an uphill struggle.

Public Spending Concerns: Summer 1981

But the main theme of the long summer of 1981 was overwhelmingly domestic: the first 'green shoots' of recovery (others were using the phrase in those days, though not the Chancellor) and the seemingly endless increase in pressure to restrain public spending, driven ever upwards by the recession.

Public spending was also generating problems of its own. For one of the most important changes that I had introduced in the Budget earlier in 1981 was the changeover to cash-based control of the bulk of public spending. To a layman it may seem strange that you could ever think of controlling expenditure except by reference to the amount of cash that you have available. But a different method had been employed almost throughout the public sector for nearly twenty years. For the Plowden Report of 1961, which was the basis of the (otherwise sensible) existing system of public expenditure control, had recommended the use of so-called 'constant' prices – that is, prices which were automatically adjusted upwards to take account of inflation. This meant that the Ministry of Defence, for example, could be confident of receiving the 100 tanks or 1000 rifles it had planned to buy in three years' time, whatever had happened to prices – relative as well as absolute – in the meantime. By means of this 'funny money' system the managers of public sector programmes were totally insulated, in theory at least, from the effects of inflation. I say in theory because in practice, even with this system, the money (real cash) could sometimes run out. Then the brakes had to be slammed on hard.

The system was a crazy one. Even the previous Labour government, encouraged by the then Chief Secretary Joel Barnett and the second permanent secretary Leo Pliatzky, had made some changes, with the introduction of cash limits. But it was left to us, under Leon Brittan's firm hand, to move as much of the system as was possible on to a cash-planned basis. From the summer of 1981, forward budgets, and bids for extra resources, were conducted upon the basis of realistic estimates of inflation for the years ahead. For the first time departments had seriously to try to live within the actual sums actually allotted. If the money looked like running out, ministers had strictly to justify demands for more. No longer were they topped up as a matter of course. It was a tougher, but much more sensible, regime.

One doubly ironic consequence of this change was to emerge when the question later arose of subjecting to the same discipline expenditure by Parliament on itself, for this was managed in a fashion that was all its own. Expenditure on the House of Commons – the building, equipment, library, restaurant, staff salaries and all other items – is managed entirely outside Treasury control by an independent House of Commons Commission. This body had always been accustomed to a relatively easy (though not wholly irresponsible) system of self-control. But now, I thought, the time had come to bring the House into the same cash-based discipline that applied to everybody else. Clearly this question was so constitutionally sensitive that it could not be left to a mere Chief Secretary. The Chancellor himself had to go personally to persuade the Commission. When I arrived at the meeting I was face to face with its senior member, Joel Barnett, the very pioneer of the system that I was seeking to impose upon him. Neither he nor any of his colleagues would hear of being subjected to a rule of this kind. Was not Parliament supreme? How could the House of Commons subject itself to Treasury control? They would do their best, of course. But, as for a rule, dear me, no! I knew when I was beaten – and withdrew.

So I took some pleasure almost exactly ten years later, when, as Leader of the House of Commons and a member of the same Commission, I was able to secure cash to finance major reforms of the House of Commons* by exercising the same authority over the then Chancellor and Chief Secretary, John Major and Norman Lamont.

For Cabinet as a whole this extension of planning in cash terms was a fresh cause of dismay. So were the continuing irritations of the Civil Service strike – more accurately, a series of selective walk-outs and one-day strikes – which ran with increasing bitterness from the beginning of March to the end of July 1981. I was close to the heart of this dispute for several reasons. I was chairman of the Cabinet's Public Sector Pay Committee (which we had set up within a few months of entering office in 1979), and we were in the middle of a very complex process of lowering the general levels of pay increases throughout the public sector (including the nationalized industries) by reference to a series of more or less consistent cash limits.

The recommendations of the Clegg Committee on comparability (we had inherited the newly created Committee from the Labour government and kept it in being, and active, until September 1980) had by now largely worked through the system. They had been expected to add

* See pp. 620–21 below.

some 6–7 per cent to the pay bill and had in fact cost 11 per cent more. So we were engaged in a battle of the first importance. And now my Treasury departments were in the front line, since the organizers of the Civil Service strike made their principal onslaught on our Inland Revenue and Customs and Excise offices, in the hope that they could destroy our cash flow. Our final problem was that the line on which we found ourselves obliged to stand was not well chosen. Our pay offer to the Civil Service stood at 7 per cent (which we could finance, with job economies, within our cash limit of 6 per cent: we were in the course of reducing the total size of the Civil Service by 100,000). Eventually, at the end of July 1981, we settled for 7.5 per cent and an inquiry, to be presided over by Sir John Megaw, a retired Court of Appeal judge, into the whole system for determining Civil Service pay. We were at least as anxious for that inquiry as were the unions, since we wanted a decisive break with comparability.

It could not be seen as a famous victory, though it fell well short of disaster. But it was the cause of serious conflict between the Prime Minister and Christopher Soames, Churchill's favourite son-in-law, then in charge of the Civil Service Department (still separate from the Treasury). He was a big man – in political status as much as build – whom I had come to like. Every job in which I had so far encountered him had been enhanced and filled out by his personality – ambassador in Paris, Commissioner in Brussels and, finally, the triumphal Governor General of independent Zimbabwe. Now he was back in a relatively humble role in a Cabinet where he felt, and one can see why, like a very big fish if not exactly out of water then at least in the wrong-sized pool of the wrong kind of water. And he and I, the Treasury (with Number 10's vigorous support) and the Civil Service department, were severely at odds. He was convinced from the outset that the claim could not be settled for less than 7.5 per cent. At that figure he was sure it could have gone in the first week of June. Margaret firmly and personally refused to sanction a settlement at that figure at that date. She took the view that it was sloppy thinking of that kind which had already taken the figure too high (up to 7 per cent) and too soon. We were really arguing about the tactics of the past, rather than the resolution of the present.

And so on and on. I remember Christopher Soames saying to me, as we walked out of yet another Cabinet at which this engaging figure (who had first served in Macmillan's Cabinet almost twenty-one years before) had received the sharp end of Margaret's tongue, 'You know, Geoffrey, the trouble with this government is that it isn't fun any more.

I don't know why we do it.' I was only just beginning to understand what he meant. Before the end I was to know only too well.

Summer Political Crisis

This was the kind of mood in which a number of colleagues were approaching the Cabinet's first formally agreed meeting to discuss economic strategy as a whole. This had been nicknamed ECOCAB and was fixed to take place on 17 June. Margaret had conceded the case for this in the aftermath of my contentious 1981 Budget. Given the continuing sluggishness of the recovery process, this particular Cabinet was in fact a reasonably straightforward occasion. Margaret and I and the Treasury team were not seeking any figure or specific conclusions but simply a continuation of broad support for our strategy. And that we secured after a couple of hours' discussion without any substantial revolt. But several colleagues, including Peter Walker, Michael Heseltine, Ian Gilmour and Jim Prior, gave fairly open notice that they were getting close to the end of their patience, at least so far as further cuts in public expenditure were concerned. The continued rise in unemployment was their overwhelming concern.

Our regular summer Cabinet on public spending was still to come, on 23 July. By then we had had to face a fearful series of urban disturbances, spread over ten days in some thirty cities, involving hundreds of arrests and thousands of police casualties. On the eve of this Cabinet meeting the Toxteth area of Liverpool had faced another night of disturbance. Much of this rioting was of a copycat, hooliganistic kind. But it was difficult to refute the argument, to which Jim Prior understandably attached importance, that it owed much to the still surging tide of unemployment (the latest figure, announced on 22 July, was 2.85 million). This was probably the chief reason why a large number of previously supportive colleagues jumped ship at the 23 July Cabinet. Michael Heseltine, with special responsibility for Merseyside, renewed – in a more specific form than before – his call for a pay freeze. He was supported by Peter Walker and Christopher Soames. Quintin Hailsham was apocalyptic in his criticisms. Only Margaret and Keith Joseph stood firmly behind Leon and myself in our insistence on the need to fix a specific target for next year's public spending total. Willie Whitelaw did his best to encourage loyalty to the Prime Minister's position, but without success.

Among the most significant and scornful defectors were John Nott and John Biffen. They had both been long-time sceptics about the Treasury as an institution. John Biffen felt liberated perhaps from his previous uneasy loyalty as a result of his move to the Department of Trade. And John Nott had probably been at the Ministry of Defence long enough to absorb something of their big-spending culture. Certainly his attitude revealed no trace of the very generous tribute he had paid to my Budget only four months before.

Margaret closed the discussion with a vigorous and effective defence of our position. But our colleagues were not in the mood for conversion. She added a promise that the debate would be resumed after the summer recess. On that basis, we were lucky to emerge unbeaten, even if unsupported, by a majority of badly shaken colleagues. The one item which united us all was the substantial package of employment measures which we had put together for announcement by the Prime Minister on 27 July. This £700 million boost to job-support could lift almost half a million people off the workless register over the next two years. That at least was good news. So was the agreement of colleagues that nothing should be said outside about the references to a possible pay freeze. That important agreement was strictly observed. But the whole tenor of the 23 July meeting had been a great shock to us. Margaret and I discussed it more than once in the days that followed. Neither of us could see any practical alternative to our broad strategy, nor indeed had any been suggested. It was this which settled Margaret's determination to undertake a more far-reaching Cabinet reshuffle before we were to meet again.

Before the House rose for the summer, I fell into one silly trap which Leon and I had largely succeeded in avoiding over many months. When the CBI's mid-summer confidence figures were published, they showed a very modest improvement, the first of its kind for almost two years. I allowed myself to proclaim the 'end of the recession'. This provoked a justified riposte from the CBI, and a much less forgivable rebuke from party chairman Peter Thorneycroft. He was, said Peter, still suffering from 'rising damp' and could see 'no sign of the economy picking up at the moment, not anywhere where I am'. Margaret and I were both very disappointed at this lapse by one of our stalwarts.

Very shortly after our return from holiday, Margaret was ready with her long-considered reshuffle. Once again I was not formally consulted at the time, although Margaret had used the opportunity of our earlier talks to share some of her advance thinking with me. I knew that she was anxious to find Cabinet places for Nigel Lawson and Norman

Tebbit, and I was glad of that prospect: they would both strengthen the Treasury voice, and Norman's approach to the union question was more in line with mine than Jim's. On the other side it was equally clear that Ian Gilmour had long been writing his own death warrant. I could not claim any enthusiasm for his semi-detached and languid negativism.

I knew that Margaret was irritated by Jim Prior's stubborn opposition to much of our economic policy, but I continued to regard him as an effective champion of an important strand in party thinking. Probably for that reason, I was not party to the exchanges which led to his transfer to the Northern Ireland Office. In itself that was a good move. Jim would be a strong Secretary of State, a worthy successor to Humphrey Atkins, who had weathered the hunger-strike and held this tough job courageously for more than two years (he took Ian Gilmour's place at the Foreign Office). Jim's experience would still be available in Cabinet. It is sad that this change could not have been achieved with less public acrimony. Jim had let it be known to the press that he would rather resign than leave the Department of Employment. Margaret had called his bluff. It now looked as though his next job would be his last.

Christopher Soames was, alas, a natural candidate for retirement from a Cabinet in which he was increasingly ill at ease. He had indeed outgrown the job. And Mark Carlisle's departure saddened me too; he was another old Cambridge friend and colleague at the Bar and felt unfairly treated (he had been Education Secretary). But he had never, as I knew, been particularly happy in Cabinet and his departure had been widely – much too widely – foreshadowed. It was good to be joined by Lady (Janet) Young in Christopher's place. She made a very effective Leader of the Upper House.

I lost two members of my Treasury team: Peter Rees, after many years on the Finance Bill Standing Committee, was glad of a change of scene to Trade, which paved the way to his later promotion to the Cabinet, back in Great George Street as Chief Secretary in June 1983. Nigel Lawson came into the Cabinet as Secretary of State for Energy: he was to make a most important contribution there – to privatization, to the North Sea tax regime and to the preparation for the inevitable confrontation with the miners' leader, Arthur Scargill. Nobody would have been able to fill the diversity of roles that he had played in the Treasury. But Nick Ridley, from my point of view, made an excellent replacement: he had a powerful reforming instinct, which I enjoyed when we had worked together on the development of the enterprise-zone idea, and was to make a far-reaching input to our tax-reform agenda.

When the irreverent Jock Bruce-Gardyne was also appointed, a few days later, that restored my Treasury team to very effective strength. It was in fact enlarged by our absorption of what was left of the old Civil Service Department. For with this there came another Minister of State, Barney Hayhoe, Member for Brentford and Isleworth. His first job had been as Jim Prior's PPS in the Heath era. So he was a genuinely useful and constructive foil to the rest of my (very) dry team. Jock Bruce-Gardyne had been a robust colleague on the economic right of the party for many years, first as Member for the Scottish seat of South Angus and then (after eviction by a Nationalist) for Knutsford in Cheshire. A natural ally of John Biffen, Nick Ridley and Nigel Lawson, he had become a critic of the Heath government – and a loyal friend of ours. He brought with him some stimulating ideas, but was prevented by deafness (for which he declined to wear any hearing aid) from fulfilling his full potential. He suffered with great courage a long-drawn-out death by cancer in 1990.

For the tasks that still lay ahead of us with this refurbished team, I was greatly heartened by the generosity of Nigel's parting letter. 'However difficult I may have been as a Junior Minister,' he said with engaging candour,

> I think you know that my overwhelming feelings towards you were those of support and admiration, admiration in particular for your sturdy resilience in the face of the most appalling pressures. . . .
>
> You have shown greater courage than any of your predecessors, and when things turn out as I firmly believe they will at the end of the day, you will be remembered as one of the few great Chancellors.

And I was certainly full of gratitude for the energy, intelligence and enthusiasm Nigel had brought to our opening partnership over five exciting years.

CHAPTER SIXTEEN

TURNING OF THE TIDE

=====

Interest Rate Rises: Early Autumn

We were swiftly to run into heavy weather. For on the very same day as the Cabinet reshuffle (14 September 1981) we were obliged to increase interest rates by two full points, to 14 per cent. The need for such a move was (rightly) perceived as a sharp setback for our economic strategy. We had now precisely reversed the rate cut which had been seen – indeed presented – as the principal early blessing of my 1981 Budget.

However much, politically, I hated having to make this shift, I had no doubt about the need for it. There were two principal reasons: first, a rapid and sustained rise in private credit demand at home (and thus in bank lending); and second, and more visibly, a sharp and apparently continuing decline in the value of the pound sterling on foreign exchange markets. From $2.37 at the start of the year, it had fallen by the middle of August to a four-year low of $1.75. In the first half of September it fell sharply against the D-mark, from 4.6 to 4.3.

Remorselessly, the markets had set the scene for the agonizing sequence of meetings of the kind that inevitably preceded a difficult decision on interest rates. The first would be held in my downstairs sitting room at Number 11 with Gordon Richardson and Douglas Wass, each usually flanked by the two key men on the money markets, Eddie George and Peter Middleton. Generally present as well on this topic were the Minister responsible for monetary policy (up to this moment, Nigel) and Terry Burns. The balance of discussion was always the same. Political arguments – the mortgage rate, the closely linked RPI figure, the fragile state of industrial confidence, even the date of the next by-election (or whatever) – invariably pointed against an increase. The economic case almost always inclined in the opposite direction: probable difficulty in selling enough gilts to fund the borrowing requirement, the fear of the pound going into free fall and so compounding the threat to the RPI from rising import prices. Gordon Richardson's advice was always measured, tempered by long, front-line experience of the need to act more rather than less decisively, above all sooner rather than later in face of unmistakable signals from the exchange markets. Theoretically, at least, the monetary figures were our only guide – and the exchange rate was free to go where it wished. But at the end of each one of these difficult days the real world was rarely like that.

Our discussions at Number 11 usually led to a second, more tense meeting next door: Margaret (and her Treasury private secretary) was confronted by the Chancellor and the Governor, sometimes Peter Middleton as well. Almost always she argued against an increase in the rate, the politics ever at the top of her mind. Often she looked for someone to blame for our problem – usually the Bank. But once she had been persuaded, then, in this field at least, she was unwavering in defence of our decision. That was particularly important on this occasion. For we had all been obliged to recognize that our benign neglect of the exchange rate and other market pressure could continue no longer. That was just as well. For just two weeks later, on 1 October, the base rate had to go up another two percentage points, to 16 per cent – only one point below the all-time high of November 1979. There were two remarkable features about this stark decision: first was the date – just two weeks before the opening of the Conservative Party Conference; and second was that it occurred when both the Governor and I were out of the country, in Washington attending together the annual conference of the IMF and World Bank. But advice from London – Bank and Treasury, orchestrated by Peter Middleton – was unanimously of the view that the markets left us no alternative.

The diversity of subsequent reactions was interesting. Our financial and banking colleagues in Washington were solidly in support. I was attending not only as Chancellor of the Exchequer but as chairman during the six months of the British Presidency of the EC's Council of Finance Ministers (ECOFIN). It was with their backing that my speech to the annual meeting contained the following sentiments:

> We must strive to achieve growth within a framework of stricter financial policies. The fight against inflation must be sustained. We have to pay particular attention to the control of monetary growth, of budget deficits and public spending. . . . There are still some critics, in all our countries,

who . . . might like to find a more comfortable approach. But it is part of our task, as Finance Ministers, to explain that there is no such option. That is the clear message which has emerged . . . from every gathering of this kind that I have attended in the last three years.

This solid backing from the financial community was not quite so evident in the British Embassy, where Nicholas and Mary Henderson had kindly offered us the hospitality of that beautiful Lutyens building. When I had preached my message to a powerfully expert lunch party, one of the more formidable guests, J. K. Galbraith, ironically urged me to prolong my 'monetarist experiment long enough for Milton Friedman to be proved wrong'. A day or two later the ambassador and his wife entertained to dinner, the new-born head of a rival team – Social Democrat leader, Roy Jenkins – while Elspeth and I were offered supper in our room. We were generously provided for and able to extend hospitality not only to my private secretary, John Kerr, but also to Sarah Hogg, then economics editor of *The Times*. Kerr was a high-flying Foreign Office man, on secondment to the Treasury, whom I had been able to hijack as my principal private secretary. He stayed on to serve Nigel Lawson and was later appointed to Brussels as Britain's ambassador to the European Union. Sarah Hogg, daughter of John Boyd-Carpenter and wife of Douglas Hogg, was a sharply independent, but not unsympathetic, reporter of our policies. We had a most congenial evening, though wondering a little at the way in which the monetarist sheep had been so clearly separated from the Social Democratic and other goats.

All this may have affected the mood at the first event on the following day. I had been invited by the ambassador, unusually, to speak to senior embassy staff about the government's economic policy. This was a good idea, since it was clearly a time when guidance would be welcome. But the tone of the occasion and substance of the first question (from one of the defence attachés) was distinctly less than friendly. This surprised my party a good deal, not least because Nicholas Henderson had been seen almost as one of the patron saints of our revolution, as the author of the insightful despatch from the Paris Embassy (entitled 'Britain's Decline' and published in the *Economist* in May 1979), which had almost defined the agenda of our election campaign. But two years' hard pounding understandably struck some people as rather longer than they had bargained for.

This impatience was certainly gathering support at home. On my return from Washington I delivered a spirited defence of our strategy during the Croydon North-West by-election campaign. (It did not prevent us losing the seat to the Liberal, on 22 October, with an adverse swing of 24 per cent.) Critics within the party were raising their voices as well, ahead of and in the margins of the Blackpool party conference. Ted Heath's supporters in this argument ranged from Geoffrey Rippon to Ian Gilmour ('If the government does not alter course . . . we Tories might be driven into . . . the wilderness for years and years'). For the first time since our entry into government, Ted brought his criticism on to the floor of the conference itself with a speech in the economic debate, to which I had to reply. 'Our party', warned Heath, 'faces its greatest crisis for fifty years. I beg you to consider a major change of direction before it is too late.'

His remarks were politely but coolly received. At the moment when I rose to reply, there was a most disconcerting distraction. For I noticed stewards moving swiftly between the rows of seated delegates, asking them to look under their seats. Another group had started, astonishingly, to dismantle the rostrum immediately in front of me and the newly appointed party chairman, Cecil Parkinson. I was totally baffled, indeed alarmed. 'What the hell's going on, Cecil?' I asked. 'You are, Geoffrey!' he replied. Unknown to me, Cecil had just made a split-second decision to discount the bomb 'warning' (timed for five minutes later), which he had received a few minutes before. He did not mention it to me until the end of my speech, by which time the scare was over.

Ted's arguments had clearly been well rehearsed in a series of broadcasts during the preceding four days. So I directed a good deal of my reply in his direction:

> I begin by saying, not just to Ted Heath but to all of you: like Ted, like Margaret Thatcher, I place myself firmly among those who see unemployment as certainly the most grievous social evil in our country today. . . . I was born and brought up in South Wales . . . the dole queue was an unforgettable part of my childhood. . . . A Chancellor of the Exchequer does not just do the sums.

If it was false and unjust for socialists to lay the blame on Ted Heath for the rise in unemployment in 1971, I suggested, there was even less cause for anyone in our party to do the same to Margaret Thatcher after 1979. I reminded the conference of what we had said in our manifesto: 'In implementing all our policies the need to curb inflation will come first, for only then can our broader strategy succeed.' Those words, I said, came not from the 1979 manifesto but from the manifesto on which we fought and won the election under Ted Heath in 1970. 'If it was true then, as it was,' I declared, 'when inflation was half as high, it is twice as true today.'

Much of my speech was devoted to an exposition of the long-term causation of our problems – the disappearance, over decades, of our manufacturing capability – and of the measures we had adopted which would take years to bear fruit. I closed with another response to Ted Heath. None of us, I said, relished the harshness of some of the decisions we were having to take and carry through. Of course, our policies had to be tempered with compassion, as they were. '"But nothing", said Ted Heath in his introduction to our manifesto in 1970, "has done Britain more harm than the endless backing and filling which we have seen in recent years. Once a policy is established the Prime Minister and his colleagues should have the courage to stick with it." I agree with every single word of that, and I invite this Conference to do the same.'

The conference responded most warmly, as the *Financial Times* reported, 'with an enthusiastic standing ovation, not for his performance or for his speech, which contained nothing new, but as a demonstration of loyalty and support for his policies, and those of Mrs Margaret Thatcher'. I was well enough content with that. So too was Margaret. She penned for me a message on a photograph of the occasion: 'A marvellous speech and a superb performance always as Chancellor'. The reception was certainly an important encouragement to the whole of the Cabinet and the great bulk of the parliamentary party.

Fracas Before the 1981 Autumn Statement

And so on to the return of Parliament and the Croydon North-West and (one month later) Crosby by-elections. By then we had been able to cut interest rates twice by a total of 1 per cent. And I had (once again) dared to assert, in the House of Commons on 19 November, that 'the worst of the recession is probably behind us'. And so, in the result and even in retrospect, it began to seem. Figures for the third quarter showed an increase in manufacturing output of 1.5 per cent, while in chemicals it was up by 6 per cent and in engineering by 2 per cent.

This had not yet brought anything like contentment to the parliamentary party, but the atmosphere in Cabinet had improved enormously over the autumn. Norman Tebbit, for example, newly installed in Jim Prior's old job at the Department of Employment, had brought a fresh, more radical approach to the central problem of trade union law reform. Norman's sardonic wisdom on this topic owed much to his own experience as a tough-minded leader of the British Air Line Pilots Association. He well understood the point, one which I had several times argued with Jim Prior at Cabinet meetings in the previous twelve months but which Jim had never been able or willing fully to appreciate. 'Too few reformers', Norman was to write, 'had faced the fact that the power of trade unions is based on the privilege of immunity from liability in tort.'[1] This was in fact the main mischief that Robert Carr and I had sought to tackle in our 1971 Industrial Relations Act. I was delighted that this message was once again to be put to work for sanity in industrial relations. Norman Tebbit's White Paper, which he produced just a week before my Autumn Statement, proposed to remove the long-standing immunity (it dated from the 1906 Act) from industrial action in support of secondary picketing, union membership clauses or closed shops. He also proposed a substantial and practically important narrowing of the definition of 'trade dispute'. This was a most useful consequence of the September reshuffle.

The changes had a similar effect on our collective approach to questions of public expenditure, which had caused such an outbreak of anguish in July. We were now confronted with much less turbulence than we had come to expect. The change in composition of Cabinet was not the only reason for this. Already the fiscal position was beginning to ease, so that we could afford some modest relaxation on the spending side. It had been well contained thanks to Leon's tenacity and to some weighty help from Willie Whitelaw, who presided over several crucial bilateral meetings with spending ministers.

Willie responded characteristically to my letter of thanks: 'I am only pleased that you felt that I was of some use to you.' We had held the line, even at the cost of yielding a little ground. I was not disposed to quarrel with the verdict expressed by somebody that the Treasury had suffered an 'honourable defeat'. But all this was much too late to save John Butcher, our luckless candidate at Crosby, when polling day (26 November) coincided with the Cabinet meeting on which we completed our public spending discussions. Shirley Williams converted the late Graham Page's majority of 19,272 into a Social Democratic equivalent of 5289. She was the first member of her party to be elected to the House.

It was now time for another Autumn Statement for me to make to the house on Wednesday, 2 December. I was beginning to realize, not before time, that this particular exercise was almost bound to be a public-relations zero, at best. For its essential structure lacked virtually all the tax-cutting or scene-shifting components that can add cheer or authority to a proper Budget. The presentational difficulty was magnified, moreover, by the press habit of describing the occasion as a mini-budget, for all that one is actually able to report is the outcome of the prolonged struggle about the scale and distribution of public spending. Even increases in expenditure – or at least the large or noticeable ones – look more like defeats. On this occasion, for example, it was hardly possible to squeeze much cheer out of the main proposals for increased expenditure: £2.5 billion to cover increased costs or deficits for local government and nationalized industries; £2.3 billion to meet pensions and increased numbers on the dole or retraining programmes, and £89 million towards an overrun in defence costs. It amounted to almost £6 billion in extra public expenditure with virtually nothing to show for it. Beyond that the announcements were largely bad news or at least half-loaves: rents and prescription charges up, student grants and most social security benefits increased by less than the rate of inflation, and worst of all, another increase of 1 per cent in employees' National Insurance contributions, to pay for the growing numbers out of work.

The *Daily Mail* comment defined the outcome with brutal clarity: 'As electrifying as an algebra lesson. The Wets and the Dries in the Cabinet seem to have fought each other to a standstill. Sir Geoffrey personifies this grinding stalemate.' The rest of the press was almost equally flat. Tory back-benchers received all this, whether in the House or later in committee upstairs, 'coolly'. At the end of the debate, which took place in the following week, there was a back-bench rebellion – the largest since 1979 – in which fourteen back-benchers, including the recently liberated Sir Ian Gilmour, abstained from supporting the government. But this restlessness was no longer evident in the Cabinet. Even on the back benches most people were ready to wait for the 1982 Budget, which was now being seen as the guiding light for the government's remaining period in office.

But my forecast of 1 per cent growth in 1982 alongside inflation still in double figures – a consequence of the weaker pound – was scarcely exhilarating.

The most startling treatment of my Statement came from next door, in the form of a last-minute row about the presentation. The Prime

Minister had been closely informed about – indeed engaged in discussing – the substance of everything that I had to say, and had not objected. But when, on the day before the Statement's delivery, she was routinely sent the full text, she protested vigorously. She delivered this presentational broadside – and she was right about the problem though short of a solution – at an early-evening meeting with me. This led me to summon a group of senior advisers and drafters to a late-night meeting in the downstairs sitting room at Number 11. We met at about 9 p.m. Some were in favour of sticking to the original text, John Kerr and some others were for revision, if only on the ground that it would be politic to make at least *some* changes.

We were still at work on this exercise when we were interrupted (and astonished) by the arrival of the Prime Minister through the connecting door with Number 10. Margaret had apparently just returned from a dinner engagement (I never did find out where) and been told by her Treasury private secretary, Michael Scholar, of the meeting taking place next door. To his dismay she decided to join the proceedings. We had no time to think of reducing the large cast present. Margaret, who was in most unprepossessing mood, proceeded to play to the gallery outrageously – more than I had ever witnessed before. Anyone who attempted to describe the reformulations on which we had agreed was shouted down. So was I. At one point she exclaimed, 'If this is the best that you can do, then I'd better send you to hospital and deliver the Statement myself.'

The storm eventually blew itself out and the lady withdrew. A shaken handful of trusties stayed on to complete our redraft. Michael Scholar and John Kerr prudently decided to withhold the product from Margaret until the morning after. It was a little shorter, and perhaps to that extent better, than the original. But it was not in substance any different from the first version or from the reformulations that Margaret had derided so fiercely. There was no further comment from that quarter until after I had delivered the Statement. By the time I got back to Number 11 there was a note in her own hand: 'Well done in a *difficult House*. We have cut the 5.30 meeting – come this evening when you are ready.* TV presentation matters more than anything else. Your quiet confidence goes over very well there, as in the House.'

I cannot recall Margaret ever coming closer to an apology than this. Neither of us ever mentioned the incident again. Nor, surprisingly, did

* I was due at Number 10 for a working dinner.

the media, save for one reference (remarkably on the *Today* programme, rather than in his own paper) by Peter Riddell, political editor of the *Financial Times*. I could only conclude that most of the amazed witnesses of the late-night fracas had had the unusual good sense to hold their peace about the occasion. It did not, even in retrospect, mark any great change in the working relationship between Margaret and myself. I suppose I have always regarded other people's personalities as largely beyond reform. Some people put the cap back on the toothpaste and some don't. Over the years I had had so many talks with colleagues about Margaret's ways of doing business, of managing colleagues, of planning strategies and the like. I do not know how far, if at all, any of them had tried to promote any change in her style and temperament. Certainly there was little evidence to suggest any significant success. But the same is true, in my experience, of most people with whom one has to deal, whether socially or professionally. For practical purposes Margaret and I were back, for the foreseeable future, to business as not so unusual.

EC Presidency at Number 11

All these Westminster dramas had been taking place at a time when the European Community was looming larger in our affairs, because we were in the middle of Britain's six-month Presidency of the EC Council of Ministers. For the Chancellor of the Exchequer this involved less burdensome work than for some other colleagues – the Foreign Secretary obviously and the Minister of Agriculture, for whom there was a continuous routine of business. The main item on the Foreign Ministers' agenda, the British Budget Question, was temporarily off the boil, between the 1980 Luxembourg settlement and its re-emergence in 1982. My periodic and fascinating weekend stints as chairman of the EMS realignment conferences (there was one such on 4 October) were part of a wider agenda, of which I shall say more in a subsequent chapter.* It was our duty to organize an informal weekend for colleagues (30–31 October). But I fear we did not lay on as exotic an occasion as the Italians had done at Taormina and Agrigento in May 1980. In April 1981 the Dutch too had had the wit to get us away, to a new setting, in the attractive township of Breda. There we had been

* See p. 276 below.

entertained to an original musical evening in Louensteyn Castle, the house of the great Dutch jurist Hugo Grotius. By comparison our London programme was very routine: a meeting in Lancaster House and an evening at Covent Garden, where we were treated to an excellent performance of *Simon Boccanegra*.

For me one of the most memorable incidents of the presidency happened on my journey to Brussels for our final December meeting of ECOFIN. As John Kerr and I boarded our commercial flight from Gatwick, snow was falling heavily, so much so that we were eventually told that it was not possible for us to take off. By the time we were offloaded back into the terminal building, train services from Gatwick had been suspended as well. But my car was still available: my all-wise driver Peter Smithson had followed his golden rule (derived from thirty years of experience in the government car service) of never departing until his master's plane had actually taken off. (Peter and I reckon we are almost the only people who receive only favourable notice in the diaries of Richard Crossman: he too was in Peter's care for many years.)

The Governor of the Bank of England, who was also due at the ECOFIN meeting, was not so lucky. His driver had departed the scene. He had to abandon his mission and spend the night at a Gatwick hotel, only to find that he was without cheque-book, acceptable credit card or sufficient cash for the occasion. It's good to know that even central bank governors are sometimes brought down to earth.

Our own fate was more hazardous. For Peter Smithson decided, after due consultation, that there was just a chance we might be able to get through by road to the Dover ferry terminal. And somehow, after several detours round blocked roads in mid-Kent, we did. Our final hurdle was on the cliff-top highway just short of Dover. John Kerr got out of the car to explain the urgency of our mission to police who were turning vehicles back at that point. Mercifully a snowplough came suddenly out of the night, spreading snow over John Kerr from top to toe, and was able to clear a path for us to the harbour. Snow-covered John made an uncomfortable fellow passenger, but we were able to join the handful of travellers who had made it to the ferry, and were met by a Brussels embassy car at Calais for an ice-strewn drive to the Europa Hotel and two hours' sleep before I took the ECOFIN chair.

Not for the first time I noticed the contrast between the way in which some ministers – the Prime Minister, of course, and Defence and Foreign Secretaries – were regularly flown around Europe, indeed around the world, in Royal Air Force jets (HS-125s or VC-10s) and the

way in which lesser mortals (even the Chancellor, who had to find the
funds to pay for it all) had to cope with travel hazards in the same way
as other mortals. I was not well placed to complain about this, for the
rules affecting such matters had been drawn up by John Kerr himself,
when he had been in charge of the Treasury's defence expenditure
division. They had been designed to squeeze departments, primarily to
stop high-ranking service officers all turning up to the same conferences
in individual aircraft. Such attempts at prudent parsimony always seem
to strike more harshly on those with the smallest initial budgets.

I may not have had access to a fleet of private jets, but I derived
pleasure enough from the use we were able to make, at all seasons, of
the splendid facility of 11 Downing Street. At Christmas particularly it
came into its own. One of the functions which we were able to
inaugurate, thanks to a suggestion from my parliamentary colleague
Michael Grylls and the Small Business Bureau, was an annual Christmas
party for handicapped children. Presents and entertainment were provided for some five or six dozen children by entertainers as diverse as
Jimmy Saville and Mickey Mouse, and the Chancellor of the Exchequer
had the opportunity of performing as Father Christmas. The photographic coverage in press and television offered a sharp contrast with
the popular vision of Chancellor as a tax-grabbing scrooge.

We were making 'corporate' use of Number 11 in other ways as well.
Elspeth had the excellent idea of laying on a grass-widow type of supper
party to match the Number 10 dinners that were traditionally held on
the eve of a new session of Parliament. For the Number 10 occasions all
ministers were on parade, together with Mr Speaker and the Cabinet
Secretary, for a ceremonial reading of the Queen's speech. (The contents
came as a complete surprise to nobody, since we had all been concerned
in preparing the text.) Everyone was expected to pay for the privilege,
for it was, curiously, a Conservative Party and not a government
occasion. The guests generally moved on (with spouses) to a Carlton
Club reception, traditionally given by the United and Cecil Club on the
same evening. So Elspeth's notion of a parallel party brought the
partners, including Dennis Thatcher, together at a conveniently handy
location. Food and drink for this occasion were produced and delivered
by the spouses themselves – much better quality, they would say, than
the fare next door; certainly much cheaper anyway, and just as much
enjoyed.

Enjoyable too were the opportunities to use Number 11 for purely
family occasions. Just three months before, on 5 September 1981, the

garden had provided a beautiful setting for the reception following our daughter Amanda's marriage at St Margaret's, Westminster, to her Cambridge contemporary Steve Glanvill. Robert Runcie, who conducted the service, was as startled as we were to see the oars of the Pembroke College rugger boat being manoeuvred through the windows of 11 and 12 Downing Street. It was just as well that our neighbours from Number 10 had a prior engagement at Balmoral.

This kind of impromptu informality was an agreeable consequence of being able to make a home of an official residence. Peter Carrington was to be comparably surprised, when he and Iona were guests at one Sunday evening dinner party. While the main course was being served Peter was holding forth in characteristic and light-hearted vein about the many shortcomings of the Welsh nation. This provoked a not so *sotto voce* exclamation from our Welsh housekeeper, Mrs King, passing vegetables along the other side of the table: 'There'll be no pudding for him if he goes on like that.' And the noble lord was, for once, reduced to silence – with a renewed respect for Welsh solidarity.

Nicholas Goodison, chairman of the Stock Exchange, was once again my host for almost the last social event of the year, the Exchange's Christmas lunch. This time I recognized the need for qualified musical accompaniment to my speech, sung in the style of Rex Harrison, so the Goodisons' guitar-playing son Adam was pressed into service. The Stock Exchange echoed with the strains of our modest rendition. The first verse ran:

> Chancellor Geoffrey Howe looked out
>   On the Feast of Stephen,
> When the snow lay round about,
>   Deep and crisp and even.
> Cannon Street shut down at noon,
>   Worse, Fleet Street stayed open,
> Westminster was full of gloom,
>   All the wets were fro-o-zen.

The Goodisons' thank-you letters differed sharply. Young Adam took a generous view of our partnership and looked forward to a joint appearance at the Wembley Arena. Father Nicholas, characteristically more bearish, commented simply, 'I think I can safely say there has never been anything quite like it.'

CHAPTER SEVENTEEN

ECONOMIC AND MILITARY SUCCESS

═══

Planning the 1982 Budget

My first journey out of London in 1982 was to give us our first experience of Chevening, the magnificent establishment between Sevenoaks and the North Downs which later became our country home for more than six years. I had decided that the process of Budget preparation would be hugely improved by giving ourselves – my full team of Treasury ministers and senior officials – the chance of a much fuller and more relaxed discussion of the options, away from the distraction of telephones and daily business. We needed the kind of weekend country-house think-in that I had advocated in a *Crossbow* leader more than twenty years before. The Treasury was nervous of adverse publicity for weekend junketing. All the options that were first suggested were forbiddingly expensive, and designed to steer me towards the mandarins' first choice – an all-day meeting in Great George Street.

This was John Kerr's chance to come to the rescue. For he knew that Peter Carrington's private office was uneasy that the Foreign Secretary was making almost no use of his official country residence. (Peter had his own estate at Bledlow on the Buckinghamshire side of London.) Their concern led them to fear undesirable press stories about wasted assets. So it was no surprise that Brian Fall (John's opposite number in the Foreign Secretary's private office) greeted John Kerr with open arms. The Foreign Office was more than willing to lend Chevening for the weekend, 9–10 January. It was ideal for our purpose, with some twenty bedrooms (including a few in the servants' wing, the village and so on), a magnificent eighteenth-century library to meet in, and spacious and attractive dining and sitting rooms – all within an hour's drive of

London. It was my idea that we should be accompanied, at our own modest expense, by our wives, who greatly welcomed the chance to see more of their husbands' workmates and of each other. It was only later that we got to know well the excellent people who ran the house and estate in most friendly fashion, under the charge of the then secretary of the Chevening Trust, General John Graham (ex-Parachute Regiment, with particularly distinguished experience in Oman) and his wife Rosemary.

Our first visit was dramatically beautiful, since the Kent countryside was thickly covered with fresh snow. This added to the drama of the parkland walks, which my Treasury team only sampled but which our wives enjoyed to the full. In these conditions the famous 'keyhole' – a rectangular aperture in the line of trees along the ridge of the North Downs above the house – was startlingly visible, looking more like a huge memorial stone, almost in the sky. On the Saturday evening I began to rediscover my army taste for billiards. But even after subsequent years of practice on the Chevening table my standard never approached that of Peter Middleton and Terry Burns at that first weekend.

The relaxed setting certainly helped to give a new lucidity and coherence to our 1982 Budget thoughts – particularly valuable when Cabinet was this year to have its first full-dress discussion of our strategy. We met as one group under my chairmanship for nine full hours. Short, largely interrogative papers had been prepared as guides round a reasonably familiar course. Three new ministers, Nick Ridley, Jock Bruce-Gardyne and Barney Heyhoe, had the chance to absorb, and to start shaping our culture. Number 10 was not represented. But Margaret was inevitably curious, so some of the more interesting conclusions were recorded in a note sent to Number 10 after the weekend. One conclusion was to have particularly long-range implications:

> The paper showing the evolution of public spending totals in the long term was frightening. It illustrated the logical consequences of giving way to the inevitable pressures and appetites for more and better services without having regard to paying for them. Options included greater privatization and higher charges for individuals. We need to persuade Cabinet and then the public that the problem existed. We must point out the danger of simply re-establishing the pledges which currently plagued public expenditure constraint.

This was the first spark of the debate that was to explode in Cabinet and at the party conference later in the year. The exercise did not produce any plainspoken public fruit for more than two years, when Nigel Lawson published his Green Paper, *Expenditure Over the Next Ten Years*, in March 1984.

Our first fully fledged pre-Budget Cabinet on 28 January turned out to be an unthreatening and useful occasion. It showed very clearly that Cabinet – certainly in its new make-up – was well able to make a balanced and supportive contribution to the debate. The test was less severe, no doubt, at a time when some of the worst pressures were beginning to ease. Margaret and her allies felt at ease in a Cabinet where they were less likely to be on the defensive. And the erstwhile wets were more at ease in an improving economic environment. Everyone round the table offered a view on the options and Cabinet agreed that it would be right to continue on the broad strategy which Government had followed hitherto. It was essential not to put at risk the objective of reducing inflation; within that the aim should be to enable the country to take advantage of the prospects of recovery. I was urged above all to avoid raising excessive expectations of the Budget, to concentrate on an imaginative approach towards enterprise and industrial recovery and to ensure that it was not necessary to undo any relief. That pointer towards 'prudence now with more later if possible' exactly reflected my own instinct.

A Cabinet meeting of this constructive kind could be entertaining as well as encouraging. One of the by-products of such occasions were the notes – often in verse form – which used to reach me, above all from my usual neighbour Peter Carrington. If I had kept them all, I could have published a small anthology. One of Peter's that dates from this period – I cannot now recall the precise cause – concerned the Defence Secretary:

> The spendthrift and bellicose Nott
> is involved in a nuclear plot;
> he's impaled on the fork
> of his Tridental talk
> and Howe has to finance the lot.

But work crowds in. After the pre-Budget Cabinet I had to go almost straight to the Commons to open a debate on economic policy in which I was able to repel without difficulty pressure from the Opposition front bench (supported, with his own proposals, by Ian Gilmour) for a '£5 billion boost to the economy'. Our own side were heartened by the glimpse that I felt able to offer of growing room for manoeuvre and of improved incentives for productivity and enterprise.

All this provoked a characteristically heartening note in my weekend box from my skilful manager, John Kerr:

> The buzz from No. 10 is that the PM thought Thursday was an excellent day. She thought Cabinet went very well; and she was singing her praises of last afternoon's despatch-box performance. Your best, for years, she said (I bet it was the impromptu bits, not the script!).

More objectively, perhaps, both Terry Burns and Cabinet Office were reported to believe that Cabinet had been 'startlingly good'. Right or wrong this was very reassuring and encouraged me in my natural wish to confide in colleagues more rather than less.

A few days later it was Elspeth's fiftieth birthday. The conventional drinks party that we gave prompted a generously charming comment from Tim Raison, at that time a Home Office minister. He expressed himself greatly reassured by the fact that Elspeth's 'half-century means no less of energy, charm or anything else. . . . We all think you are a delight to know, as well as a great prop to Geoffrey in his sterling work.' Malcolm Rutherford in the *Financial Times* made the same point a few weeks later when he observed that 'whenever Sir Geoffrey speaks in the House, Lady Howe is in the gallery, willing him on. Few other Ministers receive such open support from their spouses.' A few months later this became a more obviously two-way exercise, when Elspeth entered the London School of Economics as a mature student for a degree course in economics and social administration. The press quite soon heard of a borrowing request from the Chancellor of the Exchequer to the House of Commons Library for a first-year textbook on *The Principles of Elementary Economics*. It took some time to convince them that it was for my wife that I had been seeking such guidance.

Budget Time

By then there was just a month to go to the Budget, to be introduced on 9 March. Several factors did not operate too helpfully in the intervening weeks: inflation remained stuck at 12 per cent, industrial production sagged during the (very snow-ridden) month of December, and North Sea oil prices fell four dollars a barrel, from $35 to $31. That was good for inflation but reduced tax revenue uncomfortably. One piece of good news overrode all these, so far as Budget planning was concerned: the PSBR was, for the first time in my Chancellorship, running below the forecast figure. Largely as a consequence of this, interest rates had already fallen three full percentage points from their October peak of 16 per cent. Even after making allowance for the possibility of a further fall in the oil price – and so in my revenue – I looked like having similar room for manoeuvre on the PSBR – and so, I hoped, on interest rates – in the year ahead.

But nothing ever proceeds quite plainly. An expectant nation had to wait sixteen minutes beyond the advertised time for the start of my speech. A Labour Member, Don Dixon, had decided to take advantage of a rule of the House (the ten-minute rule) which allowed him to make a short speech introducing a Bill of his own choosing (in this case to beef up the powers of wages councils, which we had it in mind to abolish).

My speech itself started on a note of sadness prompted by the death that morning of 'one of my most gifted and distinguished predecessors . . . almost thirty years to the day since his first Budget', Rab Butler. Since his time, I said, a tradition had grown up that the Budget speech should be composed 'almost as though it were a detective story . . . with the denouement, the full picture, being revealed only at the end'. I proposed to break with the tradition and to tell the House 'without more ado that in this Budget I shall be proposing substantial reductions in taxation while at the same time reducing the government's borrowing requirement. This will be a Budget for industry – and so a Budget for jobs. But it will be a Budget for people as well.' My shrewdly observant special adviser Peter Cropper was unusually exuberant about this opening. 'A masterstroke', he wrote, 'to put that bit at the front. Something for everyone; from then on they could all sit back enjoying their lollipops, as it were.'

It wasn't all giveaway, I should add. The notion that excise duties – on drink, tobacco, oil and petrol – should rise in line with inflation was by now accepted. So was a tough tranche of measures against tax evasion. But the overall effect was a net tax cut of £1.3 billion in 1982–3, or as much as £3 billion in a full year. Even so, I was able to plan for a PSBR in the year ahead (£9.5 billion) that was £1 billion lower than in the year just ending. This was consistent with the modifications in monetary policy which I announced: the specific recognition of a diversity of targets – M1, PSL2 as well as our old friend sterling M3 – with the same target range (8–12 per cent) covering all three aggregates. We were able to persuade both Alan Walters and the markets that this broader spread was not inconsistent with the MTFS. The most decisive factor was undoubtedly our re-establishment of control over government borrowing. (The scale of the 1981 tax increases, when coupled with the firmer grip that Leon was achieving through cash control, both contributed to this.) There was still enough room for a number of modest tax reductions for people and businesses – with the emphasis on business. Income tax payers saw their allowances increased a couple of points above the rate of inflation. Business's main relief was a 1.5 per cent cut in the hated National Insurance surcharge, Denis Healey's 'tax on jobs'. This was accompanied by a very wide range of incentives to investment and enterprise. Last, but by no means least, was our fresh approach to the grievously intractable problem of unemployment.

At the start of my speech I offered a careful analysis of the way in which the many faults of our labour market had been pricing willing workers out of jobs and presented the essence of our solution: the Community Programme, we called it, carefully avoiding the more emotional notion of 'workfare'. The central idea, I explained, would be to give those who have been on the unemployment register for some time the chance to work for the benefit of their own community, while still receiving 'broadly the equivalent of their benefit entitlement plus an addition for expenses and the like'. It was, therefore, the very 'benefit plus' scheme for which people like Ian Gilmour had been pressing. Participants would remain free to take a regular job if it came along. And 'it would be for them to decide whether or not to participate in such a scheme'. This scheme was the fruit of close collaboration between Leon Brittan (for my Treasury team) and Norman Tebbit and David Young (then still at the Manpower Services Commission, to which Norman had recently appointed him).

No one could have been more startled than Norman Tebbit at the meeting in my office when he was told, by Chancellor and Chief Secretary together, that he could have more money for sensible job-creation schemes. The key official in pulling all this together in Norman's department was Donald Derx. He had once crossed Margaret Thatcher, by being right at her expense, and thus made himself unpromotable. I was to meet him years later as a colleague on the main board of Glaxo:

the public sector's loss was the private sector's gain. Unhappily the central purpose of the scheme was in the end frustrated, when we were obliged – by trade union intransigence – to pay 'the rate for the job' rather than our original idea of 'benefit plus'. This meant that the programme helped many fewer people than we intended. But it was a workmanlike and worthwhile demonstration of our positive concern. Combined with almost three dozen specific enterprise measures it helped to ensure an almost universally positive response to this, my fourth Budget. Margaret penned an instant and generous reaction: 'Just to say – *superb* – and that the troops were delighted. You should get a *very* good press tomorrow. You deserve *all* the acclaim. The economy is now set on its course for the next twelve months. Have a good night's sleep!'

She was right about the press, and the troops, from the *Mirror*'s reluctant 'His cleverest yet' and the *Telegraph*'s 'The best so far with the right dash of boldness' to Malcolm Rutherford's comment in the *Financial Times* 'Peace breaks out amongst the Tories'. Alan Walters was particularly forthcoming: 'As you know I would have preferred it somewhat tighter – but I hereby acknowledge that I was quite wrong.'

Most gratifying of all perhaps was the note from my old friend and candid critic over many years, Tom Hooson (he had yet to enter the House). 'I just want to say', he wrote, 'that I think you have gained greatly in authority this week. The more one looks back, the more the guiding principle emerges, in Shakespeare's words, "Unto thine own self be true".' Years later, after Tom's tragically early death as Member for Brecon and Radnor, I was reminded of his letter and prompted to take the Shakespearean quotation as the family motto for my lordly coat of arms, then being designed. The dog-Latin rendering, 'Tibi fidelis', seemed compact enough.

The one jest in my Budget speech, about a by-election to be held later that month, went well enough in the House on the day – but was short-lived. 'In proposing', I said, 'a rather larger percentage increase in the duty on claret than on whisky, I have at no stage had in mind adding to the problems of the candidate for the Social Democratic Party in Glasgow, Hillhead, Mr Roy Jenkins. I fancy that he may have enough troubles of his own already.' That turned out to be tempting providence too far. For although public opinion had begun moving firmly in our favour since the turn of the year* it had not yet come far enough to

---

* Gallup records that the Alliance lead over the Conservatives had fallen from 12 points in January to 2 in March (and was dramatically reversed from May onwards).

save Hillhead. Roy Jenkins gained the seat with a swing to the SDP and from the Unionists of 14.4 per cent. The SDP bandwagon continued to roll, albeit more slowly. My budget was generally perceived to have finally checked the risk of any further Tory defections in that direction.

War in the South Atlantic

Then came the Falkland Islands' invasion by Argentine forces on 2 April. I knew a little about the islands. For I had been at least partially informed when Nick Ridley and Peter Carrington reported to the Oversea and Defence Committee of Cabinet on the negotiations with which Nick was then concerned towards the end of 1980. I had some sympathy, without having thought deeply, with the lease-back proposal that was then being canvassed. But when that provoked as fierce opposition in the House of Commons as from the Prime Minister, I was not surprised that they regarded that route as closed for the foreseeable future. And as John Nott (at the Ministry of Defence) pressed, on grounds of economy, for the withdrawal of HMS *Endurance* from the region in the winter of 1981/2 it was certainly not for Treasury ministers to argue the opposite case. Nothing had ever crossed my desk which made the risk of an Argentine invasion look remotely likely.

Yet here it was, with Cabinet assembled on the evening of Friday, 2 April and the islands already under Argentine occupation. The handful of Marines who stood between the Argentines and Governor Rex Hunt and his 1700 kinsmen had surrendered in face of overwhelming force. The only question was whether or not Her Majesty's Government should take action to recover the islands. The atmosphere was one of shocked disbelief. All the normal features of government seemed for the moment to have been suspended. Here was a crisis which, if it was anything, was a crisis about foreign affairs. Yet Foreign Office ministers were, almost by definition, unable to offer any useful advice. We had before us just one document, to supplement oral 'reports' from Peter Carrington and John Nott – an intelligence assessment from the Chiefs of Staff. It was in forthright terms: a military operation to recapture the islands would be one of extreme difficulty, much more likely to fail than to succeed. Margaret (and others) were not going to be overwhelmed by that and expressed surprise at the conclusions. Rather impulsively, I passed a note to John Biffen: 'But the only surprising thing would be if any part of the substance of the intelligence report was not, on balance of probability, true?' And he replied: 'Absolutely – the bearer of realistic news is rarely welcome! See Cleopatra!!'

But when the time came for each member of the Cabinet to indicate his view of the wisdom of sending a task force to recapture the islands, John was the only one to cast his vote against. I took the view that the least relevant factor to this particular decision was the likely economic cost of the conflict – and that turned out to be right. Nobody could then have foreseen the cost of success (as opposed to the cost of conflict): the *long-run* cost of defending the islands if they were recaptured. It was no part of the Chancellor's duty at such time to argue against the use of the defence forces for the very purpose for which they had been provided – the defence or recapture of British territory. So the decision to send a task force was taken. The financial consequences were left to one side until the conflict was over. Margaret sensibly took the advice of Harold Macmillan (proffered a few days later) that the Treasury should not be represented in the small War Cabinet that she formed for this purpose. My disappointment at being thus excluded (to which Margaret refers in her memoirs)[1] was short-lived. For she took me quite often into her confidence about most of the difficult issues. The Deputy Prime Minster, Foreign and Defence Secretaries were automatic choices for membership; and Cecil Parkinson, Margaret's own creation as party chairman, was well cast as the link man with media and party.

The ten weeks of voyage and conflict were a strange time for the rest of government. I was greatly discouraged by the resignation of Peter Carrington, and I tried, on the Monday morning, 5 April, to dissuade him from going, but that morning's press had hardened his final resolve. He was, as I came to see, absolutely right to go. From this it followed naturally enough that his two colleagues, Humphrey Atkins and my old friend Richard Luce, should feel the same obligation of honour. (For Richard it was the second resignation of his life: years before, he had resigned his position as a young officer in the Colonial Service in Kenya in protest at the treatment of the Northern Frontier Provincial tribes for which he was responsible.)

The arrival of Francis Pym, who replaced Peter Carrington as Foreign Secretary, was not the most auspicious event, for he and Margaret had often before shown their incompatibility. But any other choice would have meant a series of Cabinet upheavals, which was clearly not on. One consequence of Margaret's lack of confidence in Francis was an increase in the number of occasions on which she used our Sunday-evening chats to discuss the 'progress' of his persistent, but intrinsically hopeless, search for an honourable settlement of the Falklands dispute. On those occasions, when I sensed that she felt at her most lonely, we reached possibly the high point of our relationship. It was clear to me that the Argentine leadership was never seriously committed to such an outcome.

When victory finally came there was a transformation in Margaret's standing, throughout the world even more than at home, and deservedly so. There can be no doubting the extraordinary importance, from start to end of the crisis, of her sustained courage in face of uniquely personalized pressures. There was an even more striking change in her perception of herself. The role of victorious warrior queen was one into which she grew very naturally. Her confidence in her own judgment was certainly not diminished. And her respect for the wisdom of the Foreign Office had certainly not been enhanced by the whole story. Nor, I have to confess, had mine. On the day after the invasion (Saturday, 3 April), I had had to preside over a ministerial meeting to consider the economic consequences of the conflict. The only department not represented there was the Foreign and Commonwealth Office. 'Surely', I exploded, 'they're going to send someone along to tell us whether or not there's a war on?' It was a serious question, with important legal consequences, but it went, that day, unanswered. At any rate, these changes in Margaret's perception did not bode well for the years ahead.

One side-effect of the intense publicity that was focused on Number 10 during the conflict was a sad, if inevitable, change in the nature of Downing Street. When we first arrived there, it was still very open to the public, who could walk to and fro into St James's Park. Friends could call on us with a minimum of formality. Even Alec and his friends, often coming and going at night in eccentric pop or protest-march gear, were regarded as part of the scene. By the end of the Falklands War the media had almost annexed the street as a permanent open-air news theatre. Security had been greatly intensified. Gradually, not least in face of much more serious threats from terrorists, the place became the semi-fortified enclave that stands today behind iron gates and road ramps.

Managing Margaret

For those of us who were not engaged day to day with the Falklands conflict, it was curiously business as usual on the economic front. Interest rates continued to fall throughout the summer, down to 9 per cent by November. I was speaking at each of the by-elections, which were now producing significantly better results. Tim Smith held Beaconsfield for us on 27 May and Angela Rumbold gained Merton, Mitcham and Morden on 3 June, in each case retaining the 1979 Tory percentage of the vote, while the SDP increased its share at the expense of the Labour vote (by 10 and 21 per cent respectively).

Although the Falklands loyalty factor was certainly an important influence in these results, the developing growth in economic confidence was also part of the picture. Similarly encouraging views came from the distinguished foreign visitors to London during that summer. Singapore's Prime Minister, Harry Lee Kuan Yew, a Cambridge friend, told guests at a Downing Street luncheon on 14 July of his growing admiration for Margaret Thatcher's achievements with the British economy and of his final rejection of socialism ('I used to be a socialist. And now – I'm just me!'). Ronald and Nancy Reagan came on to London from the Versailles Economic Summit, where they had joined with President Mitterrand and their colleagues in offering firm support to Britain in her Falklands conflict, then in its last three testing weeks. Margaret and the President were at their most supportive of each other at such a crucial time, with Ronald Reagan showing his consummate skill as a communicator both in the informality of Downing Street and in the splendour of the Royal Gallery in the Palace of Westminster. For most of us this was our first chance to witness at close quarters a speaker who employed the autocue glass screens, which were soon to become an all-too-regular feature of our platform trade. Elspeth, who sat next to the President at the Downing Street lunch, was struck by his choice of talking point from the Versailles Summit. He could not stop chuckling – nor indeed could I – at President Mitterrand's choice of entertainers at a late-late-show in the Versailles salon: two performing dogs, a circus seal and a sea lion.

Throughout my four years at the Treasury there were three agenda items always overhanging us. They had been from the outset on our target list, and still more emphatically indeed on the target list of John Hoskyns and the original 'Stepping Stones' team (which, as I have noted, was effectively re-formed after the 1979 election into the Number 10 Policy Unit). These objectives were, in short-hand: public expenditure, public sector pay and public ownership. There was a fourth that was not a Treasury item but was just as important: trade union or labour market reform.

On trade unions, I have already retailed the two phases of activity so far: Jim Prior's relatively modest but effective initial tranche and the more far-reaching measures now being taken through Parliament by Norman Tebbit. The packages themselves had been rather randomly put together, in much the same haphazard way that the original 'Stepping Stones' agenda had been 'managed' before the election.

John Hoskyns, I know, had been deeply worried from an early stage in the life of the government by this lack of strategic planning. In a personal note to me, written as long ago as 15 February 1980, Hoskyns had said:

> The conclusion I am coming to is that the way in which [Margaret Thatcher] herself operates, the way her time is at present consumed, the lack of a methodical mode of working and the similar lack of orderly discussion and communication on key issues with other colleagues, means that our chance of implementing a carefully worked out strategy – both policy and communications – is very low indeed. . . .

He explained that he had been fairly certain, from his own pre-election experience, that this would prove to be the case. He proposed, so he said, to take this whole matter up with Margaret again, alone, as soon as possible. But he wanted to talk it through with me first. We had had this discussion several times already and were to do so again. These were no more than an echo of the similarly frustrated (and generally one-to-one) discussions that I had had with most colleagues – certainly Willie Whitelaw, Francis Pym, Keith Joseph, Jim Prior and, of course, Ian Gow (often) on the Shadow Cabinet corridor years before.

But there never was any real improvement in Margaret's working methods of the kind that Hoskyns would have liked. As a former army officer and creator of his own business, John was always less patient than the rest of us with the messiness of politics. This was probably the final reason for his surprise early departure from Downing Street in the spring of 1982. Yet the important agenda items were being tackled, albeit in a less systematic way than he or I might have wished. I liked to think we were still staying fairly close to the strategic agenda we had first worked out in *The Right Approach to the Economy* and developed for our own 1979 manifesto. This was happening, above all, as a result of Margaret's input, authority and, sometimes, judgment. The difference from the more analytical Hoskyns – Howe approach was that her influence was deployed much more opportunistically and instinctively than we should have planned. But throughout Whitehall and Westminster her instinct, her thinking, her authority, was almost always present, making itself felt pervasively, tenaciously and effectively. It came gradually to feel, as the months went by, as though the Prime Minister was present, unseen and unspeaking, at almost every meeting. The questions were always being asked, even if unspoken: how will this play at Number 10? What's the best way of getting the Prime Minister on side for that? And so on.

I have mentioned Margaret's judgment as well as her will. For that was important too. A classic example was over the 1981 coal strike that never was. It was an occasion when the National Coal Board was on the point of executing a major closure programme. The external financing limits that we had imposed, sensibly and necessarily, left them with no alternative. The National Union of Miners threatened sustained and extensive strike action. David Howell, as Energy Secretary, was set to stiffen the NCB's resolve. But Margaret intervened to head off the conflict, which she sensed the Board, and so the government, were not going to win. On this occasion her judgment – overriding her natural long-term instinct – that it was better to fight another day was undoubtedly right. There were, of course, occasions when she was wrong – over GCHQ, for example, as we shall see,* with her reluctance ever to contemplate what was known as 'the card in the pocket solution'. If it had worked, it would have been a much better outcome, managerially as well as politically.

There was an important difference between the way in which Hoskyns and I approached the problems of managing Margaret, at least in my Treasury days, and the way in which it struck, say, Christopher Soames or Ian Gilmour. In my case, I had the satisfaction of knowing that Margaret and I were working to basically similar guidelines, even if we should not always handle the details in the same way. This sense of ideological security is what came, I suppose, from being 'one of us'. This central sympathy of purpose gave one more rather than less room for manoeuvre in the management of policies. Often indeed I was able to enlarge or accelerate actions on which we both agreed, and less often, to modify or tailor their impact so as to make them more sensitive to the anxieties of others: restraining, for example, Margaret's passionate wish to preserve the real value of mortgage interest relief or even to embark upon the replacement of the rating system.

This kind of unspoken deal is to be found, I suspect, in many

* See Chapter 23 below.

management or team relationships – is indeed essential to their survival. It becomes intolerable or unacceptable, either to the partnership itself or to the world that is affected by it, only if the relationship is manifestly or chronically unbalanced or irretrievably fissile. Margaret's most important weakness – the flipside of her strength – was the extent to which her partners were driven in the end to choose between submission or defection. Perhaps inevitably, the closer the original bonding, the longer the life of the partnership, the more dramatic the final rupture. 'I must prevail' was the phrase that finally broke Nigel Lawson's bond of loyalty and affection. Is almost all real leadership foredoomed to produce such rupture?

CHAPTER EIGHTEEN

LAST AUTUMN AT
THE TREASURY

Clash over Public Sector Pay

Through most of my Treasury days together with Margaret, I felt well able to develop our policies towards each of the three unspoken priorities on our agenda: public spending, public ownership and public sector pay. Pay, for example, fell comfortably within my purview as chairman of the Cabinet's Public Sector Pay Committee (established early in the government, in 1979). We started from the extremely uncomfortable position which had culminated in the 1981 Civil Service strike. The terms of settlement of that dispute included the establishment under the chairmanship of Sir John Megaw, a Lord Justice of Appeal, of an inquiry into 'the principles and system by which the remuneration of the non-industrial Civil Services should be determined'. This was yet another attempt to reconcile the two roles of government: its responsibility to the national economy and its responsibility as an employer. More specifically this was a clash between the long-established pattern of pay comparability (with the private sector) for the public service, and cash limits as the means of controlling public expenditure – the precise cause of conflict in the 1980–1 strike. Its management was made no easier by the terminal lack of sympathy, already noted, between the Prime Minister and Christopher Soames, in charge of the Civil Service at the time of the strike.

This was compounded by the unhappy way in which Margaret had been displeased – or as she would say, perhaps with some justice, 'provoked' – by the last (as it happened) permanent secretary of the Civil Service Department, Sir Ian Bancroft, who was also *ex officio* head of the Home Civil Service. All these tensions were eased, however unhappily for Soames and Bancroft, by the effective dissolution of the

Civil Service Department during the autumn of 1981. Most of its functions became part of my responsibility in the Treasury: a modest rump went to the new Management and Personnel Office. Janet Young, a newcomer to the Cabinet in September 1981, assumed responsibility for that, along with Leadership of the House of Lords. And my Treasury ministerial team was strengthened, as I have said, by the arrival of Barney Hayhoe with continuing responsibility for Civil Service matters, under my overall surveillance.* Both Janet and Barney were well suited to these roles, conciliatory in style but firm in substance.

Between us, and with the dedicated help of some truly subtle official thinking, mainly Peter le Cheminant and then Peter Kemp, we were able to evolve answers which very largely commended themselves to the Megaw Committee. 'Comparability' ceased to be the determining factor, and 'market forces' were given a greater role. The Megaw system itself proved remarkably resilient. It was only the resurgence of inflation at the end of the 1980s that exposed some of these more sensitive systems to undue strain. As the inflationary tide again subsided, the fruits of this work remained available for the future. Nigel Lawson was able during his Chancellorship to build on these Megaw foundations very largely through the continuing input of Peter Kemp, then deputy secretary in charge of public sector pay.

How to Privatize

'Privatization' was always a more conscious objective than reform of public sector pay, but for years it was never quite on the agenda. For most of my political lifetime the much more negative label of 'denationalization' had been in use. So I am glad to accept the tribute paid by Christopher Johnson that 'it was a master-stroke of public relations on the part of the Thatcher Government to coin and put in world-wide circulation the word as well as the concept'.[1] David Howell is credited with the invention of the word. But even with the more trendy name the idea's momentum was destined to increase only with the passage of time. This was also true of the extent to which the policy was able to command increasing political and public support. Our long-term aim was spelt out specifically in *The Right Approach to the Economy* in 1977: 'to reduce the preponderance of state ownership in our community'.

* See p. 225 above.

The key members of my Economic Reconstruction Group – Keith Joseph, David Howell, Nigel Lawson, John Nott and I – took that seriously. But our 1979 manifesto was light on specifics: we were committed to privatize only the National Freight Corporation and the 'nationalized shipbuilding and aerospace concerns'. Margaret had been fearful that a more extensive catalogue might frighten the floating voter.

By the time of my first Budget speech, the sensible disposal of the public sector assets had grown in urgency, not least as a short-term way of helping to reduce the PSBR. I set a target of £1 billion for 1979–80. But these disposals had a deeper purpose. As I explained to the House, they were 'an essential part of the long-term programme for promoting the widest possible participation by the people in the ownership of British industry'. Under my chairmanship of E(DL) Committee (established in June 1979 as a sub-committee of the Cabinet's main Economic Committee: DL was short for Disposal), it was Nigel's job to identify and bring forward assets for disposal. We started (in 1979) with a £290 million tranche of BP shares (Margaret was initially nervous of this, in an oil-sensitive world). The process gathered speed with a list of enterprises whose commercial role made them most obviously inappropriate for public ownership. Those that were privatized in 1981 included British Aerospace, Ferranti, Cable and Wireless, British Transport Docks and British Rail Hotels. By 1982 we were ready to legislate for the introduction of private capital into BNOC's oil-producing business. Widespread employee share-ownership in British Aerospace and an imaginative and highly successful staff buy-out at National Freight added to the popularity of the process.

Meanwhile, British Leyland (as it was then called: still our very own motor manufacturer) offered us a contrasting opportunity to learn on the job about the problems that were inseparable from public ownership. Sir Michael Edwardes, chairman of the company throughout our first three years in office (in fact from 1977 to 1982), confronted us with a most skilfully chosen, if very disagreeable, series of options – and lessons. At each stage it was manifestly more expensive (*much* more so) to close the business down than to retain the ownership of British Leyland, with a view to ultimate privatization – exactly when and on what precise basis we could never foresee. With equal skill, Michael exploited the mirror-image of these unattractive options to persuade the company's workforce continuously to improve its performance. Eventually there emerged at least some chunks of the company – Jaguar, Rover and Unipart – that were capable of independent existence. Meanwhile the Exchequer, under the most immediate guidance of three 'hard-line' ministers (Margaret, Keith Joseph and myself), made available to British Leyland some £990 million over two years. Keith Joseph had actually become the 'softest' of all the ministers dealing with this problem. His tremendous intellectual contribution to our work was much less evident in the coal-face decisions that he actually took in practice. I suppose I should take some comfort from Sir Michael's comment on what was probably the most crucial meeting in a long series (20 January 1981): 'Sir Geoffrey Howe's commonsense proved to be a major factor in overcoming what had the makings of a crisis.'[2]

But British Leyland was far from being the only public sector corporation that was to test my commonsense close to breaking point. Much the least predictable component in the whole of public finance during my years at the Treasury was the huge but erratic demand of the nationalized industries for cash: the Coal Board's annual subsidy in the 1980s exceeded £0.5 billion, and British Steel's worst single year cost almost twice as much.

And so it threatened to go on. This was probably the main reason why I spoke so strongly in a speech on privatization which I delivered to the Conservative free-enterprise body, the Selsdon Group, on 1 July 1981:

> It is only since the Election that the issue of privatization has moved to the very forefront of politics. Our experience since we have been in Government has convinced us . . . that the need for privatization, competition or, at least, private sector financial disciplines in the nationalized industries is even greater than we imagined in Opposition.[3]*

It was on the strength of that kind of diagnosis that we had launched early in 1981 two initiatives: first, a search for new ways of financing some nationalized industry borrowing for investment by means of private capital, thus enabling us to exclude it from the PSBR; and second, a fundamental shift in the relationship between sponsoring ministers and the boards and chairmen of industries, such as might transform their performance beyond recognition.

---

* There was in fact only one possible – and perverse – advantage in having any of these industries in the public sector at such a time of economic turbulence: the government's almost open-ended ability (if such it was) to fund short-term losses in face of strike action, until the strike was defeated. It was this consequence of nationalized status which led to management 'victories' in steel and coal in 1981 and 1984.

The Central Policy Review Staff, then under Robin Ibbs' energetic guidance, produced within a very few months an elaborate response – of objectives, performance targets, reviews, reporting structures and the like, all under the oversight of a new Cabinet sub-committee (E(NI)) under the Prime Minister's chairmanship. And I began to put this into effect in face of a less than enthusiastic response from the Nationalized Industry Chairmen's Group. The limited practical results served only to fortify the case for a more radical approach.

The other proposal (for private sector capital) ran more or less similarly into the sand. Bill Ryrie, then one of my second permanent secretaries, conducted a study of the scope for this, as did Parliament's Treasury and Civil Service Select Committee. To the dismay of the industrial lobby, they came to much the same conclusion. In the words of the Select Committee: 'The arguments put to us for greater freedom for nationalized industries to borrow more on the private market do not seem to us to be convincing.' This conclusion, from which the Treasury certainly did not dissent, put a stop to the seemingly hopeful idea of privatizing the financing rather than the ownership (the debt rather than the equity) of the nationalized industries.

The Select Committee's report was published in the same month as my privatization speech. Taken together they were seen, in Christopher Johnson's words, as 'a very clear signal to many, in Whitehall as well as Westminster, that it was time to break the mould of the nationalized industries'.[4] This all happened at a time when the key ministerial positions were held by enthusiasts for further privatization: Nigel Lawson at Energy, Nicholas Ridley alongside me as Financial Secretary to the Treasury, Patrick Jenkin at Industry and David Howell at Transport. Privatization was thus an idea whose time had come. The way was open for the extensive privatization agenda that was to find its place in our 1983 manifesto.

The privatization of British Telecom took place in 1984, as well as that of Jaguar and Enterprise Oil. Between 1986 and 1989 there followed British Gas, British Steel, British Airports and, finally, between 1989 and 1991, the water and electricity industries. One of the most successful privatizations, British Airways, was the longest to put into effect. The enabling legislation had been introduced in 1979 but it was only after protracted litigation had been settled that the sale could go ahead in 1987. I have explained that one of the main arguments driving forward this whole process, from my earliest days in the Treasury, had been the basic search for efficiency in the management of resources. The other main dynamic had been, in the words of my 1979 Budget speech, 'participation by people in the ownership of industry'. During the 1980s, both these objectives were fulfilled. Some nine out of ten of those employed in privatized concerns took up the offer of shares in their industry. The percentage of the British population who owned shares had risen from 7 to 25 per cent. We had set in train an entirely benign revolution, which I was thereafter able to commend to the rest of the world during six years as Foreign Secretary. Much of the credit for this remarkable achievement, in which many ministers played a part, should certainly go to Nigel Lawson. His career path, from Financial Secretary, on to the Department of Energy and back to the Exchequer, had put him in pole position. He made the most of the opportunity.

The CPRS Furore

The other strategic battle of my last full year at the Treasury was concerned with the long-term profile of public expenditure. At our first Chevening weekend in January 1982 we had recommended a major exercise to alert Cabinet and then the public to the dangerous equations that lay ahead. Following this up, I proposed to the Prime Minister on 5 February that the Treasury, the CPRS and spending departments should examine the likely pattern of public spending over the next decade and that I should report to the Cabinet on the whole subject in June. Within three weeks the Prime Minister had accepted my proposal. In mid-June, with the Falklands behind us and some official work to hand, I reopened this topic with her. We needed, I explained, a decisive break with the upward spending pattern of the last two decades. 'Radical changes affecting most if not all major programmes will be required. . . . This is a much bigger question than this year's public spending round. . . .' The Prime Minister agreed that Cabinet should discuss all this at a special meeting on 9 September.

In the context of this long-term agenda, the one serious mistake which I made was to propose that the CPRS should also be asked to 'point up some possible long-term options'. Or, more accurately, I had erred in allowing the CPRS to become involved on such a tight time-scale, for we had left insufficient time for any resulting CPRS paper to be edited or revised. The CPRS was under the direction of its new head, John Sparrow, a shrewd merchant banker whose City insights had been of value over a number of years but whose political experience was quite modest. One rushed attempt to revise this paper did not really improve it before it was put before Cabinet on 9 September, alongside my own more considered paper on long-term trends in public expenditure. The CPRS paper amounted to a rather alarming schedule of very radical policy ideas, many of which had been rejected several times already as 'too difficult', including private health insurance for the NHS, full-cost charging for higher education, de-indexation of social benefits, and so on.

This paper was not essential to my analysis. Even if such a document was desirable in principle, this particular text was manifestly dangerous. I should, someone should, have had the wit to see that it was quite simply withdrawn. Norman Fowler, Patrick Jenkin's successor as Health and Social Security Secretary, later commented that Leon Brittan and I must have been 'horrified' at the way this whole exercise was handled. The sad truth is that we ourselves must accept a large share of the blame.

In the result the meeting – intrinsically of fundamental importance – was a disaster. Most colleagues recoiled so fearfully from the CPRS report that they were unwilling, understandably enough perhaps, to concentrate upon the underlying message of my analysis. Several of those who did focus on that went on to question the premises in simplistic terms, suggesting, for example, that the almost over-optimistic growth assumptions were hopelessly pessimistic ('typically negative Treasury thinking' was one comment).

The CPRS paper was leaked in full within a very few days (it had been foolishly under-classified as 'Confidential', not even 'Secret' – not that that would necessarily have made much difference). The worst possible construction was put upon it by our political opponents, in our own party as much as elsewhere. Several commentators saw a connection between this paper and the speech which I had made a couple of months before to the Conservative Political Centre's annual conference at Cambridge.[5] I had there pointed to 'powerful reasons' why we should be 'ready to consider' how far private provision could supplement 'or in some cases possibly replace' the role of government in health, social security and education. The need for such reform, I had said, 'would be pressing on public spending grounds alone'. It was all true, of course, and other parties later made the same case. But it did not save me in those days from a sharp exchange of letters with Labour Shadow Chancellor Peter Shore. I had to deny that 'we are contemplating the destruction of the welfare state', describing such talk as frankly absurd.

Cecil Parkinson, appearing on *Panorama* at the start of the conference week, had to deny that we had ever been close to thinking almost any positive thoughts whatsoever. And Margaret's closing speech inevitably contained the controversy-quelling statement that 'The National Health Service is safe in our hands.'

The whole story serves to underline the problems of democracy, not only in Britain, when one tries to discuss sacred cows such as these. Even options may not be mentioned without provoking an enormous row. As a result the fundamental debate that I had hoped to start was postponed at least until after the general election, and fundamental thinking about, for example, health service reform for a good deal longer than that. Even within government any further action in this field was deferred until after the conclusion of the PESC (Public Expenditure Scrutiny Committee) round and the disposal of the autumn batch of by-elections at Southwark, Peckham and Birmingham Northfield (all on 28 October).

But nothing, from the Treasury's point of view, is ever quite as bad as it seems. On 26 November Peter Mountfield, the under secretary then logging public expenditure, recorded some useful gains. No fresh spending pledges had been given at the Brighton conference. The atmosphere for the PESC round just finished had been 'tauter' than usual. I had been able to organize special expenditure meetings during December between the Treasury trio (Prime Minister, Chancellor and Chief Secretary) and, separately, each of the chief big spenders, Keith Joseph (Education), Norman Fowler (DHSS) and John Nott (Defence). And all this, most importantly, would have helped to set the pace for our forthcoming 1983 manifesto. Of that there was at least some hope: for Margaret had placed the process of preparing that document and of managing the associated party study groups under my direction, in consultation with the party chairman, Cecil Parkinson. 'Thatcherites to co-ordinate Tory Manifesto', the headline screamed. And why not, I thought: we had come near to losing some ground which had to be held if Britain was to keep clear of the kind of high-spending abyss that is always so close in every democracy.

It may be appropriate to reflect here for a moment on the relative parts played by the various think-tanks and other agencies that were close to Downing Street at this period. The Central Policy Review Staff was the oldest, founded by Heath in the early 1970s.* In the very early

---

* For a description of its useful role at that time, see p. 73 above.

days of the Thatcher government, when it was directed by Sir Kenneth Berrill, former chief economic adviser to the Treasury, its work appeared very seldom in my sights. But under the energetic leadership of Robin Ibbs (formerly an ICI director), who took over in 1980, the CPRS became an invaluable source of analysis and advice, most prominently on our many industrial problems. Its talent was too seldom directed at the larger long-term problems of government. Robin later played a penetrating role as Margaret Thatcher's efficiency expert and in the study of the House of Commons, for which I recruited him during my last year in office (1989–90). It is a pity we did not exploit him more fully at the CPRS. Robin Ibbs' replacement, John Sparrow, seemed to have been chosen more for his commercial expertise than for multi-disciplinary analysis. The organization's diminished role did not long survive the ill-starred report on public spending. The decision to close it down, which I regretted, seems to have been taken during the 1983 election campaign, when the leaked report was ruthlessly exploited by Denis Healey and Peter Shore. There was no reason to conclude that the CPRS had been responsible for the leak.

The Number 10 Policy Unit had been set up by Harold Wilson. But there was, of course, no continuity between the one which Bernard Donoughue organized for Labour and that which John Hoskyns led for Margaret Thatcher. This outfit played a much more discreet and personalized role for the Prime Minister, all the more so when amplified by the recruitment of Alan Walters as her economic adviser. It was obviously helpful for Margaret to receive the often pithy, fundamentalist briefing notes which came from that quarter. I certainly appreciated the way in which John Hoskyns kept up the pressure of advice on the 'Stepping Stones' agenda. But sometimes too this self-contained think-tank could have the effect of a loose cannon in destabilizing the Downing Street craft. All the more reason, I told my people (in the Foreign Office as well as the Treasury) for us to keep closely in touch with the Policy Unit and other special advisers at Number 10. At some times this was less easy than at others. I have already described, for example, the way in which the report on monetary policy added to our difficulties early in 1981.*

The most recently established source of outside advice for the Chancellor was the Parliamentary Select Committee on Treasury and Civil Service Affairs, established very largely as a result of Norman St

* See p. 141 above.

John Stevas' tenacity at the beginning of the 1979 Parliament. Margaret had reluctantly accepted Norman's implementation of plans for the establishment of Commons Select Committees, originally prepared under Francis Pym's guidance. Edward du Cann, already chairman of the 1922 Committee (of Tory back-benchers) since 1972, was Chairman of the TCSC throughout my time at the Treasury. Despite intermittent efforts on both sides, this new institutional arrangment never became an easy one. I found the TCSC useful on several issues, for example with their criticism of our 'staged' management of public sector pay settlements. But they were the very reverse on some others, notably at the start of the 1983 election campaign.* This tension contrasted with the much more useful relationship (from all points of view) that I was later to establish with the Foreign Affairs Committee. Once again, we did not always agree with each other. But generally I had cause to appreciate the way in which they handled their work. The candid respect which we had for each other owed a good deal, I know, to the part played by successive chairmen of the Foreign Affairs Committee, Sir Anthony Kershaw and David Howell, my former Cabinet colleague.

Economic Progress: Autumn 1982

And so my last autumn season at the Treasury rolled on, relatively incident-free. The party conference, despite the preceding fuss about the CPRS report, went smoothly enough. The economic debate, to which I had to reply as usual, seemed to be treated as quite distinct from the public spending row, which had focused almost exclusively on the NHS. The most disturbing consequence of my speech was a protest from the French Embassy. I had been unwise enough to contrast our improving economic performance with the rigours of France under President Mitterrand. 'For socialism', I had discourteously concluded, 'it must be the positive Arc de Triomphe.' The main substance of my speech was unsurprising, with its flavour best encapsulated in the following passage: 'Tax reductions will be made only as and when we can afford them. We have not, and will not, put at risk the progress we have made towards lower inflation and lower interest rates. We are not going to pile up problems for the next government – because we intend to be the next government.'

* See page 291 below.

So through to the Mansion House Banquet on Trafalgar Day. This led me into another slight to our French friends. 'Inflation', I said, 'had shrunk like the size of the French battle-fleet at Trafalgar.' It is hard to explain, and impossible to justify, this repeated lapse into chauvinistic rhetoric, more characteristic of Norman Tebbit in his later years.

On 8 November I was able to make the first Autumn Statement which truly deserved that name. For both sides of the Budget – including expenditure plans for the next quadrennium – were fully displayed. But I still continued to incur the moderate wrath of the TCSC by declining to follow their endorsement of the Armstrong Committee's recommendation that we should go the whole hog towards a complete Green Budget at this point in the year. I was however able, as *The Times* put it, 'to reap the benefit of the courage shown in the preparation of the 1981 Budget': inflation soon below 5 per cent, base rate down by seven full points from its peak, a reduction in government spending and borrowing, and the prospect of a substantially lower PSBR in the year ahead. I was able also to announce a further reduction of 1 per cent in the employer's National Insurance surcharge. The only complaints from the press were of undue caution on my part, in unveiling too little good news, and possibly holding too much in reserve. The *Daily Mail* was more hopeful: 'What has come through is honesty of purpose; the resilience of the long-distance Chancellor. What he must now summon up from somewhere is the finishing spurt.'

The Chancellor Loses His Trousers

But that earnest statement secured much less publicity than had the disappearance of my trousers the previous week. I had been speaking at a dinner of the Manchester Chamber of Commerce and was returning to London in an overnight sleeping car. Foolishly ('I ticked him off later,' said my 'driver–bodyguard' Peter Smithson) I had not locked the door of my compartment. So my dress-trousers were extracted, cleared of £100 in cash and thrown on to the line near Nuneaton, whence they were recovered and solemnly returned to me (with a receipt to sign) at 11 Downing Street. The resultant publicity was astonishing and world-wide: from Miami to Melbourne the headlines chortled 'Minister's pants pinched', 'Top Tory's trousers taken' and so on. Radio Moscow reported the disaster, and *Pravda* made a real meal of it:

The British hope that the scandal over the Minister's trousers will teach him a good lesson. . . . Fortunately Sir Geoffrey had a spare pair of trousers and, as befits a gentleman, was able to emerge from a ticklish situation with honour. But for millions of Britons who have been left in trousers cut by the Conservatives' budgetary shears, it is much more difficult to disentangle themselves from the desperate situation.

To the cartoonists, a debagged Chancellor was irresistible. And Robin Oakley reasoned in the *Daily Mail* that this mishap might yet prove to be 'the best thing that ever happened to Sir Geoffrey Howe. He may have forfeited his pants, but he has found his personality. . . . Steadily the realization has dawned that Sir Geoffrey is one of the genuine political heavy-weights of his generation. . . . What Sir Geoffrey does possess is a degree of tenacity rare in post-war Chancellors. He is the man who has courage, and the results are beginning to show.'

It was a reassuring background against which to prepare for what was quite likely to be our last Christmas at 11 Downing Street. We had by now developed a traditional routine for the entertainment, at lunch in the large mezzanine hall, of all our family and those of my brother and Elspeth's sister, along with close family friends. Since Chequers was always Margaret's Christmas scene, we had no need to worry about disturbing the neighbours.

CHAPTER NINETEEN

TAKING THE WORLD STAGE

Group of Five at Work

My last year and a half at the Treasury had acquired an increasingly international dimension. This was partly due, I now feel sure, to the gradual easing of pressures on the domestic front as well as to my growing familiarity with the dramatis personae of the wider scene.

It was, of course, in Europe that I got to know most people best and most quickly – even though, as we have already noticed, the day-to-day business of ECOFIN was not often of overbearing urgency. The regular bilateral summits with France, Germany and Italy provided other occasions for close contact. In October 1982 Helmut Kohl replaced Helmut Schmidt, as Federal Chancellor in Bonn, to follow the similar change of cast that had taken place in Paris in May 1981. François Mitterrand's replacement of Giscard d'Estaing had led, of course, to a change of Finance Minister. The dour but business-like *garagiste* René Monory (in 1992 he was elected president of the French Senate) was replaced by the Socialist Jacques Delors – tense, earnest, easily excited and often rather academic in flavour. Quite soon after that change Margaret took a sizeable group of colleagues to Paris for a bilateral summit with Mitterrand and his government. I was asked to lead several British ministers into a discussion with Prime Minister Mauroy, Jacques Delors and others. They had just launched into a new policy of statutory price and pay control. I happened to notice that it was ten years to the day since every member of the British team – Patrick Jenkin, Arthur Cockfield, Peter Carey, Ken Couzens, myself and one or two others – had been engaged in exactly the same exercise under Ted Heath. And now here we all were, having completed three years of firmly non-statutory policy, with much greater success. It was no doubt tactless of me to bring the anniversary to the attention of Mauroy and his colleagues, but the temptation was irresistible.

In Germany, Helmut Schmidt's taut and energetic team of Hans Matthöffer and Manfred Lahnstein gave way, about eighteen months later, to the silver-haired former Chief of Schleswig-Holstein, Gerhard Stoltenberg, Helmut Kohl's first Finance Minister. All these Germans were intelligent, professional in style and easy to work with.

As well as the senior ministers of France and Germany I got to know well the Americans and the Japanese – for together we made up the Group of Five – whence came most of the leadership for the main international financial institutions, the IMF and World Bank. This tightly drawn working group (the five Finance Ministers were accompanied only by their central bank governors and one senior Finance Ministry official each, in my case usually Ken (later Sir Kenneth) Couzens) was much the most interesting and generally effective of all the regular international groupings that I ever attended. Don Regan was US Treasury Secretary from 1981 to 1985. Although not endowed with great charm, he was always straightforward and effective. For a long time he and George Shultz worked in useful harness together in Washington. His number two, Beryl (pronounced BURL) Sprinkel, was irrepressibly dogmatic, sometimes simplistically wrong – quite unmoved by the volatility of the dollar or by the scale of the US Federal deficit – which was frustrating for the rest of us. Towering over them both, intellectually as well as physically, was the immensely competent, cigar-smoking, lamppost-like figure of Paul Volcker, who as head of the Federal Reserve (a Carter appointment) was America's sheet-anchor of economic sanity throughout the decade. The most constant of the Japanese present was Central Bank Governor Maekawa, a fluent and effective participant in discussions of this kind ahead of most of his countrymen. The Finance Minister who was most involved in my period was Noboru Takeshita; he later served Japan (and Europe) well as the Prime Minister who gave his country its first VAT. (His name later passed under a cloud of alleged corruption: he resigned his seat in the Diet early in 1993.)

G5 meetings were seldom longer than a long half-day, including dinner. We were almost always able to ensure that our meeting times and places were unknown to the media, even after the event. So we were not burdened with communiqués or press conferences. We could therefore deal directly with the informal agenda, which had been the subject of preparatory work by our deputies. The meetings were usually held in the margins of larger occasions – OECD, IMF and the like – as well as once or twice a year at specific venues. Two or three were held in my time at Number 11 and several too at Kronberg Castle, near Frankfurt.

In this kind of setting we were able most usefully to co-ordinate policy on some of the really difficult questions on the international agenda: a lot of our time in those days was devoted to sovereign debt problems – Brazil, Mexico, Poland – as well as to the management and resources of the Fund and the Bank. Increasingly we came to share, not least with the French, an austerely disciplined view of the need for success against inflation and thus for firm monetary and fiscal policies – even though the Americans were for some years, regrettably and damagingly, unable to deliver on this score. Congress was much less responsive to economic leadership from the executive than our own House of Commons. Just as Jacques Delors was influenced towards a 'Thatcherite' macroeconomic policy, so I was drawn (though not the Americans) towards his enthusiasm for more stable exchange rates. The Germans were already more sympathetic as fellow members of the European Exchange Rate Mechanism. This developing consensus increasingly influenced the thinking of the other institutions, including notably the seven-power World Economic Summit meetings at Versailles (1982) and Williamsburg (1983). We were fortunate that Italy and Canada were still, in those days, ready (just) to acquiesce in their non-membership of the G5 group of Finance Ministers. But that commendable restraint could not survive the 1985 New York Plaza meeting's decision (for a second time) to issue a communiqué. So G5 was transformed into G7 and thus lost its secrecy and its intimacy (and quite a bit of its effectiveness).

There was no suggestion of intimacy at the annual ministerial meetings (in Paris, in May) of the OECD. But I found them friendly and like-minded enough (the top twenty-four industrial, non-Communist economies were members of this club) to be a useful forum for the development of shared thinking about global economic problems. The 1982 meeting was no exception. Once again I found myself engaged in hammering out common ground between Anglo-Saxon monetarism and the more sensitive, but just as disciplined, Gallic version that was being evolved by Jacques Delors. I endorsed Don Regan's view that 'there is no trade-off between inflation and unemployment' but sympathized with Delors' stress on the need for 'a balance to be struck between economic rigour and social stability . . . a balance that all of us democratic leaders have to keep in mind'.

In retrospect there was a clear risk of divergence between the naturally co-operative thinking that Finance Ministers developed in international clubs of this kind and the more isolationist approach of their heads of government. For the heads' meetings were less frequent and necessarily more political. They seldom had the opportunity, even at the annual (so-called) Economic Summits, of getting close to the nitty-gritty of economic management. Margaret Thatcher was perhaps particularly exposed to this risk for, more than at least some of her peers, she *was* interested (intensely so) in economic issues. Yet unlike, for example, Giscard d'Estaing and Helmut Schmidt (not to mention her own Chancellors) she had no personal experience of the international Finance Ministers' circuit. It is easy to see how, in these circumstances, she had less feel for the kind of co-operation that influenced both Nigel Lawson and myself towards the EMS – and in his case (less happily but perhaps *faute de mieux*) towards 'shadowing the Deutschmark'.

Commonwealth and IMF

There was a similar need for sensitivity in approaching the agenda for the annual meetings of Commonwealth Finance Ministers. Their 1982 gathering figured prominently in our diary, since it took place (29 August–1 September) under my chairmanship at Lancaster House. I had come to find this a personally friendly and practically valuable occasion. For although no less than forty-nine countries (including some remaining colonies – Bermuda and Hong Kong) were represented there, the delegations were small and the atmosphere informal and family-like. And the variety of scale and nature of the countries, their problems and their governments gave one a much broader bird's-eye view of economic stresses and opportunities than was likely to cross the desk of Don Regan, say, or even Jacques Delors.

The diversity included, from Africa, Amir Jamal of Tanzania, Bernard Chidzero of Zimbabwe and Mwai Kibaki of Kenya; from the Caribbean – where Prime Ministers were often Finance Ministers as well – Eugenia Charles of Dominica (she was her own Foreign Minister too), Edward Seaga of Jamaica, George Price of Belize (I dubbed him the only other *Welsh* Finance Minister); and from the Asia–Pacific region, as we now call it, Pranab Mukherji and Ramaswamy Ventkataraman of India, John Howard (and his young economic adviser, John Hewson) of Australia and, veteran Prime Minister of New Zealand, Robert Muldoon.

The conference had its lighter side, of course. The Duke of Kent presided over the dinner entertainment (ending with the Ceremony of the Keys) at the Tower of London. Everyone who subsequently heard that I had had the opportunity of keeping four dozen Finance Ministers indefinitely detained in the Tower has been reluctant to forgive me for missing the opportunity. And the spouses who attended the Marks and Spencer fashion show (which Elspeth had persuaded Derek Rayner to organize) were delighted, as they were bound to be, when a slender model walked along the catwalk, to shrieks of laughter – since her green and tartan dress was identical to the one that Elspeth was wearing. Elspeth gave a thumbs-up sign and was heard to whisper, 'I prefer it on the model.' And the *Bermuda Sun* next week carried the advertisement, 'Lady Howe wears St Michael merchandise – why don't you?'

The IMF itself had not less than four meetings of the Interim Committee during my last year at the Treasury. Our first meeting of the year took place in Helsinki on 12–13 May, straight after the OECD's Paris gathering. By this time the debt problems of the non-oil producers were coming to dominate the agenda. We had all of us been suffering from the grisly blend of inflation and recession that had followed the latest oil-price explosion. Falls in other commodity prices, coupled with high interest rates, were greatly increasing the pressures on the poorest countries. And the twin deficits of the United States (trade and fiscal) were compounding all these problems.

There was a striking contrast between the sun-kissed Finnish calm of the city and the tensions which arose from the need to share the conference table, and other events, with the Argentine Finance Minister, Señor Roberto Allemann, at a time when our two countries' forces were preparing for battle with each other. I had provided myself with a series of formulae with which to disengage from a potentially disagreeable encounter, if our paths should accidentally cross. Inevitably, I failed to recognize his back view as we assembled for the communiqué-drafting dinner. So I was startled by his warm expression of pleasure at some mildly jocular passage in one of my interventions, for all the world like a colleague in the Commons' smoking room. But I stuck to my plan for speedy disengagement, if only for fear of some wildly embarrassing piece in one of the London gossip columns. It would have made a fine stir in Bernard Ingham's daily press summary. Ironically the British party at Helsinki had been impressed by Allemann's own speech: he had begun remarkably sound in Treasury terms on public spending, and not least on defence. There is a frugal free-masonry that binds Finance Ministers together, even when their countries are at war with each other.

The IMF's annual meeting was at Toronto on 3–8 September. There too I had an Argentine item to deal with. By now the conflict was over, so we wanted as soon as we could to get rid of the financial sanctions that we had imposed upon each other. They did no good to the reputation for openness of the City of London. But it was too soon for us to discuss this face to face with my Argentine opposite number. We persuaded the US Treasury Under Secretary, Tim McNamar, to take it up for us. In this way we agreed that both sides would scrap their financial sanctions – but subject to the prior approval of the Argentine Air Force! It took some time for the aviators to swallow the deal, but they did. We had been offered a remarkable insight into the workings of the Argentine government.

Of even more immediately practical importance, however, was the need for adequate additional resources for the Fund and Bank, which called for early agreement by all the member-states on a substantial increase in Fund quotas. I was not to know it then, but this was to become my personal responsibility just a few months later, when in December I was elected unopposed to the chair of the Interim Committee. My successful 'opponent' at Libreville, Allan MacEachen, had stood down from the IMF when Prime Minister Trudeau moved him from Treasury to Ministry of External Affairs.

I had two positive reasons to maintain my regular autumn visits to Washington and New York (even when the Fund/Bank meetings were out of town): first, to enhance the favourable impression – now growing strongly in North America – of the economic policies of the Thatcher government; and second, to get across tactfully but firmly the extent of our concern – indeed the world's concern – with the impact on the global economy of the large and still growing US federal deficit. I spoke at two high-profile gatherings – the Council of Foreign Relations and the Economic Club – in New York, and in Washington I held meetings with Regan, Volcker and congressional leaders. I had sessions too with George Shultz and David Stockman, who was then as director of the Office for the Management of the Budget grappling directly with the problem. Paul Volcker was doing his best to head off its monetary consequences with the only weapon at his command, high interest rates. These were themselves a cause for world concern. George Shultz was always, even when I got to know him very well, delphic in his responses on this issue. He was reluctant, I came to believe, to undermine President Reagan's intinctive hostility to any tax increase for any reason – even for the sake of deficit reduction.

Margaret Thatcher saw the importance of this issue as clearly as I did. But she too was hesitant to raise it directly with Ronald Reagan. I fancy that he regarded our position as unimpressively close to a typical Democrat's 'tax and spend' philosophy – and none of us, least of all Margaret, liked to earn that label. She still went on making the point, in private, at least until she decided that it was a no-win situation. There were not many issues on which she came to that conclusion.

This deeply frustrating argument was to remain unresolved at least until Ross Perot began pressing it upon Messrs Clinton and Bush in the early 1990s. The world will long have cause to regret the lost decade of the US federal deficit.

My emergence as chairman of the IMF's Interim Committee, just a few days before Christmas 1982, was (unusually) seen by the British press in just about the right perspective. The *Daily Telegraph* saw me 'at this moment of international crisis . . . in the single most influential position apart, perhaps, from the United States Secretary of the Treasury'. The comparison was, as we shall see, more apt than I knew. The problem that faced the Fund was relatively simple to grasp. The world was one in which some twenty-five nations were unable to pay their bills on time. Brazil, the biggest borrower of all, was teetering on the brink. Mexico and Argentina were in very similar shape. They desperately needed help from the Fund and the World Bank. Those organizations, in turn, needed the extra resources that would enable them to respond. That is why I had myself urged the September meeting to secure a 50 per cent increase in the Fund's capital. It now became my task, in partnership with the Fund's managing director – by now a good friend – Jacques de Larosière, to deliver that increase. One essential component was the willingness of Saudi Arabia to make a separate and extra contribution to the General Arrangements to Borrow (GAB), whose membership comprised the Group of Ten (this time the ten major industrial nations). The question was whether the Saudis would accept this without insisting upon membership of the G10.

The current chairman of the G10, as it happened, was Jacques Delors, so once again we were working closely together. It was with his blessing that de Larosière and I set off together to Riyadh at the beginning of January. (It was a surprise for me, on my first visit to the Gulf, to wake up and see the building-site workers outside my hotel warming themselves at an open wood fire.) Our Saudi host was the still youthful but experienced Saudi Finance Minister, Mohammad Abal-Khail. Agreement was less difficult than we had feared; the Saudis were content to forgo membership of the GAB because it might oblige them to go along with decisions that could conflict with their wider (for example, Arab) interests. So our mission was a success and gave me the chastening opportunity to compare notes with a colleague whose Budget was even more dependent on the oil price than mine. I heaved a sigh of comparative relief.

The more difficult round of negotiations was still to come, with the Interim Committee members themselves. The question was: How large an increase in quotas could and should we achieve? The developing countries and political debtors favoured an increase of more than 100 per cent; I had secured the agreement of our Community partners to the concept of 'at least 50 per cent', but the United States had been reluctant to go anything like as far. This was not simply the result of personal opposition on the part of Regan and Sprinkel (and, for all I know, Reagan himself). They were all inhibited by their knowledge that Congress would be exceedingly hard to persuade. Yet we needed early agreement if the increased funds were to be in place in time. I had to decide the timing of the next moves. I judged it best to keep up the tempo and the pressure on my colleagues. I had become chairman of the Committee on my fifty-sixth birthday, 20 December 1982. Our successful visit to Saudi Arabia took place on 8–9 January 1983. After taking de Larosière's advice, I decided to fix the specific meeting of the Interim Committee (in Washington) just one month later, on 10–11 February. We, G10 Finance Ministers, met for a preliminary discussion under Delors' chairmanship in Paris on 18 January.

In order that we might address ourselves to one of the most important parts of the equation, arrangements were made for de Larosière and me, together with a representative debtor, Jesus Silva-Herzog, the Mexican Finance Minister, to meet representatives of the relevant committees in both Houses of Congress in order to expound there the immensely strong global case for a large increase in quotas: Silva-Herzog was there, in effect, to explain exactly how the poor lived. The Mexicans' plight, and their courageous response, deservedly made a memorable impression.

The crucial parts of the main meeting took place not in the Fund building but in the affluently informal setting of the F Street Club. There we met over the dinner table – before, during and after the meal.

The change of venue was thought likely to smooth the rough edges of the negotiations. I'm not too sure about that. But in the absence of simultaneous interpretation it certainly added to their length.

I was determined to achieve our 50 per cent figure, or as near as made no difference. To that end, I had struck a deal with the Chinese Central Bank representative, Shang Ming, that he would withhold his support until we mutually agreed that the likely bargain was good enough. Through most of the evening Don Regan stood firm, a long way off our centre point, claiming that it would be impossible to persuade Congress to accept a higher cash figure. Eventually, I decided to try a different tack, by suggesting that the United States might be allowed to get away with a lower percentage increase, if others were ready to go further and make up the balance. But this would, I pointed out, involve a matching reduction in the weighting of America's voting rights.

It was not long before Don Regan sought a short adjournment, so that he could confer by telephone with White House and Treasury officials. John Kerr left the room at the same time, for quite another purpose, and, when he returned, reported one remark that he had heard Regan making on the open phone just outside our meeting place. 'Those bastards', he said, 'have got us by the short and curlies.' The vivid phrase added a new dimension to the special relationship – and foreshadowed what was to come.

For very shortly Regan returned to the table and indicated his readiness to move, if the rest of us did, to 47.5 per cent. The Chinese and I exchanged glances. And when the time came for him to speak I knew, even ahead of the interpretation, that Shang Ming was content, because of the way in which, before the close of his speech, he had clapped his hand warmly on the shoulder of his Mexican neighbour, Silva-Herzog. We had achieved our objective: indeed, after taking account of the additional Saudi support, the currency resources of the Fund were effectively doubled, from $33 billion to $66 billion. I committed a modest *faux pas* when the time came, on the following day, to formalize and announce our agreement. For Marc Lalonde, the Canadian Finance Minister, pointed out that we had failed to make clear, in our communiqué, whether we were speaking of US or Canadian dollars. I compounded the offence, in his eyes at least, by saying that it was almost as serious as my failure on one recent occasion to refer expressly to the Luxembourg franc at the end of a European realignment conference.

By the time we were free to leave the IMF building to go over to the

White House and report the outcome to President Reagan, Washington was almost paralysed under two feet of snow, which had fallen in the last few hours. All public offices were closed. The streets were littered with abandoned cars. Dulles International Airport was closed. It was all we could do to reach the comfort of the Lutyens residence, there to spend twenty-four comfortable hours waiting until a return flight to London became possible.

Washington weather did not prevent the White House playing its proper role in the proceedings. For within a day or two President Reagan had written to commend my 'leadership and diligence' in bringing about the agreement, which was 'vitally important to the future health of the world economy. . . . I will do all I can', he concluded, 'to ensure that the United States will fulfil its part completely and promptly.'

Congress was very reluctant to ratify the agreement. American legislators believe – rightly, to a large extent – that the crisis had arisen because of the reckless incontinence with which the (mainly) American banks had lent dollars to the poorer countries from the surpluses piled up by the oil-producers. Why, said the Congressmen, should our taxpaying voters bail out our irresponsible bankers? One could see their point. But it was now the entire world banking system that was in danger. The deadlock was broken only when Reagan threw his whole weight behind the deal that I had negotiated. The President was as good as his word.

The European Monetary System

There was one other item of international economic business which hovered close to the agenda throughout my time at the Treasury, but which was unresolved before I moved to the Foreign Office on the other side of Charles Street: our attitude towards membership of the Exchange Rate Mechanism of the European Monetary System. Looking back on the arguments of the early 1980s, it is evident that it was an issue at *that* time of relatively little political importance and of not much greater economic significance.

For it seems clear, in the light of our later experience, that it would have been premature to have considered joining the ERM either when it first appeared (during the Callaghan government of 1978) or when we first looked at it seriously (at the time of my abolition of exchange control in November 1979). It will be recalled that in November 1978

I had told the House of Commons that the Opposition was in principle in favour of full membership of the system; and that in our manifesto for the 1979 European elections we had stated our commitment to join.* There were two reasons for delay. First, the degree of divergence between Britain's economic performance and that of our partners was certainly too large to be easily managed: our inflation was still above 20 per cent in 1979. Second, the petrocurrency factor, real or perceived, was still strong enough to raise difficulties: between May 1979 and November 1981 the pound–dollar exchange rate had moved – both ways – between a high of $2.45 to the pound in October 1980 and a low of $1.76 in August 1981.

When the question of ERM membership was actually considered for the first time under the Prime Minister's chairmanship, on 17 October 1979, those present were the Foreign Secretary (Peter Carrington), Trade and Industry Secretaries John Nott and Keith Joseph, the Governor of the Bank (Gordon Richardson) and myself. Already there was a difference in emphasis between us. We were all agreed not to join the ERM at that time. I felt that membership should remain our medium-term objective. The Governor wanted to feel that the UK was moving towards full membership. But the Prime Minister was 'particularly concerned about the potential conflict between the government's monetary targets and the EMS intervention requirements'. The matter, she said, should not be considered further – as had been planned – by OD (Overseas and Defence) Committee. There the matter rested for some time. For most of the next two years there was very little advocacy of entry into the ERM.

By the second half of 1981, however, interest in the idea was beginning to grow – largely, I think, because of the increasingly erratic behaviour of the monetary aggregates. Before Nigel Lawson left the Treasury in September 1981, he had begun to argue the case internally, as cogently as ever, on political as much as economic grounds. Curiously – or perhaps not? – I was more reluctant than he to think so soon of moving away from the central MTFS notion of steering by sterling M3. I had only just spelt out the reasoning behind this – and against exchange rate targeting – in my Mais Lecture at the City University. In addition, perhaps because of my less sophisticated economic background, I was more disposed than some others to believe that sterling M3 would rediscover its proper course. And so indeed it did. By the

* See p. 111 above.

time I left the Treasury, in June 1983, every one of the relevant monetary aggregates was performing within its target limits.

We did, however, consider the EMS case quite carefully during the autumn and winter of 1981/2. It is worth remembering that even then our inflation (at 12 per cent in November 1981) was still well above most of our partners', for example that of the Federal Republic, then at 7 per cent. I thus attached a good deal of importance to the argument advanced by Ken Couzens at that time:

> Joining the EMS at this stage, when we have clearly not won the monetary battle, would be seen not as a consequence of success in dealing with inflation but as an important change in policy, perhaps as a turning point.

Much the same argument could – perhaps should – have been advanced in respect of the date finally chosen for entry by Margaret Thatcher and John Major in September 1990.

We had the chance to consider the matter more formally on 22 January 1982, at a meeting with Margaret, Peter Carrington, Gordon Richardson and a full cast of senior officials. The Governor and the Foreign Secretary were in favour of entry to the Mechanism. I was still not persuaded: I remained unable to reconcile membership with the management of domestic monetary policy; the present Deutschmark rate was in any case too high; and, finally, people might be turned away from the Community itself if it came to be blamed for unacceptably high interest rates. (This last point was seen to have real force at the time of Black Wedneday, 1992.) Margaret concluded, no doubt with the advice of Alan Walters, that entry to the Mechanism was not for us at that time. She did not believe, so she said, that it would in practice provide an effective discipline; she was anxious about the extent to which it removed our freedom of manoeuvre; and only when our inflation and interest rates were 'much closer' to those of the Germans might the case deserve to be considered again. So we should for the time being maintain our existing 'when the time is right' position.

During the year that followed, as I have recounted, I continued to move significantly – in the IMF and G7 context – towards a more favourable view of exchange rate stability for its own sake. But I did not immediately make the connection with the case for entry into the ERM. As I have explained, it was still not a hot issue. When we looked at it again, briefly, at my pre-Budget Chevening meeting in January 1983, we concluded that it would not be sensible to make the move in advance of the 'possibly difficult adjustments in the exchange markets' which could precede or accompany an election.

But I gained some enlightening experience of the way in which the system actually worked. For there were no less than seven realignments of currency within the system during my time at the Treasury, and at almost all of these I was present to represent Britain. On at least three occasions I presided over the prolonged meetings (of Finance Ministers and central bank governors) that were necessary. As the pound sterling was the only currency that was not directly involved it was easy for me to earn plaudits for the 'skill and impartiality' of my chairmanship. More valuable to me was my growing appreciation of the way in which the firmness and flexibility of the system did indeed help to buttress the forces in each country that were on the side of counter-inflationary discipline.

In June 1982 and March 1983 Jacques Delors, then French Finance Minister, had to manage a two-stage, 20 per cent devaluation of the franc against the Deutschmark. He had to use this too as a necessary lever for an overdue tightening of French economic policy, along lines at least as tough as my 1981 Budget. The second of these two realignments took place only days after the death from leukaemia of Delors' twenty-five-year-old son. My respect for the courage with which Jacques faced this double challenge forged a bond of friendship between us that transcends any difference of nationality.

When eventually I did move to conclude that 'the time was right' – after I had been at the Foreign Office for a little time – I did so not primarily (as Margaret Thatcher and Nigel Lawson both suggest)[1] for foreign policy or for European reasons, but because I had come once again to regard as practicable and worthwhile the view which I had originally formed in November 1978. I had then expressed the hope that it would be possible (as it was certainly desirable) to achieve the best of both worlds, with a high degree of stability between currencies which had at the same time overcome the risk of internal depreciation.

But that state of affairs was not to arise before we had once again addressed ourselves to the electorate. My last Budget and the general election manifesto were even now in course of preparation.

CHAPTER TWENTY

ELECTION CALL

A Full Five Years?

My final six months at the Treasury were placid indeed compared with the turmoil of the first two or three years. The routine for Budget preparation which I had established was well settled in – and in 1983 more or less free of surprises. At our second Treasury Chevening weekend and the full pre-Budget Cabinet (in January and February respectively) there was no controversy about strategy, but there was no complacency either. Certainly, there was comfort in the opinion polls even if much of it sprang from the divided state of the opposition. The continuing strength of the Alliance alongside the shortcomings of a Foot-led, Militant-dominated Labour Party buttressed the still continuing Falklands factor. But this was by no means fully reflected in actual polling. At the Birmingham (Northfield) by-election on 28 October 1982, for example, it came as quite a shock when Labour actually captured the seat albeit with a swing of only ½ per cent. Most of the rise in the Liberal vote was clearly at our expense.

Yet this should not have been so greatly surprising, for recovery in the real economy was proving elusive. Although domestic demand had been growing, at almost 3 per cent a year in real terms, since the spring of 1981, total output in Britain increased by only 0.5 per cent during 1982. Unemployment had passed three million in September 1982 and was still rising, although the rate of increase had been slowing for two years. Inflation had fallen dramatically from its 1980 peak of 22 per cent to 5.4 per cent at the start of the year. And we had been able to let interest rates fall almost throughout 1982, from 16 per cent in November 1981 to just 9 per cent a year later. By then the exchange rate had fallen so far (from $1.90 to $1.60) that we allowed the markets to take interest rates up again by a couple of points. As Budget time approached,

markets steadied and output figures grew stronger. Even for manufacturing, the prospects began to look a little brighter.

This did not, of course, disguise the fact that even at this low point
of the recession much of the growth in domestic demand was still
reflected in growth of imports. Cabinet were under no illusions about
this. We had had to wrestle often enough with the consequences – for
the shipbuilding, steel and motor industries, for example – of earlier
decades of poor management and industrial strife. Most of us were well
aware of how far we still had to go to restore the underlying strength
and balance of our economy. This case was well represented in Cabinet,
and not only by those who were regarded by outsiders as its champions.
Jim Prior, Peter Walker and Michael Heseltine were joined by Patrick
Jenkin (Industry), the two regional Secretaries of State, Nicholas
Edwards and George Younger, and midlanders like John Biffen and
Norman Fowler in expressing a similar point of view. But only one or
two came close to questioning the central strategy.

Most important from the budgetary point of view was the greatly
improved fiscal position. The PSBR for the year just ending (1982–3)
was £2 billion below my original expectations. Oil revenues were well
up. And public expenditure, for the first time in our experience, was
falling short of expectations. We had not had to impose any extra
taxation to meet the cost (estimated at £1.8 billion) of the Falklands
War. Our prudent contingency reserve of £2.5 billion had turned out to
be too large. Falling inflation helped here, of course, but so had the
success of our new control system – cash planning. Against this
background, discussion at Chevening and in the Cabinet was largely
about the best way to deploy the modest proceeds of our reasonably
balanced position, so as to fortify our economic success and carry it into
the future. I was able, in due course, to reflect these deliberations in the
Budget itself.

I was at the same time caught up in the parallel political debate, for
the next general election would have to take place within eighteen
months. This vital topic, endlessly discussed in the corridors and lobbies,
was seldom a matter for formal consideration among ministers. It could
not appear on the agenda of Cabinet or any of the Cabinet committees
since it was party political, and officials could not be thus 'tainted'.
There was a more or less explicit recognition that it was the Prime
Minister's prerogative alone to tender advice to Her Majesty about the
date for dissolution of Parliament. So the topic arose more informally

on a miscellany of occasions, often when the Prime Minister herself saw fit to raise it, whether with groups of colleagues or with individual ministers alone.

As may be imagined, this occurred with growing frequency at my weekly bilateral meetings with her, or on Sunday evenings. Margaret's instinct had been from the outset to go for the full five years. This was partly because it made no sense even to hint at anything less and partly because Ted Heath's example in 1974 was a contrasting challenge in this respect. But Margaret was more than ready to consider realistic alternatives as well. My feeling had always been for an election after about four years, in the early summer of 1983. I had two solid reasons for this: first, I judged it by definition imprudent to go for the full five years and so leave ourselves with no flexibility at all at the end; and, second, I regarded early autumn as more hazardous than early summer, mainly because at that time of the year, as school-leavers came on to the job market, the headline unemployment figures were bound to rise, and rise substantially.

As the years and months slipped by, these well-founded instincts were reinforced by the economic prospects. The recovery to which we had long looked forward was clearly under way. By the summer of 1983 the underlying and headline figure for unemployment should be showing some downward movements, and by the end of the summer the inflation rate – by now down to 5 per cent – was expected by Treasury forecasters to be moving up again, albeit only temporarily. If this was right, an October 1983 election would take place against the background of rising inflation as well as apparently rising unemployment (because of the impact of school-leavers on the figures). There was no need to decide between the two most likely options until the end of April. But it clearly made sense to start planning for the earlier date.

It was with this in mind that Margaret asked me, at the time of the party conference in 1982, to take charge of the preparation of the party's manifesto. This, as we have seen, was to be done in consultation with the party chairman, Cecil Parkinson. Our team of helpers thus largely cast itself: from my side came my very experienced senior political adviser (who had been just as closely involved with our 1979 manifesto), Adam Ridley. Cecil was supported by the almost equally experienced Peter Cropper, who had gone to take charge of the party's Research Department after seven years as one of my advisers, the last three in the Treasury – where he was succeeded by Robin Harris. We enlisted as the principal draftsman (for the slot previously filled by Angus Maude and Chris Patten) Ferdinand Mount, the former political editor of the *Spectator* and, since 1982, in charge of the Number 10 Policy Unit.

The work had to be completed in time for us to use it for a spring election, if that was what was to be. But it had to be done without disclosing, even to those who contributed to it, the existence of any such deadline. We wanted to secure the broadest possible input of fresh thinking. So we swiftly established nine policy groups, each of which included back-benchers, special advisers and outsiders, to advise on the main areas of government policy by the end of February 1983. These suggestions were to be made available to the relevant Cabinet ministers, who were to take them on board before finalizing their own proposals. Since colleagues were preoccupied with their own day-to-day departmental work, it was important to keep all this mosaic of policy thinking on the move. So I convened a meeting of our in-group (together with Ian Gow to represent Number 10) early in February 1983, just before I left for the crucial IMF quota-increase meeting in Washington, and we finalized our work programme, so that I should be able at the beginning of April (with the Budget out of the way) to devote a whole day to working up a reasonably complete draft manifesto. Margaret and one or two others would thus be able to study it at the Easter recess.

Last Budget

Once back from Washington it was heads down for my last Budget, on 15 March. This year there was just one (very sharp) point of disagreement with my neighbour at Number 10, predictably over the tax treatment of mortgage interest relief, available at that time in respect of the first £25,000 borrowed on the principal residence. This had long been seen by fiscal commentators as a glaring anomaly: distorting the housing market almost as much as rent control, unbalancing the investment market even more than relief for life assurance and pension funds, and, moreover, unjustly favouring the better off and the south rather than the north. Even so, Margaret had long wanted it to be extended because it was of special value to 'our people'. The only contrary argument which came near to persuading me had come (he acknowledged that it was the only time he had ever lobbied me) from Peter Smithson, my driver: 'Twenty-five thousand', he said, 'would have bought a small country estate in the year when I first joined the Car

Service.' But I was unmoved and minuted Margaret three weeks before Budget Day:

I know you won't like it, but I am bound to say that I find the case against an increase in the ceiling on mortgage interest relief pretty convincing. I have discussed this with all your Treasury ministers. None of us believes that it would be right to raise the ceiling.

Margaret was unpersuaded. She thought the figure should be increased to at least £35,000. A meeting was arranged at Number 10. I insisted on bringing reinforcements – in the person of Nick Ridley. Nick's work on the principles of direct tax reform (which we were both keen to implement had we served another year together at the Treasury) left him in no doubt about our position. But even his well-founded and vigorous advocacy was of no avail against Margaret's populist instincts. We were confronted by a whole string of quotations from our own speeches in the Finance Bill Standing Committee of some five, six, seven years before, when we had all been pressing Denis Healey to accept indexation of the original figure. They had been supplied to Margaret by one of our colleagues from those days, none other than my good friend Ian Gow. (He had the good grace to apologize profusely afterwards, since he now shared our view.) Margaret threatened, if we did not accept her case, to release the earlier texts to our back-benchers and to the press – indeed even to come over to the House and read them herself! The Treasury team beat a tactical retreat. In the end, I decided to split the difference, at £30,000. The press knew pretty well how the argument had raged over this and adjudged the outcome an honourable draw. Since then the tax benefit has, in the disreputable phrase, been allowed to wither on the vine (alas, the vine of inflation).

My Budget speech itself got off to an inauspicious start: 'The longest Budget speech that I have been able to trace was given by Mr Gladstone on 18 April 1953.' The House broke into confused sub-uproar, until the Deputy Speaker, Jack (Bernard) Weatherill, gave me a chance to correct my mistake – by placing Gladstone back in his proper century. He had given a speech in 1853 that lasted four-and-three-quarter hours, as compared with Disraeli's best of only forty-five minutes. 'I cannot', I explained, 'match that; but this will be my shortest, or at any rate my shortest so far.' It came out at eighty-three minutes.

I was able to present a picture, and a set of measures, that was closely in line with the strategy that I had laid out just three years before:

government spending and borrowing all restrained and on course; all the measured monetary aggregates within their target range;* inflation, at 5 per cent, lower than at any time since 1970; and the prospect of growth of domestic output at 2 per cent during the year ahead. 'The establishment of the Medium-Term Financial Strategy', I said, 'has been more than justified by its value as a framework of fiscal and monetary discipline. . . . The need now is for steadiness and resolve. . . . The prospect is for . . . recovery. It will be gradual but it should be steady, provided anti-inflationary gains are not thrown away.'

My measures were intended 'to sustain and advance that economic recovery and to further the living standards and employment opportunities of all our people'. I raised all tax allowances some 8.5 per cent more than the year's rise in prices (Cabinet had been keen on this), to raise child benefit to its highest ever real level and to restore my earlier (5 per cent) cut in unemployment benefit. Pensions and other benefits would henceforth be increased not by reference to a forecast of the future but with more accuracy (as happened before 1976) upon the basis of what had actually occurred.

But my main help was directed towards business, industry and jobs. Employers were relieved of 1.5 per cent in total (more than half of what was left) of Denis Healey's 'tax on jobs' (the National Insurance surcharge). Small businesses and new businesses were encouraged by the conversion of the Business Start-up into the Business Expansion Scheme and substantial changes in the capital tax thresholds and other measures. The Enterprise Allowance Scheme – brainchild of Norman Tebbit and David Young and already successful in its pilot stage – was extended nationwide. Our special capital incentive schemes for information technology and small engineering firms were renewed and extended.

Some of these tax changes required a higher level of intellectual engagement than any other task I had to undertake in government. But they were worthwhile. This was certainly true of the elaborate package that I introduced for the taxation of North Sea oil operators. This set of measures was designed to sustain investment by means of extra reliefs and abolition of royalties for future fields. It was the result of very specialized hard work by the Revenue, initially under Arthur Cockfield's

---

* This was the first time this had ever happened. So I was presented with – and to my chagrin have lost – a chart to prove it, counter-signed by Eddie George (of the Bank), Peter Middleton and Terry Burns (of the Treasury) and Alan Walters (of Number 10). Those were the days of harmony indeed!

direction and, after his departure to Trade (replacing John Biffen in April 1982), John Wakeham's. The Energy Department, under Nigel Lawson, co-operated closely. So too did the industry's representatives, from UKOOA (their association) to the legendary Armand Hammer himself, who came to see Margaret Thatcher and myself at Number 10. All this effort had a gratifyingly unusual result. For when I went to lunch with UKOOA shortly after the Budget and asked what they now wanted me to do, they replied, 'Nothing, except just to thank you very much.' The consultative approach, which I had tried to extend throughout the whole field of tax policy, certainly proved its worth. For Nigel was able, during his Chancellorship, to avoid any changes in the North Sea regime, and the life of the fields seems to have stretched ahead for longer than originally anticipated.

The reaction to my fifth (and, as it turned out, final) Budget was unexcited but generally reassuring. Our back-benchers – with the exception of a handful of recidivists, like Ian Gilmour – were pleased with the balance of restrained generosity. I had been able to deal with most of the pressure points on the industrial as well as the social front, while remaining firmly within our strategic guidelines.

Press reaction ranged from predictable criticism from the *Mirror* and *Guardian*, through surprising curmudgeonliness from the *Express* ('the empty Budget Box') and *The Times* ('Sir Geoffrey Howe's stewardship of the nation's finances in the last four years deserves to be viewed with admiration; yesterday's Budget sadly does not') to a more generally supportive reaction from most of the rest. The *Sun* was nothing if not original: 'Like a stripper in the Bible Belt, Sir Geoffrey Howe had probably gone as far as he could go.' It was, said Patrick Sargent in the *Mail*, 'An electioneering budget of the modern sort . . . meant not to tickle us in our pocket but in our sense of virtue'.

It was a good moment to reflect on four years at the Treasury, before plunging into a largely electoral climate. There were two occasions which prompted this kind of review: the first was the only meeting of the Treasury Board to take place during our government – indeed the first meeting to be held since 1856. The idea was conceived by Margaret, the First Lord of the Treasury, partly as an occasion for saying farewell to Douglas Wass (who was retiring as permanent secretary to the Treasury) but mainly, I think, because it was an occasion for a piece of introspective historic spectacle. We met on 31 March in the Committee Room 'A' of the Cabinet Office. This is the enormous, square-tabled room at the very heart of Whitehall, in which are held all the most important Cabinet Committee meetings. It had been specially decked out with a magnificent array of the Treasury silver that was normally spread around Downing Street. Those present, apart from the Prime Minister, Douglas Wass and myself, were the other Treasury ministers, the Chief Whip (who is formally Parliamentary Secretary to the Treasury) and those government Whips who are also officers of the Treasury, together with Peter Middleton, Wass' successor as permanent secretary, and Robert Armstrong, secretary to the Cabinet.

We had only one substantive item of business to transact – to mark the handover from Wass to Middleton, due to take place on 15 April. When the First Lord had dealt graciously with this, I suddenly recalled that we were within a few days of a double event, namely an eightieth birthday and a golden wedding, in the life of Henry Brooke, now Lord Brooke of Cumnor, a former Chief Secretary (1961–2) to the Treasury Board, and that their son Peter Brooke was one of our number, as one of the Lords Commissioners of HM Treasury. So I suggested that we should send to Lord Brooke and his wife, Baroness Brooke of Ystrad-fellte, a message of congratulations and greeting from the Board. The basically formal occasion thus generated a piece of moving sentimentality in which I took at least as much pleasure as the Brooke family, because Henry had been one of my heroes since early Bow Group days. He had been a trustee of the Group and I had had the chance of working with him during his periods of service in Housing and at the Welsh Office.

The other Treasury occasion which fell at this time (28 March) was a dinner hosted by the Prime Minister at Number 10 at which Margaret delivered an elegant and generous tribute to Douglas Wass on his retirement from the Civil Service. This was the kind of occasion at which she could excel, almost always able to personalize attractively the speaking notes which her office provided for her. And so she did on this occasion. Though neither of us would try to pretend that Douglas had become a kindred spirit, I had certainly come to value his intellectually disciplined and orderly input into much of our work, though I found him occasionally a little disengaged from some of our wider discussions. It was only much later I learned that this was possibly a consequence of undisclosed deafness on his part, compounded by the quietness of my own voice. His economic thought-structure was certainly different from that of the government, but I never felt that this affected his willingness to commit himself wholeheartedly to the task in hand. The only real surprise came after his retirement, when he accepted appointment as president of the Freedom of Information Movement. For he had

certainly not in my experience – even when we undertook a long study
of the scope for more openness about economic policy – betrayed
comparable enthusiasm for this unMandarinesque diversion. I am not
sure, on reflection, whether this phenomenon calls for criticism or
commendation.

So how much had my team and I achieved during our four Treasury
years together? First, our tax changes decisively shifted the emphasis
from tax on income to tax on spending, and we had made the tax system
much fairer. Second, privatization, little more than a gleam in our eye at
the start of our term in office, had proceeded very widely, with growing
political acceptance of our case, in other countries as well as Britain. Our
third and most important achievement lay in our (still incomplete and
controversial) success in correcting our fundamental economic problems. Inflation, money supply, public expenditure and government
borrowing had all been brought under control, after a struggle that had
spread over several years. Our government would be the first for more
than a quarter of a century to achieve a lower average rate of inflation
than its predecessor. Interest rates too had fallen substantially. Productivity, competitiveness, profitability were all improving. After a long
recession, growth was once again clearly under way.

A question which was destined not just to feature in the coming
election but to reverberate for at least another decade was whether we
had achieved this last prize (so far as we had) at the cost of avoidable
damage to Britain's industrial base.

Conditions for industry had certainly been tough. Every industrial
economy in the world had faced similar pressures. Everywhere inflation
had been fuelled by oil-price hikes. Tight money policies had been
essential. For our manufacturers there was the additional misfortune
that we were becoming an oil producer as well. High oil prices boosted
the pound sterling and so subjected our industry to even fiercer
competitive conditions.

To make matters worse, British industry had for years been getting
less and less competitive, more and more badly overmanned – writing
its own suicide note, as I used to say. Long before we came into office,
our entire motorcycle industry and about half our automobile industry
had disappeared. There was a serious risk of losing the rest. As the
overmanning of previous decades was squeezed out, so two million jobs
were 'lost' in manufacturing between 1979 and 1983. The three million
new jobs that came into existence in the later 1980s – few of them in
manufacturing – did not start arriving until 1983.

Much of this structural change, much of the social upheaval which accompanied it, was not just inevitable. It was beneficial too. But it was grossly uncomfortable for those – mainly in manufacturing – who had to bear the brunt of change. So far as possible, I had tried to shift some of the tax burden from businesses and on to people. That was hardly a recipe for popularity. And there was a limit to what I could do.

Our principal mistake was to give less sympathy and understanding than we should have done to those who faced the upheaval. I had myself always been more favourably disposed than Margaret (or Keith or Nigel) towards organizations like the NEDC. They had been more eager to argue the case – which I accepted – for the inevitability of change than to seek economically acceptable ways of softening, without blunting, its impact. Even if one could not find such ways, it was politically important to be seen to seek them. For me, ever since the days of *Work for Wales* and *Change Is Our Ally*,* the market economy had always been a social-market economy. This was for me a perception of some importance for the continuing success of Thatcherism.

Manifesto-maker

It was this inheritance of achievement that we now had to marry to our plans for the future in the manifesto, on which drafting work had proceeded quite a long way during the Budget season. Our team reassembled for an all-day session at Number 11 on Saturday, 9 April. To avoid arousing suspicion on the part of the press that something was up, they all arrived through a variety of back doors (from the Horse Guards or through the Cabinet Office). Our core members – Parkinson, Cropper, Mount, Ridley and myself – had been enlarged to include Keith Joseph, Nigel Lawson, Norman Tebbit and David Howell. I had decided to re-engage key members of my Economic Reconstruction Group of opposition days. Norman was the only one who did not fall into that category. But since he had joined the Cabinet we had often found ourselves in alliance over questions of trade union reform and I had been impressed by his speedily perceptive approach to other topics. By 15 April a full text was in Margaret's hands. Cecil Parkinson, Adam Ridley, Ferdy Mount and I spent most of Sunday, 24 April at Chequers going over this with Margaret. She was by then well satisfied with the

* See p. 32 above.

general shape and tone. Work continued on 6 May, when Adam Ridley and I worked all night on the final draft, which was ready in time for Margaret's pre-election meeting at Chequers, just twenty-four hours later, on 8 May.

Several important issues were resolved only at Cabinet level, when we met informally to consider the manifesto the following week. Margaret was keen that our proposals for dealing with disruptive industrial action in essential services should include the last-resort possibility of invoking the criminal law. Norman Tebbit, with support from Willie Whitelaw and myself, managed to resist this. The first of two disagreements between Margaret and Michael Heseltine was resolved the other way: Margaret carried the day in favour of abolition of the Greater London and other metropolitan councils. The combined impact of Militancy and Ken Livingstone's extravagant example on the Greater London Council was overwhelming.

The third issue that went to Cabinet was, in light of subsequent history, much the most important. Margaret wanted again to renew her 1974 commitment to abolish the rates. We had managed to avoid any pledge of that kind in 1979, on the ground that 'cutting income tax must take priority for the time being over abolition of the domestic rating system' (1979 manifesto). So Margaret was certainly entitled to return to the charge in 1983. During the intervening years we had enacted two major pieces of legislation affecting the rates and had published a Green Paper on alternatives to the rating system. But the problem had not grown any easier. The Green Paper arguments against a poll tax were pretty persuasive, and there was a sensible alternative: a series of detailed proposals for the reform, control and capping of the rates. Armed with these points, Michael Heseltine and Leon Brittan (as Chief Secretary) prevailed over Margaret in our manifesto Cabinet meeting. They had been strongly supported by Willie Whitelaw, Nigel Lawson and myself. The manifesto contained no sign of any continuing intention to abolish domestic rates. In August 1983, after the election, we were to publish a White Paper recording our conclusion (which had been announced earlier) that 'rates should remain for the foreseeable future the main source of local revenue for local government'. We all believed that the issue had finally been laid to rest. But, as we know, the poll tax was later to rise from its grave with a vengeance.

When we actually went into the election on the resulting manifesto, we were accused by some critics of having armed ourselves with an unduly bland text, freer of radical promises than might have been expected. Margaret herself was later to wonder if 'perhaps Geoffrey Howe was too safe a pair of hands'.[1] That view does not sit easily alongside the three major features that were in the manifesto: extensive privatization, more trade union reform and big changes in local government. Only, I think, in the field of social services and education was there possibly any real substance in the charge, for in those fields we certainly hesitated to follow up some of the kites that had earlier been flown, not least in my CPC speech of the summer before.

There were solid reasons for this. At the 1982 party conference, both Margaret and Cecil had deliberately distanced the Party from the leaked CPRS 'proposals' for privatization of the NHS. Margaret's pledge that 'The National Health Service is safe in our hands' put a fairly comprehensive damper on radical NHS reform. There had been a similar shyness over student loans, which Keith Joseph had advised me (in a note as late as 3 May) had best be left for later disclosure, if at all, in a written answer. Even my own thinking on taxation of husband and wife had been placed in the freezer, on John Wakeham's advice that that was 'the least damaging way forward that does not prejudice the future'. One final inhibition had been adopted – at least by Margaret and myself – as a further result of the September CPRS leak: we were resolved to avoid any fresh commitment to additional public expenditure, and we largely succeeded in doing so. Existing pledges looked like being more than expensive enough. Even if Margaret was commendably cautious on the public expenditure front – and democracy does not suffer from an excess of financial wisdom of that kind – we all concluded that there was more than enough real meat for Parliament and electorate to consume. So indeed it proved.

Into the Campaign

The crucial pre-election meeting took place at Chequers on Sunday 8 May with Willie Whitelaw, Michael Jopling (as Chief Whip), Cecil Parkinson, Norman Tebbit, Ian Gow, Anthony Shrimsley and Christopher Lawson (respectively then directors of press and publicity and marketing at Central Office), Ferdy Mount and David Wolfson. As always on such occasions we were able to extend almost indefinitely the examination of the most recent entrails, the results of the local elections held on the preceding Thursday. We had done well certainly, though not quite so well as we had hoped. But the general view was that we could not afford to miss the opportunity that presented itself. (John Biffen had summed it up very neatly, 'It's no longer a question of which month but which Thursday.') This raised two international complications: the G7 Economic Summit was due to be held at Williamsburg on 28–31 May and the European Council at Stuttgart on 6–7 June. If, as seemed most likely, Margaret opted for polling day on 9 June, it would we thought be possible, advantageous even, for Margaret to attend most of the Williamsburg Summit. Stuttgart was less manageable, not least because the outcome of discussion there on the continuing British Budget Question could decisively affect our election result. That problem was solved more easily than some of us expected – although not for a week – by a suggestion from our European partners (of their own accord and not at our request) for an adjournment of Stuttgart until 20 June. So 9 June was election day. The decision became public after Margaret had called upon Her Majesty at Buckingham Palace before lunch on Monday, 10 May.

I then had to clear the decks for the campaign, in which I was inevitably bound to play a prominent – although not a directing – part, because of the relevance of economic issues. With Parliament due to be dissolved at the end of the week, on Friday, 13 May, we had very quicky to agree the shape of the Budget and Finance Bill that the Opposition were ready to allow on to the statute book. It was for Leon Brittan (the Chief Secretary generally led on parliamentary handling of the Finance Bill) to negotiate this with Labour's Shadow Chancellor, Peter Shore. We were not in a very strong bargaining position, so Labour were able to insist on exclusion (in the end, no more than delay) of all the reliefs we were proposing for higher-rate income tax, capital transfer tax and mortgage interest relief. But Labour were prepared to let the remaining proposals – many of which had already been implemented – proceed to the statute book.

The campaign was the first in which I had been engaged as a senior minister, with a continuing responsibility for policy from day to day. Happily, the Treasury (and the markets) gave rise to no serious problems during the three weeks between the launch of our manifesto on 18 May and polling day. So I was able, for the most part, to enjoy a life that was divided into four parts: my constituency (Wednesdays and Saturdays, with Elspeth working there like a dervish the rest of the time); regional tours, always including Scotland, the north-west (my Bebington political birthplace) and Wales (where on every visit I was supplied with a pound of laverbread from Swansea market); morning press conferences at

Central Office (only four or five throughout the campaign); and broadcasting studios, of one kind or another, up and down the land at almost every hour of the day. My regular helpers through this routine were William Hague (by then an Oxford graduate working for McKinsey's, poised between his days as a party conference prodigy in 1977 and his entry into the House of Commons in 1989), acting as my mobile research assistant, and Caroline Russell, my House of Commons secretary, working from a convenient base at Number 11.

There is in retrospect an ephemeral quality about election campaigns. It is hard to identify any events, victories or disasters, that can be said to have had anything like a decisive effect. Inevitably in 1983 the post-Falklands defence debate had a high profile. It played almost wholly in our favour. Labour's anti-nuclear confusion, with Denis Healey and Peter Shore trying hopelessly to offset Michael Foot, contrasted starkly with the robust clarity of Margaret Thatcher's leadership, in Cold War rhetoric as well as in post-Falklands glory. Denis Healey only compounded Labour's problems when he tried to discount the Prime Minister's reputation by alleging that she 'glories in slaughter' and was swiftly obliged to apologize.

In the economic debate the facts came through very satisfactorily on our side. Inflation – the April figure was announced on the day of our first press conference – was down to 4 per cent, the lowest figure for fifteen years. Just two weeks later, six days before polling day, the unemployment headline figure fell – for the first time for many months – by no less than 121,000, though sticking just above the three-million line.

Peter Shore struggled hard to exploit two 'secret' documents so as to make a case that I was trying to deceive the electorate. The most important of these dated back to the September leak of the CPRS report and embarrassed me not at all. The controversial policy proposals themselves had, of course, already been set to one side. Peter Shore now tried to exploit my covering minute, in which I had argued that 'It is essential that we get across to the country at large the nature of the longer-term problems of public spending and then seek its support and understanding for sensible ways of solving them.' Shore suggested that this destroyed the economic basis of the programme we were then presenting and 'exposed the central and shameful dishonesty of this campaign'. It was a sad and shabby attempt to muddy the waters, for Peter knew as well as anyone the constraints that would limit all our budgets. But the incident underlines the difficulties of trying to open up any electoral debate upon the foundations of disagreeable, but inescapable, facts.

The other economic feature of the campaign is much harder to explain. Edward du Cann was at that time still holding the two (not very compatible) positions of chairman of the Conservative 1922 Committee (the so-called 'Praetorian guard of back-benchers') and chairman of the Treasury and Civil Service Select Committee. The first role would (or should) have committed him, at least through an election campaign, to firm, complete and public support of the party and its policies. Yet in his second role he convened a meeting of the all-party Select Committee (which only a handful of members were able to attend on the last day before Parliament was dissolved) in order to obtain its authority for the publication of the draft report of the chairman of the Committee (himself).

This text, once published, was immediately hailed by Peter Shore as 'a damning indictment of the government's record' which, he said, 'revealed the dismay felt even in the Tory Party at the prospect of another five years of doctrinaire Thatcherism'. The press treated it in much the same light. Closer analysis revealed it as yet another technical study of the eternally baffling relationship between monetary and exchange rate policies. Produced in 'peace-time' it no doubt had the makings of a relevant discussion document. But why a loyal Conservative office-bearer should have hastened to get such a text into the public domain in the first week of an election campaign was very hard to understand. As soon as it was reported to me – campaigning in the east Midlands on a Tuesday morning, 24 May – I sought an explanation from du Cann, just as the press sought one from me. Du Cann's reply was as disingenuous as his original action. He found it 'very difficult', he said, 'to understand the fuss. The report is an early draft produced by the Committee's advisers. It is not the Committee's report, nor is it mine.' The original idea was that the one-page covering note would say that the draft 'represented the general line the Committee would have taken if it had had time to complete the report'. This was excised after objection from the only Tory MP present at the meeting. Yet still the report was published. It was, of course, a twenty-four-hour wonder and played no significant part in the campaign. But to this day du Cann's performance has remained hard to understand or explain.

Perhaps inevitably the campaign did bring out some personality tensions within our team – first, and most obviously, at the opening Central Office press conference. All the senior figures were on the platform: Whitelaw, Joseph, Pym, Parkinson and myself under Margaret Thatcher's chairmanship. When she was asked if she wanted a landslide victory, she replied that she wanted 'as many Conservatives to win as we can possibly get. . . . I could handle a landslide majority all right.' So, to his face, she repudiated one of her most senior colleagues, Francis Pym. For only days before, on Robin Day's *Question Time*, Francis had declared that 'a large majority is a very dangerous thing, '. Suddenly there was revealed the large and uncomfortable gulf that lay between the Prime Minister and one of her (theoretically) closest partners in the Falklands War Cabinet.

Williamsburg Economic Summit: May 1983

These underlying tensions became even clearer during what was in effect the last act of my campaign, played out, curiously, in the charming old colonial township of Williamsburg, Virginia. For this was Reagan's chosen setting for the world's ninth Economic Summit of the seven top industrial nations, between 28 and 31 May. Our team consisted of Margaret, Francis Pym and myself, and the whole affair was due to last from Saturday afternoon to Tuesday morning. This time the arrangements were more fragmentary. To reduce to a minimum Margaret's absence from the campaign, she was flown back by BA Concorde on the Monday, so that she could attend the Tuesday press conference. As Chancellor of the Exchequer at an Economic – albeit international – Summit I was left to head the British delegation for the last twenty-four hours. We had all flown out for the start of the Summit together in the one RAF VC10.

These occasions are often rather like a series of overlapping parties in which much protocol is involved in organizing an opening 'heads of delegation session', during which the Foreign and Finance Ministers conduct their own separate round tables elsewhere. We all usually come together for most but not all of the meals. Elaborate social events (or at least backdrops) are always laid on in the interstices of the meetings and meals. Williamsburg was notable for a first-class New Orleans jazz band and a high-quality string quintet, clad in eighteenth-century dress and under the leadership of an emigrated band-master warrant officer of one of our own Scottish regiments. The work programmes always go awry. The time taken to consider and approve (in different groups) the clutch of declarations and communiqués which are the product of such occasions always exceeds the planners' expectations. Alongside all this, there takes place a full series of bilateral meetings between the heads of government, exactly like a league competition in ping-pong.

In the midst of all this, a particular difficulty was to maintain the substance, or at least the appearance, of co-ordination within each national delegation, with ministers being ferried hither and thither in separate cars, often to separate venues. This was my fifth Summit; for Francis Pym it was his second. Since it was an Economic Summit, liaison between Chancellor and Prime Minister was both more necessary and more habitual. But, as between Prime Minister and Foreign Secretary, it was obvious to outsiders (George Shultz remarked upon it to me a year later) that the pattern of contact was conspicuously less spontaneous and more strained. So it was not an easy weekend. The atmosphere lightened a lot when we were able to watch relays of British television bulletins, showing the overblown stiltedness of the two Davids (Steel and Owen) at their Ettrick Bridge summit meeting. (The Liberal–Social Democrat Alliance had been seeking to proclaim its unity.)

One conversation that I had with Chancellor Kohl (curiously in the men's room at the Raleigh Tavern; thankfully there was an interpreter to hand) has stuck in my memory. It must, I think, have been prompted by his impressions of the morning heads of delegation meeting, when there had been a sharp difference beween Margaret and President Mitterrand about the legitimacy of producing political declaration ahead of the economic conclusions. 'Can you not encourage Margaret', asked Helmut Kohl suddenly, 'to be more ready to "woo" her colleagues? People like François would be much more likely to respond to that kind of approach than the argumentative one. And she is certainly well able to do it that way, if she wants to.' It was a good point and I promised to take it in. I never quoted the conversation directly to Margaret. But I did try, particularly when I became Foreign Secretary, to recall and, from time to time, to rehearse the advice. Sometimes it worked.

Consistency and quality of interpretation was, of course, another variable on these occasions, always at its most difficult when trying to cope with humour. I stood in for Margaret at the final lunch on the Monday. There were only two (and a half) English-speaking listeners around the table – Pierre Trudeau and I, and Yasuhiro Nakasone – but Reagan was not in the least discouraged from a steady fare of stories, as a means of keeping the more formal talking on the move. He told us of the astonishment of the tax lawyer who found himself, on arrival at the Pearly Gates, installed by St Peter in a luxurious mansion immediately next to a golf course, while a newly arrived pope was being installed in a remote monastic cell. 'Why', asked the lawyer, 'this difference of treatment?' 'Well, it's like this,' said St Peter. 'You see, we've got twenty-seven popes here already, but you're the first tax lawyer we've ever had.' After translation round the table into French, German, Italian and Japanese it seemed somehow to have lost a little of its original zest. But Ronald Reagan kept it up. He was a splendidly natural host, an effective and conciliatory chairman, though with a straightforward and engaging tenacity on points that mattered. There was a spontaneity about his mutually supportive attitude towards Margaret. She likewise blossomed with admiring, almost affectionate, directness towards him. It was for both of them a personally satisfying and politically supportive relationship.

It is fair to add that interpretation could also electrify proceedings. The Japanese, in the person of Prime Minister Nakasone, had arrived with a brand-new proposal of their own, for the launching of a conference on Life Sciences and Mankind. While discussing this initiative, the Italian Prime Minister, Fanfani, mentioned the recent discovery of a technique of human reproduction which operated without any intervention whatsoever on the part of the male. Those who were listening to this exposition through the kindness of an American-accented lady on our headphones were startled to hear the same voice add, 'Gee, that's absolutely the worst news I've heard in a long time!' Interpreters do not often offer running commentaries on their raw material.

The Williamsburg Summit was one of the more important of the eleven that I attended. Its most significant aspect, I think, was the extent to which it marked, under the leadership of Prime Minister Nakasone, the political coming of age of post-war Japan. For it was the first time the Japanese had committed themselves to, and actually shared in, the preparation of an important Western text on arms control and security. The communiqué was a very robust presentation of our position on INF (intermediate-range nuclear forces) deployment and negotiations, with the significant sentence: 'The security of our countries is indivisible and must be approached on a global basis.'

The economic conclusions were equally important. For, building upon the 1982 Versailles work, they committed the Seven to a pattern of economic consultation, convergence and 'group therapy' (as I called it) which was already proving valuable and which ought, in my view, to have been sustained and developed. An important objective was the greater stability of exchange markets, achieved upon a basis of convergence between disciplined monetary and fiscal policices. There is no doubt that this task became more difficult when the G5 group of Finance Ministers was enlarged to include all of the Seven. But the basic arguments in favour of such co-operation were inclining me more and more in favour of the European version – the EMS.

From the British point of view the Summit brought an added bonus. For its conclusions endorsed in every respect the economic policies and techniques which we had been applying and developing over the preceding four years. Britain was one of those countries singled out for praise for her contribution to world economic growth. We made the most of this in what was left of our election campaign.

Victory and Verdict

We entered the last week with the polls set more firmly and consistently in our favour than ever before. Already speculation was racing ahead about the way in which a victorious Margaret might reshape her Cabinet after her return to Number 10. It was said by some – not very wisely, I thought – that I had established an 'impregnable position' for myself but that I was ready to move away from the Treasury. Most forecasts had me moving to take Willie Whitelaw's place at the Home Office, which at an earlier stage of my career I had always regarded as a natural destination for a former Solicitor General. Only recently had I begun to think of the possible alternative of the Foreign Office, which I realized I much preferred. But I had deliberately not brought my own thinking to any conclusion, still less tried to talk about it to Margaret or anyone else. As a matter of fact, I never did engage Margaret in self-promotive discussion of this kind.

I don't remember seeing or hearing at the time anything of the suggestion that Cecil Parkinson was a candidate for the Foreign Office and should, I think, have been rather startled if I had. For although I had a high respect for his potential, I should not have credited him with sufficient seniority or experience for this particular position. But in light of Margaret's decision, years later, to promote the young John Major to the place I can understand how she was in fact attracted to Cecil, who had shown himself during his time in the Falklands War Cabinet to be, in the words of *The Times*, 'a consummate executor of the Prime Ministerial command'. And there are historical precedents, in 1938 and again in 1976, for young appointments to this post. I have to confess that I am not sorry – and not just for my own sake – that this plan was frustrated. For I fancy that if Cecil, and not I, had been at Margaret's side over the next six years, British foreign policy, towards Europe in particular, might have been pressed much earlier and more decisively in the wrong direction. It is, I suppose, possible that Cecil, with the benefit of the insight and experience on which he could have drawn as Foreign Secretary, might have evolved into a more independent figure in this field. But perhaps not.

I had no time for any thoughts of this kind in the last hectic days. I was at least able to be back in East Surrey for two eve-of-poll meetings (how old-fashioned that now seems!) and to spend polling day with Elspeth on our separate counter-cyclical tours of committee rooms and polling stations. (We always followed this pattern, one with our president, the other with our chairman – all meeting for lunch at a prearranged cross-over pub restaurant in mid-constituency, usually the White Hart in Bletchingley.) No one was in any doubt about the outcome, nationally as well as locally. Our Labour vote shrank even smaller than before, and although this enabled my Liberal opponent, a most able and energetic local councillor, Susan Liddell, to gain almost 3000 extra votes and so reduce my majority, my own share of the vote was unchanged at 63 per cent.*

We went on from the televising of our count to a jubilant constituency party at the home of my chairman, Margaret MacNaughton, and then, taking Amanda with us, to the turbulent festivities at Conservative Central Office. We looked, of course, for Margaret and for Cecil Parkinson, as party chairman, to offer our congratulations. As it happened they were together, aside from the main gathering, when we tracked them down. Amanda and Elspeth commented afterwards that the encounter had seemed to provoke a moment's embarrassment on their part. Not until much later did we discover the reason why.[2] Only hours before our meeting Margaret had told Cecil of her wish that he should be Foreign Secretary and he had disclosed his affair with his former secretary, Sara Keays. On the next day, Friday, Margaret first heard, from Sara Keays' father, about her pregnancy. So when we all met in Central Office that night, the Prime Minister was still considering whether she could prudently proceed to appoint Cecil as her Foreign

* Howe, R. E. G. (Con) 27,272; Liddell, Mrs S. M. (Lib) 11,836; Pincott, H. (Lab) 4249; Conservative majority 15,436.

Secretary. My own future, therefore, was still in the pending tray. The moment's embarrassment, easily explained in retrospect, was swiftly swamped by effusive congratulations in all directions.

Remarkably, I cannot remember exactly when I was asked to go into Number 10 to hear from Margaret about my position in the new government. But the suggestion of the Foreign Office was certainly no surprise. I was more than a little sad to be leaving the Treasury just at the point when things were coming right, since it would have been – or so it seemed – rather fun to press ahead with the ideas on which my team and I, perhaps particularly Nick Ridley, had been working for the previous year. But the Foreign Office offered a very different and very stimulating prospect. The idea of a fresh agenda, after no less than eight years as Margaret's Chancellor or Shadow Chancellor, was an exciting challenge.

It was a great satisfaction to have held the Treasury portfolio for long enough to have effected real change in our economic prospects. And it was good too to know that my place was to be taken by a member of the original team, Nigel Lawson, who had played such a formidable part in translating our thinking into workable practice. There had been a time when I should have been more than inclined to argue the case for Patrick Jenkin, my old Bow Group flatmate, to succeed me at the Treasury. I still had immense respect for his judgment, industry and integrity, and had been very content with our partnership during his time as Secretary of State for Trade and Industry. But Margaret's choice was always more likely to go to Nigel, who had long been close to us both and had now established his ministerial calibre after two years as Energy Secretary. I could not – and did not – challenge the view that he was likely to be the most compatible manager of my economic inheritance. As I prepared to move on from the Treasury, I was struck by the closing comments of the *Economist* on my Chancellorship:

> The key to Mrs Thatcher's emerging government lay firmly next door at Number 11, in the imperturbable presence of Sir Geoffrey Howe. While Mrs Thatcher's personality towered over the period, it was Sir Geoffrey's intellect which provided her with consistency and with argument in debate. He achieved the depoliticisation of large areas of economic policy which would have been remarkable at any time and which in a deep recession was astonishing. Sir Geoffrey's donnish manner; his openness and readiness to debate the treasury view; his presentation of economic

policy as if it were an act of God, not of the treasury; all this contributed to the single greatest miracle of the administration, the neutralisation of unemployment as an electoral issue.

Yet beneath this lay a more subtle ploy. By totally identifying treasury policy with Thatcherism, Sir Geoffrey was able to re-establish to his department a dominance over Whitehall it had not seen for a decade. He was also able to make himself virtually impregnable. To lose confidence in him, Mrs Thatcher would be losing confidence in the central spine of her own strategy.

If it was true that unemployment had been neutralized as an electoral issue, it did not mean that my – or anybody's – concern for the unemployed had diminished. It meant only that the country had come to accept the economic facts of life. It was inescapably true that I had furnished the spine of Margaret Thatcher's strategy during my years at the Treasury. It remained to be seen whether my position, and Margaret's confidence in me, would be as strong in my new role as Foreign Secretary.

PART FIVE

FOREIGN SECRETARY
1983–1989

CHAPTER TWENTY-ONE

SETTING THE AGENDA

―

Transition to FCO

One of the brutalities of political life is the way in which you can succeed to somebody else's job without retaining any clear memory of the grace, or lack of it, with which the change was effected. I am ashamed to say that I cannot now recall if I carried out any of the courtesies that should have accompanied my takeover from Francis Pym of the office which he had held, with parliamentary skill and confidence, for only fourteen testing months. I like to think I must have done so because he and his devoted wife Valerie were nothing but supportive in the months that followed.

But other more active memories crowd in, of the excitement of regrouping a new command. I was delighted when Margaret offered me Janet Young as the Foreign and Commonwealth Office's spokesman in the Lords and number two in the department. It was Janet's personal misfortune to be displaced, as Leader of the House of Lords, by Willie Whitelaw, on his long-predicted elevation from the Commons, but, granted that disappointment, I think she was as pleased to come to the FCO as I was to receive her. Two of my other ministers retained the places they had held before the election: Tim Raison was perfectly located in charge of the Overseas Development Administration and Malcolm Rifkind, the sensibly Euro-committed Scots Silk, was ideally qualified to retain responsibility for Community and European affairs: his capacity to speak lucidly and at speed in answer to a debate, however complex, without any kind of note far surpassed the best that I had ever heard. I was hopeful that my old PPS, Richard Luce (who had felt obliged to resign after the Falklands invasion), might now be able to rejoin the government; and so he was, with responsibility for two important areas of policy – the Middle East (former stamping-ground of his late father, Sir William Luce), and Hong Kong and the Far East.

Tim Renton, who came with me as my PPS from the Treasury, became a fully fledged member of the FCO team a year later, when he stepped into the vacancy as parliamentary secretary left by Ray Whitney's departure for Social Security; himself a former diplomat, Ray had been happy to end a short apprenticeship in his old department with a move to a home department. Tim and I were destined to work closely together in several different partnerships in the years ahead.

All the changing ministers were, of course, political colleagues of long standing. The switch in official entourage was much more fundamental. It was a real wrench to have to leave the Treasury team. Steadily improving economic performance had drawn us ever more closely together, so that the election victory was seen by almost all – officials and politicians – as a reward for wisdom and virtue. I could not have been served by a more professionally dedicated team during those four exhausting but exhilarating years in the Treasury.

Our new home-from-home for the next six years, at 1 Carlton Gardens in the heart of London club land, close to St James's Park, had none of the political ringside excitement and glamour of Number 11. Yet for every practical purpose it was almost equivalent: a private two-floor maisonette, with ample accommodation of all kinds, including two studies (Elspeth's LSE degree course was still under way); and two lower-ground floors with elegant and spacious public rooms suitable for official meetings and entertainment. As we had done at Number 11, we commissioned an illustrated booklet about the building, which had enjoyed an interestingly French career. Built at the same time as the Nash terraces on the Mall (after the removal by the Prince Regent of Carlton House), Number 1 had been the home of Napoleon III from 1840 to 1842. Almost exactly a hundred years later it was one of four houses which comprised the wartime London headquarters of General de Gaulle. Ernest Bevin was the first Foreign Secretary to be allowed the use of Number 1 as his official London residence, in 1945–50.

The crew that waited to receive me on Monday, 13 June 1983 certainly seemed a good deal more practically diverse than the one that I had left behind. As soon as I arrived I found myself cared for by an ever present security team of Special Branch officers, a constant feature of the life of the Foreign Secretary (as well as of the Prime Minister and one or two other colleagues). There were experts to plan and manage overseas travel (two dozen separate overseas journeys before Christmas 1983, starting with the European Council meeting in Stuttgart on my first weekend as Foreign Secretary, 17–19 June), to organize programmes and hospitality for overseas visitors (forty before the end of July), to man and manage a worldwide, top-security communications network, and so on. Beyond that there was a cluster of specialized organizations – not so large as, but seemingly more exotic than, the Inland Revenue, Customs and Excise and National Savings – GCHQ (in those days still scarcely heard of), MI6 (always known within the Office as the 'friends'), the Passport Office, the BBC External Services, the British Council and the ODA (Overseas Development Administration).

To support and guide me through all this, and to assist in the conception and execution of British foreign policy, was the mandarinate of the Diplomatic Service itself: only 4700 strong, at home and in 213 posts, 164 countries around the world – less than half the number employed by the Scottish Office. Like all elite groups in Britain they had in recent years been the subject of seemingly endless study, including at least three official reports presided over by Sir Edwin Plowden (1966), Sir Val Duncan (1969) and Sir Ken Berrill (and the Central Policy Review Staff, 1977). These critical tomes joined my summer-holiday reading material.

More immediately, I was aware of being served by people with a palpably more polished, seemingly more disengaged, more worldly-wise style than that of the Treasury. Both groups of people were the product of the same intensely competitive selection process: but the one was characterized by the flavour of Nottingham High School and the London Business School, while the other had slightly more the savour of Eton and All Souls. At once I know that this sentence is unfair to the Foreign Office. For it reflects mainly the presence on my arrival of Sir Antony Acland as permanent under secretary and of Sir Julian Bullard as political director. Acland, meticulously professional, acutely intelligent, and only fifty-two years old when first appointed, moved on (unusually) in 1986 to head our Washington embassy for five years, before becoming Provost of Eton. Bullard had already been a fellow of All Souls for seven years and went on to finish his diplomatic career with an immensely engaged and crucially successful four years as ambassador in Bonn. He later became Vice-Chancellor of Birmingham University. The principal private secretary whom I inherited from Francis Pym was Brian Fall. Not always patient with other people's shortcomings, he had even so the right kind of shrewdness to be a splendid guide through my first eighteen months in office. Peter Carrington very sensibly chose him to be his *chef de cabinet* at NATO, and he went on to represent the UK at Ottawa and in Moscow.

My first ten days in London conveyed the hectic nature of the new job well enough. Major diplomatic events crowded on each other's heels. First came the annual Queen's Birthday banquet, hosted by the Foreign Secretary for the London Diplomatic Corps and their wives: for this we were happy to inherit from Francis and Valerie Pym arrangements for the event to be held at the Royal Academy, in rooms already radiant with the Summer Exhibition. I recall vividly my shock at finding on one of the Academy walls a portrait of myself, of whose existence I had no previous knowledge, by the academician Ruskin Spear. This seemed at first a rather discourteous invasion of privacy, but later it came to seem no more intrusive, in principle I suppose, than a photograph. Ten years later, soon after Spear's death, it came up for sale at Christie's. We secured it for a modest price for our Warwickshire home. (Spear's only other painting in that sale, of an anonymous chimpanzee, fetched a slightly higher price.)

Stuttgart European Council: June 1983

The topic that was, at the end, to rupture our partnership was the one for which Margaret and I first travelled together overseas in our new relationship *à deux* – the European Community and, above all, its financial arrangements. For this was overwhelmingly the most important item on the agenda of the European Council, to be held (eight days after our polling day) from Friday to Sunday, 17–19 June 1983. It was to take place in Stuttgart, under the chairmanship of Chancellor Kohl. (The Presidency, as it is called, of the Community moves from government to government every six months.) The European Council comprised the heads of government and Foreign Ministers (but not Finance Ministers) of the, by now, ten member-states (Greece had joined in 1981). The Council met, at this time, three times each year: once before 1 July and once before Christmas in each of the two Presidency countries; and once in the spring, usually in Brussels.

The Council's importance, as the main source of authority and dynamic in the Community, has grown fairly steadily over the years. It is the Council of Ministers (most often the Foreign Ministers, but including others – Agriculture, Finance and Trade, for example – on specialized subjects) which is the lawmaking body, nowadays in tandem with the European Parliament and acting on the basis of a draft produced by the Commission. But the most difficult issues are generally resolved, and important new initiatives often launched, at European Council level. So it is a surprise – it was certainly a surprise for me attending for the first time – to discover just how informal and unportentous a body it is in practice.

There is a degree of ceremony, of course, about the coming together of the delegations, usually in a palatial setting recalling some earlier episode in European history. On this occasion we were meeting in Stuttgart's Neues Schloss, the eighteenth-century palace of Frederick I of Württemberg, largely destroyed by bombing in 1944, but restored by 1963. Heads of government arrive to guards of honour at the airport and are ushered along the roads by motor-cycle escorts (known in Germany as white mice because of their white and green leather uniforms). President Mitterrand, the only head of state as well as of government, was always allowed, or at least expected, to arrive last.

Once inside the conference room, or at meals or photo-calls together (the 'family photograph', often on some ceremonial stairway, was always the high point for badinage), Christian names were the order of the day, at least between those of equal rank. Council meetings themselves took place without any officials present, apart from two or three members of the Council and Commission secretariats. Officials outside are often deeply frustrated by their ignorance of what their heads of government might be contending – or, still worse, conceding – in the Council chamber. One of my most useful functions was to take an accurate running note of the proceedings, to be collected periodically by a British official and transcribed as just about the best evidence in Europe of what had actually occurred. It was intriguing to discover that the Foreign Secretary had to resume a task which he had performed for many years as junior counsel in court.

Even more important was to follow the proceedings closely, so as to be ready sometimes to speak myself, more often to prompt Margaret with additional ammunition – or to restrain her from intervening prematurely or unnecessarily. Sustained over ten or fifteen hours at each European Council, this was a pretty severe test of any relationship. Well managed, it could have provided – and sometimes did – an ideal setting for our 'hard cop, soft cop' double-act. Certainly there were plenty of occasions when my more regular exposure to the arguments (at monthly meetings of Foreign Ministers) made it easy for me to suggest a modest textual change that could resolve or finesse a troublesome point. Our colleagues were usually relieved to see it disposed of in that fashion.

There were other occasions when it made obvious sense for Margaret herself to deploy the strength of the British case. Almost invariably we were better briefed and more fully seized of the points than any of our peers, perhaps partly because, until her later years, Margaret exhaustively practised her arguments in debate with our officials. Though she liked to win these training bouts, she did listen to their advice – I often heard her use with skill in the Council arguments she had previously demol-ished in our own offices. All things considered, the occasions when we obviously disagreed about tactics were surprisingly few. In the last resort, I could hardly wrestle with the Prime Minister for control of the British microphone! But by the same token and for very similar reasons, we did not always make the most of our complementary qualities.

Stuttgart itself illustrated many other features of Euro-negotiation. Inevitably, the British budget question was again top of the agenda. This had last been dealt with in 1982 but only for one year, in a difficult round of negotiations that Francis Pym had had to conduct in the middle of the Falklands campaign. By 1983, however, we had a solid argument which would restore the strength of our bargaining position. Expenditure under the Community budget was now close to exhausting the total resources provided for under the Rome Treaty. The prescribed ceiling of expenditure (defined as equivalent to the yield of 1 per cent of VAT) could not be increased without the agreement of all member-states, including ourselves. We could, and in due course did, make it plain that we were not willing to accept *any* increase in that ceiling (which almost all our partners desired) unless it was linked with an equally long-term reduction in the size of the British contribution. We were prepared to open up negotiations about the future system, but only on that basis. There was a crucial condition precedent: we had to be sure of a proper reduction of our liability in any intervening year.

At Stuttgart we managed, after a long struggle, to reach agreement on the shape of future negotiations. But the French, in particular, were most reluctant to offer enough to cover the British claim for 1983. The scene then developed in a fashion with which I was to grow familiar over the years. The proceedings were adjourned for informal discussion, not once but many times. This was a signal for the two dozen or so ministers and officials present to break up into a series of small groups, sometimes in private but more often scattered round the Council room. Interpreters would weave among us trying to keep communications open, while some delegations began to talk about having to leave before long, if progress had become impossible. One moment Hans-Dietrich Genscher would open up and then break off a dialogue with Margaret

Thatcher, or Kohl with Mitterrand. Then Margaret and I, and our perceptive and tenacious ambassador to the Community, Sir Michael Butler, would huddle together to consider our next move. Quite unlike any British parliamentary or other political occasion, it was more like an assize-court lobby, with groups of counsel and solicitors trying to settle half-a-dozen lawsuits at the same time. On this occasion, Mitterrand was at first prevented by Kohl from carrying out his well-trailed intention to leave before the end. But eventually he did bow out, leaving his Prime Minister, Pierre Mauroy, to manage their retreat towards the figure of 750 million ECUs* that we felt able to accept as our rebate for 1983.

That was not, of course, the only item on the agenda. Like most European Council conclusions, those from Stuttgart run to some twenty pages, ranging from the extremely useful to the utterly banal. Probably the most striking was the solemn Declaration on European Union (based upon the earlier Genscher–Colombo Act). This text was not legally binding but 'only' declaratory; we attached less importance than most of our colleagues – less than we should have done – to this blueprint for the future.

I was delighted that the Stuttgart Summit gave me the opportunity to visit, before it was completed, the remarkable Staatsgallerie, the work of Elspeth's hugely talented brother-in-law, the architect James Stirling – who died, as a result of a surgical disaster, in 1992. I still recall Mayor Rommel's commendation of the building as undoubtedly the finest in post-war Stuttgart. The lunchtime meeting with Rommel was a further bonus, for his field-marshal father had been one of my heroes during my schooldays forty years before. It was a strange chance that introduced me to young Rommel in the same week that I had been in joint harness with Viscount Montgomery's son David, an old schoolfriend, who as President of the Anglo-Argentine Society had had a leading part to play in a series of London celebrations honouring Simon Bolivar, hailed as the Liberator, directly or indirectly, of almost every state in Latin America.

The Greek Presidency, throughout the second half of 1983, was a period of immensely unrewarding work on the crucial Community agenda to which the Stuttgart meeting had committed us. Only the Germans, generally in the person of Hans-Dietrich Genscher, were our regular allies in the overall search for budgetary and fiscal restraint. But

* The European Currency Unit, a basket of currencies used to set values for transactions within the EC/EU: at that time worth approximately 80 US cents.

as the months went by it was clear that the French, particularly when their Finance Minister (in those days still Jacques Delors) was on parade, were moving over to our side of the financial argument. For they too faced the prospect, once Spain and Portugal had become members of the Community, of joining the select band of net contributors. These were the circumstances which led Delors in the course of one Council debate to echo (unconsciously no doubt, but precisely) the phrase from my 1979 Budget speech that finance must determine expenditure and not expenditure finance. Well, one day maybe.

By the time we got to the Athens Summit on 5–6 December it had become clear that the Greeks were unwilling, under their own chairmanship, to reach any of the necessary conclusions, which were inescapably bound to be tough for Greek agriculture. President Mitterrand, having begun by now to share Delors' view of the need for France herself to achieve a rigorous settlement of the budgetary questions, was also coming to see the advantages of being able to work for such a result during the French Presidency that would immediately follow the Greek in the first half of 1984. The agenda for the Fontainebleau European Council had been clearly set by the emptiness of Athens.

Setting the Agenda

As soon as we had got the Stuttgart Summit behind us, I was able to follow up the reviews that I had already put in hand of all the main aspects of British foreign policy. I wanted to establish to my own satisfaction a framework and set of priorities for the years ahead. Less than twelve months had elapsed since the end of the Falklands conflict. Several important items were resurfacing on the active agenda: Hong Kong, the Middle Eastern peace process, South Africa and Gibraltar were prime examples. The last named was of pressing practical importance, since it could all too easily become an embarrassment in the context of negotiations for Spain's accession to the Community. South Africa was becoming urgent too, with the next meeting of Commonwealth heads of government (CHOGM) coming up in Delhi in November.

One perennial item was the management of the UK's position within the Western alliance – the balance between our special (I tried never to use the word) relationship with the United States and our place in the

European Community. I had long regarded this last as the key to all our wider relationships. There remained the dominant issue – the Cold War, East–West relations and arms control. How far could Britain play a part in tackling this?

The basic issues had at least to be identified in my first speech to the Commons as Foreign Secretary, in the Queen's Speech debate on 28 June 1983. There too I was to renew my long-running parliamentary double-act with Denis Healey. When he had ceased shadowing me at the Treasury, in 1980, Denis had moved across to foreign affairs. It was a disappointment to him that he had never been able to deploy his expertise in this field as Foreign Secretary. His speeches, like his books, were characterized by generally well-informed name-dropping on an exotic scale.

There were to be many occasions in the years ahead when I was to value Denis's bipartisan support. It was almost always accompanied by bouts of entertaining savagery, frequently at Margaret's expense. On this occasion, for example, his welcome for my appointment was accompanied by a warning that the greatest diplomatic problem I should face would not be thousands or hundreds of miles away but 'a few yards away across the street in Number 10, where he must face an opinionated and ignorant Prime Minister, who is always convinced that she knows best about everything'. Our subsequent exchanges in the debate proceeded along characteristic lines. As I thanked him for the warmth of his welcome to my new job, my mind went back to his 'dead sheep' jibe, and I said that 'to be received in that way by the Right Honourable gentleman is rather like being nuzzled by an old ram'. 'I hope', interrupted Denis, 'that the Right Honourable and learned gentleman will not spoil a beautiful friendship by accusing me of necrophilia.' I responded by deploring the injustice of his allegation that the Prime Minister was 'dogmatic and insensitive. He should know', I said, 'because no one shows more evidence of those characteristics than he.'

I was certainly not inhibited from using this particular occasion to flag up the importance which I was seeking to attach to the positive management of East–West relations. I was able to do this by quoting from the testimony offered to Congress by the US Secretary of State George Shultz two weeks before (he had just completed the first twelve months of his six years of distinguished service in that office). 'We and the Soviets', said Shultz, 'have sharply divergent goals and philosophies of political and moral order; and these differences will not soon go away. . . . At the same time we have a fundamental and common interest in the avoidance of war. This common interest impels us to work towards a relationship . . . that can lead to a safer world for all mankind.'

Although there had, at this stage, been little contact between the two of us, I endorsed his approach enthusiastically. 'That is exactly the sort of relationship that we want and we shall play a full part in working for it,' I told the House. It was to this end that key thinkers in the Foreign Office were now directing their attention. I had called them together for a theme-setting meeting at Carlton Gardens on 5 July. Along with all my ministers, the cast included my top officials, Antony Acland and Julian Bullard, two future ambassadors to Moscow (Bryan Cartledge and Brian Fall) and one to Bonn (Nigel Broomfield, at that time head of our Soviet Department), as well as Pauline Neville-Jones, then in charge of our planning staff and, in 1994, the Office's first woman political director.

We all had the sense that we were meeting at what could be an important turning point. Shultz's recent testimony suggested that the US might finally be moving away from the mode in which she had had no apparent interest in the Soviet Union except to defame her. In such circumstances, Britain, I dared to think, could hardly be better placed to take advantage of the opportunities that were opening up. Our own Prime Minister had established her credentials with the United States and her strength in the eyes of Moscow. There was, moreover, reason to hope that she might be starting to express some interest in East–West relations.

How then to approach the subject? Confronted with the theoretical choice between bare containment of the Soviets and actually attempting to roll them back, the realistic course probably lay somewhere in between. I had asked for an analysis of the options that might be open to us. It should be practically possible for Britain to play a significant part in weakening the Soviet grip on Eastern Europe and in encouraging at least some positive developments within the USSR itself. A number of ideas were suggested. We should design and follow an 'active policy' towards Eastern Europe, based on the premise that Communism manifestly does not work, especially in the economic field. And we should develop a programme for increased contacts with Soviet leaders, if possible exposing them to Western criticism and thinking. None of these moves should signal any diminution of our criticism of the Soviet presence in Afghanistan following their 1979 invasion or of their policy towards Poland. We should take care not to get too far out of line with our allies, particularly the US, but on the contrary to take them with us.

This seminar concluded with my endorsement of a twenty-point menu of proposals for specific action, which was to be worked up under the joint leadership of Nigel Broomfield and Pauline Neville-Jones. We were thus already moving ahead when Margaret indicated that she too would welcome the chance of a wide-ranging seminar on this and other foreign policy topics. This was fixed to take place at Chequers, two months later, on 8 and 9 September. We were invited to suggest a cast of Sovietology and Eastern Europe experts for one session. I had already commissioned working papers that would serve as raw material for the rest.

From George Shultz to Chevening

I was able to hear more of George Shultz's thinking on all this at first hand during a two-day visit to Washington in mid-July. Our embassy was now in the charge of Sir Oliver Wright, who had been recalled to the service just a few months after his retirement from Bonn: he and his wife, Marjorie, lived at Burstow in my constituency and had a well-deserved reputation as amateur actors. My programme included talks with all the senior members of the administration and both Houses of Congress, and a three-hour session with George Shultz and his colleagues at the State Department. Shultz, reserved at first, was an engaging man; his penetratingly pale-blue eyes signalled the alert interest of a don turned businessman turned statesman. We managed to establish a largely common approach to the Soviet-led issues. These included, of course, arms control and the NATO alliance itself. On South Africa and the Middle East our interests, though not always our policies, were similar. Flanked as we both were by at least half-a-dozen expert colleagues and advisers, this occasion did little to promote the intimacy of personal partnership which subsequently developed – and which later helped to keep us together even when we differed, for example over the nuances of Middle Eastern policy. But already our thinking about the Soviets was encouragingly like-minded.

The visit to the White House, my first, had an agreeably informal air. The entrance, through what seems like a single-storey annex, was always eased in the Reagan years by the welcoming charm of his protocol secretary, Lucky Roosevelt. One half of the call was generally devoted to a notably relaxed, and almost always useful, talk with the Vice-President. George Bush was familiar with the detail of most topics – he had travelled almost literally everywhere, and his electoral experience made him often more sensitive than the State Department, not excluding George Shultz, to the pressures of day-to-day politics.

That was even more evidently the case with President Reagan himself. Meetings in the Oval Office were much more like being received at a warmly informal Court. The President was customarily flanked by half-a-dozen supporters, including two, if not three, Secretaries of State – Shultz, Caspar Weinberger (Defense) and sometimes Donald Regan (Treasury). Our team, at least numerically, was almost as strong. But Reagan made the most of the compact, near-circular setting of armchairs and sofas to put one very much at ease. His own observations, direct and even folksy, were generally well to the point. I always felt it worthwhile using the occasion to develop some important, often slightly offbeat point which might not otherwise reach the President. One example was the extent to which Margaret and I were prepared to attach importance to the possible role in Southern Africa of Zamora Machel, chirpy President of Mozambique. This view was at one time seen as so eccentric in Washington that even the State Department, let alone the new right, was unlikely to convey it favourably to the President.

So this was a good opportunity. It enabled me too to keep up pressure 'at the highest level' against an early recommencement of US weaponry sales to Argentina. (There was frequent talk from the Pentagon about the need to resume a trickle of 'shiny toys' for the Argentine military.) 'Ah, yes,' Reagan would respond, 'Margaret would not like that, would she?'

The evening dinner party at our ambassador's residence included the two Georges (Bush and Shultz); William Casey (Director of the CIA), Paul Volcker (still at the Federal Reserve Board) and another half-dozen ministers and senators. A well-run British embassy has an extensive reach for contacts which the Foreign Secretary should exploit. On the issue that was uppermost in my mind, our attitude towards the Soviet bloc, I left Washington with the impression that my own thinking – in the direction of increased contacts – was ready to be a shade more adventurous than that of the Americans.

The summer break gave us the chance to discover more about the most desirable feature of my six years at the Foreign Office, Chevening near Sevenoaks. Our appetites had been whetted, of course, by the two pre-Budget weekends we had spent there in January 1982 and 1983. And now, as the Prime Minister reported in answer to a parliamentary question, I had 'accepted nomination as the resident of Chevening House under the terms of the Chevening Estate Act 1959'. That statute embodied the trusts prescribed by the last Earl of Stanhope, in his time a member of the Baldwin and Chamberlain Cabinets, who had died childless in 1967. The house, originally built about 1620, was attributed to Inigo Jones. It was acquired about a century later by the first Earl Stanhope and extensively refurbished. The resident, who has to be appointed by the Prime Minister, may be either a member of the Cabinet or a lineal descendant of King George VI. If none of those is appointed and the house stands vacant for six years, then it has to be offered successively to the Canadian high commissioner and the US ambassador. If both spurn the offer (they are unlikely ever to have the chance!), then it ends up under the National Trust. From 1974 to 1980 the Prince of Wales was the official resident. When he gave it up (he had found it neither suitable nor conveniently located) it was assigned to successive Foreign Secretaries, Peter Carrington, Francis Pym – and finally me. Dorneywood, near Burnham in Buckinghamshire, the other available 'entrusted' house, which had previously been regarded as the Foreign Secretary's official country residence, had been assigned by Margaret in 1979 to Willie Whitelaw.

From our point of view, nowhere could have been more convenient than Chevening, just four miles over the border from my own East Surrey constituency – and available shortly before the expiry of the lease on Henhaw, which had housed us comfortably in the constituency for almost a decade. The park surrounding Chevening – part of the 3500-acre estate whose income was intended to prevent the house becoming a charge on public funds – made it an idyllic setting for the reception of the many Foreign Ministers (and even more ambassadors) whom we entertained there.

It was for us and our family an enchanting second home. Gradually it came once again to exude a lived-in atmosphere, after many decades without children. I have subsequently been teased, I know, for having played too much the part of the country squire, who revelled in showing off this borrowed home. But, after we had been made so welcome there by both village and staff, it would have been difficult as well as churlish to avoid identifying ourselves with such a magically historic place.

One other discovery of 1983 was the villa at Montauroux, in the hills behind Grasse, which was kindly lent to us by my old friend and business colleague Bernard Audley (then still chairman of AGB Research). The sheltered terrace and pool, with breathtaking views of Callian and the Var mountains beyond, made a marvellous retreat for several weeks each summer during my time as Foreign Secretary. Workaholic as we may have been for much of the year, Elspeth and I valued enormously this annual chance to unwind completely.

The Agenda after KAL 007

The autumn of 1983 certainly started with a storm – a storm which was to bring East–West relations crashing to the top of the agenda. On 6 and 7 September all thirty-five European and North Atlantic Foreign Ministers were due in Madrid to attend the ministerial session of the CSCE (Conference on Security and Co-operation in Europe). The two following days, 8 and 9 September, had been set aside for our Chequers seminar with Margaret.

A few days before we all arrived in Madrid, the world was shocked by the news that a Korean civil airliner with 269 people aboard, KAL 007, had been shot down without warning into the Sea of Japan by a Soviet fighter aircraft. Intercepted communications between the Soviet aircrew and ground command made very clear that this was deliberate, and in compliance with the Soviet rules of engagement. But for days the Russian authorities continued to equivocate and evade responsibility. There was indeed no escape for them from the charge of brutal disrespect for human life.

With less than impressive speed or unanimity (and under pressure from the pilots' unions), the international community finally agreed on a two-week moratorium on flights to and from the Soviet Union. This was the background for my first meeting, at Madrid's Palacio de Congresos, with Russia's veteran Foreign Minister Andrei Gromyko. By the time we actually met, we had all been shocked by the brutal candour of Gromyko's speech to the Conference, just a few hours before: 'Since the trespasser did not obey the order to proceed to a Soviet airfield, an air defence interceptor carried out the order of the command post to stop the flight . . . in full conformity with the law on the USSR state border.' Small wonder, in these circumstances, that my first encounter with this man overshadowed, for me at least, the rest of my Madrid business.

Madrid gave a chance only for first impressions – formed in the least auspicious context. Even the physical circumstances of the meeting in retrospect seem bleak and cold, almost as though we were meeting in a prison cell. His aides, silently severe, did nothing to offset the blankness of his own expression, his speech laden with empty *Pravda* phrases. Our exchanges were brusque and bad-tempered. The latest Soviet statement about KAL 007, I said, was amazing and appalling in both tone and substance. 'How many more adjectives am I going to have to listen to?' interrupted Gromyko. The world, I continued, will look to the Soviets for compensation and for action to ensure that such a thing could never happen again. I've no intention, responded Gromyko, of going on to the defensive. No one is allowed to treat Soviet airspace 'as though it was his own kitchen garden'. He added, 'The American military aircraft was engaged on an espionage mission.' 'My legal experience', I retorted, 'has accustomed me to assessing evidence. Your assertion of "espionage" has no evidence to support it. To say "American" and not Korean simply ignores the facts and to say "not civilian" when 269 lives have been lost simply defies reality.'

Gromyko sought to close by switching subjects to the British and French deterrents. 'Our position on that', I replied, 'has been carefully thought through and is perfectly well known to you.' We were just able to mouth the civilities about the prospect of a further meeting in New York. But I could see why twenty-seven years of service in causes like this had given him such an unresponsive exterior. It was not an auspicious beginning to my long-haul plan for an opening to the East.

It provided a stark background for the opening, on the following morning (Thursday, 8 September), of our Chequers seminar. Michael Heseltine, lively and confident in his job after six months as Defence Secretary, and the Chief of the Defence Staff, Edwin Bramall, were there as well as Malcolm Rifkind, the Minister of State with responsibility for Eastern Europe, and Anthony Parsons, still Margaret's special adviser on foreign policy. The secretary to the Cabinet, Robert Armstrong, and Number 10 private secretaries Robin Butler and John Coles completed the in-house team. The first day was devoted to East–West relations and the first half of that day to discussion with experts on the Soviet Union: both Margaret and I had been keen on their participation. Surrounded as we were by so great a 'cloud of witnesses', she was unusually restrained and the experts were allowed to speak pretty fully to their briefs.

I had tried to set the agenda for this part of our work in a minute to the Prime Minister which I had finalized only on the eve of my departure for Madrid and just four days after KAL 007 had been shot out of the sky. In this I explained to Margaret that her own unique relationship with President Reagan and her standing in Europe and elsewhere could 'give Britain a voice in the alliance which it badly needs at a time when the Soviet campaign against INF* deployment is obviously entering its peak period'. I concluded by stressing that

> If anyone at our meeting were to argue that the shooting down of the Korean airliner makes dialogue with the Russians impossible, or shows that it is useless, I should myself wish to maintain the exact opposite, namely that this incident proves how dangerous is the state of affairs where the two superpowers talk to each other more across the floor of the United Nations than they do on the hot line.

The unpromising, impenetrable quality of Gromyko's reaction in Madrid served only to reinforce my belief that we needed desperately to search for and find other fresh ways of getting through to the Soviet leadership.

The central question before us was whether or not British policy should endorse George Shultz's aim, namely 'the gradual evolution of the Soviet system towards a more pluralistic political and economic system'. In my minute I had posed the question even more sharply. Years later, it was overtaken by events. 'What', I asked, 'in our heart of hearts do we really *want* to happen? Steady advance and Westernization or stagnation and collapse (or, more likely, reaction)?'

When we got down to discussing these specific policy questions after lunch, when the academics had departed, proceedings were less orderly. As so often with Margaret in the chair, we found ourselves being distracted from questions of long-term strategy. I was better qualified by experience than those who knew her less well to recognize this as an aspect of the natural caution with which Margaret approached any new, perhaps questionable, proposition.

Gradually our views crystallized. Notably, but not surprisingly, we failed to foresee the pace of change that was to follow in the Soviet Union and Eastern Europe. But we concluded that we should treat each country individually, encourage greater diversity, recognizing that the possibilities were severely limited. We had to take care not to induce repressive counter-action by the Soviet Union. 'One notable success', commented one official, 'had been to convince the PM that there was very little scope for destabilizing the Soviet Union or Eastern Europe.'

* Intermediate-range Nuclear Forces.

This important advance in understanding was probably to prove crucial to the successful outcome of Margaret's first encounter, still more than twelve months ahead, with Mikhail Gorbachev. The force with which Margaret later expounded this and argued the case for dialogue with Moscow was no less crucial in turning President Reagan away from the 'evil empire' rhetoric and encouraging him towards a similar relationship with Gorbachev. I sometimes think this may be seen by historians as her greatest achievement in foreign affairs. Our September seminar at Chequers was, therefore, more important than we knew.

So far as immediate action was concerned, we got the essential go-ahead for which I was looking, even if with some reluctance. Eventually Margaret agreed that, once the KAL crisis had died down, there should be an improvement in links 'as long as they did not involve herself and she had the right to veto the talks if they went too far'. That cautious conclusion was certainly an accurate reflection of the tone of the meeting. But the substance of what was recorded in the small print went more than a shade further. The UK was to build up contacts slowly, over the next few years (remember Afghanistan and KAL 007). At my next meeting with Gromyko I should invite him to visit the UK. The Prime Minister might possibly meet Andropov during the next two or three years, though not in the Soviet Union. A visit by her to Hungary was at least a thinkable idea. We should attempt to get more information into the Soviet Empire, particularly through the BBC. Trade contacts could be expanded, though never on disadvantageous terms. And, most significantly of all as it turned out, it might be possible to arrange for potential successors to Andropov to visit London. Recommendations, please, from the Foreign Office.

Our second day at Chequers was more wide-ranging and without benefit of experts apart, of course, from the Chief of Defence Staff. Malcolm Rifkind's place was taken by Janet Young, my deputy, and Richard Luce, with responsibility for the Middle and Far East. Arms-control questions, on which both Michael Heseltine and I had submitted minutes, took up most of our time, with the Prime Minister showing signs, as someone said, that she thought that Michael and I were 'ganging up on her to make concessions'. And so, in a sense, we were – with a degree of success that was later to prove its value to Margaret herself. For she accepted, at least up to a point, our case that ministerial contact with the Russians on these issues could be of practical import-ance. It was agreed too that she should take advantage of her next visit to Washington to encourage Reagan to inject a new impetus into the

US–Soviet START (Strategic Arms Reduction Talks), which had begun in 1981.

I attached importance as well to our consideration of a long list of ex-imperial 'problems left over by history'. I had considered all these with colleagues and experts in the Foreign Office, on the basis of our old *Crossbow* principle of a 'realistic appraisal of Britain's interests'. So I was especially pleased that our Chequers discussions endorsed my proposed approach virtually without comment. 'We must', I said, 'punctiliously discharge our obligations in respect of the Falklands and Cyprus' in particular 'to ensure, so far as we can, that they do not affect our wider interests – Latin America, US, NATO etc.' Beyond that over the next five years, I suggested, 'we should make a real effort to bring about solutions or at least to create the framework for solutions in those cases where this appears a real possibility'.

I cited Hong Kong as 'the chief and overwhelmingly the most important example' but listed as other possibles Belize, Bermuda, Brunei and Namibia – this last 'only in concert with our closest allies'. Gibraltar, I suggested (accurately enough), 'we probably cannot solve but we must use the EC accession negotiations as a vehicle to find a new plateau of stability in our relations with Spain, in which Gibraltar does not overshadow everything else as it does now'. Six years later we had made pretty good progress with most of this shopping list.

The same could not be said, alas, of the topic which I tried to place first on our Chequers agenda, the need to consider 'the allocation of resources to external policy, including aid and information as well as defence'. This raised two distinct questions: could the UK keep up, as we had already for several years, the same level of effort overseas, albeit from a declining resource basis? Or was there some function we could discard? Was the total being spent in defence of Britain's external interests being distributed in the correct way?

I was not looking for precise answers from the Chequers meeting but rather for the start of a process that could deliver those answers. Ideally, I said, we needed a medium-term framework that will maintain our reputation as a reliable ally, aid donor and influential member of the main international economic organizations. So should we not now take a forward look at our expenditure on all our external interests, and then decide, from a fresh base, the optimum allocation of resources between the different instruments of policy: defence, aid, diplomacy and the overseas culture and information effort? Why, for instance, did soldiers who were engaged not on conventional duty, say in the British Army of the Rhine or in Belize, but as part of the UN force in Cyprus or seconded to provide military training in Zimbabwe have to be paid for from the diplomatic and not the defence vote? If the defence forces were not provided for such diverse duties, what were they for? I did not, of course, put the arguments in quite such provocative terms. Margaret did not respond warmly to this thinking. She was suspicious, Antony Acland thought, that I was wanting to get my hands on at least a part of the MOD budget. To some extent, I was. But we did succeed in securing the establishment of a joint MOD–FCO working party to consider the allocation of resources for overseas activities. But I have to say that no significant analysis or intellectual novelty ever emerged from this quarter. Whether from the Treasury or from the Foreign Office, it always seemed impossible to open up to objective analysis the thought processes of the Ministry of Defence.

Budapest, New York, Blackpool

I was soon to have the chance of putting some of our thinking into practice. For on Tuesday, 13 September we were due to arrive in Budapest for a two-day official visit. Francis Pym, whose thinking on this topic had been on the same lines as my own, had accepted this invitation before his departure from the Foreign Office. Hungary was starting to develop a more market-based approach to economic policy and, although still strictly conformist to Warsaw Pact foreign policies, was a natural first choice. Our host for the visit was the long-serving (but fluent and adaptable) Foreign Minister Peter Varkonyi: he had been for many years private secretary and interpreter to Hungary's Communist Party General Secretary, János Kádár. Dubbed the Butcher of Budapest after the suppression of the 1956 Rising, Kádár had by now gained a modicum of popular respect. He had enabled his people to recover freedoms that were still denied, for example, to Russians, let alone Rumanians. Kádár himself, whom I met in the party head-quarters, was gnarled and bluff and forthcoming, pleased to receive a visitor from the West. He clearly realized the extent to which his less doctrinaire socialism was, and was seen to be, of advantage to his people, and he was determined to develop it. Acceptance of the Soviet military presence was regarded as a price worth paying for a degree of domestic independence. He saw Western interest as some reassurance of that.

The whole visit was a gentle introduction to the absurdities of Communist authoritarianism: the constant awareness of bugged bedrooms; the red-carpeted, flunkey-laden splendour of the magnificent parliament building, which contained no parliament; the stereotyped presentation of Sovbloc policy. But those absurdities stood alongside the reality of incipient markets and some authentic manufacturing quality. Elspeth was delighted to make her first acquaintance with Herend pottery, and with Madame Maria Hari's conductive education. And I was struck by my lunchtime encounter with a professor of economics from Karl Marx University: I realized that I might be improperly dressed for the occasion – and apologized for the fact that I was wearing my Adam Smith tie. 'No need to worry about that,' came the reply. 'If I'd known you were going to wear your Adam Smith tie, then I should have been wearing my Adam Smith sweatshirt.' Clearly we were starting to win the intellectual argument!

And so on to my first full autumn programme as Foreign Secretary, which started with three separate opportunities to begin developing our latest East–West thinking. The first was at the UN General Assembly in New York, a hectic week in what I used to describe as a diplomatic supermarket. One-on-one meetings, normally in my hotel suite, sometimes in theirs, with at least two dozen other Foreign Ministers or heads of government provided opportunities that could not easily be achieved on either party's home ground: Chile, Vietnam, Iran, Iraq, Rumania were some of the most obvious examples. In the event, my projected meeting with Gromyko in New York did not take place. The Governors of New York and New Jersey decided to deny landing rights to his aircraft. This gave Gromyko the excuse himself to reject George Shultz's offer of alternative landing rights at a suitable military airport. So the Soviet Foreign Minister, who had been uncomfortably isolated in Madrid, was able to escape from the risks of similar pariah-treatment at the United Nations.

As Foreign Minister of one of the five permanent members of the UN Security Council, I was granted the privilege of an early, and reasonably prominent, slot for my annual address to the Assembly. And I was, of course, expected to be present for the same performances by the other permanent members. It was customary for the US President to speak for his country, as host nation. The other three permanent members were represented by their Foreign Ministers: Gromyko, Claude Cheysson (France) and Wu Xueqian (China). It is difficult to imagine a less welcoming or stirring place in which to speak than the General

Assembly Hall. With 1400 seats, hugely spaced out by desks and wide aisles, it never looks, still less feels, full. For Britain's Foreign Secretary it was generally – and flatteringly – about three-quarters full; but it seemed as empty as Lord's cricket ground on the last day of a bound-to-be drawn county game.

My first speech to the General Assembly was an opportunity to spell out our developing thoughts on the position of Britain's nuclear arsenal in the arms-control debate. The Soviet Union was arguing that the British and French strategic systems should be included – unlike the strategic systems of Russia or the United States – within the scope of the INF negotiations. 'There can be no reason', I said, 'in equity or logic for such a conclusion.' But, I stressed, if Soviet and US strategic arsenals were to be very substantially reduced, and if no significant changes had occurred in Soviet defensive capabilities, Britain would want to consider how best she could contribute to arms control in the light of the reduced threat. 'The West means business over disarmament,' I concluded.

Margaret reinforced this message in Washington on the following day, 27 September. I flew up there to join her for a lunch meeting at the White House. Later in the day, at the Winston Churchill Foundation Award Dinner, she proclaimed with new clarity the need for dialogue. 'We live on the same planet and we have to go on sharing it,' she said, 'We stand ready therefore – if and when the circumstances are right – to talk to the Soviet leadership.'

Two weeks later, at the Conservative Party Conference at Blackpool, Michael Heseltine joined Margaret and me in spelling out in our separate speeches the same central message – firm but forthcoming. 'We must', I said, 'redouble our determination to negotiate and our determination to maintain the strength without which we cannot hope to negotiate successfully.' The next day, I had the pleasure of playing my part as that year's president of the National Union of Conservative and Unionist Associations (and so of the conference). This was a gratifying honour, thirty-three years on from my first attendance at a Blackpool party conference. One practical duty went with the job: I had to take the chair for the closing Friday sessions, including that in which Margaret gave her closing address.

From that occasion I remember particularly the sincerity with which Margaret underlined her commitment to the search for progress on arms control. 'As you personally know, Mr President,' she said, turning to me, the West has made proposal after proposal for arms reduction, and the day the leaders of the Soviet Union genuinely decide that they want, through arms-control agreements, to make this a safer world, they will be pushing at an open door. Until then, our threefold policy will be the same – realistically to assess the potential aggressor, firmly to maintain our capacity to defend and deter and always to stand ready to talk.

Then, as though she felt her tone might be too belligerent, she ad-libbed the next three sentences: 'As I am sure you will understand, there is no one more anxious for genuine disarmament than the person who bears the ultimate responsibility for the nuclear deterrent in our own country. I wanted to say that to you. You will understand how important it is that we try to make those arms-reduction talks succeed.'

Sitting right next to her, and able to follow her text word for word, I was struck by the real spontaneity of this addition and felt reassured about the rightness of our position. We were within a few weeks of the arrival in Britain and West Germany of the first of the Cruise and Pershing II missiles. The anti-nuclear propaganda campaign was still being waged, although it had made little impression on the outcome of the recent election. And our son Alec was still at the heart of it. I never doubted the sincerity of his commitment to a most understandable cause. So it was comforting indeed to have this first-hand insight into the strength of Margaret's faith in our own equally sincere approach to this horror of horrors.

It was something of an anticlimax to return to the routine of my London diary: an almost uninterrupted sequence of distinguished visitors to London. One of the most surprising guests of all, in retrospect, was Saddam Hussein's Deputy Prime Minister, Taha Ramadhan: his programme included, in addition to a full round of talks and a lunch at Number 10, a dinner at Carlton Gardens with the Deputy Prime Minister, Willie Whitelaw, George Younger and, of course, myself. We had all been warned that Ramadhan had a particularly unattractive reputation as Hussein's chief thug, and Willie confessed that he had found dinner-table conversation a disagreeable diversion. All three ministers assembled on the Carlton Gardens doorstep to wave farewell as the Iraqi tail-light disappeared into the night. As we did so I realized that Ramadhan had enjoyed the privilege of being entertained by Margaret Thatcher's three Wykehamist ministers. None of us had a satisfactory answer when I posed the question: 'What on earth would William of Wykeham ['manners makyth man'] have thought of such a villain being so fêted by three representatives of the Wykehamist tradition?' But in those days Iraq was still a potentially valuable export market.

One much more agreeable duty came my way that autumn. This was the ceremony conferring an honorary KBE on the distinguished Hungarian conductor Antal Dorati. The Queen herself does not normally play this role in respect of foreign nationals. Non-Britons who receive an honorary knighthood are normally decorated by the Foreign Secretary at a special ceremony in the Secretary of State's splendid office. These were occasions, on the frontier between politics and the real world, which I enjoyed greatly when they came my way: Antal Dorati was followed by Mstislav Rostropovitch. I shall never forget my astonishment when I became the recipient of one of his huge and famous hugs.

There was an exception to this routine in the case of Cap Weinberger. He received his KBE from the Queen personally because of her recognition of the quite exceptional services he had rendered, as United States Secretary for Defense, to promote the safety of British soldiers, sailors and airmen during the Falklands conflict. I was invited to accompany the Weinbergers on this unique occasion, which took place in the Queen's private sitting-room at Buckingham Palace. Jane Weinberger, restricted to a wheelchair, was especially appreciative of the intimacy of the ceremony. I felt deeply moved and very privileged to have been present. It is easy to imagine my sense of relief when four years later President Bush felt able to quash the prosecution which was so unjustly brought against Cap Weinberger for his alleged role over arms to Iran. He was a good friend of Britain, and an honourable man.

We moved towards the end of 1983 with a reasonably clear idea of our immediate agenda. With my own team I was able to plan more broadly for the years ahead, in a two-day meeting of ministers and officials at Chevening on 12 and 13 December. One practical issue that caused us a good deal of anxiety was a fresh and growing concern over the presentation of foreign policy. 'The FCO', we noted, 'did not enjoy a high reputation with press or Parliament', and tackling this should be one of our highest priorities. It was for this purpose that I set up a special Parliamentary Relations Unit, with a well-thought-through programme of contacts, designed as much to inform and persuade Foreign Office officials about the importance of Parliament as the other way around. The need for this change was identified by John Houston, my special adviser throughout my first four years at the Foreign Office.

We were delighted, of course, by the extent to which 'the policy evolved at 1 Carlton Gardens on 1 July had gained ground'. We had certainly succeeded in preparing a useful programme of work that was destined to keep me and my department more than fully engaged for the next six years.

CHAPTER TWENTY-TWO

HUMILIATION IN GRENADA

====

Caribbean Storm Warning

Planning was the easy part. It was events that kept on getting in the way. In September 1983 it had been KAL 007, the Korean airliner downed in the Sea of Japan. One month later saw two new dramas. Both came out of the clear blue sky, which Elspeth and I were sharing with other EC Foreign Ministers at the informal weekend meeting of the Greek Presidency, at Vouliagmeni, the wind-swept resort on Cape Sunium, just south of Athens.

The first was no more than a rumble that had started a few days before we left London in the RAF HS-125 that was taking us to Athens on Friday evening, 21 October 1983. It came from a place called Grenada, a Caribbean island-state of which before that time I had been no more than vaguely informed. A former British colony with a population of about 100,000, Grenada had achieved (or been thrust into) independence in 1974. Five years later the first (populist) Prime Minister, Sir Eric Gairy, had been overthrown by a bloodless coup in favour of the New Jewel Movement, led by a Marxist named Maurice Bishop. Over the following four years Bishop's People's Revolutionary Government developed on traditional Bolshevik lines, forging ever closer ties with Moscow and Cuba. This gave rise to increasing concern in many of the small Caribbean neighbour states – and, of course, in the United States. On 23 March 1983 President Reagan himself highlighted American concern at the construction in Grenada of a Cuban-built military airfield, in a speech mainly noted for his announcement of the Strategic Defence Initiative.* It was inevitable that America, Cuba-conscious as ever, should be more concerned with events in her own backyard than we in Britain. It was after all only with difficulty that we

---

* See Chapter 26 below.

had learned to refrain from post-imperial intervention in the affairs of several newborn Commonwealth states. By now we had come to regard their chequered post-independence history – from Guyana to Uganda, from Botswana to the Seychelles – as no longer directly our business. But we remained, of course, concerned. This was especially true of Grenada when, between 13 and 19 October 1983, Prime Minister Bishop and three of his fellow ministers and other supporters were executed – and replaced by a Revolutionary Military Council led by Deputy Prime Minister Bernard Coard and Army chief General Hudson Austin.

In the reaction to this violent turn of events, there developed an increasingly stark difference between our government and that of the United States. This was also to be the cause of sharp public disagreement between the United States and most European governments, and the subject of intense and emotional debate at the Commonwealth heads of government meeting in Delhi a month later on 23–26 November. Most immediately, it was to precipitate intense embarrassment for Margaret Thatcher – and above all for her (still quite innocent) Foreign Secretary. The details were later explored with some skill by the House of Commons Select Committee on Foreign Affairs. The American point of view is fully described in George Shultz's testament to his years at the State Department.[1] I shall offer here only a more personal perspective, which reveals a good deal about the much discussed special relationship.

My first perspective was shaped solely by the copy telegrams which were delivered from our Athens embassy to our conference hotel. The scene was being more closely monitored back in London, where Richard Luce was duty minister and in regular contact with the Number 10 secretariat at Chequers. During that period there was no firm proposal for action of any kind from any transatlantic source. I received precautionary advice that the West Indian guardship HMS *Antrim* was in the region, and on the Saturday evening, 22 October, I confirmed instructions (suggested by Richard Luce) that she should be diverted from Colombia to Grenada and prepared, if necessary, to evacuate the small British community. (I remember a modest feeling of grandeur at this, my first experience of authorizing a movement by one of Her Majesty's ships.) Our staff in Washington would remain in touch with White House and State Department, who were said to be reacting 'very cautiously' to the situation.

On Sunday morning, 23 October, the second thunderbolt struck. Early-morning bulletins carried the shattering news from Beirut that the

US Marine barracks and French military accommodation had each been severely damaged by terrorist suicide bombers. Both contingents in the Lebanon Multi-National Force (MNF) had suffered heavy casualties, with some 300 dead. The British and Italian detachments had this time been spared. The emergency dominated the concluding stages of the Greek weekend conference. It was agreed that the four Foreign Ministers would meet in Paris in four days' time. And we all set off for our respective capitals.

At the end of the five-hour return flight to London, I caught up with the latest news about Grenada, where nothing had changed significantly. I confirmed that I should want a meeting early on Monday morning, 23 October, of FCO ministers and officials to ensure that we were all up to speed for the meeting that would follow at 10.00 a.m. at Number 10.

We had before us reports from three places. From Barbados, there was news of the meeting on the Saturday of the Organization of East Caribbean States (OECS) (which included Grenada). That had decided to undertake military action and to seek help from friendly governments, including our own. But the promised formal request had never reached us. Meanwhile from Trinidad came news of a meeting of the more widely based Caribbean organization CARICOM, which had concluded the day before (Sunday). There the majority decision had been in favour of sanctions rather than military action. From Grenada itself came a report from our deputy high commissioner to Barbados. He had visited the island on the same Sunday, and had found the situation tense but calm. Neither the Governor General, Sir Paul Scoon, nor the British community appeared to be in any imminent danger. The Governor had made no request for help of any kind either to the deputy high commissioner or direct by telephone to Buckingham Palace, with which he had been in touch on the same day.

More important than all this were the reports direct from Washington, since it was plain that no effective military action could take place without American participation. For that very reason, our ambassador, Sir Oliver Wright, and two senior members of his staff, Derek Thomas and Robin Renwick, had been in touch with the State Department throughout the weekend. On instructions from London they had from the outset expressed our doubts about the wisdom and propriety of military intervention. 'Perhaps uppermost in their [the embassy's] consideration', the Commons Select Committee rightly observed, 'was the likely reaction of other Commonwealth States to ... the former colonial power ... taking military action against a Commonwealth

Government of which it disapproves.'[2] On the Saturday, 22 October, our embassy had been assured by Admiral Howe, director of the State Department's political–military bureau, that the US 'intended to proceed cautiously' in response to OECS requests for help and that we 'would be consulted by the US before any further steps were taken'. This assurance was repeated on Sunday, 23 October – and inspired our settled belief that no US military intervention was then planned.

This was the position that I reported to a Number 10 meeting straight after our Foreign Office meeting. The Prime Minister and colleagues endorsed our reasoning. Oliver Wright was requested once again to make clear that we were opposed to any military action. George Shultz confirms that this advice was clearly conveyed, early on the Washington Monday morning. 'Margaret Thatcher', he notes, 'preferred economic and political pressure.'[3]

This was the background to my appearance in the Commons at 3.30 that afternoon, 24 October, to make a short statement about the position in Grenada. I was questioned for not more than fifteen minutes from two points of view. Should we not, asked Russell Johnston (Liberal), be ready to accept some responsibility, unspecified, when a dictatorial group have seized power in a small Commonwealth country? This point was only modestly persuasive, since, as I pointed out, the government that had been ousted, after four years in power, was already a Marxist soulmate of Fidel Castro's Cuban government. The other anxiety expressed, from both sides of the House, reflected 'the desirability' in the words of Eldon Griffiths (a leading Conservative Americanist), of avoiding any American intervention, which Denis Healey argued 'could only make matters worse'.

'I know of no such intention' was my first carefully worded reply. We were, I added, 'in the closest possible touch with the US and Caribbean governments' and I had 'no reason to think that American intervention is likely'. I added, 'The US Government have explained that their own naval forces in the area are in that position solely because of the requirement that may arise to rescue their own very sizeable community in Grenada.'

Overtaken by Events

Less than four hours later, just after 7 p.m. on Monday, 24 October, a tele-letter from President Reagan reached Number 10. It was the first of three such letters to arrive within less than twenty-four hours.* The President stated that he was giving serious consideration to an OECS request for military action in Grenada and that the President would 'welcome' the Prime Minister's thought and advice on this matter. The Prime Minister and I were both immediately consulted and gave our initial reactions, which naturally reflected the cautious line that Her Majesty's Government had adopted throughout. Instructions were given for a draft reply to be prepared, for consideration by the Prime Minister and myself at the end of the evening.

Meanwhile, we each had separate social engagements to fulfil, ironically both under American auspices. Margaret was dining with the then American ambassador in London, John Louis – who was not seen (by either government, it must be said) as one of the more effective of emissaries. And I was due to speak at a dinner of the American Bankers' Association, where one of the guests was an old friend, the highly professional minister and deputy head of the US embassy in London, Edward Streator. In course of my speech, I had described myself, in retrospect ironically, as 'struck by the extraordinary closeness of the relationship between our two countries'. As I left the occasion, I mentioned to Ed that I was going straight back to Number 10 to consider our reply to the President's message. It became quite clear that neither he nor Ambassador Louis had heard any more about US Government intentions than we had ourselves.

When Margaret and I came together shortly at Number 10, her private secretary John Coles handed us a second tele-letter which had arrived from the White House. The President stated, briefly enough, that he had decided to 'respond positively' to the OECS request and that US forces would therefore 'establish themselves' in Grenada. We were both dumbfounded. What on earth were we to make of a relationship, special or otherwise, in which a message requesting the benefit of our advice was so quickly succeeded by another which made it brutally clear that that advice was being treated as of no consequence whatsoever? We were joined by the Defence Secretary, Michael Heseltine. We were all of one mind.

Within an hour a letter from Margaret was on its way back to the

---

* George Shultz reports (*Turmoil and Triumph*, p. 330) that 'President Reagan despatched a message to President Mitterrand about Beirut and one to Margaret Thatcher about Grenada' during the morning of Sunday, 23 October. Certainly no such message was received in London before 7 p.m. GMT on the following day, 24 October. The delay, if such it was, is hard to understand.

President. She made four points. First, the only credible justification for intervention would be the need to protect the safety of US and British citizens. Their lives were far more likely to be endangered by military action than the reverse. (This was our view of the American plea that their action was driven by concern for the safety of 1000 students.) Secondly, we had particular and express reason to be fearful for the life of the Governor General in such circumstances. Thirdly, we had received no formal request for help from the OECS, and most members of the CARICOM (which included the OECS) had declared themselves against the use of force. Fourthly, most important of all in the context of East–West relations and of the current debate about the siting of Cruise missiles in Britain, the action would be criticized as an unjustified intervention by a Western country in the internal affairs of a small independent nation.

Twenty minutes later Margaret was on to the President direct on the hot line (the secure telephone link between Number 10 and the White House). The call reached Reagan at the very moment when he was briefing congressional leaders Tip O'Neill and Howard Baker about his plans. Slightly to my surprise, Margaret was nervous of saying too much on the telephone, for fear the call was being intercepted (this particular speech channel was one of the most secure in the world). However, the essence of her message was clear enough. 'I have replied to your letters, Ron,' she said. 'You have asked for my advice and I want you to consider the points I have made very carefully indeed.' He undertook to do so but added, ominously enough, 'Margaret, I must tell you that we are already at zero.'

And so indeed it proved – well beyond zero in fact. For although the President's 'final' order to proceed was not given until 11 p.m. GMT on Monday evening, 24 October, the key decision had been taken more than two and a half days before. In the words of George Shultz, 'in the early morning of Saturday, October 22, President Reagan, with [National Security Advisor] Robert McFarlane and me at his side supporting him fully, made the decision to go ahead with a rescue operation, to be launched on Monday night or Tuesday'.[4]

Small wonder then that Margaret Thatcher's mood that Monday night – and mine and Michael's – was, in the words of her message to Reagan, 'deeply disturbed'. George Shultz described her as 'furious' and the British generally 'in a terrific uproar'. On Tuesday, 25 October, both the Prime Minister and I had to face the House of Commons, she for her regular question time and I for a second statement on events in

Grenada. Margaret was up for questions again on Thursday, 27 October. And on the intervening Wednesday, 26 October, there was a full-dress emergency debate, in which I made both opening and closing speeches for the government.

I cannot pretend that any of these were happy or distinguished occasions. For Margaret and I were both confronted with an insoluble dilemma. The United States had followed a course of action which we had both advised against. In my case I had gone further – so far indeed as to suggest, or at least imply, that the Americans were unlikely to act in that way. It was therefore difficult for us now to commend their action, as some Conservatives would have wished. Julian Amery, for example, the robust, veteran Tory ex-Minister, thought that Britain should herself have conducted, or at least participated in, the invasion of Grenada. Yet it was almost equally impossible for us to condemn the United States. For that would have done nothing for the future of Anglo-American relations, already badly enough damaged – just for the sake of disagreement over a small island in the Caribbean.

The truth is that the government had been humiliated by having its views so plainly disregarded in Washington. And the occasion provided a field-day in which Denis Healey was able, at his destructive best, completely to overshadow the arrival of Neil Kinnock as Labour's new party Leader. Our own approach throughout the week had to be confined very largely to damage limitation. Characteristically, Margaret and I set about that task in different style.

I found myself repeatedly asserting that this was a topic on which there was, as events had shown, room for more than one view – with the US and some of the Caribbean states on one side and the UK, the rest of the Caribbean plus most of Europe and the Commonwealth on the other. This did nothing to head off the taunt from the Liberal Party Leader David Steel that it was not possible for the British Foreign Secretary to hold more than one of these views at the same time – yet I had failed to choose either. In the inevitable Security Council debate, our excellent ambassador Sir John Thomson managed to distance himself amost equally from the American intervention and from the case of those who criticized it: he concluded, on instructions, in favour of a careful abstention.

Margaret likewise tried to maintain the same kind of 'statesmanlike ambiguity' – but characteristically with more gusto on all sides of the argument. She robustly defended 'everything the Foreign Secretary said yesterday, particularly his view that there are larger issues at stake between the United States and the United Kingdom'. She commended earlier American intervention of the same kind, which eight years before had secured the restoration of democracy in the Dominican Republic. But by the end of the week, in a BBC World Service broadcast, Margaret was asserting the other point of view: 'we in . . . the Western democracies use our force to defend our way of life. We do not use it to walk into independent sovereign territories. . . . If you're going to pronounce a new law that wherever Communism reigns against the will of the people, even though it happened internally, there the USA shall enter, then we are going to have really terrible wars in the world.'

In the same context I was offering similar views. Taking part in the Brian Walden *Weekend World* programme on Sunday, 30 October, I had set out our view that 'the presence of Cubans or Russians in Grenada did not provide any justification for the American invasion of the island. And on *Panorama* on the following day, I amplified that criticism. All this belated candour earned me a commendatory postcard from son Alec for my 'robust defence of key principles of international law. No doubt', he added wryly, 'you will be severely mauled in the Commons for coming off the fence.'

Anglo-American Discord

George Shultz – the President too, no doubt – was far from pleased by all this. He had been annoyed by Margaret's phone call on the Monday night, 25 October. 'We had turned ourselves into pretzels for Mrs Thatcher over the Falklands crisis,' he commented at the time. In his book, he expresses puzzlement that the British, Margaret in particular, had reacted 'so negatively' and without 'any particular concern for the "special relationship" between Britain and America'.[5] It is a fair question, both ways: how did we come so plainly to misread the likely course of events? And how did the Americans come to behave towards us as they did? These questions were among those later tackled by the Commons Foreign Affairs Committee.

The answer to the first question emerges, in retrospect, quite clearly. 'The British Government', says the Select Committee, 'appears to have remained in the dark both about American intentions and the extent of the United States and Caribbean planning for a military invasion until the early evening of Monday 24 October.' HMG, they went on, 'not being privy to the extent of the consultation between the US and the OECS' and 'being deprived of adequate information through the usual State Department channels . . . [despite] having been assured of consultation by Washington', gave undue weight to 'misleading signals' from the deputy high commissioner's reasonably reassuring interview on the same day with the Governor General, Sir Paul Scoon. We were wrong, in other words, because we were misled; and also, the Select Committee suggest, because we reacted too passively to events and signals emerging from the Caribbean itself – being 'insufficiently attuned to the political feelings' of many of their leaders. We should have taken 'positive steps to make [our] opposition clear in Bridgetown and in Port of Spain'. Our failure to do this represented, in the view of the Committee, 'a somewhat lethargic approach' because we were 'basing [our] reaction to events entirely on advice from Washington, which in the event proved to be unreliable'.[6] Not so much 'lethargy' as misplaced trust, I fear.

There we have the really uncomfortable truth. The 'special' relationship, which George Shultz thinks we had insufficiently respected, had been in practice set to one side by the US administration itself. As the Select Committee concluded, 'those wishing to pursue' the idea of military intervention in Grenada 'may well have predicted Britain's likely reaction and adjusted the information given to the British Government accordingly. *We have reason to believe that this was the case*' (my emphasis).[7] What I think we had all failed to appreciate was the extent to which George Shultz and his State Department were really the hawks, and the Pentagon and Cap Weinberger the doves, in this argument. For it is now clear, from Shultz's own book, that as early as 4.30 a.m. (Washington time) on Saturday, 22 October, he was giving guidance to State Department officials that: 'We had to move quickly before this window of opportunity closed. We couldn't let the Pentagon drag out our preparations until it was too late, which I feared they might do.'[8] Again at 4 p.m. (Washington time) on Sunday, 23 October, 'Cap again made clear his preference for a delay. . . . The debate was intense. President Reagan held firm.'[9] It is small wonder that George Shultz congratulates himself and his staff that by the Monday evening, 24 October, they had in place an impressively complete 'ten-point checklist of plans and actions ready to go'.[10]

Most interesting are the arrangements that were planned for the treatment of the Governor General. The Select Committee refer to HMG's clearly established:

ignorance of the apparent request by the Governor General for assistance. . . . Both the timing and nature of this request, which is said by the
US Government to have been a critical factor in providing a legal
justification for their decision, remain shrouded in some mystery, and it is
evidently the intention of the parties directly involved that the mystery
shall not be dispelled.[11]

The last of George's ten points may dispel a little of this mystery. For it
describes the inclusion in the American invading party of a young
diplomat, Larry Rossen, with long experience of Grenada, well known
to the Governor General and so recognizable in the middle of the night
as a 'friendly face'. 'It was important', says Shultz, 'to bring the Governor
General, whom we were assured had been incommunicado, up to speed
on the combined Eastern Caribbean US operation and assist him while
he took over. *His first public statement would be critical*' (my emphasis
again).[12]

So the operation went ahead, as had clearly been planned. And by
midday (Washington time) George Shultz was on the phone to me. His
own account of the call is interesting: Geoffrey Howe 'was my friend
and I felt terrible about his embarrassment in the House of Commons'.
He describes himself as saying, 'There was no intent to mislead you, I'm
sorry if it appeared that way. It was only early on Saturday morning that
we got the plea from OECS to intervene.'[13] But there was no explanation
of the lack of consultation in the intervening two and a half days. Nor
was there when he called again the following day (Wednesday, 26
October) to report (as we already knew) that the Governor General was
safe. I told him then that although we did not like the way the
intervention had been handled, now that it had happened, we wanted it
to succeed. Interestingly, I did not find myself holding any of this
against George Shultz into the longer future. At the time I was angry,
of course. But I could see why, in his judgment of America's interests,
he acted as he did. British *amour propre* was only an incidental victim of
his determination to outwit the Pentagon. He had taught me an
important lesson in transatlantic *Realpolitik* – and he had had the decency
to apologize for doing so.

Fall Out

In the event, the operation went relatively smoothly. By the end of the week, Grenada had been effectively taken over by the combined intervention force – at a cost, according to the United States sources, of no less than 600 casualties, including eighty-seven deaths: 134 of these were American, including eighteen fatalities. Within three weeks, the island had been cleared of some 900 Cubans, Russians, Libyans and others and the Governor General had started swearing in the Advisory Council which was to rule the island until fresh elections could be held early in 1984.

But at the end of the day, as at the beginning, the transatlantic differences were ubridgeable. The British view, held equally strongly by Margaret Thatcher, me, Denis Healey and David Steel, was flatly and instinctively opposed to the idea that Britain, the former colonial power, should appear to threaten the independence of another Commonwealth nation by taking military action against a government of which it disapproved. We could not regard it as any more appropriate for the United States to act in that way, least of all at a time when world opinion was ranged against the Soviet Union for having attempted just that in Afghanistan. What we were not to know was the extent to which the American decision was being seen, indeed treated, as part of a long-running debate between Shultz and Weinberger on 'the question of whether and when force was required and justified'[14] – a debate which was to continue long after the Grenada intervention.

It was especially regrettable in Britain's eyes that the United States should have acted as it did without any effective consultation with ourselves, notwithstanding Grenada's membership of the Commonwealth club of nations, which owed allegiance to Her Majesty the Queen. There was a special piquancy about this failure at a time when British opinion was concerned with a comparable, if more specific, duty to consult over the use of American nuclear weapons, Cruise missiles, which were just about to be deployed on British soil.

In truth, it was more disturbing even than that. For what had taken place went beyond lack of consultation and involved apparently conscious concealment of American intentions. It is scarcely credible, on reflection, that this was because the United States was reluctant to confide her plans to the well-tried channels of communication with HMG. Much more probably it was fear, particularly on the part of the

State Department and the White House, lest they stir up in Margaret Thatcher a potential ally – even if for different reasons – for Cap Weinberger and his less 'positive', more cautious approach. If Margaret had had time to weigh in directly with the President, then it is easy to see how Shultz's 'window of opportunity' might have swung shut. And that would have frustrated his hope, fulfilled as he believed, that 'Grenada, like the Falklands', would be 'a shot heard round the world by usurpers and despots of every ideology'.[15]

So George might even have been pleased to know that only a few weeks later a normally cool-headed Foreign Office planner was noting the fear that the US rather than the Soviet Union was likely to risk the use or threat of force elsewhere. The Reagan administration, he wrote, 'believes that it worked in Grenada – and it did. The risk is the thought that it can also be applied successfully in other Third World situations.' Reaction elsewhere was varied. Commonwealth countries in particular illustrated the worldwide cleavage of opinion. This was fully aired at the November heads of government meeting (CHOGM) in New Delhi under the chairmanship of Mrs Gandhi. All the Caribbean heads of government reiterated their original diversity of opinions. Eugenia Charles (Dominica) continued to champion the action with all the splendid verve that had taken Washington by storm. Most moving, however, was the nostalgia of John Compton (St Lucia). 'Grenada', he said, 'needed policemen not soldiers.' He regretted the passing of an era in which 'order could be maintained by one policeman outside Government House', and when 'you knew that a bang in the middle of the night was not a shot but a car backfiring'. The Africans too were divided in an interesting fashion. 'Zambia', said Kenneth Kaunda, 'had bought Communist arms. South Africa would welcome a pretext to invade.' His Caribbean colleagues, together with the US, had 'created a real nightmare' for him and his country. Julius Nyerere took the opposite view – at first sight surprisingly until he reminded us that Tanzania had herself supported an invasion of neighbouring Uganda to secure the removal of the Obote regime. CHOGM was probably the only international gathering that could have discussed the issue in such a mature and relaxed fashion, with the conclusion that 'emphasis now should be on reconstruction, not recrimination'.

Domestic commentators sought often to draw less useful conclusions. Paul Johnson in the *Mail on Sunday*, with his customary delicate touch, expressed the hope that 'the episode will serve some purpose if it finally goads Mrs Thatcher into an assault on Foreign Office sloth and imbecility'. So far from that, the Prime Minister conveyed a message to my Office to the effect that she was 'satisfied that from Friday night on she was kept well in touch all weekend' and that 'she thinks the FCO has done very well in this exercise. Ingham has been instructed to pour cold water.'

More straightforwardly, the *Yorkshire Post* opined that I had fallen with a resounding thump between two stools. The *Daily Telegraph* put it more kindly: 'Sir Geoffrey might have shown greater sureness of touch over the last few days, but other than wholeheartedly approving the American action, it is difficult to see how else he could have played things.' 'British governments', concluded Malcolm Rutherford in the *Financial Times*, 'have been living in a fool's paradise in looking to Washington first, and Europe second. In future, it should be the other way around.'

As the years went by Margaret and I were destined to react more and more in different ways to that conundrum. I had no doubt that we should base our future strategic planning increasingly upon the premise that Grenada, rather than the Falklands, offered the best evidence of American instincts.

CHAPTER TWENTY-THREE

GCHQ AND THE UNION BAN

Codebreakers and Strikemakers

I had known of Government Communications Headquarters, at least since my days as Chancellor, but only vaguely. Even at that point I was much better informed than most MPs and the huge majority of the public, who would never have heard of it. It was only as Foreign Secretary that I really learned anything substantial about GCHQ, its work and its problems. For in that job I became responsible for two of the nation's three intelligence agencies. MI5 – the Security Service, responsible for counter-intelligence and surveillance – was with the Home Secretary. But MI6 – the Secret Intelligence Service – and GCHQ were both within my jurisdiction.

Neither the spies of MI6 nor the counter-spies of MI5 are natural trade unionists, and in both those services union membership had always been proscribed. Nobody had ever regarded that as at all remarkable. The Attlee government in September 1950 had happily endorsed – indeed, quite possibly drafted – Article 11(2) of the European Convention on Human Rights, which affirmed the right of governments to restrict the right to join trade unions 'if necessary in a democratic society in the interests of national security or public safety'. And Michael Foot had been content to re-enact, in his 1975 Employment Protection Act (section 12(4)), a provision which I had myself designed for inclusion in the hated Industrial Relations Act of 1971, which enabled a minister by certificate to deprive specified Crown employees of any right to union membership, 'for the purpose of safeguarding national security'. It was thus widely accepted that trade unionism and intelligence and security work did not mix.

But GCHQ had developed rather differently. Founded as far back as 1927, as the Government Code and Cipher School, it became during the Second World War the most valuable of all sources of allied intelligence. British skills in interception and code-breaking, developed at Bletchley Park, a country house in Buckinghamshire, were uniquely successful and quite probably cut some eighteen months off the length of the war. During the following forty years, partnership between GCHQ and the American National Security Agency was not only an indisputably vital link in the chain of electronic surveillance which was so crucial to successful defence against Soviet bloc subversion, but also an important element in our relationship with the United States.

By now the organization, capital- and technology-intensive, employed some 7000 people. A number of these were scattered throughout a network of small out-stations in the United Kingdom and other parts of the Commonwealth. The hard core of experts in communications, linguistics and mathematics, as well as technicians and other support staff, were concentrated in a complex of industrial and office buildings at Cheltenham. Sir Austen Chamberlain, Foreign Secretary in 1927, did not think at that time of denying union membership to recruits to the infant organization. By 1979 – and for many years before that – at least half of the assorted professionals, supervisors, craftsmen and women at Cheltenham were members of one or other of the (mainly public sector) unions. That had caused no problems.

Trouble, however, came between 1979 and 1981 as a result of the clash between unions and government over public sector pay policy. The Civil Service unions, for the first time, identified GCHQ as a suitable target for selective industrial action. This is where I was brought into the picture, as Chancellor and so chairman of our Public Sector Pay Committee. I confess that the relatively isolated 'days of action' and so on at GCHQ had made much less impression on me than the prolonged squeeze which had lost us £1.5 billion in revenue at my 'own' Customs and Excise offices. But, as became apparent to me later, the GCHQ actions justifiably caused the gravest concern. For the essential require-ment for electronic surveillance is that it should be comprehensive and, above all, uninterrupted. The total loss of man-days in GCHQ over the two-year period was no more than 10,000. But there were occasions, however short-lived, when over 25 per cent of GCHQ staff were involved. And some of those interruptions in some places were seriously damaging and dangerously timed.

The then director of GCHQ, Sir Brian Tovey, had been horrified by these events, not least because of their effect on American confidence in our half of the worldwide system. As Tovey knew better than anyone else, GCHQ had failed to operate as it should during the Russian invasion of Afghanistan in December 1979. He had, as he explained in a *Sunday Times* interview, 'spent a lot of time apologizing for GCHQ's performance' at that time; and again during the Polish crisis of March 1981, which led 'to heavy and somewhat embarrassing reliance on our allies, particularly the US'.[1] If they could no longer depend on our half of the intelligence-sharing bargain, how far could we depend upon its continuance? It was then that Tovey, wisely enough, drew up plans for the deunionization of GCHQ. The unions had, in his view, 'made it brutally clear' that they regarded the organization as 'a damn good place to strike'. In the words of one union official, in April 1981, 'This is the most crucial [GCHQ] station we have hit so far. We are going to hit this department as hard as we can.'

But the small group of ministers concerned with this topic did not then take up Tovey's proposals. Indeed he did not at that time press them very hard himself. There were plenty of reasons for this. By the end of 1981 the Civil Service strikes had all been settled and I had been able, as Chancellor, to install the new Megaw-based system for public sector pay. GCHQ acquitted itself almost without interruption – and otherwise with distinction – throughout the Falklands campaign in 1982. There was a new Foreign Secretary, Francis Pym, in that year and shortly to be a new director general at GCHQ, Peter Marychurch, who took over in September 1983. And 1983 was the year in which a general election might be expected. So procrastination of a difficult issue, by ministers and officials alike, was scarcely surprising.

There was one other reason for reticence and delay. The role, even the existence, of GCHQ had never until that moment been publicly acknowledged by any government. This was not an accident. It was the considered view of Britain's intelligence community that this policy of 'non-avowal' was a valuable protection for the agencies and their work.

Nobody, of course, imagined that this could or did conceal their existence from those who made it their business to know, whether KGB agents or journalists, like Duncan Campbell of the *New Statesman*. Indeed the so-called ABC trial of that paper (in 1978) had itself involved evidence in open court about GCHQ and its work. But the convention of 'non-avowal' certainly made it easier to avoid more widespread publicity – easier too to maintain the parliamentary convention that ministers do not answer questions about intelligence matters. At a more workaday level, few, if any, of the GCHQ radio listening-posts were known as such even to their immediate communities. Those who worked in them were glad, indeed proud, to uphold that anonymity, as a buttress for the important secrecy of their actual work. This entire tradition was wholly incompatible with any changes at GCHQ that would have called for public announcement.

But all those easy assumptions were shaken – or were believed to have been – by an event which became public on the eve of the 1983 general election: the conviction, for the first time ever, of a GCHQ employee, linguist Geoffrey Prime, on a charge of spying for the Soviet Union. The gravity of his offence can be judged from the severity of his sentence: thirty-five years' imprisonment. This came as a damaging blow to confidence in the organization, American as well as our own. An event of such gravity clearly entitled Parliament to expect a statement from government. This came from the Prime Minister herself, on 12 May 1983, just two days after she had asked the Queen to dissolve Parliament with a view to a general election on 9 June. For the first time ever, the House of Commons was told the functions of GCHQ: 'safeguarding the security of our own official communications . . . and the provision of signals intelligence . . . in support of the government's defence and foreign policies'. The roof did not fall in at the disclosure. But this 'avowal' was held to mark an important stage in the transit of GCHQ from the world of darkness into light. It is precisely the completion of that transit that made the problem so difficult, when, nine months later, the time came for me to manage and present it.

The substance of the matter was, in fact, relatively easy. With the election out of the way and GCHQ now – if only in barest outline – in the public domain, management felt free to readdress the problem. So the two new Secretaries of State, Michael Heseltine at Defence and myself, were briefed, and the matter in due course came to a 'small group' at Number 10 for re-examination: the three ministers were joined at least by Robert Armstrong, secretary to the cabinet, and Peter Marychurch. The substance of the matter was relatively straightforward. The law, national (my own 1971 design) as well as international, provided for intelligence and security work to be deunionized. MI5 and MI6 already were; for reasons of historical accident, GCHQ was not, and had been put at risk and damaged by the kind of industrial conflict from which it was meant to be immune. Our vital intelligence partners, the Americans, had been as worried about this as we were, all the more so now that a fully fledged spy had been uncovered at Cheltenham. Our critics were later to suggest, quite wrongly, that we moved when we did only because of American pressure. We needed no such urging from the United States or anywhere else. Indeed there was none. We had our own reputation to restore. The appropriate action for deunionization of this security organization was ready to hand. Two successive directors of GCHQ (Sir Brian Tovey in 1981 and Sir Peter Marychurch in 1983) had decided to recommend that. All that was needed was the certificate under the Labour legislation designed for that purpose.

Going Public

The only remaining question was how best to execute this policy. So for our meeting in early December, Margaret, Michael Heseltine and I were joined by Willie Whitelaw (a former Home and Employment Secretary) and by the Employment Secretary, Tom King. Present too was Robert Armstrong, wearing an uncomfortable diversity of hats. As Cabinet secretary, he was also the Prime Minister's principal security adviser with overall responsibility to her for the intelligence agencies. But as the head of the Home Civil Service he also had responsibility in that capacity for the conditions of service and morale in those very organizations. This was exactly the kind of conundrum for which Armstrong's style of Whitehall calm had been designed.* One aspect of our work we continued to take unquestioningly for granted – the need for total security. Although we were about to bring GCHQ most controversially into broad daylight, we did not cease to treat it, until the very last moment, as though it was for ever in the dark. So our plan was hatched, without benefit of advice even from my own parliamentary and political advisers Tim Renton and John Houston, in total privacy.

From one point of view – would it work? – it turned out to be remarkably effective; for unveiled as they were by me on 25 January 1984, our proposals had within five weeks been accepted by well over 90 per cent of the staff involved. The main change was that they should no longer be allowed to belong to any trade union but could join only a departmental staff association approved by GCHQ's director. We had given a good deal of thought, or so we believed, to the sugaring of that pill. If anyone insisted on retaining union membership, every effort

---

* Only once, so far as I know, did it publicly fail him; and that is when he lashed out at a press photographer when *en route* to testify in an Australian court about the *Spycatcher* case.

would be made to find them an alternative job elsewhere in the Civil Service. If no suitable job was available, then there was the third option of premature retirement on quite attractive redundancy terms. Only if an employee tried to insist on remaining both at GCHQ and as a union member would he face, inevitably, the fourth alternative of dismissal. Those who decided to remain at GCHQ on the new terms would each receive a payment of £1000 in recognition of the withdrawal of certain former rights in the cause of national security.

This was the case that it fell to me to present in a 'surprise' Commons statement (in other words it had not been leaked or foreshadowed in any other way) on 25 January. It is possible now to look back with astonishment on the arrangements made for that announcement. The workers affected were, of course, to be informed, but only at the same time as Parliament – and almost nobody else. The two most important exceptions stand out, whom I called in to see me in the Foreign Office just hours before I made the announcement: Denis Healey and Len Murray, still then general secretary of the TUC. Both were members of the Privy Council and thus bound by the Privy Councillor's oath of confidentiality. But why them? And why so late? For one simple reason – our continuing preoccupation with secrecy. These two we felt we could trust to remain silent for the few hours that remained before the news became public. About that at least we were right. But a fat lot of good it did us, or them for that matter. Each was even more astonished by the fact of the interview taking place than by the decision itself. Denis Healey had the good sense not to question the decision, but he was beside himself with pre-emptive delight at the political hay he would be able to make.

From the moment when I made my statement to the House a huge storm of denunciation broke about my head – led (perfectly properly) by Denis Healey himself on the Opposition front bench. Why now, three years on from the last industrial action? he asked, and why no prior consultation with the unions? Why, said my colleagues, were we not even informed, let alone consulted, until you told us in Cabinet the following day? Why, said Charles Irving, the beleaguered Conservative MP for Cheltenham itself, was there not even a few minutes' prior notice to me? To this fundamental charge of non-consultation I had only one, entirely lame answer. 'It would not have been appropriate in such a matter', I said, 'to consult in such a way.'

This was our fundamental mistake. We made it because of our failure to appreciate the difficulties, the subtleties indeed, as I have put it already, of moving from darkness into light. (I was to face a not dissimilar problem five years later, when the SAS men in Gibraltar suddenly made themselves public by shooting down three IRA terrorists in the street.)* We had got used to the logic of our own thinking, and there was nothing intrinsically wrong with that. But we had got used to thinking it in secret, because we had been dealing with a topic where secrecy had been, quite properly, the habit. We had been unwilling to take into our confidence any outsiders, until we had first disclosed our secret, and we had not even made ourselves half-ready to do so. 'That his case is fundamentally a good one', said *The Times* on 9 February, 'is a secret almost as closely guarded by Sir Geoffrey as all the other secrets he is trying to protect.' The *Telegraph* put it more sharply: 'The unions are being presented with a better and more sympathetic cause than they could have hoped for in their wildest imaginings.'

For the next four or five weeks, I was engaged in a desperate struggle to recover lost ground – gallantly assisted, it must be said, by Tom King as well as by Margaret herself. We succeeded, eventually, in rebutting most of the charges. It was not American pressure that had caused us to act. We were not inventing our anxiety over interruptions in the service – although John Nott, offering some kind of reassurance as Defence Secretary in April 1981, had said that 'up to now they have not in any way affected operational capability'. We were not moving now because of our lust to introduce the polygraph (the technical name for the lie-detector) at GCHQ. (That had been recommended a year before, after the Prime case, by the Security Commission,† and was never, during my five remaining years at the Foreign Office, to get beyond very selective experimental use. Not one of us – Prime Minister, Cabinet secretary, GCHQ director or myself – ever had any real confidence in this rather unBritish device.) To my regret, I was not able completely to dispel the charge of carelessness, rather than lack of candour, on my part, in failing to make sufficiently clear the fourth option with which we were facing the hard core of GCHQ trade unionists: that if anyone insisted on trying to retain union membership as well as a job at GCHQ, then it was that job that in the end would have to go. The charge we found most difficult to deal with was that of failure to consult.

* See pp. 551–5 below.
† The Security Commission was established by the Douglas-Home Conservative government in January 1964 as a result of the Profumo affair. Chaired by a Law Lord, the Commission has power to investigate and report upon the consequences of breaches of security in the public service.

So, almost uniquely in the history of the Thatcher government, consult we did. Most unusually too we thus accepted the advice offered in a high-speed report, published on 14 February, from the House of Commons Select Committee on Employment (under the chairmanship of the astute Labour trade unionist MP, Ron Leighton). Further, on two successive occasions, 1 and 23 February, a fourteen-strong TUC delegation, under the moderate and restrained leadership of Len Murray and Bill McCall, general secretary of the Council of Civil Service Unions, came to Number 10 to present their case to Tom King, Robert Armstrong, the Prime Minister and myself. It is notable that they did not seek to challenge our basic position, but only our way of implementing it. On this, they had one specific proposal to put. It had, moreover, been tentatively recommended to us by Robert Armstrong, who had been vigorously exploring the options in his dual capacity. If GCHQ workers were allowed to remain as union members, it was proposed, the unions would themselves enter into and underwrite 'no disruption' agreements on behalf of those members.

Tom King and Willie Whitelaw both had some sympathy with this approach. I too was ready to look at the compromise. But not Bernard Ingham. 'It is a U-turn, Prime Minister,' he said. And Margaret agreed. (Part of Ingham's strength lay in his ability to articulate the Prime Minister's prejudices more crisply even than she could herself.) So our second meeting with the unions was an empty affair. But the unions, or some of them, made our final position more defensible than we might have expected. For they called a half-day mini-general strike for 28 February (the day after Parliament was to debate the topic and the day before our deadline expired) and so, in the words of *The Times*, 'provided convincing proof for the Prime Minister in her argument. . . . If the trade unions are prepared to encourage everybody else to break their contracts to give . . . coercive weight to their arguments . . . they cannot really be trusted not to do the same one day at Cheltenham itself.' There the matter rested. By 201 to 25 votes (it was an SDP motion), we 'won' the Commons debate, with a number of critics and abstentions on our own side. The ban remained in force and several public sector union conferences that summer threw out the idea of 'no disruption' agreements. (We had scarcely encouraged them to take a kinder view.)

Conflict of Loyalty

But that was very far from being an end of the matter. For throughout my time at the Foreign Office we had to cope with a small and dwindling, but tenacious, band of nonconformist employees at GCHQ. By the logic of our policy they should, of course, have been dismissed. Instead they were kept 'under constant review' by a small group under my chairmanship. They secured, at a later stage, the support of the otherwise moderate leader of the electricians' union, Eric Hammond. Whenever the prospect of dismissal loomed, as it had to do from time to time, so did the truly alarming threat of a national power strike. The left had a new four-letter word, GCHQ, with which to foment demonstrations up to and beyond the 1987 general election. Almost every aspect of the work and location of GCHQ and all its out-stations was rehearsed again and again in the press. Our most secret service had become almost the most public. There was as well a long-running saga of legal proceedings against us. On 16 July 1984 Mr Justice Glidewell declared our action invalid on the ground that our imposition of the ban without any prior consultation was 'contrary to natural justice'. This judgment was later overturned by the Court of Appeal (affirmed in due course by the House of Lords). But the case continued to reverberate for years before the European Court of Human Rights and with the International Labour Organization.

Our formal success had been close to a public relations and political disaster. For much of the early criticism I was the natural, and to some extent the proper, target. No less a target, to my greater distress, was the Foreign Office. For on this occasion certainly the department could in no way be depicted as responsible for the débâcle. The decisions had all been taken by ministers, advised only by GCHQ itself and by members of the Home Civil Service. But some of the mud flung at the Foreign Secretary was bound to splash on to our hard-pressed diplomats.

In the early days the papers were full of the notion that I should myself resign or be transplanted. On 6 February, the *Daily Mail*, and Robin Oakley, came to my rescue with a front-page two-page splash: 'Howe: I was right and I won't resign'. The fairest verdict in the end was probably that of Edward Pearce in the *Sunday Telegraph*: 'So what are a couple of bad parliamentary performances between friends? Geoffrey Howe was not hired for the talents of Cicero, but, like

Goldsmith's prospective wife, "for qualities which would last".[2] But what of my wider responsibility for the policy itself? Simon Jenkins in the *Sunday Times* credited me with being 'unique in this Cabinet in being able to think himself into Mrs Thatcher's mind without scrambling his own in the process'.[3]

So what had gone wrong on this occasion? Granted that we all had to share responsibility for the non-consultative secrecy with which we had shaped and conducted this policy – and not one of us, it must be said, had challenged that – could we not have done more to save the government from such a disastrous demonstration of unyielding hostility to trade unionism in all its forms? Well, we could certainly, and in our private discussions we did try. Tom King, Robert Armstrong and I did all canvass with Margaret the one solution that could have secured an acceptable outcome: the so-called 'card in the pocket' solution. This involved exactly the same basic prescription, with the exception that a trade unionist would have been entitled to retain his union membership, and only that. There would and should have been no union organization at or connected with GCHQ, but the basic right of membership would have been preserved. I argued the case for this by reference to my own experience. Should I have been required, for example, to abandon my life-long membership of the Bar Council if I was working at GCHQ? Why should a craft unionist's loyalty to his representative body be any less regarded than that of a professional man?

But even this concept was not one that Margaret could accept. 'The conflict of loyalty will remain,' she said, ' – loyalty to his job, on the one hand, and loyalty to the command of his union, on the other. They cannot both prevail.' It was this unflattering perception of union loyalty that caused Len Murray and his colleagues such distress. For them the charge of disloyalty to the Crown, which Margaret implied was a consequence of union membership, was equivalent to a charge of treason. It was that insult, as they saw it, which made them angry. And it was the legitimacy of their complaint that made me press as hard as we did for the 'card in the pocket' solution. Technically it would have avoided facing any individual with the fourth (sacking) option I have described. It would also have avoided the wider political disarray. It could well have worked. At least it deserved a try. But not for Margaret.

This was a case where she was at the end driven by her 'all or nothing' absolutist instinct. She could not find room in her thinking for acceptance of the parallel legitimacy of someone else's loyalty. It was probably the clearest example I had seen so far of one of Margaret's most tragic failings: an inability to appreciate, still less accommodate, somebody else's patriotism. A great patriot herself, with an enormous instinctive loyalty, she found it hard to respect or sympathize with the sense of loyalty of others, or even with the idea of a wider or different loyalty for herself. Even Welshness, I sometimes felt, she regarded as somehow beyond some unspoken pale – still more Irishness. It was their perception of this kind of instinct, I believe, that led to the progressive disenchantment of the Scottish people with the Unionist Party under her leadership, and, in the end, to her inability to reconcile the idea of European Union with the concept of national patriotism. A citizen, she seemed to feel, could never safely be allowed to carry more than one card in his or her pocket, and at GCHQ that could only be Her Majesty's card.

Her Majesty's subjects were about to be confronted with the consequences of a much more savage clash of loyalties. On 8 March the national executive of the NUM, under their Marxist president, Arthur Scargill, launched a national strike against proposed pit closures. No attempt was made to conceal the political nature of this move: it was designed to overthrow the Conservative government. In order to avoid holding a national ballot, which he believed he would lose, Scargill deployed pickets to coerce miners all over the country to stay at home. Violence and indeed riots soon broke out. But the government had been preparing for a miners' strike ever since our climbdown in face of a similar threat in 1981. Nigel Lawson (who later that month was to present his first, 'radical, tax-reforming' Budget, in which he abolished both the investment-income and national-insurance surcharges) had discreetly built up power-station coal stocks when he was Energy Secretary. So the government was now not only willing but able to resist and defeat a long strike. In Cabinet I supported Margaret Thatcher and the new Energy Secretary Peter Walker in the lengthy struggle that ensued. But as Foreign Secretary my immediate concern was with the state of East–West relations. For the Soviet Union was once again in transition, General Secretary Andropov having died on 9 February. The agenda we had set was soon proving its worth.

CHAPTER TWENTY-FOUR

HOWE'S OSTPOLITIK

Sources Close to the Kremlin

We had a secret weapon in our drive for better East–West relations – or Howe's Ostpolitik, as some of the papers were to dub it. Yet I scarcely recognized this asset when it first appeared. Not many days after my arrival at the Foreign Office Patrick Wright, then deputy secretary with responsibility for intelligence and security matters, asked if he might see me alone – without even the presence of my principal private secretary, with whom every other secret was shared.

When Patrick arrived, he handed over a double envelope of papers that I was to read in his presence and then return. The material, he explained, came from an intelligence source of the utmost sensitivity who gave us a regular insight into Soviet policymaking at the highest level. This startling claim achieved credibility when I learned that we were speaking about the KGB's then number two at the Soviet London Embassy, Oleg Gordievski. His name was not at that stage disclosed to me; he was given a codename, which changed from time to time. Even the existence of this contact was known, beyond the few MI6 'friends' who had to know, only to Antony Acland within the office. The Prime Minister was aware but no other colleague. Gordievski's existence (and most, if not all, of his advice) was, however, regularly disclosed to the American agencies. This made a most important contribution from our side of the (often unequal) Anglo-American intelligence partnership and no doubt helped to sustain it. I was later to learn more about Gordievski, much more – but only as I needed to do so. For the present, I was more than content to receive his invaluable (not least because it was so regular) commentary on thinking within the Kremlin. It played an important part in shaping our own strategy.

I did not make notes of this material, all of which was on each occasion made available in the same careful fashion. But one very powerful impression quite quickly built up in my mind: the Soviet leadership really did believe the bulk of their own propaganda. They did have a genuine fear that 'the West' was plotting their overthrow – and might, just might, go to any lengths to achieve it. This near-obsession, it became clear, was fuelled by the rhetoric (and sometimes more than rhetoric) which accompanied some of our democratic changes of political gear: for example, by the more or less simultaneous arrival in power of Margaret Thatcher and Ronald Reagan. Perversely, the shooting down of the Korean airliner, KAL 007, in September 1983 had an effect in the same direction. It took the Soviets several days to be sure that their blundering was the cause of this tragedy. But blundering it was. Yet within hours the American authorities, at almost every level, were proclaiming it a piece of deliberately calculated, cold-blooded Soviet wickedness. The principal effect of this simplistic overreaction came near to convincing Moscow, Andropov included, that the whole incident had somehow been contrived, as a cunning trap, by the CIA.

Within the next few weeks Gordievski gave us warning of another alarming example of Soviet fearfulness. From 2 to 11 November 1983 the NATO exercise 'Able Archer' was scheduled to take place. This simulated crisis was designed to lead to nuclear conflict and involved 'incidents' and active participation by senior Western ministers. Gordievski left us in no doubt of the extraordinary but genuine Russian fear of real-life nuclear strike. NATO deliberately changed some aspects of the exercise so as to leave the Soviets in no doubt that it was only an exercise. Gordievski's own reports to his nominal masters reinforced the message, and the crisis passed.

But Margaret and I had been impressed. We each found opportunities to warn allies and friends of the genuineness of Soviet fears. At the Commonwealth heads of government meeting on 23–26 November in New Delhi, Tanzania's Julius Nyerere impressed us all with his matching description of the Soviet Union. 'When the weak were frightened,' he said, 'that threatened no danger to the world. It was when the powerful were frightened that the world really felt extremely nervous, and rightly so.' And so on to his oft-cited Swahili proverb that 'When the elephants fought it was the grass that suffered.' 'So too', cracked Singapore's Harry Lee Kuan Yew, 'when the elephants made love.' 'I would prefer that,' replied Nyerere, 'for at least it would enhance the prospects for peace.' Margaret joined in to emphasize our own awareness of Soviet fearfulness, as shown by their reaction to the destruction of KAL 007. 'It is only through contact', she said, 'that we can hope to be able to influence others.' It was a useful coalescing of ideas, for which the Commonwealth offered unique opportunities. What a pity it is, I mused then and thereafter, that American leaders have no opportunity to enjoy such relaxed exchanges.

The next moves that I had in mind were along three tracks: first, my forthcoming series of meetings with Gromyko, including a visit either by me to Moscow or by him to London; second, Margaret's forthcoming visit to Hungary in February 1984; and third, the possibility of attracting a senior Soviet leader (but which one?) on a visit to the UK.

For some reason Margaret was anxious that the first formal Howe–Gromyko meeting should be in London – perhaps because her subconscious was already thinking that the first high-level visit to Moscow should be for her to make. Operationally it made more sense for me to go to Moscow: I should have the chance to size up Andropov (and to reconnoitre other possible leaders) and to carry the human-rights case on to Soviet ground; in London the reverse would happen. A passing comment by George Shultz to Margaret, when he called on each of us separately early in 1984, reinforced my preference – and it prevailed. I was in any event due to see Gromyko again a few days later at the adjourned CSCE summit. This time it was in Stockholm. The Swedish capital was uncomfortably ice and snow-bound in January. But it offered the chance of a private lunch at our Embassy with the man whom I had long seen as a champion of the most expensive kind of socialism, Prime Minister Olaf Palme. I have to confess that I was captivated by his zest and candour – and, some two years later, shocked by his still unexplained murder.

The cavernous Soviet Embassy in Stockholm provided the setting for my eighty-minute meeting with Gromyko. We were both under less pressure than we had been at Madrid, so I could get a better measure of the man. His face was surprisingly mobile, expressive even – displaying patience, then impatience, agreement, then disagreement. He spoke slowly, often softly. He seemed almost to be improvising, yet what he had to say was stale and ritualistic. I came later to describe him as an unbriefable, self-briefing machine. After twenty-seven years as Foreign Minister, he knew it all. Yet still he spoke eye to eye, with lazy but eloquent gestures. It would be easy to believe that here was a decent, sincere man, doing his best for world peace. Easy, that is, until you tried to engage him in discussion.

I found human-rights questions the surest guide to Gromyko's character. This was one of the key items on my agenda and I listed some of the most important names: Andrei Sakharov, his wife Elena Bonner and Anatoly Sharansky. Gromyko was immediately dismissive. 'You have lowered the tone of this conversation,' he said. 'I have no intention of discussing such matters with you.' On this point at least, he remained true to his word. Next time I raised the same issue, in Moscow in July, he ignored it completely: not one word in four or five hours of talking together. I returned to the charge with him a third time, at the luncheon which our UN ambassador (then Sir John Thomson) hosted for us in New York at General Assembly time in September that same year. Quite deliberately, I raised the same human-rights names with him as we left the table to take our coffee when no one else was in earshot. His reply was just as prompt and even more brutal: 'Sakharov,' he said, taking up one of my names apparently at random, 'Sakharov. That is the Russian for sugar. No thank you. I don't take sugar with my coffee.' He was grinning dismissively. As far as he was concerned, that was it.

Although his English was quite good, Gromyko normally worked through his interpreter – and did not hesitate to correct him. His man at Stockholm, Victor Sokhodrev – one of the most senior – was not afraid to answer back. He had been educated at Highgate School in North London throughout his father's war service in Britain. I have often wondered whether the curiously dated, folksy style of Kremlin English owes something to Victor's upbringing on schoolboy magazines of the era, *Skipper, Rover, Wizard* and the like.

Certainly Sokhodrev left me in no doubt about Gromyko's position. I stressed Britain's deep commitment to negotiated reduction of armaments. This I knew was Margaret Thatcher's personal wish, and I cited word for word as evidence of this her impromptu changes in her 1983 party conference speech. Gromyko's response, unchanged and unchanging, was that Washington had 'exploded' the negotiations. He had no use for the step-by-step approach, which the CSCE was meant to encourage. 'Peeping through other people's keyholes to see what they were doing' was no way, he argued, for nation-states to behave. Progress on East–West relations was going to be difficult as long as Andrei Gromyko remained in charge.

Burying Andropov

Margaret's visit to Hungary took place in the first week of February. The idea of the Iron Lady on the other side of the Iron Curtain for the first time clearly made a great impression within Hungary, and also on Margaret herself. It was a media success, and whetted her cautious appetite for more. One opportunity came only a week later, when we had to go together to Moscow for the funeral of Yuri Andropov, thus escaping for two days from the GCHQ imbroglio. The event was no surprise, since ill-health had prevented him appearing in public since the previous October. An RAF VC10 carried an unusual cargo to the Soviet capital: hastily armed with fur hats, snow-boots, thermal hand-warmers and other kit for a Moscow winter, we were accompanied by Denis Healey and David Steel, amid scenes of rare camaraderie. There was a moment in our ambassador's residence when Margaret and her party burst into a room where Denis and David were changing into their long-johns. These items were certainly necessary: for some two hours before the arrival of the funeral parade, visiting VIPs had to stand alongside Red Square on a layer of coconut matting laid directly on top of the ice.

We were a huge and weirdly diverse bunch. Yasser Arafat, dishevelled and unshaven, was only a few yards away from Margaret Thatcher, trying very hard to catch her (firmly elusive) eye. Most notable was the total absence from surrounding rooftops of the security presence which one had come to expect at the Cenotaph, or any comparable Western ceremony. The explanation was easy. The only Soviet citizens allowed anywhere near had all been bussed in, specifically to stand in the centre of the Square, as well disciplined in their compact grouping and formal variety of dress as a Bolshoi chorus. The ranks of Red Army conscripts, who marched past by the thousand, were mainly oriental and frighteningly young. But they were nothing like so disturbing as the Red Army field marshals and generals, ranged on the second tier of balconies behind us, on the Lenin mausoleum. On the top balcony stood the Supreme Soviet, led by Andropov's successor, Konstantin Chernenko. Already heavy with emphysema, he delivered a breathless, wooden commemorative address, during which he almost stumbled to a halt. The Soviet brass-hats continued throughout to smoke and chat disdainfully among themselves, like stewards at a race meeting.

Once Andropov had been laid to rest by the Kremlin wall – his coffin was accidentally dropped in the process – the assembled dignitaries had to process into the magnificent St George's Hall in the heart of the palace, to pay our respects to the bewildered widow, flanked by Chernenko and the omnipresent Gromyko. As this strange queue edged slowly up the Kremlin stairs, early-comers were racing down and away in the opposite direction. Margaret caused a stir here too, when the diminutive Mozambican President, Zamora Machel, on his way out, bounded across the staircase to greet her. As Arafat gazed upon this unlikely duo, practically falling into each other's arms, his amazed jealousy shone out.

Like all such events, this was a working funeral. It gave opportunities for Margaret and myself to meet foreign leaders, with whom bilateral meetings had not, until then, been easy to arrange, from Spain's Prime Minister Felipe Gonzáles to Pakistan's President Zia. All these encounters took place in the sound-proof secure 'bubble', a vault-like enclosure mounted on blocks between floor and ceiling in the embassy basement. (A number of our missions in especially sensitive places have one of these cabins concealed within them: a kind of diplomatic Tardis.) We also had the chance of a formal meeting with the new General Secretary, Konstantin Chernenko, in one of the gilded Kremlin halls with which I was to become so familiar. Observers noted that Thatcher had forty minutes with him, compared to Bush's twenty-five. Since half the time was needed for interpretation, each meeting was clearly too short – and Chernenko too short-lived – for it to have any real content. The significance of the occasion was that the Iron Lady had come – as she had not done for Brezhnev's last rites, hardly eighteen months before.

The most important conclusion we drew from Andropov's funeral was that Chernenko's reign would be no more than a brief staging-post *en route* to his successor. This added urgency to our search for 'the man most likely to succeed', whom we wished to invite to Britain. Nigel Broomfield, then in charge of the FCO Soviet Department, had sought advice not just from our ambassador Ian Sutherland in Moscow but from the intelligence agencies too and had narrowed the field to two or three: the Communist Party leaders in Moscow and Leningrad, Victor Grishin and Grigory Romanov respectively – and Mikhail Gorbachev, still, at fifty-two, the youngest member of the Politburo.

The last-named received timely support from a Canadian source. Prime Minister Trudeau had recently had a meeting in Tokyo with Georgi Arbatov (then director of Moscow's North American think-tank). Trudeau had told Arbatov of the way in which Margaret Thatcher was now calling (in Delhi as well as in London) for more dialogue. In answer to Trudeau's question 'After Andropov, who?' Arbatov promptly named Gorbachev. 'He is', he said, 'the youngest in the leadership, more and more involved in international affairs and very close to Andropov.'

Romanov, by contrast, 'only dealt with technical matters and was not involved'. This was only one straw in the wind, of course. But an even more authoritative view to the same effect came from Gordievski. So our considered choice fell on Gorbachev. How though to invite him, out of all the Soviet leadership, without risk of being stuck with some dim substitute? Our people hit upon the excellent diplomatic device of inviting him in his undoubted capacity as head chairman of the Foreign Affairs Committee of the Supreme Soviet, by means of a letter from his Westminster opposite number, the Conservative chairman of the Commons Foreign Affairs Committee, Sir Anthony Kershaw.

Gromyko and Gorbachev

This move fitted well into the timetable for my own visit to Moscow, finally set for 1–3 July 1984. This was the first such mission by a British Foreign Secretary since David Owen's in 1977. Our VC10 was fully laden. We had seventeen journalists and seven television crew-members on board (the Russians had not yet allowed ITV any permanent presence in Moscow). Our own communications staff were important too. They secured coverage for my closing press conference on no less than 5000 stations, worldwide from Australia to Argentina. As always on these trips, I ensured that my party included the key FCO officials. This human data-bank was obviously useful. More important even than that was for them to savour the atmosphere and personalities of the countries which they monitored. There is no substitute for having actually seen a country's Foreign Minister in action on his home ground.

As the years went by, this simple proposition was to become an increasingly contentious issue between the Foreign Office and Number 10. I shared Margaret's instinctive aversion to the overmanning of missions – and indeed the overcrowding of meetings. In this we were jointly proud of Britain's performance in the productivity league-tables of international diplomacy. At the 1986 Tokyo Economic Summit, for example, we were glad to discover that our sixty-strong delegation was much leaner than that of the other visitors, whose average was three times our size – ranging from Germany's 117 to the United States' massive 387. But the case for economy can be pressed too far, and Margaret did just that. By the end of her time she was conducting herself abroad virtually with the sole support of her own personal duo,

Charles Powell and Bernard Ingham.* On occasion she was reluctant even for our local ambassador to accompany her to meetings with 'his' head of government. There is, of course, no surer way of diminishing an envoy's standing in the eyes of his hosts. On one of Margaret's African tours, she exchanged not a single working word with the one very experienced official whom she had been persuaded – for the last time – to take with her. And at her last CHOGM, in Kuala Lumpur in 1989, Sir Patrick Wright, by then permanent under secretary at the FCO, was not invited to attend a single meeting.

My own 1984 Moscow mission offered an insight into the old-style Soviet handling of such a visit: Gromyko and his wife at the airport, complete with flowers for Elspeth; wreath-laying ceremony at the Red Army's Tomb of the Unknown Soldier; the Bolshoi Theatre; and, in the very heart of the Kremlin, shining bright and golden in the July sunshine, a visit to Lenin's flat, where the expressionless interpreter told us of his meetings with a diversity of Westerners, from 'Herbert' Wells to Armand Hammer. (H. G. Wells, like Lenin, is no longer with us. But Armand Hammer was still in evidence nine months later when Margaret and I met him in the Kremlin for Chernenko's funeral.)

The substance of my talks, almost six hours in two hard-slogging sessions with Gromyko and seventy minutes with Gromyko and Chernenko together, displayed the old Soviet Union at its most unyielding. I had a long agenda of points to discuss. Most important of all was that the Geneva talks on strategic weapons (START) had been stalled since the preceding December. The Soviet Union had walked out then, in protest against the first deployment of Cruise missiles in the West, although these were no more than a first step in matching the Soviet SS20 missiles which were already in place in the East. The most important message I had to carry to Moscow was that the Soviet negotiators should return to the talks, which they ought never to have left. Fallacious and almost wilfully perverse in all their arguments, Gromyko and Chernenko disclosed not so much as a hairline crack in their armour of self-righteousness.

Gromyko's view seemed irredeemably coloured by his judgment of Ronald Reagan. 'From the beginning,' he said, 'the American President has set out to destroy all that had been good and positive in US–Soviet

* Charles Powell was private secretary to the Prime Minister, 1984–91, in succession to John Coles. With Bernard Ingham, chief press secretary 1979–91, he came to form a fatal partnership on the frontier between Margaret Thatcher and the outside world. See pp. 396 and 147 respectively.

relations.' Time and again I stressed that the US was ready, without any strings, to open talks forthwith on the whole agenda. 'The Soviets', I said, 'have shown themselves quite unwilling even to take yes for an answer.' Our Soviet-wise ambassador Ian Sutherland reported afterwards that the ordinarily impassive Gromyko looked increasingly uncomfortable as I repeatedly stated the illogicality of the Soviet position.

But if Gromyko retained a certain fluency and adroitness in replaying his old 78 record, Chernenko did not. Bewildered and incoherent, he often turned to Gromyko for prompting or reassurance. A high-speed gabble, interrupted by stumblings (in order to breathe), indicated his lack of conviction and even, at times, a total lack of comprehension. Things were not helped by his misleading habit of repeatedly nodding his head, with a slight smile. When he did become specific, it was in the crudest of Victor Sokhodrev's dated English. 'Tell Uncle Sam', he exclaimed, 'to stop pointing his nuclear pistol at my forehead!'

The whole sequence of meetings can be seen in retrospect to represent the old Soviet Union at its most intractable. Our judgment that Chernenko had been elected on the basis that he would have no authority to interfere with policies in foreign affairs or defence was amply confirmed by his performance. I was left wondering just how one of the world's two superpowers (as we then still put it) could possibly have been reduced to such a dangerously leaderless condition.

There were some useful by-products of my visit. Although it had not been possible for me to meet Gorbachev (he was out of Moscow tending his agricultural responsibilities), I was able to deliver Anthony Kershaw's invitation, with its promise that if Gorbachev did lead a 'parliamentary' mission to Britain he could be sure of meeting Margaret Thatcher. I was able too to leave with Gromyko a list of so-called 'reunification cases' – of families that had long been divided by the Iron Curtain and its inhuman formalities. One example was particularly moving: the newly elected Conservative MP for Cardiff West, Stefan Terlezki, had left his home in Ukraine as a seventeen-year-old refugee in 1945 and had been trying to persuade the Soviet authorities to allow his aged father to visit him in the West. On this at least (and on two other similar cases) Gromyko was willing to accept my case.

I had one final reason for gratitude to Moscow: for it was there, on the verandah of our ambassador's residence looking over towards the Kremlin towers, that I was able to interview (and forthwith recruit) one of the most important pillars of the next four years at the Foreign Office, Christopher Meyer (later to become chief press secretary at Number

10), to take over as head of News Department. One of Christopher's first pleasures on taking office was to savour the movie recording the whole visit, which the Soviet ambassador Victor Popov presented to me at a private viewing in Kensington Palace Gardens. The most remarkable feature of this crudely propagandist gift is that it was made on 35mm stock film. Ambassador Popov was later himself overcome with techno-logical amazement when I played it back to him (at lunch at Chevening) from the video copy that I had had made. Such things were still unknown in the land that had launched the first man into space.

My next encounter with Gromyko, at our annual United Nations meeting in New York that September, offered no surprises. Soon after that, the Soviet parliamentary visit to Britain was confirmed for the week before Christmas, with Gorbachev in the lead. It was an exciting moment when Mikhail and Raisa Gorbachev arrived at Chequers for lunch with the Prime Minister and half-a-dozen ministerial colleagues on Sunday, 16 December. This led straight into four hours of conver-sation that changed the shape of our world: Gorbachev, Margaret and interpreters, with myself as occasional contributor and Charles Powell as note-taker.

Gorbachev was uncannily like an old steelworker friend of my father's. His famous birthmark was equally evocative of the 'blue' scar of the South Wales anthracite coalfield. I soon felt, as one sometimes does, at home with him, as though I had known him all my life. I had no idea what impression he was making on Margaret. But they slipped almost instantly into a pattern of conversation that was so spontaneous that the process of interpretation became almost invisible. Gorbachev's involve-ment in the exchanges was impressively enhanced by the use that he made of his small pocket notebook in which he had clearly written his own briefing notes.

Margaret was at her best: fluent but measured, thoughtful but shiningly and convincingly sincere. 'We don't look at you through rose-tinted spectacles,' she said. 'Our systems are very different from each other. We each believe in our own, in our own alliances – and I'm not going to try and break yours up. So you leave ours alone as well. But we do have to find ways of living together on the same planet.' That meant looking for ways in which we could make ourselves secure without making Gorbachev and his people feel insecure.

Gorbachev responded just as directly to the point. The moment when he first gripped our attention, I think, was when he rehearsed the famous Palmerston quotation: 'Britain has no permanent friends and no permanent enemies – but only permanent interests.' This was remarkable most of all for the precisely effective way in which it was deployed – and by this 'non-expert' in foreign policy. 'It is up to us', he went on, 'to identify the interests that we have in common.' Arms control was his chief example, supported by production of a full-page diagram from the *New York Times* contrasting the three million tons of explosives used in the Second World War with the fifteen billion tons now available to the superpowers. 'Once a year,' he said, quoting a Russian proverb, 'even a loaded gun can go off.' He was gravely concerned too by President Reagan's Strategic Defence Initiative.* Margaret responded by stressing her complete confidence in the peaceful intentions of the United States.

Gorbachev's interest in economic questions, though seriously constrained by the cramped nature of his past learning, was equally lively. I remember his astonishment at the diversity – the existence even – of the 'village' shops he had spotted in places like Great Missenden or Hampton – but I recall too his failure to comprehend the importance of independent management, still less ownership, as a feature of the market economy.

The importance of the occasion depended scarcely at all upon the agenda. Gorbachev had not come to negotiate but to explore and to project himself (and the Soviet case) in a new light – as much to his domestic audience as to the wider world. The high-profile programme we had arranged for him was clearly selected with that in mind, and he made the most of it at every stage. Margaret's almost instant public endorsement of him as 'a man with whom I can do business' was just the accolade for which he might have hoped. When I met him again the following morning, for three hours of talks and for the lunch at which Elspeth and I were to entertain him and Raisa at Hampton Court, he was clearly delighted by the way in which Margaret had taken to him. The instant respect was clearly mutual. Raisa too made a vivid impression. Elspeth was struck, when she showed her around Hampton Court, by the purposeful clarity of her taste in art, by her wide knowledge of classical and modern English literature – and by the commanding way in which she treated Madame Popova, second wife of the Soviet ambassador (and previously his secretary). To Raisa she was clearly a social inferior.

For his session with me, Gorbachev's party included the future

* See Chapter 26 below.

ambassador to London, Leonid Zamyatin (at the time Moscow propaganda chief), General Chervov, Chief of Defence Staff, and Dr Alexander Yakovlev, his future right-hand man. Our discussion dwelt in detail on the whole field of nuclear and space arms control, with Gorbachev displaying a complete and detailed mastery of the subject, and bringing General Chervov into play from time to time as his expert witness. Gorbachev presented most clearly the reasons for Soviet concern over the Strategic Defence Initiative and its relationship with the 1972 ABM (Anti-Ballistic Missile) Treaty, and skilfully pressed the Soviet case for bringing French and British nuclear weapons into account. When I cited a speech made by George Shultz the previous October (strength alone will never achieve a durable peace), he countered by quoting a speech made only weeks before: 'Mr Shultz had said one thing in October but another in December.' And when I got drawn into detail over the meaning of 'balance', Gorbachev reproached me with a quotation from St Thomas Aquinas.

In sharp contrast with Gromyko, Gorbachev was very ready to discuss the whole range of human-rights questions; on Afghanistan too he was quick to address the real issues. 'Britain', he observed, with a twinkle in his eye, 'has had much longer experience of wars in Afghanistan than we have done. So perhaps you would be ready to offer us some advice?' He closed by thanking me for the very candid and businesslike quality of discussion on both days. His talks with the Prime Minister had been a 'substantial step in the right direction. The ice has begun to move.'

Gorbachev's visit, which went on for the rest of the week, was as successful in Edinburgh as in London, but it was concluded ahead of time, since he had to fly home for yet another funeral of a Politburo member, Marshal Dmitry Ustinov. Meanwhile, almost straight from the Hampton Court meeting, Margaret and Elspeth and I had taken off together for Peking for the ceremonial signing of the Joint Declaration on the future of Hong Kong.

In more than one place in the world the ice had indeed begun to move.

CHAPTER TWENTY-FIVE

MAO-TAI FOR HONG KONG

History Catches Up

The Foreign Secretary's desk seemed always to be strewn with 'problems left over from history', the graphic Chinese phrase. It was almost as though my nineteenth-century predecessors had set out deliberately to design a battle-course of insolubles, from which there would be no escape for those who came later. Peter Carrington had been able to negotiate the Zimbabwe minefield, but he had been brought down by the Falklands. The Victorian puzzle that was to emerge near the top of my pile was Hong Kong.

A decade had passed since Elspeth and I first visited the Territory in 1973, as Minister for Trade and Consumer Affairs. The last of two visits during my Opposition years had been in 1978. My duties as Chancellor had not taken me to the Far East. But IMF and other meetings had brought me into regular contact with Hong Kong's tough-minded and competent Financial (and later Chief) Secretary, Philip Haddon-Cave. And Hong Kong entrepreneurs like the millionaire shipowner Sir Y. K. Pao had long been a source of parallel advice from the private sector (Elspeth had launched one of his ships during our time at Number 11). So I was suitably aware of and impressed by the Colony's burgeoning prosperity and self-confidence. Indeed, I often stressed to domestic audiences the irony that this show-place of enterprise and self-discipline was the child of two parents, Britain and China, which were at almost the same moment plumbing the depths of national humiliation: the one as the 'sick man of Europe', the other as victim of the Cultural Revolution. This prodigy had been created, in Robert Cottrell's vivid phrase, 'by Britons liberated from the obligations of Britain and by Chinese liberated from the obligations of China'.[1]

Hong Kong had been creeping up the Foreign Office pending list for some years. The ninety-nine-year lease which was the root of Britain's title to 92 per cent of the Territory was to expire on 30 June 1997. Our 'freehold' title to the other 8 per cent, which included Hong Kong Island and Kowloon, rested upon two earlier treaties of 1841 and 1860. Successive Chinese governments had rejected the validity of all these treaties as 'unequal' because imposed upon the Qing emperors by imperial force. Hong Kong's miracle was that the 'unequal' treaties had survived so long after the tables of political and military inequality had been so decisively turned. Four days in the 1940s sufficed for Japan to seize Hong Kong. For four decades that followed, China had exercised contrasting self-restraint. Small wonder that 1997 was seen by the Chinese as the date at which it was doubly right to re-establish their sovereignty over the whole Territory.

Since at least David Owen's time as Foreign Secretary (1977–9) the British and Hong Kong governments had been brooding about policy for the 1980s and 1990s, overshadowed as they were by the prospect of reversion to China in 1997. However, when we came into office in 1979, no clear game-plan for the last twenty years of the century had been evolved. This process would need to co-ordinate thinking from three different places. First was Hong Kong, in the form of the Governor and his Executive Council of officials and nominated legislators: the Governor between 1971 and 1982 was the very experienced and China-wise Sir Murray Maclehose. Second was our ambassador in Peking, Sir Percy Cradock. Percy had been an impressive president of the Union during my first year at Cambridge and was by now a most experienced China hand. Finally came HMG, led by the Foreign Secretary, the Minister of State responsible for the Far East, and Hong Kong Department, the small group of people who looked after Hong Kong affairs in London.

The absence of any forward plan on the British side had been matched by similar attitudes in Peking, at least until 1981. In both places the problem had been set aside as 'too difficult'. When Governor Murray Maclehose had tried to discuss one aspect of the matter with Deng Xiaoping in 1979 he had been told simply that investors should 'set their hearts at ease' about the future. Remarkably enough, this had appeared sufficient to hold the line for some time.

By 1982, however, Chinese thinking – about Taiwan as much as Hong Kong – had begun to develop a clear line. It had been disclosed in some detail by Deng himself to Ted Heath, visiting Peking as an old 'friend of China', just a few days after the outbreak of the Falklands War. This development could not have come at a worse time: Peter

Carrington, who had visited China a year before, had just resigned. The new Foreign Secretary, Francis Pym, was quite unfamiliar with the problem. And Margaret, who was expected to make a visit to China in September, was wholly absorbed by the Falklands conflict. Yet the new Chinese thinking certainly required consideration, if not an instant answer.

Deng's message to Ted Heath had been straightforward, if unwelcome. China, he said, intended to assert and safeguard her sovereignty over the whole of Hong Kong. All the unequal treaties would be abrogated. Britain, he implied, should withdraw completely. Special arrangements would be put in place to enable 'Hong Kong people' to maintain the prosperity of Hong Kong; its social and economic system would remain unchanged. Four words were enough to encapsulate Deng's insight: 'One country, two systems'. In this one phrase he set the scene for the next quarter of a century.

Ted reported this approach to Francis Pym within a few days of his return. He had no doubt that it was intended as a deliberate high-level message, government to government. Percy Cradock took the same view. He was anxious for the Chinese to receive a prompt British response, so that dialogue could get under way before Peking's thinking became set in stone. It was important, for example, to begin arguing the case for at least some British link – whether 'British administration' or something else – to continue after 1997. There was no reason to suppose that the Chinese had ever contemplated the notion that anything of this kind could be, as it were, detached and 'left behind', when sovereignty was recovered.

But it was not until 28 July 1982, two days after the Falklands thanksgiving service at St Paul's, that time could be found in Margaret's programme for a proper discussion of Hong Kong. Pressure of time was not the only reason for delay. No one had been relishing the idea of telling the Prime Minister, who had just triumphantly reasserted sovereignty over the Falklands, that she must now consider relinquishing it over Hong Kong. It was only with the utmost reluctance that she was eventually to accept, with her head though not with her heart, the physical impossibility of retaining sovereignty over the 8 per cent of Hong Kong to which we claimed a freehold title. This case, which was overwhelming in practice, was most persuasively put by the new Governor, Sir Edward Youde. This small, tough Welshman, himself a former ambassador in Peking, was to prove an admirably tenacious successor to the towering Scotsman whom he replaced.

On the basis of this disagreeable but inescapable analysis the realistic options available were indeed few. The Chinese clearly could not countenance independence for an integral part of China, still less renewal of our lease or any unilateral extension of British administration. Nor could we just tamely acquiesce in unilateral Chinese action to reabsorb Hong Kong as a 'Special Administrative Region'. But, if long-term confidence in the colony was to be maintained, some kind of reassurance about the future did need to be established. Doing nothing was certainly not an option.

All this was becoming clear in the days when I was still confined to the Exchequer. It is tempting to wonder, in retrospect, whether it was really sensible or necessary for such a forbiddingly difficult prospect to be tackled head on by the Prime Minister at such a time. But there seems to have been very little option about that either. Margaret's visit to China had long been foreshadowed. Most other European leaders had already been there. In Hong Kong, postponement would have been a deeply discouraging signal. So the Prime Minister's lead role on this topic was inescapable. And it was no doubt inevitable that her thinking about 'sovereignty', with all its emotional overtones, would be coloured by the absolutism of the Falklands parallel.

Yet her task was to persuade the Chinese to contemplate the unthinkable – that even after the expiry of the main (92 per cent) Hong Kong lease, there should somehow be a continuing future role for Britain in the management of the whole of Hong Kong. She did not at this stage have to win that argument. But she did have to persuade the Chinese that it made sense for them at least to consider it, to talk about it. To that end, she held, even on our own case, only two effective cards: first, our claim – which the Chinese had never accepted – to the freehold of 8 per cent of the colony; and second, our argument that 'British administration' in some form was crucial to the colony's future success. If the Chinese were ready to make concessions to us on the second point, we should have to be ready to give ground on the first. The crucial objective was to get talks under way on that agenda.

Margaret left herself, in fact, very little room for manoeuvre in her own mind. There could be no question, she felt, of conceding sovereignty over 'our' 8 per cent, unless Britain retained *control* over the whole territory of Hong Kong. The most she was prepared to envisage for the Chinese was titular sovereignty. At her Peking meeting with Deng Xiaoping on 23 September 1982, she presented this case starkly. But she had been armed with a carefully phrased formula that did point the way towards negotiations. If, she said, the two governments could agree arrangements for the future administration and control of Hong Kong which would command confidence in Hong Kong, and which she could justify to the British Parliament, then 'there would be a new situation in which I could consider the question of sovereignty'. Deng reacted sharply. The prosperity of Hong Kong would not depend on British administration. China's present leaders were not like those of the Qing dynasty (the despised signatories of the 1898 lease). He was prepared to wait one or two years to permit friendly discussions to take place, but these would be on the premise, said Deng, that in 1997 China would recover sovereignty over Hong Kong.

If it had rested there, all might have been well. The bounds had been set for negotiations. So, though less welcome, had the time frame: in Deng's words, 'one or two years' from September 1982. Margaret had, moreover, given a very strong injunction that knowledge of what had passed in the talks should be restricted to the small group of people directly involved, for fear that any wider exposure of the differences between the two sides might give rise to panic in Hong Kong. 'To maintain confidence,' she told the press before leaving Peking, 'you must also maintain confidentiality'.

Yet remarkably it was Margaret herself who returned to the treaty question in public and in terms clearly disparaging to the Chinese. In a BBC interview *en route* from Peking (and again in Hong Kong), she declared, 'I believe the treaties are valid in international law. And if countries try to abrogate treaties like that, it is very serious indeed. Because if a country will not stand by one treaty, it will not stand by another.' As Margaret herself had anticipated, the Chinese were particularly stung by these public suggestions of breach of faith and unreliability. Within days there started a Chinese propaganda campaign which was to be sustained for months to come. The effect on confidence of this public confrontation was marked and rapid. In the month that followed, Hong Kong's stock market fell by 25 per cent, and the Hong Kong dollar by 12 per cent of its value. In face of all this, Hong Kong rightly saw that the priority was to get the stalled talks back on track as fast as possible. But for some months this proved impossible.

The reason for Chinese unwillingness eventually became clear. Deng himself had apparently been greatly angered by our Prime Minister's comments on China's attitudes towards treaties. He thought they raised doubts about the sincerity of her conditional offer to consider the question of sovereignty. The deadlock was not broken until March

1983. Margaret then accepted Percy Cradock's advice that she should send a fresh message to the Chinese premier, Zhao Ziyang, making it plain that if the two governments could agree on acceptable administrative arrangements for Hong Kong's future, then she 'would be *prepared to recommend*' (my emphasis) that sovereignty over the whole territory should revert to China. This phrase went deliberately further than her original statement to Deng that she 'would *consider* the question of sovereignty', and it served to reopen the door.* Even then, it was not until 12 July that this manoeuvre (which became known as the 'first finesse') actually bore fruit, and the first 'real' talks (euphemistically described as 'the second phase') got under way. The declared object, already an optimistic one, was to persuade the Chinese to accept the continuation of British administration, as a *quid pro quo* for our acceptance of their sovereignty.

Picking Up the Threads

This was the point at which I took over from Francis Pym at the Foreign Office. It was not long before we had run into the sand again. By the beginning of September the negotiators had had to abandon the formula that the talks were 'useful and constructive'. The Chinese were making it plain, in public as well as in private, that they regarded sovereignty and administration as inseparable. They were prepared to allow Hong Kong 'a high degree of autonomy', but not to accept any kind of continuing British link. Already it was time for the new Foreign Secretary to set in hand a review of our negotiating strategy.

This topic was seemingly to dominate my personal agenda for the next twelve months. Yet it was far from being my only preoccupation. My visit to New York for the UN General Assembly gave me an early chance to meet the two most important Chinese actors. On 27 September I had my first meeting with the new Chinese Foreign Minister, Wu Xueqian; he was accompanied by the recently appointed Assistant Foreign Minister, Zhou Nan. In the months and years ahead I was to get to know both of them almost as well as my European – or even my Westminster – colleagues.

* Margaret Thatcher records (*The Downing Street Years*, p. 489) that at this point in the negotiations 'Geoffrey Howe and the Foreign Office wanted to go further.' It was only on 11 June that I became Foreign Secretary: I had apparently 'gone native' some three months before meeting the natives.

Wu and Zhou could not have been more different. Wu, born in 1921 and a veteran member of the Chinese Communist Party, had joined the anti-Japanese resistance movement in his native Shanghai while a student at an English mission school; he could still understand the language well – and speak too, but shyly. During the Cultural Revolution Wu and his wife had both been sent to work in the country, deliberately separated from each other for several years. His thinking was strikingly fresh and open despite (or perhaps because of) his background. Zhou Nan, highly educated and cultured, after twelve years with the Chinese New York mission to the UN, was apparently confident and relaxed. Only gradually did his other side emerge: highly ambitious and more than ready to do his master's ruthless bidding. It became easy to recall that he cut his teeth as interrogator of allied prisoners during the Korean War.

My New York brief encounter of course disclosed little of these qualities: but at least Wu and I were able to exchange a courteous explanation of each other's positions. I emphasized the sincerity of our view that anything less than administration would not command confidence. Wu stressed a surprising aspect of their case – that Britain 'would be able to play a great role' in the post-1997 Hong Kong, if only it could accept that administration too should revert to China. More disparagingly (and true to future form), Zhou Nan accused Britain of 'evading the crucial question' and thus of being 'to blame for the current deadlock'.

Meanwhile the British side (including Hong Kong) was torn between two views. From Hong Kong most of the unofficials, led by Sir S. Y. Chung (a wise and experienced businessman, warily but not obsessively suspicious of the 'Chinese' and supported by senior officials such as Philip Haddon-Cave (by now Chief Secretary), took the view that the Chinese were bluffing and should be pressed to accept our case, even at the risk of breakdown. They were supported, cautiously, by Governor Teddy Youde. On the other side were ranged the London China hands led by Percy Cradock. Richard Luce and I shared their view that the Chinese were not bluffing, and that confrontation would lead only to disaster for Hong Kong. This recurrent tension was dramatized when Edward Heath on 12 September visited Hong Kong and reported to UMELCO (the combined Executive and Legislative Councils) on the talks he had just had with Deng in Peking. Sir S. Y. Chung was prompted to comment, sincerely but not very tactfully, that their dinner-party guest seemed to have been 'well brainwashed' in Peking. Ted erupted and walked out. Nobody could say that the issues were not being well canvassed!

These political disagreements were accompanied by a high degree of economic turbulence. By 9 September 1983, with interest rates at crisis level, the Hong Kong dollar had fallen to an all-time low, and the slide continued into panic conditions. On the 23rd the Hong Kong dollar lost 8 per cent in a single day. It was suggested that we should endeavour to fix the exchange rate of the local currency. This raised huge potential difficulties for the pound sterling: would safety for Hong Kong put Britain's own reserves at risk? Eventually we were able to reach all-round agreement upon the answer. In mid-October it was possible to peg the Hong Kong dollar at $7.80 to the US dollar, and reasonable economic stability returned.

Further meetings to develop the British position were held in London in early October. Yet again Margaret began by hankering after the possibility of leading Hong Kong Island and Kowloon towards independence as a separate entity. But again her head recovered control of her heart. So, when we finally met again with Sir S. Y. and his colleagues on 7 October 1983, it was she who argued most eloquently the case that Richard Luce, Percy Cradock and I had been urging for some weeks. On this view, the responsible course was to find a way of exploring the Chinese position without at this stage conceding any points in our own case. Most persuasively Margaret contended that a deal *had* to be sought because the Chinese would get everything they wanted anyway in 1997. The alternative was a collapse of society. Margaret did not always thereafter stick to the logic of that analysis. But on this occasion the argument carried the day.

Within a week, on 14 October, Percy Cradock was making another call on Zhou Nan, to deliver the Prime Minister's fresh message. We still regarded continued British administration as the surest basis for Hong Kong's future. But we were ready to explore alternative Chinese proposals for autonomy and the maintenance of existing systems in Hong Kong, including a continuing role for Britain – and to see if other effective methods could be agreed in a form which the Prime Minister could recommend to Parliament. The idea of a 'continuing British role', Cradock explained, had been commended by Wu at my New York meeting with him. This did not, we had to stress, involve 'any link of authority or accountability between the government of Hong Kong Special Autonomous Regime after 1997 and the British government'.

It was upon the basis of this 'second finesse' that the official talks in

Peking got back under way and continued throughout the winter. But the Chinese remained reluctant to enter into sufficient detail about non-British arrangements for Hong Kong's future. Yet they were increasingly insistent that all these matters had to be signed, sealed and delivered by September 1984. Deng had proposed 'one or two years' for discussions at his meeting with the Prime Minister in September 1982. That timing had now hardened into a deadline. Finally, in February 1984, they proposed the establishment of a joint commission for the surveillance of Hong Kong government during the last four years of our lease.

These were the discouraging circumstances in which I decided that the time had come for me to make a personal visit to Peking. Ahead of this we had a series of intense meetings with EXCO (the Hong Kong Executive Council) in London, in order to clear my negotiating decks as far as possible. We stressed the need to get over to the Chinese our view of what might constitute a realistic agreement. Once again Margaret joined in arguing this case with some passion: the alternative was to allow Hong Kong to pass into Chinese hands with no guarantee whatsoever beyond China's own basic 'twelve-point plan'. With some unhappiness, EXCO members accepted this case. Our plan was tabled by Richard Evans, our new ambassador in Peking. The Chinese put forward their counter-proposals, including a protocol outlining the unwelcome Joint Commission. Neither side accepted the other's text. By the time we set off for Peking, with my negotiating party and camp-following journalists on board, the Anglo-Chinese situation looked about as strained as it could be. And the Governor, who joined us there from Hong Kong, reported that EXCO were getting near to withdrawing their support from our position.

Off to Peking

Peking on the afternoon of Sunday, 15 April 1984 looked very different from the city that Elspeth and I had last seen (together with Leon Brittan) in 1978. The excitable band of Hong Kong journalists were bursting to quiz me as I stepped off the RAF VC10. The old single-track, cart-obstructed airport road was now a dual carriageway. The post-Cultural Revolution Maoist cloud had lifted. During all our 'Hong Kong visits' to Peking, we were accommodated at the Diaoyutai, a group of Chinese government guesthouses set among splendid lakes and gardens in the western part of the city. All my party were in one spacious building, with communal messing – and well-placed microphones, we did not doubt.

Our talks with Foreign Minister Wu Xueqian, which started the following morning and lasted all day, took place in another pavilion on the same site. The formal banquet (all such meals are dubbed 'banquets' in China) which they gave on the second evening was in another, attractively traditional building near by.

The rest of our programme, as always with the Chinese, was not disclosed at the outset. In particular we did not know, although we had made clear that we expected it, whether I was destined to meet Deng Xiaoping himself. The second day was devoted to meetings with Ji Pengfei (former Foreign Minister and now head of the Hong Kong and Macao Affairs Office, a rather forbidding, ageing figure, still in dark Mao suit) and with the Chinese Premier, Zhao Ziyang (a purposeful, more modern man: Savile Row and Turnbull and Asser). These two meetings took place in different salons in the Great Hall of the People.

My team and I had prepared ourselves with great care for these critical confrontations. We had a series of points to make, at best to get them accepted, at worst to get them lodged in Chinese minds. But once a point had got home with one Chinese 'witness', it could be positively dangerous to repeat it with another, for he might claw back or qualify the earlier answer. One needed to diminish as much as possible the atmosphere of confrontation implicit in this forensic approach. To this end I designed a series of metaphors which might serve to range us all on the same side. In my opening talk with Wu, for example, I likened Hong Kong to a Ming vase – an object of priceless value, which we were engaged in handing over just like the baton in a relay race. If we were not to risk the disaster of dropping the vase, we simply had to get our thinking in line with each other. So at the first banquet I asked Wu the age of a particularly striking candelabra on the table. 'Not more than three hundred years old,' he answered. I proclaimed my delight with the style of this reply. 'If you had been American,' I said, 'you would certainly have said it was "Well over two hundred and fifty years old" – but each of *us*, from a greater national maturity, can afford a little historical understatement.' Even before the interpretation was half over, Wu was twinkling his acceptance of my point. It was the beginning of an increasingly open and friendly personal relationship.

My meeting with Deng – my first – was certain, I knew, to be more testing than this. At last we learned that it had been fixed for the final (Wednesday) morning of our stay and was scheduled to last two hours.

By the time we reached this critical stage, I had secured provisional Chinese acceptance – by Wu or Ji or Zhao – of: our timetable, which would enable Parliament to debate and approve (but not amend) a draft agreement before it was signed; our insistence that both drafts were to remain upon the table, with many of the vital points of substance already in place; our demand that in the final document the details should be set out in annexes that were to have the same force as the main Agreement; and my plan to unveil before a Hong Kong audience the bulk of what had been agreed so far. We were still seriously at odds, however, about the dreaded Joint Commission; and our timetable had to be confirmed.

It was a long time since I had felt as nervous as I did when we were ushered into Deng's presence. The setting, the least grand of all the rooms we had seen in the Great Hall of the People, was modest enough, with none of the atmosphere of the throne-room that characterized such encounters in the Arab world. Contrary to Chinese protocol, the visiting party was ranged along the left side of the horse-shoe – Deng's 'better' side. Once perched compactly in his chair, he looked squatter than I had expected. He had few wrinkles in a face that was almost glazed, the whole effect rather like a Chinese figurine. Chief clue to his age was his hearing: he listened with his whole body, straining to understand our interpreter, who often had to be reinterpreted by Deng's own interpreter, the admirable Madame Zhang, speaking exaggeratedly like a daughter to an aged father.

Deng may not have enjoyed a personality cult by Chinese standards but his pre-eminence was obvious, and he displayed it in mercurial style, from the moment we entered, to the well-ranged banks of Hong Kong and Western cameras and microphones: he was a master of the photo-opportunity. He commented on the titled quality of my team, as I introduced Sir Percy Cradock (still with us as adviser), Sir Richard Evans (his successor at Peking), Sir Edward Youde and myself. I decided to enhance our authority by explaining to a bemused Deng that all four knights enjoyed the extra quality of being Welsh.

The real business began when I explained to Deng what had been agreed about the timetable. He readily accepted that the British Parliament should have time to consider the matter, and he contrasted, unfavourably, the US Congress: America, he said dismissively, had three governments. Then he was off on a long detour about the problems of Korea and Germany (two still-divided countries), before arriving at his idea for Hong Kong of 'one country, two systems'. I was happy to let him run the line out a long way on this. The real points that I needed to raise were few and our allotted two hours had to be filled somehow. It was in any case fascinating to hear the author of the four-word formula illustrating just how deeply he had analysed its value as a solvent of more than one problem. In due time, I brought him back to our Agreement, and particularly to the need for detail in our final text. After some resistance, I was able to persuade him to endorse the formula that had been agreed by Zhao.

Deng turned swiftly to the next subject, his anxieties about the transition to 1997, which in his eyes had started already. All these worries, he said, underlined the need for the proposed Joint Commission that was to sit in Hong Kong. But, since the British were afraid that such an arrangement might interfere unduly in the affairs of Hong Kong, might not the group meet in Peking or London as well as Hong Kong? When I replied that we should explore ways of solving this question, Deng interrupted me in mid-sentence to shake me warmly by the hand – and announce to the astonished company that we were agreed. He was certainly a sharp negotiator, despite appearances to the contrary! For his whole style gave the impression that he was flying by the seat of his pants. Unlike the others, who had doled out long prepared texts, he uttered a sentence or two at a time, appearing to improvise and grope for the right phrase, while gesturing a lot. He interrupted himself often, with self-deprecatory comments. 'When you're eighty,' he said, 'it gets hard to tell whether you're making mistakes . . . But by ninety I could become an old devil.' As though to emphasize his points, he several times leaned over and gobbed into his white enamel spittoon.

As he was on the point of rising, Deng said that he had forgotten to mention one final point: after 1997 China would station in Hong Kong a small garrison, similar to the present British garrison. Deng's 'forget-fulness' struck me as an attempt to slip in a really fast ball at the very end of our talk. I responded vigorously, 'We do not dispute your right to do that,' I said, 'but it would help confidence greatly if you were to refrain from doing so.' Deng agreed that the point could be discussed further in the talks.

And so it was over. Within a few minutes I was on my way to the airport, accompanied in the curtained, hearse-like official car by the ubiquitous Zhou Nan. I took advantage of the journey to remove any risk of misunderstanding as a result of Deng's pre-emptive handshake. All I had agreed to do, I stressed to Zhou, was to examine constructively

Deng's latest proposal for a peripatetic joint group. And I repelled a couple of hard-nosed try-ons by Zhou Nan himself.

Very soon the VC10 had us all aloft *en route* for Hong Kong. It was at times like this that we really relished the home-coming hospitality of the Royal Air Force. Never was I more ready for a glass of champagne and cold face-towel, followed by a tea of sandwiches and cake that would have done credit to a Jane Austen vicarage.

Explanations: HK to UK

Less than three hours away was the bustle and ceremony of arrival at Hong Kong. I was less than fully prepared for the almost vice-regal reception which the Colony customarily accords a visiting Secretary of State: a ceremonial welcome from the Governor, Chief Secretary, Commander in Chief British Forces, Leaders of Executive and Legislative Councils; an immediate appearance before the huge Hong Kong battery of cameras, microphones and journalists (for *this* I had fortunately prepared a brisk and slip-free statement); the escorted Rolls-Royce drive through streets and tunnels clear of traffic; and the ceremonial hoot on the car horn and salute as we swung into Government House.

Teddy Youde and our combined staffs had to steer me through a forty-eight-hour minefield of public exposure, to EXCO first of all, to larger audiences of legislative councillors, to social and business gatherings and, finally, to my closing press conference, not just before the alert Hong Kong media but also to world press commentators, whose customers took widely differing views of this (very parochial, as some thought) drama.

EXCO paid a generous tribute to our work, if only because of their relief that we had given no ground. They had no illusions about the difficulty of the hand I had to play. 'Very often,' said one of them, 'all you can actually do is re-arrange the cards in the Chinese hand: for they hold them all.' It was always strange to hear Hong Kong Chinese ('compatriots') speak, as they sometimes did, disparagingly of those whom we all called the 'Chinese'. EXCO continued to give me wise advice and general backing for the course ahead, accepting that no more than the British Cabinet could they expect to be consulted at every turn.

The 'unveiling statement', which I made from the Governor's chair in the Legislative Council chamber, was seen by the press as probably the most momentous news about 1997 ever to have been delivered by a British minister. There can have been little surprise in my statement that 'It would not be realistic to think in terms of an agreement that provides for continued British administration in Hong Kong after 1997.' But the shock came from the bald candour of these words, actually uttered by a British Foreign Secretary in Hong Kong: they were official. Expectations were sharply lowered. The shock was deliberately cushioned by what else I had to say. Genuine negotiations *were* taking place, even if they were 'complex and difficult'. They would not drag on for ever. A workable timetable had been accepted. Both sides had the will 'to bring the work to fruition in an agreement which will ensure the stability and prosperity of Hong Kong'.

Back in Britain I was able, on 16 May 1984, to sound out Parliamentary reaction to our progress. This debate was seen as an especially important occasion in Hong Kong, since it coincided with the presence in London of a delegation of Executive and Legislative Council members, led by the indefatigable Sir S. Y. Chung. This time they came armed with a manifesto, raising quite specific and legitimate points: how would Hong Kong's British citizens fare for protection after 1997? How was it proposed to test the acceptability to the people of Hong Kong of any possible agreement? They may have felt dismayed by their welcome, if only because no parliamentary voice was raised in criticism of my approach. It was indeed commended by Denis Healey for the official Opposition. But no less than twenty-two back-bench speakers took part in a debate that lasted until midnight, all of them urging me to intensify my efforts on behalf of Hong Kong.

Several times during the next two months the Peking talks looked like stalling altogether. On each occasion I was able to reopen the way by means of a personal message to Wu. There were some public nasty moments when Deng was receiving visiting delegations in Peking. The first was when he treated delegates from Hong Kong and Macao to the Chinese Parliament to an astonishing tirade about China's determination to station her own troops in Hong Kong. The second was when Sir S. Y. Chung and Miss Lydia Dunn (her name is an anglicized version of Deng), another outstanding EXCO member, presented themselves for an audience with Deng. The straightforward style of his visitors provoked an angry harangue from the great man, in which he denied their right to represent Hong Kong – indeed the right of Hong Kong to be represented at all. It was this clash, alongside the continuing deadlock over the Joint Commission, which determined me that I had to get back to Peking if we were to have any chance of success in the three negotiating months that remained.

I managed to obtain Margaret's support for that view, with the idea that I should above all reach a conclusion about the location and timing of the work of the proposed Joint Commission. By this time, of course, I was familiar with virtually every nuance of these negotiations and was effectively in charge of them. But it was important to be sure of Margaret's backing, and useful to be able to invoke her authority. So once again I had armed myself with a letter from her to Zhao Ziyang, indicating some ultimate flexibility on this, provided we secured essential points in the Agreement itself. Characteristically, Margaret wished to be consulted before we went firm on the final shape of any possible deal.

Back to Peking and Hong Kong

On 25 July we boarded the VC10 for another journey to Peking, this time via Hong Kong. The plane is well adapted as a mobile office, so we made good use of our time in the air. I was anxious to be sure that we had an effective draft agreement on the proposed Chinese Commission (now becoming the Joint Liaison Group, or JLG): that the Group's influence should be kept to a minimum, and yet look ample enough. So, working between Heathrow, Bahrain, Colombo and Hong Kong, Percy Cradock, David Wilson, Len Appleyard, Tony Galsworthy and I got through four drafts of this text, and emerged with something very like the final text of Annex 2 of the Joint Declaration.

Our visit to Hong Kong was tense but fruitful. It was clear that EXCO members wanted to keep the JLG away from Hong Kong for as long as possible, but were not prepared to see negotiations break down on that issue. Sir S. Y. and another of Hong Kong's very talented women, Maria Tam (a barrister), pressed what they called the 'mirror-image' idea – that the Group should continue in existence for some years after the end of the lease, whereby British surveillance of some kind might continue into the twenty-first century.

Soon we were back at the Diaoyutai guesthouse in Peking: it was beginning to feel like home. The next morning we went straight into a full day of talks with Wu. The Los Angeles Olympics were just beginning and I noticed that we were sitting down with eleven on each side of the table. 'What are we going to play', I asked: 'cricket or football?' I answered my own question. 'No, we are back in the relay race, *together*. Having come this far, we have now to be sure to pass the Ming vase on without accident.' I handed over Margaret's letter and our draft text on the JLG and made a full presentation of our outstanding requirements. 'The differences between us now', I said, 'are more on how to express ourselves than on the substance.' Wu nodded vigorously at this, and I began to believe that we were on our way. At the end of the morning Percy Cradock went off for a prearranged private lunch with Zhou Nan. It was there that most of the Chinese cards finally went on the table. They were ready to abandon their own open-ended protocol and to accept our draft text on the role of the JLG, to defer its location in Hong Kong for two years (probably until 1987) and to extend its life to the year 2000. Percy Cradock pressed our case for a longer deferment, but Zhou resisted. It was clear that the Chinese were seeking now to make or break a deal.

We held our group meeting to consider this offer away from the microphones of the Diaoyutai, pacing up and down in the shade of a flowering thorn tree in the garden. (Who knows if we were 'secure' even there?) We had not succeeded in postponing the arrival of the JLG in Hong Kong as far as we had hoped, but almost everything else seemed set to fall into place. It looked as though we had carried the Chinese close to their bottom line. With some hesitation on the part of Teddy Youde, we all took the same view. I arranged for this to be reported to London. On the following day, 29 July, Margaret reacted favourably but expressed the hope that we could postpone the arrival in Hong Kong of the JLG at least until 1990. Throughout the next day hard work continued on the detailed text – not least to secure inclusion in the final text of the word 'agree'. This turned the document from a political declaration into a formal international agreement: the Chinese were reluctant to go even as far as that to acknowledge any curtailment of their own exclusive sovereignty.

The Chinese had not wanted the bargaining this time to continue to the level of Zhao Ziyang, but I decided to have one last throw when I met him the next day, 30 July. So I proposed again deferral of the JLG's arrival in Hong Kong until 1989. Zhao stuck to 1988, but eventually accepted my compromise of 1 July 1988, just nine years before the expiry of the Lease. We had, I was satisfied, pushed the Chinese to their limit. There was no need now to tackle any of the other outstanding detail. To my astonishment I was able to take most of the afternoon off, visiting the magnificent Summer Palace in the perfectly sociable company, when not on duty, of Zhou Nan. And we dined on Peking duck with a great deal of *mao-tai* (the stiff Chinese liqueur) and Ji Pengfei as our less than sparkling host.

By the following morning Margaret had accepted the outcome (though still disappointed that we hadn't got beyond 1988), and Deng had returned especially for our meeting from the holiday resort of Beidahe. With nothing substantial to argue about, he was unexpectedly discursive. 'Look how sunburnt I am,' he opened, 'like an African.' He was full of enthusiasm for the Joint Declaration. Continued investment into Hong Kong would continue, he said, since the American and Japanese governments had assured him of that – 'so there's no need to bother about all the other less important countries, Indians and people like that.' I took the opportunity to correct him. 'Capital will only come in,' I said, 'if Hong Kong retains its magnetism. And that magnetism to attract capital depends on continuing freedom for capital to move away again. Nothing said by American or Japanese governments can achieve that but only what actually *happens* in Hong Kong. That's what our agreement is all about.' I'm not sure that he understood. For he launched into one of his suspicious critiques of the way in which the Governor and other British interests were only concerned with what they could get out of Hong Kong.

But he was quickly back in generous mood. 'For we have decided,' he said, 'that we can trust the British people and the British government. Please convey to your Prime Minister our hope that she will come to sign the agreement. And to Her Majesty, your Queen, our hope that she too will be able to visit our country.' His style was suddenly very courtly, and I felt as though we had been carried back through the centuries, so that I was like some barbarian leader being received for the first time at the Chinese Imperial Court. But the invitation to the Queen was indeed a public accolade for our success that boded very well for the remaining stages of the negotiations, and for the longer future. The Chinese 'deadline', which Deng himself had originally suggested, was now only two months ahead and from now on exercised as much pressure for agreement on them as on us. For failure would surely be unthinkable after this benediction.

It was time for me to return the compliments to the Chinese negotiators, which I did with particular enthusiasm for Wu Xueqian. Then I turned to his deputy. 'The Hong Kong negotiations without Zhou Nan,' I said, 'would be like a Chinese banquet without *mao-tai*.'

With characteristic vanity, Zhou turned this back at me as we drove together to the airport. 'Tell me, Sir Geoffrey,' he said, 'did you ever find *mao-tai* too strong for you?' But with much more grace, as he said farewell to our party at the airport, he quoted an apt fragment from a poem of the Sung dynasty: 'Just when the weary traveller despairs of finding a road, lo, a village appears, and shades of willow and riotous flowers beckon.'

There was one initial hazard about our presentation of the deal in Hong Kong. On Teddy Youde's advice, we had delayed briefing EXCO on the last dizzying rounds of negotiation, as we feared that they could not be properly advised in his absence. So we gave them two distinct opportunities to take in the news: first on the evening of my arrival, and again more formally on the following morning. Sir S. Y. Chung offered thanks and appreciation far beyond our expectations: we had achieved their main manifesto objectives and the early arrival of the JLG in Hong Kong was largely offset by the prolongation of its life beyond 1997. I was deeply moved to hear him say, 'I have high hopes that the final agreement will be acceptable to the people of Hong Kong.'

That afternoon I broke the news publicly to a press conference:

We have agreed . . . the framework and key clauses of an agreement which will preserve Hong Kong's unique economic system and way of life. . . . We aim to complete our work and initial an agreement before the end of September. . . . Hong Kong's economic and social systems, its distinctive way of life and its position as a financial, trading and industrial centre will be secured. . . .

This was not yet, of course, the whole Agreement. Important work remained to be done, chiefly on land, citizenship, aviation, Chinese troops and representative government. Even so, the reception accorded to my announcement was rewarding. The Hong Kong press were enthusiastic ('all but lyrical' according to one observer), the more so no doubt because of helpful comments from Sir S. Y. Chung and other leading personalities. The long flight home in the VC10 was enlivened by the gift which I received from two of our newsmen, Gordon Martin of the BBC World Service and John Dickie of the *Daily Mail*: an American business-education tape, picked up on a Hong Kong bookstall, entitled *Successful Negotiation*.

Closing the Deal

Cabinet, which I attended within little more than an hour of touching down at Heathrow, warmly welcomed my news. There was a touching note from former Prime Minister and Foreign Secretary Alec Douglas-Home: 'I have followed your comings and goings with great interest. This is just to send admiration and good wishes.' Although the breakthrough had been achieved in the two critical days of my second visit, the negotiations had been under way for twenty-two months. Hong Kong Department of the Foreign Office had grown during that time from three to twenty-three people strong. During nine months of 1984 they had received 2300 telegrams from Hong Kong and 1700 from Peking and despatched 2400 messages to both. Work on a mountain of outstanding detail was led by David Wilson (later to govern Hong Kong) and Robin McLaren (later ambassador to Peking). The Chinese deadline continued to work in our favour. The dozen or so sentences, the 'principles', with which the Chinese had started had been gradually transformed into a comprehensive and convincing international agreement almost 8000 words long. The last exchange of substance between Wu Xueqian and myself took place as late as mid-September. This led to his accepting (within two days) my important proposal that the post-1997 Legislative Council of Hong Kong would be 'constituted by elections' and that the executive would be 'accountable to the legislature'.

On 19 September the completed text was submitted to both governments for approval. Teddy Youde and other EXCO members met with Margaret and myself, Richard Luce, Percy Cradock and the rest of Cabinet's OD(K) (Hong Kong) Committee at Number 10, where Sir S. Y. reported that the Agreement was one which he and his colleagues 'could commend to the people of Hong Kong in good conscience'. On the next day, the 20th, Cabinet unanimously welcomed it.

The draft Agreement was initialled in Peking a week later on 26 September by Richard Evans and Zhou Nan. I announced this on the same day in my annual speech to the General Assembly of the United Nations and commended our work as 'an example of what patient negotiation could do for other disputes between nations'. When I reported the deal to Parliament a month later, Denis Healey generously set the tone by hailing the agreement as 'the most outstanding achievement of British diplomacy since Lord Carrington concluded the

Rhodesian negotiations'. Denis rounded off the congratulatory parliamentary exchanges by observing that 'this unfamiliar feast of love' might not be easily repeated, and I acknowledged his warning.

There followed a full examination of the extent to which our internationally binding Agreement was acceptable in Hong Kong – not, as we had candidly emphasized, as a perfect or ideal instrument but as a very good one, the best possible, and much better than the alternative of no agreement at all but a unilaterally proclaimed Chinese arrangement. On that basis, the Special Assessment Office set up for this purpose reported near-universal, if sometimes reluctant, acceptance. And on 17 December, the day after our first Chequers meeting with Mikhail Gorbachev, Margaret and I set off for the signature ceremony in Peking. That was redolent with symbolism. We stayed once more at the Diaoyutai (including a nostalgic visit to the tree under which we had agonized over Zhou Nan's critical offer on 24 July), and paid two more visits to the Great Hall of the People. The first was for the signing ceremony, preceded by a twenty-one-gun salute to the British Prime Minister and a goose-stepping march-past by units of the People's Liberation Army, with an equally well-drilled chorus of flag-waving schoolchildren. Deng and Margaret were on their best behaviour with each other throughout. The second visit was for the gala banquet given by Zhao Ziyang (with the largest ice-sculpture of a cockerel that I have ever seen). All these events were accompanied by specially invited Hong Kongers, from Sir S. Y. to Sir Y. K., Lydia Dunn to Maria Tam. For Zhao it was 'a joyous day' and for Margaret an 'historic achievement. . . . The successful outcome of our joint enterprise'. As we flew out to Hong Kong on my fifty-eighth birthday, 20 December 1984, Len Appleyard shared with me the memory of his first exit from Peking seventeen years before, after the British embassy had been sacked and set ablaze by turbulent Red Guards in 1967. We had been working, as he used this talk to remind me, to build a defensive structure for bad times as well as for good. In 1994 he found himself back in Peking, as Her Majesty's ambassador.

The good times certainly followed. Throughout the next four years Wu and I watched over the Agreement at a succession of working meals in Chinese embassies around the world – Berne, Bangkok and Brussels – and also when he came as our guest to Chevening (the Kent police were very alarmed when the Chinese Foreign Minister got lost jogging below the North Downs). He came with me to the Port Talbot steelworks and Welsh National Folk Museum at St Fagan's. I do not know what Wu thought of the mock-Victorian schoolroom and lesson which the Museum had laid on for us, complete with uniformed teacher and class – and cane. (Chinese schools still look rather like that today.)

Royal Endorsement

We saw plenty of 'happy' Chinese schools and children during the Queen's 1986 state visit, in pursuit of Deng's original invitation. The Forbidden City, the Great Wall, the Ming tombs, Xian (for the terracotta warriors), Kunming (for Lake Dianchi and the Western Hills), Canton and, most moving of all, Shanghai. To be driven in the Queen's convoy through hundreds of thousands of peering, cheering Chinese faces along the torch-lit streets of that almost Western city, to witness the Royal Marines beating the retreat from the deck of the royal yacht *Britannia*, moored alongside the celebrated Shanghai Bund – all this was to fire an exciting sense of history.

But one media-generated incident almost marred the entire trip. In Xian, after our viewing of the terracotta warriors, the Duke of Edinburgh joined a group of long-stay British students for some tea and a 'private' chat. When one said he had already been in China for several years, the Duke exclaimed, 'Good heavens, if you stay here much longer you'll develop slitty eyes.' None of those present gave another thought to this slightly banal piece of small-talk. But by the following morning we had to think and talk of little else. For it had come as meat-and-drink to the huge royal press corps who were (predictably) deployed to escort our caravan. 'Chinese fury at royal clanger', 'Duke insults Chinese' screamed the London tabloids (or so we were told in our overnight press summary). Bill Heseltine, then the Queen's private secretary, years later recalled the anguish of our discussion about which of us should advise the Duke that the Chinese would expect an apology. In the end, we agreed that Bill would speak to the Duke and I to the Chinese. Mine may well have been the easier task. For Wu, when I spoke to him before dinner at the Kunming banquet, professed ignorance of the whole trivial affair. When I explained, he brushed it aside with the comment: 'We know that he is a sincere man.' Some of the British papers still made almost as much of the 'apology' as of the original 'incident'. It was scarcely a serious shadow over the growing warmth and intimacy of relations between Britain and China that was to prevail until almost the end of my time in the Foreign Office.

Then on 4 June 1989 came the tragedy and outrage of Tiananmen Square. Nowhere were the shock waves felt more strongly than in Hong Kong. Exactly one month later, between 4 and 6 July, I visited the colony for the last time as Foreign Secretary. For all of us it was a gruelling experience. Many Hong Kong people perceived me, for the moment at least, as the architect of their new, more fearful, future. That was understandable enough. I felt as though I had become, for millions of frightened folk, almost a lightning conductor for their sense of shock. In truth, I was no more than an agent of history. Gradually the uneasy fact began to re-emerge. Even in deeply changed circumstances, the Joint Declaration remained the safest foundation for Hong Kong's future. It was designed, as I said then, as an agreement for the bad times as much as for the good.

Since then a new generation of politicians and public servants has been bringing fresh thinking to bear on the subject of relations between China and the outside world. Inevitably they have been overshadowed by the deeply symbolic clash in Tiananmen Square. For many people, in China as well as outside, that has been seen as proof positive of the ruthlessness with which a quarter of the human race will always be denied real political reform. For many others, perhaps more in China itself than elsewhere, it has been seen as a deeply regrettable, but perhaps unavoidable, hazard of preserving the stability that is essential, if economic (and so political) progress for that quarter of the human race is to match that of the rest of mankind. In December 1992, at the invitation of our own Prime Minister, John Major, I led a delegation to China 'to discuss matters of mutual concern, including human rights'.* This debate, in and with a nation with over 5,000 years of imperial history, will not be resolved in our lifetime. It remains to be seen how far it will be influenced by the rest of the world.

* Our Report was published by HMSO in June 1993

CHAPTER TWENTY-SIX

WEST–WEST DEBATE

Atlantic Partnership

The debate about East–West relations and arms control was not, of course, conducted exclusively between East and West. Britain's national debate – reflected even within my own family – had been settled, strategically at least, by the Conservative re-election victory in June 1983. Along with other NATO partners, Britain remained solidly committed to nuclear deterrence as the basis of her defence strategy, and to the parallel search for multilateral disarmament. There was general agreement about the case for deployment of Cruise and Pershing missiles, to match the Soviet armoury of 400 SS-20s already in place. On 14 November 1983 the first Tomahawk Cruise missiles arrived in Britain, at Greenham Common, and nine days later the first Pershing II missiles in West Germany. That same day the Soviet side walked out of the INF negotiations. Within the next three weeks they had broken off the strategic (START) and conventional (MBFR – Mutual and Balanced Force Reduction) talks as well. The months immediately ahead were destined to test to the utmost the firmness of the West.

The ministerial meetings and command structures of the North Atlantic alliance provided the setting for Western partnership. There were separate meetings of Foreign and Defence Ministers at least twice yearly. On special occasions these Council meetings would take place at heads of government level. In other, narrower groupings, ministers from fewer countries worked together in *ad hoc* partnership.

The one with which I first had to deal was relatively short-lived: George Shultz (United States), Claude Cheysson (France's Foreign Minister, 1981–4), Giulio Andreotti (Italy's veteran Christian Democrat, who was in charge of their foreign affairs throughout my time at the Foreign Office) and I were jointly responsible for the so-called Multi-National Force (MNF), which had been stationed in the Lebanon in a peace-keeping role since 1982. The British contingent (of armoured scout-cars) was no more than 100 strong, in a maximum total force size (mainly US Marines) of 2100. By the time I came on the scene this venture was already destined for disintegration. George Shultz describes the withdrawal of the US Marines (in the following February) as a 'virtual stampede' and a 'rout'.[1] Certainly it looked like that from London, where Margaret and I studied the conflicting telegrams from Washington with mounting disbelief. More than once during the last twenty-four hours (6 February 1984) orders for US warships to open fire were countermanded. The last message from Washington to my Office said simply, 'The Administration had shifted into neutral and hoped we would do the same. US military would "do nothing further" and only fire if fired upon.' The various European contingents, including our own, had no option but to follow the uncertain American lead. This incident – which certainly did not enhance European confidence in the steadiness of the American decision-making process – made a more powerful impression on me, I think, than it did on Margaret. Eight months later, *en route* for Israel, Elspeth and I made what was almost a *post mortem* visit to Lebanon. We flew in by helicopter from Cyprus to take lunch with President Amin Gemayel and his young family in their fortified retreat in the hills above Beirut. The visit lifted his morale but had only modest practical value. For even then the young President had only nominal power in a nominal country.

The other small group in which Shultz, Cheysson and I met several times each year was known as the Quad – the four ministers jointly responsible, in face of the Russians, for the protection of West Berlin. The fourth member of this team was Hans-Dietrich Genscher, Foreign Minister of West Germany since 1974. This was in some ways the foreign-policy equivalent of the old G5 group of Finance Ministers. We were able to take advantage of our Berlin 'cover' to get inside each other's minds on a number of sensitive issues. This set-up was jeopardized for a time when the Italians came to suspect that the 'Berlin Four' had held an overnight meeting at Chevening, plausibly *en route* for one of NATO's regular Brussels meetings.

The sixteen ministers who normally met under NATO auspices were a diverse mixture: eleven from the European Community (minus neutral Ireland) were joined by Canada and the US from across the Atlantic, by Iceland and Norway from the Nordic bloc and by Turkey from the 'southern flank'. I was lucky to be regularly placed (on alphabetical grounds) between Turkey and the US. It was stimulating to be able to get close to our Turkish colleague, Vahit Halefoglu, who held this position from 1983 to 1987, and was a shrewd judge of Soviet thinking, after two spells as ambassador in Moscow. He offered unusual insights too because of his attendance at meetings of the Islamic Council. It was refreshing to be advised by someone who often came straight from days spent trading opinions with Arafat, Assad or Rafsanjani.

It was obviously useful too to be able to caucus, however informally, with my other neighbour, George Shultz, the head prefect of our gathering. But if George was head prefect, none of us had any doubt about the identity of the headmaster in 1983. Joseph Luns, seventy-two years old, tall, gaunt and angular, former Netherlands Prime Minister, Foreign Minister and Defence Minister, had been NATO's Secretary General since 1971 and dominated even old hands like Genscher and Andreotti. It was a piece of good fortune, for the alliance as well as for Britain, that Peter Carrington, with his talent for genial coalition management, was available and willing, after his Falklands demise, to step into Luns' shoes in 1984.

Europeans v. Americans

In addition to our regular December meetings in Brussels, NATO Foreign Ministers met each summer in a different member-state – during this period once in Washington (1984), and later at the contrasting Portuguese and Canadian waterfronts of Estoril (1985) and Halifax (1986). Quite often a mid-Atlantic fault-line threatened to divide the group. Hans van den Broek (Netherlands) once widened it dramatically, after the US bombing of Libya in 1986,* by quoting a Dutch opinion poll that showed a clear majority (59/12 per cent) taking the view that the United States was, and was ready to be, more aggressive than the Soviet Union. I could sense George Shultz simmering in the seat beside me. But he kept silent until we had all reached the ironically colonial setting of Nova Scotia's beautiful Parliament House, for a more informal lunch gathering. Once there he not merely admitted but proclaimed the truth of the charge. 'Yes, I am aggressive,' he said, 'and in defence of America's interests, I intend to go on being so – *correctly* aggressive. I value your advice and I value this alliance, of course – but it depends upon American leadership. I intend

* See p. 504 below.

to go on giving that.' Few of us at the time were exactly grateful for such candour.

This was all in the background to the French initiative, starting early in 1984, for the 'reactivation' of the Western European Union. The WEU Treaty, between the six founding members of the European Community and the United Kingdom, had been signed in Brussels in 1949. A few years later it provided the peg on which to hang the decision in favour of West German rearmament, with a British commitment to keep no less than 55,000 troops stationed in that country. But the WEU had had no real organizational role for years. Our reaction, in London as elsewhere in Europe, to this proposal – born of French domestic politics as it was – was cautious, Margaret's predictably more sceptical than Michael Heseltine's and mine. Was it to cloak some new Parisian counter to NATO? Did it not in any event pose some threat to NATO's effectiveness? After much airing at EC and other meetings, the idea nonetheless finally took root. Michael and I managed to persuade a reluctant Margaret that the idea deserved British support. The British Army of the Rhine was, after all, a key component of European defence.

London itself provided another stage for part of this West–West debate. For the 1984 World Economic Summit took place at Lancaster House between 7 and 9 June, one week ahead of polling day in the 1984 European elections and a month ahead of my own visit to Moscow. The public-relations effect of the Summit was more than slightly marred by the impact of a giant anti-nuclear rally that effectively bisected London on the closing Saturday afternoon. Lancaster House had been judged too small for the closing press presentation of the (impressively specific) economic communiqué. So this unexhilarating event had been transplanted to the City of London Guildhall, some six or seven minutes away – with the kind of motorcade that other capital cities take for granted. But not so in London. For *all* the intervening roads had been choked by demonstrators. The anti-nuclear brigade had been powerfully reinforced by supporters of the National Union of Mineworkers: the NUM's bitter strike against the Thatcher government was now in the thirteenth of its fifty-one weeks. In the result, half the heads of government and other ministers (including Margaret herself and Presidents Mitterrand and Reagan) were marooned in the London mob, for fifteen minutes or more. It was not easy at the Guildhall end to find enough small talk to preserve the tranquillity of Premier Trudeau, Chancellor Kohl and the rest.

One irony is that I had been hoping to move the 'London' Summit away from the crowded metropolis. A year before, after a detailed study of alternatives, we had come up with the idea of Gleneagles (with the media accommodated, but insulated, at nearby Stirling University). The Cabinet secretary Robert Armstrong had submitted this joint analysis to Number 10 for collective consideration. But the paper had been returned by Margaret overnight, with a curt note of her 'decision': instant (and therefore undiscussed) rejection of any innovation. There were more important causes to champion at Number 10, so I let this one pass. But this, I suppose, is one way in which authority gradually shifted towards the centre.

Michael Heseltine and I managed that autumn, however, to secure some collective discussion of defence and foreign policy with Margaret, at another Chequers seminar, formally on the subject of NATO, on 1 October 1984. One session was concerned with the rather philosophic question – extending from Nicaragua to Afghanistan – 'Is intervention ever justified?' Our supporting cast for this included several international lawyers, whose views diverged. In future years George Shultz and I, and – more tenaciously – George and Cap Weinberger between them, were to exchange speeches and papers and to hold discussions in search of objective truth on this topic. But, much as it grieves a lawyer to say so, we rarely escaped the cynical logic of the observation that 'one man's terrorist is the next man's freedom fighter'. Even when we were agreed on this aspect of a particular problem, it was not always easy – as Libya was to demonstrate – to agree on the right response.

Similar tensions, although less sharp, began to emerge in our other discussions. For the key defence questions really arose in the end from the permanent British dilemma: how far are we, will we in the future be, wise to base our security on a transatlantic or on a European foundation? And how far are we wise, and how long should we be able, to go on postponing any final choice? There was always a difference between Margaret's instinctive reaction to these questions and my own. Yet the difference was never, so far as I was concerned, an absolute one. The same was true, I believe, for my two successive partners as Secretary of State for Defence, Michael Heseltine and George Younger. None of us overlooked the historic and weapon-based bond between American and British forces, particularly in the nuclear field.

Yet we all felt, I believe – Heseltine, Younger and I – an equally strong instinct towards strengthening our European defence linkage. It was in America's interest, as well as Europe's, that Europe should pull its weight. And there always lurked the question: What if, when the balloon really went up (which God forbid), the Americans were to take a different view from Europeans about the ultimate questions? If there was logic in maintaining our own 'independent' deterrent, was there not sense in concerting our thoughts and actions more closely with those in Europe who felt the same way – most notably the French (whose deterrent was, I was ready to acknowlege, more credibly independent than our own)? Would not such thinking enable us to detach ourselves a little from some American policies, which were not always in our own national interest?

However naturally those questions might arise in my mind, it was hard to see them doing so in Margaret's. Indeed, I knew that she would instinctively recoil from them. Yet already we had shared one moment (the American invasion of Grenada in 1983), and were to share others, when the issues underlying my questions were very real.

Star Wars

At the time of our discussion in October 1984, the topic which raised these questions most sharply was Ronald Reagan's favoured notion, the Strategic Defence Initiative (SDI), which he had launched in his 'Star Wars' speech of 23 March 1983. The basic idea was that the sky over the United States (for example) could and should be so stocked with anti-ballistic weaponry (mounted in satellites and automatically brought into action) that there would be established an impenetrable shield against attack by the enemy's ballistic missiles. For Reagan, in particular, this opened up the seemingly attractive prospect, as he said in his original speech, of rendering nuclear weapons 'impotent and obsolete' and thus 'freeing the world from the threat of nuclear war'. The President's powerful instinct was to see this as a way of escape from the central doctrine of nuclear deterrence, the risk of 'mutual assured destruction' (MAD).

There were many questions that could be asked about this notion: would it ever be technically feasible? Was its likely cost acceptable? How would it deal – if at all? – with *non*-ballistic missile weapons (which never got into space at all, but were delivered by Cruise missiles or conventional artillery or even in suitcases)? And – theoretically most important of all – did not the whole line of thinking belie the ultimate effectiveness, legitimacy even, of nuclear deterrence itself?

For the Russians, the speech was particularly significant. It had been made only two weeks after the President had dubbed their country an 'evil empire', a phrase which, as George Shultz acknowledges, came to stand for 'a certain implacability in Ronald Reagan's approach to the Soviet Union'.[2] Reagan's latest text raised for them the very real fear that the US meant to shield herself completely against the Soviet's strategic nuclear threat, while retaining – even enhancing – her own nuclear sword. Russia would be obliged herself to join the space research race: could she be confident of technical success? And, even if so, could she afford it? Most far-reaching of all, would not American development of the SDI infringe the 1972 Anti-Ballistic Missile Treaty? If that treaty was to be set aside, the way might indeed be open for a nuclear-weapons race in space.

For America's allies, rather different questions arose. Suppose the USA was able to render herself immune from the Soviet nuclear threat, what assurance would America's NATO allies have that the US deterrent would still be committed on their behalf? Yet what guarantee was there that America's SDI umbrella would, or could, extend into our skies as well? Was the President not opening the way to the very notion we all feared, of Fortress America? For British (and French) nuclear strategists, in particular, the Reagan concept raised the theoretical possibility – if Russia herself was successfully to join the SDI club – of our own nuclear weapons being rendered ineffective and thus obsolete.

And so on. The miracle is that the debate remained muted for so long. By the time Michael Heseltine and I came to discuss this topic at the Chequers seminar, our experts had all come to similar conclusions about the hazards of the concept. Its main defensible feature, we all felt, was the need to keep ahead, or at least abreast, of Soviet research. Margaret was much more reluctant to express any such conclusions – not so much because she doubted the logic of the arguments as because of reluctance to side openly with Reagan's critics. She was prepared – more prepared than I was – to back research along the lines that Reagan had in mind. She had been immersed in the nuclear debate, as head of government, much longer and more deeply than I. At least since 1975 I had been contemplating such things almost entirely through a Treasury prism, which had made me technically as well as financially very sceptical about such projects. Margaret shared some of my dismay at the simplistic extravagance of Reagan's expectations. But her own scientific background made her more inclined to look positively, with more technical curiosity, on the work of fellow scientists. Certainly she was less likely than I to be wary of American enthusiasms.

Our Chequers discussion reaffirmed the broad thrust of NATO's dual-track policy for the months to come: deployment of Cruise and Pershing to go ahead, while keeping up pressure on the Russians to reopen negotiations on intermediate as well as strategic nuclear weapons. The December 1984 NATO Brussels meeting turned into a collective briefing for just that purpose, in light of the prospect that Shultz and Gromyko were to meet in Geneva in January 1985. But on the NATO agenda, we never got round, at least at that stage, to any very candid discussion of SDI. The Americans seemed almost as shy to proclaim it as the rest of us to expound our anxieties. Even Shultz (who had struggled to contain Reagan's enthusiasm for the project) was probably constrained, as I now believe, by a White House–Pentagon ruling that the US should decline to discuss SDI in any setting, for fear that that might make it a bargaining chip.

The last Anglo-American encounter of the year was one to which I was not bidden. Margaret and I had been in Hong Kong and Peking together for the signature of the Joint Declaration. From there my party returned direct to London, while Margaret took the VC10 on round the world in the opposite direction for a short pre-Christmas meeting (22 December) with Ronald Reagan at his Camp David retreat. The agenda for a three-hour working lunch had not been specifically prepared. But Margaret had two purposes in mind: to brief Reagan about our impressions of Gorbachev, and to steer Shultz into the best pro-alliance posture for his forthcoming meeting with Gromyko. After discussing our briefing across the Pacific with her Foreign Office private secretary, Charles Powell, and then in Washington with Oliver Wright and John Kerr, then a member of his staff, she was ready to focus on SDI ahead of most other topics. Ronald Reagan was accompanied by the two Georges, Bush and Shultz, but by nobody from the Pentagon. And Margaret was able, by expressing strong support for the SDI *research* programme while stressing the importance of the ABM Treaty (and assisted no doubt by George Shultz's earlier anxieties), to secure Reagan's agreement to a short, crucially important four-point statement (actually drafted by John Kerr):

First, the United States and Western aim is not to achieve superiority but to maintain balance, taking account of Soviet developments. Second, SDI-related deployment will, in view of Treaty obligations, have to be a matter for negotiation. Third, the overall aim is to enhance and not to undermine deterrence. And fourth, East–West negotiation should aim to achieve security, with reduced levels of offensive systems on both sides.

Margaret later came to believe that George Shultz was dismayed that the Americans had conceded too much in this wording.[3] That certainly was not the case. In his own words he regarded it as 'an excellent statement: it differentiated between research and deployment and gave me [Shultz] some running room at Geneva'.[4] For Britain and the European allies, it went a long way towards drawing the most disturbing teeth of the SDI programme.

Despite the initial negotiating success of the Camp David four points, Margaret and her government – partly because we backed the attempts of British defence contractors to win a large share of SDI research work – became more and more identified with the very different case for the SDI that was being presented by Richard Perle and other Pentagon hawks. I grew increasingly worried that we were effectively consenting to the next stage of a nuclear-weapons race in space.

On 20 February 1985 Margaret (accompanied by Michael and myself) gave her much vaunted address to both Houses of Congress. Using Churchill's words, she proclaimed the importance of nuclear deterrence. She emphasized the ABM Treaty and warned that SDI deployment would have to be negotiated in accordance with that. But she left her audience in no doubt about her final position. 'I used my speech,' she says, 'to give strong support for SDI. I had a terrific reception.'[5] Like many others in Europe, I was dismayed that the central anxieties on which I had thought we were all agreed were being overlooked. A gap was opening up between our objective assessment of the arguments and our publicly stated position. Eight years later it became much clearer that Margaret was already fretting at the concept of collective policymaking in this field. For she has explained how the pressure of Michael Heseltine and myself cramped her style when she talked and lunched with Reagan on that day. 'I did not bring them again,' she concluded.[6]

So, not surprisingly, I decided to correct the balance, by stressing the more interrogative view of SDI which we had formed in the run-up to Camp David. About a month later, on 15 March 1985, the Royal United Services Institute offered a suitably expert London audience. As required by Whitehall rules, we sent a final draft copy of my speech to the Private Offices of Michael Heseltine and the Prime Minister.

Michael's office signalled that he was content with my text. Number 10 had not replied before Margaret and I had to set off together to Moscow for Chernenko's funeral (on 13 March). But on our return to London there came a letter from Charles Powell recording – to our slight surprise, it must be said – that the Prime Minister 'had seen and approved' my speech.

My clear starting point was the Camp David four points. Research into defensive systems is permitted by the ABM Treaty and made necessary and prudent by the scale of the Soviet research effort. But, like all research programmes, this raises many questions. (Although I did not know it then, many of them had been asked by George Shultz – but not answered – before the President made his original SDI speech.)

What should happen, I asked, if and when decisions are required on moving from the research to the development stage? Would the supposed technology actually work? Would it ('as Mr Paul Nitze* has noted,' I added), provide defences that not only worked but were sensible and cost effective? Could members of NATO be sure that the US nuclear guarantee to Europe would indeed be enhanced as a result of defensive deployment?

Credit for my most headline-grabbing point ('there would be no advantage in creating a new Maginot Line of the twenty-first century in space') should be given to Michael Pakenham, the head of our Arms Control Department, who contributed incisively to the crafting of the original speech. Ironically, exactly the same point had been made two years before, by the Assistant Secretary for European Affairs, Laurence Eagleburger, to George Shultz as they studied an early draft of Reagan's original Star Wars speech. But that did not prevent a transatlantic explosion as soon as the text of my speech was released. The most violent (and public) reaction came from Assistant Defense Secretary (nicknamed in Washington the 'Prince of Darkness') Richard Perle, who happened at the time to be due in London for a conference. The very intemperance of Perle's reaction ('Sir Geoffrey's speech has proved an old axiom of geometry that length is no substitute for depth') deterred the White House from their original instinct of expostulation to Margaret. She had in any case reacted by instructing Charles Powell to inform Ronald Reagan that the speech 'had not been made with her authority'.

My RUSI speech, as it came to be known, made a powerful impact.

* Veteran US arms-control and strategic expert.

It provoked *The Times* to a leading article of massive length and unbalanced ferocity: 'The Foreign Secretary's speech . . . may have done untold damage . . . at a critical juncture. . . . Mealy-mouthed, muddled, negative, Luddite, ill-informed.' Almost everywhere else in Europe, East as well as West, it was warmly received. On my visit to Czechoslovakia three weeks later, I was startled to find that the text had been broadcast in full on Prague radio. That was not quite the audience that I had had in mind. But thereafter I was increasingly perceived on both sides of the Iron Curtain as a usefully independent participant in the East–West debate. And I had successfully pointed up a British alternative to Margaret's technique of influencing American thinking by starting from a premise of loudly proclaimed loyalty. More and more Europeans were coming to feel that, when it came to the crunch, their governments had no real influence on America's strategic thinking and that established NATO mechanisms for consultation risked becoming unidirectional. There was a corresponding interest in strengthening the European half of the alliance. Hence the moves towards revitalizing the Western European Union, in which Britain was taking part. Ian Davidson, in one of his thoughtful *Financial Times* pieces, on 1 April 1985, shrewdly highlights some of the wider implications of this discussion: 'Sir Geoffrey's speech suggests that British loyalty is no longer as unconditional as it once was thought to be. Who knows, perhaps even the British government is starting to think of itself as a European power among Europeans.'

The Number 10–FCO Axis

My speech also highlighted the tensions that were developing between the Foreign Secretary and Prime Minister. Even during my time at Number 11 some friction had, of course, occurred occasionally. But on most big issues (the 1981 Budget) or tactical questions (the timing of interest rate changes) differences were generally ironed out either by fuller debate or by the passage of time. Contact between us and our private secretaries was easy and frequent, because of the connecting door between our two houses, which were also our offices. And we always shared a unity of purpose on the main thrust of economic policy. Foreign affairs were never likely to be so easy. 'There is nothing so difficult or delicate in the management of government', wrote Harold Macmillan, 'as the relations between the Prime Minister and the Foreign

Secretary. They must really be like brothers in a partnership'.[7] During my four years at the Treasury the Thatcher–Howe partnership had something of that sibling quality. But it became very different during my six years at the Foreign Office, not, I think – at least initially – for personal reasons but largely because of Margaret's profound antipathy towards the Office.

. 'Like all human institutions,' writes Robert Rhodes James, 'it [the Foreign Office] has its weaknesses, but it is a machine of great power and influence abroad which several Prime Ministers have not only ignored but on too many occasions despised and distrusted.'[8] This was certainly Margaret's attitude, and it had not been softened by her Falklands experience. More even than for most other departments, she strove always to keep the FCO – and thus to some extent the Foreign Secretary – at arm's length. Because of absences abroad, my regular meetings with her, as distinct from committees and 'small group' occasions, often failed to keep up even the weekly timetable that was our aim.

The tendency for our thinking to drift apart was increased too by the growing volume of solo foreign travel. For Foreign Ministers that was part of the job. In today's crowded, jet-linked world the habit seems to make sense for heads of government as well. But it becomes less satisfactory if a President or Prime Minister gets into the habit of dealing on his (or her) own with ministers of an important country. A certain tension in this particular relationship is perhaps inevitable. Sir Nicholas Henderson has noted 'the customary ill humour' of Foreign Secretaries 'when accompanying the PM on visits abroad, which is nevertheless nothing to their mood if there is any suggestion of their being left behind'.[9] Certainly I was never too happy to be travelling as Margaret's number two – not least, I suppose, because of her unquenchable tendency to play second fiddle as well as first. But like other Foreign Ministers, not to mention my own predecessors, I feared that separate summitry on her part might lead to divergence on key questions. Sometimes too it could diminish the authority of the Foreign Secretary. George Shultz had told me, after all, how his perception of the gap between Margaret and Francis Pym had prompted him to discount the latter.

No serious problem of this kind was yet arising between Margaret and myself. But the SDI issue was only one of several on which it was going to be important to reconcile our two approaches, or if necessary to play them both in a joint strategy. There were some topics (over and

above the European Community) on which it would have been positively helpful to exploit our differences of emphasis in a properly
orchestrated approach. But we too seldom consciously partnered each
other in that fashion. This is because Margaret was too often looking
for a way that did not leave her dependent on Foreign Office advice –
hence her tendency to invoke the authority of '*my* people' in support of
her own approach. 'Her people' extended from men like Brian Crozier,
David Hart, Alfred Sherman, Woodrow Wyatt at one extreme to more
orthodox figures like Henry Kissinger, Julian Amery or Franz Josef
Strauss. There was nothing wrong in this. The danger came from the
tendency to invoke these voices in deliberate counterpoint to the FCO's
(often more rounded) analysis, without enabling '*my* people' even to
know or test the validity of Margaret's own sources. This meant that on
some occasions my office and I had to spend almost more time on
managing, informing or finessing Number 10 than on getting the whole
of the rest of the world into line. It is easier now to see exactly why that
was so than it sometimes was at the time. For Margaret Thatcher's own
words now make plain the difficulties of our task. 'Laid back generalists
from the Foreign Office,' she writes, ' – let alone the ministerial muddlers
in charge of them – could not be relied upon.'[10]

Crucial figures in managing this sometimes uneasy dialogue were the
private secretaries at Number 10 as well as in my own office. Their role
was infinitely varied and required the utmost personal sensitivity and
political shrewdness. A good private secretary should be able to react to
a thousand difficult situations with an almost intuitive sense of how his
'boss' would want him to react. Yet he would need to know just when
he could not safely rely on his own judgment, so that his Secretary of
State or Minister would need to be consulted. The other requirement is
to know when and how to advise his Minister about issues that need a
special professional insight and which could not safely be handled by
political instinct alone. The propriety, as well as the effectiveness, of
government was especially the province for the good private secretary.

The Foreign Secretary's Private Office (about two dozen people in
all) was in the care of three private secretaries with diplomatic experience, ranging from the youngest in his or her early thirties to the senior,
the principal private secretary (PPS – not to be confused with the
similarly initialled parliamentary private secretary, who was invariably
an MP), some ten or fifteen years older. At least one, sometimes two,
came with me on overseas trips, while one remained in charge of the
office. Relations with Number 10 were normally handled by the PPS.

The Number 10 Private Office was headed by the Prime Minister's PPS (conventionally an under-secretary from the Treasury or Home Office – at this time Robin Butler of the Treasury), while all her foreign business, with occasional very important exceptions, was handled by the one diplomat detached from the Foreign Office to serve – conventionally for two to three years – as her foreign affairs private secretary.

Private secretaries, in all departments, were appointed only with the personal approval of and after interviews by the Minister concerned. Departments naturally took some care to offer the highest-quality choice, not least when putting names forward for the Number 10 slots. I had had to make two important choices in the autumn of 1983, as replacements for Brian Fall, as my own PPS, and for John Coles,* at Number 10. Among those whom I interviewed were Len Appleyard and Charles Powell. The Office, I understand, had intended the first of these for Number 10 and the second for me. But I knew Appleyard much better, from the time that he had spent on secondment to the Treasury during my Chancellorship. I was confident from that experience that he was the right man for me. So Charles Powell, without any kind of shadow against his name, remained free to go forward for Number 10. As is well known, he went on to serve Margaret well – perhaps too well – in that capacity.

It was after a year in that office that he found himself having to cope with my SDI speech and to write first to my office with the news that the Prime Minister had seen and approved the text, and then, a few days later, to the White House, with a message to exactly the opposite effect. Most of the books say the confusion arose because Margaret herself had fallen asleep over the text of my speech, on the flight back from Chernenko's funeral. It is very hard to believe the other suggestion – sometimes made – that it was Powell himself, and not Margaret, who faltered in that way.

History might have been very slightly different had my own speech been intercepted by Charles Powell on its way to delivery. But it might have been a good deal more different, I fancy, if Charles Powell had been intercepted by me on his way to Number 10.

* Coles succeeded Sir David Gillmore as permanent under-secretary at the FCO in August 1994.

CHAPTER TWENTY-SEVEN

THE FONTAINEBLEAU
SOLUTION

Home Thoughts from Abroad

My personal centre of gravity had soon shifted a long way from the Treasury base, where it had been rooted for so long. I was probably airborne for at least ten hours a week and overseas for much longer than that. This was bound to have an effect on my personal position in the political spectrum – on the Westminster stage, in the public eye, in my relations with colleagues.

Certainly the day-to-day intimacy between Number 10 and 11 was no longer sustainable, as I have shown. And Margaret's and my instinctive responses to a European or an American bugle-call would no doubt have been different, even in those days. That would have been true, at least in degree, of our reactions to initials like ANC and PLO. But we shared a positive view of Britain's role in East–West dialogue. None of the old Commonwealth issues – from Hong Kong to Gibraltar – quite threatened to tear us asunder, though South Africa was to come close to doing so.* And neither of us was so directly and passionately engaged in the politics of the Middle East that the Finchley factor (Margaret had a large Jewish element in her constituency) could create an unbridgeable divide between us. We discussed such questions, sometimes in preliminary fashion on journeys in each other's company, and resolved most of them sensibly enough at our talk-ins at Number 10. That is not to say that it was easy. Our discussions often followed a prolonged exchange of minutes or notes between our offices (and with other colleagues, when necessary). Meetings of ODP (Overseas Defence Ministerial Committee) were relatively few and were frequently

* See Chapter 32 below.

concerned with weapons-purchase decisions: in themselves full of hazard, as Westland was to show.

This limited involvement with colleagues in foreign affairs was matched, naturally enough, by the scale of my own insulation from Cabinet consideration of domestic affairs. Even pre-Budget discussion was a remarkably relaxed occasion for me in 1984, and apparently for Nigel as well. In course of the proceedings, on 9 February, I passed him a note: 'Lucky chap! You're dealing with a much more economically literate Cabinet than I started with!' This evoked the flattering reply: 'You have been the greatest educator in political history!' I was not so sure about that. But I was certainly determined to remain engaged in the domestic debate, and throughout my six years at the Foreign Office I generally devoted at least one weekend a month to travel and speech-making in different regions of the UK. The planning and management of these tours was one of the most important functions of my special advisers, in those days John Houghton and Adam Ferguson.

Often enough events at home brought me back to the Commons despatch-box. News that Arthur Scargill was seeking cash help from Colonel Gaddaffi for the miners' strike added fuel to the flames of that controversy. Later in the year I intervened again in that dispute. On two occasions I had cause to rebuke Ambassador Popov for similar Soviet interference: first Afghan trade unions (as though such things had an independent existence) and then Soviet miners had been caught sending cash assistance to Scargill's increasingly beleaguered strikers.

But no task absorbed as much time as my meetings with fellow Foreign Ministers of the European Community. This meant at least that we got to know each other's negotiating style, personality and national characteristics. Now was the time to put some of this accumulating knowledge to good use, for the twelve-month time limit set at Stuttgart, in June 1983, for finding an answer to the British Budgetary Question was fast running out – as indeed were the existing resources of the Community. The Athens Summit on 5–6 December 1983 had made no effective impact on any of these questions. Now everything was up to France, which took over the Presidency of the Community for the first half of 1984, ending with a meeting of the European Council at Fontainebleau on 25–26 June. It had become clear that President Mitterrand had recognized the need to grasp this nettle. The Community would need more resources when Spain and Portugal joined in the following year, and those extra resources would be made available only if Britain cleared the way by declaring herself satisfied with future budget-sharing arrangements. France also had a major interest in the outcome, since she was about to join Germany and the UK as a net contributor to the budget. And France, like Britain, was one of those nations that took the Community seriously.

Roland Dumas, France's European Affairs Minister and one of France's top trial lawyers (Mitterrand and Picasso had both been clients), was a tough, shrewd negotiator and an engaging advocate. The time had come when he and I should get together to seek out, if we could, a generally acceptable solution. Chevening offered the ideal setting for this kind of hard-headed, entirely private negotiation. So over two separate weekends he and I – with our David Hannay and his opposite number from the Quai d'Orsay, Guy Legras – gathered round the huge centre table in Chevening's magnificent tapestry room and put together the elements that went to make up the ultimate solution.

There were three fundamental questions. How should we measure the scale of British grievance? To what extent should it be remedied? And over what period of time? Our continental partners – those who were prepared to acknowledge we had a problem at all – wanted to determine the scale of Britain's grievance at a fixed annual sum, declining from year to year and lasting for a strictly limited number of years. Their baseless theory was that the problem was and would be self-correcting. Our case was exactly the opposite: we needed a solution which automatically reflected the probably growing scale of the imbalance and which 'would last as long as the problem would last'.

The French were ideal negotiating partners for this closing stage of the battle. For they, better than most, could recognize the strength of our determination in defence of a national interest. Moreover, they had the intellectual agility to identify, and argue with skill, the points where negotiation could oblige us to temper the strength of our case. We were aiming together to find an answer which the French Presidency could then sell to the other partners and table for acceptance at the Brussels meeting of the European Council on 19–20 March 1984, *en route* for the Fontainebleau Summit in June.* For that we needed a clearly stated formula. The figures to be inserted into the formula would still be for agreement by heads of government. And that, as experience proved, would be a hard enough task for them. As Brussels drew near, we thought – Hannay and I – that we had arrived at an answer which

---

* In those days the European Council used regularly to meet three times a year; the frequency was cut by the Single European Act 1986 to two a year.

Dumas and Legras were ready to buy, and sell. But, for reasons which we could only guess, they had not tabled it by the time proceedings started in Brussels on Monday, 19 March.

For the two working dinners at the Palais d'Egmont on the first evening – Foreign Ministers and heads of government – there was thus no fresh material available on which to base discussions. Margaret had already told the earlier plenary session of our willingness to accept the gap between VAT share and expenditure as the basic measure of the scale of our grievance. (Few, if any, of the other heads of government had understood the point: but Dumas and I knew well enough what she was talking about. It referred to a modest, and diminishing, UK concession in the method of measuring our payments to the Budget.) So at dinner Margaret and I could only sit tight and privately urge the French to table our 'agreed' solution for consideration the next day. We Foreign Ministers had other topics on our dinner agenda. By the time we had exhausted these, and each other, it was already 10.30 p.m. 'Were the heads ready to go home?' we asked. Apparently not. They were deep in argument. What about? The budget question, we were told, with Margaret reportedly in full flood. This did not augur well.

There followed an hardly believable scene. For the Foreign Ministers were not free to go home, in case – as was still theoretically possible – they were summoned to join the heads for a (probably less than lucid) late-night discussion. Yet we had nothing left to say to each other – not surprisingly after days (and weeks) in each other's company. So we found chairs and *chaises longues* on which to rest in the hall of the Palais. Very shortly the place began to look like a wartime waiting room at Crewe station, with ministers strewn round snoring, though without soldierly kitbags on which to rest their heads. I was more wakeful than most, since it was my boss who was, apparently, prolonging the agony. So I assumed the responsibility of telling the word-weary interpreters that they at least could go home to prepare for a long tomorrow. Around midnight the heads emerged, sleepy and bad-tempered, to make for home. Back in ambassador Michael Butler's house (where we were both staying), Margaret explained that she had been propounding the case for the VAT share–expenditure gap, to the increasing irritation of her largely uncomprehending and certainly unsympathetic colleagues. It was hard to understand how or why she had got into that quite unnecessary argument.

We had to hope that their irritation would have subsided by the following day, and we put together a plan on that basis. Margaret would see Mitterrand, ahead of the Council meeting, and once again press the French to table a proposal that reflected my long talks with Dumas. By lunchtime on the Tuesday, 20 March, this had happened. But it was too late for delegations to be properly briefed. Discussion was inevitably confused. Chancellor Kohl began to get impatient (it was his turn – just as it had been Mitterrand's, with Kohl in the chair, at Stuttgart). Craxi, of Italy, had never got over his irritation of the previous evening. Eventually Kohl made a half-baked proposal – in effect an extension of the 'temporary' Stuttgart system – at 1000 million ECU a year to Britain. That met nobody's long-term needs. Time ran out. And Brussels had solved nothing.

The Fontainebleau Summit

So Dumas and I were back to our drawing board – but not entirely, for we knew our components were basically right. They needed, the French felt, to be substantially simplified for Fontainebleau, to be held on 25–26 June. Word reached me, via Robin Renwick (who had taken over from David Hannay), that Dumas had an exciting new idea he wished to share with me privately and informally. So we proposed dinner together in Brussels on the eve of the next (June) Foreign Affairs Council meeting, at one of the city's best restaurants. The food was first class, certainly, and the conversation lively enough at first. But oh, the service was slow. So what, I said finally, of our great work? What indeed? came the reply. As we waited for our dessert, it became clear that Dumas had nothing to say: on a Sunday evening that we should both have preferred to be spending with our families, the small talk ran out. And so, as soon as we decently could, did we. Only months later did I find out that Dumas had accepted my invitation on the strength of an identical misunderstanding – that *I* had a brilliant new thought to share with him. It was the blindest date that either of us had ever endured.

But at Fontainebleau itself we were able to get a French paper before the Council that contained the simplified essentials: an automatic mechanism for the retrospective abatement of Britain's contribution by a simple proportion of our VAT share–expenditure gap. And the duration of the system was to be 'linked' to the duration of the proposed increase in total Community resources, to which we had agreed – in principle at Stuttgart – as a condition of securing our own settlement. All that remained to be fixed was the percentage refund. Suddenly the close seemed near. We had been seeking something over 70 per cent. Kohl shifted from 50 to 60. Margaret assembled our team, Michael Butler, David Williamson and myself, in one of the little salons that surrounded the palatial conference room. We were all of one mind. It was time to settle. Margaret saw Mitterrand, who was ready to offer 65. We still wanted two-thirds. Mitterrand said you'll have to persuade the whole Council to give you that. Margaret accepted his challenge – and got the figure up to 66 per cent. That single extra percentage point was, over the next ten years, to be worth at least £150 million to the United Kingdom.

So it was easy to justify the toughness with which we had argued our corner, when we had to do so. Whether such tactics always work is a different question. If used as a matter of course rather than in exceptional cases they can store up counter-productive resentment in others. But this was certainly not the time for mutually critical reflection. For we had ended the long tussle to place the Community finances on a more settled basis, and solved, at last, the British Budget Question. The Commons gladly gave Margaret great credit for our success, when she reported the Fontainebleau outcome on 28 June.

The Palace of Fontainebleau had itself offered one revealing insight into the cultural balance of French life. This magnificent sixteenth-century château seemed to be wholly without toilets. And no one had briefed me about the range of point-to-point-style portaloos that had been installed in one of the salons. So, off on a search of my own, I had found my way to a rather splendid, fleece-carpeted, gold-plumbed toilet suite. On leaving I was greatly embarrassed to walk almost into the arms of the President, approaching his own private facility. He was as relaxed then as he had been throughout the entire Council, over which he had presided with some skill.

At lunch on the last day, in the Salle des Colonnes, Mitterrand expounded with enthusiasm his plans for the enhancement of Paris. 'It is a President's duty, and his pleasure, to add to the architectural grace of his country's capital city. And,' he stressed, 'with the world's *best* architects.' He surprised us all, I think, by his willingness to put his pet projects – later to become the Louvre Pyramid, the Grande Arche de la Défense and the Opéra Bastille – out to entirely unrestricted international competition. This certainly challenged our view of traditional French chauvinism over matters of taste. And it was remarkably successful. For within five years of that Fontainebleau lunch, when we were back in Paris for the Economic Summit and Bicentennial celebrations in July 1989, the three splendid buildings he had had in mind were not merely designed but actually in place. The contrast with the story of the British Library, say, or the Bridge Street extension to the Palace of Westminster could hardly be more dispiriting. The completion of Britain's not so *grands oeuvres* seems to require as many decades as the French need years.

European Identity

So it was a pleasure to host, the day after Fontainebleau, on 27 June, an impeccably British function in one of our most attractive royal palaces. For I had arranged for this year's Queen's Birthday banquet in honour of the Diplomatic Corps to take place in the Great Hall at Hampton Court, by chance on the last day of the Islamic Ramadhan fast. The sun went down just soon enough for our Muslim guests to join us in eating the main course. I could look back on an eventful few weeks: the month that ended at Fontainebleau had started with the London Economic Summit. In between, on 14 June, we had managed with remarkably little fuss, our second round of direct elections to the European Parliament. For this election (as later in 1989) the production of the Tory manifesto, *The Strong Voice in Europe*, had been managed under my chairmanship, in harness with our experienced leader in the European Parliament, Sir Henry Plumb. It had been a low-key campaign (with a 31.8 per cent poll), in which we had lost seats, but still retained an overall UK majority of nine.

The Irish took over the Presidency of the Community for the second half of 1984 and it was, in that context, a quiet six months. I spent an enjoyable day in Germany on 19 September with Hans-Dietrich Genscher, visiting some of the 66,000 British troops permanently stationed in that country, who were taking part jointly with the Bundeswehr in the major NATO manoeuvre, 'Operation Lionheart'. I returned a month later to make an important speech in Bonn. 'In the first place,' commented *The Times*, 'Sir Geoffrey stated with unmistakable clarity that Britain's commitment to Europe is "profound and irreversible". This cannot be said too often in a place where it is so often doubted.' I was indeed seeking to demonstrate, explicitly, the range of Britain's European commitment and, by implication, to suggest that the

Franco-German relationship should not be seen as the only cornerstone of the European Community.

I left my audience in no doubt of my own view of the importance of that relationship. For only two months before Elspeth and I had visited, twenty kilometres from Limoges, the sacked village of Oradour-sur-Glane, where 642 innocent French civilians (men, women and children) had been brutally put to death by German SS troops four days after D-Day, on 10 June 1944. The fire-stained ruins had been a chill reminder of the central purpose of our European endeavour. In my Bonn speech, I stressed that Britain would indeed be helping 'to build the common European identity to which we all aspire'. The same message was implicit in the warm reception given, a week later, to President Mitterrand when he spoke during his state visit to Britain from the same spot in Westminster Hall as President Charles de Gaulle had done, thirty-four years before.

The year's end saw a general post in the membership of the European Commission. The unremarkable Presidency of Gaston Thorn, the former Luxembourg Prime Minister, was drawing to a close. It had been firmly, if informally, agreed that it was Germany's turn to fill the top job. Like others, we had been encouraging Helmut Kohl to find a 'good German' – a personality of sufficient strength and quality for this position. Once again the Germans had not really tried to fill the bill. Mitterrand's first suggested French alternative, Claude Cheysson (his own Foreign Minister), did not appeal to Kohl any more than he did to us. The French second choice, Jacques Delors, was much more generally acceptable. I had developed considerable respect for his performance as the fellow Finance Minister who had tamed French Socialism. Margaret was ready enough to join the consensus in his favour. As though to emphasize the strength of French commitment, President Mitterrand pressed ahead with the nomination of Cheysson to fill the second French slot. This left the way clear for Roland Dumas, Mitterrand's own man, to take over at the Quai d'Orsay.

Both the serving British Commissioners were also retiring: Ivor Richard, our Labour man, after only four years; Christopher Tugendhat had done a full eight years, the first four as Roy Jenkins' junior partner and the second as the senior Conservative Commissioner.

On appointment as a Commissioner, the individual is expected to abandon any national or party loyalty and to give his collegiate allegiance to the Commission itself. And that is what, for the most part, they do. But inevitably there are occasional conflicts of instinct, if not of loyalty, on particular issues. Margaret took a straightforwardly severe view of these. Whatever the Treaty might say about the Commissioners' theoretical position, she looked – particularly to the Conservative Commissioner – for unwavering commitment to the wishes, if not the commands, of Her Majesty's Government. This Christopher Tugendhat had, quite rightly, not been willing or able to give. How could any Commissioner expect his voice to carry weight with his colleagues if he was thought always to be acting as no more than the agent of his own national government? Yet Margaret came close to expecting that kind of relationship, and so to blaming Christopher whenever he failed to convince the Commission of 'our' case. It was worse still, of course, if he went so far as himself to reject it. He stood convicted, in her eyes, of having 'gone native', unforgivably. In truth he had never been forgiven for having taken the job in the first place without Margaret's blessing and at Jim Callaghan's direct invitation.

So in seeking a successor to Christopher, Margaret naturally looked for someone entirely after her own heart – for 'one of us' in the familiar phrase. We had a strong candidate for this slot in Arthur Cockfield. His singlemindedness in our cause, particularly during his seven years as one of my Treasury colleagues, had been exemplary. I shared the view that Arthur would be a robust and energetic Commissioner. But I never imagined that we should be able to command his constant loyalty once he had moved to Brussels. I knew, from my experience of his earlier commitment (under my suzerainty) to the chairmanship of the Prices Commission, that his sense of integrity would soon generate its own allegiance to his new role. Even so there was a good case to be made for having a British Commissioner who was likely to be as committed to his job as he was competent. Cockfield's fellow Commissioner was to be the former Labour junior minister, Stanley Clinton-Davis.

Nineteen-eighty-five was the year in which we were able, now that the budget problem was out of the way, to make a powerfully distinctive contribution to the 'relaunch' of the Community, for which the new President Jacques Delors was looking. This turned above all on the appointment – for which we had worked – of our new Commissioner, Arthur Cockfield, to the crucial internal-market portfolio. Arthur seized this opportunity with characteristic zeal and mastery of detail. Within months he had secured publication by the Commission of the White Paper, *Completing the Internal Market*. This identified some 300 measures needed to achieve, by a 1992 target date, the establishment of the full 'Common Market', the originally declared objective of the Treaty of

Rome. It was endorsed by the June 1985 European Council in Milan and was a commitment with which Margaret could identify as much as any of us. For a moment Arthur succeeded, because of their common enthusiasm for the single market, in winning the simultaneous admiration of both Margaret Thatcher and Jacques Delors. It was a short-lived achievement: for very soon it was Delors, and not Margaret, who was able to rely on Arthur's tenacious commitment to his cause.

There was general support too for the negotiations for enlargement of the Community, to include Spain and Portugal. Talks had dragged on for years, with the most intractable problems arising over fishing and agriculture. They fell to be resolved when the veteran Italian Giulio Andreotti was in the chair of the Foreign Affairs Council. Several times already Italian Prime Minister (most recently at the Tokyo Economic Summit, in 1979) and long gossip-linked to the Mafia, he had returned to their Foreign Office at the same time as I had first arrived in ours. Intelligent, laconic, hump-backed and dark-suited, with a sharply witty tongue, he attended Mass every day, wrote a column for *Oggi* every week and a book almost every year – he made more from his writing, so he told me, than from his politics. Every time we met each other in Italy or Britain, Andreotti presented me with a bunch of elegant Gucci ties. He had exactly the stamina-laden temperament necessary to conclude the negotiations with Portugal and Spain.

The complex deal was concluded in time for the Accession Treaty to be signed in both countries on a single hectic summer's day, 12 June. I remember that as a revealing, informal twenty hours of Europeanism at its most relaxed – and most exhausting. Britain's signing formalities were in the hands, literally, of her two chief European Wykehamists, Michael Butler and myself. Flown by RAF HS-125 from Heathrow at 6.00 a.m., we were received (with other heads of government and Foreign Ministers) by Prime Minister Soares on Lisbon's Tagus waterfront at the Torre de Belém. The signing ceremony itself took place in the sun-drenched cloister garden of the Jeronimos Monastery. We enjoyed an almost picnic lunch in the cloister itself. The RAF carried us to Madrid for a more ceremonial evening at the Palacio Real. The signing in the Salon de Columnas was followed by a dinner and champagne reception hosted by the King of Spain. The earlier spontaneity of the Portuguese Republic contrasted with the restrained grandeur of the Spanish ceremonial, engagingly offset, as it was, by the relaxed style of the Spanish monarch and his consort. We retired at a suitably late Madrid hour, for a (very) few hours' sleep at the Ritz. We left early enough to be back at Northolt by 08.15 – in time for Cabinet on the morning of Thursday, 13 June.

My British team claimed, privately, a little special credit for this success. It could have been completely derailed had we not been able to clear the way for Spanish membership of NATO as well as the Community. That was made possible only with the strenuous help of my opposite number, Fernando Moran, with whom I had found at least a partial solution to the historic Gibraltar dispute. After fifteen rough negotiating months we had the previous February signed an agreement for the reopening of Spain's land border with the tiny colony (it had been closed by General Franco in 1969) and laid the way for talks about the sovereignty of the colony. Anglo-Spanish relations were greatly enhanced by this understanding. By 1988 each of the two monarchs had made a state visit to the other's country, and Margaret Thatcher herself paid a notably successful visit to Madrid.

Milan and a Failed British Initiative

Beneath all this apparently plain sailing for the Community another important issue was about to break surface: was there a need to amend the Rome Treaty itself, if we were to make headway even on our own basic British objective of the single market? Agreement on some of our most cherished aims was proving impossible because the existing Treaty required unanimity on the necessary legal decisions, and that was constantly being blocked by one protectionist country or another. Yet the Treaty could only be amended – as the UK might, in this respect, desire – after the holding of an Inter-Governmental Conference (IGC). But, once an IGC had been convened, any and every possible 'constitutional' amendment could be proposed and discussed. Pandora's box would indeed have been opened.

Eventually I thought we had found a way of squaring this circle: let us propose the acceptance of a constitutional 'convention' – a concept more familiar to Anglo-Saxon than to continental minds – whereby the written Treaty would remain unchanged; but there should be agreement, written but not legally binding, that in respect of all the single-market agenda we should proceed as though the unanimity rule had been set to one side and been replaced by rules for qualified majority voting. This would be the obverse, I explained, of the so-called Luxembourg Compromise – invented and insisted upon by General de Gaulle, whereby a country could insist (whatever the rules said) on unanimity on 'a matter of vital national interest'. Many times I explained this informal 'British' approach to groups of bewildered continental parliamentarians, for whom charters, declarations, solemn acts, single acts, constitutions even, were their real *raison d'être*.

However sincerely I might present this argument in European dress it was bound to strike many of our partners, accustomed to think of 'British negativism', as simply a new way of projecting our old stance. If it was to have a chance of carrying conviction it needed to be backed and flanked by a comprehensively positive attitude on most, if not all, the other European questions. Remarkably Margaret had by now been persuaded, on the surface at least, quite positively in that direction. Already she was a genuinely enthusiastic protagonist of the single-market agenda. Now we were able to persuade her also to accept the case for some movement on foreign policy. There existed some arrangements, that had been working quite well, for political co-operation between the Ten. The time had come, thought my advisers and I, for these to be codified and brought together in a new framework for European Political Co-operation – a kind of precursor of the Common Foreign and Security Policy of the later Maastricht Treaty. So we drew up the text of a free-standing agreement, a draft treaty if you like, which embodied little, if anything, beyond a codification of existing practice.

I was able, with the help of advisers in the Cabinet Office and of Michael Butler in Brussels, to persuade Margaret that she should be the one to produce this on the European stage. Indeed better than that, I thought: she should use it as a way of persuading Helmut Kohl to team up as a joint sponsor of the scheme. (I still had at the back of my mind Kohl's advice, in the Williamsburg washroom, that I should urge Margaret to 'woo people' more openly.) So Kohl was invited, unprecedentedly, for a Saturday afternoon and evening at Chequers. The intimacy of the occasion was underlined by the absence of any matching invitation to Genscher. In due course Margaret put forward the proposal. 'I am putting it to you personally like this, Helmut,' she said, 'because I want it to be a genuinely joint endeavour, between the two of us. It will be a useful partnership – and, anyway, it's a good idea.' The Williamsburg romantic was not, I have to say, much in evidence in the Chancellor's response. Certainly Helmut did not seem to have appreciated the importance of the exchange. But the paper was tucked into his briefcase and he promised to look at it. His advisers must surely have seen the point.

Margaret was ready to undertake one more initiative ahead of the June Milan Summit, as part of our campaign to convince people of our seriousness. She agreed to circulate a discussion paper, outlining all the positive features of our approach, entitled 'Europe: The Future'. I developed the same themes and was able to make some real headway, most notably at the Italian 'informal' at Stresa. But all this was badly blighted by the fate of Margaret's attempt to 'woo' Kohl. For not only was there was no response from him, just a few days before the Milan meeting on 28–29 June 1985 there appeared reports of a 'new' Franco-German proposal for a Treaty of European Union. The section on political co-operation bore a close similarity to the text that Margaret had given the Chancellor just one month before. She was furious, and so was I. We have never received a word of regret or explanation from Helmut Kohl or anyone on his behalf. The incident can hardly be said to have done a lot for Anglo-German relations. Not that it did much for the Franco-German axis either. Even the French press saw the Treaty as 'a device for patching up relations' and 'an attempted last-minute coup', and were deeply wary of its substance. *Le Matin* wrote of 'the spectacular evolution of the British position . . . which will confuse those critics normally sceptical about Britain's European enthusiasm'.

The Milan conference venue, when we finally did get there, gave a characteristically Italian impression of having been thrown together like some scene-stealing film-set. Prime Minister Craxi's briefing and chairmanship had something of the same quality. The Council was long and increasingly bad-tempered on all sides. Margaret, with more excuse for tetchiness than usual, contrived to get us emotionally aligned with Papandreou at his worst. Craxi made no effort to seek consensus, rather relishing the conflict on his Milan home ground. For the first time at a European Council meeting, the chair pressed for a decision by majority vote rather than by consensus. We had certainly not anticipated this. On the narrow issue – to hold or not to hold an IGC on Treaty amendment (with an open agenda) – Craxi was technically entitled to do so. But the temptation for him to behave in such fashion was building up steadily as a reaction above all to the sharp tone of British leadership.

Milan had in truth been a miserable experience, hugely typical of the switch-back emotions of European Community politicking. Only a week or two before it had looked as though we might be on course for a strikingly successful outcome, with a great deal due to imaginative British input. But the result was very different. Bad temper on all sides, some poor judgment on our part, even more selfishness from the Italians had us now on course for what looked like a bruising, open-ended battle all the way to Luxembourg. Who could know where and how that would end? One thing was for sure: it meant another grinding round of hard work, with no assurance of success. One was tempted almost to turn one's back on the whole thing. But it was too important for that. Europe, like Parliament, even like democracy itself, had this 'unique' capacity to infuriate and yet to keep one ensnared. Downcast and dismayed I might feel today, but duty would call again tomorrow. In any event, hope was glimmering on another horizon. Just a few months later we would be signing an historic agreement with the Republic of Ireland.

CHAPTER TWENTY-EIGHT

ANGLO-IRISH AGREEMENT

First Dealings with the Province

The Anglo-Irish Agreement of 1985 is among the most enduring monuments of the years in which Margaret Thatcher and I shared responsibility for the foreign policies of the United Kingdom. How did we find ourselves, how did Margaret Thatcher, in particular, find herself, drawn towards this remarkable development?

Neither she nor I entered politics with any special concern for Northern Ireland. During our early years at Westminster there was no need for either Margaret or I to cast our eyes across the Irish Sea. I have one recollection from the days of the first Wilson government, which catches the mood of the time. George Thomas, the Member for Cardiff West and later Lord Tonypandy, was at the despatch-box when I wandered late one evening into an almost empty House of Commons. He was then a Parliamentary Secretary at the Home Office and replying to a crushingly routine debate about Northern Ireland. 'And so,' said George, 'I can tell the House with some confidence that conditions in the colony—' His slip of the tongue stirred the little cluster of Ulster Unionists into contrived uproar. 'Oh dear, Mr Speaker,' said George, 'what have I said?' – and, with his lilting Welsh accent, that was the only apology that the Minister needed to give. For in those distant days the 'colony' still seemed at peace with itself and the rest of the world. The atmosphere was to grow very different over the next decade.

My role as Shadow Chancellor (1975–9) and then Chancellor of the Exchequer (1979–83) took me to Ulster three or four times, principally to expound our economic policy and to absorb Ulster's views about its impact. The Chancellor is one of the few UK ministers with any direct responsibility in and for the Province. So I made it my business to visit the Ulster headquarters of Customs and Excise, for 'my' tax-collecters were often in the front-line of attack by terrorists. I called too on the ill-starred DeLorean automobile enterprise and had the disturbing experience of a test-ride in one of their gull-wing cars – unequipped with lights as dusk was falling! The whole project struck me, as I recorded at the time, as 'conceived on extravagant and wasteful lines'.

This underlined the feature of Northern Ireland policy that could not escape the notice of either the Chancellor or the First Lord of the Treasury herself: the prodigious and mounting cost of the Union to the British taxpayer. Net transfer of funds to Ulster from the rest of the Kingdom (*ex*cluding defence costs) rose from under £1250 million in 1979–80 to almost £2500 million in 1991–2 – equivalent to some £4500 a year for each of the 530,000 households in Northern Ireland.

This had had no effect, however, on the broad continuity of our policy towards Northern Ireland during the first eight years of Margaret Thatcher's leadership of the party. It was based firmly upon the maintenance of the Union. The few paragraphs that I included in our 1983 manifesto made only the most modest concession towards Jim Prior's eighteen months of work as Secretary of State for Northern Ireland. As with the 1979 manifesto, the key sentences were cleared with Number 10 through Ian Gow. Ian acted not only as Margaret's massively conscientious PPS from 1979 to 1983, but also, on this front – as Jim not unnaturally complained – as the equally strict guardian of her Unionist conscience. She wanted, as Ian knew, to remain faithful to the legacy of Airey Neave, whose brutal murder by the IRA had deprived her of one of her closest advisers. Her Unionist instincts, like those of Ian, were constantly refertilized by his regular liaison – with Margaret's knowledge, if not on her behalf – with Enoch Powell, who had now for ten years represented the Ulster constituency of South Down. (My own earlier enthusiasm for Enoch had been sadly but remorselessly eroded long before he got as far as Ulster.)

For all these reasons I had not, from my Treasury eyrie, been very sensitive to the modest (and more or less subterranean) fluctuations that had taken place in Margaret's thinking. In December 1980 I had gone with Peter Carrington, Humphrey Atkins (then at the Northern Ireland Office) and the Prime Minister to an unprecedented Anglo-Irish Summit in Dublin Castle. This was at the time of Margaret's initial – and surprising, if short-lived – affection for Charles Haughey, during his first spell as Taoiseach (Irish Prime Minister). I say 'surprising' because

Haughey's Fianna Fail Party, the Republic's largest, was strongly nationalist and generally regarded as the least flexible on constitutional questions. So it was a real achievement for Haughey to secure from Margaret a future commitment to give 'special consideration to the totality of relationships between these islands'. Nothing substantial, however, emerged from that in Haughey's time. All that I can now recall about the 1980 excursion is an exchange with the Irish Treasury official who was my lunchtime neighbour: 'How do you like this claret, Sir Geoffrey?' 'Very well indeed,' said I – perforce. 'And so you should,' came the reply, 'at £84 a bottle.' Treasury officials are much the same the world over.

Garret FitzGerald's brief first spell as Taoiseach (in 1981) was not long enough to engage my attention. And for most of my remaining time at the Treasury, Margaret's view of Ireland appeared to be largely dominated by the impact of hunger-strikers (ten had starved themselves to death in the Maze prison, during Humphrey Atkins' gruelling two years as Ulster Secretary) and by her renewed coolness – to put it mildly – towards Charlie Haughey, following his government's foolish (but sustained) support for Argentina over the Falklands conflict.

The intractability of Ireland's problems (and personalities) had therefore – for the moment and not for the first time in history – taken them off the British Prime Minister's action list. It was thus all the more strange that Margaret chose that moment (September 1981) to hand responsibility for Northern Ireland to one of her most action-oriented (and then still ambitious) ministers, Jim Prior. But if that was strange, it was also characteristic that Margaret had made this change not for the positive reason that she wanted him to direct his energies to this new, and thus far intractable task. On the contrary, Jim had been sent to govern Northern Ireland for much the same reason as some predecessors had been sent to govern New South Wales – to get him out of the Prime Minister's hair.

But he was not to be so easily disposed of. For very soon he was engaged in the preparation of a fresh plan of direct rule: a form of 'rolling devolution', which could (if it went well) lead to the emergence of a genuinely local assembly. In the result it was boycotted by the SDLP – John Hume's constitutional Republican Party – and so failed to get off the ground. But the incident is remarkable mainly for the extreme reluctance with which Margaret allowed Cabinet approval for Jim's Bill – and for the openness with which my old friend Ian Gow (still then Margaret's PPS) seemed to enjoy virtually complete freedom to lobby the parliamentary party against the Bill. The lobbying was not successful: but it was for Jim an infuriating example of Margaret's determination, on occasion, to have her cake and eat it – more than once if she could.

FitzGerald Opens a Door

Jim Prior was still at his Ulster post when I moved in June 1983 from Treasury to Foreign Office – and so to take up a share of direct responsibility for Anglo-Irish affairs. By this time the topic had become one which I was glad to take in hand. For although my work as Chancellor had not exposed me greatly to the domestic aspect of Irish affairs, their international aspect had begun to engage my interest significantly. This was a direct result, I came to understand, of the way in which Irish and British ministers found themselves working alongside each other within the European Community. As Chancellor I had come to appreciate the absurdity of ignoring the practical case for partnership, between the peoples and governments that shared the British Isles, within the wider concert of Europe. All this had predisposed me, without my fully realizing it, to the approaches that were soon to come from Garret FitzGerald, who in December 1982 had returned to power in Dublin. After Margaret's re-election with the towering majority of 144, FitzGerald took advantage of their first meeting (at the Stuttgart European Summit) to propose substantive talks on Anglo-Irish relations. She was, says FitzGerald, 'immediately receptive' to the idea. And so, certainly, was I.

He was lucky to find ready to hand not just the machinery but also the people who would be able to turn his agenda into action. For in his previous existence, at the November 1981 Summit meeting with Margaret Thatcher, he had secured the establishment of a body that was to play a crucial part in the months ahead: the Anglo-Irish Intergovernmental Council. It was crucial because of its composition: the Steering Committee – which reported directly to the two Prime Ministers – was under the joint chairmanship of the two Cabinet secretaries. On the British side this had the particular advantage of ironing out, in advance, the dispute that would otherwise have been certain between Northern Ireland and Foreign and Commonwealth Offices over which should be the lead department on this sensitive topic. Even though the two ministers involved, Jim Prior and I, both took the same positive view of developments, that would not in itself have ensured harmony at the official level.

More important even than that was the presence in the driving seat of the negotiations – for that was what lay ahead – of a man with exactly the right qualities for the task: Sir Robert Armstrong. For this infinitely sensitive and patient subject he had the ideal temperament – and previously engaged experience. We were even more fortunate that the senior Foreign Office deputy secretary then in the Cabinet Office was precisely suited for this very work. David Goodall was a deeply reflective and industrious Catholic, descended from an old Anglo-Irish family in County Wexford. His experience in diplomacy had included serving the Prime Minister during the Falklands War. So he enjoyed the unusual advantage of being trusted on both sides. The Irish official team was hand-picked and of comparable quality.

But even this galaxy of skill could not have carried these negotiations forward without the inspired tenacity that Garret FitzGerald brought to his mission. Margaret deserves real credit too for being ready to rise to the historic challenge involved – and still more for the way in which she subsequently championed and upheld the outcome. She never for a moment forgot her overriding concern to achieve a more secure, less violent, future for the Unionist community. She did become intensely engaged in the negotiations, but at no stage was she the pro-active partner. It was for the Irishman to make the running.

The first full meeting of the two regular teams took place at Chequers on 7 November 1983. Armstrong, Goodall and I were with Margaret at all the meetings over two years. The third ministerial slot was occupied successively by Jim Prior, Douglas Hurd and Tom King. FitzGerald was throughout accompanied by his Tanaiste (Deputy Prime Minister) Dick Spring and his Foreign Minister Peter Barry: Spring was the barrister who led the Irish Labour Party and Barry a tea merchant from Cork. Garret was at his most persuasive best in the spacious comfort of Chequers, where Margaret too was often at her most relaxed. It was here that he achieved the first breakthrough, by persuading Margaret that the *status quo* was unacceptable and that, if no progress was made towards a political solution, there was real danger that Sinn Fein would replace the SDLP as the main voice of nationalist opinion – with the inevitable consequence that violence and terrorism would increase. It was this last point that always drove Margaret most strongly: security, success against the men (and women) of violence, was her main preoccupation.

FitzGerald's hardest task was to persuade her that, even on that score, the way forward lay in securing greater minority acceptance of and involvement in the political, legal and security processes in Northern Ireland. This was the point on which, time after time, the two premiers fell out – often over the meaning and use of the word 'alienation'. For Margaret, it always had a Marxist ring. For Garret, it conveyed very clearly the sense that the bulk of the minority community in Ulster was simply unable to identify with, or accept the legitimacy of, the British forces and institutions of justice and order. As a Welshman, I found much less difficulty in grasping this concept. I was and am no narrow nationalist and am generally the first to bridle at Cymric parochialism when I encounter it in Wales. But I have still not forgotten the atmosphere of English strangeness, hostility even, that for many years I used to sense on stepping out from the Red Dragon express on to the streets of Paddington. So I could see exactly what FitzGerald was getting at. It was his genius that he was able to offer Margaret some real insight into that – and more. For he persuaded her too that if 'alienation' was to be overcome ('I do wish you would stop using that dreadful word, Garret,' she would cry), then it was necessary to establish an 'Irish dimension' – involving *some* kind of formal role for the Irish government in the affairs of Northern Ireland.

That first Chequers meeting triggered a year's intensive work in which the two sides struggled to find common ground. The Irish made clear that they were seeking a role amounting to 'joint authority', in return for which they were prepared to hold a referendum to seek approval for amending Articles 2 and 3 of the Irish Constitution to remove their territorial claim to the North. For our part we made clear that we were not able or willing to concede the Irish a role that went beyond 'institutionalized consultation'. Much of the discussion throughout 1984 was taken up with scaling down Irish expectations on that point, and with deciding whether what we could offer could be regarded by them as enough for constitutional amendment.

The same trio of ministers, Margaret, Jim and I, met regularly with Armstrong and his official colleagues. Another long in-house meeting at Chequers in January enabled us to develop proposals for which we obtained Cabinet approval in March 1984. Margaret was notably cautious throughout. Most guarded of all our colleagues was Quintin Hailsham, whose family's Ulster background made him a constant reminder of the Unionist case. For different reasons, prompted by his own robust and chastening experience, Willie Whitelaw also took a very wary view. But in principle he was always strongly supportive of our endeavour. And Jim was tenaciously and sensibly positive. The point to which he and I repeatedly returned was that 'the risks of doing nothing are currently greater than the risks of any attempt to achieve political progress'. If we wanted more effective cross-border security co-operation from the Irish government – as we all did, and Margaret most of all – then they had to be able to demonstrate an enhancement of their political role in the affairs of the Province. This less than heroic argument enabled us to keep both Prime Minister and Cabinet sceptically in step and supportive of the continued search for a balanced package.

The routines of the European Community continued to offer opportunities to keep the show on the road. Peter Barry and I were able to share insights or defuse tensions on minor issues at our regular monthly meetings and half-yearly informal weekends. In October 1984 we went with all our colleagues from the UN General Assembly to Costa Rica. By offering Peter Barry a lift in the small plane that we had chartered for my return flight from San José to Miami, I created the chance for another useful talk with him. We had with us a packet of Barry's tea, which I had commissioned before departure – so that we could make Peter feel really at home. Unhappily the aircraft offered us no means of boiling water in-flight.

Garret had his own Euro-chances to keep up his dialogue with Margaret. A talk at the Fontainebleau Summit on 25–26 June paved the way for another over lunch at Downing Street on 3 September. FitzGerald was in London on that occasion as Mitterrand's successor in the Presidency of the EC Council of Ministers. European business was fortunately light, and talk over the Downing Street lunch table had provoked Dick Spring and me into a series of Welsh and Irish courtroom anecdotes. This prompted me to remark that we were among the few nations in the world, certainly the only two in Europe, for whom the whole idiom of such private jokes was mutually and completely intelligible. FitzGerald responded by telling us of the night that he had spent, years before, in one of the children's bedrooms at Jo Grimond's home. 'Nine out of the ten books,' he exclaimed, 'were ones that I had read in my own childhood. See just how close we are to each other in so many ways. All the more reason, Margaret,' he concluded, 'for us to seek ways in which our peoples can share their lives together more peacefully.' It was agreed that the next Anglo-Irish meeting between the two ministerial teams would be at Chequers on 18–19 November.

Attacks and Setbacks

By that time two important events had intervened. Most dramatic was the IRA's bombing of the Grand Hotel, Brighton, in a bid to murder the Prime Minister and other members of her government just before 3 a.m. on Friday, 12 October 1984. The main conference hazard for me was over, I thought, by 4 p.m. on the Thursday. My closing speech in the foreign affairs debate had gone well. A long evening of broadcast interviews, parties and receptions stretched ahead, until past 1 a.m. Elspeth had been glad to hear from my principal private secretary, Len Appleyard, that he'd kept the night's papers to a minimum. 'Just one box,' said Len. 'He deserves an early night.' Once finally back in our suite, next to the Prime Minister's on the first-floor sea-front of the hotel, Elspeth went straight to bed. I spent an hour or so on my papers at the desk in the sitting room. For some reason I forgot my usual routine of drawing open the bedroom curtains, just as I got into bed at about 2 a.m. Within minutes I was asleep. And moments later, it seemed, I was awakened by a loud combination of vibration, thump and clatter. Budget began barking. Elspeth, hard of hearing but woken by the vibration, sat up in bed. 'I think it's a bomb,' she said. Suddenly the curtains fluttered as the wind blew from the sea through the shattered windows. An alarm began ringing somewhere. And automatically, but in a daze, we began to dress. Elspeth looked for a moment on to the landing. A figure, peering through a cloud of dust and smoke, told her that we should get ready to leave. 'Where's Budget's lead?' said Elspeth, and moved to open the door to the sitting room. It wouldn't move – and then we saw that the lintel had fallen out of place. Clearly the bomb had done damage on the Prime Minister's side of our suite.

Very swiftly the three ministers on our side of the first floor – Home Secretary Leon Brittan, as well as Margaret and myself – were together with our spouses in her private office. Soon we knew that everyone on our floor was safe. And quickly we learned (wrongly, as it turned out) that the bomb had gone off in the hotel foyer. A night porter, it was said, had been trapped beneath the rubble. It did not occur to us that serious damage had reached our floor, still less those above. By now the police were ready to start leading us out. Thick dust covered everything in the lobby. We saw broken furniture but mercifully no signs of people – dead or alive – as we threaded our way towards the back entrance of the hotel. The chill danger of the moment suddenly struck home when

Elspeth noticed a police marksman covering our exit from the roof above. Within minutes police cars had rushed us all to Brighton police station. The Whitelaws, the Gummers and Charlie Price, the American ambassador, were soon on the scene. Still we had heard nothing of any injuries to other ministers or conference delegates. After a swift council of war with those directly responsible, Home Secretary, Chief Constable and party chairman, Margaret took the only decision that mattered. Willie Whitelaw and I were of the same view. The conference would go ahead uninterrupted. The 9.30 a.m. debate, on Northern Ireland, would start as advertised.

Where now to spend the rest of the night? Chevening was only about fifty miles away, along the M23 and M25. So a high-speed police convoy swept us there, in time not for sleep but at least for a bath and a change in our own home. Still there was no news of casualties. It was only the first television news bulletin that started to disclose the dreadful truth. It was the sight of Norman Tebbit, being agonizingly inched out of the rubble, that really brought home the shock. Elspeth made speed to telephone each of our children, to report that we were safe and well. And the first daylight pictures of the damaged hotel made it all clear. The victims of the blast, five dead and dozens grievously injured, all fell through a collapsed section of the building – which included the sitting room of our own suite. Margaret's bathroom was on the other side of the chute. One of my Foreign Office black boxes came back from the rubble weeks later, battered but not destroyed. My hand-held tape-recorder, badly dented, was still inside. Every time I use it, to this day, it is a reminder of the brutalities of that night. Had I been at my desk an hour later – as I had been the night before – I should almost certainly have died. I had reason to be grateful to a thoughtful private secretary.

As the hours slipped by, we heard from the radio the number and identity of other colleagues like John Wakeham, Tony Berry and their wives who had been trapped or killed. I am not sure whether that news, had it come earlier, would – or should – have altered Margaret's decision to stick to the published programme. But I am glad we did, and glad too that this savage tragedy did not perceptibly alter the Prime Minister's approach to the talks with FitzGerald – save to reinforce the dominant importance which she already attached to closer security co-operation.

Much less dramatic, but also potentially disturbing for the future, had been the changing of the guard in the Northern Ireland Office on 17 September 1984. That was the day when Jim Prior carried through his plan to leave politics for good and to start a new career as chairman of

GEC. I say 'his' plan – but in truth the timing, perhaps the decision itself, was Margaret's. She had no wish to prolong Jim's life as a leading member of her government. From a very narrow point of view I could see why. He was almost always, so far as she was concerned, a member of the awkward squad. Indeed, I had had my own difficulties with him as Chancellor. Yet he was a substantial figure, with whom it was possible for many Conservatives – and non-Conservatives too – to identify. His services, his contribution to the breadth of a government, could have been retained for many years had Margaret so wished. But that kind of lateral thinking, which would ironically have helped to consolidate her own achievements, was too seldom part of her temperament.

So our policy towards Ireland had to undergo the jolting of change when Jim's place was taken by Douglas Hurd, in his first Cabinet post. His previous experience – as a career diplomat, then one of Ted Heath's closest advisers, a successful author (fiction as well as history) and, most recently, as a Minister of State in Home and Foreign Offices – qualified him well for the Irish minefield. Yet for me there was still something evocative of the tousle-haired, serious-minded undergraduate with whom I had shared Cambridge Union debates more than thirty years before. But even Douglas needed a learning curve, and naturally his initial tutors included the traditionalists in the Northern Ireland Office whose views Jim Prior had had to deflect or qualify. It was perhaps inevitable that senior members of the Northern Ireland Office who carried the day-to-day responsibility for administering the Province should have been more concerned about the risks of destabilization and violence there, if an agreement were reached with Dublin, than about the hypothetical longer-term benefits such an agreement might bring. These concerns shaped the impression Douglas Hurd created, intentionally or not, during his first visit to Dublin on 25 October, two weeks after the Brighton bombing. Certainly his feeling at that time, that the gap between the two sides was too great to bridge, communicated itself to Irish ministers. At almost the same moment Margaret became 'very pessimistic' about the exercise and doubtful whether it could be taken much further. She was tempted to think again in terms of a much more limited agreement – confined to security co-operation and possibly border adjustment (this was an idea to which she reverted from time to time, but it was never raised with the Irish).

Happily another EC opportunity for clearing the air presented itself just two days before the Chequers Summit. For on 16 November I was in Dublin for a meeting of EC Foreign Ministers with our opposite numbers from the ASEAN countries (South-East Asia) and so was able to talk with FitzGerald and Barry about the prospects. Garret stressed a recent opinion poll which showed that a sizeable majority of Irish opinion acknowledged the need to set aside the idea of Irish unity for the foreseeable future. He (rightly) took credit for lowering Irish expectations on that point. This encounter gave me a fresh chance to encourage Margaret (and Douglas) to press ahead. 'We should not give up the attempt,' I urged, 'unless we are convinced that there is no hope of reaching agreement.'

That was, in effect, the only conclusion of the November Chequers meeting itself. The two protagonists took very differing views of the occasion. For Margaret it was 'the best discussion we have ever had . . . tackling the problem in detail for the first time'. Garret, on the other hand, was more disturbed by the 'combative . . . negative' character of the encounter. But they did, in the end, agree that 'an enduring settlement was worth going for', though 'it had to be a realistic one'. So – to my intense relief – the Armstrong–Nally* talks should continue.

None of us should perhaps have been surprised by the disaster of the two divergent press conferences that followed – Margaret Thatcher's at Downing Street, first, and then Garret FitzGerald's at the Irish embassy. The fat was thrown in the fire by just one of Margaret's answers. Almost at the end, she was asked to comment on the options offered by the report (by then six months old) of the New Ireland Forum, which Garret FitzGerald had set up in Dublin to canvass the views of all the Irish constitutional parties on the problems of Northern Ireland. Two of the three options originally suggested in that many-sided discussion document – a united Ireland and an all-Irish federation – had already disappeared from the effective agenda; and the third – joint authority – was no longer being pursued in its original form. The Taoiseach was still pressing for a greater degree of Irish government involvement in the administration and policing of Northern Ireland than we could accept. But the Irish proposals in this respect had been considerably scaled down.

Yet this was another of those occasions on which Margaret rose to press questioning with exactly the same unqualified vigour as she had been dealing with the points for months, and even that very day, in private discussions with Garret FitzGerald. At the back of her mind also

* Dermot Nally, secretary to the Irish government, was Armstrong's opposite number in Dublin.

was probably a doubt about the extent to which Garret – the ever-reasonable face of Irish nationalism – represented the 'real' views of the Irish political establishment. So there emerged her celebrated 'Out . . . out . . . out!' reply, in which each of those three Forum options was brutally hit out of the ground. It is easy to understand why the press presented this performance to the Taoiseach, just a few minutes later, as conclusive evidence that the negotiations had in effect collapsed. And it is easy to understand his acute discomfiture.

FitzGerald's considered response to this humiliating episode is a measure of his statesmanship. The drastic lowering of expectations which it had produced in the Republic, although damaging to Garret personally in the short term, was not wholly unhelpful; and he judged it probable that the very intemperance of Margaret's performance ('this débâcle', in his words)[1] would evoke, even in Britain itself, a reaction that might eventually serve to get the negotiations back on to a constructive course. But for this to happen he had himself to refrain from any critical public response to the scathing attacks that were launched upon him by Charlie Haughey and the rest. This was, he thought, a 'short-term price worth paying for a possible long-term advantage'.[2] In this he was right. For within a week he had received a conciliatory letter from Margaret. Two weeks later she came close to making public amends, at a press conference after the Dublin meeting of the European Council (be it noted another EC-prompted occasion). 'I have a weakness', she said, 'when people ask me direct questions, of giving direct answers.'[3] Within a month she had made it plain to Ronald Reagan's anxious – if not unprompted – inquiry that she had no intention of just standing pat on her public position.

The scale and nature of United States involvement in all this needs to be seen in the right perspective. Only rarely were we under direct pressure from the other side of the Atlantic specifically to change our policies. But we were continually aware of a very resistant strand in American opinion of deep misunderstanding of Britain's role in Ireland. So we were constantly having to establish, indeed re-establish, the legitimacy of the presence of British troops, the validity of the electoral system, the fairness of the legal system – and the extent to which all these took proper account, as far as could be, of the 'Irish dimension'. We did all this, as much as anything, in the overall British interest: to undermine American fund-raising for terrorism, to strengthen American willingness to extradite those wanted for trial.

So we certainly did not stand pat. After the careful reconsideration of our position that followed the Chequers–Downing Street performance, we came forward in January 1985 with a proposal that became the core of the final settlement. This involved a regular and continuing institutionalized role for the Irish government in Northern Ireland (in deference to Irish sensitivities the term 'consultation' was avoided). This role was to be serviced by a joint secretariat, located in Belfast. With Irish hopes for 'joint authority' definitely dashed by Margaret's November press conference, the possibility of securing amendment of the Irish Constitution was abandoned.* Even so, it took many months to work the package into final shape, with recurrent sticking points over which failure sometimes seemed all too likely.

There were two more turning points before the end. The first was again on a European stage. FitzGerald and Thatcher were due for another of their regular bilaterals, to take place in the course of the June 1985 Milan European Council. (It is a miracle that opportunities could ever be found for moments of Anglo-Irish calm in the midst of these pan-European dramas, but found they generally were, even during the Milan-Craxi punch-up.) In Garret's own words, 'I must go in with all guns blazing, using more forcible language than I had ever previously used.' And so he did, fearful all the time that he might have 'gone over the top'.[4] There was, he stressed, a grave danger of ending up with an Ireland which was under hostile and sinister influence. He was ready to take great risks to prevent that, and was no less anxious to prevent Unionist revolt. He and the Prime Minister were the only two people able to reach an agreement. If they failed, the opportunity would be lost, possibly for ever.

Garret's advocacy, sustained with manifest sincerity over meeting after meeting, could not have been more effective. Margaret's reply, on other occasions as well as this, may even have surprised her and was couched in remarkably similar terms. She and the Taoiseach both had the same problem in mirror-image. Each was worried that they had gone too far and would lose support. But it would now be very damaging not to go ahead with the proposed Agreement. The meeting closed – and here was the breakthrough – with the two premiers discussing a date and place for possible signature of a final agreement. 'The important thing,' said FitzGerald, 'is that it should be signed in Ireland.' On 25 July 1985 Douglas Hurd and I were able jointly to present to Cabinet a draft of

---

* It resurfaced, of course, as an important feature of the 1993 Downing Street Declaration.

the Agreement that was emerging. Cabinet concluded that it was right to accept the risk involved in carrying the negotiations forward: this was preferable to continuing indefinitely with the existing situation, 'without sign or hope of change'.

The 1985 Anglo-Irish Agreement

One further obstacle lay ahead – and that was the second change within twelve months in the leadership of the Northern Ireland Office. On 2 September 1985 Douglas Hurd was appointed Home Secretary and his place in Belfast was taken by Tom King, until then Secretary of State for Employment. I did not regard this change as either necessary or desirable. In the first place, it arose only because of the decision – which Margaret had not discussed with me – to move Leon Brittan to the Department of Trade and Industry and away from the Home Office, after only two years in that job. I had regarded his appointment there (in 1983, straight from the Chief Secretaryship) as premature, but his exceptional ability had by now enabled him to acquire much of the experience and status appropriate for a Home Secretary. I felt that those who had been responsible for the original over-promotion (Willie Whitelaw as well as the Prime Minister) should now be ready to stand by it. The parallel case for not giving Northern Ireland a third Secretary of State in such fast order was, if anything, an even stronger one. There was everything to be said for leaving in place, to implement the Anglo-Irish Agreement that was now so near to completion, the Northern Ireland Secretary who had helped to shape it. But that was not to be, and Tom King went to Dublin for his first introductory meeting with Peter Barry on 17 September.

Ten days later, without any consultation with me, the new Secretary of State sent a long minute to the Prime Minister to express with 'some reluctance' his 'serious concerns' about the content and balance of the Agreement. I minuted the next day from Ottawa (where I had gone after the UN General Assembly in New York) to warn that if we were now, at this late stage, to begin proposing further significant or unexpected adjustments in the Agreement, there was a real risk that the whole venture might founder. There followed a series of meetings between the three of us in which Margaret, while ready enough (as I was) to consider purely linguistic changes, basically upheld my side of this unwelcome argument. Tom continued, however, to press his case (even before he arrived in his new job the Unionist case had no doubt been strongly pressed upon him by Ian Gow).* He extended his dissent by starting to argue for the removal from the Agreement of the (already highly qualified and hotly contested) commitment to the consideration of joint courts. As a result of these late dissents from the newly appointed Northern Ireland Secretary, we had to arrange two additional ministerial meetings (of Howe, King, Barry and Spring) – one in London and one in Dublin.

At the end of the second such meeting (on 6 November, just nine days before the date agreed for signature) Irish ministers were manifestly exasperated and depressed by what they perceived as Tom King's 'negative' performance on our side of the table. The issues were only finally resolved in a last-minute exchange of messages between the two Prime Ministers on 11 November. Margaret reaffirmed our agreement with the pre-King positions. Tom had not exactly endeared himself to any of us in his first few weeks; but that may have been scarcely his fault – and his courage and firmness later, when he was inevitably exposed to all the assaults and pressures that went with his job, were to win him widespread respect. At least we were all ready to fly to Hillsborough for signature of the Agreement on Friday, 15 November 1985.

I had no doubt about the historic importance of the occasion. It was underlined in curious ways. Hillsborough Castle itself – as well as my own few personal memories of the place – was so shot through with Ulster history that it seemed an unnatural stage for trumpeting a new-found Irish dimension. (It had been chosen because the Irish wanted the scene set in Ireland. We wanted it in the North. Stormont was too 'Unionist' for the Irish. So Hillsborough emerged as the natural compromise.) Garret FitzGerald and his ministerial and official colleagues were clearly not in their natural habitat. Nor for that matter were we. I was almost as disturbed as Margaret herself to be the object of hostile demonstration from Unionists who had long been natural participants at our party conferences.

Most dispiriting of all, for me as much as for Margaret, was the news that Ian Gow – her most intimate and devoted supporter and my oldest and dearest political friend – remained determined, as a result of our decision, to resign from his proud position as a Treasury minister. Margaret, I knew, had already done her best to dissuade him. Now it

---

* Gow had served as one of King's ministers at Environment until the September reshuffle; when Tom moved to Northern Ireland, Ian went to the Treasury.

was my turn to try – in a long telephone call after the signature but before the announcement of his decision. But he was already as firm – and as fair – as he was later to be in the speech which he made in the Commons debate eleven days later: 'I disagree profoundly with the new policy. . . . I fear that this change will prolong and not diminish Ulster's agony. With all my heart – it is quite a big heart – I pray that I am wrong.' All my words were in vain, on this issue. But we remained close personal and political friends.

And still the Agreement has not brought peace to our troubled islands. Was it then all in vain, wrong-headed? Emphatically not. The two Prime Ministers took immense care to present the accord at Hillsborough with a single voice – their briefing, even their thinking, had been consciously co-ordinated to avoid any fresh misunderstanding. They pledged themselves and their governments to work 'with determination and imagination' not just in improving co-operation in combating terrorism but in 'helping to reconcile the two major traditions in Ireland'. The Agreement provided, as I stressed in a speech a few days later, 'not the "answer" to the Irish question, nor a "solution"', but 'the opportunity for a new and more hopeful phase'. 'It is no more than that,' wrote Malcolm Rutherford in the *Financial Times*: 'an opportunity. It is also no less.' It was, in the words of *The Times*, 'A ship of hope' – a ship of hope, as I saw it and was always at pains to explain, that would reach its destination not years but decades, even centuries, ahead.

During the months and years that followed, the familiar ghastly sequence of violence placed our relationship and the Agreement under recurrent threat. Never more so, perhaps, than after the murderous tragedies at Milltown and Andersonstown in March 1988: at the first, three IRA mourners in a crowd of 10,000 were killed by 'loyalist' pistol and grenades; and at the second, two English corporals were dragged from their car by a mob, beaten and shot dead. Those were months, I said a few weeks later, in Derbyshire, 'of the kind with which the Anglo-Irish Agreement was designed to deal. And it has withstood the strain. We are still talking to each other. Let us keep it like that.' Since then the Agreement has remained the cornerstone of good relations between London and Dublin.

No doubt Margaret and I did not see our achievement in quite the same light. She had been concerned, for example, to maintain British 'sovereignty' over the North. I had ceased thinking of that as a commodity which could or should be measured and upheld in so many vertically designated packages. I was more concerned to provide for the interpenetration of influence between the several communities that have to share the British Isles together. Ian Gow had protested, in his resignation letter, against 'the involvement of a *foreign* power'. In my speech to that Derbyshire audience I replied, as I do today, that 'we cannot treat each other as strangers, as "foreigners". . . . Two civilized peoples must be able to find ways of living peacefully together. If France and Germany can do it, then why not us?'

The Agreement was thought to be against all Margaret's instincts. Her 'Out . . . out . . . out!' had rung all too true. She was publicly denounced by our mutual friend Enoch Powell for 'treachery'. It took a gigantic struggle by many far-sighted people to persuade her; but, although her head was persuaded, her heart was not. Her respect for Garret's integrity was tempered by misgiving at his success in persuading her to compromise with an Irish nationalism for which she had neither sympathy nor understanding. But despite the dismissive tone she adopts towards him in *The Downing Street Years* it was the personal chemistry between herself and Garret FitzGerald which was decisive at the time. 'He was,' said *The Times*, 'a standing rebuke to the cynicism which infects so many in the business of politics.' It was that quality, that transparent sincerity, interacting with her own determination to improve security and save lives, which finally moved Margaret to the right conclusion.

But she has confessed to having second thoughts, going so far as to describe the results of the Anglo-Irish Agreement as 'disappointing'. 'It is surely time,' she has said, 'to consider an alternative approach.'[5] I remain convinced that there is no alternative, and I hope that Margaret may once again be ready to accept her share of the credit for having opened the way.

CHAPTER TWENTY-NINE

SHEVARDNADZE'S ARRIVAL

Iron Curtain Excursions

Ninety-eighty-five was the year in which I became closely engaged in the revolution that was to overthrow the Soviet Empire. My planned tours of the five loveless republics of the Warsaw Pact started on 8 February 1985 with visits to Rumania and Bulgaria.

Ceaușescu's Bucharest was the most inhospitable city I have ever visited. The pavements were solid with frozen snow. For our meeting with the characterless Foreign Minister, Stefan Andrej, we sat huddled in our overcoats in an office without heat (and almost without light). The dinner at which we were 'entertained' in the Intercontinental Hotel (one of their most courageous out-stations) was uniquely depressing. We saw Ceaușescu himself in his first-floor office in the Central Committee building. The dictator, a very mechanical-seeming creature, was perched none too grandly in a gilded ballroom-like place, a kind of poor man's Versailles. The posturing pretentiousness of his 'independent' foreign policy setpiece was matched in absurdity by the triviality of the barter trade deals that he wished to discuss. I had never to forget that the most dismal disaster in Anglo-Rumanian history had been the state visit for which Ceaușescu had been mistakenly invited – or had somehow invited himself – during the days of the Harold Wilson government. I had to ensure that not a word passed my lips that could conceivably imply royal willingness for a return engagement.

I had never expected our arrival in Sofia, the capital of Bulgaria (10–11 February), to feel like a return to freedom. But after the sullenness of Ceaușescu's regime indeed it did. There was an impressive dignity about the evening wreath-laying ceremony, except that the military band broke into the National Anthem prematurely, obliging me to freeze to attention when only halfway across the flood-lit parade ground. The same informality characterized my talks next morning with

Foreign Minister Mladenov. Against a background of sunshine rather than snow, a sudden gust blew open the window and lace curtains of our meeting room. At every subsequent meeting Mladenov reminded me of my instant comment that 'A wind of change is blowing through the Iron Curtain.' And so it must have seemed. For this was indeed the first ever visit to Bulgaria by a British Foreign Secretary, after a full century of diplomatic relations between our two countriess. My message was a constantly positive one: the West is serious in its wish to see progress on arms control; likewise on economic and human relations, provided you in the East start playing your part. Why not press the Russians harder to get them back to the Geneva negotiations? (The point would be reported back to Moscow, of course, so it was worth making.) And why not take more seriously your own human-rights obligations under the Helsinki Final Act? (Its tenth anniversary was coming shortly.)

Bulgaria's President Zhivkov was certainly the most entertaining dictator I have ever known. His palace, the Boyana Residence, was cement, glass and carved wood, but with an airport-terminal sparkle about it. He kept our formal talk short and thigh-slapping, quickly merging it into a spacious lunch for the whole of my party. Zhivkov was at pains to explain how Bulgaria's typical command economy had nothing to learn from market economies. 'How do you decide which industries, which enterprises, deserve new capital?' I asked him. 'We have more than one state-owned bank to whom they can apply,' he said. 'And if one says no, they are free to ask another.' 'And for new enterprises?' I asked. 'How is their case recognized?' 'We have a special bank', said Zhivkov, 'for new enterprises of high risk.' Lukanov, financial adviser and fluent in English, had the last word: 'You see, Sir Geoffrey, this is our "venture capital market".' I decided to try a new tack: 'How do you decide where to invest, in what industry? How do you know what you need? Do you have anything resembling market research?' Wearing for a moment my old market-research hat, I explained my question. Zhivkov's good humour faltered not for a moment: 'Ah, you see, we have no need of that. You remember the way in which the British Empire worked, Sir Geoffrey – with the colonies serving as the markets in which you could dispose of all the surplus produce for which Britain herself had no need? Well, for Bulgaria,' Zhivkov chuckled, 'Russia has long served the same purpose as your colonies.'

A month later, 12 March 1985, I was across the Iron Curtain again, for my second Soviet funeral in twelve months. Chernenko had come to

his predictably early death. He had been succeeded, as we had anticipated, by Mikhail Gorbachev. The occasion was by this time almost
routine. The weather was if anything even colder than a year before.
But the new leader's funeral speech was a good deal brisker, though
equally content-free, and the crowd of visiting dignitaries significantly
larger. Many were curious to meet the first Soviet leader for a long
time whose health seemed likely to sustain him for more than a year or
two.

The style of Margaret's and my late-evening meeting at the Kremlin
with Gorbachev and Gromyko was to the point and friendly. Scheduled
for only fifteen minutes, we were there for almost an hour. Margaret
enthused over Gorbachev's recent London visit ('one of the most
successful ever'). 'We must', replied Gorbachev, 'continue to meet and
talk to one another.' 'People in Britain', concluded Margaret, 'took great
pleasure in Gorbachev's appointment and would be pleased to see
Gromyko in London.' Gorbachev chuckled. 'Mr Gromyko', he said, 'is
waiting for the London fog to clear.' The bonhomie was not quite
universal. One hard-boiled Foreign Office official who read the note of
the meeting expressed himself 'bothered' that 'the PM seems to go
uncharacteristically weak at the knees when she talks to the personable
Mr Gorbachev'. He need not have worried. Certainly the two leaders
were attracted to each other, relished each other's company. But neither
Margaret nor Mikhail ever completely lowered their guard.

The second leg of my Central European tour started less than a month
after Gorbachev's takeover from Chernenko, and before anyone had
started to take in the significance of that shift. East Berlin and the
German Democratic Republic, as we arrived there on 7 April, lived up
to their reputation as the most austerely sombre and disciplined of the
satellites. I used my meeting with Erich Honecker (already fourteen
years in office) to make very clear the message for the first ever visit by a
British Foreign Secretary: Britain was impatient for progress in arms-
control negotiations and eager for an expansion in trade; but serious
progress depended on advances in human freedoms within the Soviet
bloc. I described the 1975 Helsinki Final Act as the 'trumpet call' which
could help bring down the walls which divide Europe. I stressed that
the artificial division of Germany, one half free and the other enslaved,
could not continue for ever. It was indeed in West Berlin and West
Germany that my message was most immediate.

But it was in Prague, on the first visit by a British Foreign Secretary
for twenty years, that we felt most poignantly the contrast between the

regime's intolerance and the natural spirit of the people. My vivid personal memory of Dubček's Prague Spring (1968) contrasted sharply with the ruthlessness with which political dissidents were kept away from my programme. The personality of the Foreign Minister, Bohuslav Chnoupek, seemed itself to encapsulate the Czech dilemma. He was an intelligent extrovert, shrewdly able to understand the anomalies of his country's position. My recent RUSI speech (on the Strategic Defence Initiative) intrigued him greatly.* I disabused him of any notion that a wedge might be driven between the US and her European allies, then asked why there could not be similar open-mindedness in countries like his own. His main recreation was bear-hunting and, when he was unable to tell me the national origin of the frontier-roaming bears, I teased him that the animals of Eastern Europe had more freedom of movement than the people. At the official luncheon, I delivered, said *The Times*, 'one of the strongest attacks on human-rights abuses in the Communist world heard from any British spokesman for a considerable time'. Prague was the only city in which we actually caught Communist eavesdroppers redhanded. One member of my party (staying at the Intercontinental Hotel) walked by mistake into a room next to her own. The headphoned couple crouched on the floor beside their recording equipment were even more startled than she was.

One of Chnoupek's more bizarre routines (I learned later of its regularity) involved taking guests round his official apartment at the top of the Foreign Ministry. The purpose, astonishingly, was to show off the bathroom – and its window – from which Chnoupek's non-Communist predecessor, Jan Masaryk, had 'jumped' or 'fallen' so tragically to his death, thirty-seven years before. Like some guide to a French château, Chnoupek pointed to the bath. 'Here', he said, 'is where Masaryk lay for a while after taking the drugs which drove him to take his own life. He leaped from this window.' My response was shamefully inadequate. 'As you know,' I said, 'we have a different account of what happened.' Chnoupek said nothing but continued with his guide-prattle. A year or more later I heard from the outspoken and engaging Danish Foreign Minister Uffe Ellemann-Jensen, a television journalist by trade, that he had been given the same tour and had reacted much more effectively. 'Don't give me that crap, Chnoupek!' he had exploded – at which the Czech Foreign Minister had remained as bland as he had with me.

* See pp. 391–3 above.

On each visit I sought to establish contact with opposition spokesmen, Helsinki rights monitors or dissidents. Most active in Prague were the Charter 77 group. They rightly feared that public contact could precipitate retaliation. But they were ready to meet my senior officials – political director Derek Thomas and head of East European Department John Birch – in a private venue. This engagement coincided, conveniently enough, with the musical supper party (another of his routines) to which Chnoupek treated me and my party at the Seven Angels gipsy wine cellar. I had been warned that the visitors would be expected to offer a choral response to Chnoupek's Czech music (he was a cheerful and intriguing host). So I went equipped with a clutch of 'hymn-sheets', photocopied by the embassy. The British understood better than the Czechs why I opened our performance with my Welsh favourite 'Cwm Rhondda'. What opening line could have been more appropriate for my mission? 'Guide me, O thou great Redeemer, pilgrim through this barren land.'

Towards the end of the evening, we were joined by Derek Thomas, fresh from his encounter with Charter 77. Derek was seen by our hawk-eyed hacks to exchange a scribbled note with me. The presumed text ('Mission accomplished') quickly achieved inaccurate, but worldwide, immortality. Derek's note had actually read: 'Doesn't the gipsy fiddler remind you of Ernest Borgnine?' And my reply: 'Rather more like Nigel Lawson, I think?' Next day's *Express* headline was characteristic: 'Howe's amazing Czechmate foils reds.'

The next morning ended with the almost empty formality of a meeting with the dour Soviet-puppet, Gustav Husák, who had been ruling the Czechs for seventeen long years, since the deposition of Dubček. The contrast with my first call of the morning could not have been sharper. Elspeth and I had gone with a small party to see the eighty-five-year-old Cardinal Tomasek in his palace near the castle. He and his dwindling band of bishops and priests had been for years besieged by the authorities. The state consent that was necessary for new Church appointments had been systematically refused. There were no less than ten out of thirteen bishoprics now waiting to be filled. Yet, as the challenge grew, so did the Cardinal's courage. He was sitting alone in the room when we entered. Rising firmly to his feet, he looked straight at our photographer and BBC microphone, and said forthrightly, 'I want to welcome you in the name of the Catholic Church and of the Czech people. It is of the highest importance that in your visit to my country you have come to see me, as the representative of the

Church whose very existence is now in danger. In the name of God, I welcome you most warmly.'

The Cardinal was obviously heartened by our call. I was deeply moved by the vigour and courage of his response. The occasion had an impact far beyond the small room where we had met. For all Eastern Europe, more than I had dared to hope, was following my visit closely on BBC, VOA (Voice of America) and RFE (Radio Free Europe). The news that a Western statesman was carrying the case against religious persecution into the heart of Soviet Europe was more important even than we had thought.

Our last three days, 11–13 April, were for Poland. Immediately the atmosphere was less oppressive, though still far from free. Most of the leading actors whom we met had more than one side to their character. Foreign Minister Stefan Olszowski had himself been a teacher. His hardline support for President General Jaruzelski's regime, and its oppression of academic freedom, had a nonetheless soft edge to it. And the welcome from the Primate of Poland, Cardinal Glemp, for my emphasis on human rights was given an extra dimension by the fact that in Communist Poland the Roman Church did enjoy a certain tolerance.

This less oppressive atmosphere was sustained even during my meeting with Jaruzelski himself. First impressions were entirely supportive of the image of the beleaguered, narrow-minded dictator: military uniform, dark glasses, heavily curtained room and a voice that was sometimes almost inaudible. But Jaruzelski was different. His presentation of standard Cold War rhetoric faltered early in face of my statement of the need for courage to tackle the arms-control deadlock. 'You are right to stress that case,' he said. 'Your country is the one that can do so, for your country has trodden the path of greatness and mine has not. So yours can do so again, and lead the way. Not that I am ashamed of my country,' he added more confidently. 'I am proud of my own country, proud of Poland. But we have never enjoyed the opportunities that your country has done.' It was one of those conversations that one recalls as vividly as if no interpreter was present. The General listened attentively as I went on to expound, respectfully, the need for tough economic policies if Poland was to stand a chance of deserving more support from her friends in the West; and then to argue the case for democracy, for partnership with Solidarity, if the Polish people were ever to be reconciled to the necessary hardship of reform. None of this did he reject out of hand. The impression grew on me of a man who was a genuine patriot, seeking the best way forward for his people.

A few months later, when a girl student at a sixth-form conference that I had been addressing asked me to name the three most interesting statesmen that I had met, I surprised myself by including Jaruzelski as the third, alongside Gorbachev and Deng Xiaoping. I still believe that I might have been right.

That was certainly not the view of the Polish people in 1985. Yet it was, I suppose, symptomatic of the more tolerant nature of this dictatorship that I was able on the same day to meet a group of senior Solidarity supporters – in the margins of the large party given that evening at the residence. We met some of them again, at Elspeth's suggestion in the same small ante-room, when we returned to Warsaw almost exactly eight years later, in the spring of 1993. They had included free Poland's first Prime Minister, Tadeusz Mazowiecki.

The Polish authorities tolerated too the most publicly dramatic event of my entire Iron Curtain tour, a pilgrimage to the church of St Stanislaw Kostko and the grave of Father Jerzy Popieluszko, the pro-Solidarity priest murdered by the Polish police. They had perhaps little option about this. This particular trail had been blazed not long before by my Minister of State, Malcolm Rifkind. I had insisted that the programme of my visit – the first by a Western Foreign Minister since the 1981 imposition of martial law – should be at our discretion and not theirs. Our secret-police escort was ostentatiously withdrawn for this off-limits mission, undertaken after darkness had fallen. As we reached the entrance to the churchyard we were surrounded by a 500-strong crowd, carrying blazing torches and shouting, 'Viva Anglia! Viva Anglia!' As our embassy driver, George, reminded me eight years later, several were leaning forward to kiss the Union Jack on our car. I can still feel the freezing hand of the small girl who met us at the church gate to present a small posy of flowers. The crowd burst into patriotic song, surged round and carried me forward to the graveside, where I laid the flowers and placed a lighted candle in memory of the murdered priest. The secret police (who still turned up, ostensibly for my protection) struggled – it was not easy – to make themselves invisible. The tears welled up in my eyes. Neither Elspeth nor I could speak as we were led round the church.

The emotional impact of the occasion, publicized worldwide by press, radio and television, was overwhelming. And the Poles were prepared to be tolerant. For next morning, Foreign Minister Olszowski happily reappeared to welcome me at Warsaw's rebuilt royal castle, before my return to London. On my next visit to their Portland Place Embassy the cheers of the crowd outside prompted the ambassador to observe wryly, 'You see, Sir Geoffrey, when you come to the Polish Embassy, even the demonstrators are on your side!'

My tour behind the Iron Curtain had delivered a strong message from Britain to Europe. It was an uncoded statement of the importance that Britain attached to human rights. 'Sir Geoffrey', commented *The Times*, 'has sounded the first note on the trumpet. Will others follow?'

There was soon a fresh collective opportunity for just that. Celebrations were due in Vienna on 14–15 May for the thirtieth anniversary of the Austrian State Treaty, the remarkable agreement of the Khrushchev era, which had led to the withdrawal from Austria of the armed forces of the four occupying powers, most notably the Red Army. This had established Austria's independence and neutrality, and above all secured her freedom from the circle of Soviet satellites. It was very hard, even in retrospect, to work out what could have prompted Khrushchev and Molotov (in his closing years as Foreign Minister) to authorize this voluntary curtailment of the Soviet Empire. Certainly it was an occasion worth celebrating.

The principal participants, apart from the Austrians themselves, were the representatives of the four powers which had signed the original Treaty: Gromyko, Shultz, French Foreign Minister Roland Dumas and myself. (Although we did not know it, this was to be Gromyko's last appearance at a major international event.) George Shultz was seeking, without looking like a *demandeur*, to advance the prospects of the promised Soviet–US Summit. My own last bilateral meeting with Gromyko was notable less for its content than for the fact that my PPS, Len Appleyard, forgot to remove from the Soviet embassy table my brief and speaking notes for the meeting. It was a very sheepish PPS who returned a few minutes later to reclaim my papers – which were mercifully innocent of any compromising material.

The commemorative ceremony in the Belvedere Palace was suitably musical and grand, making the most of Vienna's imperial splendour. Roland Dumas startled us all, and stretched to the limits of credibility even his formidable forensic skills, by devoting his speech to the heroism of the Austrian resistance movement. It was fun to have my only photo-call with Dumas, Shultz and Gromyko on the same balcony where Molotov, Dulles, Eden and Pinay and had stood for theirs thirty years before.

Gordievski Goes, Shevardnadze Comes

Soon the other, secret strand of Anglo-Soviet relations received a sharp tug in the wrong direction. Until that moment Gordievski had been offering an increasingly crucial insight into the dawning of the Gorbachev era. At the start of the year he had been summoned to the KGB Centre to learn that he had been officially confirmed to take charge of the London Residency in May, when the acting Resident, Nikitenko, was due to return to Moscow. Our source was going to be more highly placed than ever before. Then came disturbing news: on 17 May he was recalled at short notice to Moscow for confirmation of his position and 'further briefing'. He was able to alert us to his shadow of anxiety about exactly what was happening and why. This turned out to be well-founded. For his absence from London appeared to be of indefinite duration. Our friends were fortunately able to maintain occasional contact with him in Moscow. But not even Gordievski himself could get any clear idea of his future. Soviet investigation of his position seems to have been less than conclusive.

A couple of weeks later his wife Leila and their two daughters, Maria and Anna, were also called home from London. Then came six weeks more of alarming uncertainty. For some time a plan had existed which would offer us at least a chance of being able to get Gordievski out of the Soviet Union to safety. It was for him to trigger it, if ever he felt it necessary, and if he was still free to do so. On Saturday, 20 July this final message reached me. Two senior officials (one from the FCO, the other from SIS) attended upon me at Chevening. And I gave authority for the plan to go ahead. Even today it would not be prudent to say more. At several points there was grave risk of discovery, and not just of Gordievski. So it was with a huge sense of relief that I heard the news on Monday, 22 July that for the first time in Soviet history a KGB officer already fingered as a Western spy had escaped across the Russian border. Some time was to elapse before news of this coup became public. But I found an early opportunity for a face-to-face meeting with this remarkable man. Already we had begun to worry about Leila, Maria and Anna. Oleg Gordievski had gained his freedom but lost his family: they were not reunited until November 1991.

There was a family footnote to this drama. One of Elspeth's fellow students throughout her three years at the London School of Economics was Kurt Stengl. A married man in his early thirties he came, so he said, from Austria, with a previous career as a refrigeration engineer. He was a hard-working, intelligent member of the class, in which he had enrolled before the wife of the Foreign Secretary. Elspeth had found him a congenial classmate, regularly achieving good upper-second results. Kurt had visited Carlton Gardens for student parties with Elspeth on more than one occasion. Elspeth frequently borrowed his notes and, like others, sought and valued his advice. Their final exams started on Thursday, 30 May, yet meticulous Kurt did not show up for the first exam. He was never seen again. In his flat, where the fridge had been switched off, but where all his family's possessions had been left behind, was a note to his landlady: 'I have had to go away at short notice for a few days but will be in touch.' A few weeks later a postcard arrived from Vienna, but bearing no address, to say that he had taken advantage of an unbeatable job opportunity with the United Nations. But no independent evidence ever became available to confirm that story. And no wonder. For what we now know is that, during Gordievski's first two weeks back in Moscow, action was taken by his superiors to pull out most, if not all, of the existing KGB 'illegals' in Britain. (An illegal is an agent with a false identity controlled by clandestine means.) Kurt Stengl was indeed one of those. It was purely by chance that he found himself working so close to the Foreign Secretary's wife. On the only occasion he met me, he seemed slightly embarrassed by the encounter.

Only a week after Gordievski's dramatic escape to freedom came the next gathering that was to bring together Foreign Ministers from East and West – at Helsinki from 30 July to 1 August to celebrate the tenth anniversary of the Helsinki Final Act. But there had been a dramatic change in the leading roles. For on 3 July, Andrei Gromyko had been translated to the honorific position of President of the USSR and replaced as Foreign Minister by a man with no experience of foreign policy, First Secretary of the Communist Party of the Republic of Georgia, Eduard Shevardnadze. Helsinki was a challenging stage on which Gromyko's virtually unknown successor had to make his debut. If there was any European city where there might be built a broad-based resurgence of respect for human rights, it was here. George Shultz took the opportunity to offer a warm public gesture of welcome for Shevardnadze, which was widely appreciated. George's perceptive wife O'bie, with whom Elspeth had struck up an easy and enduring friendship, was equally determined to take Nanuli Shevardnadze under her wing. So for much of the slightly hazardous sightseeing of their programme, the three wives – O'bie, Nanuli and Elspeth – formed a mutually supportive troika, determined to ensure that not one of them should slip or stumble in view of the myriad watching cameras.

My first face-to-face meeting with Shevardnadze was at the residence of our ambassador, Alan Brooke-Turner, an attractively placed hill-top house originally built for Princess Yousoupoff. From the moment of his first appearance Shevardnadze's style and temperament were in complete contrast with those of his grim-faced predecessor. His most striking feature, his smile, at this stage signalled nervousness as much as confidence. He began shaking hands with almost everyone in sight in the hallway. Once gathered round the table, I tried to identify some kind of common ground by comparing his Georgian origins with my Welsh. And Shevardnadze pitched in with two messages. First, the Russians did not look at everything through a US–Soviet prism; Russia's relations with the UK were important in themselves, especially those between Gorbachev and Mrs Thatcher. The visit by the parliamentary delegation under his leadership had been 'of profound significance'. Shevardnadze's more personal message was that the most important task facing 'the present generation on this planet' was to 'prevent the militarization of space'. Every country has its own voice, and Britain's voice mattered because 'your country has a vast experience of international affairs'. I told him how Margaret and I had early concluded that our most important long-term task was the improvement of East–West relations. All my travels had been directed to that purpose and not to 'converting East European leaders to membership of the Conservative Party'.

Often during our talk Shevardnadze looked from side to side for signs that his team approved the line he was taking. He was obviously grateful when I renewed my invitation for him in Gromyko's place, to make an early visit to Britain. But he was ready too to talk tough – on human rights, for example. He responded to my plea for Sakharov, Sharansky and others with a grim refusal to accept my list of names. But unlike Gromyko he was ready to debate the issue, with an onslaught on the human-rights implications of the 'hardship' we had inflicted on the miners and their families. 'But I do not propose', he said firmly, 'to hand over any lists of names.' When he was doorstepped on leaving the house by the BBC's Russian-speaking Tim Sebastian, Shevardnadze responded with a smile, eager for the opportunity to get himself across.

There were to be plenty of clouds over the relationship in the months and years ahead, for example when he found out about Gordievski. (At the outset, we were playing diplomatic poker. I did not know at this time whether he knew of Gordievski's case or not, and he must have had similar doubts about my knowledge. It was certainly not mentioned.) But already I felt that we had here the beginning of a fresh approach to Soviet Foreign policy. He was clearly Gorbachev's man. They had worked together in the Communist Youth League almost forty years before. Shevardnadze had impressed by his tenacity. He had served as Communist Party boss in Georgia for thirteen years, appointed to that post by Brezhnev in 1972, after seven years as Interior Minister of the small, proud republic. The more I was later to learn about Shevardnadze, the clearer it became that he was no ordinary apparatchik. He had acted fiercely, but fairly, against the party's rampant corruption and nepotism. Long before it was fashionable, or even safe, to do so (some say as early as 1979) he had approved – encouraged even – the making of the controversial film *Pokayanie* ('Repentance'), an allegorical denunciation of Stalinism, a first sign of the cultural thaw that was just beginning.

Even in his private life, Shevardnadze knew his own mind. His wife, Nanuli (she had worked as a journalist on a Georgian women's magazine) refused his first proposal of marriage. She was, she had warned him, the daughter of 'an enemy of the people' and was fearful that the liaison might harm his party career. He was undismayed, quit his party job, re-presented his case to Nanuli – and was accepted. Fortunately for all of us, he was able to resume his party career.

Not long after this first meeting I obtained a fascinating insight into the way he was tackling his new job. At his first Moscow meeting with the Foreign Minister (later President) of Mozambique, Joaquim Chissano, Shevardnadze scrubbed the Bolshoi from the programme and spent the entire evening asking Chissano to tell him what *he* thought was wrong with Soviet foreign policy in Africa. Chissano had been sufficiently impressed to tell me the story at our next meeting. During the years ahead we were all to have chances of playing our part in Eduard Shevardnadze's foreign-policy learning curve. He was to play a fundamental role in steering his country, and the world, towards a startlingly different future.

Just six weeks after the Helsinki meeting (on Thursday, 12 September 1985), the news finally broke of Gordievski's defection and escape to London. We had by then completed our appraisal of the action to be taken against the KGB spy network in Britain. On that day Soviet ambassador Popov was summoned to the Foreign Office and given the names of twenty-five 'diplomats' who were given three weeks to leave Britain because of 'activities incompatible with their status' (the standard formula). My decision was expressly attributed to information received from Gordievski. 'It is quite clear from his account', we said, 'that despite action as recently as April this year' (we had expelled five Soviet personnel), 'KGB activities have continued on a deplorably large scale.'

This was the most dramatic action of its kind since Alec Douglas-Home had expelled no less than 105 Soviet agents in 1971. In the past Moscow had usually responded to such action by expelling a small number of Western personnel: this took account of the lower level of Western representation in Moscow. Now, however, Gorbachev gave a clear demonstration of his support for the KGB both inside and outside the Soviet Union. He adopted a strict tit-for-tat policy. Within forty-eight hours our new ambassador, Bryan Cartledge, was shocked by the news that a precisely equivalent twenty-five Britons had to leave Moscow. When we responded two days later by expelling six more Russians, six more Britons were forthwith ordered in the opposite direction. On each occasion we followed the line that had been established by Alec Douglas-Home in 1971 and reduced the ceiling on the total permitted number of Soviet 'diplomatic' personnel in Britain.

No other NATO country pursued such a tough policy. It did serve to keep some kind of lid on the scale of more or less overt Soviet spying in Britain, but we were now reaching the limits of its feasibility. For our ceiling applied only to Soviet officials while their much narrower figure applied to the total number of British residents. And though we were always able to show that our targets were indeed engaged in espionage, the Soviet side had no such scruples. As a result of this difference between the premises on which each side was operating, our own tough policy was now clearly beginning to hurt us more than it hurt them. For by this double-barrelled exchange of expulsions we had reduced the ceiling on Soviet officials in London – but *only* officials – from 224 to 193. Yet in Moscow the ceiling on Britons of *all* kinds, including businessmen and journalists, was cut from 103 to 72. At a stroke, the British press corps in Moscow was more than halved, from fourteen to six.

It was not easy to put a very cheerful face on all this at the small 'party' that I subsequently held for the expellees. We had had to consider too the impact of such a tough line on the chance of an improved relationship with the new Soviet leadership. But the continuing scale and tenacity of Soviet espionage activities (which were still well authenticated by Gordievski) left us with no alternative. Even the Americans, who did not operate a ceiling policy, were faced with comparable problems. For when they decided, twelve months later, to evict about eighty Soviet spies from the United States, Moscow was unable to identify anything like that number of equivalent Americans to be expelled from the Soviet Union. But the KGB were soon able to find a 'suitable' response. They sharply reduced the number of locally engaged Russians allowed to work in America's Moscow embassy and gravely disrupted day-to-day working there. Gorbachev was leaving us in no doubt of his continuing commitment to the KGB, whose support had certainly played an important role in his own arrival at the head of the Soviet Empire.

This factor continued to cast a dark and curious shadow over relations with the Soviet Union right to the end of my experience in this field. And it seemed to live in a completely separate dimension from all the rest of our relationships, personal as well as political. This was true when I next met Shevardnadze, in his UN Embassy in New York, at General Assembly time two weeks after Gordievski's defection became public. Our meeting was certainly frostier than our initial encounter in Helsinki two months before. An entirely separate, hard-nosed segment of the discussion was triggered by a harsh protest from Shevardnadze at our wickedness in having suborned one of his diplomats. On this occasion there was at least some justice in the charge. For certainly we had had something to do with Gordievski's exit from the Soviet Union. But he was equally unashamed when he denounced us as the guilty party for having expelled two dozen of his conscientious and innocent officials. His 'anger', even so, fell well short of conviction. I only hope that my response – which *was* based upon hard evidence of sustained KGB misbehaviour – was rather more convincingly angry than his. But the whole episode did not prevent us dealing in a routine and civilized way with the rest of our agenda. On this occasion at least (as indeed on most others) it had proved possible to maintain the unavowed fiction that neither he nor I was directly responsible for our intelligence and security agencies. This meant we were able face to face to act simply as channels for the transmission of mutual complaints about the activities of these semi-detached organizations.

The following July, 1986, we were able to introduce Shevardnadze to London – and, by helicopter, to a working lunch at Chevening. As we started our flight back to London, Zamyatin, who had replaced Popov as Soviet ambassador in London, surprised me by saying that in his country it was quite unknown for government leaders to travel in that way. I never discovered whether this rather special helicopter-phobia was on grounds of security or of aircraft unreliability. Our talks with Shevardnadze – for he was received at Number 10 as well – continued the process of opening still wider his already fertile mind. Only once did he surprise us – me certainly. When we were continuing our formal talks in the relatively remote setting of Lancaster House, proceedings were from time to time disturbed by some dissident loud-hailing. Those were still the days when Soviet visitors could expect hostile demonstrations. Despite the distant modesty of the noise, Shevardnadze suddenly broke off in mid-sentence to protest with startling severity at the 'intolerable' discourtesy of such hectoring. It was almost the only time I had seen his regular smile completely suppressed to make way for a snarl. For a moment, Eduard the prospective peacemaker had been replaced by Shevardnadze, the old-style Communist boss who had dominated Georgia for thirteen years.

CHAPTER THIRTY

THE SINGLE EUROPEAN ACT

Summer and Summit

Two weeks after news broke of Gordievski's defection, I flew to New York for the UN General Assembly. This year there was a special meeting of the Security Council on 27 September, to mark the fortieth anniversary of the birth of that institution. The permanent representatives had stepped aside to allow the fifteen member-states to be represented by their Foreign Ministers. Because it was Britain's turn to be in the chair throughout the month of September, it was my privilege to preside over this rather awesome occasion. Most of the speeches, generally about the role of the UN itself, were reasonably constructive. Wu Xueqian and I saluted each other across the hall and made something of our maturing partnership for the future of Hong Kong. George Shultz was vigorously positive and set the scene well for me to close the proceedings – according to *The Times* as the 'star' of the occasion. 'Sir Geoffrey', said the paper's UN correspondent, 'made the ultimate diplomatic gesture. He wove the speeches of his colleagues into his own and made them sound brilliant.' Our own ambassador, Sir John Thomson, was less surprised by my parliamentary technique of extracting nuggets from the prepared statements of virtually all my colleagues. Perez de Cuellar, on the other hand, apparently described it to his *chef du cabinet* as 'a virtuoso performance the like of which he had never seen in the Council before'.

This unexpected impact of my more or less routine performance – for a parliamentarian – does illustrate the way in which Britain's representatives on the international stage can often box above their weight. The near-universal understanding of the English language means that we can perform on such occasions with an informality, an intimacy even, that is not possible for others. Sir John Thomson himself was later able to capture the attention of the Council in much the same way. For at the very moment when news came through of the assassination of Indira Gandhi, John was actually addressing the Council, without arousing much sympathy, on our case over the Falklands. He immediately broke off and, drawing upon his intimate knowledge of the Gandhi family after five years' service as British high commissioner at New Delhi, paid a spontaneous tribute to the murdered Indian leader that has shone in the memory of all those who heard it. The English language, and the ability to use it spontaneously and effectively, is still one of the most potent diplomatic instruments in the world.

Despite all these activities abroad, I managed during the summer to catch up with some of the domestic agenda. I was never completely detached from this because of the strictness with which I sought to follow Margaret's entirely sensible rule that Cabinet meetings should be given the highest possible priority, even by the Foreign Secretary. By this time, the year-long coal strike, which had started early in 1984, had run its tragically triumphant course. For all its unhappy impact from time to time in my native South Wales, I had given Margaret my steady support throughout this struggle, which had been long foreshadowed by the all-too-turbulent history of this brave but grisly industry. I had indeed cut short a trip to Brazil in order to give Nigel Lawson my backing at that summer's public expenditure Cabinet. One major item (of national as well as international significance) had also been commanding a good deal of my attention throughout the previous twelve months – the delicate process of shaping the Anglo-Irish Agreement. Nigel's second Budget, inevitably less dramatic than his first, had been intelligent, reforming and restrained.

But the government was still far from basking in popularity. There had been three by-elections in Tory-held seats in the year since June 1984. We had held the seat in Southgate and lost in Portsmouth South and Brecon and Radnor. Most poignant for me was the loss of Brecon and Radnor on 4 July 1985 with a swing from ourselves to the Liberals of 16 per cent. For that by-election had followed the tragically early death, from cancer, of one of my closest political friends, Tom Hooson. The seat had been Labour held for decades until 1979, when Tom's dedication to Welsh Conservatism helped him to victory. As I said at his memorial service, it was one of the great sadnesses of Tom's early death that his service to that constituency had been so curtailed.

By this time I was sufficiently at ease with the foreign affairs portfolio to make fairly regular contributions to wider political debate, with a major speech on domestic or general affairs about once every six months.

On 16 July I spoke to a Young Conservative audience at Westminster.[1] My remarks there were seen as having 'moved the Tories off the defensive', not just by exposing Neil Kinnock's failure to disengage his party from extremism but also by stressing the extent to which the government's policies represented what I called 'mainstream thinking in the industrialized world'. The Labour alternative, I argued, faced Britain with the threat of a major reversal of policy, just at the moment when Britain was regaining not only her economic feet but also her position in the world stage. I tried constantly to stress the link between economic and foreign policy success, and the extent to which our own position, so far from being dangerously intemperate, was near the international centre of gravity. 'This', I had stated clearly – and in those days without fear of contradiction – 'is a European-minded government.' Milan I was able already to dismiss as 'a temporary delay in progress' towards our objectives.

I carried this theme through into my speech to the 1985 party conference at Blackpool. The policies of government, I stressed, were based upon the belief that 'by history and by inclination, by geography and by self-interest', Britain was required 'to play a critical role . . . in shaping the political and economic future of democratic Europe'. I closed with an account of the moving scene at Popieluszko's graveside, earlier that year, when 'a throng of people for whose freedom we went to war in 1939 were chanting "Viva Anglia! Long Live Britain!"' It was that reputation and those values, I closed, which our government would steadfastly uphold.

One sad feature of this conference was the absence from government, for the first time in many years, of my old Cambridge and Hampstead partner Patrick Jenkin. Margaret had asked him to give her room for new faces in the Cabinet. We were both sad. 'You and I have soldiered together for so long', wrote Patrick, 'that it is difficult to believe that we can no longer do so – at least in the same way.' He took it more philosophically than I did. I was myself dismayed to see him go, since I saw him as one of a number of colleagues whose ability to shape the collective wisdom of the government had been diminished, and finally lost, by too frequent job changes and premature disposal. A government that is long in office does, of course require refreshment from time to time. And loyal, sometimes long-suffering, back-benchers need to see credible prospects of advancement. That is one reason why I regretted the reluctance to put forward British political candidates for international positions, simply for fear of by-elections – at least when our majority was as large as it was in those halcyon days. I certainly regretted, as I say, Margaret's tendency towards extravagance in dispensing with colleagues who possessed talent that had been strengthened by experience. When Margaret tendered her resignation on 28 November 1990, less than half her 1987 Cabinet was still with her and only three had survived since 1983. This is one reason too why John Major's Cabinets perforce seemed short of heavyweight experience.

There was one change in my own departmental team at this time as well. I was sad to lose Richard Luce, whose always alert wisdom on Hong Kong and the Middle East I had come to value most highly. Richard was, however, being promoted (albeit not into Cabinet) to a job that he relished and was destined to perform to everybody's satisfaction – Minister for the Arts. Tim Renton (himself later to take that job) was promoted within the Foreign Office to take Richard's place as Minister of State. And for a long-serving stint as Parliamentary Secretary I acquired Timothy Eggar. He turned out to be perceptive as well as energetic – the only minister I met, during thirteen years in Cabinet, who set himself six-monthly work programmes and then reported (to me) his performance. This is why I was all the more surprised and sad that it was during his time as Energy Minister that John Major and Michael Heseltine, seven years later, ran into the great coal-industry disaster of October 1992.

There were two pieces of nostalgia in the story of that summer. I decided to hold the Diplomatic Banquet in an old haunt that had dazzled me during my younger days at the Bar. For several years I had boosted my early earnings by giving lectures on civil law to young officers at the Royal Naval College, Greenwich. It was to the Wren–Hawksmoor Painted Hall there that we now invited our 1985 diplomatic guests. It was even more magnificient than I remembered, and determined me to seek out each year a fresh – and, I hoped, even more striking – setting for this agreeable fiesta. I recall too a much more modest, but very cheering, event: the fortieth-anniversary dinner which was largely organized by my VE-Day companion Jackie Lowry for all those who had been with us on our Royal Signals short course at Exeter in 1945. Remarkably, some eighteen out of twenty-three originals were able to reassemble for this occasion – held in Admiralty House, since Carlton Gardens was being refurbished for most of that year.

There was a much less cheerful event to recall: the death, while we were on holiday in Spain, of our cherished Jack Russell, Budget – still less than six years old. He was killed by a farm vehicle while on holiday in Devon with Amanda and her in-laws. She agonized before deciding to give us the news while we were still away, and Elspeth was equally shattered to receive it. Happily, Budget's daughter Tara soon produced a litter from which we chose another charming dog, as intelligent as Budget, though not so good at football. But what to call him? Marcia Falkender, in the *Mail on Sunday*, ran a competition for the name best suited to symbolize my move from Treasury to Foreign Office, and came up – unkindly – with Fudge-it. Elspeth, with unusual lack of imagination, first thought of Carly (after Carlton-Browne of the FO): but eventually we made the happy choice of Summit.

Soon the irritations of Milan faded into history. Although the UK still formally challenged the need for any Treaty changes at all to emerge from the forthcoming Inter-Governmental Conference, we were in truth eager to hammer into place the Cockfield single-market programme, along with our own proposals for closer political co-operation. We were also at the point of 'changing the guard' in our crucial Brussels embassy. Michael Butler was to be replaced by another Wykehamist, David Hannay. 'I can hand over', said Butler in his valedictory despatch, 'in the certain knowledge that there will not even be a faltering moment as the baton passes.' He was right. The much maligned British Civil and Diplomatic Services have never been given due credit for the sustained quality of those who serve the United Kingdom in our Brussels mission to the Community. Drawn from the whole of Whitehall, the eighty or so men and women weld into an effective and united task force, to a far greater extent than most other countries' permanent representations. This kind of team work perhaps comes most easily in a post like Brussels, where all are kept busy on interesting, challenging work, producing a flow of real, often important decisions. Ministerial colleagues had given me the same message, in rather different terms. 'Your British people', they would say, 'are like the Kremlin. They all always say the same thing.'

Michael Butler was ready to pay similar tribute to Prime Minister and Foreign Secretary. Meetings with Mrs Thatcher, he rightly observed, were not for the faint-hearted or the ill-briefed, but she seemed, in his eyes, 'positively to welcome serious argument and to have a high regard for those who argued with her most effectively'.[2] I was grateful too for Michael Butler's envoi to myself: 'good humour, hard work, patience and negotiating skill which brings us a higher than average degree of success. My Community colleagues', he concluded, 'make no secret of their envy.' His own tenacious record of vigilant and dynamic service to Britain's interests in the Community is unlikely to be surpassed for many years.

Missing the Boat on the ERM

The last three months of 1985 were destined to bring two of the most important EC decisions that we were to take during my eleven years in Margaret's government. The first concerned our membership of the Exchange Rate Mechanism (ERM) of the European Monetary System (EMS). Our policy remained, as it had for six years, that we were ready to join 'when the time was right' or 'ripe'. (Neither Nigel Lawson nor I can cast any light on how or why or when this word was changed – if indeed it ever was officially.) But none of those close to the heart of . economic policy had been disposed to press the case during our first term. Nigel has reminded us that he began to argue the point just before leaving the Treasury in 1981.[3] But the rest of us regarded the argument as premature for so long as the petrocurrency factor continued to maintain the volatility or the strength (or both) of the pound sterling. The strictness with which we were pursuing our monetary targets – and indeed our success in that direction in 1982–3 – was another argument for holding our hand.

By the time I left the Treasury in June 1983 I was, however, becoming increasingly attracted by the case for ERM membership on economic grounds. Our work in the G5 group of Finance Ministers had been leading us increasingly towards exchange-rate stability. The conclusions of the Versailles and Williamsbury Summits (1982 and 1983) in my time could be seen as pointers towards the agreements made at the Plaza (1985) and the Louvre (1987) in Nigel's. Countries already in the ERM appeared to be deriving real benefit from exchange rates that were much more stable than our own. Particularly was this the case at a time when the pound rate against the dollar had sunk to an all-time low of almost 1:1. In the UK itself the monetary aggregates were proving increasingly less reliable indicators than the exchange rate.

I knew, however, that the Chancellor, whatever his own view, had had to deal with a sceptical Treasury and a cautious central bank. The new Governor, Robin Leigh-Pemberton, whom I had invited into that office in December 1982, had by now eased the Bank into a more positive attitude. That was important. For there had been no prospect of raising the issue constructively with Margaret until Nigel had got all his ducks in a row. A voice from the Foreign Office would in any event be heavily discounted. So I was content to leave the judgment of the key economic factors very largely to Nigel. We kept in touch, of course. He knew that this was an issue on which he would be able to count on my support, whenever he judged the time was right.

And by 1985 he did. In a series of discussions and meetings throughout the year (13 February, 30 September and others, which are fully described in his own book),[4] Nigel set about leading Margaret in that direction. His principal, though not quite his only, opponent, Alan Walters, was at that time offstage, working in Washington as an academic economist at the World Bank and Johns Hopkins University. But he remained one of Margaret's most persistent 'voices'. Even Walters' influence seemed, however, to be waning. For on at least one occasion during 1985 I caught her speaking of 'when' and not 'if' we joined the Mechanism. Mainstream Conservative opinion had also moved firmly in that direction. David Howell (as ever a sensitive barometer) identified 'a broad section of opinion' now favouring entry. 'We should move into the ERM', he wrote, 'quickly, ideally now, before the next dollar storm breaks.'[5]

So the crucial meeting at Number 10, on the morning of 13 November, seemed to be well timed. Most of the participants chose themselves: the Deputy Prime Minister (Willie Whitelaw), the Chancellor, the Foreign Secretary, the Trade and Industry Secretary (Leon Brittan) and the Governor of the Bank. Margaret had chosen three additional ministers: the party chairman Norman Tebbit, the Chief Whip John Wakeham and the Leader of the House of Commons John Biffen. (The last was the only one whom one could confidently identify as an opponent of entry to the Mechanism.) There were officials too: Peter Middleton and Terry Burns from the Treasury, Eddie George from the Bank and Brian Griffiths (now in the Number 10 Policy Unit). Their voices counted for little on an occasion of this kind, but all the officials (except Griffiths) were by now in favour of entry.

It was the balance of ministerial opinion that mattered: Nigel had tabled a powerful set of papers in favour of entry and he secured early support from Leon as well as myself. Leon's thinking, which started in 1983 from the same Treasury base as myself, had very closely followed my own. And he had been fortified at the DTI by the strong view of most of the industrial leaders with whom he worked there. Norman Tebbit, later one of Margaret's closest allies in opposition to things European, was the big surprise. Speaking as party chairman, but also influenced no doubt by his experience at the DTI, he too spoke in support of the Chancellor. So did John Wakeham. Both he and Tebbit believed that a decision to enter would be positively helpful in fending off party critics of the government's economic policy. Robin Leigh-Pemberton expressed the Bank's by then clear view in favour of entry – and only John Biffen spoke, as expected, in the opposite sense. Willie's traditional role was to ease the way towards Margaret's likely conclusion. This time he clearly felt that whatever she thought – and I don't know how far he had sounded her out – the verdict was clear. 'The Chancellor, the Governor and the Foreign Secretary', said Willie, 'have all spoken in favour of joining the EMS. And the politics point in the same direction. For me that should settle the question.'

I think he was as surprised as I certainly was by Margaret's instant reaction. She spoke, briefly for her, and made it very plain that she could not and would not accept that view. She brought the meeting quickly to a close, leaving us all wondering where on earth we went next. Nigel invited Willie, Norman and me to join him next door. We were all downcast as well as dumbfounded. What had been the point of the meeting, we asked ourselves, if Margaret was unwilling to heed our collective judgment? The Prime Minister, we knew, was *prima inter pares* but this was the first time that any of us had contemplated her exercising a veto of this kind – and against the very principle of a government policy that we had all been proclaiming for years. Nigel's first (under-standable) instinct was to resign. Equally predictably, we all urged him to hold his hand. And he did. For, rightly or wrongly, we all felt that Margaret's position could not remain unchanged for ever. Yet, for longer than any of us might have thought possible, it did. The influence of a distant professor (for Alan Walters' undisclosed advice had indeed been decisive)* had effectively removed the topic from the agenda of collective discussion for the foreseeable future. To change that state of affairs we should, I think, have needed to go almost off the constitutional map.

As subsequent history made clear, Nigel's resignation alone would not have sufficed. It would have been taken, as four years later indeed it was, in Margaret's stride. Had two or three of us come together to threaten the same course, we could perhaps have carried the matter

---

* Nigel Lawson points out that Walters had by this time passed to the Prime Minister (but not to the Chancellor) the relevant, deeply hostile, section of his forthcoming book, *Britain's Economic Renaissance* (OUP, 1986).

forward. But even that method, after careful and perfectly proper preparation of the kind that Nigel and I gave it in 1989, was capable, as events again showed, of being out-manoeuvred. And the topic was, of course, the most difficult of all to handle in that way, since almost every aspect of the discussion was so intensely market-sensitive.

So, not for the first time, Margaret's ministers had to regroup as best we could and press on with our next items of 'business as usual'. Were we wrong to do so? David Howell probably wrote more perceptively than he knew, in the article already quoted:

> The penalties for not [entering the ERM at this time] will be very great, both in the near term and further ahead. Perhaps the error of a negative policy will not be immediately apparent. Perhaps, as is often the case, those who commit it will neither recognize nor worry about the mistake. But there is a longer view as well, the one which history takes.[6]

For I am now free to take the more historic view that, if in 1985 we had buttressed our faltering monetary discipline with that of the Exchange Rate Mechanism, we should have avoided or substantially abated most of our later mistakes of economic policy. Nigel Lawson has himself acknowledged, indeed argued, this. I agree with his analysis as far as it goes,[7] and would go further. I believe that, by joining the fixed but adjustable system that the ERM then was, we should have achieved more stability not only with the exchange rate but also with monetary and, quite probably, fiscal policy too. For membership of the Mechanism would have enabled us to avoid the unsatisfactory halfway house of 'shadowing the Deutschmark', which Nigel for some time adopted *faute de mieux*. This would itself have delivered a more restrained monetary policy and quite probably steered us away from the Lawson Boom – and consequent inflation and inevitably recession. Finally we should have been able, as more mature, streetwise, members of the system, to play a much more credible and thus fuller part in shaping the Delors Report and managing the (inevitably difficult) response to the shock of German unification. In the result, accession to the EMS mechanism – still under Margaret Thatcher's Premiership but five years too late and in far less favourable economic circumstances – came only after years of divided counsels over UK economic policy had sown the seeds of conflict that eventually precipitated Margaret Thatcher's own downfall.

But I suspect that the only chance – at the time of which I am writing – of averting the long sequence of subsequent disaster would have been achieved, if at all, not by some different pattern of ministerial coercion of the Prime Minister but by a more sustained and engaged attempt (and opportunity) to challenge or neutralize the effect of Alan Walters' remote control of Margaret's thinking. Her final 'conversion' (if such it was) came only in September 1990 – and at a time when others already regarded the pound–Deutschmark exchange rate as unsustainably high. The task of making the policy sufficiently credible to the markets was thus much harder than it need have been. So the way was paved to sterling's ignominious exit from the ERM on Black Wednesday 16 September 1992.

One much earlier instance of Sir Alan Walters' wide-ranging imagination deserves to be recalled. Shortly before Christmas 1983 I received a personal note from Walters, then still at Number 10, with which he enclosed his own draft document entitled 'An Economic Solution for the Falklands'. It had, he explained, been originally designed in April–May 1982 – when the task force was still on its way – but never at that time put forward. One can see why. It was certainly an ingeniously simple idea. After the cessation of hostilities and withdrawal of Argentine forces (an important condition precedent), Britain, suggested Walters, should give Argentina a chance to buy out the sovereignty of the islands, almost as in a contested corporate takeover bid. The Argentines could choose what figure to offer to every Falklander – man, woman and child. Walters gives the example of £50,000. The islanders would then, suggested Walters, 'vote on a plebiscite whether they wished to take their £50,000 per head and receive Argentinian sovereignty, or whether they reject both the compensation and sovereignty. . . . If the Argentinians really want sovereignty then they will bid high in the compensation stakes. . . . I suspect more than two-thirds of the islanders would be willing to settle at £50,000.' But, if not, the plan continued, Argentina might be allowed, after a suitable interval, to make a further bid. 'Granted the acquisivite obsession of the Argentines, their second bid would be likely to be raised to heights which the Falklanders could hardly refuse.'

In his letter to me (of 16 December) Alan explained why he did not put this plan to Margaret in 1982: 'for quite obvious reasons, I did not even intimate that I had such thoughts. But now it seems . . . this sort of solution is slightly less impossible' and 'would be widely welcomed – now that Argentina has a less odious government – especially in the United States. It would do quite a lot to repair the rift caused by Grenada.' He asked me, finally, to consign his note to the WPB if I thought he was being 'merely silly or, worse, unrealistic'. I replied to the effect that Walters' plan compared well, as indeed it did, with most of the other 'unthinkable' solutions that had crossed my path. But I felt that, whatever might have been its earlier merits, the proposed cash offer would at that stage provoke accusations that the islanders were being encouraged to 'sell a birthright for which some of their country-men had died'. That, I advised him, would not be acceptable. And that was the last that I heard of the idea.

The incident is revealing I think, for several reasons. First, Walters was willing to share his plan with me on a personal basis because, as he said, 'I can be quite frank with an old friend.' For that was no exaggeration of our relationship in those far-off, just post-Treasury, days. Secondly, it shows that at that stage even Margaret's closest personal advisers were not 'bunkered' in the way which they later became: for he had tentatively shared the idea not with her but with me. Finally, it is interesting that one of Walters' prime motivations was his wish to 'repair the rift' with the United States; for even when he was on our side of the Atlantic his heart often beat to an American rhythm. This is one reason why he may later have found it so difficult to allow Margaret to lean towards things European as much as most of her Cabinet colleagues might have wished.

Our Falklands policy, and so our attitude towards Argentina, did in fact remain virtually unchanged throughout the rest of my time in office. We welcomed the emergence in December 1993 of Raoul Alfonsín as a democratic successor to the defeated dictator Galtieri, and much later took heart from the country's return to economic stability. But the restoration of diplomatic relations had to await the Major–Hurd era.

Luxembourg Inter-Governmental

Meanwhile in the real world we were into the Inter-Governmental Conference that was due to culminate in Luxembourg on 2–3 December 1985. There have been only two such proceedings in the history of the Community. The second ended at Maastricht, in December 1991, and produced the Treaty of that name. Inter-Governmental Conferences are clearly important events. It is only this way that changes can be made in the basic Treaty, in effect the constitution of the Community. Unanimity is required at the Conference itself. The resulting Treaty has to be ratified by each member-state, in accordance with its own constitution:

for some countries – Denmark and Ireland, for example – that means a referendum.

Granted the importance of an IGC, its procedure was strikingly informal, not to say chaotic. Perhaps everything that is being done for the first time is like that. The prime reason for disorder here was the entirely open-ended agenda for the Conference: any proposal for any change that had the backing of any one of the twelve member-states had to be placed on the 'order paper'. As though to emphasize the breadth of the canvas, the European Parliament had already given its approval to a completely new constitution, known (after its principal author, an Italian Communist MEP) as the Spinelli Treaty. And, the European Council itself, at Stuttgart, had given its blessing to the broad-ranging declaration which flowed from the Genscher–Colombo Plan.

The task of distilling all this into a manageable agenda now fell to the Luxembourg Presidency, in consultation with the Commission and Foreign Ministers, meeting almost every week. We depended greatly on the Secretary General of the Council of Ministers. That job – even more important than that of Britain's Cabinet secretary – was performed for fourteen formative years (1980–94) by an immensely effective, calm and intelligent Dane, Niels Ersbøoll, the kind of Eurocrat without whom the Community would long since have ground to a halt. We had the backing for this exercise of the tiny but immensely efficient Luxembourg machine. A small government has much fewer problems than a large about internal co-ordination: often one man does the job of five elsewhere. In the four working months since the Milan Summit, culminating with a full weekend's 'conclave' before the European Council met on Monday, 2 December, we had distilled the task into a huge agenda paper with dozens of alternative proposals for heads of government to debate and choose between. And, sitting with their Foreign Ministers alongside them, they devoted themselves to this gruelling marathon for no less than twenty-seven hours in two working days – finishing at midnight on Thursday, 3 December.

Margaret Thatcher complained – and still does – of the time wasted in this process, attributing the blame either to 'talkative males' or to 'garrulous Europeans'. Some other commentators regard it as absurd for heads of government to be directly involved in such detailed drafting of a treaty text. But when one reflects on the sensitivity and importance of many of the issues underlying the words it is difficult to see any workable alternative: it is only at the highest level of national authority that crucial concessions can be made or bargains be struck.

Contrary to the impression that she has subsequently tended to generate, Margaret Thatcher addressed the four or five key issues – as we saw them – directly and positively. On two issues agreement proved reasonably easy to find. Strengthened co-operation on foreign policy was quite quickly agreed upon the basis of the proposals which, Margaret pointed out, we had put forward before the Milan Council. The text of Part III of the Luxembourg Treaty (the Single European Act as it became entitled) was indeed very close to that which the British Prime Minister had handed to the German Chancellor at Chequers on 18 May 1985. Nor was it difficult to reach common ground on a modest extension of the role of the European Parliament. This is an issue on which there was a particularly wide gap between the national posturing of some heads of government and the positions which they were finally ready to adopt – after a certain amount of 'grandstanding' in the Council for the sake of their national press. Most of Margaret's colleagues – particularly Mitterrand, Kohl, Craxi and the Benelux premiers – found it popular (at least at this stage) to present themselves as champions of the European Parliament. Margaret Thatcher on the other hand (especially in the House of Commons) was tenaciously dismissive of the European 'Assembly', as she insisted on calling it until the very moment when its legal title was changed by the Treaty now under discussion. Yet in truth all the heads of government had a common interest in maintaining their own joint and several authority, as represented by the powers of the European Council. At Luxembourg, Margaret expressed this balance candidly and well. MEPs, she said, are democratic representatives. So are we. We have to take decisions for our own countries and in the Council for the Community as a whole. We must find the right institutional balance – one that does not make that process slower or more difficult. And so, in effect, it was agreed.

We had a tough battle on 'economic and monetary union'. This undefined concept had long been an 'aspiration' of the Community, at least since the adoption of the Werner Plan in 1971. Most of our partners were now anxious to establish it as a formal Treaty objective, with at least some initial detail spelt out. We did not want this. Better by far, said Margaret, to concentrate on practical steps – the liberalization of capital movements, the wider use of the ECU. The incorporation into the Treaty of the EMS, she argued, could change the basis on which it had developed satisfactorily so far. (This was, of course, a positive view which I could certainly endorse.) On this firm position we understood that we had the support of the German government. But, we had equally been led to understand, their support might be less than rock-solid. And so it proved to be. There was thus one harrowing break in the proceedings when Helmut Kohl, Margaret Thatcher and I caballed in one of the corridors. He was torn between pressure from his coalition partner, Foreign Minister Genscher, on the one hand, and, on the other, his near commitment to his own Bundesbank as well as to ourselves. In the result, he cracked, but only a little: the Single European Act contains the first Treaty reference to economic and monetary union – but only vaguely defined.

The remaining questions were all about how far we should be ready to accept majority voting (in place of unanimity) on proposed extensions of the scope or application of Community law. Quite literally they raised the question of our willingness to extend that manifestly 'federal' aspect of the Community – though the word was not much used at that time. We were enthusiastic protagonists of this where it could be seen as necessary for the effective operation of the single market. (This was indeed our chief campaigning cry – 'Thatcherism on a European scale' was one of the catchphrases.) But just as we were keen for this kind of progress, so were we anxious to preserve important exceptions to the concept of a single, frontier-free Europe. Most of these sprang naturally from our geographical position as an island – for example, tight, frontier-operated controls on immigration, terrorism, dangerous drugs, rabies and the like. These 'insular' arguments often commended them-selves, understandably, to the Irish and sometimes the Danes. Broadly we relished the idea of a Europe that was frontier-free for goods, services and capital, but not for (criminal or non-European) people nor for (dangerous and infected) animals and plants. It was always going to be difficult to design a continent-wide set of rules that could be seen to deliver this mildly schizophrenic compromise. But in the end we obtained agreement at Luxembourg on a framework that came as close as possible to achieving that prospect.

There were arguments, of course, about how far it was right to go on presenting Community-wide standards on, for example, the health, safety and other conditions of employment (they were to echo through later debates on the Maastricht 'Social Chapter'). This provoked a memorable clash between Margaret Thatcher and one of her less loved colleagues, Giulio Andreotti. We were anxious, then as now, to avoid burdening small businesses. Margaret Thatcher argued this case by citing her own experience. 'I should know,' she said, 'I once worked in a firm that employed only three people.' At which Andreotti offered the typically sardonic comment: 'I wonder what happened to the other two? I suppose they must have died from an occupational disease?' One would like to think it was an aside. But it found its way through the interpretation system. Whether or not it was intended as a joke, it roused Margaret to snap back, 'This is becoming very discourteous.' She continued to seethe beside me for several minutes.

Of much more importance was our success in maintaining the unanimity rule for any taxation proposal. Tax structures would thus remain primarily a matter for national governments. Cockfield had already become a champion for the other 'harmonizing', 'unifying' side of this argument. But we all felt – Margaret, Nigel and I – equally strongly that Arthur had been pressing this case too far; and that any market distortions arising from tax diversity would iron themselves out through fiscal competition in due course. With that view we were able, happily, to carry the day.

Reactions to the Luxembourg agreement, to the Single European Act, were generally favourable – certainly at home. Whitehall reactions, which I reported to Cabinet on 6 December, were that our success in winning 'all the points which were of real importance' was a 'remarkable achievement'. The parliamentary reaction, with the usual handful of predictable dissenters, was equally favourable. The Prime Minister had no anxiety, and we had no difficulty, about securing the passage through the Commons of the ratifying legislation under a guillotine motion after a total of six days' debate, starting with my second-reading speech on 25 April 1986. By contrast, the President of the Commission, Jacques Delors, was downcast. He commenced the formal proceedings of the Foreign Affairs Council – when we met in Luxembourg on the morning after the agreement, to tidy up the nuts and bolts of the draft Treaty – with a sustained cry of woe that the Conference had achieved so little. When I responded in the opposite sense and urged him to look at the half-full glass rather than the half-empty one, I was warmly supported by most, if not all, my colleagues.

The Single European Act was to achieve most of what we had hoped of it. The Cockfield single-market programme was all put through pretty well on time and we were enabled to carry the free-market case into other fields – further than many of our partners had expected. On the other hand we found ourselves facing on some social and environmental matters a more extensive use of Community powers than we had regarded as foreseeable or legitimate. Both these trends can probably be attributed to the impact of the Single European Act upon what might be called the 'culture' of the Community and its institutions. The habit of working together, of sharing sovereignty, of give and take, which we had so strongly urged for the single market was not something that could be ruthlessly confined. In this case, as in others, we have learned that the impact of Community membership is as much part of a process as it is an event.

There was one consequence of the Single European Act that I had certainly not fully anticipated, namely its impact on the so-called 1966 Luxembourg Compromise. This convention of the Community constitution – for such it was and probably still is – entitles a member-state, on an issue which it regards as affecting a vital national interest, indefinitely to resist an adverse majority vote. When reporting to the Commons on the effects of the Single European Act, both Margaret Thatcher and I insisted that the Luxembourg Compromise remained 'in place untouched and unaffected' by the Single European Act. As a matter of law that was undoubtedly correct, for the Compromise was itself a creation not of law but only of convention. And the convention itself was never unanimously endorsed. For that very reason, the scope, effectiveness, survival even, of the convention remains the subject of lively debate. Even before the 1985 change (when majority voting was less frequent) the Compromise was not often formally invoked. But the threat of its invocation always hovered in the background – credibly enough. Now that majority voting has become the habit over so wide a field, occasions for invoking the Compromise seem to arise less often. This has encouraged some commentators to write its obituary. Practitioners in the field remain confident, however, that the influence of the Compromise was ever present, for example, on France's behalf in recent discussions affecting the end of the GATT Uruguay Round. It would certainly be imprudent to conclude that the Compromise has melted away.

No subsequent meeting of the European Council – at least before Maastricht – could begin to compare in importance with Luxembourg, 1985. Two days after this most decisive event in the European history of her administrations, Margaret Thatcher found herself having to grapple with the most serious challenge so far to her domestic authority. The Westland saga was destined to unfold very largely upon her own Downing Street stage.

CHAPTER THIRTY-ONE

WESTLAND TURNING POINT

Politics Goes On

For the Foreign Secretary, Number 10 was less often a place of work than a kind of hospitality suite, to which I repaired most frequently for talks, working meals or banquets with visiting Foreign Ministers and heads of government. As Chancellor, I was a member of almost every Cabinet committee and 'small group' of ministers, which were a growing feature of Thatcher governments. Margaret had not invented them – Ted Heath too had found them useful. Even in his day, small meetings, informally minuted only by Number 10 had been much less likely to leak. Margaret liked them too because membership of each group could be chosen to suit her own thinking.

My more limited participation as Foreign Secretary allowed me a welcome detachment from the day-to-day turmoil of parliamentary fracas, public sector pay disputes and quarrels with local government. I could stay strategically in touch with the domestic scene through the weekly Cabinet meetings and daily press summaries. While at Number 11 I had got my name on to the circulation list for the highly personalized digest that was prepared each day for the Prime Minister by Bernard Ingham. I stayed in that particular loop for the rest of my time in government. It was useful, sometimes startling, to be able to share Margaret's idiosyncratically edited view of the world. I took care to add a wider perspective through weekly 'prayer' meetings with my own ministerial team, their PPSs and our special advisers, and drink-and-chat sessions with back-bench MPs (at least once a month). I also kept up my life-long habit of speaking regularly to business, university and party audiences in the provinces as well as in London. My regional tours, as they were rather grandly called, were planned for a year ahead, and almost invariably included a factory or other industrial visit. At much shorter notice I managed to register an appearance in the great majority of by-election campaigns throughout my time on the front bench.

By-elections were to provide a drum-beat of disappointment through most of our time in office. Poor opinion-poll figures were an almost equally constant background. It was only modest comfort to know that we shared that experience with most democratic governments around the world. At least until the summer of 1986, this was not manifesting itself in the form of support for Neil Kinnock's Labour Party. But the Liberal–SDP Alliance – with Steel and Owen still apparently in brother-hood – we saw as more troublesome. The loss of Brecon and Radnor with an adverse swing of 16 per cent, in July 1985, was followed by a swing of 19 per cent in Ryedale (8 May 1986). And economic recovery, which had actually been under way since mid-1981, remained masked by the high level of unemployment. Only in July 1986 did the figures start to fall from a peak of 3.2 million.

In Parliament there was important progress with the privatization of British Telecom (1984) and, later, British Gas (1986). Measures of this kind, desirable on their merits, had the political advantage of increasing the numbers of those with a vested interest in our success. On the other hand, a huge amount of political goodwill – and energy – was expended on the destruction of the Greater London Council and other citadels of the 'loony left'. Yet local government seemed always to elude control. Policy was seen to falter on a number of other fronts. Educational reform, which had seemed a natural for Keith Joseph, became enmeshed in 'industrial action' by the teachers, and he proved unable to sell to our back-benchers the first tentative moves towards a student loan scheme. There was something of a revival of 1981-style Tory dissent, from voices as disparate as Harold Macmillan and Francis Pym. The latter's uncharacteristic attempt to foster a party within a party (Conservative Centre Forward) was predictably more short-lived than the impact of Macmillan's sparklingly unsenile maiden speech in the Lords, which was subsequently repeated, like some much loved cabaret turn, before a diversity of audiences.

In September 1985 Margaret reacted to the growing unease with another reshuffle of her Cabinet (the eighth since 1979). The unwise (and unjust) notion that Leon had to leave the Home Office was probably the core decision.* He replaced Norman Tebbit at the DTI – in his third Cabinet job in three years. He was the eighth of twelve

* See p. 424 above.

ministers to share responsibility for that department during eleven Thatcher years. No one was fooled, least of all Leon, by Margaret's suggestion that no demotion was involved. Norman, who did his best to conceal shrewd judgment with crude rhetoric, was charged as party chairman with the mildly implausible task of furbishing the party's human face, in time for a general election, now less than two years away. Leon's slot at the Home Office was filled by Douglas Hurd. In itself this was an excellent idea, save that it meant a second change within twelve months in Northern Ireland. Despite his later success, Tom King's settling-in period in Belfast was a difficulty we should have been spared at this time. This reshuffle was also the start of Kenneth Baker's high-speed transit through the Cabinet – four jobs in less than seven years, with just nine months as Secretary of State for the Environment.

A Tale of Two Ministers

One player who kept his place was Michael Heseltine, Secretary of State for Defence since January 1983. After almost four years at Environment he had quickly and credibly established himself in the foreign dimension of the Defence job. We had worked together overseas for some two and a half years, sharing very similar views about Britain's role in Europe, in East–West relations and more generally. Though our partnership was not as continuous as that which I had shared for almost as long with Leon Brittan during his time as my Chief Secretary to the Treasury, I counted them both among my closest friends in politics. They were both long-standing Bow Group colleagues. We had jointly and severally been partners in many enterprises. And each has formidable political talents – Michael's the more histrionic and Leon's the more cerebral. Michael's gesture politics was sometimes impulsive: during my Treasury days he was always calling for dramatic pay policies which he would have been the first to find unworkable. At this particular time, when Leon's self-confidence must have been dented by his move from the Home Office, Michael's was riding high. He had just pulled off a notable coup in establishing the European Fighter Aircraft as a joint venture between the United Kingdom, Germany, Spain and Italy. Michael would have been less than human had he not derived some pleasure from the identity of his two opponents in this coup: first, the French, who had refused to take part unless the specifications were closer to their own and had failed to secure German support for this view; and second, Margaret Thatcher herself, who had wanted an Anglo-American or all-British aircraft. On each of these fronts Michael had enjoyed support from both Nigel Lawson and myself. Unusually, the Treasury arguments were in line with those of European policy.

Nothing like this harmony was to prevail on the question that hit the Cabinet shortly before Christmas 1985. The future of the Westland Company, Britain's only helicopter manufacturer, was at stake. It was a company that I had visited a couple of times over the years. It had never struck me as very well managed. Throughout 1985 its future had been in jeopardy – and largely dependent on the prospect of support from the Ministry of Defence and of a largely ODA-financed order from India. It was an all too familiar situation. HMG were struggling to leave the future of a business to the market-place. But it was a market-place in which, directly or indirectly, we were the crucial customer. A takeover bid for the company by Alan Bristow (whose successful helicopter-operating company was headquartered at Redhill in my constituency) had been made and then withdrawn. Westland acquired a new chairman, Sir John Cuckney, very able and worldly-wise, and he had succeeded in finding a new private sector bidder for Westland – the American United Technology Group, manufacturer of Sikorsky helicopters.

Apparently galvanized by this prospect, and inspired perhaps by his recent success with the European Fighter Aircraft, Michael Heseltine then renewed the search – almost at the eleventh hour – for an alternative European future for Westland. He rested his hopes on the possibility of support from the European National Armaments Directors (NADs). This was forthcoming in the form of a strongly worded, though not conclusive, declaration issued on 29 November. This fortified Michael's wider concern that acceptance of the Sikorsky deal and acquiescence in an American partnership could well damage more widely the prospects for collaborative European defence production. The House of Commons Defence Committee later recognized this anxiety as well founded. They also expressed the view that Michael's efforts in the European direction had 'accomplished an extraordinary amount in a very short time'.[1]

These issues came before three ministerial meetings at Number 10 in the first ten days of December 1985. Two meetings of a 'small group' – the Prime Minister, Willie Whitelaw, Heseltine, Brittan, Nigel Lawson, Norman Tebbit and myself – failed (on 5 and 6 December) to agree a solution. So three days later it was considered by a specially convened meeting, on 9 December, under the Prime Minister's chairmanship, of the Cabinet's main economic sub-committee, E(A). The regular membership (of mainly economic ministers) had been augmented by the presence of others, including Michael Heseltine and myself. Unusually Sir John Cuckney was invited to attend a part of the meeting. His advice clearly favoured early acceptance of the American bid. Even so, there was continuing support for the possibility of a European alternative. Margaret summed up our interim conclusions. The sub-committee 'was not ready yet' to reject the NADs' recommendations; a 'number of Ministers' (including Norman Tebbit and myself, as well as Michael Heseltine) would 'have a clear preference for the European alternative, if it could be developed into a form which the Westland board would regard as preferable to the Sikorsky arrangement.' But time was short. If the European consortium had not produced 'a package which the Westland board could recommend' by 4 p.m. on Friday 13 December, the government would be obliged to reject the NADs' recommendation.

Here was the origin of the first – Heseltine – bone of contention in the Westland affair: 4 p.m. on Friday, 13 December had been set as the deadline for Westland's approval of a European alternative to the Sikorsky deal. The Cabinet committee minutes do not record any decision or agreement for a further ministerial meeting to be held before that 4 p.m. deadline. Michael Heseltine believed that the need for such a meeting had been agreed. Certainly officials did 'ring round to see whether people would be available if a further meeting was called',[2] But no such meeting took place. Even so, a firm proposal from the European consortium (which Michael Heseltine put together) was transmitted direct to the Westland board on Friday, 13 December. It was supported by a number of other documents from Michael. The Westland board met that evening. They decided nonetheless to approve the alternative of a capital reconstruction, along the lines proposed by Sikorsky – now with support from Fiat. This seems, today as much as it did at the time, to have been the decisive moment. For it was the board of Westland that took the vital pro-Sikorsky decision. This should not have been surprising, for John Cuckney throughout had a clear preference in that direction. That was not diminished even by the skill with which Michael Heseltine had got together the alternative. Cuckney's 'profound scepticism about the feasibility of a European deal' had been expressed some weeks before.

Michael Heseltine still enthused over the European option. He thought that he – and we – had been robbed of a great prize. He blamed this upon Cabinet Office machinery – and so on the Prime Minister.

The 'cancellation', as he thought, of the Friday afternoon meeting-that-never-was deliberately deprived him of the chance to press the superiority of his European case. But there is only scanty evidence to support this theory. He had sought in Cabinet on 12 December to challenge the 'cancellation' – without success. No colleague shared his recollection of an arrangement for a meeting. Margaret certainly did not. So too in Cabinet on 19 December, when the Prime Minister again summed up government policy: it was 'for Westland to decide what was the best course to follow in the best interests of the company and its employees'; given that that was the policy, 'no minister was entitled to lobby in favour of one proposal rather than another'; questions on the subject 'should not be answered in any way which favoured one group proposal rather than another'. On the same day, Westland announced their financial results and the proposed Sikorsky-based reconstruction of the company. And that for the moment appeared to be that.

I still had some sympathy for Michael. Like him, I believed the long-run national interest required us, if possible, to secure a European anchorage for our helicopter industry. I did not feel that every one of us had tried as hard as we should to that end. Margaret's heart certainly had not been in the right place. Even Leon's had disappointed me. But any temptation to maintain that argument was wisely discouraged by my experienced PPS, Len Appleyard. The case was not clear cut. On any commonsense view, the Christmas break should allow the dust to settle on the scene as it had been set by the decision of Sir John Cuckney and his colleagues. My heart remained with Michael, Leon by now had my head. Just as I was reluctant to enter the lists against either of my old friends who had become thus embroiled, so I refrained from lobbying either of them. Number 10 I left strictly alone.

To my dismay the New Year triggered a fresh outbreak of hostilities. Margaret fired the first salvo, to Sir John Cuckney on New Year's Day. She set out to reassure Westland of HMG's support in face of any possible European hostility. This letter had been 'cleared' for accuracy not only with Leon and Michael, but also with Sir Patrick Mayhew, the Solicitor General. None of that prevented Michael from publishing, two days later, on 3 January 1986, a fresh exchange of letters – between himself and Lloyds Merchant Bank – designed to undermine the assurances contained in Margaret's earlier letter. She was predictably furious at this challenge to her authority – and not without reason. So too was Leon, who was now campaigning jointly with Margaret against Michael's attempt to recover ground that had been irretrievably lost. In place of collective ministerial responsibility, we now had civil war within the Cabinet.

Margaret moved swiftly on Saturday, 4 January. She required Leon to ask the Solicitor General, Patrick Mayhew, to consider the accuracy of Michael Heseltine's most recent letter. Later in the day Mayhew expressed the provisional view that the Heseltine letter was materially inaccurate and required correction. By the same Saturday evening Margaret had asked the Solicitor General to consider expressing that opinion in writing to Michael Heseltine. By noon on Monday Mayhew had re-examined the papers – and signed and delivered to Heseltine a letter which identified material inaccuracies in Heseltine's of 3 January and advised him to correct them forthwith. Copies of the Mayhew letter reached Number 10 and Leon Brittan's office at about the same time. So by about 1 p.m. on Monday, 6 January one fateful objective had been agreed between Leon, Margaret and all their relevant officials. As Margaret said later in Parliament:

> the fact that the Defence Secretary's letter of 3 January was thought by the Solicitor General to contain material inaccuracies, which needed to be corrected, should become public knowledge as soon as possible and before Sir John Cuckney's press conference [due to take place less than three hours later, at 4 p.m.]

The 'fact' referred to by the Prime Minister – that is to say, the Solicitor General's opinion that Michael Heseltine's letter was materially inaccurate – was accordingly disclosed to the Press Association. It was published on their tapes by 3.30 p.m. It has ever since been clear, in the words of the House of Commons Defence Committee Report, that 'the method of disclosure that was adopted, the unattributable communication of tendentious extracts from the letter, was disreputable'.[3] Worst of all, of course, was the simple fact of disclosing, without his knowledge or consent, the advice tendered by a law officer – even disclosing the fact that he had advised at all. Such disclosure was contrary to almost every rule in the book. This was the second – Brittan – bone of contention in the Westland affair. Who was to carry the can for this serious impropriety?

Leon Brittan was the only minister directly involved. As ill luck so often has it in the whirlwind of ministerial life, he was lunching away from his office when the matter arose. So it was only in course of a hasty mid-lunch phone conversation that the question was put to him by his private secretary: should we or should we not publish the fact and substance of Patrick Mayhew's advice? And if so how? Leon replied, in the little thinking time that was available, that his officials should discuss with Number 10 whether the disclosure should be made; and, if so, whether it should be made from Number 10, as he would prefer. Failing that, Leon authorized disclosure through the DTI's Press Office but, he emphasized, 'all . . . subject to the agreement of Number 10'. It is clear, and accepted, that he expressed no view about the precise method of publication and was probably not even asked about it.

Discussion then followed between Leon's private secretary John Mogg and Charles Powell, who was dealing with the affair in Number 10, and between Colette Bowe, Leon's press officer, and her opposite number at Number 10, Bernard Ingham. It was quite quickly 'accepted' on all sides that the only practicable way of getting the key facts into public domain was the method actually adopted. Indeed it seems unlikely, given the time constraint, that any alternative was seriously considered. It was only when it came to giving 'authority' for this disclosure that Number 10, in the person of Bernard Ingham, appears – after a fashion at least – to have demurred. The Prime Minister told the Commons on more than one occasion* that DTI officials acted as they did 'in good faith, in the belief that they had the agreement of my office . . . and cover from my office'. The word 'cover' here seems to have been given special force, if only for the purpose of cloaking the extreme ambiguity of the role which Number 10, in the joint persons of Bernard Ingham and Charles Powell, had succeeded in playing throughout this transaction. The Defence Committee put their finger close to the truth when they suggested that 'Mr Ingham realized very well that what was being sought was not agreement but authority for the disclosure, the authority of Number 10 and so of the Prime Minister.' Undoubtedly, they thought, he 'realized the implication of what was about to take place and wished to distance the Prime Minister from the consequences'.[4]

Michael Walks Out

The parliamentary and other manoeuvres over the next three weeks concentrated in the end on just how successfully that had been done.

* On 23 and 27 January 1986.

But first the Heseltine half of the drama had to reach its conclusion – three days later in Cabinet, on 9 January. Westland was first on the agenda. For Margaret had at last determined to restore order, in place of the chaos for which she was herself in large part responsible. A long disussion ensued which did not take us away from the conclusions we had recorded before Christmas: it was for the company and its bankers alone to decide, without further intervention of any kind from ministers. Michael stuck quietly and tenaciously to the case he had tried to make from the outset – that there had been no proper collective discussion of the merits of the case. The earlier validity of his argument, for there had been some, seemed to grow less and less as Michael's presentation became more apparently obsessive. The more he seemed faintly reminiscent of Tony Benn, and occasionally he did, the less he commanded our sympathy.

So Margaret felt able to carry the dialogue, for such it was, on to procedural ground. She pressed for a self-denying ordinance even more severe than in December: from now on, all statements or replies by members of government in relation to Westland, including replies which confirmed statements already made, should be cleared through the Cabinet Office. It was on this point that I recollect, though nobody else seems to do so, making an intervention. 'Surely,' I said, 'we can at least be trusted, without further checking, to confirm statements already made?' Both the combatants swept on regardless. Even then, I had not expected the clash to end in anything but a draw. For we had seen it all before, when others had occasionally engaged in hand-to-hand combat with the boss. And always – even for my own occasional jousts – the steam would go out of the fight, if only to be recalled to fuel the next. But not this time. Margaret 'summed up', as so often, in line with her own arguments. Michael briskly closed his folder, with a reprise of his argument: there had been no collective responsibility in this matter, there had been a breakdown in the propriety of Cabinet discussions, he could not accept the decision recorded in the Prime Minister's summing up. 'I must, therefore, leave this Cabinet.' With that he left the room. No one moved to stop him.

The Prime Minister broke the ensuing silence by proceeding directly to deal with routine business: foreign affairs, Community affairs and Northern Ireland business. Then only was the meeting adjourned for an unusual coffee break of thirty minutes. Margaret carried through the immediately necessary changes. George Younger went to Michael's job at the MOD. And I was asked to release my excellent Minister of State,

Malcolm Rifkind, to take over the Scottish Office. For him at least it was a lucky break: he well deserved a Cabinet place. But Margaret regarded him as too left-inclined and pro-European to let him in easily. The sudden void in the Scottish Office was his heaven-sent opportunity.

But none of this could make up for the loss to the government of Michael Heseltine. I had found him an imaginative and effective partner in our frequent double-acts on the NATO or WEU stage. And in our earlier jobs we had worked closely together on the creation of enterprise zones and on keeping the poll-tax at bay – indeed, we had thought, laying it to rest in 1983. And the party generally had derived enormous benefit from his personal flair and rhetoric, not least in the great defence debate over Britain's nuclear deterrent. I still don't know whether Margaret or he had actually planned for this shock. But I don't think either of them was totally unprepared for it. Margaret's swift repair job on the Cabinet was matched by Michael's near-instant twenty-minute statement to the press about the causes of his departure. Each of them had become too self-centred a personality for coexistence to be easily tolerable. Yet that was no basis on which to make the most of the front-rank talents available for any government. Michael's latest campaign certainly had gone over the top. I still believe that he could and should have been preserved as an effective member of the team, had that been seen by Margaret as an important objective. But she perceived him, in truth from almost the outset, more as a challenger than as a partner. During his final weeks in the Cabinet he had come to be seen more and more as an enemy who had to be defeated. If that meant disposing of him for good, then so be it. My advice or intermediation was never sought. My view would certainly not have been so casually dismissive.

Shouldering the Blame

Nor in normal times would Leon have been so committed to conflict of this kind. Initially he had indeed tried to hold the ring between competing 'Europeans' and 'American' solutions. But his confidence in his own independence had been seriously eroded by his shock removal from the Home Office. If that weakness tugged him ever more closely on to Margaret's side, then Michael's tenacious campaign had done nothing to offset it. He had been drawn ever more deeply into the fray. And so, as visibility improved of the circumstances in which the Solicitor

General's letter had been so recklessly exploited, it was poor Leon who emerged as the Minister with the smoking gun in his hand.

There followed a series of parliamentary occasions, in which Leon and Margaret were obliged to alternate at the despatch-box for two full weeks, in the presentation of an increasingly ragged case. On such occasions the House of Commons can be ruthlessly unfriendly – on both sides. The greater the success of the Opposition in exposing government misconduct the more severely ministers are beset by their own back-benchers. If error has to be acknowledged, then all the more reason to identify a scapegoat who may be discarded with least harm. All too predictably the luck began running against Leon in that role. In his first parliamentary appearance, on 13 January, he was trapped by Michael Heseltine into equivocation about the existence of a confidential letter from Sir Raymond Lygo, chairman of British Aerospace. Before that day was out, he was obliged to face the damaging (and gruelling) experience of apologizing for having misled the House. In debate just two days later, British Aerospace records again appeared to challenge Leon's account of events. His forensically skilful rebuttal of the charge later appeared to have slightly shaky foundations. Leon had not been in office long enough to establish a substantial lobby of personal support in the Commons. Yet his sheer ability had carried him so far and so fast up the promotion ladder that jealous critics, some with malodorous streaks of anti-semitism, were never too far away. His position was not unlike that of Nigel Lawson, with the added disadvantage that he had already been dislodged downwards from his premature peak at the Home Office. So the cards were stacked against him. And he was caught in the crossfire between two protagonists of equal ferocity.

And now it was Margaret's turn to think of her own skin. The Attorney General, Sir Michael Havers, had reacted explosively to the original leak of his confrère's letter. He had threatened to mount his own investigation of Number 10 for possible breaches of the Official Secrets Act. Margaret had responded by appointing the Cabinet sec-retary, the ever useful Robert Armstrong, to conduct an official leak inquiry – into events which had been almost entirely orchestrated from within her own Private Office. She had now (22 January) to decide how to handle the conclusions of Armstrong's report. It was from that document, she has ever since insisted, that she learned for the first time of Leon's role in authorizing the leakage of the Solicitor General's letter. Margaret had known about, indeed initiated, all the earlier steps in this story. She personally had sought the Solicitor General's opinion. When she learned what it was likely to be, she personally suggested that he should write about it to Michael Heseltine. She personally had used Leon Brittan to communicate her wishes to the Solicitor General. Margaret's own actions had thus secured the production of a letter whose contents she wanted to see in the public domain as a matter of urgency. That is what had happened, with the full knowledge and consent of two senior officials in her own office, Charles Powell and Bernard Ingham. They imposed only one restraint upon the whole process. Ingham ensured that the deed was not done by himself but by Leon's press officer, Colette Bowe.

The question that remained is how far he succeeded in doing so. Margaret Thatcher asserts to this day that at the time she remained ignorant of two key facts: the exact method whereby her declared objective was achieved and Leon Brittan's endorsement of what occurred. No less than three times in two weeks (on 15, 23 and 27 January), the Prime Minister had to convince the House of Commons of her own innocence. The gravity of the offence was acknowledged. 'I deeply regret', she said on the 27th, 'that this was done.' On the 15th Margaret and Leon shared the task of replying to the first debate. That round they were able to survive. It was only when Sir Robert had completed his report, on 22 January, that Leon Brittan became fully aware of the risk to his own position.

With Michael Heseltine already removed from the scene, my personal loyalties were no longer pulling in two directions. Leon and Diana, his staunchly supportive wife, lunched with us at Chevening on the Sunday after Michael's resignation, 12 January. I was glad to help Leon in trying to shape the words with which Margaret reported Armstrong's findings to the House. For the draft statement that Margaret had to make on Thursday, 23 January, there was a brisk overnight tussle. In the result she did acknowledge that when Leon's officials disclosed the letter, 'they were right' and did have 'cover from my office'. These were the words on which Leon understandably insisted.

But the statement did not convince the House of the innocence of any of the participants. Somebody still had to take the rap. The offence was not yet so great that a Prime Minister had to go. So the 1922 Committee meeting that evening turned upon Leon. Next day *The Times* concluded, in reserved terms, that it 'would be better now for his government and his Party if he were to give in his resignation'. He and Diana consulted both Elspeth and myself at Carlton Gardens more than once that miserable morning. But the decision could only be for Leon. He concluded, rightly as Elspeth and I believed, although to our intense regret, that he had to go. Leon was the victim of a row that was not of his own making. Over-enthusiasm and under-confidence had led him into an untenable position. The Government could ill afford the loss of another of its most able members.

Only three days later Margaret, by then alone on the bridge, had to face her third Commons ordeal. Leon was now free, if he so wished, to disclose much more of what had passed between them in the past two weeks. But Margaret, in her letter accepting his resignation, had expressed the 'hope that it will not be long before you return to high office'. He was torn between anger at having so far had to shoulder the blame and yet hope of early return to government. So it was important – for both of them – that Margaret's speech should not provoke Leon into hostile candour.

Negotiations about this final text continued well into the eleventh hour. The debate was due to start at 3.30 p.m. Yet as 2.30 approached, Willie Whitelaw, John Wakeham and I were astonishingly assembled in the small private secretary's room at Number 10 – with Powell, Ingham and Nigel Wicks, nominally their senior, in and out of the room – discussing the text. The formalities of meeting in the Cabinet Room next door or upstairs in the study had been abandoned. For we all needed, like so many printers' devils, to be near to the stone where the final text was being cast. Margaret too was in and out. Leon's last words, which I had just brought to the meeting, were finally accommodated. It was to this random audience, distractedly and to nobody in particular, that Margaret blurted out, 'I may not be Prime Minister by six o'clock tonight.'

There was a rumble of dissent. But none of us actually said anything, for the forecast was not beyond the bounds of possibility. Certainly my own heart missed a beat. For this was, if anything, the 'number 11 bus' – so often talked about but never credibly foreseen. Even to my cautious eye it was not possible to identify any successor in those circumstances but myself. And I had just been expending my best endeavours to prevent such an outcome. The very next day, as it happened, Ladbrokes reported that I had replaced Peter Walker as the betting man's favourite to take over if anything should happen to Margaret.

Margaret's worst fears were not fulfilled. Her speech contained a degree of candour, even a touch of contrition. Neil Kinnock, who had to make the all-important opening speech, famously missed the opportunity. David Owen, who spoke after Margaret, tried to press her on some of the questions that Kinnock had missed. But by then Margaret was past the worst, and she felt bold enough to ignore Owen's interrogation. The storm began to blow itself out.

With it went the frightening thought that I might suddenly find myself taking Margaret's place. I was probably never closer to real power than at that moment. It did not seem like an incredible prospect, but it was certainly short-lived, for by the end of the day's debate the crisis had passed, and Margaret was back in command.

The Saga's Impact

Even in retrospect it is possible to take different views of the importance of the Westland drama. In Willie Whitelaw's opinion – expressed when Margaret was still in office – 'Despite the furore at the time, it had no lasting impact.' It seems to me now, however, to have been probably the turning point for Margaret Thatcher's administration. The first moral was immediately clear. Ministerial colleagues were expendable, and not as a result of carefully considered choice or leadership but as a by-product of error or misjudgment.

There was never, of course, much love lost between Margaret Thatcher and Michael Heseltine. Intermittent conflict was inevitable, because of their similarities as much as their differences. Our tasks were large enough to benefit from both their talents. Yet Margaret became reckless of the consequences of his possible departure – ready indeed to welcome it. None of the rest of us – not even, as he admits, Willie the great conciliator – realized just how far each of them was prepared to go in pressing their case. Leon's position was rather different. Unjustly as Margaret had behaved in demoting him from the Home Office, she still valued his ability (rightly so, in light of his subsequent Brussels triumphs). But throughout this episode she used Leon – and he, too, loyally, allowed himself to be used – on a mission that was fraught with constitutional danger. And, when the unwisdom of such conduct made it inevitable, she was equally ruthless in letting him go. Her own survival became the only imperative.

So two of our strongest talents were casually cast away. The Cabinet was beginning to look more like a Catherine wheel than a council of colleagues. Better man-management, less antagonistic policymaking, could have prevented it. But it was becoming clear that we were set in the opposite direction.

It is easy enough – and fair enough – to load the greater part of the blame for this centrifugal state of affairs on Margaret's shoulders. But inevitably one has to ask whether we, the colleagues, could not together have taken more active steps to prevent it. Certainly we talked in twos, and sometimes threes, about our worries and woes, but seldom with constructive effect. Nigel Lawson and I, for example, laid plans for the discussion of the ERM – and twice at least got the topic on to the agenda. But whether in a larger group (as in 1985) or *à trois* (as in 1989), we secured at best only modest progress, at the cost of massive disharmony. It is fair to notice that Jim Prior, Peter Walker and Ian Gilmour – addressing similar problems five years before, when I was inside the policy laager and they were not – had found it equally difficult. They 'would run the risk', so Prior says, 'of being castigated immediately as conniving together against leadership'.[5] Nigel Lawson and I were to experience this after Madrid – with a notable acceleration of the Catherine-wheel effect.

The second lesson of Westland was, perhaps, the more important. It was not yet the most obvious. The inner core of the Thatcher administration was consolidating in unorthodox and dangerous mode. The crucial decision to leak the letter would not have been taken but for the willingness of two men in Downing Street, Bernard Ingham and Charles Powell, to join Leon Brittan in riding roughshod over the rules. They did so – all three of them – because they had come to regard the Prime Minister's passion as entitled to prevail. Her word was indeed their command. Leon Brittan paid the ministerial price of resignation. What of the responsible officials in Downing Street? 'She must ask herself', said *The Times*, 'whether those who took such decisions are the right people, in the right place, with the right powers if she is to overcome problems like this in the future.' David Owen was more blunt. 'It is inconceivable', he said, 'that they can continue to advise the Prime Minister.' Yet they did, both of them, until the end.

Loneliness is part of the price of leadership. Any head of government must want to offset that handicap with the comforting continuity of an inner core of advisers. This is why the 'kitchen cabinet' exists as often in the White House or the Elysée as in 10 Downing Street. Such agreeable arrangements can all too easily become reinforcements of mutual error. Something like the Westland affair can easily establish a sense of mutual solidarity, which becomes ever harder to break. The British system, working properly, is designed to head off this risk of a developing bunker mentality. Whitehall convention normally provides for a regular turnover, every two or three years, of the civil servants who work in most intimate, private-office partnership with a minister – even a prime minister. This is not designed, as some frail ministers occasionally suspect, to ensure that they remain continuously subject to the departmental will. It is sensibly intended to ensure that the innermost councils of government are regularly exposed to independent professional advice. If such independence is to be assured then it cannot indefinitely live in-house. It was neglect of that commonsense rule which landed Margaret Thatcher in the Powell–Ingham triangle that was by the end to play an important part in her downfall.

Bernard Ingham had already been at Number 10 for almost seven years. This 'mild, insignificant, modest, quiet, unassuming Yorkshire-man' – to borrow David Owen's irony – already enjoyed a role more dominant in the government's information service than that of any Prime Minister's press secretary this century. By now he had been in joint harness for almost two years with Charles Powell, the Foreign Office private secretary at Number 10. Alongside corresponding secondees from Treasury and Home Office, the holder of this post was subordinate to the principal private secretary. That official had changed since Powell's arrival. High-flying Robin Butler – he had become secretary to the Cabinet in 1988 – was replaced at the end of 1985 by an equally talented, but more diffident, Treasury official, Nigel Wicks. Powell – intelligent, fluent and immensely hard-working – had by then achieved a dominant position, which his nominal superior was never to recapture. Almost always at the Prime Minister's side, not just on her frequent journeys overseas but throughout most weekends at Chequers as well, Powell's influence was to spread well beyond its prescribed sphere. Westland itself was a good illustration of this. For it was being considered by Cabinet's Economic Committee and not by OD. So it should have been handled by the Treasury and not the Foreign Office private secretary at Number 10. But not so.

As the years went by, Charles Powell's increasingly exclusive role became a matter of serious concern throughout Whitehall as well as in Cabinet. In the ordinary way it would have been for the permanent secretary at the Foreign Office, in consultation with the Cabinet secretary (and, of course, the Prime Minister and myself), to arrange in due time for Powell's onward posting (and no doubt promotion). Successively,

Sir Robert Armstrong and Antony Acland, Sir Robin Butler and Sir Patrick Wright applied themselves – with my support – to this task. Twice they thought they had been successful in reaching the necessary agreements, with the Prime Minister and Powell alike.

It was agreed, first time round, that Powell should be appointed Her Majesty's ambassador to Switzerland: he was to take up his post (after seeing the Prime Minister through the general election) in January 1988. But when the time came, both sides of the Number 10 equation seemed to be equally dismayed at the inconvenience of fulfilling the commitment – and it was dropped. Second time round, agreement took that much longer, and the proposed posting was that much grander: Madrid, to be taken up (once again after seeing the Prime Minister through the CHOGM in Kuala Lumpur) before the end of 1989. But this deal too, even when supported strenuously by all Whitehall's top brass, was not to prevail. When the time came for Margaret Thatcher to resign, Charles Powell and Bernard Ingham were still part of the crew that she left behind. Meanwhile the tensions exposed by Westland were to be aggravated within months by discord over South Africa.

CHAPTER THIRTY-TWO

ARGUING ABOUT
SOUTH AFRICA

═══

The Horror of Apartheid

South Africa could be counted on to provoke instinctively different reactions from Margaret Thatcher and myself. The tension was often obvious. Yet our taut partnership did, I think, play its part in prompting positive change.

The factors that shaped our attitudes could hardly have contrasted more. Two years' Swahili-speaking army service in Kenya and Uganda, leadership of a Cambridge protest committee against the Attlee government's banning of Chief Seretse Khama in 1949, sponsorship of the Bow Group's first (1952) pamphlet on *Coloured People in Britain*, campaigning to persuade Macmillan to 'Free Hastings Banda', membership of the Street Committee (on anti-discrimination legislation), whose report trail-blazed for Roy Jenkins' 1968 Race Relations Act: all this was background to the unauthorized visit that Elspeth and I made to Soweto in 1975.

I said that this was an unauthorized visit: it was certainly clandestine. That characteristic aspect of apartheid lives in my memory. Our Soweto call came at the end of a week in South Africa (just after my appointment as Shadow Chancellor) as guests of the South Africa Foundation. Frustratingly, and suspiciously, every proposed meeting or contact with any of the leaders of the black community had fallen through. We faced the prospect of leaving the country without having spoken to a single black man or woman. In desperation we contacted the Johannesburg agent of Colin Eglin's Progressive Reform Party. He arranged to drive us to the edge of Soweto, where large notices forbade the entry of whites (or any others for that matter) who were not in possession of a pass. There we were picked up by a woman community leader from

Soweto (I remember only her Christian name, Constance) and she drove and walked us through this closed all-black community. My most vivid recollection is of the way in which we had to turn our car away down side-streets whenever we saw any South African military or police vehicle approaching. We did not want to risk confrontation with them. I was by no means confident that my membership of the British Parliament would be seen as an excuse for being caught without a pass in Africa's largest black city.

The real tensions of apartheid were conveyed to me in those few minutes: the fears and hatreds of a system in which the upholders of the law were almost entirely drawn from a community other than the one they sought to police; and in which, even in our company, our guide was obliged to behave almost as an alien in her own country. It was the impact of this experience that prompted Elspeth to write a report to the Equal Opportunities Commission, eerily foreshadowing the horrific massacre that occurred only a few months later.

This was some way removed from Margaret Thatcher's approach, derived mainly, I suspect, via Twickenham and Gleneagles (the golf-course not the Agreement) and her own well-remembered broadcast expression of fear (in January 1978) of Britain's cities being 'swamped' by coloured immigrants. Since 1979 she had, of course, enjoyed much wider experience of the Commonwealth than me: the Lusaka (1979) and Melbourne (1981) heads of government conferences and, most of all, the unexpectedly successful Rhodesian/Zimbabwean settlement. But the few occasions during my time at the Treasury when together we confronted race-related problems – the Brixton riots, for example – did not persuade me that her outlook had much changed.

This remained another area where she seemed to find it difficult to identify personally with the real anguish of some of the deprived or oppressed. I often wondered how she so clearly and sincerely identified with the suffering of, say, Soviet Jewry or Solidarity in the 'evil empire', yet could not do so at all in the same way with the hardships faced by young blacks in Soweto or by Palestinians in the Gaza strip, still less by the Nationalist minority on the Bogside. Why? The answer is to be found, I think, in the fact that each one of the three groups I have mentioned can be loosely identified with a 'terrorist' campaign: ANC, PLO and IRA. The terrorism is of course deplorable. But surely that should not colour one's view of the group in question to such absolutist extent? Yet as late as her Vancouver press conference after the CHOGM in October 1987 Margaret's readiness to dismiss the ANC as a whole as 'a typical terrorist organization' was to show that absolutism still held sway.

Official Dealings

During my first two years at the Foreign Office the point scarcely arose in practice. My first Commonwealth outing with Margaret had been for the New Delhi CHOGM in November 1983. A week or two earlier, on 15 November, I had spelt out our South African policy in a long speech to the Royal Commonwealth Society in London. But in practice Grenada and the Cold War were the immediately pressing and substantial issues for discussion in Delhi: South Africa did not dominate the plenary sessions.

During the next twelve months I had two meetings directly linked to South Africa. On 2 December 1983 the South African Foreign Minister Pik Botha visited London in course of a European tour. (Number 10 was not able to find time for the Prime Minister to see him – confirmation that South Africa was still on the back-burner.) But I enjoyed my first encounter with this long-running, lively if sometimes erratic character. He had spent all his working life at the South African Foreign Ministry, first as a legal adviser, then as UN representative and finally, from 1977, as Minister; he survived in this post until the end of the de Klerk era in 1994. The nickname Pik, by which he is always known, is taken, so he told me, from the Afrikaans word for 'penguin' – because he was thought, as a boy, to walk like one.

He had a disconcerting tendency, even in the small Carlton Gardens salon where we met, to conduct a private conversation as if it was a public meeting, and he was sometimes carried away by his own performance. He spoke more angrily than I had expected of those parts of my Commonwealth Society speech where I had spoken bluntly about apartheid and denounced South Africa's 'punitive military raids' on her neighbours. But when I reminded him that it was probably the most understanding foreign speech he had read in many moons he agreed that my 'frank speaking' had 'lanced the boil'. His views were far from comfortable: the Zimbabwean Prime Minister Robert Mugabe, he thought, was 'doomed'; Mozambique would remain a target for South African destabilization, but 'only in response to provocation'. South Africa herself would change but only at 'her own' speed. Yet through all this prickly defensive talk I thought I detected a man with real insight into the imperative need for his country to change – and to change fundamentally. My judgment has, I think, been confirmed over subsequent years in which we came to know each other well.

Pik was in much more restrained mode on our next meeting, at Chequers on 2 June of the following year, when he flew in with P. W. Botha for lunch and talks with Margaret Thatcher and myself. I had suggested the encounter when news reached me that the South African Prime Minister was visiting Bonn, in the course of a wider European tour. This was the first visit to Britain by a South African premier since Verwoerd had come in 1961, to announce South Africa's departure from the Commonwealth. I was under no illusions about the likely strong public reaction. But Britain had a greater interest in promoting peaceful change in South Africa than any other country. Apartheid had one day to come to an end. If it was to do so only as a consequence of prolonged violence and civil war, then up to one million South Africans who were entitled to British citizenship would arrive here as a flood of refugees. Angola, Mozambique and Portugal offered the precedent that we had to avoid. We had to be prime advocates of change, and actively engaged in the debate.

Chequers was our chosen venue not because we wanted to flatter the two Bothas with intimacy, but because a helicopter flight direct from Heathrow to Buckinghamshire was the best way of keeping them clear of the mass protest rally planned for inner London. Margaret left Dennis Thatcher and me to greet the flight not, as some speculated, for subtle protocol reasons, but because, as she said when she urged us down the drive, 'The helicopter will make a fearful mess of my hair.'

Talks before, after and over lunch lasted for five hours. The Bothas were probably surprised to be pressed by Margaret, but sympathetically, on all the key issues: apartheid must go, Mandela (and others) be set free and the front-line states no longer exposed to attack from South Africa. Forced removals (of black city-dwellers) had also to come to an end. We commended the Nkomati accord for regional peace, recently struck between Botha and his Mozambican neighbour, Zamora Machel. P.W.Botha, almost ill at ease in the outside world, was courteous but dour. There was no give in any of the major South African positions, but we had succeeded in improving the atmosphere a little – the first stage in the long process of attempting to affect perceptions and policies at the highest level within South Africa. And Botha knew that at least one Western leader had some recent insight into his problems.

Some months later I revealed to Sir John Leahy, our former ambassador in Pretoria, what I had not dared tell him or anyone else at Chequers – that the anti-apartheid marchers in Whitehall that afternoon had included our son Alec. I was comforted by the news that Leahy's own daughter had also been on parade. We were both reassured to know that we were engaged, in a very different mode, on the same mission as our more militant offspring.

The name of Zola Budd provoked an unexpected diversion during the spring of 1984. This talented young South African athlete became a cause of controversy following her application to Leon Brittan, still in his first year as Home Secretary, for registration as a British citizen. She was entitled to apply for this because her grandparents were British, and she had done so because registration would entitle her to run for Britain at the 1984 Los Angeles Olympics, from which South Africa was excluded. The only way in which this could happen in time was if Leon was willing, quite publicly, to give her application exceptionally speedy treatment. This he did, even though the whole question of sport and South Africa was a political minefield (every round of correspondence was being copied, exceptionally, to Number 10). He had been pressed by the *Daily Mail* and its editor, Sir David English, to whom an assurance had apparently been given already that the case 'would be considered with sympathy'.

In retrospect it is hard to understand why I did not press Leon harder to change his view on this (immigration questions are in the first instance a matter for the Home Secretary's discretion). I suspect now that it was for fear that if he had appealed, as he was entitled to do, for backing from Number 10, he would almost certainly have got it. It was the kind of issue on which the *Daily Mail*'s voice carried a lot of weight. I did not wish to court the risk of near-certain defeat on what seemed like a relatively minor question. I was wrong in that judgment of the importance of the issue, but probably right in my assessment of Margaret's likely reaction. That is no excuse for not having tried.

Almost every one of Zola Budd's subsequent appearances was a source of controversy and protest. I had some sympathy for her: she was a keen athlete, and I suspect that the politics had not been her idea. The affair certainly did not make any easier the task of managing the South African question in a Commonwealth context during the next few years. It provoked widespread boycott of the Edinburgh Commonwealth Games. It was also the cause of a blazing row between Elspeth and Alec which disrupted our holiday that year. Elspeth was shocked by Alec's support for those who were demonstrating so violently against Zola Budd.

Divisions at the Bahamas Conference

By the time we came to the next Commonwealth heads of government meeting held in October 1985 at Nassau, capital of the Bahamas, the crisis in South Africa was growing ever more serious and repression was intensifying. All our Commonwealth colleagues were convinced that further action of some kind to promote change was urgently necessary. This was manifestly desirable, but Her Majesty's Government – and Margaret and I were at one on this – did not believe that such action should sensibly take the form of, in the stock phrase, comprehensive economic sanctions. We were not the only government to take that view. The Reagan administration, though not the US Congress, argued in favour of their own policy of 'constructive engagement' – the antithesis of political and commercial isolation. Within Europe, the Portuguese and Federal German governments took the same view, although Foreign Minister Hans-Dietrich Genscher was sometimes an uncertain factor in the German equation.

But around the huge Bahamian conference table, of forty-six national delegations (forty-one heads of state or Prime Ministers, with Prime Minister Sir Lynden Pindling in the chair) we had few effective allies. Botswana, Lesotho and Swaziland, geographically tied to the South African economy as closely as any hostages, were silent supporters. Harry Lee Kuan Yew of Singapore was, as so often, a brilliantly wild card, who could sometimes be helpful. But in terms of willingness to argue the case in broad principle we were effectively alone. Our advocacy clearly needed to be robust, but if it was to be effective over the long term with such a large group of opponents, however friendly, then it needed to be thought through and handled with the utmost sensitivity.

All the more was this the case in the particular setting of a CHOGM meeting. For as was the habit on such occasions, the most difficult and thorny question was again reserved for consideration by heads of government on their own at their 'private' retreat – this time in the exclusive grand luxury of the Lyford Cay Club. Here Margaret's style of argument was incorrigibly calculated to provoke the rest. For the others apartheid called for outright condemnation without any possible quali-fication. The core grievance was the exclusion of black South Africans (by force whenever necessary) from anything like a fair share in the resources of their own country, and from any share whatsoever in its government. Margaret would see and present it in much less absolute terms. She would point out that mixed marriages, for example, were now lawful, that job reservation was on the way out along with the Group Areas Act, and so on. All this signalled, in her words, that apartheid 'was if not dead at least rapidly dying'. For the others it was scarcely beyond the beginning of the process of change. There was a fundamental difference of view.

In the same unconsciously partisan fashion Margaret would, quite rightly, denounce the violence of ANC terrorism, but without ever acknowledging, even by tone of voice, that the whole white-controlled repressive structure of the apartheid legal system was bound itself to provoke inter-racial conflict. Most irritating of all to the majority was her tendency to rest too much of her argument against sanctions or the harm they did to the economic interests of South African blacks. This stirred two hostile reactions: first, the suspicion that she was making much of black economic hardship only as a means of safeguarding our own British interests; and second, the thought that it was hardly for us, in the comfort of our European homes, to dismiss the judgment of those in Sowetan slums and shanties. They were after all ready not just to advocate but to face the hardship of sanctions, as at least some kind of non-violent protest against the greater harshness of apartheid. Ironically enough Margaret would inveigh with special ferocity against the immorality of those who argued, as she would put it, 'from the well-paid comfort of Western conference centres and hotels', in favour of measures that would bring unemployment and poverty to hundreds of thousands of South African blacks. But this charge of insincerity could just as easily be pointed in the opposite direction: for by definition all outsiders – including those who were seen as soft on sanctions and thus on apartheid – were arguing from the same sheltered berth.

The most decisively irritating feature of all this, for me at least, was that most of the arguments we had to advance were in themselves sound enough. But this was classically yet another issue where style was so important as to be almost a point of substance in itself. So it was at the Lyford Cay Club. We had been able to assemble a list of no less than nine 'measures' against South Africa that had already been imposed by most countries, including our own, from the arms and oil embargoes to the Gleneagles ban on sporting contacts (agreed in 1977). Our partners were demanding as many as ten further measures, from the breaking of airline links to a ban on agricultural imports. One important positive proposal was common ground: the appointment of a Group of Commonwealth Eminent Persons (the EPG, as it became known) to conduct an investigative and mediatory mission to South Africa.

Margaret was able to limit any fresh commitment to immediate additional measures to bans on the import of Krugerrands and on government funding for trade missions, fairs or exhibitions in South Africa. But this was accompanied by a commitment to consider, if the so-called EPG was unable to secure 'adequate progress', 'the adoption of further measures'. If this reluctantly conceded compromise was to be upheld, it was vital that we should cast no doubt upon the good faith of our commitment to *consider* – even if in the end to argue against – further measures in due course. As so often in international – or even domestic – relations, the conclusion had to be hailed as a victory for neither side but only for compromise and common sense.

In a disconcerting repeat of the post-Chequers Anglo-Irish press conference,* Britain's Prime Minister very quickly exploded that notion, seriously undermining confidence in our good faith.

Before the world's television cameras, Margaret set out to present not the successful achievement of a concerted Commonwealth policy for change in South Africa but only the triumphant insignificance of the concessions *she* had had to make to achieve it. With forefinger and thumb only a few millimetres apart and contemptuously presented to the cameras, Margaret proclaimed that she had moved only 'a tiny little bit'. With four little words she had at one and the same time humiliated three dozen other heads of government, devalued the policy on which they had just agreed – and demeaned herself. She had certainly ensured that things would be a good deal less easy at any future such meeting. Even I could scarcely believe my ears.

I was, of course, sitting beside Margaret throughout this performance. So, it may be asked, if I felt so strongly about it what, if anything, did I subsequently say or do about it? I was certainly one of the very few people perhaps in a position to do so: the others would have been her private and press secretaries, Charles Powell and Bernard Ingham. Certainly on the VC-10 flight back to London none of us said anything critical. The atmosphere was scarcely conducive. For we were all both relieved and exhausted at the end of an ordeal successfully (for so it was, in the broadest sense) surmounted. And almost forthwith we were on to preparations – severally as much as jointly – for the next day, the

* 19 November 1984. See p. 421 above.

statement in the House and such sleep as we could fit in before Heathrow loomed. So some time was to elapse before I could take up the topic as directly as was necessary. This I did on the eve of the following summer's London Conference, which was called specifically to review this very question.

Nine months on from Nassau, storm-clouds were once again massing over South Africa. The bright intervals in the intervening months were occasionally and generally short-lived. Most of them arose from the anticipation or the actuality of the work of the Commonwealth Eminent Persons Group (EPG) established at the Nassau Conference. Margaret Thatcher at one time had the outlandish notion that I should serve on this Group, which was to spend weeks at a time on the road in Africa. Her original motive for this was, I think, probably innocent enough. She really did believe that my presence with the Group would be the best way of feeding Britain's view into the process. I pointed out that the role could not possibly be handled alongside my normal job. Margaret reacted by claiming that she could easily cope with the Foreign Secretaryship as well as the Premiership. I believe that, as she spoke, she really meant it, in the sense that she saw no need for any separate ministerial opinion alongside her own in the field of foreign affairs. She has indeed said as much elsewhere.[1] And other Prime Ministers (Chamberlain, Eden, Macmillan) have felt, and sometimes said, the same. In the event, she was easily persuaded to drop the idea. I had only to begin reciting my future engagements for the weeks and months ahead. She was soon convinced that even if one mind might easily fill both roles, there was no way of avoiding the need for two bodies.

We chose instead the former Tory Chancellor Tony Barber as the British member: he had banking experience of Africa, as chairman of Standard Chartered, and had recently done good service as a member of the Franks Committee on the invasion of the Falklands. The chosen joint chairmen of the Group, General Obasanjo, former head of government of Nigeria, and Malcolm Fraser, former Conservative Premier of Australia, managed the mission well. Tony Barber played a highly praised role in helping them to develop a group personality and to shape proposals with which to seek a middle way. Tony tells a moving story of his meeting, together with Malcolm Fraser, with Nelson Mandela, after twenty-seven years in his prison cell on Robben Island. Almost the first question Mandela posed to the pair was, 'Tell me, is Don Bradman still alive?' They were able to report that Australia's most famous batsman (born in New South Wales in 1908) was still in very good shape.

Early in February 1986 I had a useful opportunity to bring minds together when I was one of only three European ministers who was able to attend a conference in Lusaka of (theoretically) all the European Community Foreign Ministers and their opposite numbers from the six front-line states of black Southern Africa. This valuable occasion exposed some of our more simplistic EC partners to the practical arguments for moderation on sanctions that came from front-line countries like Botswana, Swaziland and Mozambique. This put into perspective the tearful rhetoric of Zambia's Kenneth Kaunda (his huge white handkerchief was much in evidence during his opening address). I had found it possible to maintain the essentials of the British case without provoking the wrath of any colleagues, black or white.

A month later, during the EPG's first full-scale visit to South Africa, P. W. Botha responded sensibly, on 3 March, by lifting the state of emergency (which had been a cause of mounting international anxiety since its imposition in July 1985) and announcing a number of other liberalizing measures. But in the second half of May, the whole process went sharply into reverse. While the EPG was present in their country, South African armed forces launched raiding attacks across the borders of Zambia, Zimbabwe and Botswana. As I told the Cabinet on 22 May, these had no sensible practical effects. Their only possible purpose was to mollify Botha's right-wing critics. The identity of their instigator was never established. Coming as they did when the EPG was actually in South Africa, they demonstrated very clearly that there was no chance of a united, still less a positive, response from the Pretoria government to the Group's proposals.

Conditions in South Africa thereafter went rapidly from bad to worse. Margaret herself was very bitter about what she saw as P. W. Botha's perfidy in allowing the raids to happen. And the EPG quickly and unanimously (on 12 June) concluded that there was 'no genuine intention on the part of the South African government to dismantle apartheid' and 'no present prospect of . . . dialogue leading to the establishment of a non-racial and representative government'. This was the signal for both the international organizations to which we belonged – the Commonwealth and the EC – to reconvene, inevitably with a view to considering 'further measures'. The European Council was due to meet under Dutch Presidency on 26–27 June and the seven Commonwealth heads of government six weeks later in London on 3–5 August.

Mission Impossible

So I prepared a paper for consideration by OD Committee (as always under the Prime Minister's chairmanship) on 24 June and by Cabinet on the following day. I reminded colleagues that the government had earlier agreed (in the EC as well as at Nassau) that in the absence of sufficient movement by the South African government we would be ready to consider further measures.

One new notion was introduced into the discussion by the Prime Minister. It sprang from the fact that Britain took over from the Dutch the Presidency of the European Council for the second half of 1986. The idea was that I might, as President of the Foreign Affairs Council, undertake a ministerial mission to South Africa, treading as it were in the footsteps of the EPG. In retrospect, it became clear that one of Margaret's motives for suggesting this was the hope of postponing still further any final decision on further measures, if possible even beyond the August Commonwealth review meeting. I regarded such an outcome as improbable in the extreme. I took much the same view of any other prospects of success for such a mission. Even with the added authority of the EC, how should I succeed where the EPG had only just failed? How indeed could I be confident even of getting a hearing either in South Africa or with her neighbours? And, if I failed, would not the pressure for comprehensive sanctions be stronger than ever? One argument pointed quite strongly the other way: the possibility of such a mission had already been widely trailed – quite probably, I guessed, as a result of a leak from Number 10. It would be very damaging, for the UK in particular, for me to appear unwilling to accept responsibility of this kind.

The OD discussion was confused and we came to no conclusion. My own final, finely balanced advice to Cabinet the following day was that I should be prepared to go, but only if asked by the European Council to do so. 'I shall need to be assured', I said, 'that colleagues will be prepared to support further measures, if necessary, in the event that my mission failed in its purpose of promoting progress in South Africa.' This essential condition was accepted by Cabinet. It was subject only to one gloss. Margaret and I at the European Council would seek to defer final decisions on any fresh negative measures. If we could achieve some postponement there, that would leave us rather more room to manoeuvre at the subsequent Commonwealth meeting.

At The Hague European Council meeting on 26–27 June, with support from Portugal and Germany for our general position, we did in fact achieve just that result. Further measures were to be introduced by all twelve EC states, but only after a delay of thee months: bans on the import from South Africa of gold coins, iron, steel and coal (we had headed off a ban on fruit and vegetables) and a voluntary ban on new investment in South Africa. The delay was to allow time for my proposed mission to South Africa, which I was to undertake alone but on behalf of the entire Community. By this time, a number of commentators (and of our EC colleagues) had detected some difference between Margaret's enthusiasm for this mission and my own more sceptical approach. Some sections of the press and, so it would later appear, some aspects of Number 10's press briefing were reluctant to acknowledge any weakening in Margaret's hostility to sanctions of any kind. But I was determined that this would not diminish the wholeheartedness of my commitment.

My Foreign Office team and I had to put together, within the month that remained before the Commonwealth London meeting, the programme and arrangements for a mission that would have to take in not just South Africa itself but at least the key front-line states – Zambia, Zimbabwe and Mozambique (the third was important if we were to hear more than one black view on sanctions). I also had to fit in, on the afternoon of 16 July, a half-day emergency debate in the Commons on the whole principle of the mission. This gave me the opportunity to reaffirm in Parliament (for the second time in little more than a month) the government's commitment (confirmed in Cabinet on 25 June) to consider further measures. 'If the mission does not procure tangible and susceptible progress in South Africa,' I told the House, 'I would regard agreement on further measures as likely to be necessary.' I had seen Margaret that same morning and got her to agree to that commitment. That statement of our position was not questioned in Cabinet the following day. On Friday, 18 July, before I set off for the second time to South Africa, Geoffrey Smith in *The Times* underlined the importance of this 'critical development – a change not of objectives but of assumptions'. As Mr Botha seems unlikely to oblige, added the *Economist*, 'Sir Geoffrey has been wise to prepare a space for Mrs Thatcher to reverse into.' Yet even on that day the *Daily Express* reported, 'Sanctions – No U-turn by Maggie', and said that any contrary impression was 'due to wrong interpretation of Sir Geoffrey's Commons speech'.

So it was no surprise that we faced initial difficulties in persuading Kaunda and Mugabe that it made sense for them to receive me at all.

The South Africans were even more reluctant. It was only after a strenuous private meeting with their excellent and liberal London ambassador, Dennis Worrall, that President Botha agreed to receive me – and even then not before the second half of July. Eventually my journeying fell into two halves: in the first leg I visited the three senior front-line heads of government, Prime Minister Mugabe and Presidents Kaunda and Machel, and on the second leg at the end of the month, South Africa itself and the three lesser front-line states, as well as a second call on President Kaunda.

From Robert Mugabe and Kenneth Kaunda the public message was the same, although the method very different. For both of them sanctions were inevitable and 'right' (even if they 'couldn't' apply them themselves). Mugabe saw me in a tiny study, whose sombre, enclosed style matched his quite unyielding tone. Following Zimbabwe's own example, he gave firm backing to the ANC's armed struggle. My own mission ('approaching South Africa with a white flag') he dismissed as 'useless'. This was the message that was released to the media on his behalf.

Kaunda's performance was altogether more histrionic. On each of my two meetings with him (9 and 24 July), our talks, well balanced and sensible, took place in his cosy, souvenir-lined den. But that was only after he had subjected me to trial-by-ordeal before world press and television in his large reception salon. His performance on the second such occasion lives in popular memory, certainly my own. He did not welcome me in my capacity as Britain's Foreign Secretary, he explained, 'because my dancing partner has been kissing apartheid'. (Mrs Thatcher and he had famously danced together at the Lusaka CHOGM in 1979.) On that account, he would have excluded me altogether from State House. But he was prepared to receive me as 'a human being', because of his 'love and respect' for Her Majesty the Queen, and as President of the EC Foreign Council. All this he delivered, with tear-sodden handkerchief in hand, in portentous tones, like some indulgent headmaster. At least it lasted long enough for me to think out my reaction. Many, I know, would have walked out well before the end, well laden with protests and expostulations. I consciously rejected the thrill of escalating public rhetoric. Once again I placed on record the important purpose of my EC mission – as one journalist described it, in 'sharp but nevertheless restrained language'. Diplomacy, I explained afterwards, 'is not about walk-outs. It's about talks-through. Just because it's difficult is no reason to give up.'

The Botswana, Lesotho and Swaziland visits were dubbed by our travelling press corps the Heineken leg of the trip, as we hopped between airfields at Gabarone, Maseru and Mbabane, parts previously unreached by any similar mission. Guided by a practically sensible Foreign Minister, Dr Gaositwe Chiepe, Botswana was a restrained supporter of sanctions. From the other two I received the same message, quiet and clear: sanctions would ruin us, we cannot ourselves be heard to condemn them – so please keep doing your best to hold them at bay.

That was the theme expressed, though more brashly, by President Machel and Foreign Minister Chissano in Mozambique. The visit to Maputo (formerly Lourenço Marques) was fascinating on its own account. The state guesthouse to which Chissano escorted us told its own story. It was a spacious Mediterranean villa, one of many overlooking the Indian Ocean riviera, that was well stocked with furniture, antiques and pictures mainly from Macao or from Portugal. All of this, we were matter-of-factly informed, had been the property of some well-to-do (now refugee) Portuguese family. It was as though we were being invited to join a very upmarket squat. Less comfortable still was the contrast with the disintegrating structure of the rest of the once lovely city – and with the hard-pressed government service, crushed between the effects of residuary Marxist theory on the one hand and resurgent (South Africa-backed) Renamo terrorism on the other.

In Machel's eyes, Pik Botha *did* favour positive change within South Africa. But the South African military stood in the way, just as they continued to menace Mozambique. Britain should do everything possible to dissuade them from that. And he, Machel, would do all he could to persuade the ANC and the front-line states to take my mission seriously. The most widely reported feature of Machel's cheerful performance was his gift of a consignment of huge prawns. 'Do British women know how to cook these?' cried the President. 'Well, *my* British woman does,' I replied, 'and will be delighted with your gift.' It was just as well that Elspeth was out with Señora Chissano visiting one of Maputo's nursery schools at the time when that exchange took place.

The real contrasts were to be found in South Africa itself. All too many of the black leaders were unwilling to meet me, including Bishop Tutu (who had served for some time as a curate at Bletchingley in my constituency), the ANC and Nelson Mandela himself. Even those who agreed with us about sanctions were worried that the ferocity of our opposition to them prompted many to see us as the sole defender of apartheid. Aside from that important advice, I was glad to have our

general position reinforced by Colin Eglin and the redoubtable Helen
Suzman, as well as by the extremely clear-sighted but firmly independent
Zulu leader, Chief Buthelezi. But all were clear that our rhetoric was out
of line with the balance of our case.

More than twelve hours of my time was spent with one or other or
both of the Bothas, P. W. and Pik. Most revealing was one long evening
alone with Pik, in a government guesthouse in Pretoria. We started over
drinks, perched on tall stools at a private bar, then enjoyed a most
hospitable meal on the other side of the room, and resorted finally to
armchairs for coffee and brandy. We were uninterrupted throughout the
evening. Pik's mood and tone swung from one end of an emotional
spectrum to the other. At one moment, 'people say that I'm a kaffir-
lover – and I am, and proud of it'; at the next, 'If sanctions are applied,
we shall make damn sure our neighbours suffer, and suffer a damn sight
more than we do!' But he did manage to convey the tensions within the
government, between those like him who saw clearly what was needed
and those who thought they could continue indefinitely to dictate the
pace, extent and form of change. Sooner or later, he felt, pain and
suffering would cause blacks and whites to come to agreement, but only
after millions in surrounding countries had died of hunger. 'Abandon
your tragic mode,' I urged him. 'The prospect you've just painted is so
apocalyptic that it must be right to risk the alternative of fundamental
but peaceful change.' He desperately wanted to agree, but he could not
see how.

After my two meetings with his President I could understand why.
P. W. Botha received me for two hours on 23 July and for as long again
on the 29th, in a room that, despite its size, seemed curiously cramped
and free of natural light. The setting and atmosphere immediately
reminded me of the room in Warsaw where one year before I had been
received by General Jaruzelski. The talks were tense, quite often heated.
He was dismissive of my mission and 'would not have received you but
for my regard for your Prime Minister'. He showed no willingness to
comprehend, let alone accept, any view of the world but his own. He
betrayed no understanding of the gap between such changes as he had
(just) contemplated and what the world expected. He produced, rather
angrily, a bizarre pie-chart to prove that Bishop Tutu's views were
representative of almost nobody in South Africa. He gave every sign of
believing this.

At our second meeting, P. W. was even more ill-tempered than at our
first. Almost beside himself, he denounced 'damned interfering foreign-

ers' and gave no ground at all. A sadly narrow shaft of light came at the very end of this last talk. P. W. B. did say that he accepted Britain's good faith but 'was more doubtful of that of some other European leaders'. In his press conference immediately afterwards, he described his own plea to me that South Africa should be left in peace and denounced my Commons speech (of 16 July) as 'nothing but a threat against our country'. You won't, he said, 'force South Africans to commit national suicide'. I still do not know which was the more testing experience: being harangued by President Kaunda in public or by President Botha in private.

But if there was little hope of change at that level, there were strong signs elsewhere in National Party ranks. Finance Minister Barend du Plessis had a very clear insight into the economic imperatives which dictated the need for early reform; so too did Education Minister Dr Gerrit Viljoen. Plainly it was for the South African government to find a formula which made Mandela's release a real possibility. Most surprising of all was Professor J. P. de Lange, the Rector of Rand Afrikaans University. I was introduced to him not in that role but in his much more daunting capacity of President of the Broederbond. I had expected to meet someone to the far right of the Ku Klux Klan. On the contrary, this spokesman for 15,000 Afrikaaners told me that there had been surprisingly little negative reaction to his own recent meeting with the ANC. Many members of the government saw the absolute need to get the ANC to the negotiating table. The problem was to get Botha out of the corner into which he had painted himself. In words that thereafter remained as relevant in Northern Ireland today as ever they were in South Africa, de Lange stressed that any peaceful settlement needed to 'bring in the extremes'. It was essential, he closed, 'to get this insight into the mind of P. W. Botha'. The farewell note I received from the other Botha was quite different in tone. 'I know you speak as a friend,' wrote Pik. 'This we never doubted. . . . We may still move forward in the months ahead.'

At home and abroad, my month-long mission evoked a remarkably sympathetic reaction. Robert Mauthner in the *Financial Times* coined the phrase 'punch-bag diplomacy' to contrast my approach with 'those who felt that the only way to make their point was with a sledge-hammer'. George Shultz conveyed thanks from Reagan and told me he shared my sense of 'frustration over how we and you are seen mistakenly as friends of apartheid. How', he asked, 'can we break out of this box? Elevating our dialogue with the ANC may prove to be a positive first step in this direction.' George Shultz was already well ahead of Margaret Thatcher on this point. More and more often I found that he and I were thinking along similar lines.

Difficulties with Number 10

But there was still real uncertainty about Margaret's position. Margaret records her belief that I had been not just reluctant but 'deeply angry' about being set up by her for this mission. Reluctance I have already acknowledged (Margaret agrees that this 'proved justified').[2] But my anger was directed not at the mission itself but at the frequency with which Margaret and her people had been undercutting the strength of my authority for the role. Even during my last days in South Africa the *Sunday Telegraph* on 27 July had carried an interview which recorded that she 'had not shifted at all' on sanctions. Would my mission be backed up in good faith or shown as a sham? On my return, the Cabinet offered their thanks for the dignified and persuasive way in which I had conducted my mission, expressed their 'deep dismay' at P. W. Botha's 'discourtesy' towards me and reaffirmed their support for policy conducted in recent months by the Prime Minister and the Foreign and Commonwealth Secretary on the question of South Africa. More specifically, we were instructed how to proceed at the Commonwealth meeting that was due to start in a couple of days. We should not stand out against measures already identified by the European Community, if at the end of the three-month period allowed for my mission other EC members wished to impose them. Any such measures were to be prescribed not as 'designed to promote progress' but as 'a signal of disapproval'. On that basis we were, I thought, firmly in the position for which I had been consistently working. But I had reckoned without Margaret Thatcher's reluctance to steer away from conflict, and Bernard Ingham's matching enthusiasm for fireworks.

For by the time I got back to my office at the end of the morning it was clear that the press had received from Number 10 a quite different picture of the Cabinet's conclusions. Their briefing had started indeed at 8 a.m. that morning – an hour before any ministerial meeting – when the *Evening Standard* was told by Bernard Ingham of a 'unanimous Cabinet decision to back the Government's policy on sanctions'. The government, it was later clearly explained, was 'not in the business of further sanctions' beyond the thirteen already in place. This line, intended no doubt to preserve the impression that the Prime Minister had once again 'won the day', was very far removed from the deliberately open position that had been endorsed by the Cabinet. It was small wonder that Fleet Street was soon buzzing with false reports – we were never able to trace these definitively – that I was on the point of resignation. This sharply conflicting press briefing was fully reported by the *Scotsman* on the following day, 1 August. The Foreign Office and Number 10, said that paper's leader-writer, could not both be right and it was a matter of regret that most would conclude, 'simply from previous experience, that Number 10 is the guilty party'.

The argument between my News Department and Number 10's went on running strongly in the context of how best to handle the forthcoming Commonwealth meeting in London. Bernard Ingham made it clear that he would welcome a 'break-up' of the Review Meeting with 'emotional outbursts from Kaunda, Mugabe and company'. The British press, he argued, would 'crucify' the Prime Minister 'if she was seen to make any concessions to blacks'. He proposed to go on briefing in a very rigid sense, while leaving a 'tiny' loophole in case some measures had to be conceded. When he was reminded of my statement to the House on 16 July ('further measures likely to be necessary'), he made it very plain that he regarded those words as 'an albatross of which he was reminded every time he spoke to the lobby'.

All this was brought to my attention by the deputy head of my News Department (its head Christopher Meyer and my private secretary Tony Galsworthy had both gone on leave on our return from South Africa). The crisis was essentially a political one. My two available political advisers on that Friday were Richard Ryder and John Houston. After long and anxious discussion I decided that the matter had to be raised with Margaret personally before the Conference began. Most unusually I decided to write to her in my own hand, taking only one copy for my own files. But with the hindsight of history the letter can now be seen to have foreshadowed much longer and more enduring problems. So it is worth recording the text in full:

1 August 1986

My dear Margaret,

I want to let you know about my extreme concern at the way in which matters have been managed in relation to yesterday's OD discussion about South Africa and the Commonwealth Review Meeting. I am taking the unusual course of writing personally because it is both the quickest and most confidential way of alerting you to my anxiety and I am not sure when we shall have a chance to discuss it.

There are three aspects to my anxiety: the first concerns what has already happened; the second relates to the handling of the conference this weekend; and the third is of more fundamental long-term importance.

On the first my concern arises from the way in which the OD/Cabinet discussion was presented to the lobby by the Number 10 Press Office, specifically by Bernard Ingham. I say this principally for two reasons:

– When my office – and later in the afternoon when I myself – took with the press the deliberately noncommittal line which we agreed after Cabinet, we were greeted with *complete* disbelief. For a number of those to whom we spoke reported that the Number 10 line had remained sharp and specifically hardline, dismissive of the Commonwealth as 'irrelevant' – and all in very intemperate terms. Bernard was described by someone as having gone 'right over the top' in briefing which would, according to another, 'have been sensational if it had been on the record'. Someone else today described him in terms as 'briefing against Geoffrey'.

– Consistently with this last point, throughout the second half of Thursday morning we received a number of inquiries asking for confirmation of my resignation. In face of the briefing that had provoked this story, we were still having to refute that – by reasserting our agreed line – until the end of Thursday afternoon.

The net effect of all this has been, of course, to destroy the value of the common line we had specifically agreed; and to reaffirm – through the press and in the eyes of others coming to the weekend meeting – an entirely unsympathetic position.

That brings me to the second main point: the handling of the press side of the Commonwealth meeting (I am sending you a separate note about the meeting itself). I have no doubt that the whole thing will require immensely sensitive handling if we are to steer it – as I think we *should* be able to, with luck – to a sensible conclusion that we can accept. This means that the press briefing – throughout, as well as at the end – will have to be equally sensitive if it is not to provoke others to try to push us further than they otherwise would. But here too I am fearful – on the strength of what I have heard about his comments in the last day or so – about the effect of the line that Bernard is likely to take. He is said to have made it very plain that as far as he was concerned a bust-up of the meeting would be by no means unwelcome – and would 'probably add another 5 points to the PM's popularity' (today's MORI poll* suggests rather a different picture). In my judgment our best chance of getting an agreement that will stand us in good stead is to think not in terms of a quick PR *éclat* of Bernard's kind – but to be aiming for a 'victory' not for you or for me or for Kaunda or for *anybody* else – but for something that will be seen as a victory for common sense, and so a satisfactory result for all. I believe OD's brief – handled in public as well as at the table in a balanced fashion – should allow us to achieve that: but not if it is handled, before and after, on the basis of Bernard's approach.

And so to my last more fundamental point. We have worked together closely, and I like to think successfully, for more than eleven years. I want to continue serving in your government, and thus playing a part in helping to win the next general election. That means that we must continue to have confidence in each other: the partnership – for example, this weekend – is too close to survive without that. And that kind of confidence cannot survive unless I can have the assurance that decisions taken by Cabinet and Cabinet committees affecting the policies for which I share responsibility are truthfully reflected by the Number 10 Press Office.

We know that the task of press secretary at Number 10 is one of the most sensitive and demanding in Whitehall. Not only is the press secretary the Prime Ministerial spokesman, he is also the channel for relaying governmental decisions and policies, and in that capacity is the servant of the government, although directly accountable to you. There should be no scope for painting personal glosses, setting department against department, Minister against Minister – or other self-indulgences of the kind civil servants are instructed to avoid.

And my bigger worry thus goes beyond my concern about the forthcoming conference. I fear that the Number 10 Press Office, in its present style, is (and has been for some time) undermining our chances of securing a third term, by causing friction in Whitehall, and so giving the impression to the outside world of government (and party) disunity – destroying what should still be the party's secret weapon.

This is, I know, a question that goes beyond what we can tackle this weekend. But it is of the highest importance and must be taken seriously

---

* The MORI poll published in *The Times* that day (1 August) gave Labour a 9 per cent (41:32) lead over the Conservatives. The percentage who thought government policy was 'not tough enough on the South African government' had risen from 42 to 56.

if we are to be able to continue working together in confidence: without that we shall not be able to get through to Tuesday night, let alone the general election!

I have kept only one copy of this letter, for myself: I hope we may be able to find a chance to talk about it.

Yours ever
Geoffrey

The letter (in a 'strictly personal' envelope addressed by me) went across to Number 10 by hand the same day, together with other papers about the weekend Conference. The Prime Minister and I met only briefly before we went into the ensuing roundabout of meetings. I took one opportunity to say that I looked forward at some stage to a chance of discussing my letter about Bernard, to which she replied (as she had done previously, in face of milder complaints to the same effect), 'Bernard isn't like that. But we can't talk about it now.'

London Review Conference

The Review Group of Senior Commonwealth Prime Ministers assembled at Marlborough House in London on 3–5 August 1986. The meeting convened at 3.15 p.m. on the Sunday afternoon. Our first purpose was to hear the report of the Eminent Persons Group (appointed after the Nassau Conference a year before) on the outcome of their mission to South Africa. Those present, under the chairmanship of Sir Lynden Pindling (Bahamas), were President Kaunda and Prime Ministers Gandhi, Hawke, Mugabe, Mulroney and Thatcher. The meeting proceeded without any sign of change in Margaret's approach.

Her own account of the proceedings speaks for itself: 'it was back to more irrationality. . . . the formal discussions were every bit as unpleasant as at Lyford Cay'.[3] They need not, of course, have been so. Margaret's own statement to the press at the end of the Conference indicates the common ground which could from the outset be identified. 'We have been able', she said, 'to reach agreement on how, in our different ways, we should register our abhorrence of apartheid and the urgent need for further reform in South Africa.' So there was no argument that the EPG mission had achieved any real progress. Further action was still necessary. Margaret continued, 'If . . . the European

Community decides to introduce the measures mentioned in the Hague Communiqué the United Kingdom would accept and implement them.'

The first of her conclusions – the urgent need for further reform – was the clear conclusion of the EPG, which had been reported to the meeting by the joint chairmen, General Obasanjo and Malcolm Fraser. I had been invited to follow them with my own assessment, in light of my recent mission. As Margaret well knew, I had no alternative but to confirm the EPG's judgment. Even so, she had been concerned to make the most of the changes that had been made in the outer ramparts of apartheid. Yet there was no escaping the conclusion that the Botha government had still not made the quantum leap for which we all looked: Mandela and his colleagues were still in gaol, and the ANC and its parallels were still banned. On those central questions, there was no room, or need, for the argument which Margaret insisted on provoking.

There remained room for discussion about the measures that should then be put into effect. Even here the difference need only have been one of degree. Clearly our Commonwealth partners would wish to press ahead with the package of measures that had been agreed at Nassau but postponed to await the outcome of the EPG mission. But the UK was now more positively placed than we had been a year ago. For, as Margaret Thatcher's closing press statement made clear, we were now ready to join our EC partners in implementing the more modest package of measures that we had provisionally agreed at The Hague in June. That, of course, was the result – two parallel packages of further measures – that was eventually announced late on the evening of Monday, 4 August. It was a pity that on the way so much effort had been expended and bad blood shed unnecessarily. The proceedings ended, so far as I was concerned, on a lighter note. Bob Hawke had shown me during the turbulence of the day an Australian newspaper cartoon, depicting Margaret as a beached whale, with me trying to shove her back into the sea. He sent me a kind note on his return to Australia, together with the original of the cartoon to add to my collection.

There was, of course, the unfinished business of the letter that I had written to Margaret Thatcher on the eve of the Conference. Did I ever get a further reply? Did I ever raise the issues again? I fear that the answer to both questions is no. For as soon as the London Conference came, mercifully, to its conclusion, wild horses could not have held us back from the holiday that Elspeth and I had planned for our usual retreat to the wooded hillside above Grasse. And on my return the scene had moved on. The detail of my complaint had become stale and there were fresh things to fret about. The possibility, of course, remained for Margaret Thatcher to offer a discussion about the issues that I had raised. She did not do so.

Certainly the questions were big enough, important enough and strategic enough to require proper attention. For a Cabinet minister to have written in such terms about such a central issue should have rung alarm bells in Margaret's mind. The larger questions were, at the end, close to the reasons for her ultimate demise. I have later wondered whether, if I had pursued them more deliberately, that demise itself might have been avoided. But they were at the heart of the way in which Margaret organized her own close-knit ménage. And this was the set-up which, earlier that year, had brought her to the brink of disaster over Westland – and the set-up which had also steered her away from that débâcle. In the last resort the questions that I had raised were questions for her to consider.

Coda

The South African story continued, after as well as during the rest of my time in the Foreign Office, in much the same vein. President P. W. Botha suffered a stroke in January 1989 but remained in office until he was succeeded as President by F. W. de Klerk in August 1989 – just one month after I moved from the Foreign Office. During that time the dismantling of so-called petty apartheid had moved slowly forward. But the breakthrough implied by Mandela's release, the unbanning of the ANC and the promise to end the state of emergency had to wait until these were announced by de Klerk in February 1990.

By then there had been no less than two more CHOGMs, the first (which I attended) at Vancouver in October 1987 and the second (John Major's baptism of fire) at Kuala Lumpur in October 1989. Each of these occasions saw a widening of the rift between Britain and her Commonwealth partners. For the first time at such a meeting heads of government held a separate press conference at Vancouver to dissociate themselves from Britain. And we were dropped – or rather dropped ourselves – from the inner group of Foreign Ministers that had for years sought to co-ordinate Commonwealth policy towards South Africa. Not inappropriately perhaps, it was when we were in Vancouver that news first reached us of the unforecast hurricane which did such tragic damage to the forests and woodlands of south-east England – including those which gave such enchantment to the views around Chevening. Vancouver itself closed with another unhelpful aside from Margaret Thatcher to her closing press conference. It was there that she suddenly lashed out at the ANC – which we had for years been trying to get unbanned – as 'a typical terrorist organization', and once again set back the prospect of dialogue between us and their leadership.

One development in our relationship with South Africa during this period was strongly positive – the appointment in 1987 of Sir Robin Renwick as our ambassador to that country. Gradually his sheer professionalism enabled him to secure access to those inner recesses of Botha's National Party, whose existence had been disclosed to us by such people as Rector de Lange. He achieved close contact too with the leadership of the ANC and of the townships, so that our message, in all its aspects, began more effectively than ever before to get through to all shades of South African opinion. We were able to encourage Margaret Thatcher to embark on more than one successful journey to black Africa, in which our anti-apartheid message was not overshadowed by the ferocity of her presentation of the case against sanctions.

I was to make a further visit to Mozambique in September 1998. President Machel's death in an air crash had led to his replacement by my less flamboyant opposite number Joaquim Chissano. I took the opportunity to visit Magude (on the Limpopo line) and so to see the British-equipped rail facilities and British-trained troops. I was joyfully greeted by a huge throng of refugees fleeing from Renamo terrorists. In answer to their grateful spokesman I made a short speech which I closed by raising my hand as he had done and shouting 'La lutta continua!' – an innocent enough courtesy. The photograph taken on that occasion was subsequently displayed by right-wing critics to underline my Marxist tendency! Less attention was paid to the fact that in Maputo, at the end of the same day, Elspeth and I were granted an audience with His Holiness Pope John Paul II. It was a strange setting for such an encounter.

All these developing contacts made it easy for Margaret, when she was in Zimbabwe a few months later, to fly with President Mugabe to a meeting with President Chissano at Nyanga on the Mozambican border. She was able to make another important and well-timed call at the end of this tour. For she ended up on a 'surprise' visit (that is to say unknown in advance to the press) to Windhoek, the capital of the newborn state of Namibia – on the very day, 1 April 1989, of its independence (at last) in compliance with United Nations Security Council Resolution 632.

In that setting (in her own words, 'the right person in the right place at the right time') she was able to play a crucially important part in helping the UN authorities to avoid serious conflict between the Namibian (SWAPO) troops of Sam Nujoma (the future Namibian President) and the South African Defence Force. Foreign Minister Pik Botha was fortunately also on hand to help in the same delicate task.

The sadness is that Margaret Thatcher, right to the end, persisted in her often ill-concealed antipathy towards most of our Commonwealth partners as also towards the Foreign and Commonwealth Office and all its works – as though it had nothing to do with the devoted and detailed work that so many people put in on her behalf.

Others were ready to spread their thanks a little more generously. Soon after Nelson Mandela was set free, there came two public events that he and I both attended together: the first was at the Royal Commonwealth Society in London in the summer of 1990 and the second was the deeply moving Conference on a Democratic South Africa (CODESA) at Johannesburg in December 1991. On both occasions, Mandela saw me almost as soon as he entered the hall and strode directly across the dividing space to salute me. I was glad of his recognition that I had been able to play some part in generating the changes that had led to his freedom, and sad that over the years this had involved so much unnecessary tension between Margaret Thatcher and myself, and even between Margaret Thatcher and so much of the rest of the world.

CHAPTER THIRTY-THREE

TERROR AND DIPLOMACY

Diplomatic Terrorists and Transgressors

It was regrettable that Margaret Thatcher sometimes found it difficult to come to terms with nationalist movements around the world. But her dismay in face of the worldwide terrorist threat was only too legitimate. Terrorism in one form or another had been part of the backdrop of my life almost from the first moment of entering government in 1970. The hazard had grown immeasurably both in scale and complexity since those days of Leila Khaled and the Angry Brigade. The Irish element, as I have shown,* was ever present. But the threat was now diverse and international. All too often acts of violence were clearly the result of state sponsorship.

The gravest of these – and the first during my time at the Foreign Office – occurred on 17 April 1984, when gunfire from the Libyan People's Bureau (Gaddaffi's Orwellian name for an embassy) in St James's Square killed Woman Police Constable Yvonne Fletcher, on duty alongside an entirely peaceful demonstration in the street outside. This dreadful crime prompted intense parliamentary concern about the abuses of diplomatic immunity that had enabled such events to occur. They arose essentially from the fact that many Libyan 'diplomats' were now armed revolutionaries. The government which they purported to represent was equally ready to authorize or condone violence against foreigners, including diplomats, within Libya itself. So when action was taken in London to remove from the Libyan 'embassy', and then from Britain, those responsible for this crime, retaliatory action against our embassy and staff in Tripoli quickly followed. And some of the 10,000 Britons then living or working in Libya were effectively taken hostage. Ours was at that time the second largest West European community in

* See pp. 411–27 above.

Libya. The British embassy itself was set on fire, though not destroyed. The Americans in 1979 and the French in 1980 had been less fortunate. Both their embassies had been burned down.

Even in face of such outrages, however, neither France nor America had broken off diplomatic relations. The actual severance of relations happens only very rarely. Only three times since 1945 had Britain done this: with Albania, with Uganda, in each case after actions not far short of war, and, of course, with Argentina. Never before had any government broken off relations on grounds of breach of diplomatic immunity. This was not just a matter of international nicety. As I explained to the House of Commons after the Libyan affair, our embassies and diplomats are deployed around the globe for the furtherance of Britain's interests, not least the protection of British subjects. In all too many places the conditions they have to face are anything but safe. 'It is precisely in such places', I said, 'that the protection of Her Majesty's Government is most necessary.'

Despite these considerations – and thousands of Britons remain at work in Libya, to this day – Libyan conduct in this case was rightly regarded as uniquely shocking. So we decided nonetheless upon complete severance of relations. The whole episode stimulated an illuminating examination by the Commons Foreign Affairs Committee of the legitimacy and acceptability of the provisions of the 1964 Vienna Convention on Diplomatic Relations. Its sensible purpose was to protect legitimate diplomatic activity against interference by an intolerant host country. But the Convention was seen by many people as the root cause of the problems – as an unjustifiable licence for mischief and abuse.

Such anxieties were not diminished by another deplorable incident that occurred only a few months later. On 5 July 1984 a former minister of the deposed Shagan government of Nigeria, Umaru Dikko, was abducted on a London street. He was later found concealed and heavily drugged in a crate that had arrived at Stansted Airport, *en route* to Lagos from the Nigerian high commission. With him in the crate was another man, conscious and armed with drugs and syringes. A Foreign Office lawyer had responded promptly to an anguished phone call from Customs and Excise offices at Stansted. 'Are we entitled', they asked, 'to open this diplomatic bag' (it turned out not strictly to qualify as such), 'in which we think there may be a human being?' 'Yes,' she replied, 'for you have an overriding right, indeed duty, to preserve and protect human life.' The lawyer deserved the congratulations that came her way, for the precise situation facing her was without precedent. Yet she had instinctively appreciated the correct legal principle.

The three men responsible for that abduction, two of them Israelis, were later tried (in Britain), convicted and jailed. The Nigerian high commissioner denied any involvement in the affair but refused to allow police to interrogate his staff. In light of other evidence, I decided to expel two members of the commission – and to make it plain that we should not welcome the return to London of the high commissioner. (He had already been recalled to Lagos for consultations.) 'Tit-for-tat' measures were taken by Nigeria against our high commission in Lagos. There was, of course, no justification for this. More than a year was to elapse before I could restore our high commissioner to his rightful place.

The outcry which followed these events provoked a call for substantial amendments in the Vienna Convention – even for me to repudiate it. Why, the cry went up, are we obliged to tolerate such 'diplomatic' misconduct on our territory? Why may we not throw 'them' out? All this I was able to discuss with the Foreign Affairs Committee. I wanted their help, not just in rejecting foolish advice but in formulating sensible alternatives. The Committee concluded that we were right not to concentrate on amendment of the Convention. Instead, they favoured – as we did – internationally concerted action against nations which flouted the rules, particularly those which were in the business of promoting or condoning terrorism or other cross-frontier violence.

Within the United Kingdom we were indeed able to tighten substantially the disciplines contained within the Vienna Convention, to the benefit of public order. Diplomats accused of serious criminal offences had in the past often had their misdeeds overlooked. Now we took a much sterner line. Particularly with drug offences we looked to an offender's government to waive immunity, so that he or she could face trial here. In other cases we were much more ready to declare the offender *persona non grata*, that is to send him home. We even gave notice that such action would follow automatically in respect of repeatedly unpaid diplomatic parking tickets. The scale of this abuse, which provoked public and press outcry out of all proportion to its gravity, was dramatically cut, from 109,000 tickets in 1984 to 7800 in 1989.

But the real malefactors were not so easily curbed, Libya and Syria particularly. Two days after Christmas 1985, terrorists had opened fire on passengers in transit at Rome and Vienna airports. Seventeen were killed. The gunmen were from the Abu Nidal group, to which Syria's President Assad had previously lent support. Libyan praise for this action was quickly forthcoming. This set off a series of American actions against Libya, from economic sanctions to intensified patrolling in the Gulf of Sirte. Predictably we were urged to give our opinion on the proper scope for such 'retaliation' or 'deterrence'. Because it happened the day after Michael Heseltine's Westland-induced resignation, the Prime Minister was pressed on this by a group of American correspondents. Her reply – not referred to in her own book – was unequivocal. 'I must warn you', she said, 'that I do not believe in retaliatory strikes that are against international law.'[1] Once you start going across borders, she concluded, 'I do not see an end to it.' There should have been nothing surprising in this. For we had all faced the same question in the same way many times before – not in this context, of course, but with reference to the possibility of raids in 'hot pursuit' across the Ulster border, by British forces, or across the South African border, whether by ANC guerrillas or by South African Defence Forces. In both those settings, and more generally, the advice was certainly right.

The US Strike Against Libya

Three months later there was a fresh Libyan test of our patience – and of the law. On Saturday night, 5 April 1986 a terrorist bomb exploded in an American nightclub in Berlin, killing two people and injuring 230. One of the dead and at least fifty of the injured were American. Both British and American intelligence left no room for doubt about Libyan responsibility for the attack. Our own intercepts confirmed that Tripoli had congratulated their Berlin agents – and asked for more. Three days later, on 8 April, an evening message from President Reagan came into Downing Street. As it happened, the Prime Minister, George Younger (Defence Secretary) and I were all there, at the end of a dinner for the South Korean President Chun. So we considered the text together. The President was asking for our support for the use of American F-111s based in Britain in strikes against Libya. No objectives or targets were precisely specified. And he wanted our answer by noon the following day. He did not receive it. Margaret signed instead, within two hours, an interrogatory message which conveyed all our initial anxieties: What targets? What would be the public justification? Won't this start a cycle of revenge? What about Western hostages? And so on. On one thing only were we reasonably clear: the use of UK-based F111s would maximize the accuracy of targeting, minimize the risk of 'collateral' damage and minimize US casualties (carrier-based aircraft were less accurate and other land bases were almost too far away).

Margaret Thatcher's own account of our subsequent reactions to Reagan's request tends to oversimplify the position.[2] I am described as opposed to the move, but publicly supportive once we had established our position. George Younger is said to have 'supported it from the first'.* In truth we were much closer to each other than that, in the evolution at a series of meetings over several days of a broadly common response. We were helped in this process by the advice of the Attorney General, Michael Havers, who joined us for our second meeting on Wednesday, 9 April and subsequently through to Sunday, 13 April. We *all* started out from the premise that Margaret herself had publicly identified only three months before – that it would be very difficult to justify action of the kind proposed. But, now that the request had been made, the political difficulties in refusing it became equally apparent.

That was the dilemma with which we wrestled for several days. The argument was by no means as polarized as on other occasions. Gradually we all convinced each other – and, in due course, our Cabinet colleagues – that we had defined the action proposed in terms consistent with the right of self-defence and Article 51 of the UN Charter. Our initial reaction ('probably too negative',[3] said Margaret seven years later) was indeed cautious, as was apparent from the questions that first flew back across the Atlantic. And the Attorney's advice strengthened our insistence that the action had to be justified on grounds of self-defence or not at all. This was always an unsteady concept for American minds: a society where there are 24,000 murders a year (and one hand-gun per head of the population) seems to think more instinctively of a 'suitable response' – in plainer language, 'retaliation'. As distinct from self-defence, this is not a legitimate concept under any Western system of law.

George Younger was in Scotland throughout the weekend (12–13 April), so that only Margaret and I were available to see Reagan's special envoy, Ambassador Vernon ('Dick') Walters on the Saturday. He argued his case vigorously, as always – and saw too the force of the points which we had to make, particularly as they might affect European opinion. By the end of that weekend the Prime Minister and her key Secretaries of State (Foreign and Defence) were of one mind. The White

---

* He is said to have expressed his anxieties publicly on Scottish radio: see Hugo Young, *One of Us*, p. 476.

House was told that we could allow US aircraft to fly from British bases for action consistent with the right of self-defence 'against specific targets demonstrably involved in the conduct and support of terrorist activities'.

The subject was brought to a special meeting of Cabinet's DOP (Defence and Overseas) Committee, which was convened under Margaret's chairmanship on Monday, 14 April. Neither George Younger nor I was there: George could not escape a previous Scottish commitment; I had to be in The Hague for an EC Foreign Ministers' meeting. Margaret, with support from Willie Whitelaw, whom we had kept informed, had an uphill task persuading DOP colleagues to endorse our decision. Norman Tebbit was particularly upset that he was being consulted so late. Eventually, he agreed with Nigel Lawson, John Biffen and Paul Channon (who had succeeded Leon Brittan at the DTI) that there could be no question of qualifying or withdrawing our agreement, 'despite misgivings about the likely effectiveness and possible consequences' of the US action proposed. With my colleagues at The Hague (some of whom at least knew quite as much as I did about American intentions, which had been widely leaked), I had to speak and behave as though the options were still rather more open than by then seemed likely. But no more than them could I be sure, since no final presidential decision was notified to me before the end of the day.

The US air-strike took place that night, 14 April.* The targets chosen were restricted, reflecting our concerns. But only some of the specific Libyan targets were hit. So too were a number of civilian buildings, including the French embassy in Tripoli. The bulk of European, including British, opinion reacted very critically to the American action (though Mitterrand told me, when I met him at an OECD reception in Paris on 17 April, that the French had found their own decision – not to allow US aircraft to overfly France – 'extremely evenly balanced and difficult to take'). Cabinet meetings on Tuesday, 15 April and again on Thursday, 17 April were long and deply uneasy – for all the reasons which had originally caused Margaret, George and myself to consider the case so fully with the Attorney General. News of the death in Beirut of two British hostages, Leigh Douglas and Philip Padfield, added gloom to the proceedings. On the same day, British television

* So too did the shock defeat in the House of Commons of the government's Shops Bill, designed to legalize Sunday opening. Seven years were to elapse before John Major felt able to reintroduce the proposal, in modified form.

journalist John McCarthy was kidnapped in Beirut, to be kept in captivity for five dreadful years. It was also dispiriting to learn that public phone calls to the Foreign Office were critical of our decision, in the proportion of ten to one. On 17 April, no one challenged our basic decision: but I was instructed by Cabinet to ensure that the US administration recognized the political difficulties which HMG faced as a result of our support for American action – and (once again) to urge the Americans to justify that action on the basis of self-defence.

And so I did, exactly as Margaret and I had both done in the emergency debate in the Commons on Wednesday, 16 April. I have to say that I did so, and have done so since, with ever mounting confidence in the legitimacy of our case. When I first agreed that we had to support the American action, I was doing so as Foreign Secretary – because the alternative of dissent was (in Margaret's overblown word) 'inconceivable'. As a lawyer, I was at best persuaded only that we had a good enough defence to argue that it would be dangerous for a jury to convict. At least one Foreign Office lawyer (the one who had given such wise advice about the Nigerian in the crate) was so shocked even by that proposition that she felt obliged to resign the Service.

But as the days and weeks passed by, I became increasingly convinced of the legitimacy of our case, as I had argued it in the House, just forty-eight hours after the raid. There was, I had argued, a plain right of states to defend themselves and their citizens against attacks and against sustained threat of attacks directed from, promoted and organized by another state. The right of self-defence should not be seen as an entirely passive right. 'It plainly includes', I said, 'the right to destroy or weaken the capacity of one's assailant, to reduce his resources, and to weaken his will so as to discourage and prevent further violence.' Even that tenacious critic Hugo Young comes a good way towards conceding the point. Although it was, he says, some time before it became apparent, the Colonel 'behaved like a man who had been taught a lesson'.[4] Libyan-inspired terrorism was much reduced in the months that followed. In Geoffrey Smith's words: 'It is ... difficult to maintain a burning sense of indignation against an act of deterrence that appears to have deterred.'[5]

Looking back now on this analysis, I do not find it easy to believe that we were wrong. Our conclusions had resulted from a synthesis between Margaret's political instinct and my own legal intuition. It was an effective example of our partnership at its best. Ironically it produced two swift and very different dividends. The first, which delighted us both, was the long-delayed acceptance by the US Congress (on 17 July 1986) of the Extradition Treaty, which was of such importance to us in our battle against Irish terrorism, and for which we had been pressing the Americans over a period of years. Reagan argued specifically, and successfully, in its favour because Margaret Thatcher had 'stood shoulder to shoulder with us . . . against Gaddaffi's terrorists'.

But a fortnight later I was much less pleased when Margaret insisted on a reciprocal favour for Ronald Reagan. The International Court of Justice had just ruled against America's support for the action of some Contras in laying mines in Nicaraguan waters. It had been Britain's consistent policy (only recently endorsed by the Prime Minister) to uphold ICJ judgments as a matter of principle. So when the UN Security Council came to vote on 31 July for 'full compliance' with the Court's decision, I had no doubt that we should support that proposition. The US after all could always veto the resolution; indeed it did just that. But Margaret insisted that rather than vote against the wishes of President Reagan himself we should abstain. It was hardly a major issue. But I was nevertheless disconcerted by the strange sequence of events: first, Britain supports US action against Libyan terrorism; second, US supports Britain in action against Irish terrorism; third, Britain condones US-sponsored 'terrorism' against Nicaragua. This was yet another occasion on which Margaret insisted on carrying the 'special' relationship perhaps one bridge too far.

Against the Bomb and the Bullet

Syria was the other leading Middle Eastern sponsor of terrorism. With suitably dramatic timing her most serious offence in Britain came to light three days after the American bombing of Libya. Only five weeks before, Tim Renton had told the Commons, after a visit to London by the Syrian Foreign Minister Farouk Al Shara, that our relations with this country were 'sound' and problem-free. Yet on Thursday, 17 April 1986 one Nezar Hindawi was charged with attempting (by the cowardly use of his pregnant Irish girlfriend as an unwitting bomb-carrier) to blow up an El Al aircraft that was due to leave Heathrow with some 400 passengers on board. Syrian involvement in the case became clear when Hindawi sought refuge at the Syrian embassy and stayed in one of the staff apartments there. The embassy refused to allow police questioning of three staff members. They were accordingly expelled. In retaliation the Syrians expelled from Damascus three of our people, including the defence attaché.

Six months later, Hindawi faced trial at the Old Bailey. The Syrian ambassador, Haydar, was reported by the BBC's John Simpson to be 'upset and nervous'. And understandably so. For Hindawi's conviction was accompanied by conclusive evidence of Syrian official involvement in the offence; Syria was and remained for some years the 'home' of the extreme Abu Nidal terrorist group. Hindawi was sentenced to forty-five years' imprisonment, for a 'monstrous and inhuman crime', and I was obliged to sever completely our relations with Syria. I use the word 'obliged' advisedly. For I knew that by taking that step I was closing our eyes and ears in Damascus, where they could still have had a real value in the search for British and other Western hostages. But the House of Commons shared the feeling of 'deep universal repugnance' which I expressed when I announced our decision.

These events were part of the background to the vigour with which the British government took the lead in pressing for concerted international action against state-sponsored terrorism. Our European partners were seldom as enthusiastic as we were for such action: the smaller states were perhaps less often exposed to terrorism than we were; and some of the larger ones (France, for example) were more temperamentally inclined towards 'striking a deal' in such cases. After the Hindawi affair, for example, I needed two EC ministerial meetings to persuade colleagues to ban arms sales and high-level visits to Syria and to tighten security on Syrian Airlines; I could not persuade them to withdraw their ambassadors from Damascus, even temporarily. The United States, however (with direct access to the same intelligence material as ourselves), withdrew their ambassador from Damascus at the same time as we did.

This same Anglo-American partnership had already promoted the single most important conclusion of the Tokyo Economic Summit, held on 5–6 May 1986. President Reagan arrived there, less than a month after bombing Libya, with a tough anti-terrorist draft communiqué in his pack. This had been watered down substantially by the multinational sherpas. Margaret and I therefore put forward a much stronger British draft, which finally formed the basis of the Summit's robust conclusions. The list of measures which the Summit nations there agreed to apply against 'any state which is clearly involved in sponsoring or supporting international terrorism, and in particular Libya' was headed by: 'Refusal to export arms to states which sponsor or support terrorism'. That was the policy to which Her Majesty's Government maintained its unqualified commitment at all times when I was responsible for or aware of policy on this matter. It is clear in retrospect that the same was not true for the United States. For although the facts about Irangate (the supply of American weaponry in exchange for the release of hostages) did not become public until they surfaced in a Beirut magazine, *Al Shiraa*, on 4 November 1986, it is now well known that transactions of that kind had been taking place at least since May 1985.[6]

The suggestion has since been made by responsible commentators[7] that Her Majesty's Government had sufficient explicit intelligence of some of these activities to have been aware of the essentials of Irangate, not just at the time of the Tokyo Summit but even a month before, ahead of the American bombing of Libya. If this had indeed been the case, our conduct at Tokyo (if not on both those occasions) can be seen as disingenuous indeed. Margaret Thatcher's book does not refer at all to these issues. But she does report and (rightly) take credit for the Tokyo Summit's conclusions on terrorism.[8] So too does George Shultz, albeit in a curiously fragmented way: in one passage he deals solely, and enthusiastically, with the anti-terrorist communiqué;[9] at a later page he describes the messages which reached him in Tokyo at the same time, suggesting that his own country was at least dangerously close to supplying arms to Iran.[10] In the end, however, he claims to have been reassured that there was no foundation for this fear. If the American Secretary of State remained in this state of innocence until, as he claims, the start of November 1986, it would seem hard to impute any higher state of knowledge to the British Prime Minister or Foreign Secretary.

One continuing anxiety, about which Margaret Thatcher and I both knew – and cared – a great deal, however, was the long-running plight of British hostages, and indeed of other Britons unjustly or unjustifiably languishing in gaols or detention around the world. There was always, of course, a fair number of British subjects quite lawfully serving prison sentences or awaiting trial in foreign countries. I was responsible, as Foreign Secretary, for arrangements to ensure that these were properly visited, advised and cared for. But the category that was of special concern were the hostages proper, for the most part people who had been snatched by unknown gangs while going about their lawful business in places like Beirut – such as John McCarthy and Terry Waite. Some others in this group had been detained by a foreign government either without trial or after some manifestly unjust or artificial trial procedure: two examples, in prison throughout much of my time as Foreign Secretary, were Ian Richter in Iraq and Roger Cooper in Iran.

As the American experience underlines, there is probably no aspect of policy that causes more pain to policymakers than this. Reminders of the plight of our fellow countrymen would reach me almost every day. Often as I travelled round Britain, on regional tours for the party, I was confronted – very often on the way into or inside broadcasting studios – by grieving relatives of a British detainee or hostage. 'What are you doing about our William?' (or whatever), they would ask in real anguish. I got into the habit of briefing myself, before visiting a region, on the names whose families I might encounter. This was important not just because it enabled me to show that each individual case had not been forgotten but because it served also to keep the problem close to the front of all our minds.

The plight of the hostages and their families caused me great anxiety, but at the same time I had no doubt about the wisdom of our policy. No deals with terrorists or kidnappers, whether over hostages or anything else, could be tolerated, in the long-term interests of all British subjects. This was the hard lesson I had learned from the days in 1970 when we agreed under duress to the release of Leila Khaled, the Palestinian hijacker. Other nations had not drawn the same conclusion, with predictable results. Middle East kidnappings rose from under ten in 1981 to almost fifty in 1985. During the months in 1986 when Irangate produced the release of three Americans, the same number of fresh American hostages were taken: as George Shultz pointed out, this was the way to 'commerce without end'. But it was far from easy for hostages' families and friends to accept this analysis. Who can blame them? So it was important to convince them all that we were not 'just sitting there'. I made sure that every opportunity of contact, direct or indirect, was always used to remind and inquire. Whether for a meeting between our defence attaché in Cairo and his opposite number or between Margaret Thatcher and King Hussein, the topic was always on the agenda. I was always on the look out too for openings for what I called 'unconventional diplomacy'.

One of the most grotesque charges I had to rebut was that the government sought to 'avoid embarrassment' by seeking to create 'the impression that the hostages were presumed dead'. We had, in fact, no more evidence than anyone else with which to establish a positive conclusion either way. We tried to share the little knowledge that we had with those most closely concerned, hostage families and Lambeth Palace alike, and so to assess the grimly fluctuating balance between hope and despair. I was particularly comforted, on my departure from the Foreign Office, by two notes: one from the Archbishop of Canterbury's public affairs secretary, the late John Lyttle, expressing admiration for and confidence in the way I had handled the hostage issue; and the other equally kind from Terry Waite's brother David – still bravely confident to Terry's return.

The doors finally began to unlock in Douglas Hurd's time at the Foreign Office. There were two principal reasons for this: the ending of the Iran–Iraq War and its replacement by UN action against Saddam Hussein; and John Major's replacement of Margaret Thatcher. These changes enabled us to reopen diplomatic relations, first with Iran, now our ally against Iraq (my own successful attempt to achieve this had been brought to naught by the Rushdie fracas), and then with Syria. Margaret Thatcher had never been willing to close the book on the Hindawi affair and blocked attempts by Douglas as well as myself to move in that direction. But when the new Gulf War persuaded Damascus too to shift towards the West, John Major was ready to make the most of that opportunity. It has since then been a source of great joy to me to witness the return to freedom of each one of the brave British men who had so long to endure without cause the hardship and indignity of often solitary detention.

One man remained still a prisoner in his own country: the author Salman Rushdie. I confess that I had not begun to appreciate his significance, even if I had heard of him, when Ayatollah Khomeni of Iran issued his notorious *fatwa* against the author of *Satanic Verses* on St Valentine's Day 1989 – and a few days later reaffirmed explicitly the continuing threat to the author's life. This was rightly perceived, almost throughout the world, as an attack not only on the author and publishers but also upon most fundamental freedoms: the freedom of expression, religious tolerance and the rule of law. It was particularly galling for me since only a week before I had had my second meeting with Iran's surprisingly reasonable Foreign Minister, Ali Akbar Velayati, to reaffirm our decision of a few months before to restore diplomatic relations between our two countries. There was now no option but to put that relationship back into the icebox.

The Western reaction to my call for support was on this occasion swiftly and unanimously positive. *All* the EC governments agreed to withdraw their ambassadors from Teheran and to restrict Iranian diplomats in their own country. It was Voltaire who pointed out that in India and China they believe that a prophet will come out of the West, whereas people in Europe expect their sages to come from the East. We still need both our prophets and our sages today: and the world should be big enough for both.

These are only some of the fault-lines on which members of the diplomatic service, among others, have to fashion their lives. I have almost surprised myself by the frequency with which I have had to describe diplomatic upheavals which obliged our missions to discontinue operations and decamp at short notice. But such upheavals were not, alas, the worst hazard to confront those with whom I served for six years in the Foreign and Commonwealth Office. Not long before I arrived there, two of our ambassadors in European posts, Sir Richard Sykes in The Hague and Christopher Ewart-Biggs in Dublin, had been killed respectively by a terrorist bullet and a bomb. In 1984 two more murders occurred: in Athens our British Council cultural attaché, Kenneth Whitty, was shot and died immediately; so too our deputy high commissioner in Bombay, Percy Norris (both killings were in the end attributed to the Beirut-based Revolutationary Organization of Socialist Muslims).

There is now at the foot of the grand staircase in the Foreign Office a memorial plaque which I unveiled on 4 November 1985 in memory of these victims of today's violent diplomacy. And in Bombay there is another dedicated to Percy Norris, which I unveiled there on 30 March 1986. The tiny congregation for that ceremony consisted only of our Bombay mission staff and of the travellers in our VC-10 aircraft. I drew attention then not only to the diplomats but also to the even larger number of journalists and broadcasters who had fallen on active service in remote places – each helping, in their own way, to bridge the gaps between the peoples of our world. It is uncomfortable to belong to this particular club – of those whose lives are officially at risk. But the burden of boredom, as well as risk, must be much greater for those who guard than for those of us who have been specially looked after.

CHAPTER THIRTY-FOUR

MY LAST ELECTION CAMPAIGN

Palaces and Parsimony

Life in the Thatcher administration may have been turbulent. It was still an exhilarating adventure. Lawyers are bad witnesses to the quality of a relationship. Too often they see only the pathology. So too with historians and biographers. The casual outside observer often gains an opposite impression. The official round *can* look like a jet-setters' junket: from summit to banquet, from concordat to Concorde, from GATT to Great Wall. And so it sometimes was. Whether in the Hogsnorton Parish Council or in Peking's Great Hall of the People, official life means official entertainment. The mayor may not need a Rolls-Royce. But he has to have a parlour. Striking the right balance between conspicuous extravagance and self-defeating parsimony is impossibly hard. We British seem to find it harder than most.

We can point to some special reasons for this. One is the sheer scale of our heritage. Another is the sense of economic decline which has for years been part of our political common ground. Comparisons are inevitable between the cost of feeding a geriatric patient in Tower Hamlets and the hospitality for President Reagan in Downing Street or between council housing in Toxteth and the ambassadorial residence in Paris. Margaret Thatcher and I were more than ready to use such arguments in support of tight public expenditure when we came into office in 1979. Undoubtedly our attitudes changed, and for good reasons – up to a point. I think I was still Chancellor when Margaret first began asking why so many buildings close to Downing Street were permanently shrouded in plastic sheeting. Generally the answer was 'public spending cuts', dating sometimes even from before our own entry into government! All too often these 'economies' had been achieved by bringing building projects expensively to a halt. Even for us the seemingly imperative tide of current expenditure was always much harder to curb.

We never did find a satisfactory general answer. But we were more or less shamed into lifting the dead hand in 'exceptional cases'. The attractive refurbishment of Parliament Street and Richmond Terrace, just opposite Downing Street, was allowed to proceed. So too the complete restoration of the complex originally occupied by the Home, Foreign and Indian Offices – all today the Foreign and Commonwealth Office. At seemingly vast expense (£80 million was the cost intitially agreed), these long-neglected buildings started to get back to a standard which Paris would regard as routine. The beautifully restored Locarno Suite and magnificent Durbar Court provide facilities that can match the best.

We reached, eventually, very similar conclusions about many of Britain's magnificent embassy buildings around the world. Many are where and what they are for historical reasons. Vienna, for example: I once invited all the NATO Foreign Ministers to a working breakfast in our magnificent Habsburg-era residence there. As they were leaving, Uffe Ellemann-Jensen, the Dane, characteristically asked me, 'Is this building, Geoffrey, a monument to Britain's future? Or to Britain's past?' 'It is, I think, Uffe,' I replied, 'a monument to Austria's past.' The scale of all the older missions in Vienna had been determined in Imperial days – and it wasn't for Britain to lead the downward trend. Harry Lee Kuan Yew of Singapore helped us to learn the lesson, by literally refusing permission to scale down the striking Eden Hall in which our high commissioner resides. 'I will not allow you', he said, 'to give such a misleading signal about Britain's "decline".' And he was right. Similarly, we should save very little hard cash by 'relocating' from the magnificent Lutyens embassy in Washington or from Pauline de Borghese's palace on the Rue du Faubourg St Honoré in Paris. But we should surely be accused of diminishing the credibility of our claim to permanent membership of the UN Security Council.

There was occasional scope too for similiar gestures of domestic self-confidence. Margaret Thatcher, like Ted Heath before her, developed real style in her management of Number 10. It is a tremendous privilege to live in one of these great houses. One should be forgiven too a modest pride in seeing that they are put to positive use – and properly cherished. This is why I procured the production of illustrated booklets about all but one of my official 'homes'. It is no less legitimate to exploit assets of this kind – and indeed to exploit important events – in support of impressive or novel features of the nation's history. Margaret contrived two such occasions some eighteen months from the end of her second administration. In December 1985 she staged a truly sparkling dinner to mark the 250th anniversary of Sir Robert Walpole's establishment of Number 10 as the Prime Minister's official residence. To have assembled all her living predecessors, from Ted Heath to Harold Macmillan, as her guests was in itself remarkable. Even more gracious was the presence of senior members of the family of every twentieth-century Prime Minister, from Lord Avon's widow to Ramsay Mac-Donald's daughter.

Two months later it was not the past but the future that Margaret Thatcher was celebrating – with an unlikely partner, François Mitterrand. Duplicate ceremonies had been arranged, one in Lille and the other at Canterbury, to mark the signature, by Roland Dumas and myself, of the Treaty governing the construction of the Channel Tunnel. I never ceased to be surprised by Margaret's sudden enthusiasm for this quasi-Napoleonic, Ted Heathian project. Plainly she regarded private sector financing of the tunnel itself as much more than a fig-leaf of respectability. But the consequent need to find a path for high-speed trains through the Kentish countryside and suburban London has presented her successors with a formidable IOU. This may be why the project, originally visualized – or so it seemed – as a monument to the Thatcher millennium, receives only one oblique mention in her memoirs.*

There was in fact a parallel ambiguity about the celebration, which took place in the shadow of the Westland drama. The City of Lille, on 20 January 1986, threw itself enthusiastically into a bunting-decked, Marseillaise-led ceremony, under the leadership of their mayor – and Mitterrand's Prime Minister Pierre Mauroy. Three weeks later, on 12 February, in Canterbury, the presidential motorcade was slowed by politely protesting demonstrators and the ceremonial was distinctly non-municipal. The Treaty was signed in the Cathedral chapter-house. Lunch was taken in the Deanery. Elspeth's old family friend, Charles Mozeley, the inimitable illustrator, gave the giant menu cards a truly Chaucerian flavour:

---

* 'On that day [13 March 1984] it so happened that I was due to see Ian MacGregor about the Channel Tunnel – a quite separate matter in which he had an interest' (*The Downing Street Years*, p. 345).

Things thought impossible by everyone,
Things which you'd swear could never, ever be,
Shall yet be brought to pass, though on a day
That happens once a thousand years or so.

It must be a mammoth Freudian slip that denies this project a place in Margaret's history book.

But in the early months of 1986 we were into another difficult patch. The near-coincidence of Westland with the bombing of Libya had provoked an upsurge of anti-Americanism – just when we least needed it. For this was a moment when the troika of Thatcher, Lawson and Howe were still together on the main thrust of economic policy. The ERM fault-line was at an early stage. With most colleagues, we were still seeking ways to rein back, if not reverse, the growth of the public sector. So we were attracted by the prospect which suddenly opened up of privatizing the bulk of the Rover–Leyland motor vehicle business. Two American companies were the prime movers: General Motors put in a bid for the Leyland truck and Land Rover–Range Rover businesses. This was soon followed by an offer from Ford for the volume-car business. Both were made in confidence, of course. But by the start of February 1986 they had found their way into the press. Paul Channon had only just taken over from Leon Brittan at the DTI. He was beset by back-bench protest at both prospects. With the jobless figures still rising, this was amplified into Cabinet by the two West Midland ministers Norman Fowler and Peter Walker. We were obliged to recognize discretion as the better part of valour. Two years were to elapse before a fresh bid – this time for the entire business, from British Aerospace – was to prevail.

Consolidation or Advance

This was not the only check on the domestic front. On student loans, state pension policy (SERPS), water privatization and elsewhere we had had to moderate our pace. But neither this nor our level-pegging one-of-three position in the opinion polls did any great damage to our confidence. I kept up my contributions to the wider political debate. My speech to the London School of Economics Conservative Association on 26 February was one that attracted attention. It was no coded message. Geoffrey Smith, in *The Times*, got it right. The Foreign Secretary, he said, is not one of those Conservatives 'who believe that it is time to pause, either to consolidate or to modify' the substance of policy. 'He wants to press ahead with the strategy' of lower inflation, lower income tax, wider ownership of property and further privatization. I deliberately put this message in the context of the three-party debate. The consequences of voting for the 'SDP – Liberal hybrid . . . [offering] moderation without conviction', I warned, involved the grave risk of losing all that had been gained. Either a hung Parliament or an extreme-left Labour government by default would be equally damaging. The programme had been 'first identified by the early Bow Group generations and subsequently filled out and developed by organizations like the Institute of Economic Affairs'.

But there was, as Geoffrey Smith observed, 'a critical distinction' between Margaret Thatcher and myself. 'She speaks', he said, 'as if she is building a new Jerusalem.' Sir Geoffrey, on the other hand, tries to 'make the country seem more comfortable with the present strategy', to 'make the same broad approach seem not so much daring as natural'. The moral, concluded the *Daily Telegraph*, when Sir Geoffrey reminds the party-political world that he is there, 'is simply that this is after all not a one-woman government. Mrs Thatcher would not disagree that that is not a bad uncoded message to get across.' At that stage in the relationship between us, I like to think it was still Margaret's view.

We were soon within a year of the general election of 1987, destined to be the only campaign which I had to combine with active service as Foreign Secretary. I was about to plunge into my whirlwind tours of Southern Africa. So it was fun too to be able to enjoy some more relaxing features of Foreign Office routine. Entirely frivolous, first of all came the annual cricket match in June between the Commonwealth Secretariat (based in London and since 1975 led by Guyana-born Sir Shridath (Sony) Ramphal) and the Foreign and Commonwealth Office, staged at Blenheim. I had never before dared to expose my cricketing incompetence on these occasions, not even in the so-called Gentlemen's match (the Players' was the more serious affair). But on this occasion Elspeth (she had captained the Wycombe Abbey eleven) batted a magnificent five overs not out, and Amanda (for two years a half-blue at Cambridge) put in a spirited performance as wicket-keeper: they more than vindicated the family reputation.

On a more serious note, I said farewell at about the same time to three notable diplomats upon whom I had come to rely. Sir Antony Acland had been permanent secretary since 1982. He was not strictly retiring, but moving on to become our ambassador in Washington. He was handing over the London headship of the diplomatic service to Sir Patrick Wright. The two truly departing veterans were Sir John Graham, for two years our man at NATO, and Sir Oliver Wright, recalled for four years' post-retirement service in Washington. His farewell letter struck a most encouraging, and not untypical, note:

> To have arrived here in the afterglow of the Falklands and to leave in the afterglow of Libya is not the usual fate of HM servants abroad. To have been present at the arrest of the decline in our national economic performance and to be then able with conviction to trumpet the resurgence of Britain has been an exhilarating privilege. In over forty years' service, I have never known the all-round reputation of Britain stand so high in the world. The 'Thatcher Revolution' is working: there is much still to be done, but it is happening.

If even hardened professionals were prepared to think in these terms, then we politicians were entitled to look for some rallying of electoral support. But Margaret was leaving nothing to chance. I could not expect to play the lead role in preparing the manifesto for the forthcoming election. It would have been impossible to combine sufficient knowledge of domestic policymaking with my endlessly travelling role. On this occasion the Prime Minister eventually assumed effective control herself. But by way of preliminary she set up in June 1986 a Strategy Group, consisting of the Deputy Prime Minister (Whitelaw), the holders of the 'three great offices of state' (Howe, Lawson and Hurd), party chairman and Chief Whip (Tebbit and Wakeham), and a series of supporting policy groups, under the chairmanship of departmental ministers. But the Strategy Group, although we met weekly and were publicly identified as the '"A" Team', was never entrusted with any seriously coherent role. The actual manifesto work was done by three party officials – Brian Griffiths and Stephen Sherbourne in the Number 10 Policy Unit and Robin Harris, head of Research Department at Central Office. Towards the end, when they complained about lack of ministerial guidance, John MacGregor (then Chief Secretary) was placed in charge. But the final content and style were essentially imposed by Margaret herself, with the other apparatus serving essentially, as she acknowledges, 'to make the Party feel involved in what was happening'.[1]

From my foreign vantage – or disadvantage – point, I felt frustrated by my inevitable exclusion from the details of the domestic policymaking process. But, as I had indicated in my LSE speech in February, I was broadly more than content with the main thrust of our agenda on housing, health and education. Economic policy was safe, or so I was entitled to think, in Nigel's experienced hands.

But one area had caused me anxiety, though not as much as it should have done – the re-emergence of our pledge to abolish domestic rates and replace them with the Community Charge. I had last looked closely at this topic at the end of my Treasury days and had then seen it, as I thought, finally disposed of, dead and buried, in our White Paper of August 1983. I knew, of course, that the topic had been forced back on to the agenda by the furious Scottish backlash against the rates in 1985. George Younger had always been a powerful, and attentive, champion of that point of view. So I was not over-surprised to learn that the search for the Holy Grail had been resumed – and resumed, I knew, by some of the ablest minds around: two of Ted Heath's old think-tank maestros, Rothschild and Waldegrave. All this dulled my absentee mind – for I was not on any of the relevant economic committees – into a sense of false security. Most remarkably of all, I do not recall any alarm call from my most embattled – indeed almost my only embattled – colleague, Nigel Lawson. (For our earlier ally in support of the rates, Michael Heseltine, had quit the domestic scene for the Ministry of Defence – and in January had departed from the government altogether.)

The system was such that almost the first sight I had of any key working papers was on the eve of the Cabinet meeting which actually approved Kenneth Baker's Green Paper unveiling the Charge, on 9 January 1986 (the very Cabinet meeting at which Michael Heseltine had so dramatically resigned). Even Nigel Lawson, as I recall it, registered no vigorous opposition at that stage. He had already done his best almost single-handed. I had come to assume that the array of talent that had been engaged in the search for over a year must indeed have found some relatively bug-free version of the Charge. So it is extremely unlikely that any kind of last-minute intervention on my part could at that stage have halted this particular steamroller in its tracks. The entire experience convinced me, in retrospect, of the need for every senior Cabinet Minister to have not one but two special advisers; one would have to be expressly charged with surveillance of the wider non-departmental front. But, for this Thatcher government, the fatal poll-tax die had now been cast.

End of Year

The last meeting of the European Council before the 1987 general election took place under Margaret Thatcher's Presidency at the Queen Elizabeth II Conference Centre in Westminister on 5–6 December 1986. It was in any case an uneventful meeting, not least because Chancellor Kohl – like ourselves, with an election coming up – was unwilling to contemplate any difficult decisions on the restraint of farm expenditure. Our most notable achievement was the enactment or agreement of a record number of single-market measures. We had been able, in other words, to exploit to the full the steps agreed at Luxembourg for the enlargement of Community authority at the expense of 'sovereign parliaments'. It was an achievement worth recording, not least under this Presidency.

It was also the occasion of the infamous brush between Jacques Delors and Margaret Thatcher at the closing press conference. Delors, as President of the Commission, was on the podium alongside Margaret and myself. We all had, at least theoretically, speaking parts on such an occasion. But the opportunity seldom arose. Suddenly Margaret ended one of her answers to a press question by inviting Jacques Delors for his comment – and he was at a loss for anything to say. Nothing is easier than for a non-playing participant to cease listening to a speech at a press conference, particularly if it is in a foreign language. My guess was (and is) that Delors had nothing to say quite simply because his concentration had faltered, which was no doubt embarrassing enough. But in Margaret Thatcher's view 'he refused to say anything. . . . I continued to urge him, but to no avail. "I had no idea you were the strong, silent type",' was her concluding comment to Delors.[2] The misunderstanding was complete. She thought he was being perversely silent. And he thought, as I learned afterwards, that she had more or less deliberately set out to humiliate him before a largely British audience. Neither side ever really forgave the other for the 'offence' which neither of them had wittingly committed. It was a serious step along the road to deeper misunderstanding.

Later that month, on the 20th, we held our most memorable party, my sixtieth birthday. Alec revealed himself with a startlingly perceptive and witty toast to his father. More generally the Welsh flavour was dominant. A veritable *gymanfa ganu* of Welsh and other hymns and carols was capped by Geraint Evans' superb rendering of 'Dafydd ap

Garreg Gwen'. The cabaret by Christopher Cooper and the Loose Chords concluded with a specially composed chorus from Alistair Sampson, to the tune of 'Men of Harlech'. A few lines will give the flavour:

> Poor Sir Geoffrey down at Chevening
> See him on a Friday evening
> Boxes ruddy, in his study,
> Maggie's light his guide.

The Reykjavik Summit Fall-out

And then we were into the last lap for the general election. The dates we had chosen for Margaret's first official Moscow visit at the end of March 1987 were geared to the prospect of an election before many months had passed. In the previous eighteen months the lead in East–West diplomacy had fallen naturally into the hands of Shultz and Shevardnadze. At successive meetings of the NATO Council, Shultz meticulously and skilfully maintained the confidence of his allies in the hand that the Americans were playing at the Geneva negotiations. Following our Halifax meeting in May 1986 I encapsulated the NATO view by calling upon the Soviets to respond positively to our proposal for 'bold new steps' in the cause of disarmament.

With remarkable speed such action did indeed follow. For at the Reykjavik Summit between Ronald Reagan and Mikhail Gorbachev in October both sides were quite startlingly prepared to agree far-reaching arms-reduction proposals. In most respects this was entirely good news. Agreement was close upon a 50 per cent reduction in strategic nuclear weapons and on a reduction of intermediate weapons (INF) that would cut by more than 90 per cent the Soviet SS-20s then targeted on Europe and Asia. Beyond this, two further, even more fundamental steps were in contemplation: President Reagan declared himself ready to eliminate altogether within ten years the entire range of strategic ballistic missiles. Gorbachev, for his part, tried to press Reagan to limit any further SDI work to laboratory testing only. This would have gone a long way towards spelling the end of SDI, and would, of course, have taken a huge load off the Soviet space research programme, to Moscow's immense relief. Reagan was ready to confine his SDI work to development and testing so far as that was compatible with the ABM Treaty, and indeed to prolong his commitment to that Treaty for a further ten years. But further than that he would not go. So the Summit broke off without agreement.

There were very different reactions to this outcome. For some (including George Shultz, at least according to his book)[4] Reykjavik was a near triumph, which failed only because Gorbachev tried to press Reagan a notch too far over SDI; correspondingly the President's insistence on keeping the whole SDI programme sowed the seeds of the Soviets' failure to keep up the pace of research – and thus eventually of their economic collapse. On the other view (with which Margaret and I, Mitterrand and most other Europeans agreed) President Reagan had narrowly avoided falling into a Russian trap, which would have led to American abandonment, within ten years, of their entire strategic deterrent. We should have moved, via Reagan's dream of a nuclear-free world, into a nightmare world where the notion of deterrence – the key to Western defence policy for decades – had been suddenly discarded. There was one supreme irony about the whole dilemma: the only reason why Reagan had hung on to his own strategic deterrent (which the alliance cherished) was his deep attachment to the SDI programme (which many in the alliance deeply mistrusted). When George Shultz came to explain all this to bewildered NATO Foreign Ministers in Brussels the next day he made, characteristically, as good a fist of it as he could, and secured our warm appreciation and continuing support.

But not far below the surface there had been a curious shift in the debate. Until that moment the French and British nuclear deterrents had quite often attracted some gently critical attention from our European allies. They tended to feel (but did not always say) that we should be more ready than we were to 'bring our nuclear armoury into the negotiations'. To that extent at least, our bombs used to be seen as almost a threat. But after Reykjavik no longer. The Alliance had been more than slightly scared by the spectre of an American President who might actually take seriously the prospect of a nuclear-free world. The real anxiety sprang from the fact that a US President had come so close, without any effective transatlantic consultation, to striking a deal of such far-reaching importance. Some of us, in France as well as in Britain, began to think even more seriously about the need, and the scope, for partnership between Europe's two nuclear powers: not in rivalry to the United States but as a strengthening complement. The thought was to take a long time developing.

Margaret Thatcher, of course, was at once alert to the danger, if less responsive to the opportunities. All of us in London were particularly conscious of the threat to our own Trident programme, because the new generation of missiles for our new generation of submarines depended for their very existence upon the completion of the United States' strategic modernization programme. Underlying all those assumptions there was the long-standing doctrine of nuclear deterrence, now in doubt. So, with my full support, Margaret was very shortly off for a second solo visit to President Reagan at Camp David, 14–15 November. I had no reservations about her mission on this occasion. George Shultz was very ready to endorse our bid before Margaret presented it to an equally understanding Reagan. So she was able to return from Washington having effectively salvaged from the Reykjavik upheaval the essence of earlier alliance strategy. Nuclear deterrence 'based upon a mix of systems' was preserved. Disarmament objectives were agreed (and endorsed at the December Foreign Ministers' meeting in Brussels). Margaret Thatcher also secured, crucially, the President's support for 'arrangements made to modernize Britain's independent nuclear deterrent with Trident'. These would proceed in line with the United States' own strategic modernization programme.

This was an important outcome, which served Britain as well as it served the alliance. Clearly George Shultz was not sorry to see the fundamental doctrines reaffirmed, in a fashion that was not incompatible with his President's more far-flung vision. In some ways it suited him that Margaret was such an absolutist proponent of the nuclear argument, to the point of being much more closely identified with the bomb than was sensible – or necessary – for her. 'What's so good about a world where you can be wiped out in thirty minutes?' he used to ask. Shultz had never learned to love the bomb.

Sweeping Through the Soviet Union

By the same token, it suited Margaret Thatcher's book to be credited in Moscow with this kind of influence in Washington. It was in this spirit that she prepared herself with characteristic diligence for our pre-election visit to Moscow from 28 March to 1 April 1987. But already it had become a fairly solitary process, increasingly like a royal tour without the household: in twelve pages of her autobiography devoted to this journey, Margaret makes no reference to any other British member of the entourage.[5]

Margaret's Moscow programme was largely along familiar lines: an evening at the ballet, an excursion to the splendid Orthodox monastery at Zagorsk, a formal dinner at the Kremlin, a meeting with dissidents at our embassy and an informal evening over dinner with her hosts. What was unusual was the length of her one-to-one with Gorbachev himself, which undoubtedly did offer useful insights into and chances of opening the General Secretary's mind. Certainly my own long evening session over dinner with Shevardnadze and two or three of our personal staff, including Bryan Cartledge, our ambassador, was a fascinating opportunity. For I had decided to use the occasion, if I could, as a kind of seminar on Soviet foreign policy outside the NATO area. Shevardnadze was more than happy to respond in the same spirit. Only once did he bridle, and that was when I asked him what value the Soviets thought they got for their $2000 million 'investment' in Vietnam, apart that is from their base at Cam Ranh Bay. 'There you go again,' he cried, 'criticizing our bases, of which we have only a handful, compared with the dozens with which you in the West ring the Soviet Union.' 'It's a fair point,' I replied, 'except that I wasn't criticizing you but simply inquiring for your own view.' He soon calmed down. Across a wide informal agenda – from Korea to Cambodia, from Japan to Jerusalem – Shevardnadze proved himself an excellent and perceptive listener. Consciously or unconsciously, we had, I think, advanced the mutual understanding that was later to help us to work more closely together on the UN Security Council.

It was marvellous to behold the impact which Margaret herself had on ordinary Russians whose path she happened to cross. The three Soviet television journalists who interviewed her for the long, uncensored interview which they broadcast had never encountered anything like the whirlwind that swept them aside. The nationwide television audience loved it. This was indeed reflected in the reaction of Russians in the streets of Moscow and, even more, of Georgians in the streets of Tbilisi. When Margaret decided, as she did on more than one occasion, to make an unconventional exit from her Zil limousine to greet passing pedestrians, she was instantly overwhelmed by enthusiastic recognition and acclaim. 'Margaret Thatcher', said the *Mail on Sunday*, 'has become, internationally, our best-known Prime Minister since Churchill. Her driving personality puts her head and shoulders above anyone else on the world stage.'

In the closing hours of our day in Georgia, I was deeply moved by the radiant enthusiasm of the young woman who showed us the ikons and religious silver in the State Treasury. Was she, I wondered, fired by Communist learning? Or by Christian faith? Or by pride in her own Georgian nationalism? Surely, I felt, by a mixture of the last two rather than the first. The passion and harmony of the Georgian male-voice choir which sang for us during our last supper on that visit to the Soviet Union, evocative as it was of the Welsh chapel choirs of my youth, certainly carried some signs of a nation in the making. So Georgia's dash for independence on the disintegration of the 'evil empire' did not surprise me when it came. Nor did Eduard Shevardnadze's brave decision four years later to return to Tbilisi, for his ill-starred struggle to reunite his people.

Campaigning Again

But as we took off from Tbilisi on our four-hour flight through the small hours to Heathrow, Margaret's thoughts were not, I guess, all that much about Georgian nationalism. Already they were bounding ahead to the prospect of a fresh appeal for support from the British nation, which might not now be long delayed. The election date remained uncertain until Margaret held her first meeting with senior colleagues at Chequers on 10 May. But the steady progress of the economy was encouraging. Inflation at 3.6 per cent was as low as it had been for many years. The rate of growth was the highest in any major European economy. Unemployment had begun to fall steadily. And the accompanying improvement in the opinion polls (our support rose to 44 per cent at the end of January) augured well. So Margaret decided to go to the country on 11 June.

My domestic speech-making programme too had been increasingly election-dominated. On 25 January 1987 I had been in Cambridge again to make a pre-emptive strike on a forthcoming Alliance policy document. Theirs, I said, was a 'Partnership for Paralysis',[3] which offered 'at worst a back-door route to power for Labour and at best a recipe for national inertia'. The real Liberal tradition, I claimed, remained 'alive and active' with 'many of its best elements inspiring the policies of the modern Conservative Party'. Geoffrey Smith in *The Times* later contrasted my approach with that of Norman Tebbit. We were both right, he said, to avoid detailed analysis of Alliance policies because they had no chance of being put into practice. Far wiser to point, as Norman and I had both been doing, to the possible practical effects of voting

Alliance. But how best to do so? 'While they both make the same points,' said Smith, 'Mr Tebbit manages to sound like a political assassin,' while Sir Geoffrey gives the impression of having been forced to his conclusion by careful analysis.' I was convinced that this was the tone most likely to persuade the crucial floating voter, who might like much of the substance of Thatcherism but recoil from the harshness of the rhetoric. 'Every time they hear a savage attack on the Alliance,' Smith rightly concluded, 'it confirms what offends them most about the Conservatives.'⁶ It was just this argument that I largely succeeded in getting across to those who were drafting the manifesto.

One other matter needed consideration ahead of the election: did I have any preferences, if I was given a choice, for my role in a re-elected Thatcher government? It was probably symptomatic of a slowly widening gap between us that Margaret and I never found an opportunity for discussing this directly. The question was raised with me more than once, however, by Willie Whitelaw and Ian Gow. Each of these I knew to be gossiping regularly with Margaret on this kind of topic. Ian (no longer Margaret's PPS and no longer in government) retained that very close relationship until his death. Long experience had taught me that he was often a more effecitve route into Margaret's mind than any form of direct advocacy. What did I think, came the question more than once, of a move to the Woolsack? Quintin Hailsham, now in his twelfth year, was surely due for retirement: who next? My view was that Margaret herself would be most inclined to offer the place to Michael Havers. It was the least he was entitled to expect after eight years' unswerving loyalty as Attorney General. For some non-political critics in the legal profession it was, I knew, the very unswervingness of that devotion that was seen as a disadvantage for the Lord Chancellorship. I did not expect Margaret to be influenced by that kind of consideration – and I was right. Michael's fast-declining health was another important factor. Contrary to some commentary, this could actually work in his favour. Even a few weeks on the Woolsack would qualify him for the generous pension which went with the job.

But I still had to be clear about my own reaction if, contrary to my expectations, the job was offered to me. Helpfully or not, the press had been offering advice. The *Daily Mail*, in a complimentary piece on 28 April about my recent plain-speaking in Australia, New Zealand and the United States, saw the Lord Chancellorship as 'a noble culmination to a fine career'. Even so, their preference was for me to stay in my present post, 'a very good Foreign Secretary, well on his way to becoming a great one'. Even more persuasive was a personal letter to the same effect from Patrick Wright, my permanent secretary at the Foreign Office, claiming to write on behalf of most of his colleagues in the Service.

In fact I needed no prompting, for two concurrent reasons: in the first place, I was greatly enjoying my present job, and, more important than that, I was still reluctant – however foolish it might be – to give up all hope of succession to Margaret. The Lord Chancellorship would spell an end to any such prospect. In the result the question did not arise, for the job went, as I had expected, to Michael Havers. And the question was postponed – though, as it happened, for no more than four months. Havers' health obliged him to retire in October. He was replaced by the Scottish Law Lord James Mackay. By that date I had no time, nor reason, to rethink my own position. I am fairly confident that if I had decided, at the moment of Havers' departure, to abandon any bright political ambition and to go for the Woolsack, I should probably have been taken in preference to Mackay (the job had never before gone to a Scotsman). But in truth the question went at that time very largely by default in my own mind. Margaret seems not, on this occasion, to have considered any alternative to myself for the Foreign Office. A brief phone call, quite soon after our election victory, was enough to confirm that understanding. 'I'd like you to carry on at the Foreign Office, Geoffrey,' said Margaret – and that was enough.

As always, I had enjoyed the campaign. Two days a week in my own constituency, with Elspeth doing the bulk of the work, were less domestic than usual, because of the foreign journalists keen to follow the Foreign Secretary's trail. Guests at a wine-tasting luncheon in Limpsfield were startled to find their Conservative candidate pursued through the room by a mini-herd of ladies from Lebanon. Travelling from end to end of the country, I never became deeply involved – apart from two press-conference appearances – in the daily tribulations at Central Office. I was out of town on 'wobbly Thursday' and steered clear of the row between Margaret's squabbling seconds, Norman Tebbit and David Young. I never myself lost the sense of solid electoral support. The nearest I came to immortality was when canvassing a bus-queue of pensioners in Ilkley, with our member for Keighley, Gary Waller. With more enthusiasm than sense, Gary sought to shake hands with a Yorkshire terrier just as I was greeting its owner. Some trick of camera angles caused the resultant savage snarl to be for ever recorded as directed at me. I appeared in this foolish dog-provoking role on the lead-in to every ITN Election Special for the rest of the campaign.

My more serious message was based on the foreign view of Britain's recovery in our eight years of power. I quoted often from two French papers. 'Britain', said *L'Express*, had pursued 'a foreign policy which has made the British proud of themselves again, and has anchored them to Europe'. 'Some time ago,' said *Le Point*, 'to talk of Britain's economic success seemed frankly burlesque. . . . Now her economic politics are seen from abroad as a model to follow.' The message seemed to carry conviction.

For the last four days of the campaign I was scarcely able to play even a nominal role. For the G7 Economic Summit was convened under Italian chairmanship at Venice on the three days before polling day, 8–10 June. Margaret judged the importance of the agenda well by attending for no longer than was necessary to fit in the photo-calls. But I had to man the UK seat at the table from beginning to end. The RAF HS-125 got me back to Gatwick only just in time for two well-attended and cheerful eve-of-poll meetings at De Stafford School, Caterham and St Peter's Hall, Limpsfield, in my constituency, which was conveniently alongside the airport. And then, astonishingly, I was straight back to Gatwick for another flight. This time we were bound for Reykjavik in Iceland for the first half of a two-day meeting of the NATO Foreign Ministers' Council. We had important work to do on the handling of intermediate nuclear weapons in the arms-control talks.

So I spent the most unusual polling day of my life. We reached Reykjavik at three o'clock in the morning, in broad daylight. We were locked in conference all day. On the plane back to Gatwick that evening, I said to my aides, 'Well, at least you all know what you'll be doing tomorrow – which is more than I do.' I reached the count, taking place as usual in the Oxted County School, about 11.15 p.m. At 12.21 a.m. the result was announced: I was the only candidate ever to have spent the whole of polling day in Reykjavik and yet to have increased both his majority and his share of the vote.* Next time, I mused, I might be better advised to spend the entire campaign away from the constituency. But although I did not know it then, there was not going to be a next time. I had reached the end of my last election campaign.

* Howe, R. E. G. (Con) 29,126; Anderson, M. A. J. (Lib) 11,000; Davis, M. J. (Lab) 4779; Newell, D. R. (GP) 1044; Conservative majority 18,126.

CHAPTER THIRTY-FIVE

BRUGES REVERSAL

Back to the Budget

Re-election meant Cabinet changes, and so changes in my own team. Janet Young's decision to retire after eight years in government was understandable, but sad. I had drawn heavily upon the wisdom she had honed in her much respected service in the Lords. Timothy Renton too was on the move – to broadcasting in the Home Office: that would test even his even-tempered subtlety. They were replaced by Simon Glenarthur in the Lords and David Mellor, with me for a one-year stop-over *en route* from the Home Office to Health. Chris Patten, remaining in semi-autonomous charge of Overseas Development, was fast maturing towards Cabinet rank. My other survivor, Lynda Chalker, was equally effective – and popular – in black Africa and in the European Community. She was the lady alongside me during most of the routine Foreign Affairs Council meetings, sensitive to every nuance of the discussion but never wavering in her effective presentation of our case.

But the big issues were, as always, reserved for the European Council meetings, where Margaret was my half-yearly table-mate. So within three weeks of our general election victory, on 29 and 30 June, we were back alongside each other in Brussels, under the chairmanship of the Belgian Premier Wilfried Martens. The long and complex paper before us (on agricultural expenditure and the Community budget) had been hammered out over months with a large British input. On the day before the Summit when we Foreign Ministers had licked it into pre-final shape, several of my colleagues had rounded on Leo Tindemans, our Belgian chairman, for having produced an 'Anglo-Belgian paper'. So in the full Council we started ahead on points. But Martens' chairmanship was time-consuming. Soon we were sitting at the uncleared lunch table on the afternoon of the second day, already into 'injury time'. The air-conditioning had failed: impatience grew as the temperature rose.

A Commission official was called in at this unlikely stage to explain some mysterious aspect of the green currency system. 'How can we possibly instruct farm ministers', demanded an exasperated Mrs Thatcher, 'if we ourselves don't understand the details?' Others responded by urging Margaret to look more closely at the guidelines on the table, which were already 'a compromise in your favour'. There were only two points on which Britain needed to secure significant change. Given reasonable debate, it should have been possible to sort them out in less than an hour. But Margaret was fiercely unwilling to narrow our objectives in that way. She proclaimed her readiness 'to remain all night, if necessary, to get the right text'. It was this prospect that led the other eleven heads of government to chorus, 'Well, we're all prepared to sign the paper that is before us: why not you?' Martens, in the chair, accepted with alacrity the proposal from Spain's Felipe González that everyone should do just that.

Britain ended once again in the eleven-to-one minority position from which we had hoped to escape for good at Fontainbleau. It was ironical that a Council marked by the ineptitude of the Belgian Presidency should break up in disagreement because of a sudden accession of authoritarianism on his part. Martens' failure to give our key points a hearing was a serious misjudgment. They were certainly capable of resolution. But the failure was not his alone. A calmer approach from the British corner would almost certainly have avoided the impasse. For underlying the final drama there was a high degree of accord, on the basis of a largely British text. Yet sadly, as at least one commentator observed, 'the Thatcher style had been brutally confirmed – and the rest had surprised themselves at how much they were prepared to agree'.[1] A dangerous, and unnecessary, precedent had been set.

Before the end of the year (on 4–5 December) the same European Council cast was around a huge Copenhagen table, under the chairmanship of the benign but very effective Danish (Conservative) Prime Minister Poul Schluter. The agenda had not changed. But six months' work by the Agriculture, Finance and Foreign Ministers and their officials had made it a great deal more precise, even if no more simple. Even so, at the end of two days agreement still eluded us. With strong support from Ruud Lubbers and Hans van den Broek, the Netherlands team, we had made good progress and were ready to do business, on the basis of revised texts which Schluter had produced. But the French and the Germans were not: both had difficulties with agriculture. Their elections were due in the spring. The meeting would be resumed in the New Year in Brussels under the German Presidency.

Then, suddenly, President Mitterrand asked for the floor. He spoke gravely. His voice was laden with foreboding. We had come to the end of the road, he said. The brightest hopes had been blighted. The dreams of the founding fathers would turn to dust. Perhaps a Community of twelve nations could never be made to work. And so on, for ten minutes or more. This semi-spontaneous epilogue, as may be imagined, cast something of a pall over the proceedings. Then, to my surprise, Margaret Thatcher leaned forward and asked to speak. 'Come on,' she said brightly, 'it isn't as bad as that. We've made a lot of progress. But we haven't finished today. Don't you remember just how gloomy things looked in Brussels in 1984? Yet three months after that, at Fontaine-bleau, under your brilliant chairmanship, President Mitterrand, we did reach a major agreement. And I am quite sure that, under Chancellor Kohl's chairmanship in a few months' time, we can do the same. So', *very* brightly, 'cheer up, President Mitterrand, *cheer* up!' And President Mitterrand, catching the mood of the occasion, replied, 'I begin to wonder whether Madame Thatcher isn't even more intriguing when she is saying yes than when she is saying no.'

All those present at Copenhagen were indeed heartened by the tone of Margaret's closing remarks. We were still all on the same side, they felt – and I hoped – whatever the difficulties from month to month. This was reflected in the continental press. The French, Italian and Belgian newspapers spoke of Margeret Thatcher's 'goodwill', portrayed her as 'restrained but firm' and commended 'the clarity and consistency of her views' and particularly the way in which her 'soft approach' contributed to showing divisions among others. It showed very clearly what *could* be done.

The difficulties were clearly in evidence at the resumed meeting in Brussels on 11–12 February 1988. Even by the standards of European Councils, it was a gruelling and bafflingly complex affair, but after a special meeting of Foreign Ministers ten days later, a deal was finally hammered into place. As a result farm expenditure came under much stricter control. Food surpluses began to fall. Thereafter the proportion of the Community budget spent on agriculture fell sharply: from more than two-thirds at that time to half in 1994.

Economic and Monetary Union

The 'main' Summit of the German Presidency, at Hanover on 27 and 28 June 1988, raised the curtain on the drama that was to dominate Community politics for the next five years – economic and monetary union (EMU). I often found myself wondering why the European agenda seemed always to be unfolding at such breakneck speed. Why this now, when so much earlier business remained to be concluded? In domestic politics one had at least the feeling of being able to influence the speed and manner in which policies developed. But in the Community we often seemed to be on a remorselessly moving carpet – bringing forward, in A. J. P Taylor's words, 'one damn thing after another'. Some leaders of European opinion certainly did appear to be almost personally driven from one 'initiative' to another by the fear that if ever they came to a halt they might risk falling over. This is the impulse, I believe, that tends to prompt the production of endless documentary symbols of progress – of charters, of Acts, of draft treaties and the like. Britons have little time for such things. We have no written constitution and tend to be proud of the fact. We like to leave it to others to be enthused by solemn texts of that kind.

But not all the European agenda was driven by such emotion. The economic imperatives imparted a much more practical impetus to certain topics. The single market itself, which Margaret Thatcher and I had done so much to promote in unproclaimed partnership with Arthur Cockfield – *and* Jacques Delors – strengthened that thrust. Financial transactions in a single market, from trade to tourism, would undoubtedly be much easier, more profitable, if they could be concluded in a single currency – as in the United States. In the absence of a single currency there would be real advantage in achieving a more or less stable set of exchange rates between the different currencies in use in the market.

This is why the member-states of the European Community had already committed themselves, on a number of occasions, to moves in that direction. The objective of economic and monetary union had been agreed and proclaimed on a number of occasions: in the Paris Communiqúe of October 1972, when Edward Heath was Prime Minister; on the establishment of the European Monetary System in 1978, when James Callaghan was Prime Minister; and with Margaret Thatcher's authority in the Stuttgart Declaration on European Union, on 19 June

1983; and in the Single European Act, at Luxembourg in December 1985.

It is true that the meaning of the term had not at any time been expressly defined. Margaret Thatcher has always rested her case on what she describes as the 'studied ambiguity' of Article 20 of the Single European Act, which purported to define EMU as no more than 'Co-operation in Economic and Monetary Policy'. But it was apparent that the real choice had to lie between two alternatives. Either we continued with something like the existing EMS, whose Exchange Rate Mechanism offered the prospect of reasonable currency stability. Or we committed ourselves to the establishment of a single currency, embracing more than one – and, one would hope, all – of the national economies.

It was this set of options that had produced what was in effect a three-way split at the heart of the British Cabinet. Margaret Thatcher and Nigel Lawson both opposed the idea of a single currency on principle. They regarded that as synonymous with single government, involving an unacceptable 'surrender' of national sovereignty. Nigel Lawson and I, on the other hand, both endorsed the concept of the Exchange Rate Mechanism for currency stability, which we had for nine years been committed to join 'when the time was right'. Margaret alone remained hostile even to that. And I was alone in regarding a single European currency as a desirable medium-term goal. I did not – and do not – regard it as impossible for a group of countries, still retaining their own political identity, to agree arrangements for the establishment of a single currency, which they all use in substitution for their own. But I concede that important problems have to be solved if the economies so linked are to coexist without facing disruptive (and acceptable) pressures for 'regional revaluation'. That, of course, would spell the end of the union. So the problems are by no means purely technical – they are political and emotional as well as economic. California may be ready to face recession while Texas enjoys a recovery, for the sake of the wider union. Spain (or Britain) may not feel quite so ready to face hardship for the sake of East Germany. In the long run success depends on a shared perception that we all have interests in common.

All this was for the Hanover Council to consider. It had been on the active agenda for months already, with a proposal to establish a committee of experts to study methods of approaching the topic. Now the German Presidency had enlisted the support of their own arch-sceptics, Karl Otto Pöhl, the President of the Bundesbank, and their

Finance Ministry. So we concentrated, sensibly and without fuss, on securing a committee composed not of 'experts' but of all twelve central bank governors, including our own Robin Leigh-Pemberton. It was to be chaired by Jacques Delors himself and to report in time for consideration at Madrid a year later. The terms of reference excluded any specific mention of a European Central Bank. Margaret had been particularly anxious to avoid any such prejudgment of the issues. Skilful chairmanship by Kohl and a general wish to put the emphasis on joint endeavour rather than disagreement inspired harmony. The British Prime Minister was able to put a good face on the decision to extend Delors' Presidency of the Commission. No other candidate's name had been put forward. So Margaret gracefully seconded the proposal that Delors should be invited to continue. It looked as though economic and monetary union was set for calm analysis in the months ahead.

The Speech

There followed a welcome break in formal Community activity. But one change in British representation in Brussels did distress me. Lord Cockfield's four-year term as a Commissioner was due to expire at the same time as Delors'. Margaret was determined that his term should not be extended. She had, of course, been irritated by some of the positions he had taken up as a Commissioner. Most notably we had viewed his campaign for tax harmonization as a tiresome nuisance. On the other hand Cockfield had almost single-handedly imposed and carried well on the way to fulfilment the entire single-market-programme. This was one of Britain's top two or three priorities. He had, moreover, by his sheer enthusiasm and professionalism, established himself as one of the most effective Commissioners. He had done a good job for Britain as well as for Europe. But for Margaret his work for Europe had been too much. He had 'gone native' – and had to be replaced. That was not a verdict that I had accepted without argument, not least because Arthur had been a notably loyal and effective colleague in our Treasury days. There was, however, one comfort in all this. Arthur Cockfield's loss was to be Leon Brittan's gain. I suggested Leon. He would do the job with no less independence than Arthur – and he would do it well. Margaret made it plain that he had no prospect of early return to the Cabinet. But she was ready to back this choice. So too, eventually, was Leon.

And so to the Greek Presidency of 1988. It was virtually as content-free as had been its predecessor in 1983. The Council meeting in Rhodes on 2–3 December produced eight pages of prose, which on this occasion well deserved the label 'Euro-guff'. But almost all interest centred on Prime Minister Papandreou. He was simultaneously recovering from a well-publicized course of heart treatment in a London hospital and conducting an even more widely noticed affair of the heart with the comely air hostess who was destined to become his third wife. The 'well-informed' medical intelligence had even doubted whether he would be able to manage the ordeal of presiding over the Council. He more than got by, through a combination of guile and inertia. In later years he seemed to go from strength to strength, and on to triumphant re-election as Prime Minister at the age of seventy-four in October 1993.

But this, alas, was the moment when the British domestic outlook upon Europe was suddenly to become more turbulent. The cause was twice to spring from the recently re-nominated Jacques Delors himself. He chose to offer to the July 1988 session of the European Parliament his view that within ten years '80 per cent of our economic legislation, perhaps even fiscal and social as well', would be enacted by an embryo European government. This bombshell was dropped on the eve of a radio interview of Margaret Thatcher by the redoubtable Jimmy Young. She roundly dismissed Delors as a fantasist and his exaggerated claim as airy-fairy and extreme.

The whole episode starkly coloured a process already in train. The Prime Minister was due to deliver a major speech in late September at the College of Europe in Bruges. I had myself suggested this, months before, as a suitable platform for a 'positive' speech. So various drafts had been prepared in the Foreign Office. But as the date drew nearer there was some hesitation about submitting them. Somebody noted on 28 July, 'The Jimmy Young Show shows that the Number 10 market for constructive language on the Community may still be poor.' Texts were nevertheless exchanged during August, and by 1 September comments were invited on a draft produced by Charles Powell in Number 10. Some of my own initial notes speak for themselves:

> The draft tends to view the world as though we had not adhered to any of the Treaties. A stronger Europe does not mean the creation of a new Euro super-state but does, has and will require the sacrifice of political independence and the rights of national Parliaments. This is inherent in

the Treaties. . . . Reference to decisions reached by sovereign governments overlooks the Treaty provisions for majority voting.

On 7 September my principal private secretary (by now Stephen Wall) sent back a revised version, taking account of comments from me and others.

The next day, 8 September, Jacques Delors turned up in Brighton to tell the TUC that collective bargaining should henceforward take place at European level. The standing ovation which he received from the brethren fuelled the flames at Number 10. So the next revision from Charles Powell provoked another reply on my behalf. The latest Number 10 edition, said the accompanying note to my office, 'buys some 80 per cent of the suggestions in our 7 September version, which was strongly endorsed by the Chancellor and Lord Young. In the attached draft we are, in effect, trying to secure another 10 per cent. The remaining 10 per cent don't matter (and concern areas where Number 10 are probably incorrigible)'. At that point my people had to give up the tussle. I had myself departed for a tour of East and Central Africa on 10 September.

The speech as finally delivered contained a number of sections where the original Powell draft of 31 August had actually been strengthened. One well-known sentence will convey the toughening flavour of the changes. The 31 August draft, 'we have not embarked on the business of throwing back the frontiers of the state at home, only to see a European super-state getting ready to exercise a new dominance from Brussels,' had become, by 20 September, 'We have not successfully rolled back the frontiers of the state in Britain, only to see them reimposed at a European level, with a European super-state exercising a new dominance from Brussels.'

It was just this kind of phrase that underlined the negative impact of the speech when it was delivered on 20 September. In its description of the actuality of the ambitions of the Community the speech veered between caricature and misunderstanding. The picture of a 'European identikit' being imposed, 'ossified by endless regulation' (when very often a single Community regulation replaces twelve national ones) through 'decisions taken by an appointed bureaucracy' (when decisions are in fact taken by the Council of Ministers), was sheer fantasy. And to talk of the alternative of decisions being taken through 'willing and active co-operation between independent sovereign states' was to mis-understand or misrepresent the Community as it already existed and to inhibit its future in defiance of the texts that we had ourselves negotiated.

I was, of course, deeply dismayed by the Bruges speech. Its impact, at home as much as abroad, far exceeded my initial fears. At first I had thought, or at least hoped, that the gap between the rhetoric (at Bruges) and the pragmatic performances (from Copenhagen to Stuttgart) could and would go on being resolved in favour of practically sensible policies. But the effect was much closer to that illustrated in Dukas' overture to *The Sorcerer's Apprentice*: where Margaret had drawn the first bucket of Euro-scepticism from the well, others were only too ready to follow. Arguments which had been exposed as without foundation in long debates about accession, almost twenty years before, suddenly acquired renewed respectability. Margaret herself began to return, again and again, to the well which she had reopened. She began readopting arguments which she and I had had no difficulty in rebutting in debates over the Single European Act only a couple of years before.

I was driven finally to conclude that for Margaret the Bruges speech represented, subconsciously at least, her escape from the collective responsibility of her days in the Heath Cabinet – when European policy had arrived, as it were, with the rations. Keith Joseph had waited only six months from our election defeat in 1974 before making his Preston speech, in which he detached himself from the economic policies of the Heath government in which he had served. But Margaret had waited almost fifteen years to display her own distaste for the European policies which she had accepted as a member of that same government. I began to see her – and I do so even more clearly now – as a natural member of the gallant but misguided back-bench group of Enoch Powells, Robin Turtons and Derek Walker-Smiths, who had fought so long and hard against the European Communities Bill in 1971. Yet her deeds from day to day generally continued to belie that analysis. For she went on acting, for the moment at least, as though she was indeed the Prime Minister of a member-state of the European Community. And we had to continue conducting business on that basis. It was, I imagined, a little like being married to a clergyman who had suddenly proclaimed his disbelief in God. I can see now that this was probably the moment at which there began to crystallize the conflict of loyalty with which I was to struggle for perhaps too long.

Recounting this story offers a fresh insight, which I can appreciate now more deeply than I did then, into the increasingly curious way in which policy was being adjusted within government – most of all on the major questions. No longer did we have widely representative seminars or other gatherings of ministers and outsiders, on the basis of papers prepared by or for ministers. Such discussion did occur, of course, on nuts and bolts, day-to-day decisions about expenditure and legislation, but not often, if at all, on the broad-sweep questions of foreign or defence policy. George Younger (or Michael Heseltine before him) and I would meet pretty regularly and organize joint studies from time to time – but seldom now, on these large topics, with Number 10. And the relaxed Sunday-night talks at Number 10, an important way of comparing notes, which I had enjoyed as Chancellor, had ceased – either with me or with Nigel Lawson. So the Prime Minister had progressively curtailed Cabinet debate and cut herself off from private discussion with her principal ministers. This was one of the reasons, I realized in retrospect, why this pre-eminent question about our attitude towards the Community was being argued out through subordinates for the purpose of constructing a speech. Whoever was making the speech had the last word. No wonder 'coded messages' were coming into vogue.

I was not the only one to be baffled by what was going on. So too were the rank and file of the Conservative Party, in Parliament and in the country. Ever since Harold Macmillan's original commitment in 1962, the party leadership – Home, Heath, even Thatcher – had been taking and persuading us more and more firmly to a sensible European course. By contrast with our Labour opponents, who had twisted and turned on the issue for decades, we *were* the 'European party'. But, if that was the case, where were we going now? Was it conceivably possible to tap a vein of populist and nationalist opinion in the opposite sense, while staying true to our entrenched commitments? That was the question which I had to face directly in less than a month's time, when I replied to the foreign policy debate at our party conference in Brighton, on 13 October 1988. It was the last such debate to take place before the European election, due on 15 June 1989. The motion chosen for debate was unequivocally supportive of the pre-Bruges faith.

Predictably Ted Heath spoke and was very critical of the Bruges speech. He ridiculed the idea that Britain would lose its identity in an integrated Europe and dismissed the notion that a united Europe would be corporatist. I decided I had to tackle the central question directly, by trying to identify continuing common ground, and by interpreting the Prime Minister's speech in that sense, so far as I could. The task which I now had to perform in the field of foreign policy was a precise echo of that which I had attempted as Chancellor after Ted Heath had spoken in the economic debate at the 1981 conference. I began with one of the better quotes from Bruges: 'Our destiny is in Europe, as part of the

Community. That's what the Prime Minister said in Bruges. And that's why the shape and direction of the Community is of such importance to us all.'

But what sort of Europe? I asked. That's what the Bruges speech and Ted Heath's speech were all about. I addressed Ted directly: 'This conference knows that Ted Heath and I, and the rest of his Cabinet' (no need to mention Margaret by name), 'worked together to achieve our membership of the European Community. I helped steer through Parliament the legislation, but I did it as you did' (looking at Ted) 'from a conviction of where our country's interest lie. And the nation owes him a great debt of gratitude for that.' Ted was more than entitled to the round of applause that followed. I went on to explain, as Ted Heath had pointed out, that Margaret Thatcher and I together had negotiated, only three years before, the significant changes in the Single European Act which had bound Britain ever more closely into the Community. 'I made similar judgments'. I said, 'as a member of Ted Heath's government and I make them today as a member of Margaret Thatcher's. . . . The central goal remains the same, the one that has always succeeded in uniting our great party, to see a strong Britain in a strong Europe.'

I ended with a call for solid backing for our candidates in the European election, not just because Europe is where our home market lies, not just because our defence and security depend on a strong European pillar of the North Atlantic alliance. But 'above all because we need to shape the Europe-wide decisions which are going to affect directly the lives of our children and their children as well. Archimedes once said, "Give me a firm spot on which to stand, and I will move the world." For Britain,' I concluded, 'Europe is that place to stand.'

It was my last platform speech to a party conference. As with every such speech as Foreign Secretary I had offered a passionate but reasoned exposition of Britain's commitment to the European Community. And like every such speech it was received with a standing ovation. But Margaret had not been there to hear it. This must explain her sadly uncomprehending statement that she had never heard me define what she described as my 'misty Europeanism . . . an almost romantic longing for Britain to become part of some grandiose European consensus'.[2] For she had established the habit of attending the Thursday-morning debate and so supporting the Chancellor – in my day as in Nigel's. But Thursday afternoons, when foreign affairs were usually debated, she generally missed. It was the last daytime chance she had to work on her own speech for the following day. A couple of weeks passed before I had the chance to speak to Margaret about the Bruges speech, at one of our regular bilateral meetings, on 26 October. There were real risks, I said, that the speech was being interpreted as implying a new hostility in our attitude towards the Community. She did not accept this analysis. Her confidence in her fresh approach was growing fast. What the speech actually said, Margaret insisted, was rather different from some of the interpretations that had been placed upon it. Strictly speaking that may have been true. But in truth it was what the speech did say that was actually doing the damage. Even then, I was by no means alert to the full gravity of the change that was taking place.

CHAPTER THIRTY-SIX

FROM WEU TO IRA . . .

===

Cautionary Thoughts

The success of Margaret Thatcher's pre-election visit to Moscow, following the mould-breaking Reagan–Gorbachev Reykjavik Summit in November 1986, had pushed forward dramatically the frontiers of candour and debate in East–West relations. Mikhail Gorbachev's *glasnost* had been seen at its most convincing during Margaret Thatcher's uncensored fifty-minute interview on Russian television. But there remained a mass of detail to be conquered if solid progress was to be achieved on arms control or other practical issues.

For all this footslogging the West's undoubted leader, after Britain's initial role in helping to open the door, was the tireless George Shultz. In April 1987, within two weeks of our return from Moscow, Shultz was back in the Kremlin for three solid days' work. He was seeking to clarify and consolidate the many gains – on human rights and regional questions as well as on arms control – for which Reykjavik had pointed the way. Shultz had set out on this particular trip in face of declared opposition from 70 out of 100 members of the US Senate. NATO Foreign Ministers, to whom he reported in Brussels at the end of the week, were, in contrast, elated by the results of his Kremlin talks. An agreement for the worldwide elimination of INF weapons was now within reach.* It was to take the Shultz–Shevardnadze partnership most of the year to put a complete package together, just in time for the Washington Summit on 8 December.

Meanwhile there was much need for thought within Western ranks. How far would detente, if it came, call for changes in the balance of our

---

* At that stage it was not clear whether the INF agreement would cover only those of longer range (1000–5500 kilometres) or take in those of shorter range (500–1000 kilometres) as well. Over the next six weeks or so opinion hardened in favour of the simple conclusion LRINF *and* SRINF.

own alliance? How should we react, given the new Soviet attitude, to other chronic world problems, from the Afghan conflict to the Iran–Iraq War? As soon as the British election was out of the way, I had published, in booklet form, the texts of four controversial speeches* which I had made in the first half of the year on East–West relations. These were esentially designed to clear the way for NATO's four-point arms-control package, which we had been working out in 1986: a 50 per cent cut in superpower strategic nuclear weapons; a worldwide reduction (and later a ban) on medium-range (INF) nuclear weapons; a total ban on chemical weapons; a commitment to reduce the East–West imbalance of conventional weapons. I was confident that economic constraints would be a near-decisive influence on Gorbachev's policymaking. 'The God of War', I said, 'must eventually bow to the God of Mammon.'

I did not shrink from warning the United States of hazards that they had to avoid. They should take no precipitate action, I said, over the deployment of space weapons which might jeopardize the 1972 ABM Treaty. 'We have to accept', I said, in an echo of my 1985 SDI speech, 'that not everything technically possible may be affordable or prudent.' On chemical weapons too, Britain had put forward an inspection scheme that was more acceptable to the Russians than to the Americans – but none the worse for that. US critics had been roused by both these ideas: my old friend Cap Weinberger with characteristic restraint, and my former sparring partner Richard Perle with no less characteristic ferocity. I had no objection to that. It was, as Chris Meyer, my head of News Department, used to say, 'good de-poodlification': it directly challenged those who saw the Thatcher administration in some mistaken sense as Reagan's poodle.

The European Defence Pillar

My other theme at this time had emerged most clearly in my Brussels speech on 16 March: the need for Europe to be thinking and doing much more about its own defences. 'Europe no longer dominates American thinking', I said, 'as much as it did in the past.' We need to be alert to transatlantic trends which 'might diminish our security – perhaps not today or tomorrow, but possibly in the longer term'. Closer

* In Brussels, Chicago and London, between 27 January and 7 May 1987. Published as *Down to Earth Diplomacy* (HMSO for FCO, 1988).

European defence links, I emphasized, should not be seen as an alternative to NATO but as a strengthening of the European pillar of the Atlantic alliance. George Younger, Defence Secretary since West-land, was as ready as Michael Heseltine had been to identify Western European Union as the vehicle for closer defence co-operation in Europe. And he backed my plea for increasingly close partnership between Europe's two nuclear powers, Britain and France.

This part of the Brussels speech had to be closely negotiated with Number 10, for Margaret could never be trusted not to snort impatiently whenever the three letters WEU crossed her path. By the time of her Bruges speech, on 20 Septemeber 1988, she had relapsed, and was warning expressly 'against any development (as a result of Franco-German initiatives) of the Western European Union'. But eighteen months earlier, at least for an interval of time, we had secured her reluctant consent to my Brussels commendation of a growing role for WEU. This, said the *Independent* on 19 March 1987, was 'an important development in British policy'. So indeed it was – or should have been. But it had not evolved as a result of any orderly collective discussion between ministers. It was the outcome of a fragile bargain about the contents of one speech, albeit one of some significance. It was an uneasy way to determine a nation's most important strategic choices.

The very issue was to recur more practically within a matter of months. For one of the topics that had been upon the international agenda now for eight years was the bloody conflict between Iran and Iraq. The United Nations was the world's best weapon – almost the only one – for tackling this, but its effectiveness very largely depended on the extent to which the five permanent members (including ourselves and France, as well as the two superpowers and China) were able to work together. Some progress towards such partnership, which was historically rare, had been made during the past year. This was the result of a move by Britain's UN ambassador Sir John Thomson. He had invited the permanent-five ambassadors to an unscripted private gather-ing in his apartment. Out of this there had developed over the months a regular informal meeting of the five, under British chairmanship. (Only after two years did the French, not too surprisingly, suggest that this informal 'world presidency' should not be in British hands in perpetuity. So the 'office' began to rotate.)

This initiative led to an even more significant meeting, in the margins of the UN General Assembly meeting of 1987. I attended (with our ambassador, Crispin Tickell, who had recently taken John Thomson's place) the first meeting for at least fifteen years of the Foreign Ministers of all five permanent members of the Security Council. It took the form of lunch in the office suite of the Secretary General, Perez de Cuellar. The function had been first suggested, with my authority, by the British ambassador. It had all the awkwardness of an impromptu occasion. It was by no means clear who, if anyone, was 'in charge'. George Shultz and Eduard Shevardnadze were at ease with each other. There was a certain awkwardness between Jean-Bernard Raymond (Chirac's Foreign Minister) and myself: was I to take the chair, in succession to our ambassador? Or was he, since France was – by chance – in the rotating chair of the Security Council that month? Or Perez de Cuellar, since he was hosting the lunch? The Chinese Minister Qian Qichen and I were natural partners, with Hong Kong as our engagement ring.

In the upshot it was more like a Quaker meeting than anything else, with nobody in charge. We weren't even sure who was taking the record. But we were able to hammer out agreement that the Security Council's call to end the Iran–Iraq conflict (set out in UNSC Resolution 598) should now be reinforced by an arms embargo. Somehow it became my job to carry away to an expectant world the piece of paper recording the agreement. A full year was to pass before a ceasefire began to take hold. But throughout those twelve months I often derived pleasure from my memories of that messy meeting. It was a moment of history when the five of us groped our way uncertainly, across an informal polyglot luncheon table, towards the establishment of at least some sort of world authority for peace.

At a more modest level of things it was by no means so easy. During the spring and summer, Iran had been stepping up attacks on international shipping by laying mines in the Gulf. Britain, France and, primarily of course, the United States had been pressed to provide a mine-sweeping force to keep the Gulf waters clear. We were at first reluctant. Our Armilla patrol – normally one destroyer and two frigates – had been escorting British shipping through the Straits of Hormuz and in the southern half of the Gulf for most of the 1980s. But Margaret Thatcher, George Younger and I all had some doubt about engaging the Royal Navy in a joint operation of this kind. There was recurrent anxiety about American judgment in face of provocation from Iran.

In mid-August, however, another American supertanker struck an Iranian mine. More mines were being found throughout the Gulf. I was on holiday in France but in constant touch by telephone. We decided we needed to despatch two mine-sweepers, if only for the peace of mind of our own shipping. So, shortly afterwards, did the French. We followed through a plan which George Younger had discussed earlier in the year with his French and Dutch opposite numbers. The whole European participation was now transformed into a Western European Union operation. The WEU Fleet would have a separate identity and a separate command from the United States. The idea quickly attracted comprehensive WEU support. Belgians, Dutch and Italians would join the French and British in providing sweepers. German sweepers, constitutionally banned from deployment outside the NATO area, filled some of the gaps others had left in NATO ranks. And land-locked Luxembourg provided cash. Command of the WEU contingent would rotate from nation to nation.

Everyone in European capitals, including our own Defence Ministry, was well pleased with the swift launch of this first WEU joint operation. But the pleasure was short-lived. Margaret Thatcher promptly took umbrage at these arrangements. For her the notion that any Royal Navy ship should be under command of any 'foreigner' – unless he were an Anglo-Saxon – was quite unthinkable. We explained to her that this was no great novelty. 'NATO allies', she was told, 'often operate under mixed command structures. The Royal Dutch and Royal Navies, in particular, are virtually one service for such purposes.' But all in vain. At the cost of much goodwill the arrangements already accepted had to be unstitched. Happily all the other contingents, except the French, were prepared to enlist under Royal Naval command. So the WEU operation retained its identity. But it was another of those moments when the Thatcher touch was less sensitive than it could have been in a European context. A lot of the psychological benefit of this joint operation had been dissipated.

December Drama

Shultz and Shevardnadze were able to avoid such contretemps. Throughout the autumn of 1987 their teams were hard at work in Moscow, Geneva and Washington. The two Foreign Ministers spent many days in face-to-face negotiations. By the beginning of December the INF Treaty, which provided for the complete elimination of intermediate nuclear weapons, was ready. Gorbachev and Shevardnadze set off for the Washington Summit. *En route* on 7 December they had a short stop-over in Britain, at Margaret's invitation, at the RAF station at Brize Norton. Margaret and I each had short talks with our opposite numbers. Kenneth Baker made a bid for international status by being on hand to escort Raisa Gorbachev to a local primary school. And we all had lunch together. The occasion helped to underline the part played by the Gorbachev–Thatcher relationship in bringing the two leaders together for the enormously successful Washington Summit.

At the end of the week, on 11 December, the NATO Foreign Ministers met for their annual Council in Brussels. The INF Treaty signed by Gorbachev and Reagan in Washington was one for implementation by the whole alliance. So with the Foreign Ministers of the other 'basing countries' – those where American INF missiles were deployed (UK, West Germany, Belgium, the Netherlands, Italy) – a supplemental treaty had to be signed. This gave the Soviet Union the right to conduct on-site inspections of Cruise missile sites in Britain. The INF Treaty was indeed an agreement without precedent: the first occasion in history when two rival alliances had agreed to destroy an entire class of weapons.

The following week was marked by two traumatic domestic events. The first was an act of God, the second self-inflicted. On 14 December Willie Whitelaw was at a carol service at St Margaret's, Westminster, when he suffered a minor stroke. He was seventy years old. The medical advice was inevitable, and Willie, wisely encouraged by his wife Celia, did not hesitate to take it. By the following Sunday evening (as it happened my sixty-first birthday), the Whitelaws were able to receive Elspeth and myself at their London house off Cadogan Square. Willie himself was surprisingly well – shaken but already evidently relaxed by his own decision to resign. Two Wykehamists are not necessarily very good at communicating with each other on such an occasion. But I hope we left Willie in no doubt of my debt of gratitude for his support so often in the past. Particularly in my Treasury years, Margaret and I were often the joint beneficiaries of his support. But increasingly, as the years went by, it was his cautionary voice that steered us away from reckless proximity to rocks. We did not always agree, and his view did not always prevail. But time and again he provided that mixture of ballast and yeast which secured second thoughts – and often ensured that they were fruitful. The consequences of his self-confessed reluctance to intervene in the Westland drama were ample warning of how much the government would miss him in the future. For he was unable to fulfil his own hope of injecting occasional wisdom in the years that followed his retirement. He never had been a natural member of Margaret's inner circle, and once out he did not find it attractive or easy to reinsert himself. The virtually total loss of Willie Whitelaw's wisdom was a grave and unavoidable blow to the fortunes of the Thatcher government.

The second blow, however, was one that the government had long been determined to inflict upon itself. For on Thursday, 17 December, I responded, without giving it any special thought, to the three-line Whip which required me to support the second reading of the Local Government Finance Bill – the poll-tax bill. So it was that, as one of the government majority of seventy-two, I helped to launch Margaret Thatcher's ill-fated 'flagship' – the Community Charge. The poll-tax was not an issue on which Willie had been playing an especially cautionary role. For the idea had been born and was still keenly supported (by Conservatives) in Scotland, Willie's native land. It is ironic that almost the only occasion when Margaret Thatcher allowed herself to be swayed by Scottish opinion was the time when her populist judgment went most seriously astray. From this innocent and unthinking enactment of the poll-tax grew the domestic storm which was blowing at gale force by the time my own European drama came to a head almost three years later.

Second Soviet Visit

Meanwhile, on the Eastern front, progress continued. And the alliance was holding together well. My second official visit to the Soviet Union as Foreign Secretary, on 14–17 February 1988, was this time to take in Kiev as well as Moscow. My talks with Shevardnadze – more than ten hours altogether – greatly extended the range of topics we could discuss in particularly frank dialogue. Elspeth and I (and interpreter) enjoyed the intimacy of supper *en famille* with Eduard and Nanuli Shevardnadze in their official Moscow flat. This occasion was without precedent, but became part of the Shevardnadze style of hospitality extended later to the Shultzes and the Genschers. Shevardnadze talked a lot about his time as state boss in his native state, where he had encouraged schools to teach in the several minority languages of Georgia.

My two and a half hours with Gorbachev next day in the Kremlin's St Catherine's Hall were equally candid and generally friendly. But there were moments of tension. More than once Gorbachev spoke to me as though I was the 'hard cop' half of the Thatcher–Howe team. It was an unexpected role reversal. He was upset, for example, by parts of my speech at Shevardnadze's lunch the previous day. It had been fully reported in the Moscow press (*glasnost* at work). He disliked the firmness with which I pressed Russia to quit Afghanistan and reproached me for missing their anouncement the previous week that withdrawal would start in May. (I had seen the report, of course.) I had also provoked him on the subject of chemical weapons. The Russians had recently disclosed figures about their stocks of such horrors. Our intelligence people – and the Americans – had no doubt that these figures were much too low, by a factor of five or six. I put this to Gorbachev. He reacted angrily. He plunged his hand into the zip-up leather folder in which he kept his notes. He pulled out a bundle and stabbed at the papers with his other hand. 'I asked my people for these figures specifically,' he said, 'since I know you are always making this point. And I can assure you that these figures are the correct figures, as given to me.'

There was clearly a limit to my licence to accuse the Soviet head of government of not telling the truth. But to this day I have wondered: was Gorbachev deceiving me – or was he being deceived? He was certainly a powerful witness. I ended by emphasizing how much Mrs Thatcher was looking forward to his promised return visit to Britain. I agreed with him that it would need careful preparation. 'Because', as I said, 'you and Margaret Thatcher are both like Stakhanovites – determined to squeeze the maximum out of every minute of your time in each other's company.' (My one term's Russian history at school, more than forty years before, had armed me with the word: Stakhanov was a miner in the Stalin era, whose name came to symbolize hard work because of the incentive scheme he had invented.) Gorbachev laughed heartily. 'I like the word "Stakhanovite",' he said. 'That was well chosen – and a good note on which to end our very useful talk.'

Before leaving Moscow we saw a little more of *glasnost* in action. My television interview with Russian journalists was broadcast uncut. We had meetings with dissidents and refuseniks – less reassuring than I could have wished. Places of worship were still tightly controlled, but more and more of these brave people were being allowed to leave the country. And Elspeth and I led our party on a late-night visit to the fledgling Bluebird Jazz Club. We didn't feel tempted to take the floor.

For our journey to Kiev we were accompanied by our ambassador and his wife, Bryan and Ruth Cartledge. Ruth had been a member of my Bow Group research team on the Welsh economy thirty years before. Bryan was one of our top Sovietologists, playing a key role in maximizing the Thatcher–Gorbachev relationship. In Kiev, we were all put up in a *fin-de-siècle* government guesthouse, midway between the Central Committee hotel and the Supreme Soviet ('Parliament') building. I could never get used to the contrast between the grandeur of certain Russian buildings and the 1940s 'utility'-style barrenness of their furniture, fittings and service. And here it was again.

My courtesy call on the council of Ministers was dominated by a very sterile twenty-five minute 'briefing' from Deputy Prime Minister Mrs M. A. Orlik. Ukraine's veteran Prime Minister Scherbitsky – the man responsible for the massive open-air museum of military hardware and the grotesque skyscraping 'statue' on the outskirts of Kiev – was away in Moscow. Mrs Orlik half-apologized for the length of her remarks. I assured her that she had no need to worry. 'I feel entirely at home,' I said. 'I have, after all, been sitting in the same position directly opposite a woman Prime Minister in London for the last nine years.'

Our visit to the Maxim Gorky Machine Tool factory took me back to the dark untidy chaos of a British steel works forty years before. I asked a drab meeting of collective managers, 'What message would you give to Mikhail Gorbachev, if you had the chance?' 'Give us more freedom', they said, 'to take more decisions for ourselves.' I might have hoped to hear the same thing from Archimandrite Filaret, head of the Orthodox Church. He received us in St Vladimir's Cathedral – not unlike my first encounter fifteen months later in the Bishop's Palace at Wells with the next Archbishop of Canterbury. The Archimandrite, inevitably black-bearded, looked and sounded like Jehovah. His Church was just celebrating its millennium. We expected a historic discourse. But no. He launched forthwith into another Kremlinologically correct lecture on the West's exclusive responsibility for the Cold War, the coming nuclear winter – and the rest. We were moved, however, by the liveliness of worshippers, young and old, in the breathtakingly beautiful cathedral. And it is hard to forget the tone in which one sharp but dispirited Kiev lady told us, 'You must understand that when we Russians describe ourselves as such, we are identifying not a nationality but a fate.'

Death on the Rock

I returned to London to find myself caught up in events of high and unwelcome drama. Intelligence had reached me quite early in the year that an IRA 'active service unit' was planning a murderous strike against British troops stationed in Gibraltar. The small, inexperienced Gibralter police force needed and asked for specialist help against a threat of this kind. After carefully considering expert advice, I authorized the necessary SAS presence in the colony.

The IRA plan unfolded as we had been led to expect. The target was the Tuesday morning guard-mounting ceremony, which regularly involved about fifty soldiers before a sizeable tourist audience in the close vicinity of the Convent (the quaintly named government house) and of a school and an old people's home. By about 3 p.m. on Sunday, 6 March the three known IRA terrorists, who had been under surveillance (two of them had previous terrorist convictions), had convened around a white Renault car, which one of them had earlier that day parked in the area where the guard-mounting usually takes place. At that time, some sixty-four kilograms of Semtex high explosive were stowed not in the white Renault but in a white Ford Fiesta still over the Spanish border in Marbella. The IRA have never denied that their 'active service unit' intended this massive charge, in one or other of their vehicles, for explosion on the parade ground on Tuesday, 8 March. (A bomb half this size had four months before killed eleven and injured sixty at a Memorial Day Parade at Enniskillen.) One of the terrorists had already been observed making adjustments to the parked Renault. The SAS men, who were now following the terrorists' movements closely, had every reason to believe that that was the car which contained the would-be fatal charge. There was also good reason to fear that these unscrupulous and dangerous terrorists would be armed and would have no hesitation in using their weapons.

That is the background against which I told the House of Commons, in course of a statement on the following afternoon, Monday, 7 March:

> All three left the scene and started to walk back towards the border. On their way ... they were challenged by the security forces. When challenged they made movements which led military personnel operating in support of the Gibraltar police to conclude that their own lives and the lives of others were under threat. In the light of this response, they were shot. Those killed were subsequently found not to have been carrying arms. The parked Renault car was subsequently dealt with by a military bomb-disposal team. It has now been established that it did not contain an explosive device.

The detailed candour of my statement, made exactly twenty-four hours after the incident, deserves to be noted. It was the essential foundation of the case made by and on behalf of the SAS men when their conduct came to be examined in detail by the Gibraltar coroner's inquest, some months later – and it was that case that was upheld by the jury's verdict of 'lawful killing'.

There is a second, more curious, reason to note the terms of my statement. In one respect, it was totally at odds with the facts of the matter as they had been understood by almost everybody (and reported by the media) during the preceding twenty-four hours. Almost until I spoke, everyone had believed the initial press report that the Renault had contained a bomb. That is what I myself had believed when I had left my office after approving the first draft of my statement earlier that day – and indeed until the moment, just before 2 p.m., when I returned to my office to check the final draft. Only then did I first learn that there was, as yet, *no* bomb. (It was not until the following day that the Marbella stock of Semtex was finally discovered.) My statement had to be frantically recast. It was inevitably delayed. We could not comply with the rule of the House to get a copy of my text to the Opposition spokesman George Robertson (the intelligent and responsible MP for Hamilton) by 3 p.m. It was only as we were entering the Commons Chamber together at 3.25 p.m. that he received his copy of my final text – and from me personally, in a brief oral exchange, the true facts.

How on earth did it come about that we – the 'authorities' – had been unaware of those facts for so long? Because, unbelievably, we had not put in place before the event a sufficiently foolproof communications system to ensure that the full official truth came through to London from those on the ground in Gibraltar. We had all seized on, as truth, the first unofficial media 'news' that had hit the air – plausible as it was ('there was a bomb in the car'). The story illustrates, although in a slightly different way, the same dilemma as I experienced over GCHQ: there is nothing more difficult than the public relations handling of an operation or activity that involves 'moving from darkness into light'. Literally, until the SAS shots were fired, we had been – and had rightly been obliged to remain – in the complete darkness of a total security black-out. Then suddenly the story was on every news bulletin around the world – and, to make it worse, the story as it emerged was *wrong*. We had made no plans for the arrival of 'daylight', first for the establishment and then for reporting of accurate facts. Once again, and for psychologically understandable reasons, we had thought too little about the right way of publicizing a secret. We thus appeared to be incompetent as well as inaccurate. It is small wonder that we were suspected too of deliberate (even if quite pointless) deceit.

Trial by Television

Now it was for the facts to be established and judged by the Gibraltar coroner's court. But, before that court had been able to complete its work, Thames Television, with the approval of the Independent Broadcasting Authority, transmitted on 28 April a programme entitled *Death on the Rock*. This forty-three-minute programme purported to cover exactly the same ground as the inquest: was the killing of the terrorists lawful or unlawful? It was put out in defiance of my request to the IBA that it should certainly not be broadcast before the conclusion of the inquest.

In the real court, which did not record its verdict until 30 September, the proceedings were conducted on the basis of a clear exposition of the law to the jury. Lord Hailsham, the former Lord Chancellor, quoted the key passages in the subsequent Lords debate:

– A person may use such force as is reasonable in the prevention of crime. . . . No criminal liability is incurred even though such force results in the death of another. . . .
– In determining whether the force used was reasonable, the court will take into account all the circumstances . . . including the seriousness of the evil to be prevented and the possibility of preventing it by other means. . . .
– The reasonableness of the force must be assessed in relation to facts which the defendant knew *or believed* to have existed.[1]

The inquest jury's verdict was given only after evidence had been given, very willingly, by each of the SAS soldiers concerned – and after all the other evidence had been tested by cross-examination on their behalf. And the verdict of the properly instructed jury was quite clear: opening fire upon and killing the IRA's self-styled 'active service unit' (whose intentions, in the later words of Baroness Warnock, were 'totally lethal') constituted, in the circumstances of this case, a justifiable response within the rule of law.

I could not, of course, have been sure of such a favourable verdict when I had to react (in April 1988) to the advance news of the Thames programme. But I had no doubt that it should not be allowed to go ahead. So I wrote, in confidence, to Lord Thomson of Monifieth, chairman of the IBA, requesting a ruling to that effect.

First, I pointed out, if the inquest had been taking place in the UK, then Thames Television would have been *obliged by law* (on the ground of contempt of court) to postpone the broadcast until after the inquest. Since news, indeed tapes, of the broadcast were bound to reach Gibraltar (and so the jury), there was an overwhelming moral and practical reason to apply the same rules in this case. Second, the production of this programme would be directly contrary to the recommendations of the Salmon Committee, which had been appointed to consider television coverage of the background to the 1967 Aberfan Tribunal (before which I had appeared). Salmon had reported that 'the Press, Television and Radio have always considered that once any type of tribunal has been appointed' – in the present case of course an inquest was already on the way – 'it is inappropriate for them to conduct anything in the nature of a parallel inquiry. . . . We regard it as of the utmost importance that this restraint should continue to be exercised.'[2]

I could not then, and cannot now, see any answer to either of these arguments. But the IBA were unimpressed. And so too, to my surprise and dismay, was the panel, Lord Windlesham and Richard Rampton QC, later appointed by the IBA to consider the case in retrospect. For, as Robin Day later pointed out, the programme *was* 'unfair and unbalanced',[3] contrary to the Broadcasting Act – and bound to be so. There is no doubt that it pointed to the opposite conclusion from the inquest – in Windlesham's words, to the 'real possibility that the terrorists had been unlawfully killed'. And it did so for the unsurprising reason that not one word of evidence was recorded from any of the soldiers who stood accused. That was quite simply because neither government nor SAS soldiers were in a position to give evidence to any *pre*-inquest television programme, for so long as the soldiers faced a possible verdict of unlawful killing and the consequent risk of prosecution for murder. Those responsible for the transmission had made – and been determined to make – the programme without having heard half of the evidence and at a time when they could not have had it available. I cannot for the life of me understand how the result can possibly be regarded as responsible. Nor to this day do I see any possible, let alone reasonable, rebuttal to my argument that Thames Television (and the IBA) ought voluntarily to have postponed *Death on the Rock* until after the inquest.

The strength of my feeling on this point explains the vigour of my initial reaction to the Windlesham Report (published on 26 January 1989), which I described on the *Today* programme as a 'report of television, by television, for television'. As I later made clear to these two authors, I did not intend this as an attack on the integrity of either of them; but I still share the view expressed by many others that it was hardly propitious for the making of such a report to have been led by someone formerly so closely engaged in the television industry.*

When faced with terrorism, the security forces, the courts, the governments – of all challenged societies – have hard choices to make. 'Their decisions', as I said shortly after the murderous tragedies of Milltown and Anderstown, 16 and 19 March 1988, 'are open to challenge, debate and appeal. Not so those of the terrorists. They act as self-appointed judges, jury and executioners. There is no Court of Appeal from their verdicts, no reprieve from their sentences. Our response to terrorism is governed by law and not by political convenience.' Is it too much to hope that in the same context the response of the media should be governed by self-restraint? Robin Day has reminded us that:

> a wise jurist† once said that there were three great domains of human conduct. The first is where our actions are limited or forbidden by law. Then there is the domain of free personal choice. But between these two is a third domain, that in which there is neither law nor unfettered freedom. This is the domain of 'obedience to the unenforceable' where people do right although there is no one and nothing to make them do right but themselves.

Day himself commented, 'That is the spirit which should govern television and should decide its responsibility to society, particularly to a society threatened by unreason, by violence and by terrorism.'⁴ Are not those who risk their lives for our safety entitled to expect, from media and public alike, the kind of support without which there can be no certainty of success against terrorism?

* Lord Windlesham, a former Bow Group chairman and Cabinet colleague (in the Heath government), had been managing director of Grampian Television (1967–70) and managing director, later chairman, of Associated Television (1974–81).
† Lord Moulton (1844–1921), Liberal MP, Lord Justice and later Lord of Appeal [Robin Day's footnote].

CHAPTER THIRTY-SEVEN

... FROM NATO TO KGB

Change at the White House

Within a fortnight of my return from Kiev, Margaret Thatcher and I were in Brussels for the first NATO heads of government Summit for six years. The proceedings fell into two distinct halves. On the first day we wrestled with a real issue: how far should NATO, would NATO be able to, retain any non-strategic nuclear weapons in Europe? The INF Treaty was going to eliminate all missiles with ranges of between 500 and 5500 kilometres. We were resistant to the idea of phasing out all the short-range nuclear weapons(SNF) as well. For this 'third zero' would, as we then believed, deprive the alliance of any real flexibility of nuclear response to a Soviet threat. If this narrowing of choice was to be avoided, it would be necessary at some early date to modernize or update the alliance's short-range nuclear weaponry.

The West Germans – or at least some of them – were unhappy at this prospect, for many such weapons might well be stationed – and used – only on German soil. The practical politics of this dilemma intellectually divided the West German coalition. Christian Democrat Chancellor Kohl was ready to recognize – and, if necessary, affirm in public – the need for modernization. Free Democrat (Liberal) Foreign Minister Genscher would far rather postpone, better still avoid, the recognition of any such need. The Americans, of course, agreed with us on this. So too, more or less, did the rest of the alliance. But, as so often, they were reluctant to say so. On the first day, the search for a communiqué formula that could accommodate this range of opinions had not prospered.

So, again as so often, the purely social and well-wined dinner of Foreign Ministers had to continue the work into the night. Most of the cast were silent, if not somnolent – and anxious to call it a day. But Shultz, Genscher and Howe felt compelled to keep up the search for compromise. Shultz and Genscher didn't always find it easy to achieve that. So it fell to the British to mediate. On such occasions the 'master' of the negotiating language, English, was always regarded as a walking thesaurus of suitable synonyms. Our three placements at the long table were miles apart from each other. Verbal attrition eventually produced a toneless compromise: 'a strategy of deterrence based upon an appropriate mix of adequate and effective nuclear and conventional forces, which will *continue to* be kept up to date *where* necesary'. The settlement finally depended upon our inserting the words 'continue to' and 'where' in place of 'if'. Such is the raw material of history!

Next day, the heads of government had only to endorse our text. And the morning was free for a fascinating, and in the end very moving, debate about the future of democratic Europe between the sixteen elected leaders of the Atlantic world. Inevitably it fell to Ronald Reagan to wind up the proceedings. As that moment came, the President – sitting next to us – laid aside his customary little stack of prompt cards and whispered something to George Shultz: 'I think I'll take this one on the wing, George.' As George told me after the meeting, he was for a moment anxious. He needn't have worried. For Reagan's ten-minute extempore tribute to the unique quality of our democratic alliance and its potential strength for world peace was of a quality that I could not possibly reproduce. Shultz may have been, indeed was, the brooding intelligence behind American foreign policy. But Reagan's stock of principle, and his ability to express it, should not be discounted. An audience of some of the hardest-boiled politicians and most conference-scarred diplomats in the world was deeply and visibly moved. I noticed several handkerchiefs being put away. We all felt a new spring in our step as we left for our aeroplanes – and a fresh respect for the Great Communicator. The world had needed his leadership if Mikhail Gorbachev's courage was to receive a sufficient response.

President Reagan was back in Europe only three months later, on 30–31 May 1988, for his Moscow Summit with Gorbachev. The public aspects of this, in particular, built skilfully on Margaret Thatcher's success of a year before. There was no spectacular breakthrough, but the START negotiations were kept on course, and Gorbachev and Shevardnadze were encouraged with the important new international thinking that they were to unveil in speeches in the UN General Assembly later in the year. Regional questions from Afghanistan to Angola, from South-east Asia to the Middle East were all being nudged towards solution. And seeds were sown for the vast and unforeseen European changes that were yet to come.

Back in London after Moscow, the Reagans were entertained soon after arrival to a small 'family' dinner at Number 10. As the inevitable photo-opportunity was taking place at the start of our meal, Ronald Reagan was clearly at ease. 'As our Lord said at the Last Supper,' he joked to one of the television crews, 'if you want to be in the picture, you'd better be on my side of the table.' The next day saw him performing in quite different style to a distinguished audience in Guildhall. Six years before, in 1982, he had told a packed parliamentary audience in the Royal Gallery, Westminster of the long haul which he foresaw in relations with the 'evil empire'. Now he was reporting back to a City audience the opening up of the East, towards freedom and partnership. It was a characteristically confident, yet modest, performance. The President of the United States was deservedly acclaimed in the heart of London.

The first half of 1988 was marred by the sudden death of my brother Colin, still a teaching consultant at King's College Hospital. He had been a widower for eleven years, with all four of his children now through university. Some happy instinct had prompted us to invite him to Chevening for lunch on the Sunday before he died. This last link with our common past was broken at a time when world events were slowing a little. The East–West agenda certainly moved less quickly as the US Presidential election came to dominate the rest of 1988. Peace of a kind finally began to take hold in the Iran–Iraq conflict. The ceasefire called for by UNSC Resolution 598 came into force on 20 August 1988. William Waldegrave had just taken over from David Mellor the delicate task of overseeing this hopeful development.* Meanwhile the British economy seemed to be going from strength to strength, with Nigel Lawson's second tax-cutting Budget in the spring of 1988. I had felt no need to become any more engaged than I had been in the Budget-making process, at a time when all the indications seemed to be set fair. Tax cuts of £6000 million, dramatic as they seemed, looked safe enough alongside a Budget surplus that was twice as high. I was drawing upon this record of apparently unalloyed success to preach Britain's economic example around the globe. We had all begun, I fear, to make speeches which sounded a little as though we had learned to walk upon water. But, beneath the surface, monetary growth and inflation were moving sharply up. A day of reckoning, with which we had ourselves failed to reckon, could not be indefinitely delayed.

---

* The ceasefire and its consequences furnished the background to the prolonged public inquiry subsequently undertaken by Lord Justice Scott in 1993–4.

With 1989 came the Bush administration. We had all got to know George Bush during his eight years as Vice-President. I liked him and respected him. Already he had a formidable record of public service. At one time I had hoped that a new Presidency might signal a fresh, more robust, approach to America's burgeoning federal deficit, for George Bush had several times agreed very strongly with my suggestion that the deficit simply had to be reduced. But that notion had been decisively buried on the Bush campaign trail. The new President's encouragement to voters to 'watch my lips – no new taxes' struck me as a reckless, and probably unnecessary, curtailment of his own room for manoeuvre. We expected no surprises in the field of foreign policy. The departure of George Shultz was something that I regretted enormously, for his rock-like, thoughtful stability had been the keystone of the alliance. But no more than Ronald Reagan could he be expected to last for ever. And we had already come to know his successor, Jim Baker, as a member of the Reagan administration – first as White House Chief of Staff and then as Treasury Secretary. So here too it looked as though continuity would be the order of the day.

But we reckoned without three developments. In the first place George Bush – and Jim Baker – wanted to escape from the shadows of their predecessors. One perceived part of that inheritance, so it was said, was Ronald Reagan's tendency to take almost too serious note of Margaret Thatcher's instincts and anxieties. US administrators had seen – or displayed – examples of that on several occasions, from Grenada to Libya, from Camp David to Zamora Machel. George Bush would want to establish himself as his own man. Even in human terms, it would have been surprising if his reaction to Margaret's style of conversation had been as compatible as Ronald Reagan's. Reagan was indeed one of the few men with whom Margaret's tendency to orate was tempered by deference. Gorbachev was another. George Bush was deferred to much less often, if at all.

The second reason for difference was a real conviction on the part of US policymakers that relations with Europe could not sensibly be too dependent upon the compatibilities of Anglo-Saxon instinct. The United Kingdom was only one of five medium-sized European nations, and by no means the most successful – or influential in continental politics. So neither Bush nor Baker was likely to accept the thesis, which Margaret Thatcher has re-enunciated, that 'the ties of blood, language, culture and values which bound Britain and America were the only firm basis for US policy in the West'.[1] The third factor that was different was Jim

Baker's own personality. He was a more pragmatic, intuitive and restless – even impatient – man than George Shultz. He was more inclined, by temperament, to be looking for a 'deal'. And where more natural to do so than over problems with allies?

These new factors quite soon became manifest. The first European leader to visit President Bush in Washington was not Margaret Thatcher but Chancellor Kohl (Margaret had actually seen President-elect Bush not many weeks before on a farewell Washington visit to outgoing President Reagan). It was not long before President Bush referred in public (in Mainz, on 31 May) to the 'partnership in leadership' between Americans and Germans. It was no use our reacting to practically understandable nuances of this kind as though we were being jilted.

New Thinking at NATO

We still had to manage the same issues within NATO as we had been able to finesse at the Brussels Summit in 1988. But, not least because of the steady improvement in the East–West climate, Margaret was becoming increasingly isolated personally in her commitment to the view that short-range (less than 500 kilometres) land-based missiles (SNF) were essential to the flexibility of NATO's defensive response. Our own soldiers – and George Younger himself – were becoming steadily less attracted by tactical nuclear weapons of this kind. Their role could be performed, for example, by Sea-Launched Cruise Missiles or Tactical Air-to-Surface Missiles or indeed 'ordinary' bombers. So the intellectual argument against the total elimination – or non-replacement – of short-range land-based missiles (the 'third zero') was becoming ever less convincing. Yet Margaret persisted in attaching huge importance to the continuance of land-based nuclear weaponry. The alternative she described as the 'denuclearization' of Europe – an event which she would denounce as vigorously as Denis Healey used to warn of the hazards of 'nuclear winter'. They were not comparable.

So NATO's centre of gravity was shifting rapidly. It was due to be tested quite early in the year, for on 7 March talks between the two alliances on conventional armed forces in Europe were due to open in Vienna. It was my function there (my name had been chosen by lot) to speak first on behalf of the whole of NATO immediately after Shevardnadze's opening speech for the Warsaw Pact. The main part of my speech was quite straightforward. Each side was laying out a substantial opening bid for conventional-force reductions. This was the start of months of negotiation.

Shevardnadze, however, had introduced a second element, skilfully designed to split NATO wide open. He proposed immediate, separate negotiations on the reduction of tactical nuclear weapons in Europe. I made it clear in my reply that this topic was right outside the Conference's terms of reference. 'The military carousel could not be slowed down,' I said (for the moment echoing Margaret), 'by hastening the denuclearization of Europe'. On behalf of all NATO members I made plain our determination to go ahead within two years with modernization of tactical nuclear weapons. But already this position – agreed upon by NATO less than a year before – was looking fragile, all the more so when Hans-Dietrich Genscher, the very next day, said that his country would be ready to endorse early separate negotiations on short-range nuclear weapons. It was going to be very difficult to hold the position at the next NATO Summit at the end of May.

The Vienna meeting, the first of two that spring, was the occasion for much wider-ranging East–West discussions and prediction. We decided to mark the occasion by the publication of the Cyril Foster Memorial Lecture on Soviet Foreign Policy, which I had given in Oxford not long before.[2] Among other things, I had suggested ways in which Soviet 'new thinking' could help to create 'the conditions for a genuine "common European home"' – of which Gorbachev had been speaking – 'instead of a Soviet-dominated "common European dacha"'. Three of the points I made deserved another look: readiness to tear down the barriers to the movement of people, including the Berlin wall; real willingness to eliminate massive Soviet stocks of chemical weapons; an end to KGB subversive activities: their 'secret offensive overseas', I said, 'continues unabated and has even perhaps intensified'.

These last two points aroused fresh Soviet anger at the line being taken by 'hard man Howe'; and the first provoked the *Guardian* to denounce me for reckless fantasy-mongering. I have to confess that even I did not, in my wildest dreams at that time, expect to see the Berlin Wall laid low before the end of the year. I had long been an established critic of what I called the 'Jericho School' of diplomacy. Vienna gave me the opportunity too to challenge my Rumanian opposite number, Ioan Totu, on a particularly bizarre aspect of his country's policy. One of the worst-treated dissidents in Rumania, Mrs Doina Cornea, had long looked to Britain for support against oppressive measures directed against her. And our ambassador had been calling upon her quite regularly to remind both her and the Rumanians of continuing Western concern. Now the Rumanian authorities designed what they regarded as a foolproof way of keeping the ambassador out. They erected a 'No Entry – One Way Street' sign at both ends of the street in which Mrs Cornea lived. 'This', I said fiercely, 'is a gross violation of the Helsinki Agreement provisions for "Freedom of movement of people".'

Spying for Gorbachev

Relations with the Soviet Union too were still subject to squalls, sometimes of a much more serious nature. In the first half of 1989 high-level diplomacy and espionage interfered quite sharply with each other. A visit by Gorbachev to the UK had been in prospect but was postponed from December 1988 because of the earthquake in Armenia. In mid-January 1989 the fresh date for his visit had not been fixed. At almost the same moment (7 p.m. on 15 January) we knew that a meeting was due to take place in London between a double agent (whose movements were known to our people) and a Soviet embassy KGB man, Kuznetsov. And we had also established beyond doubt the identity of a further dozen fresh KGB men whose expulsion was highly desired. We were on the point of expelling those people, including Kuznetsov.

But we felt unable to implement those plans when Soviet ambassador Zamyatin (Popov's successor) booked a call to see the Prime Minister at almost exactly the same time as the Kuznetsov meeting was due to occur. As it happened, Zamyatin could not offer any fresh date for the Gorbachev visit. But the KGB man, Kuznetsov, was able – in exchange for documents – to hand over £6000 in cash (making a total of £26,000) to our double agent. The KGB had placed their contact on to a very professional basis. I decided that the expulsions that I had in mind could not be any longer delayed. The sooner they were over, I thought, the less they were likely to affect the prospect of an early date for the postponed Gorbachev visit.

Yet before *that* decision could be implemented, news came, on 18 January, that Gorbachev would now be able to visit us between 5 and 7 April. Margaret Thatcher and I discussed this turn of events on the next day. Both the intelligence services and I were still inclined to press ahead. Margaret took the opposite view. Given our interest in 'avoiding a major embarrassment to Gorbachev', she wanted any expulsions deferred until after the visit. With some reluctance I accepted this, and the visit went ahead on 5 April.

I was with Margaret at Heathrow to meet Gorbachev and Shevardnadze and their wives when they arrived direct from Cuba, late at night. Gorbachev was quick off the mark. As he greeted me, he said, with simulated anger, 'Ah! Here's Sir Geoffrey, who's been making life difficult for us by going on again about chemical weapons and the KGB.' He was as well briefed as ever – and not serious. But my reputation as the British hitman was still intact.

The visit went well. Margaret Thatcher and I each conferred with our opposite number. It was my fifteenth meeting with Shevardnadze – and we had five hours together. Our dialogue was by now very informal but very direct. We could not by ourselves advance the Vienna agenda. But Shevardnadze seemed increasingly confident that modernizaton of short-range nuclear missiles would be prevented – by public opinion in West Germany rather than by anything that he might say. One bone I had to pick with him was the recent Russian sale of fifteen advanced SV-24D bombers to Gaddaffi's 'unpredictable' Libyan regime. Shevardnadze countered with an attack on our large (but scarcely comparable) supply of arms to Saudi Arabia. It was a sharp exchange. But, as Shevardnadze told the press, the fact that we could have a deep disagreement without falling out 'reflected the maturity of the relationship'. This was true too of the comprehensive and thoughtful speech which Gorbachev made from the same Guildhall platform as Reagan a year before. Finally both ministerial parties enjoyed lunch with Her Majesty at Windsor Castle. Mikhail Gorbachev was probably nearing the high point of his own undeservedly short but remarkable reign.

Within two weeks Margaret was told by the director general of MI5 that the level of KGB and GRU (Soviet Army intelligence) activity remained high and the case for expulsions as strong as ever. Indeed similar action was now to be recommended for a group of Czech diplomats. On this basis Margaret accepted my view that expulsions could and should go ahead about six weeks later. So Ambassador Zamyatin was summoned to the Foreign Office on 19 May to be told that eleven of his people would be expelled and three others declared *persona non grata* and not allowed to return. But I was determined, as I had been on earlier occasions, to avoid over-dramatizing the confrontation. So we went to most unusual lengths to try to cushion the blow.

Margaret wrote a long personal and confidential letter to Gorbachev to explain our approach. This was a decision, she said, which we had 'hoped not to take'. The expulsions we had effected in 1985* had been intended to remove 'once and for all' the obstacle of Soviet intelligence activity in Britain. But the KGB had 'step by step reconstructed their staff in London'. So we were 'left with no alternative but to require the removal of certain intelligence officers'. But once again, stressed Margaret, we should be looking and hoping for a fresh start consistent with our search for an overall better relationship. So we were not going to propose any further reduction in the ceiling on Soviet posts. (On that point, of course, we were making virtue out of necessity, given the difficulties we had experienced since 1985.) Finally, wrote Margaret, 'I have given instructions that publicity for the removal of your intelligence personnel is not to be given by any British official.' This last condition was one on which Margaret had particularly insisted. But it was no surprise that knee-jerk press criticism of this 'misjudgment' was directed against me and the Foreign Office. 'Pre-emptive Cringe', screamed the *Evening Standard* and 'Howe Dare He?' demanded the *Sun*.

We might as well never have bothered with such anxious courtesies. Less than thirty-six hours after Zamyatin had received our list of miscreants, our new ambassador in Moscow, Rodric Braithwaite, was presented with a precisely matching list, including three British journalists, whose independence was beyond question. The Soviet authorities also attempted, although they later abandoned the idea, to impose a much harder general restriction on the total number of Britons in Moscow (a reduction from 375 to 205). Against the background of all the trouble we had taken to handle this particular package in a different way, it was galling to hear Gerald Kaufman (Denis Healey's replacement as Shadow Foreign Secretary) trying to make capital out of our 'incompetence'. Naively he asked why the problem 'could not have been sorted out directly during the visit of President Gorbachev to Britain last month'. The folly of this charge became plain when I was obliged, only three days later, to take further tough action, by expelling four members of the Czechoslovak embassy: their misbehaviour had been exposed by a defector from their own service.

A couple of weeks later we heard from the Soviet London embassy that the expulsion had been taken very badly by Gorbachev. He had apparently 'gone through the roof' and 'taken it as a personal insult'. Margaret's message had apparently done nothing to assuage his feelings. For it was Gorbachev, so we were told, who had himself ordered the

* See pp. 439–40 above.

retaliation and the imposition of a fresh ceiling on British numbers in Moscow. The conclusion which I reached was that, whatever other changes Gorbachev might succeed in making in the Soviet Union, the last citadel to fall would be the KGB. It can have been no coincidence that one of the leaders of the plot to overthrow Mikhail Gorbachev in August 1991 was Vladimir Kryuchkov, whom he had appointed to head the organization in October 1988. Even today there are lessons to be learned from this story.

Anchor to Windward

At the end of May 1988 came George Bush's first NATO Council meeting. There were no new issues to be tackled, but the divergence between the British and German views on SNF negotiations stuck out like a sore thumb. There was no really credible way of bridging the gap by face-to-face negotiation. So Bush (more probably it was Baker's idea) put forward a judgement of Solomon, with little, if any, consultation – at least with our side of the argument. They proposed much deeper and very swift conventional-force reductions, which had the prospect of being implemented by 1992 or 1993. After that the prospect of SNF negotiations still opened up – 'early' as the Germans would say. Meanwhile, Margaret Thatcher was able to reassert the existence of the modernization pledge. But, if the conventional reductions did indeed take place, the case for a new generation of tactical nuclear weapons would virtually have disappeared. Alliance 'unity' was thus restored, and Margaret's objective appeared to survive. But so did the Germans' – more convincingly. George Bush certainly meant well by saying that this outcome would not have been possible 'without an anchor to windward'. But that did not strike me as a particularly useful or flattering role to have occupied. He rubbed salt in the wound by the reference, at Mainz on the following day, to the leadership role of Germany. The further Britain seemed to move herself away from the heart of the European debate, the greater the risk of her being disregarded in the transatlantic debate as well. Events were beginning to develop in the 1990s in a way that threatened to fulfil the warnings given two and three decades before by Alec Douglas-Home and Harold Macmillan.

CHAPTER THIRTY-EIGHT

ROAD TO MADRID

High-Water Mark

Domestic politics at least should have been relatively plain sailing after our 1987 success at the polls. We had, as I told a Cambridge Summer School twelve months after the election, taken the crucial step from a period when the reversal of the Conservative revolution always seemed possible to one where it was almost inconceivable. There was, I said – with more than a degree of hubris – 'no political, moral or intellectual challenge in sight' to the policies with which we had released the spirit and the talent of the nation.[1]

The wide-ranging reform programme, foreshadowed in our 1987 manifesto, was set in train. I was particularly pleased that Nigel Lawson had at last been able, in his 1988 Budget, to implement the plans on which we had both been working, for the genuinely independent taxation of married women. The previous system had long been resented as unfair. As long ago as 1980 I had published the first Green Paper proposing action to remedy this. Nigel published a second, more fully developed set of proposals in 1986. But Margaret had always been inexplicably hostile to this reform, as to a number of others demanded by her own sex. Nigel suggests that this was because she attributed the whole notion to my 'feminist' spouse, Elspeth.[2] I had in fact been personally committed to the idea, at least since 1968. For in that year the Cripps Committee, of which I was a member, had recommended just such a change in our report, *Fair Share for the Fair Sex*.* This is a not untypical example of the pace of the reform process in our country: virtually two decades of sustained effort by people, including Nigel and myself, each with a well-considered personal commitment to the change.

---

* See p. 526 above.

At least the process, in which Inland Revenue taxation experts had been throughout engaged, did in the end deliver a carefully considered, popular and workable system.

Almost every aspect of the welfare state was similarly on the agenda – not for destruction but for reform. This had been a constant theme of my own domestic speeches. 'We must be ready', I had told a Conservative Political Centre audience at Cambridge as long ago as 3 July 1982, 'to consider how far private provision and individual choice can supplement, or in some cases possibly replace, the role of the government in health, social security and education.' Seven years later I was still explaining in a lecture to the newly formed Radical Society* that these changes were designed not just 'to tackle the mentality and mechanics' of what I had called (in a Bow Group essay in the mid-1960s) the 'Waiting List Society'.[3] We had even more ambitious objectives. We wanted certainly to extend 'the benefits of choice, competition and accountability to the consumers' of health, welfare and education. But we wanted also to give the suppliers of these services a better chance to improve their own working environment. These people, 'who take decisions about how public money is spent', I said, 'should have greater responsibility, enjoy greater motivation'. In the process, they would 'both have an added incentive to improve standards and be subject to enhanced public accountability through consumer choice'. The two most conspicuous examples of this kind of thinking were Kenneth Clarke's NHS reforms and Kenneth Baker's Education Bill.

Without Margaret Thatcher's restless determination on both these fronts these important proposals would never have taken effective shape. They were aspects of the government's record which were well in line with my own long-term thinking. I was glad, as Foreign Secretary, to find how closely they were being followed abroad – often admired as well, sometimes in surprising places.

So there were still a good many things going in the right direction during 1988 and 1989 – and some high spots to remember. Perhaps the most symbolic was 24 January 1989. For that was the day on which I qualified for the *Guinness Book of Records*. After more than five years and seven months in office, I became Britain's longest-serving Foreign Secretary for seventy-three years, since Sir Edward Grey stepped down in 1916. After 2055 days I had overtaken the previous record-holder, Ernest Bevin. Much of the resulting comment was predictable. Some

* On 19 July 1989, five days before I was moved from the Foreign Office.

was statistical: seventy-five countries visited, 700,000 official miles in the air – equivalent to circumnavigating the globe once every eighty days. It was at about this time that I received a gently warning text from an old psychiatrist friend, Professor Hugh Freeman. In a paper on 'The Human Brain and its Adaptation to Modern Politics',[4] he warned people like Margaret Thatcher and myself that though we might perhaps enjoy 'an inherent need for relatively little sleep' and be 'superficially unaffected by the kind of travel which the average person would find prostrating', nobody could be sure that our judgment and health were unaffected by the load. He contrasted our huge volume of paperwork – and worldwide agenda arriving by several satellites simultaneously – with Baldwin's six-week holidays in France and Asquith's annual visit to his Scottish constituency. I later worked out that during six years at the Foreign Office I took home, to work through overnight while others slept, no less than twenty-four tons of paper: three boxes a night, six nights a week, forty weeks a year. Six o'clock was my normal time for getting up. My average bedtime was about four hours earlier. George Shultz found life in Washington no different. 'Being Secretary of State', he used to say, 'is like trying to get a drink out of a fire-hose.'

Some of the criticism of my long service record was on familiar lines: 'aggressively uncharismatic and passionately wooden' said Richard Heller in the *Mail on Sunday*;[5] Sarah Hogg in *The Times* had spotted 'lack of attack' as my 'greatest political defect'[6] – and so on. More kindly, Andrew McEwen, in *The Times*, thought that I should be seen as the Foreign Secretary in whose time Dean Acheson's famous jibe ceased to be true.* During the Thatcher–Howe years, he wrote, Britain 'has re-established a place at the table of the super-powers, as a medium-sized power whose voice can no longer be ignored'.[7] For one ambassador, who retired at about that time, I had 'created a sense of purpose in our diplomacy and a sense of family within the service. It was great fun.'[8] It was the word 'fun' that I most liked. I echoed it with a touch of conceit in my letter of thanks to Patrick Wright: 'It's all – or almost all – been great fun, so far. . . . Now for Grey, Genscher and Gromyko!'†

But now the shine was beginning to wear off our economic perform-ance, and other troubles were building up. Nigel Lawson's 1989 Budget had to be a much more cautious affair. Despite the prospect of another substantial surplus in 1989–90, he could not risk any substantial tax

* See p. 66 above.
† They served as Foreign Minister respectively for eleven, twelve and twenty-seven years.

cuts. For rising inflation, which he had initially described as a 'blip', was taking more serious hold. During 1989 the underlying rate reached 6 per cent and the headline figure topped 7.5 per cent. A year later it peaked at 10.9 per cent. Interest rates had been moving in the same direction, up to 14 per cent by May 1989. Yet bank and building society lending had expanded during the previous year by no less than 25 per cent. This overheating was inevitably reflected in a growing current-account deficit. What came to be known, fairly or not, as the Lawson Boom – to be followed, as night followed day, by the Major Recession – was under way.

Also under way was the developing disaster of the poll-tax. I remember being astonished when, some time after leaving the Foreign Office, I came upon an earlier working document about this tax: for this made it clear that, even before the adventure had started, it was forecast that – *all* other things being equal – the reform would make at least 50 per cent of households and individuals worse off. By the spring of 1989 the average Charge looked like exceeding £300 per head (up by more than 50 per cent on original estimates). By the autumn of that year, as Margaret Thatcher herself reminds us, Kenneth Baker (by then party chairman) was predicting that the percentage of individuals and households likely to be made worse off was between 73 and 89 per cent.[9] A reform that was going to have such a foreseeably unpopular impact needed to deliver some massively obvious benefit if it was ever to justify itself. But it never was going to – and never did.

Gloom had by no means reached this pitch as the time approached to mark the tenth anniversary of Margaret Thatcher's accession to power. The most recent by-election result – to fill the vacancy left at Richmond, Yorks by Leon Brittan's departure for Brussels – had been held short of disaster by our excellent candidate, William Hague. He had been the party-conference prodigy of 1977 and had served as my own election helper in 1983. He held the seat, on 23 February 1989, against a 24 per cent swing to the Liberal Democrat, with a greatly reduced majority of 2634. I had one startling experience during my own visit to the constituency. When canvassing one village street, the occupants of Numbers 1 and 3 told me that I had to call at Number 5 because the lady there was a particular fan of mine. And so it proved. For the lady opened the door to my knock and threw her arms heavenwards. 'Oh!' she cried. 'My little teddy-bear!' There was one vote at least that William could count upon – and he was going to need them all.

A Diet of Brussels

The malaise that was developing that spring had triggered a good deal of speculation about the need for the Prime Minister to 'strengthen her team' by appointing somebody specifically in place of Willie Whitelaw, struck down by ill-health at the end of 1987. The *Mail on Sunday* decided that the Prime Minister stood in real need of such a deputy, someone 'above the herd', someone 'with the respect not just of the Party but of the country'. They concluded that such a man existed 'in the affable – but highly expert – frame' of Geoffrey Howe.[10] I was appreciative, of course, of the constancy of the *Mail on Sunday*'s support, under the editorship of Stuart Steven.

But I felt myself that Bruce Anderson's judgment in the *Daily Telegraph* was closer to the truth. The relationship between Margaret and myself had come, he felt, to resemble 'one of those marriages which any stranger witnessing for the first time would think was headed straight for the divorce court – if not the homicide court'. Certainly the Prime Minister could – and did – become very rude. She was often exasperated by my tenaciously quiet brand of advocacy. When the crockery had stopped flying, I was still there waiting for the interruption to end. This, argued Anderson, was one reason why British foreign policy had been, since 1983, 'more successful than at any time this century'. The 'creative tension between the two positions' – the Foreign Secretary's rationalism and the Prime Minister's impatience – had been 'of immense value'.[11] This was a rather idealized description of what was becoming an increasingly tense relationship. Certainly it did not suggest that either of us would find it easy to translate me into a Willie role. For so long as I was Foreign Secretary, with an independent power base of my own, I could and did have real leverage over what the government actually said and did. But once translate me into a non-operational slot and I should find it, I thought, very hard to persuade Margaret to follow any political instinct but her own. Yet when this theoretical prospect became a reality, in July 1989, I was to disregard my own warning instinct.

On 4 May 1989 came the tenth anniversary celebration dinner at Number 10. Only Cabinet ministers, the Cabinet secretary and Margaret's parliamentary and private secretaries were present, with spouses. I was the senior of three survivors from the 1979 Cabinet (Peter Walker and George Younger, at Wales and Defence respectively, were the other two). So it fell to me to propose Margaret's health. It was an occasion for camaraderie rather than candour. So I sadly discarded the not so light-hearted verses which Adam Fergusson had supplied for me. Instead I contrasted the fast-changing decade – four Japanese Prime Ministers, eleven Italian governments, forty-seven Cabinet colleagues, 416 Cabinet meetings – with the immutability of the Prime Minister. Elspeth (and some others) thought I was being too generous. But if the late Peter Jenkins could write, as he did that day, the words with which I closed my after-dinner remarks, then none of us could in fairness say less:

> History will surely recognize her achievements as Britain's first woman Prime Minister, a leader with the courage of her convictions, who assailed the conventional wisdom of her day, challenged and overthrew the existing order, changed the political map, and put her country on its feet again.[12]

But, even as I spoke, the foundations of that success were becoming increasingly insecure. On the same day as the dinner, the Vale of Glamorgan by-election, in a seat that had for almost four decades provided a secure base for the veteran Welsh Conservative, the late Sir Raymond Gower, was catastrophically lost to the Labour Party with an adverse swing of 12 per cent. It was a poor augury for the European election campaign. The domestic reasons for this débâcle were ample enough: rising inflation and high interest rates, the poll-tax, and the coming 'privatization' – so it was widely, though wrongly, alleged – of a highly respected NHS hospital in the constituency. All these causes of discontent were fanned by recurrent reports of disagreement within the Conservative Party – indeed within the Cabinet itself – about government policy towards Europe.

Our internal conflicts within the Cabinet were to become increasingly obvious. For we were about to start the campaign for elections to the European Parliament. Polling day, occurring automatically in the same week every five years, was on 15 June. The press conference at which we were to launch our manifesto was on 22 May. Margaret had put me once again in charge of the preparation of that document, which I undertook with a widely drawn team of collaborators. This included Members of the European Parliament and ministers (and their advisers) at Westminster.

The same arrangements had five years before been warmly commended by all possible factions. The drafting was excellently carried out by Chris Patten, with the help of my special adviser, Anthony Teasdale. By March we had the Prime Minister's unqualified endorsement of the text. Her Private Office minuted, 'She thinks it very good.' Subsequently she has sought to dismiss it as 'nicely written' but 'unexciting'. Geoffrey, she explains, 'had tried to reach a consensus'.[13] So indeed I had, not excluding a specific pledge (for the umpteenth time) to join the ERM 'when the time is right'. Predictably, Margaret was questioned about that at our opening press conference. She could not wait to get away from the agreed compromise position. We would not be joining until we had inflation under control – and, she added, 'maybe not even then'. She followed this up with a dismissive critique of the very Exchange Rate Mechanism that we were pledged to join.

This was a trailer for her attitude throughout the campaign. She found it impossible to conceal her contempt for the European Parliament itself. Her own quasi-Gaullist pronouncements increasingly imprinted on our campaign a crudely embarrassing anti-Europeanism. Our candidates and party workers were more and more baffled by the hostility of this 'Europe of the saloon bar', as Joe Rogaly was to characterize it.[14] The ultimate confusion of our message was summed up in the main Conservative poster: 'If you don't vote Conservative next Thursday, you'll live on a diet of Brussels.' The text was literally obscure. But certainly it conveyed a feeling of hostility towards the whole European venture. This misguided invitation was launched by Central Office, in response to an assessment there of the likely wishes of the Prime Minister.

Our European successes over the three previous decades had flowed from the party's positive commitment to Europe – under Macmillan and Heath and Thatcher alike. The discordant populism which now confused and undermined our candidates, our workers and our voters was the new note that had been struck in the Bruges speech. The party was effectively being split by the defection of its own leader.

During the three weeks of the campaign I travelled more widely than any other Cabinet minister. In the Borders constituency where we lost a good member, Alisdair Hutton, I had the chance to take a charmingly leisurely tea with the former Prime Minister Alec Home and his wife at the Hirsel: it was my only visit there and the last time I was to see Elizabeth Home alive. Mrs Margaret Daly MEP gave me the chance, in her Somerset constituency (which she held), of a meeting with the new Bishop of Bath and Wells, George Carey: the discussion of South Africa with a group of churchmen which Margaret Daly had arranged may not have won many votes, but it gave me a good chance of getting to know the next Archbishop of Canterbury. None of my encounters with voters in any part of the country gave me any electoral encouragement. The divisions within the government were all too clearly observed. The electoral consequences were inevitable. There was a little more public interest in this European election than in its predecessors. Thirty-seven per cent of them voted in 1989, compared with only 32 per cent in 1984. But our own party's share of the total vote, at 34 per cent, was the lowest at any national election since the beginning of universal suffrage. We lost thirteen of our forty-five seats, giving Labour for the first time a majority of our Strasbourg representation.

Divide and Rule

Looking back now on my last year at the Foreign Office, it is remarkable just how fragmented relationships had by then become between the Prime Minister and each one of her three senior colleagues – Nigel Lawson, Douglas Hurd and myself. This was above all true on important questions of European policy. The Bruges speech of September 1988 had been the subject of detailed, though inconclusive, negotiations between Charles Powell and my officials. Most of my major speeches were by now being similarly handled. So too the manifesto. The final fragment of text, about possible entry into the ERM, which Nigel Lawson and I had worked up together in a meeting on 16 March, had been settled in a brief exchange between draftsman Chris Patten and – unusually for a civil servant – Charles Powell.

Nigel Lawson and the Prime Minister had been conducting a long-running parallel debate about exchange-rate policy – at least since the time of their initial row about 'shadowing the Deutschmark'. For a time they had been able to manage this face to face. But that too came to an end not later than 3 May 1989 when, as Nigel explains, Margaret sought to insist in terms that she 'must prevail'.[15] The topic which fuelled this tension more and more was the timing of accession to the EMS. Since 1985 Nigel and I – and many of our colleagues – had been of one mind about the need to find an early opportunity for this. There was no doubt that Douglas Hurd would take the same view, but he had no departmental interest in or responsibility for the topic.

It was in this context that early in 1989 Hugo Young was provoked to comment on the undignified plight of this talented trio: Lawson,

Hurd and Howe. This 'nap hand in brain-power', as he described us, respectively exhibiting 'technical self-confidence, political astuteness and an accumulated relentless mastery of complex detail of every kind', was nevertheless without real power or significance. 'Three people of unusual political qualities' had allowed themselves to become, in his view, 'painfully subordinate figures . . . victims of the Prime Minister's utterly insatiable desire for domination.'[16] He was uncomfortably close to the truth. How had we allowed this to happen? And what, if anything, could we have done about it?

Essentially we had fallen into the trap of dealing too much on a one-to-one basis with Number 10, taking advantage of the arguments that we could win in private – and discounting those that we had not. The only escape from such a pattern of behaviour was a wholly new kind of partnership between the three of us. Nigel and I were indeed prepared, in the end, to work together in this way. And I had spoken to Douglas, as well as to Nigel, about the possibility of establishing a wider three-handed team. The difficulty was to establish a plausible agenda. In any case, once we had begun trying to construct one, Margaret would certainly have smelt a rat. If we were then to have a chance of 'prevailing', we should need to have pre-emptively agreed that an attack on any one of us would be treated as an attack on us all. We should need, in other words, to have thought through to the end all the consequences of a fully fledged 'conspiracy'. For such that would have been. And it was that which we never did. Even Nigel and I in our subsequent partnership ahead of Madrid quite clearly never reached that point. Each one of the trio of 'brain boxes' remained in his present job 'during the Prime Minister's pleasure'. Perhaps it was ever thus.

The question of our own membership of the ERM had in fact made no headway since the last full meeting of ministers considered it in November 1985. On the Community agenda, we had (at the Hanover Summit in June 1988) allowed the wider topic of economic and monetary union (EMU) to pass into the hands of the Delors Committee, which was due to report in the spring of 1989. Sterling's relationship with the other EC currencies, particularly the Deutschmark, had been, of course, the subject of recurrent conflict between Prime Minister and Chancellor. Since this had finally broke into the open in March 1988,[17] the open secret of their disagreement about ERM entry was a matter of continuing public comment.

I deliberately left it for Nigel to take the lead with Margaret on this topic, since it was essentially an economic question – and they were constantly in touch about such matters. But inevitably I was asked or obliged to speak about it from time to time. I found that the agreed formula, 'when the time is right', was sounding less and less convincing. Audiences were scarcely able to take it seriously. Increasingly often it was greeted with open mirth, particularly on the continent. After six or seven years with the bare formula, I began heading off the risk of laughter by adding the phrase 'and I know we can't go on saying that for ever'. At least one example of this oft-repeated remark (at a meeting with the Conservative Group for Europe) found its way into a prominent *Times* report ('Warning by Howe on the EMS').[18]

By 1988, however, when Margaret and Nigel were almost publicly at each other's throats, even my casual remarks began attracting rather more attention. On 24 March, for example, in a speech at Zurich,* I discussed the growing interest of G7 Finance Ministers in exchange rate stability. I added that this was 'necessarily coming to play a more significant role in both domestic monetary discussions and international policy co-operation'. Significantly, this glimpse of the obvious was seized upon by both Margaret and Nigel as evidence of my engagement in the argument. Margaret saw me apparently from at least that time as 'making mischief' of the issue 'in cahoots with' Nigel: Geoffrey, she says 'was more ill-disposed towards me personally'.[19] But I wanted not to move the Prime Minister out, only to move the policy forward.

Even so, I suppose one should not be too surprised at her reaction to another entirely innocent coincidence. On Friday, 23 May 1988 I was replying to a general European debate at the Scottish Conservative Party Conference in Perth. I had put out a five-page press release of most of my remarks. Deliberately I had included nothing about the ERM or EMS. In the end I could not avoid saying something about it, for several MEPs and Euro-candidates had pressed me in the debate for clarification of our policy. More than one speaker actually mocked the 'time is right' formula. It was, they said, well past its sell-by date. So I responded, in a necessarily ad-lib section of my speech, with my customary coda: 'We cannot forever go on adding that qualification to the underlying commitment.' This time, however, the press pounced on the phrase. For on the previous day Kinnock had cornered Margaret (and so Nigel) on that very topic. With more care I might have realized the risk that my standard line could this time attract more than usual attention. Certainly the press thought I had widened the rift between Prime Minister and

* Delivered before the Swiss Institute of International Affairs.

Chancellor. Even then I did not bargain for the near-paranoid quality of Margaret's reaction.

For on the following day I telephoned her, in all innocence (but in her view 'imprudently'), to suggest a meeting between the three of us to find, if we could, a way of settling the 'semi-public dispute' that was now threatening real damage. I was astonished by the ferocity of her reaction. 'No, I shall certainly not see the two of you together about this,' she said. Her own account is even more graphic – and revealing – than my own recollection:

> I told him [that is me] three times – since he did not seem to take it in and persisted in his attempt to contrive a meeting at which he and Nigel could get their way – that the best thing he could do now was to keep quiet. We were not going into the ERM at present and that was that.[20]

This was almost a year ahead of her statement to Nigel that she 'must prevail'. But each occasion offers a real insight into the way in which Margaret was now dealing with her most senior colleagues.

The Delors Report

So we were anything but a close-knit team when the time came for Her Majesty's Government to react to the final report of the Delors Committee in April 1988. We had all of us earlier had some hope that the Governor of the Bank of England, Robin Leigh-Pemberton, would be able to concert an acceptable position with his German opposite number, Kark Otto Pöhl. But Pöhl had disappointed us all, and Leigh-Pemberton had not felt able to dissent on his own. The report therefore took the form of a single linked plan that would take us, if accepted, irreversibly through three stages towards full monetary union, based upon a single currency and European Central Bank. While I certainly did not exclude the eventual possibility of EMU, neither Margaret nor Nigel was prepared to go that far. They were opposed to EMU in principle. But Nigel, like myself, was ready to accept Stage One: this involved completion of the single market, closer European monetary co-ordination, development of the ECU – and, crucially, membership of the ERM for *all* member-states. We had varying reactions to the intermediate Stage Two. But Europe did not yet have to decide about that.

The crucial objective for Margaret, Nigel and myself became the removal – or emasculation – of paragraph 39 of the Delors Report. This sought to provide that the 'decision to enter upon the *first* stage should be a decision to embark on the *entire* process'. We all three objected to this automatic link between the ERM (Stage One) part of the plan and full-blown EMU. The divide between Nigel and myself on the one hand and Margaret on the other was simple. Nigel and I were sure that if we were to succeed in resisting the automatic nature of the pararaph 39 link to full EMU, then we had to be ready to demonstrate beyond doubt the good faith of our commitment to join the ERM in Stage One. Ideally, we should be willing to do that now. But how on earth were we to get Margaret over this long-standing hurdle? And particularly now that Professor Alan Walters had returned from the far side of the Atlantic to her side in Downing Street, even more sure of his own wisdom and even less discreet than before.

Nigel and I had been considering these issues jointly for some time before the arrival of the Delors Report itself. We met without officials on three occasions between mid-March and end April 1989. We were clear that we needed to tackle the Prime Minister, jointly, on the subject of ERM membership. Initially we had expected to rest our case essentially on domestic, economic policy: ERM membership would lower the costs of counter-inflationary policy. When we met on 26 April, however, Nigel had become less confident of winning on those grounds alone. Now that we had seen the Delors Report, the key argument, we felt, had become the need for an early UK move on ERM, at Madrid, in order to prevent the Eleven convening an immediate Inter-Governmental Conference to draft EMU amendments to the Treaty.

One of the more remarkable features of this whole process was the Anglo-Dutch 'Summit' meeting which then took place on 29 April, at Chequers. I had concluded that the most likely 'outsider' who might influence Margaret away from her continuing 'gut' hostility to the ERM was the Dutch Prime Minister, Ruud Lubbers. A conservative, intelligent, good-looking and unfanatically tenacious, he was one of the few European statesmen whose company Margaret almost enjoyed. And he had all the right pro-market, Atlanticist prejudices. By good chance we needed his support at this time – or so Margaret believed – if we were to get the right 'modernization' result from the forthcoming NATO Summit on 29–30 May. So Lubbers was accompanied to Chequers by both Foreign and Finance Ministers: Hans van den Broek and Onno Ruding. Margaret naturally spent a good deal of time on the NATO issue. On this the Dutch were among the soundest of the allies.

But eventually Nigel was able to introduce Ruding on the subject of the ERM. Van den Broek and I had agreed, ahead of the meeting, that Foreign Ministers would lie low on this topic. We both felt that financial arguments were more likely than political to carry the day. And Ruding did well. The chances of resisting any automatic move to EMU, he said, would be vastly improved by a British commitment to early ERM membership. Lubbers added his weight to the argument on strictly practical grounds. Margaret responded by laying into the Dutch, with ferocious gusto. Nigel was taken aback by this. I was well used to it – and so were the Dutch – from their experience of Margaret at European Councils. But that experience too left them in no doubt that their arguments had made little impression. The experiment in cross-frontier Cabinet government had been in vain. But it was well worth the attempt. I was most grateful to our good Dutch friends.

Work now started in earnest on the joint minute to Margaret that Nigel and I had in mind. The first outline draft was actually produced in the Treasury and then jointly honed between Tim Lankester in that department and John Kerr in mine. The essential purpose, we said, was to convince our EC partners to tackle the Delors agenda step by step. If we were to persuade them then to concentrate on Stage One and leave over for later decision the rest (including any possible Inter-Governmental Conference), then we had absolutely to convince them of the good faith of Britain's commitment to Stage One. They had to know that the time truly *was* becoming 'ripe'.

Both Lankester and Kerr originally felt that actually naming a date for British entry into ERM would be a bridge too far for Margaret and in any case not necessary to take the trick at Madrid. Events were in the end to prove them right. But the text that went to Number 10 on 14 June did propose a non-legally binding undertaking that sterling would join the ERM by the end of 1992. This, we suggested, should be subject to a condition that all the major states would by then have abolished all exchange controls, as already provided for by the Capital Liberalization Directive. The pound, we said, should enter with wider margins, as the Spaniards had themselves stipulated for the peseta. We would also, of course, want to ensure that our inflation rate was on the way down again. But that was a matter for us – and something we were determined to achieve anyway. 'Could we', we concluded, 'discuss this with you?'

That closing question was in itself very revealing. 'As usual before European Councils', writes Margaret Thatcher, 'I held a number of preparatory meetings with ministers and officials.' The purpose, she explains, was to ensure that she 'was thoroughly briefed' but also 'to sort out with colleagues our precise objective on each issue'.[21] This had indeed been her practice in earlier years. The passage which I have just quoted precedes Margaret's description of the Athens Summit in December 1983. But by 1989 her habits had changed a great deal. For no such meeting with ministers had been, or was being, planned by Number 10 ahead of Madrid. Yet the agenda, above all the Delors Report, was of far-reaching importance. The Foreign Secretary and Chancellor of the day would have been lamentably failing in their duty if they had not sought a meeting with the Prime Minister at such a time. Yet it was only with the utmost reluctance and ill-grace that Margaret accepted the idea.

Only much later did we learn the extent to which she had already been taking her own counsel about the Madrid agenda. On 19 June she had held a meeting of all her Number 10 advisers (including Alan Walters and Brian Griffiths) to consider the matter in depth. This was the equivalent of her previously routine pre-Summit meetings. The important difference was that her ministerial colleagues (and their senior advisers) were the only ones to be excluded. In ourselves seeking to discuss these questions with the Prime Minister, we had in her view organized a 'cabal' and 'mounted an ambush'.[22] So far had her thinking departed from the notion of collective responsibility.

We were eventually granted an audience on the day after her private briefing and just six days ahead of Madrid, on 20 June. The Prime Minister was uncompromising and resistant to our thinking. She wanted simply to play Madrid by ear. Eventually she agreed formally to 'reflect further' on what we had said. But not for long. For within twenty-four hours we received from her office a counter-proposal for 'Madrid conditions' going far beyond anything that could have been seen as relevant to Delors Stage One and the ERM itself. We now know – what then we only suspected – that this 'ingenious suggestion' (from Alan Walters, of course) was seen by Margaret as possibly 'the only way in which' she 'could resist the pressure from Nigel, Geoffrey and the European Community for early entry' to the ERM.[23]

Clearly the matter could not be left there. The line now suggested from Number 10 was calculated to produce exactly the wrong answer: an early Inter-Governmental Conference to draft an EMU Treaty – and almost no chance of holding back the Delors route to a single currency. So on 23 June Nigel and I wrote a second joint minute, requesting a further meeting. Margaret struggled angrily to avoid this. She offered separate telephone calls with each of us. But Nigel and I were determined to leave her in no doubt of the strength of our opinions. Eventually she agreed to meet us both again at 10 Downing Street early on Sunday morning, 25 June – the very day she and I were due to fly to Madrid.. No outsiders were present. It was a stiffly formal occasion. I spoke first. If she remained totally unwilling to move forward on the ERM along the lines we suggested, I said, then 'I should no longer be able to remain a member of the government.' Nigel spoke briefly, but firmly, to the same effect. What Margaret describes as this 'nasty little meeting',[24] between three old friends and colleagues, ended in empty silence. The matter was wholly unresolved. Nigel and I withdrew together to Number 11 for a few moments. But we did not reach any fresh conclusions.

There had been no ulterior motive to our manoeuvres, no personalized conspiracy. Nor would there be. We were engaged in a joint exercise, jointly conceived – and with a single legitimate purpose. We both felt strongly the need to influence for the better Margaret's handling of Madrid, and specifically to do so by a clear tautening of the 'time is ripe' formula. We had agreed that, if this case was to make any headway at Number 10, it needed joint presentation (how right we were!). And we had agreed to back our view with a seriously intended statement of our willingness to resign, if the case was brushed aside. We had done just that. Nigel was now to stay in London and I to go with Margaret to Madrid. We each had next to see what happened there.

CHAPTER THIRTY-NINE

DISMISSED FROM THE
FOREIGN OFFICE

The Madrid Summit

The Prime Minister and I met again just five hours later, Sunday afternoon, 25 June, in the VIP departure suite at London Heathrow South Side. We boarded the Royal Air Force VC-10 together for the flight to Madrid. Margaret and her entourage were in the front section of the aircraft and I with mine in the second compartment. The buff curtain across the gangway between the two remained drawn. John Kerr, ever with me on these European missions, had prepared two alternative speaking notes for the Prime Minister's opening remarks – one assuming success, and one failure, at the earlier Number 10 meeting. Our encounter, more like a goalless draw, did not fall into either category. But nothing ventured, nothing gained. So I asked John to pass the 'success' version through the drawn curtain to the Prime Minister.

We travelled separately to our respective suites in the Ritz Hotel. The British ambasssador and his wife, Nicky and Mary Gordon-Lennox, were expecting to entertain our party at an informal open-air supper with senior embassy staff. But the Prime Minister, Charles Powell and Bernard Ingham declined to attend. They all remained in their hotel rooms incommunicado until the following morning. It was a strange, but strangely relaxed, supper party. Nobody outside the Number 10 team saw a final draft of the Prime Minister's speaking notes. She and I next met in the delegation suite at the Palacio de Congresos, where the European Council meeting was to take place. Conversation was brittle and businesslike – but unrelated to the ERM–EMU part of the day's agenda. The atmosphere was like that of a household on the morning after conjugal conflict, for which neither partner has the least intention of apologizing. And so it remained, as we took our places alongside each other at the enormous conference table.

Proceedings opened with the usual homily from the President of the European Parliament, our very own Henry Plumb. Economic and monetary union came next. The general expectation was that Margaret Thatcher would object lock, stock and barrel to the whole thing. She bided her time. Delors, Kohl, Lubbers and four or five others said their pieces. When the British Prime Minister finally started to speak, her Foreign Secretary still had not the least idea what she intended to say. He was as expectant as everyone else at the table. It was an unusual experience. Equally unusual was Margaret's speaking style: calm, quiet, measured and sticking closely to her script. Even more unexpected was the substance of what she had to say.

The Hanover European Council (of 27–28 June 1988), she said, had agreed that there should be concrete stages leading to the progressive realization of economic and monetary union, and we should be pragmatic. The Delors Report was right to go for a staged approach to EMU and its analysis was valuable. We were ready, she said, here and now to make an early start on Stage One with effect from 1 July 1990. In some respects she hoped the Community would go further than Delors had proposed, for example in the use of the ECU. She had always made clear that we would join the ERM when the time was right, but this would have to be carefully judged. Speaking very deliberately, she declared, 'I can reaffirm today the United Kingdom's intention to join the ERM.' This must be done in conditions which would strengthen the ERM and provide assurance that an enlarged ERM would be sustained. The timing, she said, would depend on progress in the UK against inflation and progress in the Community on the single market (scheduled for completion in 1992), particularly on the abolition of exchange controls (agreed for 1990).* The timing, of course, was for HMG alone. As for the later stages, Two and Three, we had serious difficulties: the adoption of a single currency would not be acceptable to the House of Commons. Finance Ministers should, however, undertake preparations for Stage One as a matter of urgency. The Delors Report had been valuable. Its long-term proposals needed further study but its recommendations for early action should be implemented.

---

* These, and only these, were the conditions suggested in the 'success' speaking note that we had passed to the Prime Minister through the VC-10 curtain on the flight out.

The effect was electrifying. As soon as the morning session was over and as we walked into lunch, a number of colleagues came over to commend the new, strikingly calm presentation of a much more positive position: Genscher, van den Broek, Ellemann-Jensen and Tindemans were among the first. Jacques Delors himself was delighted. 'Congratulations, Geoffrey,' he said, 'on having won the intellectual argument within the British government.' I explained to him that it was probably not quite as straightforward as that – and so it proved. But, although the Prime Minister had avoided giving any specific date for British entry into the ERM, we had made the essential breakthrough. Our commitment in principle could no longer be doubted. The Madrid conditions, which led – with some modification – to entry within fifteen months, had been set. And President Mitterrand found himself isolated later in the day when he tried to secure a commitment to an early IGC. We were able easily enough – though whether wisely is a different matter – to avoid any commitment by Britain to participate in future discussion of the proposed Social Charter. The whole occasion was perceived as a victory for the United Kingdom, and two days later presented and received as such by Margaret Thatcher to the House of Commons. It was as close to the outcome for which Nigel and I had been pressing as we might have hoped.

So it was seen too as a victory achieved because of a significant, but entirely sensible, shift in position by Number 10. 'Our leader', wrote Hugo Young, 'has made her compact with the real world. . . . It can only do her quite a lot of good.'[1] Here in Madrid, wrote Peter Jenkins, 'we have heard quite a different tone of voice and seen her pursue, for the first time, a constructive diplomacy aimed to ensure Britain's proper part in the shaping of the future'. Almost without exception the press echoed Jenkins' conclusion that 'Britain, at long, long last, may have found itself a valid role in the construction of Europe.'[2] The only ambiguity was about the way in which Margaret Thatcher viewed the event. For in her memoirs she gives gleeful prominence to the way in which, for the following Thursday's Cabinet (29 June), she 'stood in the doorway – waiting. But there were no resignations.' Nigel and I had thus, in her eyes, acknowledged her 'victory'.[3] For, whatever else she had conceded, she had avoided setting a precise date for sterling's entry into the ERM. I have to say that the significance of this piece of retrospective theatre, if such it was, was completely lost on both the other actors in the drama: neither of us had noticed or have since been able to recall any change in Margaret's routine. Certainly we were both satisfied that the synergy of our earlier confrontation with the Prime Minister had produced a result that was good for Britain, and one with which all three of us could be content. So, for a time, it seemed.

We were all together, Nigel, Margaret and myself, for the next major international event, the Economic Summit. It was being hosted this year by France on dates (13–16 July) that coincided with the 200th anniversary of her own Revolution. The days (and nights) were alive with immense parades in the Place de la Concorde and Champs Élysées and magnificent fireworks on the banks of the Seine. Most moving of all was the mass of solitary Chinese cyclists stopping to ring their bells in a floodlit Place de la Concorde – in modest, mournful memory of the very recent victims of Tiananmen Square. The only gauche note was struck, alas, when the British Prime Minister challenged the French claim to have 'invented' the rights of man in 1789. Even our American cousins were reluctant to accept that the English had got it all right – ahead of the Colonies as well as the French – with our 'Glorious' Revolution of 1688. But Margaret collected good marks from her European colleagues for her suggestion that the Community should take the lead in organizing the delivery of economic assistance to the Soviet Union. From beginning to end of our stay in Paris there was no serious tension or difference within the British delegation. The Prime Minister appeared to be approaching the summer recess in a more relaxed and tranquil mode than we had seen for some time.

Not only on the overseas front was that a relief. For at least since the start of the European election campaign on 22 May 1989 the press had been making intermittent forecasts of my demotion in a summer Cabinet reshuffle. Margaret had conspicuously not laid these rumours to rest. On Sunday, 28 May the *Observer* forecast that the Chancellor or the Foreign Secretary (or both) were due for early removal, because of 'increasing tension particularly over Europe and entry to the EMS'. This 'informed guess' gained real substance a couple of days later. The Prime Minister was given a specific opportunity to quash the speculation. In answer to a question from the *Glasgow Herald*, she answered, 'Nigel is a very good Chancellor. Geoffrey is a very good Foreign Secretary – I'm not going any further.' So far from killing the story, she had given it a powerful kiss of life.

It was not long before I was receiving conflicting advice from unexpected quarters. No one had a steadier temperament and wiser head than one of my former special advisers, Peter Cropper, who delivered a bolt from the blue. 'The Sunday papers', wrote this retired Director of the Conservative Research Department, 'seem to be fairly sure, no doubt on Bernard Ingham's advice, that you are going to be relieved of the Foreign Office and given a sinecure. May a humble retired adviser beg you not to accept another post in this loathsome administration.' He went on to argue his case. It was my most startling insight so far into the mounting dismay of some of our heartland supporters. At almost the same moment, on 5 June, conflicting advice came in a disarming note from, of all people, Alan Clark. 'I know I irritate you from time to time,' he wrote,' – it's part of the fun – but I remain a staunch fan.' His message to me was that I should 'hang in there', for two reasons. First, because I was 'the only person with enough cross-faction support to block Michael [Heseltine] if/when "something should happen"'. Alan did not want that option closed off. His second reason was more immediate. He was a great believer, he said, in the theory of Hegelian tension. 'Thesis and antithesis are necessary in order to bring about a benign synthesis' and 'your role here is crucial', thought Alan, at least for as long as Margaret remained at the helm.

I did not, however, need to brood long on this conflict of advice. For a week or two later, the Chief Whip, David Waddington, called on me in the Foreign Office for one of our occasional chats. He told me then that the Prime Minister had decided, following strong advice from the Whips and officers of the 1922 Committee, against making any change in the top three members of the Cabinet – Hurd, Lawson and myself. I realized, of course, that the pre-Madrid spat with Margaret might have cast a blight upon that understanding. But the dust seemed to be settling quite smoothly, not least in light of the generally perceived success of Madrid itself and the tranquillity of Paris.

Even so, I was prompted to check the position twice in the next week. On 19 July the *Daily Mail* carried a story that Margaret was thinking of giving me a 'high-powered deputy' at the FCO, a second Cabinet minister with special responsibility for Europe. So when I saw Margaret later that day for a routine (and fairly straightforward) bilateral, I said to her as I was leaving that I stood by for consultation, if necessary, about any possible changes in my team. The Chief Whip already had my thoughts about new recruits, if any were needed. Margaret did no more than take note. Three days later, on Saturday, 22 July, I rang David Waddington specifically to secure confirmation from him that there was no foundation for the 'European supremo' story. There was no question, he confirmed, of any change at that level. We should be in touch in due course about possible changes in my junior team. He added nothing to suggest any change since we had discussed the whole topic in the Foreign Office some six weeks before.

I Am Asked to Leave

So when I heard on Monday morning, 24 July, that the Prime Minister wished to see me at Number 10 at 09.10, I had no special anxiety. Elspeth and I agreed, of course, to discuss anything that might emerge. But we did not regard any change of post as either sensible or likely. I had a similar exchange in the office with Stephen Wall, my principal private secretary, before walking across to Number 10 through the Cabinet Office back entrance.

I saw the Prime Minister alone, in her study. She was courteous, welcoming even, but businesslike. Our conversation was fairly brief. 'I'm making some changes, Geoffrey,' she said, 'and they will involve the Foreign Office.' Parliament was moving into the television age. So the Leadership of the House (with the Lord Presidency of the Council), which she wanted me to take, would be very important. There was, of course, the alternative of the Home Office to which I could go, 'though I don't think', she concluded, 'you've expressed any strong interest in that.' I responded by saying that I hadn't really contemplated either of those changes: was not the Foreign Office still the right place? 'That option,' said Margaret, 'is not open.' 'Why not?' She felt there was a need for change there, for a younger face. 'Who do you have in mind?' I asked. But she was not prepared to say yet, since she had not set about proposing the other changes she intended. The suggestion that the change was prompted by our pre-Madrid exchanges certainly entered the conversation. The Prime Minister made it clear that it was a factor in her mind, though it was not stated to be the reason for the change.

We had some further discussion about the Home Office. I indicated that I had certainly not been thinking of that as an alternative, since all the key problems there had already been tackled. 'It's a job', I said, 'that I might well have liked at an earlier stage. But I've moved so far away from what had at one time been a natural agenda for me, I feel little enthusiasm for it now.' There was no mention of the Deputy Prime Ministership, but Margaret did make clear that I should be presiding over the same Cabinet committees as Willie Whitelaw, including, if necessary, the Star Chamber (the key public spending Cabinet committee).

One other topic was volunteered by Margaret in this first conversation. 'I shall be asking Nigel to give up Dorneywood,' she said, 'so that you can move there from Chevening.' This kind of detail had not, of course, entered my mind. Nor would I have thought of raising it. Chevening had become so much part of the Foreign Office during my time that I should never have thought of suggesting any separation of the two. The Prime Minister asked me to say nothing of this to Nigel. 'I shall want to do that myself,' she said.

So I had now a full picture of what the Prime Minister had in mind, all clearly thought out well ahead of this conversation. The word 'shock' cannot do justice to my feelings at the way in which this was sprung on me, after ten years as one of her closest Cabinet colleagues. Certainly I was to leave the Foreign Office, with the prospect of a move either to the Home Office or (as seemed more likely to both of us even by then) the Leadership of the House of Commons. There remained the third alternative of leaving the government altogether – which neither of us had mentioned at that stage. I closed by saying that I could not give an answer to her proposals without a chance to talk them through – particularly, of course, with Elspeth.

I left Number 10 as I had entered, through the Cabinet Office, and reported events to Stephen Wall before returning to talk with Elspeth in Carlton Gardens. We were joined there by my former PPS, Richard Ryder (by now a junior agriculture minister). I spoke on the telephone to Leon Brittan in Brussels and Nigel Lawson at Number 11. (I said nothing to Nigel, of course, about Dorneywood.) Each one of them was greatly shocked by the news. Nigel was clear that I should accept neither office. We agreed to keep each other posted about any further developments. But neither he nor I suggested any kind of alliance or revival of our pre-Madrid partnership. So much for our 'conspiracy', even 'cabal'. It might have been better had we been thinking in such terms, but we were not. Leon Brittan and Richard Ryder, as well as Elspeth, were all inclined towards resignation. I then returned to my office. Stephen Wall and Anthony Teasdale – my clear-sighted and tough-minded special adviser – had there been considering the prospects with David Harris, my PPS, who had just arrived by morning plane from his St Ives constituency.

They were much more inclined to the view that I should stay in government – but only with proper authority as Deputy Prime Minister. I was, they thought, a natural insider and would retain a stronger position within the government than on the back benches. My departure from office would seriously damage the government and would not be understood or forgiven, even by some of my own supporters. The Number 10 propaganda machine would highlight the offers I had turned down, so that my defection would seem churlish. If I was to stay on, however, it would have to be plainly agreed that I did so as Deputy Prime Minister, with all that that implied in terms of committee chairmanships, oversight of policy, presentation and so on.

Meanwhile, a draft letter of resignation, which I had penned at Carlton Gardens, had been typed up by my Private Office. As we were pondering my decision, I asked to see the Chief Whip, David Waddington. There was initial resistance to this, but I insisted. At about 12.30 p.m. he arrived. In Anthony Teasdale's words, he looked 'ashen-faced' as he entered my office. I told him I was inclined to leave the government and let him see my draft resignation letter. The text – which looks more persuasive with the wisdom of hindsight than it appeared at the time – was as follows:

More than fourteen years have passed since you first asked me to serve as Shadow Chancellor. Since then we have achieved a good deal together. Hence my surprise at the suggestion, made this morning for the first time, that I should now leave the Foreign and Commonwealth Office, at a time when major matters are in train in our relations with China over the future of Hong Kong as well as with the Soviet Union and our NATO partners. The European Community, of course, is at a crucial phase of its development.

You indicated that you had some lack of confidence in our continuing partnership as a result of differences in our approach which became most manifest in the run-up to the recent Madrid Summit of the European Community. As you know, I am convinced that Britain must play a positive and leading role in the Community and all its institutions.

Given that background and my own developing anxiety at the way in which decisions are taken in the Government, I do not think it would be in the best interest of either of us, nor the Government as a whole, for me to remain a member of your Cabinet in the circumstances you now suggest. I am, of course, very sad that our long years of service together should have to end in this way. It has been a great privilege to serve under your leadership at a time when we have been able to change Britain's future so much for the better. I shall, of course, maintain my support for your Government in following policies to that end.

David Waddington, obviously alarmed by the prospect, argued strongly against my departure from government. During this conversation he did his best to apologize for the way in which he had misled me. He had known when I telephoned him on Saturday morning, he said, of what was afoot, but 'I had been sworn to secrecy, Geoffrey.' There was no point then in reproaching him, for he had faced a real conflict of loyalties. But our relationship with each other could never be the same again. I returned to the business in hand. 'If I am to stay in office,' I said, 'then the terms on which I hold the Deputy Prime Ministership will be of crucial importance.' He agreed to relay these thoughts to Number 10.

There was then a brief, and in the circumstances bizarre, return to 'business as usual'. For I was due to attend a military police lunch in Rochester Row, in order to present a long-service medal to one of the officers who had escorted us on overseas missions, Staff Sergeant David Humphries. This was an engagement which was by then of much more importance to everybody else than it was for me. I carried it through as best I could. But I often wondered just how Sergeant Humphries and his family would look back upon the occasion, if it later turned out that I had already left the government by the time he had received the award from my hands.

On the way back to Whitehall, I called briefly in to my Commons office. The usually busy Foreign Office tie-line had been silent all morning. My secretary, Arabella Warburton, with four years' experience of the onerous parliamentary workload, had already sensed the impending change. In answer to her inevitable question about the choice I faced, I said, 'I think that I shall probably stay in there.' 'But only if you're sure that's what you really want, ' she replied, with more loyalty than conviction. 'It hardly makes me happy,' I said. 'But I have no real choice. I still believe I have a role. I don't think I can relinquish it.' I was moving towards a decision. By the time I got back to the Foreign Office David Harris, Anthony Teasdale and Stephen Wall had been joined there by Elspeth. Soon afterwards David Waddington rang to say that, if I did stay on, the Deputy Prime Ministership would definitely be part of the package. Further discussion led to the conclusion that my decision should rest on just how far Margaret was ready to accept my description of the Deputy's job. So I returned, again via the Cabinet office, for a further talk with the Prime Minister.

There was only the one issue for discussion: the terms on which I should agree to serve. The possibility of my accepting the Home Secretaryship had already been dismissed. And the position about Chevening and Dorneywood had been made explicitly clear at our first meeting. So there was no 'bargaining' to be done about things like that. If I was to stay on as Deputy Prime Minister, I said, then that would have to be made clear – not just in formal terms but to the extent that I should be assuming the role previously occupied by Willie Whitelaw. There was no problem about the actual positions that I should hold. But the rest, said Margaret sensibly enough, would depend on how far we were able to recreate confidence in each other. For Willie had been 'a very special kind of person'. 'That confidence', I replied, 'has been greatly damaged by today's events.' Margaret demurred and said the problem was mutual. It was illustrated, I replied, by the fact that she had not, even now, told me whom she had in mind as my replacement at the Foreign Office. She could not tell me, she said, 'since I haven't yet warned his boss'.

The whole conversation, as we should both perhaps have seen more clearly at the time, was scarcely an encouraging foundation for renewed partnership. I left on the basis that I should give the Prime Minister my final decision as soon as possible. At least she was free to approach her new Foreign Secretary. I returned to the Foreign Office and reported there to Elspeth, David, Anthony and Stephen Wall. Anthony Teasdale worked out more quickly than the rest of us the reference to the new Foreign Secretary's 'boss'. 'John Major?' he said. 'It can't be,' was our immediate reaction. Then after a pause, 'It must be,' I said: for the Chief Secretary was the only Cabinet Minister who had a 'boss'.

We then returned to discussing my own position: we concluded that I had done everything possible to define the terms of my new position, and that I should go ahead on that basis. Stephen Wall passed that answer back to Charles Powell at Number 10. A little later Charles Powell rang me, before any announcement had been made. The Palace, he said, had had a little difficulty in accepting the official description 'Deputy Prime Minister'. They were proposing to follow the precedent of Eden with Churchill and use the form of words: 'Sir Geoffrey will act as Deputy Prime Minister.' Was that all right? I replied that so long as the job was presented along the lines already agreed, with details of Cabinet committee chairmanships and so on, I should be content with that precedent.

Elspeth and I returned to Carlton Gardens to begin the reconstruction of our domestic arrangements. Two constants at least remained in that part of our lives: Mrs King, our treasured housekeeper at four different houses; Peter Smithson, my government car service driver for eleven years, and a constant source of wisdom, practical advice and sheer loyalty. Elspeth was due to leave the next morning, with Cary and grandson Christopher, for the start of our holidays in Montauroux. I was due to join her later in the week. Meanwhile, Alec would have to start moving out of the terrace-house in Camberwell that we had acquired as a London *pied-à-terre* a couple of years before.

The whole family was shell-shocked by the suddenness of the tremendous upheaval ahead. Elspeth was as angry as I was at the ruthless lack of candour with which the 'coup' had been planned and carried out. More than I did, she had inclined to the view that I should have left the government. But she was, as always, ready to back my decision and to carry on managing the mainstream of our family life. The first *Daily Mail* that she saw after her arrival in France carried another of those articles (this time a not unsympathetic piece by June Southworth, headlined 'Behind those smiles – the secret hurt of Elspeth Howe') which depicted her as 'the real Iron Lady of Cabinet politics'. She had 'pushed her husband hard through high office for more than a decade' and was now off for a working holiday in France to 'replan a campaign that would have done Napoleon proud' – and so on.[4] Neither of us could ever recognize this picture. 'Formidable' may well have become her Homeric epithet, from which she cannot escape: it is now part of our family-teasing vocabulary. For Elspeth has achieved a distinguished career in her own right. But so far from her having been the actor-manageress of my life in politics, the relationship has always been one of partnership. At no time was Elspeth's support more important than in the weeks of readjustment that lay immediately ahead.

Fifteen months later, when I finally left the government, Stephen Wall wrote to me reflectively. 'I have often thought', he said, 'of the grim day when you left the FCO and whether you should have followed what was clearly your instinct then – to resign. How anyone can be expected to make such a judgment, in two hours and under maximum stress, I don't know.' He was right, of course. That is why I allowed my instinct to be exposed to at least some outside advice, and over 'so many' hours. Yet even today it is hard to be sure which course would have been best in the interests either of the government, the country even, or of my own future contentment. The resignation letter which I wrote, but never sent, was certainly an accurate reflection of my feelings.

Why then did I not follow those feelings into practice? Probably, I think, because I felt in my bones that that would be the beginning of the end of such influence as I might still have over the political future. No one else who left the Thatcher government – before or since, from Heseltine to Lawson – had any significant effect, once and so long as outside the system, on the practical conduct of affairs. So why should my case have been any different? I don't think my reaction was at all driven – let alone as much as outsiders might think – by purely personal considerations: will life be more tolerable, better paid even, away from all this turmoil? Will I be more or less likely to climb the last step on the political ladder by reclaiming my 'independence' now? The first question was probably too simple to be decisive – and the second much too difficult. So I settled, in effect, for the option that I thought I could best comprehend: the one that involved the least transformation at impossibly short notice in a life that was already facing violent upheaval. If I had followed my instinct and left Mrs Thatcher's government at that time, that might have given the Howes a more settled life. It is still impossible to be sure about the wider consequences of such a decision.

News Management

The political fall-out of my dismissal from the Foreign Office was more substantial even than the personal. It was more complex, more far-reaching and, I should guess, very different from anything that either Margaret Thatcher or I might have expected.

The Prime Minister's most overt aim would have been to strengthen, or at least to freshen the appearance of, her government. Less explicitly, but more importantly, she would have been wanting to reshape her Cabinet so that it would more readily respond to her will. We know today (but did not know then) just how firmly determined she was, after Madrid, to 'move [me] aside for a younger man'.[5] 'Never, never . . . again'[6] did she mean to.be as exposed to pressure from her Chancellor and Foreign Secretary as she had been before that event. None of the other Cabinet changes was headline stuff. David Young, John Moore and Paul Channon were being replaced by Peter Brooke, John Gummer and Norman Lamont. Most interesting was the promotion – at last – of Chris Patten, shrewd and rising star, in place of almost the last of the respected veterans of her first Cabinet, George Younger. But Margaret's key objective must have been to secure as positive a response as possible to the arrival in the Foreign Office of John Major, alongside my own return to the domestic scene. And my own interest, once having decided to remain in the government, would not have been very different: I too should have wanted the most positive construction to be put upon my new domestic role, to offset the impact of my 'demotion' from the Foreign Office. So both sides should have had an interest in presenting the change in the best way possible, with the most being made of my new role.

But that is exactly what did not happen. The 'lead stories' in Bernard Ingham's press digests for the Prime Minister on the next two days say it all:

> Positive reception for reshuffle overshadowed by disclosure of offer of Home Office to Sir Geoffrey Howe. Presentation in ruins because of briefing. (26 July)

> *Sun* says you blame Sir Geoffrey for turning the Cabinet reshuffle into a fiasco. It has seriously damaged his standing in the Party. (27 July)

The quotations well illustrate the singular style of Ingham's press digests – the readiness to find an outside scapegoat for bad news and a preference for tabloid sourcing. But the central message was unarguably right. Three things had seriously damaged the impact of a story that was never going to be an easy one to get across. First, the news that I had first been offered Douglas Hurd's job – and that there had been prolonged negotiation about my role; second, the devaluation of my new position as Deputy Prime Minister; and, finally, the unfounded suggestion, carried in one paper under the headline 'Howesey Housey' that I had launched a process of 'bargaining' about Chevening and Dorneywood.

Most serious of all was the absurd notion that it was I – or more precisely my 'friends' – who had been, deliberately, the source for all these stories. This would have been wholly contrary to my own interests. It was also wholly contrary to the truth. My people – specifically David Harris, himself a former chairman of the Lobby (of parliamentary correspondents), and Anthony Teasdale – first heard public mention of my refusal of Douglas Hurd's job from journalists on the Tuesday morning, 25 July. By then Number 10 had told the Lobby in terms that 'Sir Geoffrey had seen the Prime Minister twice before Mr Major had arrived.' The press could, therefore, have deduced that I might not have accepted the first job offered to me. We know too that Number 10 sources had talked freely, on the evening of the reshuffle, 24 July, about Geoffrey Howe having no reason to feel 'hard done by', since he had been offered other jobs. So far from emanating *from* my people on that Tuesday morning, the key story was actually being put *to* them by the press.

So too with the Chevening–Dorneywood story. That had only entered the agenda, and then the public domain, because preconsidered arrangements were put to me by the Prime Minister at my first meeting with her. I had not requested or bargained about Dorneywood or any other house: indeed given the shocking impact of what the Prime Minister had said to me such ancillary details scarcely registered. Though Elspeth and I had made the most of Chevening, as a superb adjunct of my job – and much though we had enjoyed it – we had no grand illusions about the duration of our ephemeral tenancy.

The final irritation was the way in which the Deputy Prime Minister-ship was 'rubbished' at Bernard Ingham's Lobby briefing next morning. As the *Daily Telegraph* reported: 'those close to Mrs Thatcher' were describing the role of Deputy Prime Minister as 'a courtesy title with no constitutional status'. The *Daily Mail* quoted 'Downing Street' as suggesting that the new job was 'constitutional fiction'. One other tale gives curious corroboration to this insight. Willie Whitelaw's regular place in Cabinet had been on the left side of the Prime Minister. On the day before my first Cabinet in the new job, Margaret asked me if I would mind leaving Nicholas Ridley in that place, where he had sat since Willie's departure. After a little reflection, I felt it would be more sensible for me to move into Willie's place. If it had been worth Margaret asking me about it, it was worth getting the answer right. And so I did. But not before the Press Association (and several papers) had reported the whole story, with my 'fierce rearguard action' ensuring that I was 'firmly ensconced in Lord Whitelaw's old place'. How absurd it was to see internal public-relations battles being fought about such trivialities! Certainly the 'rubbishing' story reached and, in the words of the *Independent* on 27 July, 'distressed a considerable swathe of Conserv-ative back-benchers'. This was only the last of many factors which secured the worst possible press reception for the reshuffle.

It is scarcely perhaps for me to say so, but it should not have been too surprising that even the substance of what the Prime Minister tried to achieve did not naturally arouse widespread acclaim. The point was very simply put by a writer whom I do not often quote, Richard Ingrams.

Perhaps in ordinary times, he said, it would not matter much who is Britain's Foreign Secretary. But we are living not in ordinary times but amid momentous events. All the more extraordinary, wrote Ingrams, that 'our man on the world scene is . . . completely lacking in any experience of, or evident interest in, foreign affairs by comparison with a predecessor who now seems like a giant of statesmanship'.[7] Bernard Ingham had indeed commended the changes to the Lobby with ruthless candour from Number 10's point of view. John Major, he said on 25 July, 'came with no baggage of previous pronouncements on foreign affairs'.

A Well of Goodwill

I felt indeed desperately sorry for John, for whom I had developed some respect in his first Cabinet post, as Chief Secretary. He was now being pitchforked into a formidably multidimensional job, where he would have to cope directly with a boss who regarded herself more and more as having less and less need of the services of a Foreign Office, let alone a Foreign Secretary. By contrast, I was immensely heartened by the generosity of the Foreign Office's farewell to me. On the day after I left the Office, a party was by chance taking place to say goodbye to the outgoing Chief Clerk, Sir Mark Russell. The host, Patrick Wright, insisted that I should still go to this. Mercifully before arriving there, I had received from Arabella one of her characteristically perceptive green-ink notes: 'This is just to warn you of the sheer scale of goodwill and emotion that is likely to overwhelm you tonight.' Even then I was less than prepared for the depth of feeling (one wrote of the 'disappoint-ment, dumbfoundedness and disillusion which has engulfed this office') and warmth of kindness that awaited me.

On the following day, I was three times surprised in similar fashion. I was due in the afternoon to attend a Buckingham Palace garden party and then to go straight into the Palace for my first Privy Council meeting as Lord President of the Council: as I was walking alone through the crowd towards a side entrance of the Palace, I was astonished to realize that a sudden outburst of applause was directed not at one of the royals but at me. Later that same evening, as I gave Alec dinner at the Garrick Club, arranged weeks before, we were surprised when we were served with a bottle of champagne 'with the compliments of the centre table' and then, the third surprise, with two balloons of brandy from another group of diners. 'At this rate,' said Alec, 'I think we should stay here all night.'

But that could not be, for I was due to meet John Major in the House of Commons at 10 p.m. to give him the first of several briefing talks that I had promised. It was a strange encounter, at which John conducted himself with great understanding and modesty. I genuinely wanted to help – to help John handle an immensely challenging agenda, and to help British foreign policy exploit a no less promising one. The Iron Curtain was about to crumble. Britain was poised, almost for the first time, for a positive role within the European Community. Five-power leadership was at last making a reality of the United Nations. Apartheid, though we didn't know it then, was close to surrender. Yet here was I, six years into this task, about to offer advice to a successor who came to the job, in Ingham's brutal words, 'with no baggage of previous pronouncements on foreign affairs'. The paradox was bizarre. John Major, flattered by his preferment, was also a little forlorn. The occasion was doomed to be little more than a generous exchange of courtesy and bewilderment. John knew he had my blessing; he well understood that, for the challenges that lay ahead, he needed all the blessings he could get. My own need for benediction was hardly less compelling, and I needed time, too, to think about the implications of my fractured future. Both of us faced a bemusing prospect.

Even more startling was my experience as Leader of the House the following day, 27 July. I had at 3.30 p.m. to face for the first time the regular Thursday-afternoon barrage of questions about the business of the Commons. This followed straight after the Prime Minister had finished her Thursday question session. When I had to answer my first question as Leader of the House, the House was full and she was still in her place. As I rose to my feet, there came a deep-throated roar of applause, such as I had never heard before, from both sides of the House. ('Loud, continuous and triumphant applause (as Pravda would call it),' wrote Edward Pearce in the *Daily Express*). It seemed to go on and on, for one full minute at least, with me standing at the despatch-box and Margaret sitting on the bench beside me. The *Evening Standard* headline, 'Howe brings the House down', underlined that this outburst was as much a reproach for the Prime Minister as it was a greeting to me. I was so moved that, when it became possible for me to make myself heard, I was barely able to manage an emotional croak. It was good to know that I had friends on all sides of the House, where I had now to refurbish my relationships.

Alan Cochrane, writing three days later in the *Mail on Sunday*, was one of several who noticed how Margaret Thatcher had 'catastrophically under-estimated . . . the well of goodwill' towards me, not just in politics but in the country at large. By treating me so shabbily she brought forth 'an amazing display of warmth towards him and hostility towards her'. Prophetically, he concluded, the previous week might well come to be seen by historians as 'the watershed of the Thatcher years, the moment when it really began to go badly wrong'.[8]

For me it was the moment for another change of role, and for reflection on more than six years' work as Foreign and Commonwealth Secretary. There was no shortage of valedictories from all round the world. Two among many touched us deeply. Jacques Delors wrote in French 'because the words spring naturally from my heart'. He thanked me for 'the precious and comprehensive support' that I had given him in his early years as Finance Minister and, 'on behalf of many in Europe', for bringing 'the same spirit to bear in helping the Community over many obstacles'. George Shultz expressed himself baffled by the significance of my change of post. But, he said, 'You have done a simply extraordinary job for your country and for the free world. You have been solid as a rock on the basic principles that we share and must stand by. You have been a gifted participant in ministerial meetings. You have been the "glue" of the joint efforts of the alliance to move ahead on all fronts.' From no one did I value such kindness and respect more highly.

Elspeth, I know, was especially touched by a card that came, a few weeks later, from some of her special friends among the wives of EC Foreign Ministers, all *en route* to an informal weekend *rendezvous* at Chartres. Marie Delors, Anne-Marie Dumas, Alice Ellemann-Jensen, Barbara Genscher and Josee van den Broek all wrote to say that they were 'missing us terribly'. Europe had forged many real friendships for us both. And we roared with laughter at a bread-and-butter note for supper in Paris that arrived soon after my departure, from twelve-year-old Duncan Burns, son of my last head of News Department, Andrew Burns. Duncan's letter carried a touching postscript, which said it all: 'P.S. Sorry about the job.'

The press, as always in our free society, was mixed. Adrian Hamilton in the *Observer*, for example, took almost as dim a view of me as he did of the Foreign Office. 'One of the least imaginative and least impressive

Foreign Secretaries for many decades' had failed to find a vision for a Foreign Office which 'has lost its way hopelessly in the modern world' and 'hasn't come to terms with the present'.⁹ It was hard to recognize the same subject in the appraisal by Nicholas Ashford in the *Independent* of 'one of the most effective Foreign Secretaries since World War Two', primarily because I 'saw quite clearly that Britain's influence depended essentially on two factors – the strength of our economy and our membership of the EC.'. The interesting question, on which Ashford ended his piece, was whether, as some argued, I had been too deferential in my dealings with Margaret Thatcher. His judgment, based on the facts of my recent demise, was that if I had tried to be more robust in standing up to her, I would probably have been moved aside sooner. 'Sir Geoffrey', concluded Ashford, 'did his diplomatic best to temper her impetuosity and for this we should be grateful.'¹⁰

That daunting assignment did not end with my departure from the Foreign Office.

PART SIX

=====

LEADER OF
THE HOUSE
1989–1990

CHAPTER FORTY

STALKING-HORSE

Nigel's Exit

My last fifteen months in government were to be the least satisfying. I was not without interesting and worthwhile opportunities. Leadership of the House of Commons offered a long, and often neglected, agenda for reform. But I found myself away from the turbulent mainstream of a government that was running off course. Most of the real work was being done in ministerial groups chaired from Number 10. Denied the opportunity of doing so, I could only rarely make an input into the management of key issues. Yet, even semi-detached, I remained too big a figure simply to be dropped, but too recently committed to be able to resign. Margaret apparently wanted it that way. This separatist structure clearly did not make the most of my experience. Less obviously perhaps than that, it can be seen to have paved the way for a dramatic end to our relationship.

Some of the tensions for my own position very quickly became apparent. Within days of my change of job, David Harris was obliged (during my absence in France) to proclaim my loyalty to the Prime Minister and to deny a report that I was 'plotting a coup'.[1] In the middle of August I issued a stinging attack on the Labour Party – 'the longest postcard in history,' somebody said. It was a signal of my return to the domestic political scene. And in my first week back from holiday Brian Walden was pressing me, on his Sunday lunchtime programme,[2] to accept the role of licensed dissident. I was going to be, in his words, a 'deeply active, robust Deputy Prime Minister', because I could now regard myself as 'quite unsackable. . . . She can't get rid of you.' I would not accept my role as he described it, of course. But he was reflecting a widely held view. Indeed it was one that many colleagues had commended at the time of my change of job. Two of my former PPSs, for example, were pleased with the prospect. Ken Clarke extended 'congratulations on your guts'. Statesmanship, he thought, was needed in domestic as well as foreign affairs, so he was encouraged to see me 'installed at the centre of things'. Virginia Bottomley, 'speechless about events of the past month', was nevertheless comforted by the thought that I was now 'uniquely in a position to be a major force for the good'. In an ideal world they were certainly right. But all would depend upon the quality of my partnership with the Prime Minister.

The next public test came at the party conference, in October. It was the first since 1973 at which I was not to answer one of the principal debates. The Deputy Prime Minister was not responsible for any subject that earned a separate place on the agenda. So my most conspicuous engagement was a long-standing fringe commitment to address the Bow Group. In my forty-minute talk I tried hard to strike the right balance. The special quality of Margaret Thatcher's governments, I said, had been 'an overall and, above all, sustained sense of purpose'. I traced this back to our original Bow Group agenda. That is why 'it must remain our principal task to maintain the successful momentum of the revolution' of the previous decade. But we had, I said, a serious task of political persuasion ahead. We had to choose a style to match the country's changing mood. That did not mean staunching the flow of ideas which gave the government its intellectual cutting edge. 'But it does mean making sure people recognize us as a listening party, just as much as a crusading one.' The Conservative case had to be put carefully and with caution about 'superlatives, hyperboles and absolutes'. Above all, we needed to show that 'we are good, not just at winning battles, but at winning arguments and winning friends'.

This carefully calibrated message made the front-page lead of the *Evening Standard* as an expression of 'growing concern', a 'coded warning' and the like.[3] Other papers followed this lead. It was a measure of the extent to which my every word would be scanned, more than ever before, for any signal of 'revolt' from the Deputy Prime Minister. I was being eased into a position of 'responsibility without power' – and I did not find it a comfortable process.

There was another side to this problem – the extent to which I was seen, nevertheless, as sharing responsibility for aspects of policy in which I was not engaged. The poll-tax was the most striking example. As Foreign Secretary I had not been at all involved in this. But nor was I even in my new position. The 'small group' of ministers managing this problem, under Margaret's chairmanship, had long since acquired a jargon-laden life of its own. It was much too late for me to be admitted to the club. Yet I found myself increasingly sought out by individual colleagues (even some who *were* in the 'small group', like Chris Patten, who sensed the impossibility of his own position) as a kind of one-man court of appeal. My concern with the tax far exceeded even theirs. Most of them were to some extent case-hardened. I was not. And I was dismayed by my total inability to offer any kind of respectable reply to even the simplest complaints about the tax from my own constituents. Never before in my political career had I found myself wholly un-equipped with any intellectually credible explanation for what we were trying to do. The case that was often impossible to explain was the imposition of a standard double charge on a single-income family.

This kind of dilemma steadily eroded the confidence of ministers in themselves and each other. Nigel Lawson, I know, felt bitterly about the wider political and economic consequences of this ill-judged fiscal upheaval. He sent me a note after one particularly fruitless talk about the subject, on 21 September 1989. Money spent on making the Community Charge 'slightly less appalling', he said, was not only 'bad value for money objectively' (that is compared with the spending of lesser sums of public money on more carefully chosen objectives). It was also 'money spent to save her face', since Margaret's personal enthusiasm for the Charge was well known. 'I do not', he concluded, 'regard that as a worthy cause. Do you?' My reply was pragmatic: 'Her face? Well, yes – certainly. But our bacon as well, surely? Though even there we have to compare prices.'

This exchange might seem to imply a pattern of intimate consultation between Nigel and myself. But that was never so. We were always ready to talk things through candidly. But we had, for example, done no preplanning ahead of my demise from the Foreign Office. Nor did we do so in advance of Nigel's resignation from the Treasury, on 26 October. I knew certainly that his task had been made steadily more difficult as a consequence of the return, the previous May, of Alan Walters as Margaret's economic adviser. By the time of the party conference in Blackpool, on 10–13 October, the rising rate of inflation (and level of overseas interest rates) had obliged Nigel to raise our own bank rate to 15 per cent. This grisly political task was made no easier by recurrent reports of Walters' conflicting advice. I was myself questioned about this when I was deputizing for Margaret Thatcher – as I did whenvever she was away at Prime Minister's questions – on 19 October.

Nigel and I had the chance to discuss these problems briefly when we came together on the following Monday, 23 October. For the Institute of Economic Affairs had invited us both to speak informally at a dinner to celebrate the tenth anniversary of the abolition of exchange control. It was a good occasion. We were among friends whose economic radicalism had done much to shape the politics of the last decade. Nigel and I had been privileged to play leading roles in putting them into practice, and Margaret Thatcher had provided the political authority which had made that possible. What Nigel and I knew – but our friends at the IEA did not – was just how badly frayed now were the bonds that had once bound the three of us together. The situation, Nigel told me that day, was becoming 'preposterous' and he was 'close to the end of his tether'.

I realized his frustration, of course. In a different way it matched my own, but I did not have the impression that a resignation decision was imminent. I assumed, I suppose, that like the rest of us he would soldier on. So I was astonished, three days later, not only by Nigel's departure but by the way in which I learned of it. On that particular afternoon I had a string of duties which kept me in, or close to, the Commons Chamber. My regular Business Questions had to follow a long report from the Prime Minister on the Kuala Lumpur Commonwealth Confer-ence (at which she had treated John Major with ill-concealed contempt). Next came a three-hour guillotine debate, which I had to open and then follow closely. The resignation news reached me from my own office in the House, as I sat on the front bench. Only moments later Dennis Skinner was on his feet in the Chamber, demanding a statement: 'Why is there no one on the government front bench ready to explain what has happened?' It was a good question. One answer was that the Leader of the House was even then posing the very same question. 'Why on earth', I was asking, 'have I not been told what is going on?' A minute or two later a handwritten note arrived from Number 10:

Dear Geoffrey,
    I am the bearer of bad news. Nigel has decided to resign as Chancellor and I have not been able to dissuade him in spite of intensive efforts. It is a great *shock* – he has been such a good Chancellor.
    I have just seen John Major whose appointment will be announced shortly – as the new Chancellor.
    I will see you soon after the vote if you are available.
        Yours ever,
        Margaret

It was not an answer to my question, of course, particularly since it soon emerged that Prime Minister and Chancellor had been discussing his proffered resignation since 9.00 a.m. that day, and I had sat alongside her from beginning to end of that morning's Cabinet meeting. Margaret does not appear to have discussed the topic with any ministerial colleague until after she left the House, when I took her place at the despatch-box at 4.30 p.m. That was the moment when she asked John Major, three months old at the Foreign Office, to step into Nigel's Treasury shoes. Kenneth Baker, the party chairman, seems to have been the only minister to join her at Number 10. The Chief Whip, David Waddington, and I were by then pinned down in the chamber, struggling to resist demands for a statement about Cabinet changes, while impressing upon Number 10 the urgency of the need to make one. The mounting hubbub persuaded the Deputy Speaker that 'a brief cooling-off period' was desirable. So he suspended the House for ten minutes. By then I had found an opportunity to speak by telephone to Margaret at Number 10. She was still uncertain – or purported to be – about the choice of John Major's successor at the Foreign Office. She perceived Tom King as an alternative to Douglas Hurd. But it took her almost no time to agree with me – she may well already have been persuaded – that Douglas was pre-eminently the right choice. To succeed Douglas at the Home Office, she had no doubt about David Waddington as the right man.

Only, I think, for the choice of the new Chief Whip did my voice carry real weight. My former PPS, Tim Renton, had, I thought, many of the right qualities. Calm under fire, balanced and wise, he had also (years before) resigned from my Treasury team on grounds of principle that Margaret and I could both respect. She came later, and unjustly, to regret this choice. More generally, I was more than dismayed that it was only at this eleventh hour, and then only by chance, that she received any advice about the crisis from her Deputy Prime Minister. Elspeth said as much to Kenneth Baker, when he turned up a little later at my room in the Commons. It was no consolation that it fell to me, in a few minutes, to announce the changes in the House. Later in the evening I did in fact join Margaret for a few minutes over a drink at Number 10. 'I cannot understand', she repeated, 'why Nigel has resigned.' And so indeed it appeared.

'Calculated Malice'

Clearly the Chancellor's resignation, now that it had actually come, was a great shock. He had been a tremendous source of strength and intellectual inspiration during my eight years as Shadow Chancellor and Chancellor. By the end of his time at the Treasury, I was inevitably discomfited by the way in which his inflationary 'blip' had ballooned into something much bigger. (The year-on-year headline rate had by now reached 7.5 per cent.) None of us could escape some share in responsibility for this. For we had all been carried away by our own success story and, in the words of CBI director general John Banham, had 'taken our eye off the inflationary ball'. It is hard to resist the feeling that Nigel's own 'animal spirits' had carried him further towards optimism than my own less adventurous instincts might have allowed. But probably the most important single cause of the inflationary boom was the long-running failure – 'at the highest level of government' – to resolve the chronic conflict over economic policy between the Prime Minister and her principal colleagues. The question of ERM membership had not been openly and collectively addressed since Margaret had closed down discussion at the meeting on 13 November 1985.* From now on it would have to be tackled without the benefit of Nigel's experience and wisdom.

But at least John Major was back in a department where he had some reasonable grasp of the issues and looked at home. And the Foreign Office (with which John had struggled manfully) was back under the command of a man almost uniquely qualified for the task. From now on Margaret's management of the Madrid conditions for ERM entry was shared with Major and Hurd. No longer were her ministerial colleagues to be outbid in authority by a transatlantic guru. This was the crucial, plainly stated reason for Nigel's departure. The only useful by-product of losing a Chancellor was the near-simultaneous resignation of Alan Walters himself.

Certainly my own exposure on this topic had not diminished. Only two days after Nigel's resignation, I was due in Bath to give a keynote speech at the first meeting in Britain of the Anglo-Spanish Joint Conference (or Tertulia).† As I reflected with David Harris and

---

* See p. 450 above.
† This was the body that I had been glad to establish (with much help from Ambassador

Anthony Teasdale on the morning after Nigel's departure, I realized that this was an occasion at which I should be expected to address the principal European issues, not excluding those which underlay Nigel's departure from government. The thought of resigning from the government, as it were in Nigel's wake, came into my mind for a minute or two and was almost as quickly dismissed. But, if I was to carry on, it had to be with a real purpose and to good effect. That pointed the way for my weekend speech. For what better opportunity could there be to reaffirm, before an Anglo-Spanish audience, the continuing validity of the commitment and the conditions that Margaret herself had spelt out in Madrid? Those certainly were unaffected by Nigel's departure from government, and the sooner somebody said so, the better.

So Anthony Teasdale and I set about putting together a short speech to that effect. I cleared the important passages by telephone on the Saturday morning, 28 October, with John Major and Douglas, to whom I delivered a copy at his Oxfordshire home on our way down to Bath. The text was distributed immediately to their two departments as well as to Number 10 and released to the press from my own office. (It would not have been appropriate to use Conservative Central Office for this non-party occasion.)

I delivered the speech in the elegant setting of the Pump Room at Bath with Chris Patten, the local MP, ensconced at my side. I repeated the Madrid conclusions – 'on which the Prime Minister, Nigel Lawson and I all agreed' – almost verbatim. That remains, I said, the position today. 'It is of the highest importance that Her Majesty's Government is seen to remain committed to that position, clearly and in good faith . . . not just for the credibility of our European commitment, but for the economic health and strength of Britain herself.' Almost as a grace note, I added a valedictory tribute to the departing Chancellor, Nigel Lawson. Margaret was later to cite this praise for Nigel as evidence that my speech was one of 'calculated malice'.[4] But my language was certainly no more fulsome than that which the Prime Minister herself used in her Walden interview on the following day: Nigel had been 'Brilliantly successful . . . extremely able . . . unassailable . . .'

Press reaction to my remarks did, however, underline the extent to which ERM membership remained a fault-line within the government. The *Sunday Times* headline for my remarks, 'Howe throws down

---

Puig de la Bellacasa and Lord Thomas of Swynnerton) as an equivalent of the Anglo-German Königswinter Conference.

gauntlet', was bizarrely offset by the briefing from Number 10 that featured in the same report: 'The Prime Minister is said to believe that her Madrid statement pushed the issue into the future and that by the time the British criteria have finally been met, the nature of the EMS may well have changed.'[5] This reported view was dramatically corroborated by the transmission that day of the Prime Minister's own views, prerecorded with Brian Walden on the Saturday morning. There was almost no limit to Margaret's multiplication and extension of the Madrid conditions.* Walden was right when he summarized what she meant in practice, 'that we shan't be going into the ERM for quite some time'.[6]

The debate continued for the next week. First Douglas Hurd broadened the issue with an unequivocal assertion that 'the trend towards European collective action was many-fronted and inexorable'. He also confirmed, to *The Times*, that both he and John Major had been consulted by me about the text of my Bath speech.[7] Then John Major, in his first speech as Chancellor (which, he pointedly said, the Prime Minister had not seen in advance), asserted in the Commons that 'the Madrid commitment must be seen to have been made in good faith'. Finally Nigel Lawson, in his powerful resignation speech, made the link between Alan Walters' presence in Number 10 ('the tip of a singularly ill-concealed iceberg') and the gulf between the Prime Minister and most of her colleagues. He put the key ERM issue crisply: 'For economic and political reasons alike, it is important that we seek the earliest practicable time to join rather than the lengthiest for which a tolerable case can be made.' Norman Tebbit, more objective and shrewder then than he later became, delivered the prophetic judgment: 'It is dangerous for a captain to appear semi-detached from her team.' The process of detachment still had some way to go.

The Challenge

Nigel's battle with the Prime Minister had been conducted largely out of the public eye. Only towards the end did the titanic clash become obtrusive. Other tensions had been building up below deck. But never

---

* 'We shall join the ERM', she said, 'when there are no foreign exchange controls, when there's freedom of the movement of capital, when their financial services . . . are run as openly and freely as ours are and when we have fair competition and the subsidies are gone. . . . Other countries have to catch up a long way before it happens'

before now had they threatened to manifest themselves in a challenge to Margaret's leadership. This had been a theoretical possibility in each of the thirteen years since her first election in 1975. But only in 1989 did the idea bubble towards the surface. The thought that Margaret Thatcher might actually be defeated was never seriously considered. But there was something to be said, thought some, for a demonstration of her political mortality. So various names began to be canvassed as so-called 'stalking-horse' candidates against her. These included ex-ministers such as Barney Heyhoe, Ian Gilmour and David Howell.

The man who had in the end the courage for this kamikaze task was the sixty-nine-year-old baronet, MP for Clwyd North-West, Sir Anthony Meyer. After Eton, he saw four years' war service with the Scots Guards, three years at New College and twelve in the diplomatic service. He held the marginal seat of Eton and Slough for the same time as I did Bebington (1964–6) and was one of the last four on the Reigate short-list from which I was selected in 1968. He went on to hold Nigel Birch's old seat in North Wales. Gentle and a bit of a loner – but always supported by his wife Barbadee – Anthony had earned the respect of constituents and House of Commons alike by his principled champion-ship of Britain's role in Europe. But his candidature against Margaret Thatcher, though almost by definition forlorn, was more broadly based than that might imply.

My own reaction to the emergence of a challenge was more sympath-etic, no doubt, than it ought to have been. The recklessness with which Margaret had been ready, within the last three months, to downgrade or discard two card-carrying foundation members of Thatcherism had done nothing to endear her leadership to me. Yet there was no evidence to suggest that any credible alternative was likely to emerge. So what advantage could accrue to country or party from any weakening now of the authority of her experience? These were the terms in which I was thinking, without reference to the possibility of any personal role. I had thought of myself, of course, as a potential successor to Margaret and, for all that the opportunity might never arise, I still did – but never, at least until then, as a credible potential *challenger*. Yet now there were several ready to press that case seriously. Joe Rogaly, in the *Financial Times*, for example, commented that I saw it as a 'very important purpose in my life' to ensure that 'Britain does not once again miss the European boat'. That required me, in his view, to resign and challenge Margaret Thatcher in this imminent leadership contest. It would, he acknowledged, be 'the biggest gamble of my life', and he did not think that I should find the boldness now that had eluded me at the time of my removal from the Foreign Office.[8]

The most persuasive advocate of such boldness was former MEP Will Hopper. His impressive credentials included the fact that he had attended upon me, almost nine years before, to offer powerfully pre-emptive support for my 1981 Budget. He urged me now to stand against Margaret not as 'a wet European, calling for membership of the EMS etc', but for much the same reason as he had backed me in 1981. The present inflationary, high-interest-rate cycle, he argued, called for 'a return to economic virtue as exemplified by your own period as Chancellor'. With this he would have had me couple 'a more collegiate . . . and more compassionate style of government, including a strong attack on homelessness' and 'a more constructive approach to Europe'. (All of this was well in line with my own thinking, as expressed in recent speeches to the Bow Group and the Radical Society.) Hopper went on to echo Rogaly, in arguing that I would 'take everyone by surprise' because 'no one thinks you have it in you'. Finally, he addressed the factor that worried me most: 'You need have no concern about accusations of disloyalty. Loyalty is after all a two-way business. The Leader's recent total and public lack of consideration relieves you of all responsibility on that score.'[9]

I was attracted by the analysis and by the advice. I took very much my own counsel about it. In the end I rejected it, because I felt constrained, as I explained to Hopper, very largely by the loyalty factor. 'Certainly,' I wrote, 'loyalty is a two-way business – and has not been seen as such by the other party; but I have allowed myself to proceed, since last July, upon the basis of a continuing commitment which it would, I judge, have been impossible to break at this particular eleventh hour.' This was far from a ringing declaration of loyalty, but it was, as I believe, more than just an alibi for lack of courage. Looking back on it now, I think I still felt that the long-run joint endeavour (which Margaret and I and others had all been carrying forward) was more likely to stay afloat if I remained on board, trying to influence the course, than if I jumped ship, having first tried in vain to challenge the captain. Above all, I could not now so swiftly repudiate the commitment of continuing service which – wisely or not – I had given less than four months before.

So, like Michael Heseltine, Kenneth Baker and Willie Whitelaw, I issued a statement urging parliamentary colleagues not to 'force the party into a leadership election'. The Prime Minister, I said, 'commands the overwhelming support of the party'. That judgment was not entirely vindicated by the result on 5 December. After an energetic Thatcher campaign – masterminded by two Wykehamists, George Younger and Ian Gow – Margaret secured 314 votes and Anthony Meyer 33. Twenty-seven MPs abstained from voting. The result fell very far short of a vote of no confidence. But the scale of dissent was a significant warning for the future. Over a late night drink in my room at the House Ian Gow expressed the view that Margaret would do well to draw the right conclusion from the sixty votes not cast for her. George Younger did well to advise her of the wisdom of moving Messrs Powell and Ingham away from Number 10 to pastures new. For in Kenneth Baker's words 'their combined influence was resented by many Tory MPs'.[10] The advice went unheeded. I probably compounded the mischief by inviting 'the whole Cabinet', at its next meeting on 7 December 1989, to 'join in congratulating the Prime Minister on the outcome of the leadership election' – which was, I said, a recognition of the achievements of the last ten years under her leadership. I had to acknowledge that in such circumstances loyalty could not easily be given in half-measures.

CHAPTER FORTY-ONE

HOUSE LEADER

My New Job

The Leadership of the House of Commons – coupled in my case, as it often is, with Lord Presidency of the Privy Council – involved an astonishingly broad range of duties. On 4 September 1989, within six weeks of appointment, I was on the platform in Westminster Hall for Her Majesty the Queen's opening of the Centenary Conference of the International Parliamentary Union (IPU). No less than 111 nations were represented there. And only a few weeks later I was answering parliamentary questions about women's hairdressing facilities and toilets in the same Palace of Westminster.

I was on parade about once a month for meetings of the Privy Council. The Queen herself would almost always preside, normally at Buckingham Palace but occasionally – depending on the royal calendar – at Windsor, Sandringham or Balmoral, even on the royal yacht *Britannia*. Four or five other ministers would generally be present, sometimes, among other things, for new recruits to take the oath of loyalty. The whole routine, conducted in settings of informal grandeur, would last no more than thirty minutes – unless lunch was being served, a treat reserved for the country residences.

The only State Opening of Parliament with which I was concerned was at the commencement of the 1989–90 session and the very first to be televised. It is strange now to recall the flurry of anxiety, even alarm, that was occasioned by that belated innovation. Most of the practical arrangements for televising had already been made before I arrived, by the special House of Commons Select Committee under the chairmanship of my predecessor John Wakeham. But there remained scope for a good deal of hostility between Members and broadcasters as practical details began to be perceived: too much heat, too little light, poor sound, obtrusive cameras, unflattering shots, incompetent editing – the scope for complaints was endless. I was fortunate in the membership of the Committee. All my colleagues shared my wish for a non-confrontational relationship with the broadcasters. We were helped by the benignly professional good sense of the first director of broadcasting, John Grist.

The first day's coverage got Commons Television off to a good start. For two of the most TV-sceptical parliamentarians, Margaret Thatcher and Ian Gow, turned out to be great screen hits: the first because she had dressed for the part in a striking electric-blue suit and had taken a great deal of trouble to modulate and vary her speaking style; and the second because he had remained his superbly unchanged, mildly pompous, gently self-mocking self. The hazards soon became apparent too. It was not long before the *Daily Mirror* claimed to have seen me 'nodding off' beside Margaret Thatcher in full flood. Another correspondent protested when I appeared 'wearing the tie of the Garrick Club, which has replaced the wispy beard as the uniform of the left-wing intellectual'. Bright-eyed, bushy-tailed – and no flash ties – became the order of the day.

There was one other curious aspect to relationships between the Leader of the House of Commons and the media. This arose from the convention that, when the House is sitting, the Leader should meet all the parliamentary Lobby correspondents at about 4.30 p.m. (after Business Questions) every Thursday afternoon. This took place in the small Lobby Briefing Room in one of the upper-floor corners of the Palace of Westminster. The Leader appeared there traditionally – or so I understood – in the presence of Number 10's chief press officer, at this time Bernard Ingham. My PPS, David Harris (himself a former journalist and chairman of the Lobby), would come too. I found this a most unnerving and unfruitful experience, and not just because relations with the Number 10 Press Office were almost as hard to manage as relations with the Lobby itself. I was glad to learn, from their own books, that most, if not all, of my predecessors had been similarly nonplussed by this fixture.[1] The whole affair was 'off the record' and 'unattributable'. But the timetable was so well established that any thinly disguised indiscretion reported in Friday's papers was automatically attributed by one's colleagues to the Leader of the House. And it was only the indiscretions that were worth reporting. I was glad of the fact that Bernard Ingham stopped coming to my Lobbies after a week or two, leaving it to a junior to take his place.

The 'Howesey Housey' story returned to haunt us again, I'm afraid, and once again through no fault of our own. Within a few weeks of leaving the Foreign Secretary's official residence at Carlton Gardens, we were reasonably installed in our own small Camberwell house. But the security authorities remained acutely anxious. Careful evaluation of evidence which always underlies these 'threat assessments' led them to the conclusion that I was almost as much at risk in my position as Deputy Prime Minister as I had been as Foreign Secretary. (Later evidence established beyond doubt that they were right about this.) They were insistent that I should once again be found accommodation that was less off the beaten track and more secure than was then possible for our own home.

The authorities quite quickly came up with the suggestion of a rather oversized MOD house in Atterbury Street, not far from the long-closed and still empty Millbank Military Hospital. I was naturally curious about its normal use. More than anybody else we needed to be sure that there was no snag. Was it really available? What had happened to the previous occupant? The Cabinet Secretary, Robin Butler, and Permanent Secretary of the MOD, Michael Quinlan, both responded most helpfully. The normal occupant, the Director of the Army Medical Service, had been living elsewhere, while the empty house was done up. He could be asked to continue to do so in order that the house might be used to meet our immediate security difficulty. There was absolutely no problem. Why else would the authorities have suggested our going to the house? It seemed reasonable enough, if we had to move yet again. And we were told we had to.

So, reluctantly, Elspeth and I were back to tea-chests and suitcases. No sooner had we made the move than a fresh storm broke. 'Howe to get army house in London', screamed the headlines. Senior army officials were said to have 'reacted angrily' to what they saw as 'the eviction of the Commandant of the College of the Royal Army Medical Corps from his traditional residence'. It was reported that the Major-General and his wife, on the point of moving in, had already ordered the decorations, the specially printed notepaper and so on and had been looking forward to Christmas in residence. On this basis, they were understandably upset. So indeed were we. For, as a result of this unexplained misunderstanding, we found ourselves once again presented as house-hungry schemers. Indeed we were furious, but totally frustrated, for by then the damage had been done. It was only compounded by recollection (and reporting) of the fiction that I had 'bargained for' and secured Dorneywood, in exchange for Chevening.

All this made it sadly difficult to appreciate the charms of Sir Courtauld Thomson's fifty-year-old gift to the nation, and the kindness of the small staff who looked after Dorneywood and its occupants. We came to grasp the full meaning of the phrase *embarras de richesses*. The final irony is that none of the *richesses* belonged to us. But we had always been glad to share our relatively short-lived enjoyment and use of these splendid tied 'cottages' with as many people as possible, not least with the journalists and broadcasters whose media were now so ready to join in denouncing us. It is a strange way of encouraging people to accept the risks and responsibility, as well as the opportunity, of high office.

Happily the parliamentary aspect of the Lord President's work opened up a wide vista of reformist opportunities. I found some of the tiny staff in my new 'department' – no larger in total number than the private office alone in either of my previous jobs – who were very keen to make something of them. So were some in the Cabinet Office, the very centre of the Whitehall web. It was enlightening to discover the reality of parliamentary 'characters', people whom I had known for years – but never really knew, until I had to work with them on parliamentary committees. 'Radicals' like John Biffen or Tony Benn turned out often to share a deep conservatism; and 'conservatives' like Peter Shore or even Mr Speaker Jack Weatherill turned out to have an encouragingly radical streak. And there was still Denis Healey, now finally retired to the Labour back benches. Predictably he extended a warm welcome to my appearance in yet another role. Receiving his greeting, I said in reply, was like 'being cherished by a dead savage'.

There were plenty of complex opportunities for trying to mobilize all-party reformist zeal. One such was the problem of relations between the House of Commons and the European Parliament. More than in any other national parliament, British MEPs were still treated by their Westminster colleagues almost like pariahs, strictly forbidden to enter any of the working parts of the Palace. The Commons had for too long seen itself as engaged in hostile competition with Strasbourg for management of the EC's 'democratic deficit'. I wanted to steer it more towards partnership in the control of European law-making institutions. With the helpful support of my Labour opposite number, Dr Jack Cunningham, I secured a new set of specialist committees for just that purpose. This ended the absurdity of keeping the whole House up for late-night debates on detailed EC legislation. We also moved the six-monthly European debates to a couple of weeks before each European Council, so that MPs could raise topical issues at the best times. Almost more important psychologically was agreement that MEPs should be allowed much freer access to the bar, restaurants, libraries, lobbies and corridors where much of the Commons daily business is played out. So too I was glad to be able to procure for Members of Parliament free telephone (as well as postal) access and travel rights to and from the European institutions in Brussels, Luxembourg and Strasbourg.

Voting Procedures

All the legislative and debating procedures of Parliament stand in equal need of reform, though I did not have time to tackle these problems strategically. But one important opportunity for innovation arose in connection with the handling in the Commons of the Human Fertilization and Embryology Act. Originally this Bill embodied only the pioneering recommendations of the Warnock Committee on these sensitive subjects. At the end of its parliamentary journey the Act also included some very useful and hard-fought compromises on the law of abortion.

This was, initially at least, a most unexpected outcome. Governments of both parties had traditionally regarded abortion as the province of back-benchers, and the subject had been explicitly left to one side by the Warnock Committee. If passions ran high on embryo research, those who were opposed to abortion and those who sought to defend the present law were even more implacably opposed. In the summer of 1989, pro-life MPs had lobbied for government time to be provided by allowing an amendment on abortion law to be included in the forthcoming Warnock Bill. There were serious risks that, if abortion were admitted to the Warnock agenda, it could all too easily swamp the rest of that legislation. One or other of the sharply conflicting abortion pressure groups might seek to filibuster and, perhaps in the end, wreck the Bill itself. On the other hand Parliament would not improve its status in an age of televised debates by failing to reach a decision on a major topic of this kind. (The exploitation of seemingly arcane procedural devices had been a feature of earlier debates on these issues.)

All these questions had arisen before I arrived on the scene – and remained unresolved. I decided – with the keen support of the Chief Whip, Tim Renton, and the Health Ministers, Ken Clarke and Virginia Bottomley (all three had at one time served as my PPS) – that we ought to have a go at getting everything settled.* So, as a first step, the Bill was introduced with a long title whose wording gave a signal that it would be possible for abortion to be debated.†

The pro-life group had indicated that their strategy was for abortion to be taken once the Bill reached the Commons. When this was clear, the veteran Labour peer (and my constituent) Douglas Houghton introduced on 22 November 1989 a Private Members' Bill which aimed to give effect to the recommendations of the Lords Select Committee which had reported in 1987.² This offered in effect a minimum-change option, which aimed to clarify the law and introduce a time-limit set for nearly all cases at twenty-four weeks. This point was the consensus of medical opinion, in the light of the latest neonatal science, on when a foetus was capable of being born alive. That Bill, which was presented as a better way of dealing with abortion through keeping it separate from the embryo-research issue, passed all its stages in the Lords after a division on the second reading on 22 November. The real battle, however, about abortion time-limits then remained to be fought in the Commons.

So far we had grasped the nettle of allowing Parliament to debate the abortion time-limits question. Now we were faced with how best to handle it so as to minimize the risk to the rest of our legislative programme. This was the cue for another constitutional novelty. We decided that it was sensible for me, as Leader of the House, to table a core clause as a basis for discussion and to assist the House in reaching the decision which had so far eluded it. In fact the new clause, which, like the alternative provisions for embryo research, was discussed in a Committee of the Whole House on 24 April 1990, closely resembled the provisions of Lord Houghton's Bill, which by then had completed its Lords proceedings. I made it absolutely clear that this government new clause was being tabled to allow orderly debate and not because it represented the position the government wanted to reach. In other words, we were making no departure from the traditional position of neutrality on abortion, which governments had adopted since the 1967 Act.

Ken Clarke, as Secretary of State for Health, tabled a series of

---

* This account of our proceedings is based upon the article, 'Legislating on Human Fertilisation and Embryology', by R. L. Cunningham in *Statute Law Review*, 1991, pp. 214–27; he was closely concerned with the Bill as an assistant secretary in the Department of Health.

† The important phrase was 'and the subsequent development of an embryo'.

amendments to 'my' new clause: his amendments embodied a range of alternative time-limits ranging from eighteen (as in David Alton's 1987 Bill) to twenty-eight weeks (the *de facto* current position). Again the purpose in moving these alternatives was to assist the House to reach a decision. To ensure that the issue did not take so much time in debate that it endangered the remaining proceedings on the rest of the Bill, I had proposed beforehand a complex timetable motion and this had been agreed with all the main interested parties. The outcome, a time-limit in nearly all cases of twenty-four weeks, was reached by a system of pendulum voting with sucessive votes narrowing the gap from the extremes of eighteen and twenty-eight weeks – finally, after rejecting twenty-two weeks, settling on twenty-four, the figure in the original new clause.

There was one other novelty in our procedure – the production of a number of voting guides for MPs: these tried to explain in plain terms the actual effect of voting for one or other group of amendments. An 'official guide' was produced and circulated by my office; much nearer the time, rival guides were prepared by the main pressure groups and also, on a neutral basis, by the government Whips' Office, which attempted to present the issues in a simplified form.

There were one or two accusations that some MPs had by mistake voted against their stated intentions during the long succession of votes on the abortion time-limit question. But these were not sustained. So the careful handling strategy which we had evolved had been successful in helping Parliament to reach clear-cut decisions. Parliament could take some satisfaction in having dealt clearly with two highly emotive and, in the case of abortion time-limits, complex legal issues. It was important for the Commons that it succeeded in reaching decisions, since the Private Members' Bill procedure had previously proved an inappropriate vehicle for this kind of reform. The painstaking way in which agreement was reached in advance with all the main interested parties had clearly paid a significant dividend.

The problems which had led to these procedural innovations struck us at the time as possibly unique, with no immediate parallels. But we had at least shown that government could help Parliament reach decisions on difficult ethical issues within the framework of a government Bill. And we had done so by using existing parliamentary techniques in ways which, while perhaps not individually remarkable, were, taken together, an important development of the legislative process. We had successfully handled a new situation forced upon us by the imperatives of science and medicine.

Ceremony and Reform

Encouraged by this success, I felt able for a day or two to switch my attention away from Westminster and down to Winchester. For I had been invited back to my *alma mater* to be accorded, on 5 May 1990, the highest honour that the school can bestow – the ceremony of being received Ad Portas. This takes place in the central quadrangle of William of Wykeham's fourteenth-century buildings, known as Chambers Court. The assembled company includes the Warden, fellows, headmaster and staff and, most important of all, the 500 boys. The speaking role, apart from that of the honorand, is played by the Prefect of Hall. He is the most senior of the seventy scholars. Let me for a moment hand over the narrative to the eloquent speech made, in my case, by the Prefect of Hall, Richard Lea:

> This College is a place of many traditions, of ceremonies that set it apart and bind it together. These are often puzzling to the Wykehamist and incomprehensible to the outsider. . . . And perhaps strangest of all is this rare ceremony. A distinguished person walks in through Middle Gate. The Prefect of Hall welcomes him with a speech, perhaps in Latin, and he replies in whatever language he feels appropriate. . . . Most importantly, we gather here for Ad Portas to celebrate the achievements of a leading figure and by so doing to honour the purpose of our founder.

Richard and I both opened and closed our speeches with a few sentences of Latin. (I was fortunate to have yet another classical scholar, Tim Sutton, as my private secretary in the Lord President's office.) I tried, in my reply, to set my work in context. The last Wykehamist to serve as Foreign Secretary, who was also received Ad Portas, had been Lord Grey of Fallodon. On that occasion he described how, in 1914, he saw the lights going out all over Europe. 'It has been my privilege', I said, 'to serve in the same office at a time when the lights of freedom have been coming on again throughout Europe, East as well as West.' I commended the style of the three most recent Wykehamist Chancellors (Stafford Cripps, Hugh Gaitskell and myself): 'none of us . . . was easily tempted to flinch from the need for economic discipline'.

I contrasted that with the 'slightly gentler tradition' which I shared with the last politician to have been received Ad Portas, Willie Whitelaw. Successive deputies to Britain's first woman Prime Minister, we had each played 'a subordinate but much less than menial role' in helping to carry through programmes of reform that 'might have daunted even Wykeham's radical zeal'. We had tried to do so, I hoped, 'in a fashion that has served the widest social interests of the nation, in accordance with the precepts of reason and good faith'. I was claiming perhaps too much success in that respect. But at least we had tried.

My last thought was one suggested to me by fellow Wykehamist Ian Gow, in the words of a prayer regularly used in the Temple Church – and which his own career was destined to fulfil, alas too well. Long may Winchester continue to play its part, I said, in ensuring 'that there may never be wanting a due supply of persons well qualified to serve God, both in Church and State'.

I suspect that the person to whom I owe most thanks for this opportunity for modest glory was the then Warden of the College, my brilliant – even in that setting – contemporary Sir Jeremy Morse. His notable career in the Bank of England, the world Bank and as chairman of Lloyds Bank qualified him as the best Governor of the Bank of England we never had. But there are many races in life that cannot be won by every one of those who may be qualified to win. It was time for me to return to duty at Westminster.

There was one rather larger parliamentary nut to be cracked. I became acutely aware, during my time as Leader of the House, of the difficulties involved in improving facilities and services in face of the multitude of decision-making bodies in the House. The 'senior' body was, I suppose, the House of Commons Commission, under Mr Speaker's chairmanship and with five senior Commons members, including Leader and Shadow Leader. As the Liberal member of the Commission, Alan Beith, pointed out in one debate, 'responsibilities are so widely diffused that it is often impossible to know who is answerable for what'. There was no difficulty in discovering the agenda for action. Accommodation was 'abysmal'; staff facilities 'squalid and dangerous'; accountancy and management methods 'a complex anachronism'; the places where some people try to work in the 'Palace' of Westminster almost as cramped, congested and scruffy as the cupboard-sized cubicles in which Hong Kong boat people had to survive.

This chaotic state of affairs convinced me that we had to take a fundamentally fresh look at the whole pattern of management of the House and its facilities. I persuaded my Commission colleagues to appoint a five-person review team led by Sir Robin Ibbs. Formerly an ICI director, the head of the CPRS, he had recently retired from his position as Prime Ministerial adviser on efficiency in government. The key remedies were clearly prescribed in the masterly report that was in this way commissioned, prepared and approved – all within less than six months. Within three months of my resignation from government, the Ibbs Report had been debated and adopted by the Commission and effectively by the rest of the House authorities. From this there followed the establishment of a totally new, purpose-designed finance and management system, with radically revised committee structure. No statutory changes were required. What was crucial was the actual exercise of power and responsibility by the existing Commission, under the Speaker's chairmanship.

There was and is a huge backlog of work waiting to be done, to repair, modernize and reorganize buildings and services. The 'new' buildings to be constructed on the site opposite Big Ben, long half-derelict, finally got under way, in time for the fullest use to be made of the opportunities offered by the construction of the new Jubilee Line station. All this – and the prospect of much better management and better-quality facilities for Parliament and public alike – is a direct consequence of the work of Sir Robin Ibbs and his team. I count the commissioning and implementation of his report as the most important achievement of my year as Leader of the House.

CHAPTER FORTY-TWO

THE RIFT WIDENS

———

Making Laws

I have been surprised by many of the things that Margaret Thatcher has said about me. I dare say the same is true in reverse. But nothing startled me more than her belief that 'he' (that is me) 'never really put his heart into the Leadership of the House'.[1]

For, as should by now be clear, that was the part of my last year's life in government that I enjoyed a lot. That may have owed a good deal to the fact that I could get ahead with much of it without reference either to Number 10 or to anybody else. The Prime Minister's opposite understanding of my enthusiasm may have derived from the context in which my parliamentary duties actually impinged upon her. It became increasingly clear that we took different views about the place and pace of lawmaking in our political programme. That was bound to give rise to trouble, for I was in charge of the planning and management of the government's legislative programme.

I discovered there, when I came to look, a huge and growing gap between promise and performance. When I had given, way back in 1977, an address to the Society for Conservative Lawyers I had proclaimed that 'we must make fewer laws and make the laws fewer'.[2] Before we came into office in 1979, Margaret Thatcher had specifically endorsed the same objective. Since I left the Treasury in 1983, I had not been much concerned with this topic. Now was the time to re-examine our record. I was shocked by what I found. The annual average number of pages of new legislation (excluding Scottish statutes and election years) enacted by the Labour government between 1975 and 1978 was 1177 pages. For our Conservative government (on the same basis) the average between 1980 and 1989 was 1788, peaking at 2170 in 1988 and no less than 2581 in 1989. That last figure surpassed the Attlee government's all-time high of 2288.

Not only had we been increasing the quantity of legislation, we had also been reducing its quality. This could be judged by the number of amendments that had to be made to Bills once they had reached the House of Lords. This figure had risen from an annual average of 1106 during our first four years (1979–83) to 2668 in our last three years (1987–9). One last figure shook me particularly: the number of Bills affecting local government that had been introduced since 1979 was 141. No less than seventeen of these affected local government finance. The connection was too simple, I know. But the rising tide of poll-tax discontent that was now sweeping the country, culminating in some ugly riots, seemed a poor reward for all this lawmaking activity.

There was only one clear conclusion to be drawn. The government had to recall its original instinct – make fewer laws and make laws fewer. Sometimes we *had* to legislate – to deal, for example, with new technologies, like embryology or satellite broadcasting. Even then, we should take great care to get it right first time. For the rest, the message from my office to Prime Minister and Cabinet was loud and clear. Fewer Bills, shorter Bills, better Bills, properly thought through. No more lawmaking on the hoof. That last was bound to be seen next door – for the Lord President's office in Whitehall is directly linked, through the famous Cabinet Office connecting door, to Number 10 – as a not so oblique crack at hasty lawmaking, on everything from football supporters to dangerous dogs. Sadly it added sourness to another aspect of working contact with the Prime Minister. This had one further consequence. The less the Prime Minister and I impacted upon each other in any policymaking process, the more we were perceived to be doing so through our speechmaking, broadcasting and public activities.

As the second senior member of the government, I retained a substantial programme of that kind. The message which I tried to preach was consistently clear. The *Financial Times* political editor Philip Stephens could be relied upon to get it right. 'Howe's not for turning' was the headline on his feature 'Monday interview' with me on 26 March 1990. Perhaps symbolically enough, this was the day on which I paid a visit to Canary Wharf on the Isle of Dogs – escorted by young, rapidly rising Thatcher acolyte Michael Portillo, then Minister of State for Transport – to mark the tenth anniversary of my 1980 Budget announcement of Enterprise Zones.

It was only a week or two after the disastrous Mid-Staffordshire by-election, in which Labour's middle-of-the-road magistrate Sylvia Heal had trounced Jim Prior's nephew Charles with a straight swing to

Labour of 21 per cent. I had spoken, as always, in course of that campaign, with a warning (almost more severe than his) of the forthcoming toughness of John Major's first Budget. My warning may have been delivered tenderly. But my 'mellow tones', said Stephens, certainly did not signal that I had 'gone soft' on 'Thatcherism'. We had, I acknowledged candidly, to 'shoulder our responsibility for allowing inflation to get a grip again'. So, as before, there was 'no alternative' to current high interest rates. Our radical, market-based agenda remained to be completed. But if we were to press ahead with it sensibly, we had to take care to carry opinion with us. That was why we had to recognize the key role of manufacturing industry. But that kind of intelligent dialogue did not require us to don Labour's – or even Michael Heseltine's – corporatist clothes. It was 'only' on Europe and, symbolic of that, on the European Monetary System and EMU that the views of the Prime Minister and her Deputy substantially diverged. And even then we had, or ought to have had, a *modus vivendi*, based upon the Madrid conditions.

On this basis, my contributions to public debate attempted to defend some deeply unpopular policies. We were expecting to have a rough passage in the May 1990 municipal elections. By some standards we certainly did. Labour scored a net gain of 277 seats and Conservatives a net loss of 172 (we had gained a number from the Alliance parties). But this was much better than the net loss of 600 seats that had been forecast. In places like Wandsworth and Westminster we actually made significant net gains. Our opponents attributed this to the government's favourable treatment of those boroughs. But Kenneth Baker was able, skilfully exploiting selective success, almost to turn defeat into victory. I gave loyal support to this view and went on defending the essential austerity of the government's message. A week later, I reminded the British Property Federation that getting the economy back into balance required a tight fiscal policy and a tough monetary policy with high interest rates. 'There is', I said, in an unconscious echo from the past, 'no alternative to this combination and in time it will have the desired effect.' They did not give me a standing ovation!

Nobody could complain that I was not giving strong support to the Prime Minister – and on a difficult part of the front. Indeed my message was, if anything, harsher than any from Numbers 10 and 11. Any such differences in tone led all too often to my being cast as offering an alternative style of leadership. That certainly did nothing to diminish the signals emitting from Number 10 that could be seen as attempts to downgrade my role. One such example occurred when it was reported that the Prime Minister had invited John Wakeham, then Energy Secretary, to resume responsibility for the co-ordination of government publicity. Neither the party chairman, Kenneth Baker, nor the Leader of the House was apparently considered worthy of this task, as each of their predecessors had been. So there sprang a rash of reports and counter-reports along the lines of 'Howe denies his future in doubt'.[3] The *Daily Mail* shrewdly commented that my 'denial of a rift with Mrs Thatcher was raising more questions about [my] future than it was designed to settle'.

War Crimes Bill

Before long there was a real rift to report. Predictably it arose from the legislative programme. The cause was the War Crimes Bill. This topic had been making its way through our agenda for more than two years. In February 1988 we had set up inquiries to consider allegations, then circulating, to the effect that some war criminals of the Second World War had years ago taken refuge in this country, and were still at large. The retired DPP Sir Thomas Hetherington and his Scottish opposite number Thomas Chalmers were invited to investigate, to assess the evidence and to recommend whether the law should be changed to establish jurisdiction in such cases. This course had been, or was then being, considered in the United States, Canada and Australia at the invitation of the Wiesenthal Institute. In June 1989, the inquiry concluded, to my surprise and dismay, that sufficient evidence was indeed available to mount a number of criminal prosecutions for clear violations of long-standing international law. More surprising still to me was the recommendation that British law should now be amended to give our courts jurisdiction over offences committed almost fifty years ago, and in countries other than our own.

When Cabinet considered this report (on two occasions, in July and December 1989) it was agreed that both Houses of Parliament should debate the principle involved, but that the government should take care to avoid committing itself to any course. The Commons, by a free vote of 348 votes to 123, on 12 December supported the principle of legislation. In the Lords debate eight days earlier no vote had been taken. But the great majority of speakers had been against the principle. The Bill was thus introduced. On 8 March 1990, the Commons gave it a second reading by 273 votes to 60, again on a free vote. I noted that less than half the membership of the Lower House had actually been ready to support the Bill. The critical point arose on 4 June, when the Lords refused the Bill a second reading by 207 votes to 74, also on a free vote. The principal arguments which had swayed their Lordships – and which impressed me – were reluctance to extend British jurisdiction, extraterritorially as well as 'retrospectively', and to do so for the sake of bringing proceedings, on the basis of evidence that was bound to be shaky because ancient, against defendants who were already in the twilight of their lives.

We then faced a choice between two courses. Either we could make use of the Parliament Act 1911 (as amended by the 1949 Act) so that the Commons should make their view prevail over the Lords. Or we could accept our defeat in the Lords, on the basis that it would be unwise in principle to try to enact a statute that could require jurors to convict a person under a law which had been decisively rejected by one House of Parliament. Whatever view one took of the main question, I was quite clear that the use by a Conservative government of the Parliament Act, in order to override the view of the Upper House in this way, would be a constitutional step of great significance. It would be entirely without precedent, and it would give the green light to any future non-Conservative government to behave with exactly the same disregard of the Upper House. For both the reasons I have suggested, I took the clear view that the Bill should be abandoned. But I readily agreed in Cabinet, on the day after the Lords vote (Tuesday, 5 June), that we should need to reflect carefully before coming to a final view. On this basis, the matter would be remitted for reconsideration by the group of ministers that had been handling this matter, under my chairmanship, ever since 1988.

The shock came at the following Monday's usual small pre-lunch meeting of ministers at Number 10. Margaret suddenly committed herself strongly to the view that we should certainly make use of the Parliament Act to overrule the Lords, and so to reintroduce the Bill in the next session. I responded swiftly that we had yet to consider the matter properly, and that my ministerial group would be reporting in due course. Quickly there flared up a row between the two of us, with the few colleagues present all holding their peace. The clash faded as quickly as it had started, and we both accepted, or so I thought, that the question would be considered more formally at a later stage. I knew even then that I had the support on this issue of the two other Secretaries of State most closely concerned, Douglas Hurd and Malcolm Rifkind (Secretary for Scotland, where many of the alleged offenders were thought to be). The Home Secretary David Waddington was, however, by now a champion of Margaret's view. So the very next day the story was all over the front page of the *Evening Standard*, 'Nazis Bill Splits Cabinet: Thatcher and Sir Geoffrey at loggerheads'.

It was nine days later, on the 21st, that the matter came back before full Cabinet. The tone of the meeting was very different from the caution of our discussions a year before. Margaret, now with the bit between her teeth, dominated the discussion. The numbers supporting the Bill, even in the Commons, had progressively diminished. But in her mind the opposing arguments were now uppermost. It was tempting to think that these were mainly fanned by the 'Finchley factor'. But it is fair to remember that it was only two weeks since Margaret had visited Babi Yar in Kiev, the memorial to the 30,000 Jews whom the Nazis had murdered there. She appeared to be particularly provoked, however, by the fact that it was the Lords who were standing in her way. That argument would not have carried such weight during our earlier years in office. Now, however, Margaret discounted arguments, much heeded in the Lords, from champions of tradition and justice such as Lords Shawcross, Home, Hailsham and Whitelaw. The last two were no longer in her Cabinet. How we missed their voices on an issue like this! Cabinet loyalty to principles which they felt instinctively seemed to have departed with them. The discussion concluded, predictably, in accordance with Margaret's wishes.

This was a signal for press speculation about my future to run riot. It was boosted, it must be said, by Elspeth's participation in a National Sleep-Out week (4–11 June). She was photographed, with such well-known undesirables as Esther Rantzen and Paddy Ashdown, sleeping out (with Summit) in a dustbin liner. This charitable exercise had raised £30,000 in 1989. The 1990 target, intended to help get roofless people out of the 'cardboard cities' which were increasingly disfiguring our streets, was £500,000. The campaign was sponsored by, among others, the CBI's Business in the Community (Elspeth was chairman of their Women's Initiative), and by Kingfisher plc, of which she was a non-executive director. Many of her business colleagues were also committed to take part. Reports of her participation were linked, of course, to the baseless 'Howesey Housey' saga. The inevitability of that was probably the only plausible argument against Elspeth's public participation in the campaign. But criticism from such 'friendly' critics as the *Sun* – and

Terry Dicks MP – had the effect only of strengthening her support for a cause to which she had committed herself in good faith.

The press speculation naturally focused on my future. Headlines like 'Maggie and Howe told to make up or break up',[4] 'Maggie and Howe: The Angry Silence'[5] and a full page in the *Sunday Times*, 'Lonely ordeal of accident-prone Howe'[6] told their own story. The analysis – and advice to the Prime Minister as well as to me – was as diverse as that which came from my friends and family. The number urging me to 'throw my hat in the ring' as a challenger to Margaret was growing smaller. Will Hopper was far from the only one to reassert this view. But my changed public profile since leaving the Foreign Office, and the consequent flow of hostility from Number 10, had taken its toll. 'Many Conservative MPs accept that he would be a good Prime Minister,' wrote the *Economist*. 'But they . . . want someone who will win the next election and Sir Geoffrey would not be good at that.'[7] Since becoming Deputy Prime Minister, wrote Alan Watkins, 'he has also, by an apparent paradox, lost his old status of being what is called "the bus candidate"'.[8]

I was not disposed to disagree with that view. Nor indeed was Elspeth. Mythology presenting her as the most persistent of those urging me to nurture my ambition, to maintain the struggle to replace Margaret, is and was deeply misleading. Elspeth was nothing if not a realist. Her analysis, like that of most others, was now directed to the question: should I soldier on with a continuing challenge to the Prime Minister to 'sack' me if she dared? Or should I resign, and if so when and in what circumstances? Elspeth understandably tended to think more of the practicalities than of matters of ideology. So too, not surprisingly, did the Chief Whip, Tim Renton. Knowing Margaret and me as well as he did, he could foresee the near-certainty of eventual break-up. With a party manager's instinct he wanted this, when it happened, to be a controlled explosion. And, as a friend, he wanted me to be hurt as little as possible by the fall-out. I could see his point, of course. But I was deeply reluctant to play a part in allowing the government (and the Conservative Party) to slip still further, as I saw it, in the direction of Prime Ministerial domination. Least of all did I relish the prospect of ever-mounting hostility towards a balanced view of Britain's role in Europe.

One of the arguments that did most to persuade me to stay and fight my corner was the suggestion, by Margaret's supporters in the press as well as in Parliament, that my views were prompted by 'disloyalty'. The stories appearing – by telling coincidence, at the same time as the first news of the 'War Crimes rift'[9] – did little to conceal their source. 'Howe is accused of disloyalty as rift grows wider', headlined the *Express*. The *Daily Mail* was more specific: 'Downing Street has only one word for the reason Sir Geoffrey is in the doghouse: Disloyalty'. It might, I suppose, strike some observers as 'disloyal' to have argued, as I had done two days before, that we should pause a while before accepting the Prime Minister's view that the House of Lords should be steamrollered into submission. But 'disloyal' to whom – or to what? I did not feel that on that issue or any other I was obviously lacking in loyalty to the principles of the party which Margaret Thatcher and I had tried to serve together 'for perhaps too long'. I was fortified by a note which came at that time from a former private secretary – most unusually quoting Horace: 'Neither the people's passion for the pleasure of a scandal nor the glare of the tyrant, can shake the peace of mind of a just man who holds firm to his cause.'*

Ridley Has to Go

No more did I feel that I was being 'disloyal' by keeping up my end of the European argument within our party. It was after all the position to which the government and the party had been committed as the very basis of Harold Macmillan's application for membership of the Community, as long ago as 1962. I was not, however, being offered much opportunity of doing that inside the government itself.

Momentous events had been unfolding within Europe since my departure from the Foreign Office. The Berlin Wall had been torn down. Eastern Europe was setting itself free. The prospect of a reunified Germany had forced itelf on to the agenda. Special European Council and NATO Summit meetings were convened to question or to control, to acknowledge or to legitimize, these developments. Margaret Thatcher had been as dismayed by President Bush's emphasis at the NATO meeting on the cause of 'European integration' as she had been isolated elsewhere in her 'resolve to slow up the heavy pace of developments'[10] on German unification. Within the European Community successive

---

* Odes, III, iii. 1:
  Justum et tenacem propositi virum
  Non civium ardor prava iubentium,
  Non vultus instantis tyranni
  Mente quatit solida.

Dublin Summits (28 April and 25–26 June 1990) endorsed the proposal to convene an Inter-Governmental Conference (IGC) on political union, in parallel with that already agreed for economic and monetary union: the Maastricht foundation stone was being set in place. Within the wider Europe the 'two-plus-four' talks (the two Germanies and the Berlin Four Powers) paved the way to the CSCE Summit, Margaret Thatcher's last, in Paris in November 1990.

Very few of these topics were ever directly addressed in Cabinet. It was amost equally rare for the Cabinet's European Committee (OD(E) under the Foreign Secretary's chairmanship) to consider such broad questions. It was only with some reluctance that I had been readmitted to membership of this Committee. Questions affecting ERM membership were not discussed in this Committee. Nor were they ever raised between the Prime Minister and myself. I knew that Douglas Hurd and John Major were gradually making headway on that.

In particular, John Major had been able on 20 June to persuade the Prime Minister to agree that he should that day, with the blessing of the British government, launch in public what had become known as the 'hard ECU' plan. The idea of this was that the existing European Currency Unit (essentially no more than a unit of account) should develop into a medium of exchange, with a life of its own. It would not replace national currencies, but would be interchangeable with them, and would in that sense become a new, thirteenth (and in the long run potentially single) 'European currency'. One of the principal progenitors of this idea was our former ambassador to the EC, Sir Michael Butler, now prominent in the City. He was supported in this thinking by the British Invisible Exports Council. He had taken great care to keep key figures in Whitehall, including myself, in touch with the thinking. He made at least one attempt to sell the plan to the Prime Minister. But it was only now, through the agency of the Chancellor himself, that the idea had made at last a significant breakthrough. John Major spelt it out in a speech that night five days before the second Dublin Summit. 'The ECU', he said, 'would become a *common* currency for Europe. In the very long term, if people and governments so chose, it could develop into a *single* currency.'[11] With this skilful intervention, the United Kingdom had at last acquired the right to be seen as a realistic, even if still slightly outlandish, player on the field of economic and monetary union.

I had played no part in the governmental process that had borne this fruit. So it was inevitable that my views on European and other foreign-policy questions should surface as often at engagements with the outside world as they did around the Cabinet table. I presided, for example, at the Inaugural Session in Westminster of the British–Irish Parliamentary Body on 26 February 1990 and was able there to welcome this consolidation of the Anglo–Irish Agreement. And I travelled more frequently to conferences in continental Europe. Helmut Schmidt and I made the two keynote speeches at the Foundation for International Studies, St Gallen University in Switzerland on 28 May. The concrete situation of a united Germany had presented itself much more rapidly than anyone could have foreseen. But 'the workings and the dynamic evolution of the Community', I pointed out, 'were designed precisely with such contingencies in mind'. The coming together of sovereignty excluded and was meant to exclude the tragic and traditional philosophy of dominance and subjugation, of power and conflict which had 'too often characterized Europe's history' for centuries past.

I developed similar themes in an important lecture on 'Sovereignty and Interdependence'[12] at the London School of Economics on 8 June 1990. I was at pains to emphasize that 'sovereignty should be seen as divisible – and exploitable in the interests of the nation' by being used in partnership with that of others. 'Sovereignty is not like virginity', I said – 'now you have it, now you don't.' I commended instead the analogy of a rope. The EC represented 'the coming together of twelve different skeins of silk, each of which retains its unique quality, but all of which gain in strength by being engaged with each other'.

At a more practical level, I had circulated to Cabinet, in advance of the second Dublin European Council on 25–26 June, a long comment on Douglas Hurd's proposals for our approach to the forthcoming IGCs. Unusually he had sought written reactions from all Cabinet colleagues, a rare exercise in collective dialogue on Europe during the last eighteen months of Margaret Thatcher's premiership. My central message was simple. Any ideas that manifestly aimed to stall integration or deliberately limit the emerging role of the Community were likely, I argued, to fall on deaf ears. 'We must play from within,' I said, 'with the grain of the European process, with positive proposals likely to attract others.' Echoing almost precisely the sentiments of the letter that I wrote forty years before,* I endorsed Douglas Hurd's argument that 'a purely negative reaction . . . would harm us domestically, in Europe and with

* See pp. 21–2 above.

the Americans'. And I took it virtually for granted that 'early entry into the ERM would be an important indicator of the UK's good faith'.

Such brief discussions about foreign policy as did occur in Cabinet generally arose either in the context of Douglas Hurd's regular weekly reports or when the Prime Minister spoke about her own international encounters. With some sadness I must now record that the courage of many pro-European colleagues often faltered, so that they remained silent in face of remarks from the chair that were usually hostile to most of what was in prospect. Some ministers – not always the overt 'anti-Europeans' – were only too keen to report on items of EC business which the Prime Minister could treat as half-volleys and hit out of the ground. And Nick Ridley would play with growing conviction the role of Greek chorus to the Prime Minister. It was not surprising that I was from time to time provoked – much less often than I might have been – to offer some remarks in opposition to the irritatingly recurrent tone of Euro-scepticism. Nor then, I suppose, was it surprising that 'Mrs Thatcher's allies' were often reporting to the press that 'the Deputy Premier hardly makes any contribution to Cabinet debates and is generally negative when he does'.[13]

I have for years been fond of quoting the legal aphorism that 'even in an affidavit the truth will out'. The same is sometimes true of newspaper interviews. The point was amply proved by the *Spectator* report of Nicholas Ridley's talk[14] (at that time he was still Secretary of State for Trade and Industry) with its editor Dominic Lawson. The headline aptly summarized Nicholas' views: 'an impassioned denunciation of a country he accuses of trying to take over Europe'. The EMU was a 'German racket', German behaviour was 'absolutely intolerable', Kohl would 'soon be trying to take over everything' – and so on. The interviewer's comment was almost more damaging. 'Mr Ridley's confidence in expressing his views on the German threat', said Lawson, 'must owe a little something to the knowledge that they are not significantly different from those of the Prime Minister.' This needed little corroboration. A day or two later it came in the form of a leaked record of a seminar on Germany that the Prime Minister had recently held at Chequers. Even though skilfully sanitized by the note-taker, Charles Powell, the note could hardly be described as enthusiastic.

Taken together, the two episodes served to confirm the scale and passion of Margaret Thatcher's 'anti-Germanism', as it was already well known to those Germans whose business it was to know. This was perhaps the main reason for the ferocity of the critical reaction to the

Ridley interview. Probably for the same reason the Prime Minister did not initially want him to go. After two or three days, however, she had no option but to accept Nick Ridley's departure from her Cabinet. He was in effect drummed out by the reaction of a broad majority of Conservative MPs. Douglas Hurd had spoken for many besides himself when he described the interview as 'poisonous'. It was difficult at the time to think through the implications of this débâcle for the future of government policy towards Europe. Peter Jenkins saw the whole thing as 'a blow to the Bruges faction'. He thought that the 'tasks of involving Britain in the next chapter of European development and saving the Conservative Party from a catastrophic split' had been made a little easier by Nick's departure.[15] I was by no means so sure.

Elspeth and I were both much saddened by the personal implications of the affair. Twelve or thirteen years had passed since Nick and I had first started working closely together, in the Opposition Treasury team, on the notion of Enterprise Zones and on privatization. In the second half of my Chancellorship he had brought stimulating sparks of fun to the whole process of tax reform. There had been long periods (intermittent in my case) when we were the last two surviving smokers in Cabinet. For a week or two I felt relief that his troublesome voice was absent. But within a month I was writing to him (from a brief holiday retreat at Bedarra on the Barrier Reef) to express sadness at his departure. I thought, I said, that we had always been agreed on three objectives – 'restoring enterprise, beating inflation and leading Europe'? 'The last two,' he replied, 'conflict with each other. You can't beat inflation with a fixed exchange rate.' We agreed to differ.

Ian Gow

We were soon to suffer a far more shattering blow. On the first Monday of the recess, 30 July, I was sitting at my desk in Dorneywood when the radio brought news of the kind that was never far out of mind. But this time it was about my oldest and closest political friend, Ian Gow. He had been brutally murdered by the IRA, a bomb wrecking his car just as he was moving away from the Dog House, his Sussex home that we knew so well. His wife Jane had reached his side as he died. My mind was filled with anger, with grief, with disbelief. Elspeth was equally shocked. Minutes passed before we made any practical reaction at all. Then within hours, Margaret and Denis Thatcher, Elspeth and I –

suddenly drawn close to each other by our common grief – had joined the circle of friends that came together to offer support for Ian's family in those days of tragic darkness. His words, in the last Queen's Speech debate on 21 November 1989, were ringing in our ears: 'Our resolve will never weaken, those who choose the bullet and the bomb will gain no concessions, their campaign of terror is as odious as it is futile.' Every word was true, but no comfort in our present grief. For each word had heightened the risk to his own life.

Yet the deeply convincing Christian faith, in which Jane and Ian had built their lives together, was a real support through the following weeks. Not just for their family but for a whole series of wider communities, the Gows had been a constant inspiration. The intimate informality of St Luke's, Stone Cross (where Jane played the tiny organ), the packed civic Mass at St Saviour's, Eastbourne on 8 August, the essentially parliamentary comradeship of St Margaret's, Westminster on 22 October: these diverse occasions all testified to the depth of anger at this wanton killing of one of the most courageous, warm-hearted and respected politicians of his generation. They demonstrated too the extent to which Ian, despite his relish for controversy, had been one of the great forces for concord in our body politic. Margaret Thatcher had read one lesson at each of the main services. At Eastbourne, Peter Ball, then Suffragan Bishop of Lewes, spoke of Ian with deep affection and insight.

At St Margaret's, the corresponding privilege and duty fell to me.* I began by recalling Ian's signet ring. Elspeth and I had spent a day with Ian some thirty years before, on holiday in France. Bathing in the pounding breakers of the Atlantic coast, near Arcachon, Ian found that his signet ring – it had belonged to his father – had been wrenched from his finger by the Atlantic swell. So he procured an exact replica of it and cherished it dearly. Several years later, he was entertaining our own young twins with a tremendous snowball fight in our garden. Suddenly, unbelievably, his ring was lost again, deep in the snow, and undiscoverable. This time, when the long snows had melted, the ring *was* found. 'Ian's joy', I said, 'knew no bounds. He could teach us all how to rejoice. He was doing so almost every day of his life. . . . Deep Christian conviction was at the very centre of his life – his life with Jane, Charles and James, and his wider family.'

I tried to follow this theme through Ian's immensely full, and varied

* The full text of my address is at Appendix I.

career: Wykehamist, soldier, solicitor, church warden, lay reader and Member of Parliament. He was indeed 'a faithful servant of Church as well as State'. In his beloved Eastbourne, I said, his conscientious response to people's needs, his truly magnetic sincerity, had won the affection of an entire community. So too in the House of Commons. He had made his maiden speech in Denis Healey's first Budget debate. Douglas Jay, Labour's veteran Wykehamist, who spoke immediately after Ian, observed with some prescience that Ian had 'shown a capacity to disagree with his own party which would endear him to both sides of the House'. And so indeed it proved. 'Ian was totally incapable of any kind of deceit. And the House knew that. So too did people, as time went by, in every corner of the nation. And, perhaps, above all, in Ulster – the province that had enlisted his devotion ever since he had soldiered there.'

Yet, as we all knew, it was Ian's love for Ulster that had destroyed not only his own life but also the political partnership with two of his closest colleagues, Margaret Thatcher and myself. Dismayed by the Anglo–Irish Agreement, he felt obliged to end his all-too-short ministerial career by tendering his resignation. We both sought strenuously, in friendship and with respect, but in vain, to dissuade him. Ian closed his resignation speech with a restatement of his conviction that we were embarking upon the wrong course. He concluded, 'With all my heart – it is quite a big heart – I pray that I am wrong.' It was 'that massive openness of heart', I said, 'that truly granite integrity, which were at the very core of his bubbling personality. . . . we may be sure – he may be sure – that Ian's oh-so-full life was not in vain.'

I finished as I began: 'Like his own signet ring, when the snows had melted away . . . Ian's witness will endure for ever, in the faith of Christ.'

As I returned to my place in the pew behind Margaret Thatcher, she turned touchingly to murmur thanks. Even more striking – within an hour or two – were the generous notes from Opposition leaders, Neil Kinnock and John Smith. 'His political opponents', wrote Neil, 'mourn him and despise his murderers for taking a good man.'

But the loss to British politics as a whole, great as it was, was as nothing compared to the impact of Ian's death on some of the fragile relationships nearer the top of the Conservative Party. Few people understood these better than my former special adviser Peter Cropper. 'History', wrote Peter at that time, 'may tell how much Ian did to lubricate the relationship between PM and Chancellor between 1979 and 1983. It was in the highest tradition of Wykehamist subtlety.' Ian's good offices had continued long after both Ian and I had left Downing Street. The devotion of his loyalty to Margaret, forged during his years as her all-time-model PPS, was closely matched by the loyalty of his long friendship to me: fifteen years had passed since he had helped to run my own leadership campaign in 1975. Ian had been keenly aware of the gap that was opening, during my years as Foreign Secretary, between Margaret and myself – above all on Europe. So he took care to see a good deal of each of us. In my room in the House, after the Commons had risen, we would often linger over a glass of whisky, trying to make sense of our common dilemma. The 'Gow factor' – which kept me so often late at night and which Peter Smithson, my long-suffering driver, knew so well – became ever more evident in my year as Leader of the House.

By instinct himself a Gaullist, Ian's heart would lead him to follow Margaret most of the way towards Bruges. But he perceived too the force of reason behind my case. He sensed the validity of the European-ism that had been shaped by his other heroes, Macmillan and Churchill. And his unique position as a personal confidant to Margaret as well as myself enabled him, I think, to sense the wider symbolism of our continuing relationship. If we were to drive apart from each other, Ian's loyalties were not the only ones that would be intolerably strained. It was that insight which caused Ian to argue, right to the end and in contrast with Tim Renton, that I should for as long as possible stay with the government. Even when Ian was gone, that remained my view. But his brutal disappearance did not make the future any easier – for any of us. Who knows how differently history might have unfolded had it not been for the assassination of Ian Gow?

CHAPTER FORTY-THREE

RESIGNATION

We Join the ERM ·

In the days between Ian Gow's death and his funeral service, the world was transformed by fresh shock. Saddam Hussein's Iraqi army stormed into Kuwait on Thursday, 2 August. Margaret Thatcher was by then with President George Bush at Aspen, Colorado. The vigour of the President's response to this flagrant aggression owed a good deal to Margaret's proximity and instant reaction. To his credit France's President Mitterrand was ready to follow suit. The rest of Europe faltered badly. But within days we had mobilized the UN Security Council into a united response.

For almost the only time I had to preside, as Deputy Prime Minister in Margaret's absence from London, over meetings of the Oversea and Defence Committee of Cabinet. But if Churchill was always in effective command during the Second World War, then all the more so was Margaret from the outset of 'Operation Desert Storm'. Modern communications would in any case have ensured that. In the weeks that followed, British forces were assembled in the Gulf, beginning with two Tornado squadrons of the Royal Air Force. Parliament was recalled for 6 September. Worldwide sanctions were the first UN response. Margaret made clear our readiness to use ground forces, if necessary, and there was overwhelming support for that policy. Economic sanctions did not mature into armed conflict until the third week of January 1991.

I was able in the following week, 9–12 September, to fulfil a series of European engagements. Everywhere I was able to speak to the same agenda as Margaret would have done – though not always to the same effect. On the Gulf crisis, I argued in Strasbourg that the uncertainties and hesitation of 'some of our partners' underlined 'the need to give Europe a stronger foreign policy identity'. On economic and monetary union, I could now point to John Major's 'hard ECU' proposal as 'a good-faith contribution designed to help find agreement, not a delaying tactic or wrecking manoeuvre'. Only on the future role of Germany in Europe were there signs of divergence. In a television interview on 9 September the Prime Minister disclosed to David Frost her anxiety that 'the more Europe was federated, the more Germany would be dominant'. This certainly contrasted with my assertion in Frankfurt the following day that further development of 'sovereignty-sharing in the EC was the way to ensure that a united Germany remains firmly anchored in Europe'. These remarks reflected my concern that Margaret was drawing quite the wrong conclusion from German reunification. They were little noticed at home.

It was the reassertion of Margaret's 'Iron Lady' role against the repellent Saddam Hussein that was making an impact. This served for a time to boost her position in domestic politics. But, as MPs began to reassemble at the end of the recess, the sense of economic and political unease began to reassert itself. Constituency hostility towards the poll-tax was continuing to erode morale at every level. Inflation had risen to an eight-year peak of almost 11 per cent. The economy was clearly turning down. 'If it isn't hurting,' John Major was later to say, 'it isn't working.'[1] Interest rates stood at 15 per cent. As the Bournemouth party conference approached, it was this last fact that was worrying the Prime Minister and her Chancellor most. That was the context in which they were once again considering (with the Bank of England and Foreign Secretary) the timing of sterling's entry into the ERM. Work on this topic had been proceeding at an increasing tempo, particularly since the Chancellor's launch of the 'hard ECU'. Astonishing as it may seem to any outsider, I was still not engaged in or informed about any aspect of this. In the middle of June 1990, however (as is now clear),[2] Margaret had finally told John Major that she 'would not resist sterling joining the ERM'. But timing still had to be settled. A few days later the Prime Minister decided to enlarge the circle of those who were considering these matters.[3] She added the one Cabinet member who was still most resolutely opposed to the entire idea, Nicholas Ridley. (His resignation came a month later.)

I became aware of the actual decision to join the Exchange Rate Mechanism only in circumstances that should have been as embarrassing for the Prime Minister as they were for me. For on the critical day, 5 October – the Friday before the party conference – I was due to attend a meeting of the Privy Council at Balmoral. Together with the Secretaries of State for Energy and Health, John Wakeham and William

Waldegrave, the Attorney General Nicholas Lyell and the Clerk of the Privy Council, Sir Geoffrey de Deney, I had to take a morning flight by RAF HS-125, from Northolt to Aberdeen. While I was airborne, someone (presumably at Number 10 or in the Treasury) realized the need for me to 'know' what was going on. But the telephone message that awaited me at Balmoral did not reach me before my first encounter with Her Majesty. In almost her first words, she asked for my opinion of the morning's news. It did not take many moments to guess the point she had in mind. But long enough, I feel sure, for Her Majesty to have realized my state of ignorance. She must have thought it a little odd that the only member of her Cabinet who had been dealing with the subject since 1979 (apart from the Prime Minister) was apparently the last to hear of the government's decision. It was a dramatic signal to me personally of the impossibility of securing the sort of effective working partnership with Margaret for which I had genuinely hoped when I decided to stay in the government in the previous July.

The Prime Minister could at least take some comfort from the 1 per cent reduction in interest rates that was, at her insistence, announced on the same day. I was genuinely able to take pleasure in the ERM decision itself. Four days later I tried to explain, to a fringe meeting at the Bournemouth conference, just why. The decision should be seen, I said, as all of a piece with the central thrust of the government's economic policy over the preceding ten years. Price stability remained our central objective. But the exchange rate now assumed a more prominent role, 'not as a substitute, but as a buttress, for monetary and fiscal policy'. The new link should certainly not be seen as some 'fresh surrender of British sovereignty to the dominance of the Deutschmark' but rather as 'a firm commitment to share in the management of a wider system'. I was at pains to emphasize that this was anything but a soft option. Rather was it a reassertion of the disciplined philosophy which had inspired the Medium-Term Financial Strategy that I had unveiled a decade before. 'That', I said, 'was a strategy we designed for ourselves.' We should now 'play our part in designing and developing the new, wider system' for Europe as a whole. On one crucial, final point I registered agreement with Margaret Thatcher.[4] 'Depreciation is no longer an option,' I said. 'Governments have been obliged to choose between . . . realignments . . . or tighter monetary policies.' And *that* choice – including the tough option of realignment – still remained. But more generally, I concluded, 'there should be "no turning back" from this historic commitment'.

There was here, I thought, and intended, ample common ground between us all, that could now be fashioned into a long-term solution of this unduly protracted problem. Later in the week, as in the previous year at Blackpool, I delivered another long think-piece to the Bow Group. The politics of the coming decade, I forecast, would be internationalist in foreign policy and economically conservative and socially liberal at home. There would be continuing emphasis on sound public finances, and market-led reforms, with increasing moves to give greater choice and opportunities. Any government which ignored these imperatives would do so at its peril. If Conservative governments were to succeed in implementing radical policies, as I would wish, for example, in health and education, then, I said, a 'step-by-step' approach was necessary. 'No turning back' was not the same as 'bash on regardless'. (The No Turning Back Group was a parliamentary pressure group whose message had been growing increasingly naive.)

But this was not the feature of my two speeches at Bournemouth that attracted most attention. For I had given my second Bow Group speech just one hour after the Chancellor of the Exchequer had wound up the economic debate. He had appeared to draw a line under ERM entry. 'Joining the ERM', he said, 'does not mean that we are now on a road leading inexorably to a single currency.' I spoke not of a road but of a railway: 'The next European train is about to leave, for a still undefined destination, but certainly in the direction of some new form of EMU.' Shall Britain this time, I asked, 'be in the driver's seat? Or in the rear carriage?' Our European Commissioner, Leon Brittan, in a Bournemouth speech on the same day, pressed the same point. All that was necessary for success, he argued, was for Britain to accept that John Major's 'hard ECU' plan not only *could* but '*would* lead to a common currency in the future and that Britain wanted that to be so'. The central point on which we both agreed was that it would certainly be unwise for Britain to pass up the chance of sharing control of the joint arrangements that were now likely to emerge. We should not, as I said, 'opt out emotionally from the club'.

Remarkable as it appears in retrospect, the decision to join the ERM seems to have stirred up rather than quelled the underlying arguments. More sympathetically handled the decision could and should have been seen as offering an opportunity to establish a much more harmonized approach within the government and with our European partners. But that was not to be. The party conference proceeded instead to an unexciting conclusion. Margaret made – on her sixty-fifth birthday – a closing speech that broke no new ground. Her section on Europe simply boiled down the themes she had been running for two years since Bruges. The most memorable sentence, unfortunately, was the parallel she tried to draw between comedian John Cleese's 'dead parrot' joke and the new emblem of the Liberal Party which he supported.

For we were now within two weeks of the by-election that had to take place in Ian Gow's former constituency. Jane had made a very courageous appearance at the conference, displaying Ian's signet ring defiantly as she held her hands high above her head. I went straight from Bournemouth to Eastbourne to spend Saturday with Ian's old electorate. I was not reassured by the experience. Over fifteen years, Ian had built up his personal majority (16,923) to one of the largest in the country. But on his local Council the Liberals had remained strong. The seat looked almost tailor-made for a Liberal gain. The outcome was in the same mould as Crosby (1981), Ryedale (1987) and, most recently, Mid-Staffordshire (March 1990). There was a swing from Conservative to Liberal of 20.5 per cent. Our candidate, Richard Hickmet (previously a Lincolnshire MP), was in the wrong place at the wrong time. He paid the price for the party's misfortunes.

These were only too apparent when Parliament reassembled in the following week. The by-election result renewed the post-recess depression of many members. The business managers, John Belstead and Bertie Denham in the Lords, Tim Renton and I in the Commons, were struggling to complete the passage of an overload of legislation. Right up to the last day of the two-week 'spill-over' session (Wednesday, 31 October) ill-digested Lords amendments for the registration of dangerous dogs were being passed to and fro ('ping-pong' was the parliamentary slang expression) between the two Houses. None of this improved the climate for the reception of deteriorating economic news. The unstoppable flow of poll-tax complaints and a sense of exasperated boredom with an all-too-familiar Prime Minister combined to keep spirits low. Yet even those discouraging omens foreshadowed exhaustion rather than explosion.

Roman Intemperance

So no one, I think, foresaw quite how dangerously clouds were gathering round the government in the autumn of 1990. Troubles certainly were predictable. But the two most worrying European items seemed to have been, for the moment at least, safely tucked away. At long last the pound sterling was snugly enfolded in the Exchange Rate Mechanism – and holding pretty steady. And the Chancellor seemed to have devised a formula that would keep the peace, at least for the time, on the single currency. (No matter that only the experts could begin to explain it.) There had been only the most modest of parliamentary revolts against these decisions. Tony Favell, MP for Stockport, had resigned from his position as the Chancellor of the Exchequer's PPS, and on 23 October eleven Conservative MPs had voted against the ERM.

True, the Italians had decided to call an extra Summit. This was set to take place on Saturday and Sunday, 27 and 28 October – halfway through their Presidency. On that Sunday I was myself due to do another interview with Brian Walden on his lunchtime programme. That did not look, at the time I took it on, as though it would pose any unusual problems. Nor did the Italian Summit itself look as though it would consist of much more than an opportunity for grandstanding. Indeed the British quality press, notably the *Economist*, had been urging the Italians to take their Council Presidency more seriously. Prompted by these rebukes perhaps, they decided to quicken the pace.

Led by my guileful former colleague, Giulio Andreotti, the Rome authorities suddenly sparked into life. It became clear (in London and elsewhere), as the week preceding the Summit drew on, that the Presidency was aiming for substantive decisions on EMU at Rome. On this occasion – in contrast to the Milan Summit in 1985 – the British Prime Minister and her Foreign Secretary, Douglas Hurd, at least had some few days' notice of what was afoot. Despite that they were unable to persuade their eleven colleagues to refrain from asserting highly detailed pre-emptive conclusions on key questions that could only be resolved at the Inter-Governmental Conference that had yet to meet.

In these circumstances, the British delegation wholly reserved their position on such questions. On at least two earlier occasions during my time as Foreign Secretary,* Margaret Thatcher and I had had to follow a not dissimilar line. We had later been able to resolve the questions thus left over in a way that we were able to accept. It was far from being the best way of doing business, but it had worked before. Once again there was no alternative. So that was the way in which Margaret Thatcher and Douglas Hurd handled proceedings at the Summit itself.

* Milan, June 1985, and Brussels, June 1987.

A suggested starting date for Delors Stage Two was postponed from January 1993 to January 1994. And the British position – 'the UK delegation prefers not to pre-empt the debate in the IGC' – was sensibly recorded. That too was the entirely practical basis upon which the Prime Minister herself, two days later, formally reported the proceedings to the House of Commons.

But much was to happen before then. First of all, in Rome itself, Margaret Thatcher, so soon as she was outside the conference room, became, more dramatically than ever before, a quite different personality. In media interviews, she decisively hardened her position on EMU. The Community, she said, was 'on the way to cloud-cuckoo land'. The British Parliament would 'never agree to a single currency'. We should 'veto the very idea', and any subsequent treaty, because 'we shall block things which are not in British interests'.

At almost the same time as Margaret was waxing intemperate, I was due on air with Brian Walden. I had been kept in touch with happenings in Rome, and with much that Margaret had been saying. So I realized that I should need all my skill if I was to prevent Brian making much of a 'Cabinet split' on this issue. I stuck to precisely the 'hard ECU' line that John Major had presented, with Margaret's and Douglas' approval, before the Dublin Summit. 'The hard ECU, which Britain proposes, would become a common currency and, if peoples and governments so wished, could become a single currency.' Eventually Brian accepted the point. But then he put the corollary: '*You* may believe that. *And* the Foreign Secretary. *And* the Chancellor. But *she* doesn't. And *she's never* going to have a single currency.' At least we were clear now where the split in the Cabinet was to be found. That did not prevent the appearance in next day's Ingham Press Digest to the Prime Minister of the telling sentence: 'Sir Geoffrey Howe felt to have signalled differences over EC in Govt.' I did not think it was I who had been doing the signalling.

For it was the Prime Minister herself who was breaking ranks with her own government, with a clear view that Britain would *never* participate in any EMU arrangements. I was most unhappy about the situation now emerging. Margaret's declared policy was bad for Britain. If she persisted, my own position would be – and increasingly would be seen to be – untenable. I consulted my team, particularly David Harris and Anthony Teasdale. They confirmed my own instinct to wait until Tuesday afternoon, 30 October, when Margaret Thatcher would make the customary Commons statement about the Rome Summit.

Neil Kinnock had the chance to question her about my position even before she reached that point. Would the Prime Minister, he asked, condemn those Tory MPs who had 'publicly insulted her Deputy simply for expressing his views' on the future of the European Community? 'Does she not owe it to her Deputy', he repeated, 'to say that he enjoys her full confidence?' Margaret's reply smacked a little of that with which she had sought, a year before, to distance herself from Nigel Lawson. 'The Deputy Prime Minister', she said, 'is too big a man to need a little man like the Right Hon. gentleman to stand up for him.'

Then she moved on to her Summit statement itself. This lasted about twelve minutes and subsequent questioning for another hour or so. The contrast between the two parts of her performance had never been so startling. On economic and monetary union, for example, her opening text 'stressed that we would be ready to move beyond the present position to the creation of a European monetary fund and a common Community currency'. The Prime Minister actually repeated – it was the first time from her lips – the full Major 'hard ECU' formula. The possibility of an emergent single currency was actually admitted, by Margaret herself. She was back on side. Or so I thought.

But the effect was soon swept away. Once through with the carefully prepared text, Margaret let herself go – as she had never before been heard in public on this subject. Most striking was her direct attack on President Delors. He wanted, she said, 'the European Parliament to be the democratic body of the Community . . . the Commission to be the executive . . . and the Council of Ministers to be the Senate'. To this she cried, 'No! No! No!' She did not hesitate to undercut the British 'hard ECU' scheme itself, which she had earlier purported to commend. 'In my view, it would not', she said in answer to a question from Labour Euro-phobe, Nigel Spearing, 'become widely used. . . . I do not believe that [it] will happen.' Each answer was more reckless than the last. The Commission was 'striving to extinguish democracy', others were planning to take us through 'the back door to a federal Europe', and 'we have surrendered enough' to the Community. She seemed to be feeling for the crudest pressure points she could find. It would be 'totally and utterly wrong' to agree to 'abolish the pound sterling, the greatest expression of sovereignty'.

Anti-Europeans on our back benches were cheering loudly by now and beginning to infect their neighbours with their enthusiasm. It could hardly be 'unsound', they began to think, to respond positively to such strong signals from one's own Prime Minister. The whole process was mutually intoxicating – and filled me with foreboding. I was seated beside Margaret on the bench, in full view of the television cameras. I could not, even if I had wanted to, feign enthusiasm for this stuff. So my discomfiture was obvious. No less so, I thought, was the increasingly nationalist crudity of the Prime Minister's whole tone. Was she, I began to wonder, talking herself into the mode in which she intended, consciously or unconsciously, to fight the next election?

Later that afternoon, David Harris, Anthony Teasdale and I considered the implications of her performance. The Prime Minister had not expressly repudiated my position. But, emphatically, she had not made it any easier. My presence was no longer restraining her dangerous anti-Europeanism. We broke without conclusion. On television that night, pride of place was accorded to the 'No! No! No!' sequence. Next day's Ingham Digest presented the message even more starkly: 'You get a good press for your defiant act in the Commons yesterday. . . . Conclusion: you are prepared to make Europe an Election issue.' Then, quoting Peter Jenkins in the *Independent*, 'Throw the question to the country . . . Maggie Thatcher or Jacques Delors? . . . The more you let go yesterday, the more you warmed to the idea.' And finally: '*Sun* says Sir Geoffrey Howe has lost the support of his Cabinet colleagues. . . . *Mail* says Sir Geoffrey may have to go for the sake of unity.'

Time for Decision

It was during that day, 31 October, that I came to the regretful conclusion that it was time for me to leave. I attended my last Privy Council meeting as Lord President and went on to lunch with the BBC's veteran political writer John Cole. Later he reminded me, without reproach, of the story that I had kept from him at that lunch. I discussed my final reaction with David Harris, Anthony Teasdale and Arabella Warburton in my room at the House, and in the evening again, together with Elspeth, at Atterbury Street. Already I had made a start at drafting a resignation letter. Elspeth was still hesitant about the decision. By then I had no real doubt, but it was prudent to sleep on it.

In the meantime, Arabella had been addressing herself to the thousand mundane questions that would arise. Before the end of that day she had completed the first of many notes of practical advice, which were to help enormously through the difficult weeks ahead. 'Immediate thoughts about this agonizing time . . .': she checked calmly through the agenda. Where to live? When to move? My room in the House? Anthony

Teasdale, unfailingly committed: 'He insists that he will be beside you to tide you over the next few months whenever needed.' Her own position: 'I confess the whole prospect fills me with personal panic as to my ability to deal with you alone. . . . We have very little choice other than to take the days as they come.' (Arabella rose to her own challenge magnificently, even in the darkest hours.) And the politics, she went on: 'We must, of course, be quite prepared for the attack from Number 10. . . . your final draft of letter must cover every angle . . . without having to resort to further clarification after the event.' Her note contained, finally, the best contemporary insight into my own thinking: 'GF (our accountant and friend Geoffrey Fox) still has his Pimlico flat on ice for you. . . . Perhaps best not for either of us to get in touch with him until we are absolutely certain that the final price must now be paid, and that news has been announced.'

Overnight we all gave thought to my draft letter. I sought advice too from Richard Ryder, my ex-PPS, who had always remained closely in touch. My team met over breakfast in Atterbury Street and then worked in my room at the House putting together a near-final draft. I was due in the Chamber for the Prorogation Ceremony at 9.30 a.m. I was now quite sure about my decision. But I was not ready to disclose it until practical details were properly sorted out – and my letter was ready. The timing remained under my control. So I took my place alongside Margaret on the front bench. We did not speak much. Neil Kinnock and Jack Cunningham, Shadow Leader of the House, sat opposite us. A handful of other members were present. In a few moments we were all summoned by Black Rod to follow Mr Speaker to the House of Lords for the closing of the session. It was the last parliamentary ceremony that Margaret and I were to share together.

Within a few minutes, we were alongside each other again in Number 10, for my last Cabinet. There was nothing but routine business to transact. I had only one matter to raise. Two or three of the Bills that were due for introduction on the first day of the next session were still not ready. One, I recall, was the Transport Bill on which Cecil Parkinson had been so insistent some weeks and months before. I had only one purpose in raising this trifling matter. I wanted a Cabinet 'chop' on the need for departments (and parliamentary counsel, if necessary) to get their act together – and quickly. Margaret had only to utter four or five words to meet my point. Cabinet minutes would do the rest. But to my astonishment she turned on me: 'Why aren't these Bills ready? Isn't it the Lord President's responsibility to see that this kind of thing has been done?' And so on. Colleagues were as amazed as I was by the outburst. But, I thought, what the hell? This is positively the last time. Everybody else could see that the complaint answered itself. And I could see from the Prime Minister's diary card, displayed on the table between us, that she was due to be in Number 10 in the early evening. Time enough then, I thought, to bring all this to an end. So far from being the last straw, this final tantrum was for me the first confirmation that I had taken the right decision. For others, it was perhaps another revealing insight into life as it was now being lived in the Thatcher Cabinet.

I went back to the House to finalize my letter – and to a last-minute message from Elspeth, via Arabella: 'She worries about timing. She wonders if it would be better tomorrow rather than today. . . . General opinion seems to be sooner the better: it will be truly ghastly whenever it happens. . . .'

Back in the Lord President's department there were still one or two loose ends to tie up: a meeting about the insurance of MPs against risk of accident, and another to ensure that instructions *were* given for completion of the Bills that had triggered Margaret's last flurry. By about 4 p.m. the final revision of my letter and I came together for signature. It was now time to trigger the final arrangements. My private secretary, Tim Sutton, called Number 10 with the news that I wished to see the Prime Minister 'on a personal matter of some importance'. They agreed to call me as soon as she was back, between 5.30 and 6 p.m.

I could now start telephoning the few people who needed to know before they heard it on the news. Our children and my constituency agent and officers came first, of course. And I wanted myself to tell the Chief Whip Tim Renton, as well as the Foreign Secretary Douglas Hurd, since it was on his patch that any policy backlash was most likely to come. Tim was harder to trace. On the first afternoon of the short recess he was out walking the South Downs, which lay behind his house. When he returned, he made immediate contact. He was surprised only by the timing but not by the substance of my news. He had known it would come sooner or later and had hoped indeed to manage it more peacefully. Douglas was rather more surprised. For a minute or two he tried to dissuade me. He said it would make the position of pro-Europeans in the Cabinet more difficult. But he very quickly gauged the seriousness of my intent. I was sorry to be leaving him to play such a difficult hand without my support. We both wished each other well.

Handshake at Number 10

The Prime Minister's return to Number 10 had been delayed. She had been visiting the Gulf War Communication Centre, in the basement of Marsham Street. When she did get back, I was invited to walk through to Number 10 from the Privy Council office. She already knew the nature of my mission. Tim Sutton had told her Private Office, who had been dismayed at my insistence on seeing her between her late return and an impending reception, that my purpose at the meeting was to resign. I entered her study at Number 10 soon after 6 p.m. She was alone. She was obviously shaken by the event, now that it had actually come. 'Is there', she asked, 'anything we can do that would cause you to change your mind?' I thought not, I said, and the point was not seriously pursued. There followed instead a short but gracious discussion of the many things we had been able to achieve together. Then we turned to practicalities. 'How to inform the press?' I asked. The Palace came first, replied Margaret.

We were joined by her private secretary, Andrew Turnbull. I gave Margaret my letter, which she started to read. 'It's very generous,' she said at the end of page one. 'Better wait', I replied, 'until you've read it all.' 'Yes,' said Margaret at the end, 'I can see now why we shouldn't be able to change your mind. You've obviously thought a lot about it.' So it was agreed that the news of my resignation would be released by 7 p.m., with the text of our exchange of letters a little later: her own, after all, had still to be written. Margaret's manner had been courteous, shocked and practical. We parted in curiously formal fashion – with a handshake. It was, I think, the first time we'd ever shaken hands. It was a strange prelude to the exchange of letters that followed:

1st November 1990

Dear Margaret,

I am writing to explain some of the reasons for my decision to resign from the Government.

I do so with very great regret. Almost sixteen years have passed since you asked me to serve as Shadow Chancellor. Since then we have done so much together, against the odds, to rebuild the economic and political strength of our nation. Your own strong leadership has been of crucial importance in making this possible. It has been a privilege and an honour for me to have contributed to that success.

Our work has been based on common values and shared beliefs – for economic and personal freedom, for a responsible society and for greater British influence in the world. Although our principles have been sorely tested by opponents of the Government at different times over the last eleven years, I have always tried as best I can to uphold and advance those principles in a way that united our Party and served the best interests of Britain.

It gives me all the more sadness, therefore, to acknowledge the growing difference which has emerged between us on the increasingly important issue of Britain's role in Europe.

As much as you, I have wanted to make the most of Britain's influence in the world, to deploy Britain's sovereignty to the best advantage of our people. Ever since our original application to join the European Community in 1962, that has clearly involved Britain's firm, practical commitment to the historic process of close European partnership.

I was proud to have steered Britain's membership through the House of Commons in 1971, and prouder still to play my part promoting Britain's national interest in Europe, first as your Chancellor of the Exchequer, and then as your Foreign Secretary, for ten hard and rewarding years.

My vision of Europe has always been practical and hard-headed. I am *not* a Euro-idealist or federalist. My concern is less with grand schemes than with immediate realities, as they affect our well being and prospects as a nation. Like you, I have fought too many European battles in a minority of one, to harbour any illusions on that score.

Our conduct of policy on the crucial monetary issue in Europe – first on ERM and now on EMU – has given me increasing grounds for concern. We did not find it easy, in the run-up to last year's Madrid Summit, to establish the conditions for the UK's entry into the ERM. I felt at that time that my continued membership of your Cabinet could help maintain a united approach on this issue.

Now that we are finally inside the ERM, we have a great opportunity at last to shape Europe's monetary arrangements in the years ahead. We can only do that by being and staying firmly on the inside track.

We must be at the centre of the European partnership, playing the sort of leading and constructive role which commands respect. We need to be able to persuade friends as well as challenge opponents, and to win arguments before positions become entrenched.

The risks of being left behind on EMU are severe. All too much of our energy during the last decade has been devoted to correcting the consequences of our late start in Europe.

It would be a tragedy, not just for our financial institutions and our industrial strength, but also for the aspirations of a younger generation, if we were to risk making the same mistake again, by trying to draw an arbitrary line under our engagement in the European process.

I am deeply anxious that the mood you have struck – most notably in Rome last weekend and in the House of Commons this Tuesday – will make it more difficult for Britain to hold and retain a position of influence in this vital debate.

Of course, there are still huge questions to be considered and resolved in this discussion. None of us wants the imposition of a single currency, but more than one form of EMU is possible. The important thing is not to rule in or out any one particular solution absolutely. We should be in the business, not of isolating ourselves unduly, but of offering positive alternatives that can enable us to be seriously engaged.

Cabinet government is all about trying to persuade one another from within. So too, within the unique partnership of nations that is making the European Community. Plain speaking certainly – but matched always by mutual respect and restraint in pursuit of a common cause.

The need to find and maintain common ground on the European issue within our own party will be crucial to our electoral success and the future of the nation. In all honesty I now find myself unable to share your view of the right approach to this question. On that basis, I do not believe that I can any longer serve with honour as a member of your Government.

I am, of course, very sad that our long years of service together should have to end in this way. The close of this Session of Parliament seems an appropriate moment for me to leave. It has been a great privilege to serve under your leadership at a time when we have been able to change Britain's future so much for the better. I shall, of course, maintain my support for your Government in following policies to that end.

Yours ever

Geoffrey

1 November 1990

Dear Geoffrey,

Thank you for your letter telling me of your decision to leave the Government and the reasons for it. As I told you when you came to see me earlier this evening, I very much regret your decision, coming unexpectedly after we have worked together for so long. I shall for ever be grateful for your distinguished service and your sturdy and unflinching support in difficult times.

Your contribution to the philosophy of modern Conservatism and to the policies which we brought to Government in 1979 was great indeed. It helped to ensure that we came to office with a clear and radical programme for changing Britain and reversing the decline of the Labour years. As Chancellor of the Exchequer, you took the main burden of implementing our economic policies: and you did so with courage and fortitude in the face of many attempts to push us off course. The foundations of Britain's economic success in the 1980s were laid in those earlier years, and in particular by the budget of 1981.

As Foreign Secretary from 1983, you built on that economic success to restore Britain's standing in the world. Together we succeeded in obtaining a fair settlement for Britain's budget contribution to the European Community. Your patient negotiations with the Chinese Government secured Hong Kong's future: and you subsequently applied the same skill to the negotiations with Spain over Gibraltar. You played an important part in building up our relations with the Soviet Union and with the countries of Eastern Europe, as they emerged from the shadow of communism. In all these activities, you won the highest respect and admiration of your Foreign Minister colleagues.

Your time as Lord President enabled us to put on the statute book many of the domestic reforms which you did so much to formulate and inspire.

Your letter refers to differences between us on Europe. I do not believe that these are nearly as great as you suggest. We are at one in wishing to preserve the fundamental sovereignty of Parliament. We want Britain to play a leading part in Europe and to be part of the further political, economic and monetary development of the European Community. As I made it clear in my statement to the House, our aim is to find solutions which will enable the Community to go forward as Twelve. I believe the party is united behind these aims and demonstrated that very clearly in the House on Tuesday: we have always been the party of Europe, and will continue to be so.

Finally, may I say how saddened I am personally at your decision to move to the back benches. Your steadiness has been a source of great strength to the Government for more than eleven years. I am grateful for your assurance of continued support.

May I also add a particular word of gratitude for the contribution which Elspeth has made. Denis joins me in sending our best wishes to you both.

Yours ever

Margaret

It was time now for the press, radio and television to start their analysis. I was impressed at the speed, the scale and technical proficiency with which they set about it. I myself had been able to escape from a speaking engagement that evening with the higher management of Customs and Excise. Richard Ryder, now himself Paymaster General, with responsibility for Customs and Excise, was willing – and well qualified, in more than one sense – to relieve me of that. I was immensely grateful for his help in this way, as in so many others. Elspeth was not so lucky. For she insisted, characteristically, on fulfilling her commitment to attend, as guest of honour, at the prize-giving for the Hackney Free and Parochial Secondary School. 'Despite the turmoil of the preceding few hours,' said the parish newsletter, 'Lady Howe proved a most collected guest and impressive speaker.' It was only when we rejoined each other at Atterbury Street, a few hours later, that I was able finally to acknowledge the unquestioning calm and loyalty with which she had helped me through the turbulence of the weeks and months that had just passed. For the days immediately ahead at least I was determined to hold my peace – so we should be able to reflect a little on the future that might lie ahead.

PART SEVEN

═══

BACK-BENCHER
1990–1992

CHAPTER FORTY-FOUR

SPEECH

=====

Loyal to a Fault?

There was an accidental tidiness about the timing of my resignation. The trigger had been the Prime Minister's report on the Rome Summit. But the consequences coincided with the end of the parliamentary year. The seven-day recess between the two sessions provided a useful natural break. I had plenty of time to reflect on what, if anything, I should offer by way of further public comment. Following Nigel Lawson's experience the previous year, I decided that my first elaboration should be given to the House of Commons. That was a matter both of courtesy to colleagues, to whom I owed it, and of calculation. It would ensure that my explanation was reported clearly and on my own terms.

The next parliamentary business would be the Queen's Speech debate, starting the following Wednesday, 7 November. That offered me a choice of four or five days on which to speak, if I wished. Good fortune provided one additional blessing. For during the night after my resignation I found that I had lost my voice, more completely than ever before or since. My self-imposed vow of silence had been physically, and decisively, reinforced. The Friday after my resignation had long been earmarked for a constituency day. So when Elspeth and I emerged early that morning to an Atterbury Street full of journalists and cameras, I was literally unable to answer a single question. I pointed to my open but noiseless mouth. 'I'm afraid he's lost his voice,' said Elspeth. I doubt if at that moment a single one of them believed us. Disbelieving microphones predictably followed me almost throughout the day from the fascinated tots at Woodlea First School in Woldingham to the by-pass protesters at a Felbridge evening meeting. They still heard nothing from the local Member of Parliament.

But they were able to report what the *Guardian* described as a 'constituency chorus of approval'.[1] Political opponents, said one report, 'savagely described him as a man of charm and integrity'. This certainly captured the spirit of constituency reaction during that first day of freedom from front-bench responsibilities. People were shocked by the news certainly, but not much worried about the issues that may have prompted my resignation. 'We're not a bunch of Euro-fanatics,' said one constituent, 'but we're not little Englanders either.' Supporters were in fact ringing my association office all day, 'just in case there was any risk of his resigning as an MP, to assure him of their support'. The same message was echoed on the streets of East Surrey and through my own office in the Palace of Westminster. Popular reaction to my perceived personal clash with the Prime Minister seemed to be substantially in my favour. One former constituency chairman rang to say that he 'looked forward to the next announcement being the PM's departure'. A former agent put the same point less kindly in a telephone message: 'About time that bloody woman got her come-uppance. When is she going to realize she will lose us the next election?' There were some who took the opposite view, of course. But that certainly was the dominant flavour of the many hundreds of letters and messages that reached me during the next few days.

Colleagues' letters were the most perceptive. 'I quite understand', wrote Willie Whitelaw, 'why in the end you felt you had to go.' 'The temptation to go on fighting inside the organization . . . is always very strong,' wrote Arthur Cockfield, 'but the point must ultimately be reached when the fight can only effectively be carried on from the outside. . . . Tuesday's tantrums clearly marked the parting of the ways.' Support and understanding came from every quarter of the party – from Ken Clarke to Alan Clark, from John Biffen to Robert Carr. It came too from scores of others in every part of the political spectrum, from the distinguished columnist Peter Jenkins to the former TUC general secretary Len Murray. More than understandably, my former PPS (and Margaret's then Chief Whip) Tim Renton was especially sorrowful at his 'failure' to prevent the rift between me and Number 10; but perhaps, he said, 'the gap was unbridgeable . . . and goes back a good deal in time and history and predilection'. Tim was right, of course. For my European 'commitment' was now more than forty years old. Robert Sheaf, the friend to whom I had written my definition of Britain's European destiny way back in July 1950, wrote to me on 2 November 1990: 'You have been loyal to Mrs Thatcher to a fault. But enough is enough.' He was far from the only one to pose the loyalty dilemma.

Many expressed sympathy with my endurance and forbearance.

Robert Rhodes James, historian as well as parliamentary colleague, saddened though not surprised by my decision to leave, wrote, 'You have been very badly and disloyally treated over the past year.' Patrick Mayhew expressed himself in forthright terms:

> You and I have often talked wryly – and in my case with fury – of your treatment over the years by the Prime Minister in council. Personally I should never have had the stamina, nor the sense of duty, to put up with it. For that reason alone you would have been fully justified long ago in resigning. It has been a truly shameful blemish on her record, and your toleration of it has been a no less admirable achievement of your own.
>
> There must come a time, however, when if public ineptitude is heaped on private slights a breaking strain is imposed both on toleration and on party loyalty. I think you were absolutely right to go: and by doing so you have jolted many in the party into acquainting themselves with what is already inherent in our adopted policy on Europe. It is *just* possible that Margaret will now realize what it is about her that turns off millions of voters, and do something about it.

'To your friends,' wrote Robert Runcie, still then Archbishop of Canterbury, 'it's been sad to see someone so fundamentally loyal so sadly provoked.' Most widely perceptive of all, perhaps, was Canon James Mansel, the man who had been my house tutor at Winchester, then Ian Gow's housemaster and later domestic chaplain to the Queen at Windsor:

> I'm sad from my heart to read of your resignation. . . . But proud too to think that, together with Ian, you have laid down high office . . . for the sake of principle. . . . To know that you *both* have cared for nothing except doing what *is right* is . . . 'a cordial for drooping spirits'.

The press on 2 and 3 November was more divided. Not one paper doubted that I was right to go. They all acknowledged my length of service – the last to leave Mrs Thatcher's 1979 Cabinet – and my tenacity: 'A conviction politician who showed rare endurance' (the *Guardian*); 'Tireless traveller with love of unpredictable' (*Financial Times*); and – with some prescience, 'The wrath of a patient man' (The *Independent*). Even those which sought to play down the significance of my departure had some kind words to offer. For the *Sun*, I 'deserved to be remembered as a constructive Chancellor'; for *The Times* as 'a figure of competent reassurance, liberal, sensitive, balanced, the best sort of British politician'.

The *Financial Times* was one of the several papers which saw my resignation as endangering Mrs Thatcher's survival: it was 'yet another signal, after so many, that the Thatcher edifice is falling apart', wrote Joe Rogaly. For Julian Critchley, writing in the *Guardian,* it was 'a severe blow to government and party', and for the *Mirror* 'a very grave loss . . . from which she may never recover'. *The Times* took a simplistically opposite view: 'Mrs Thatcher's leadership remains robust, undaunted and unchallenged.' Even Hugo Young, so often endowed with more foresight than others, felt that sudden departures had by now become 'such a hallmark of the Thatcher years that Howe's is no longer one capable of shaking the Thatcher world'.

No Conspiracy

There was plenty more of the same kind of analysis for me to brood over with friends and colleagues in the days that followed my resignation. Even at that time, there was still a fair amount of speculation that my decision might be seen as part of a wider scheme of things. This increasingly conspiratorial view of the world may have been encouraged by the fact that BBC Television was at that time showing, on three successive Sunday nights, a serialization of Michael Dobbs' first political novel, *House of Cards*. Other actors on the scene began, of course, to carry forward their own thinking. Nobody – outside the tiny group of my own personal team – had been given any advance warning of my intention to resign. Michael Heseltine, with the rest of the world, learned only from the Thursday-evening news bulletins. He telephoned me on the Friday, 2 November, and began by saying that he was sorry, but by no means surprised, to hear of my resignation – and to wish me well for the future. He had after all blazed that trail himself, almost five years earlier. He went on to tell me that he was on the point of departing for a short, long-arranged visit to the Middle East. He now intended to issue, on Saturday, an open letter to his constituency chairman. This would start with a commendation of my resignation and go on to offer some general observations on the outlook for the government. I confirmed to him (as already reported on television and in the papers) that I had no intention of standing against Margaret Thatcher for the leadership. He said that that remained his present position as well. We agreed to keep in touch over the days ahead.

The timetable for any possible leadership contest was set in place by the 1922 Committee chairman, Cranley Onslow – to a tighter schedule than the previous year. Nominations had to be in by noon on Thursday, 15 November. First-round voting was on Tuesday, 20 November. There was still time enough for any decision to be taken. Meanwhile the reactions to my own resignation were becoming more varied. Mrs Thatcher's initial comment was disclosed by Number 10 immediately. She had received my resignation, it was said, 'more in sorrow than in anger'. There were many who saw this 'generosity' on her part as distinctly 'patronizing and self-righteous'. I tended to agree. Her response to my resignation letter had similarly tried to make light of the difference between us. Kenneth Baker took up the theme in his comments as party chairman. The difference, he said, was one not of policy but only of style. A day or two later both Douglas Hurd and John MacGregor were echoing the same line. All this was strengthening my instinct to explain my resignation to the House. If my former colleagues really did believe that my resignation was based solely on differences of presentation and not of principle, then the sooner I set the matter beyond doubt the better.

Meanwhile, and quite independently, the pressures on Michael Heseltine to stand against Margaret Thatcher were multiplying. His open letter to his constituency chairman had been less than a resounding success. His critics wondered first why he needed to intervene at all at such a sensitive time. They questioned his wisdom in doing so just as he was about to leave the country. The press began asking Michael's constituency officers for their response to his missive. They felt obliged, with some misguided help from a Central Office agent, to prepare a less than enthusiastic reply. This was widely seen as a rebuff to their own Member. Bernard Ingham unwisely added to the pressure. 'He'd better put up', reported the press, 'or shut up.' The effect of all this, whether Margaret Thatcher herself had willed it or not, was to increase the pressure on Heseltine to take up the challenge. Less and less could he be seen to chicken out.

By the second half of that week, Michael was once again in touch with me by telephone. His thinking had moved on from the previous Friday. If he did decide to stand against Margaret, he asked, would I be ready to give him my support in the ballot? He emphasized that he had not yet taken any such decision. I should need, I replied, to think very carefully about my answer to that question. And I did, consulting my closest team. On Saturday, 10 November, I returned his call. I told him that I did not feel able to give him any advance assurance of the kind he hoped for. Michael was disappointed, naturally enough. But he understood, I think, why I felt that my position was best left uncluttered by any such commitment. I had it in mind now to explain myself to the House, just as I had done in my letter. I should certainly make it clear that policy substance more than presentational style was at the centre of my concern. To continue following our separate, but often very largely parallel courses was probably as helpful for the future as any other alternative. If I had any further message to convey at any later stage then I should be sure to do so. There we left the matter. I was determined to remain innocent of any charges of conspiracy or concertation. I could not be seen to act in a way that implied, quite falsely, that I might have resigned to catapult Michael into the leadership.

On the next day, Sunday 11 November, Michael's increasing inclination to let his name go forward received a further boost from two separate pieces of news. His constituency officers had looked again at the effect of their first reply to his ill-fated open letter. They were now anxious to give a fresh reply, which amounted to a ringing endorsement of Michael's position. The Sunday papers also reported that a private poll of Tory MPs suggested that he could count on the firm support of over a hundred members of the parliamentary party.

I had myself been receiving much advice. One school of thought still cherished the hope that I might let my own name to go forward as Margaret Thatcher's principal challenger. Certainly there were plenty of ordinary people who wanted to see me win such a contest and who had written to say so. But the closer my supporters were to the only electoral college that mattered, the 372 members of the parliamentary party, the less ready they were to encourage me. My keenest parliamentary advisers knew, as I did, that my position was now much weaker than it had been in July 1989. Fifteen months in the ambiguous role which Margaret had forced on me had taken its toll. The most beguiling argument was that I was 'everybody's second choice' or 'the ideal compromise candidate'. But, for that to be relevant, one had to get enough first-choice votes to reach the last two. That was quite clearly beyond reach. David Harris, Anthony Teasdale and I discussed whether to revisit my initial, instinctive refusal to stand, announced by David to the media in Whitehall on the evening of my resignation. We all concluded that that judgment had

been right. Only one real question remained to be answered: what kind
of resignation speech should I make?

What Kind of Speech?

Events were already offering a clear pointer towards the answer. My
mood was best articulated in a letter that reached me three or four days
after I had stood down. It was from Vernon Bogdanor of Brasenose
College, Oxford. 'It seems to me', wrote the academic author, 'that if
one feels sufficiently strongly to resign from a government one ought to
press the issue on which one resigns, especially when . . . it affects in so
fundamental a way our relations with other countries.' Like many others,
he emphasized the extent to which former colleagues were arguing that
my differences with the Prime Minister were 'based only on style and
not on principle'. But the argument, I knew very clearly, was far more
fundamental than that.

For many Conservatives it had long been an article of faith that
Britain should play a full part in European unification. During the long
years of Labour hostility to the EC, it was our party which had kept
that flame burning in Britain. Were we now to see those roles reversed?
The Prime Minister's increasingly narrow nationalism had removed her
from the centre of gravity of her own Cabinet. It was she who was
largely responsible for the political turbulence, which had made my own
position untenable. In so doing, she was splintering a rock upon which
we had for decades together been building our party's success and our
nation's future. Was all that now to be cast away? That was the context
in which I saw the full force of the argument in Bogdanor's letter:
'There is no point in a "civilized" resignation which is soon forgotten.'[2]

Another correspondent, Alan Bristow, offered the same conclusion:
faced with a choice between family, friends and colleagues and 'loyalty
to country and . . . principles', he had no doubt which should come first.
So, he concluded, 'make your resignation count, really count'.[3] I had
already been moving towards a similar conclusion, in even simpler
terms. My speech, I knew, would be treated either as a 'sensation' or as
a 'damp squib'. Try as one might, there was almost no chance of striking
a perfectly balanced position. On an issue of this importance, it was the
'damp squib' verdict that had to be avoided.

The structure of a speech was beginning to take shape. The choice I
had made would have to be crystal clear. I was no longer able to share

the Prime Minister's view of the right approach to the European question. That had become of greater long-term importance to the future of the country, the government, the Conservative Party than my long-standing personal bond with Margaret Thatcher. 'On that basis,' as my letter had said, 'I do not believe I can any longer serve with honour as a member of your government.' The notion of conflict of loyalty was already clear.

As so often, spectators had already seen most of the game. What, asked Alan Cochrane in the *Mail on Sunday*, had been the proper role of the Deputy Prime Minister? 'The main function of the post was to be loyal,' he wrote. 'Yes, but loyal to what or to whom?'[4] Was I not, in the words of the *Financial Times*, 'a founder member of the loyal order of Thatcherites'?[5] Or of the *Daily Mirror*, 'her most loyal, most long-suffering, most stable Cabinet Minister'?[6] To others, of course, I was 'openly undermining the Prime Minister'[7] and had 'been too disloyal for too long'.[8] For the *Independent*, it was Margaret who 'had behaved with casual disloyalty' towards me.[9] Clearly the issues by now transcended questions of purely personal loyalty. It was on policy that matters now had to turn. If the Prime Minister truly was and chose to remain 'on so many issues – especially Europe – in a minority of one in her own Cabinet',[10] then one conclusion was likely. But a quite different outcome was possible, if the Prime Minister could only 'demonstrate to her supporters that she comprehends and accepts the responsibility to provide a form of leadership around which her party can unite'.[11] More than one conclusion at this stage remained possible. For Margaret Thatcher herself, as well as for her colleagues in Cabinet and in Parliament, there were still different choices that could be made for the future.

On the Back Benches

Parliament assembled for the State Opening and the Queen's Speech on Wednesday, 7 November. It was the first such occasion for fifteen years in which I had no formal front-bench part to play. Where did I sit? How to bag a place? How soon to go into the Chamber? David Harris guided me through it all. It was like going back to school, as a new boy after years as a prefect. The first two front-bench speeches would be made by the Leader of the Opposition and the Prime Minister. Those I had to hear, not just as a matter of courtesy, for it would be surprising if neither referred to my departure. Neil Kinnock did indeed do so. In a conscious echo of Margaret's comment a week before, he described me as 'too big a man to endure any more of her disloyalty to him and her contempt for his convictions'. Margaret replied initially in courteous – indeed generous – terms. But then she returned to the familiar theme: 'If the Leader of the Opposition reads my Right Hon. and Learned friend's letter, he will be very pressed indeed to find any significant policy difference on Europe between my Right Hon. and Learned friend and the rest of us on this side.' As soon as I left the Chamber I conferred with my team. It was clearly desirable to counter the Prime Minister's bland dismissal of my resignation. So I issued a brief statement. 'When I come to speak,' I said, 'I shall be dealing with matters of substance as well as style.'

I had no need to appear in the House again until the time came for my own intervention. I decided to speak on the Tuesday, 13 November. With luck the House would be reasonably full – after Prime Minister's questions – while not overloaded with heavyweight competitors. I had only two public engagements before then (all others had been cancelled). The first was Remembrance Sunday. Ever since 1979, I had been one of the great and the good on parade at the Cenotaph. This year, I was able to return to my constituency. The sun-blest ceremony at Godstone's thirteenth-century parish church was just as moving. So too was my other duty: a call to Buckingham Palace, before lunch on Thursday, 8 November – to take leave of Her Majesty, at the end of my time as a Minister of the Crown. The Queen was full of discreet sympathy and immensely kind. A long chapter had drawn to a close.

I penned the first manuscript version of my speech on Saturday and Sunday, 10–11 November. The main structure of the final argument was in place from the start. It was intensively revised over the next two days. The text from which I finally spoke on 13 November, for nineteen minutes, was the fifth or sixth typescript. All these emerged from the memory of Arabella's machine, which she had transplanted to a make-shift office at Atterbury Street. I sought advice from some of those who gave most regular help with my speeches: Anthony Teasdale, my special adviser, David Harris, my PPS, and Adam Fergusson, the ex-MEP and former special adviser. Instant mythology gives Elspeth credit for writing the whole in ten minutes. In fact she played no part in the writing process. 'Geoffrey,' she said, when she first read one of the later drafts on Monday, 'are you sure you need to go that far?' She sought to test but not to challenge my line. With the house under siege from zoom lenses and microphones almost throughout the night, Anthony and Arabella worked with me on successive drafts until about 3 a.m. – and then again from 8 on the following morning. Arabella produced the final version shortly before lunch on the day. And even then I was marking it up with last-minute stage directions.

Very late in the day there was a change in the circumstances in which I spoke. I had been expecting to speak, as Nigel Lawson had done, in course of the ordinary Queen's Speech debate. That would have meant waiting until after the two main front-bench speakers. On this particular day, even they were to be preceded by a long statement from Peter Lilley about telecommunications. Some claimed that this was a deliberate move to delay my speech and reduce its news impact. On this basis, I would not have been on my feet until about 5.15 p.m. By then, the House would be almost empty. So how did I come to speak an hour earlier than that, and to an almost full House? The answer was pure procedural chance. For just before noon Mr Speaker's office telephoned me with a surprise message. The subject appointed for the fifth day of the Queen's Speech debate, they said, was education. Although formally I could speak on a general subject, if I insisted – as the Queen's Speech debates were an indivisible whole – it would set a bad precedent, particularly for an ex-Leader of the House, to disregard the subject heading for the day. The authorities had, however, an attractive answer to their own problem. 'You're making a resignation statement, aren't you? So there is no reason why you shouldn't do that as a personal statement, at the start of the business.' And what if I speak for as long as twenty minutes, I asked. Will that still be in order? That, I was assured, would be all right. 'But not more than twenty.'

So I readied myself to take my place that afternoon, on the third bench back below the gangway. This was the near-traditional spot from which Nigel Lawson had spoken a year before. I had asked Nigel to sit beside me, partly to give moral support, partly to show the Prime Minister that her former ministers had a common view on the key questions. I was in my place in good time, to hear Prime Minister's questions for the first time that session. A curiously pointless note reached me, only moments before I rose to speak, from one of my back-bench Conservative colleagues, Michael Grylls, MP for Surrey North-West: 'Good luck – you've a difficult task. *Please* do not damage the Prime Minister to whom you have been Deputy. It will damage England *and* yourself.' I could only react by ignoring it. It is hard to see how anything else could have been expected. At nineteen minutes past four, my long and rather nervous wait came to an end. Mr Speaker rose to remind a full and expectant House that a resignation statement is heard in silence and without interruption. I was launched into my first speech from the back benches for more than a quarter of a century.*

Almost at the outset, I was able to break the ice of the moment and put some people at ease. I joked about the idea that I had resigned solely because of questions of style, and not at all on matters of substance. 'If some of my former colleagues are to be believed,' I said, 'I must be the first minister in history who has resigned because he was in full agreement with government policy.' Even the Prime Minister could join in the laughter at that, perhaps without realizing its double meaning. I then paid extensive tribute to the government's many achievements under her leadership; and referred to the thirty international summits and 700 Cabinet or Shadow Cabinet meetings that we had shared alongside each other during the previous eighteen years. 'Something more than simple matters of style', I suggested, 'would surely be needed to rupture such a well-tried relationship.'

So I turned to the Exchange Rate Mechanism of the EMS. This had been the cause of Nigel Lawson's resignation almost exactly a year before. With him sitting beside me, I revealed for the first time that we had both threatened to resign before the Madrid Summit of June 1989, unless the Prime Minister was there ready to strengthen Britain's commitment to join the ERM. This caused the first serious reaction from the House as people realized the divisions it signified. 'Today's higher rates of inflation', I went on, 'could well have been avoided had the question of ERM membership been . . . properly resolved at a much earlier stage.'

I moved on to 'wider questions of European policy'. We were, I said, perfectly entitled to question the Delors Report, to criticize the Italian Presidency 'plainly and courteously' and, 'if necessary, alone'. Like the Prime Minister, I had 'fought too many European battles in a minority of one to have any illusions on that score'. But it was crucially important to conduct those arguments upon the basis of a clear understanding of Britain's true relationship with the Community. It was here that the Prime Minister was 'leading herself and others astray in matters of substance as well as style'. The Prime Minister too often presented to herself and the nation 'an oversimplified choice, a false antithesis, a bogus dilemma, between one alternative, starkly labelled "co-operation

---

* The full text is at Appendix II.

between independent sovereign states" and a second, equally crudely labelled alternative "centralized federal super-state", as if there were no middle way in between'. Winston Churchill's perception of Europe was a good deal more convincing than 'the nightmare image sometimes conjured up' by a Prime Minister 'who seems sometimes to look out upon a continent that is positively teeming with ill-intentioned people scheming, in her words, to "extinguish democracy" or to "dissolve our national identities".' I had chosen to quote back words she had used in the Commons two weeks before.

Then I returned to economic and monetary union and the Prime Minister's reporting on the Rome Summit. The real risk, I said, was not that we might have a single currency imposed upon us but that we should find ourselves 'with no say in the monetary arrangements that Europe chooses for itself. . . . That would be the worst possible outcome.' That was why we had to be seen to be part of the same negotiation. It was to that end that the Chancellor and the Governor of the Bank of England had been putting forward Britain's 'hard ECU' proposal. It was disturbing in those circumstances that the Prime Minister, when reporting to the House the other day, had 'casually' dismissed the whole idea – 'even of a common currency, let alone a single one'. How on earth, I asked, are the Chancellor and the Governor 'to be taken as serious participants in the debate against that kind of background noise?' As I spoke those words, I heard a sharp intake of breath in all parts of the House.

This was even more audible when I moved on to my cricketing metaphor. I believe, I said, that 'both the Chancellor and the Governor are cricketing enthusiasts, so I hope that there is no monopoly of cricketing metaphors. It is rather like sending your opening batsmen to the crease only for them to find, the moment the first balls are bowled, that their bats have been broken before the game by the team captain.' Gasps mingled with laughter on all sides of the House. For in offering a cricketing metaphor, I was responding to the previous night's provocative foray by the Prime Minister, in her annual speech to the Lord Mayor's Guildhall Banquet. Margaret had been dressed for that occasion in enormous white collar and long black train, like an assertively self-confident Elizabethan monarch. There had been no mistaking her challenge. Likening herself to a batsman, she had said, 'I am still at the crease, though the bowling has been pretty hostile of late. And, in case anyone doubted it, I can assure you there will be no ducking the bouncers, no stonewalling, no playing for time. The bowling's going to get hit all round the ground. That's my style.'

I had seen this performance on *News at Ten* the previous evening. It had been featured widely in the day's newspapers. The cricketing metaphor had immediately suggested itself for my own speech. It had made a powerful impact. It caught the mood of the moment. So I came towards my concluding remarks:

> The tragedy is – and it is for me personally, for my party, for our whole people and for my Right Hon. friend herself, a very real tragedy – that the Prime Minister's perceived attitude towards Europe is running increasingly serious risks for the future of our nation. It risks minimizing our influence and maximizing our chances of being once again shut out. We have paid heavily in the past for late starts and squandered opportunities in Europe. We dare not let that happen again. If we detach ourselves completely, as a party or a nation, from the middle ground of Europe, the effects will be incalculable and very hard ever to correct.
>
> In my letter of resignation, which I tendered with the utmost sadness and dismay, I said: 'Cabinet Government is all about trying to persuade one another from within.' That was my commitment to government by persuasion – persuading colleagues and the nation. I have tried to do that as Foreign Secretary and since, but I realize now that the task has become futile: trying to stretch the meaning of words beyond what was credible, and trying to pretend that there was a common policy when every step forward risked being subverted by some casual comment or impulsive answer.

Almost every half-sentence of this last passage seemed to evoke another gasp from the House.

> The conflict of loyalty, of loyalty to my Right Honourable friend the Prime Minister – and, after all, in two decades together that instinct of loyalty is still very real – and of loyalty to what I perceive to be the true interests of the nation, has become all too great. I no longer believe it possible to resolve that conflict from within this government. That is why I have resigned. In doing so, I have done what I believe to be right for my party and my country. The time has come for others to consider their own response to the tragic conflict of loyalties with which I have myself wrestled for perhaps too long.

The reaction as I sat down was quite unlike anything that I had ever before experienced. No 'hear, hears' from my own side. But no hubbub from the other side either – just bemused silence. And then a mounting babel of noise, as Members began talking to each other, in astonished reaction, on their way to the exits. Of my own reaction I remember nothing – save that of sheer relief. David Harris, sitting just in front of me, was the first to speak. 'Not', we agreed, 'a damp squib.' Some of my colleagues seemed almost unsure if they ought to be seen talking to me at all. Then into my hands came a second note – this time from Robert Jackson, a former MEP, now Member for Wantage and a junior minister: 'Well done: dignified, moving and altogether at the level of the occasion.' It was a rather donnish compliment but one I appreciated.

This note was to be the first of thousands that were to pour in during the next two weeks. None of us, I think, reckoned on the effect of the televising of Parliament on the impact of my performance. It was broadcast live on BBC and replayed *in extenso* on the news. It was reprinted in full in most quality papers. I decided that, as after my resignation twelve days earlier, I would not respond to any of the bids that had piled up for broadcast or press interviews. My speech was intended to speak for itself.

CHAPTER FORTY-FIVE

THE PRIME MINISTER FALLS

Another Challenge

The audience most immediately affected by my words was the Conservative parliamentary party. Within forty-four hours they would know if there was going to be a challenge to Margaret Thatcher's leadership. Upon their reactions would depend successive tidal waves of public opinion – in the Conservative Party, in the country at large and in the wider world. The first wave had followed my resignation and the second my speech. Within two weeks we should know if there was to be a third. I was destined to be a spectator rather than an actor through most of this. My part had largely been played.

As always the press, on 14 November, had the first chance to shape the ensuing debate about Margaret Thatcher's future. 'The issues at stake, both in terms of Europe and in terms of her conduct of the leadership, are too crucial to be buried – Michael Heseltine, after this, has no option but to run,' said the *Guardian*. That was almost the universal verdict. Some, like the *Express*, still contended, even now, that 'if [Geoffrey Howe's] speech made anything clear, it was that his main difference with Mrs Thatcher *is* primarily over style rather than policy'. But for Paul Johnson, in the *Daily Mail*, 'Howe put his finger on the real weakness of Mrs Thatcher's premiership – her inability to unite the party over Europe, or even to convince it that she is doing her best to keep it together.'

The key decision now rested with Michael Heseltine. He was not intending or expected to stand against Margaret Thatcher in 1990. His long-planned bid for the leadership was not meant to happen until 'the time was ripe'. But suddenly it was. The morning after I had spoken, Michael Heseltine announced his candidature. The ballot had to take place on Thursday, 20 November. The rules were complex. The winning candidate needed to gain two targets: a majority of the 372 Tory MPs who were entitled to vote, that is to say 187; and a winning margin over the nearest rival of 15 per cent of the total, that is to say 56.

I played no part in the public campaign. But by now I was myself sure that we needed a change of leadership – and that Michael was the man for the job. Even so, I was surprised by the *breadth* of the opposition to Margaret. There was no doubt about the commitment of the hard core of Thatcher loyalists – Norman Tebbit, Peter Morrison (her PPS), John Moore, Cecil Parkinson, for example. But that was seriously offset by the diversity of reasons for disenchantment. The poll-tax, her mounting unpopularity on the doorstep, personal dismay at her whole 'style of government': all these came ahead of concern about her attitude towards Europe. They combined to strengthen the belief that Margaret was becoming unelectable. This feeling was all the more corrosive for being quite widely shared, though not proclaimed, in all ranks of the government. The dependability of the 'payroll vote' had to be the foundation of Margaret's strength in the first ballot.

Not only in retrospect, I felt that her team placed too much faith in that loyalty. On the other hand, they were able to count – much more than I should have guessed – upon an almost offsetting distaste for Michael Heseltine. His Westland walk-out (and the memory of his having seized the Commons mace well over a decade ago) still raised real doubts for many about his 'reliability'. Even so, these were over-estimated by the Thatcher camp, who were misled by the strength of their own prejudices. So, much more than I had expected, the first round became a contest between negative factors.

George Younger had warned, after Sir Anthony Meyer's challenge a year before, that the sixty who then declined to support Margaret Thatcher were only a fraction of those who were losing faith in her leadership. This may even be one reason for his own less committed role in 1990. The most serious loss to Margaret's team was the murder of Ian Gow. He would never have allowed her to misjudge her own vulnerability. Possibly the plainest evidence for this was her business-as-usual approach to the whole contest. This meant that for the final thirty-six hours she was not – like Heseltine – at Westminster campaigning for the last handful of votes. She was instead in Paris, for a CSCE Summit meeting. In 1983 and 1987 Margaret had been more than ready, for the sake of elections, to trim down ruthlessly her attendance at the Williamsburg and Venice Summits. But, this time, Paris was given priority. So it was in the splendour of Her Britannic Majesty's embassy on the Rue du Faubourg St Honoré that the Prime Minister heard the first ballot result: 'Michael Heseltine 152 votes, Margaret Thatcher 204 votes'. She had failed by four votes to secure the 56-vote majority over Michael that was necessary for an outright win.

I was among the millions who were watching these critical moments on television. We scarcely had time to take in the figures before Margaret Thatcher herself was on our screens. The embassy doors burst open. Margaret, with Bernard Ingham in the thrusting lead, rushed down the steps almost as though to ambush the television reporters. Her statement straight to the cameras seemed typically impulsive. 'I am naturally very pleased', she said, 'that I got more than half the parliamentary party, and disappointed that's not quite enough to win on the first ballot.' Then, without a pause, 'I confirm it is my intention to let my name go forward for the second ballot.' We have subsequently learned that this formula had been carefully considered for just such a situation. That was not the impression given by the almost instant outburst on the embassy steps. How characteristic, thought many people, that she hasn't even given herself time to consider the significance of the figures that have just been announced. But it was probably well past the point when anything that Margaret – or, for that matter, Michael – could do would have much effect on people's well-established prejudices.

I took no part in the frantic lobbying and canvassing of the next thirty-six hours. Nominations for the second ballot had to be in by noon on Thursday, 22 November. There was no doubt about Michael Heseltine's determination to press ahead. But what of Margaret? Or any other contender? One impression came through clearly. The solidarity of Margaret Thatcher's payroll vote was quickly disintegrating. The impact of the first-ballot figures on many of the 120 ministers and PPSs, who must have made up almost half her first-round vote, was dramatic – and progressive. The fact that no less than 40 per cent of the party had by now withheld support from Margaret reinforced the doubts that many already harboured. Their loyalty to the leader who appointed them would have kept all but a possible handful of secret dissenters in line thus far. But what prospect now, they began wondering, of being able to regroup the party with any chance of electoral success under Margaret Thatcher's increasingly beleaguered leadership? If even within the parliamentary party her 'electability' had diminished so far, what were the chances of it prevailing with the general electorate? Quite apart from their own personal reactions to the leader whom they had come to know so well, did they not owe it to the party to consider a change?

As Wednesday, 21 November drew to a close, the voices of doubt grew ever louder and more numerous. 'Five members of the Cabinet', said the gossip that ran like wildfire around the Palace of Westminster, 'have told her that they won't support her.' And so on. When David Harris, Anthony Teasdale, Arabella Warburton and I met early the next morning in my small panelled office, the rumour was specific: 'She's going to resign.' And soon after 9.30 a.m. the news was official. Unsurprisingly, the least noticed statement of the day was my own tribute to 'the Prime Minister's courageous decision'. I saw it as an 'act of statesmanship, which the nation will respect'. She had opened the way for the party to unite around a new leader, who could 'ensure continued success upon the foundations laid by her governments'. Later that day she treated the Commons to a dazzlingly confident display of Thatcher rhetoric. Her personality shone through, as she seemed to revel in the prospect of freedom from responsibility. And the Leader who had just lost the confidence of her own party secured the rejection of a no-confidence motion in the House of Commons by 369 votes to 247. Three nominations had been filed for the contest to take her place. By the appointed hour of twelve noon the names of Douglas Hurd and John Major stood alongside that of Michael Heseltine. I had little difficulty then in rejecting the advice of those – none in my immediate entourage – who once again urged me to let my name go forward. Most persuasive of these was Nigel Lawson: he saw me as a champion of 'Thatcherism without Thatcher'. But he readily accepted my view that there was a limit to the number of roles that I could play.

Major's Win

The second-round campaign, like the first, was five days long, with the result due at 6 p.m. on Tuesday, 27 November. The disappearance of Margaret Thatcher's name from the lists liberated many voters from earlier commitments. But one new pledge seems to have come into existence. One of the outgoing Prime Minister's last acts in Cabinet was apparently to secure from her colleagues a commitment to 'stop Heseltine' at all costs. I can understand the importance which Margaret attached to that. But I never had the impression that every other former colleague felt the same overriding antipathy towards the man who had worsted her. Significantly, the only Cabinet minister who missed the last meeting – David Hunt was on a trade visit to Japan – was the only one to declare for Michael Heseltine. The remainder divided their support between Douglas Hurd and John Major – whom Margaret Thatcher had by now identified as her heir apparent. Many different factors determined the way in which loyalties were divided. At least two colleagues, who had been close to me during my long march to resignation and beyond, abandoned Michael Heseltine for Douglas Hurd in the second ballot: one was driven primarily by hostility towards Heseltine in his constituency party and the other by his own carefully reasoned comparison of their merits, as he saw them. One or two of John Major's supporters were equally unexpected.

Michael Heseltine and I met for the first time for some weeks on the Wednesday afternoon. This provided one of the tensest moments of the whole contest. He came to my room (on the main corridor between the Speaker's office and the back of the Chair) immediately after calling upon Kenneth Baker. Norman Tebbit had just taken Margaret Thatcher for a belated tour of the tea room. Arabella and Anthony were self-appointed sentries outside my room. As Norman and Margaret rounded the corner on their way back to her room, my door started to open. Arabella intervened just in time to prevent Michael plunging straight into the arms of Margaret and Norman as they were walking by. In my talk with Michael, I had made it clear that he would have my open support in this final stage – so far as he wanted it and it was sensible to receive it. There were no deals of any kind about any possible place in a Heseltine administration. We agreed that one strong feature of his case was his ability, if successful, to retain Douglas Hurd and John Major in their present jobs. And I agreed to seek for him support from two of the old guard, Peter Carrington and Nigel Lawson. By the end of the week Peter Carrington had confirmed that he would declare for Michael. Peter and I had both shared NATO experiences with Michael as Defence Secretary. We were in no doubt about his international competence and standing. When I spoke to Nigel Lawson, he too was ready to back Michael. He saw him as the most likely election-winner of the three on offer.

So the Sunday papers were able to give prominence to the three-barrelled boost for Heseltine from Carrington, Lawson and Howe. I decided to amplify this with a press statement which urged Tory MPs to consider eight questions:

> ∗ Who is most likely to inspire the party with conviction of its ability to win, and so promote unity with the impetus of political success?

* Who is best qualified to enable the party to reach out to new electoral groups, as well as regain the support we need in Scotland and the regions?

* Who has the most recognizable and attractive political identity in terms of both policy and personality?

* Who is best equippped to dominate the House of Commons?

* Who has been most truly tested by experience, in and out of office?

* Who has the most impressive record of effective innovation and radical policy thinking?

* Who has the most freedom to reshape policy and presentation, and not only on the community charge?

* Who, in short, can offer us a fresh start, while drawing on all that is best in the past?

Both Douglas Hurd and John Major have very substantial talents, which must be given full weight. After careful reflection, however, I have concluded that Michael Heseltine is the leader most likely to carry our party forward as a popular, innovative and successful force throughout the 1990s, and so give Britain the government she needs.

But the outcome was to depend as much on personality and semi-tribal loyalties as on rational analysis. Michael's vote had peaked in the first round, when his was the only home for those who wanted Margaret out. Douglas' campaign, intelligent and principled as it was, always had an air of hesitation about it. Forty years had passed since I had first enjoyed his seemingly effortless performances in the Cambridge Union and as one of my successors in the chair of the Conservative Association. Twenty years later, experience as a diplomat had developed the polish and worldly wisdom which made him a first-class political assistant to Ted Heath at Number 10. Another two decades later, his Cabinet service in Northern Ireland and as Home Secretary made him an excellent, all-round professional – a wicket-keeper's wicket-keeper. If I was looking for reactive advice, I would look no further. Almost his only shortcoming was a lack of that thrust that would make him anything but a reluctant leader. The leadership contest did nothing to conceal that amiable flaw. I had called on Douglas shortly after Michael came to see me, to express my sadness at not feeling able to support him. He was courteously philosophic in his response.

John Major's star, by contrast, was still on an upward trajectory. My own personal experience of his style and substance had been very limited. As Chief Secretary, his performance had seemed second only to that of Leon Brittan – the best of the five with whom I had dealt in Margaret Thatcher's government. No judgment could fairly be based on his brief, almost probationary, sojourn at the Foreign and Commonwealth Office. During twelve months back on familiar ground at the Treasury he had made an impressive start as Chancellor. Not the least of his successes then had been, at last, our entry into the ERM. I had seen something of the same tenacity in his dealings with me as Leader of the House.

But all that said, neither Douglas nor John could, in my view, match Michael when measured against the eight-point yardstick by which I had invited colleagues to judge the field. In the first ballot, Michael's strength – formidable but not quite enough – had lain in the fact that he *wasn't* Margaret. And, in the second, John's strength – untested and surprising as it was – sprang from the fact that he *wasn't* Michael, and that he *was* Margaret's preferred alternative to that – for some – unacceptable prospect. John rode those twin horses with skill, integrity and charm, and he did much to vindicate the ticket on which his sponsors, John Gummer and Norman Lamont, had nominated him: 'candidate most likely to unite the party'. This is certainly the reason why he attracted so much more support than Michael or Douglas from party activists away from Westminster. John came to deserve this success.

The figures, declared on Tuesday, 27 November, were John Major 185, Michael Heseltine 131 and Douglas Hurd 56. John needed only two votes for an overall majority, and Michael Heseltine immediately withdrew in his favour. In my subsequent exchanges of congratulation and commiseration with the three protagonists, Douglas characteristically offered the shrewdest comment:

> I am content that I had my hat in the ring and perhaps helped to keep the contest within bounds. You too had a difficult role. Although I tried to dissuade you, looking back I now think you were right to resign. You did not plan the avalanche which followed, but if the landscape had to change, better now than next year.

So within four weeks of my resignation from Margaret Thatcher's Cabinet, the man who had joined that Cabinet only three years before had been elected leader of the Conservative Party – and thus Prime

Minister of the United Kingdom. The most reassuring judgment came from the *Daily Telegraph*: 'It is a tribute to the democratic process and to the individuals involved that, in the past month, Conservatives have been able to act upon their belief that the time had come for a new leader, and thus a new Prime Minister.'[1] On 4 December at the Queen Elizabeth II Centre, the formal 'coronation' ceremony took place at a meeting of Conservatives from both Houses of Parliament, under the chairmanship of Willie Whitelaw. Emotions and perceptions were still very confused. An elderly peer asked me why the apologies for absence were apparently being read out by the chairman of the Young Conservatives. He didn't believe me when I said that the 'young' reader was the new Chief Whip, my ubiquitous ex-PPS Richard Ryder. Keith Joseph, a close colleague in policy research for more than a quarter of a century – and Margaret's original sponsor – turned courteously but firmly away from me, with the words, 'I'm sorry, Geoffrey: we're not friends any more.' Three full years were to pass before Keith and I were again to engage in more than formal conversation.

CHAPTER FORTY-SIX

AFTERMATH

═══

The Reactions

Tension and conflict of this kind was symptomatic, alas, of those turbulent weeks. From the moment of my resignation through to John Major's formation of a Cabinet, my postbag displayed with dramatic clarity the clashes of loyalty that had been opened up. Arabella, on that first day, had forecast, 'No doubt it will be hell for the next few weeks.' That was the understatement of her life. I had never seen or heard views more vehemently expressed. Bitter charges of treachery, cards bearing the simple word 'Judas', even some bags with thirty pieces of cupronickel, arrived by almost every post.* So too did paeans of praise from unknown homes in every corner of the land, as well as from colleagues and friends around the world. We hastily recruited helpers to cope with this torrent of mail. The initial flow, immediately after my resignation, was strongly supportive. The popular tide turned briefly the other way after my speech. But as the days went by my supporters regained the majority. Certainly they seemed, to us at least, to make a case that was characterized above all by reason. Many of Mrs Thatcher's champions seemed much more emotionally, even crudely, partisan. But then loyalty is often like that.

The European question, original cause of the dispute, was quickly flanked by all the other causes of complaint and reasons for fidelity. One articulate critic found my speech 'marked by spite, vengefulness and distasteful sententiousness'. My 'assault' on the Prime Minister was 'astonishingly inappropriate' for one who had been 'an assiduous member of her government for eleven years'. I doubt if his wrath was assuaged by the copy which I sent him of a City clergyman's letter (it had arrived by the same post as his) paying tribute to the 'vigour,

---

* The money received went into a collection box for guide dogs for the blind.

humour, human sympathy, courage . . . decency and goodness' of my speech in the House. My parliamentary colleague David Amess (archetypal 'Essex man') wrote, in anguish on the day of Margaret's resignation, of my 'spiteful act of treachery', which had 'destroyed our party . . . and plunged our country into turmoil'. He was generous enough to say that he 'greatly appreciated' my letter in response. Less than two years later his triumphant re-election in marginal Basildon was the first unmistakable signal of John Major's success in the 1992 general election. A quite different view was expressed by Geoffrey Rippon, my leader on the European Communities Bill of 1971. 'You spoke for many of us', he wrote, 'who have been in despair at the PM's recent conduct of affairs. There are indeed higher loyalties to be considered.'

Nicholas Ridley pointed the way towards reconciliation in a typically generous note: '1979–83 was the best period we had for economic policy – and the credit is due to you. I see it as ironic that you had no exchange rate policy then, but it is exchange rate policy that eventually led you to part company with the government – in part at least. . . . Even though we may appear on opposite sides of the argument, we will at least be being true to our convictions.' In reply, I expressed the hope that we had now 'reached pretty well the end of the reasons for writing about each other's most recent piece of drama'. I agreed with Nick that the days we spent together at the Treasury were among the best – personally as well as for policy – and 'they were actually fun – which seems a long time ago, just at the moment'.

For we had moved uncomfortably, as it seemed, from fun to history. Unsurprisingly, Roy Jenkins was one of those to make the point. 'As the last Deputy to resign over Europe,' he wrote, 'I send you a slightly belated word of salutation. . . . It is not a road, as you know very well, which tends to lead to 10 Downing Street, but I have never regretted my 1972 decision.' It was good, I replied, to be 'welcomed so warmly to our rather exclusive club!' The road, I agreed, was not the most encouraging, 'but it is, as *you* know so well, more important to try to be right'. Another connoisseur from the ranks of Tuscany, Tam Dalyell, wrote, 'Yours was in a different league from any other resignation speech – and a hundred times more impressive and convincing than George Brown. I wonder what Ian Macleod would have thought!' From our own benches came another letter from Eden's biographer, Robert Rhodes James: 'Well. Even I do not remember Leo Amery's May 1940 speech . . . but its impact can hardly have been as great as yours. . . . My only worry is that others may benefit from your courage and integrity.'

I acknowledged that the experience had been 'quite an ordeal'; but it had been important 'not to allow the resignation to trickle away. . . . Eden's omission to follow through, as well as Amery's intervention – both were in my mind.'

The most startling historical excursion arose from a letter from Cedar Rapids, Iowa, and purported to come from Lord Acton. The name was, of course, familiar as that of the Victorian author of the aphorism 'Power tends to corrupt, and absolute power corrupts absolutely.' The letter came from the great-grandson of the nineteenth-century historian, hitherto unknown to me, a lively independent peer, with a business (and a marriage) based in Iowa. He had been exercising his right to sit in the Peer's Gallery of the Commons on the day when I made my speech. 'There will be those in your party', he said, 'who will condemn you for ending Mrs Thatcher's Prime Ministership. I believe that you articulated the view of the nation and . . . will be revered in history for telling the truth.' He closed by drawing my attention to a less well-known sentence on the relevant page of his ancestor's text: 'There is no worse heresy than that the office sanctifies the holder of it.' Not every comment that came my way was quite so courteous – or so apt.

Just one aspect of the whole sad story aroused my unqualified fury. That was the treatment accorded by some commentators to Elspeth's role. The high point of calumny was reached in a *Sunday Telegraph* profile, 'The Other Woman', published under the name of its (then) editor, Peregrine Worsthorne. The piece was topped by a caricature of Elspeth as Lady Macbeth and does not deserve quotation. Its character may be judged from one sentence: 'Howe happens to be a four-letter word and Lady Howe is two four-letter words.'[1] A number of mutual friends wrote, without our knowledge, to denounce the article. One described it as an 'essay in vindictiveness, distortion, intention to wound and dreary old-fashioned anti-feminism'. Worsthorne, who had been a friend since we had worked as colleagues at the launch of the *Sunday Telegraph* thirty years before, replied baldly that 'Lady Howe has been so vitriolic in public about Mrs Thatcher for so long that we thought she herself might be the target for some criticism. If we went over the top, please bear in mind that there was much provocation.'

Three days after the publication of this 'profile', I was due to speak at the *Spectator* lunch, where I was to receive one of their annual prizes for having made the parliamentary 'Speech of the Year'. Worsthorne was among the many journalists present. I took the opportunity to set the record straight. I expressed my extreme sadness that 'some whom I had counted as colleagues and friends for many years, in Fleet Street as well as in Parliament', had taken this as an occasion for launching, 'not at me but at my wife, wild outpourings not of reason but of crude abuse – of mindless vulgarity'. Elspeth and I, more than most people, I said, 'are very ready to be held accountable, each of us, for our own actions'. Insofar as we do have influence upon each other – and that was inevitable – 'that is always in the direction of reason and restraint'. I hope, I concluded, that others might from now on 'try to keep this same principle in mind'.

One final sadness for me was the impact of the controversy on long-standing bonds of loyalty and friendship, which had been forged over years of partnership in the field with hundreds of Conservative Party workers. These were stoutest of all in my own East Surrey constituency, but strong too in South Wales and Merseyside, where I had fought my earliest campaigns. Even through the toughest of times, the message had always been coherent and simple. Loyalty to party leadership, to party policy and to member of Parliament (or candidate) had always been one and the same – three sides of the same coin. Now, here was I, the steadfast standard-bearer, apparently trying to tear one apart from the rest. No wonder there was confusion among some of my erstwhile friends. In the nature of things, some of the most strident critics were among the party's keenest supporters. And some of my strongest champions were those near the margin, whose support was just as important.

Inevitably opinions were divided, even among my own constituency's senior officers. This was reflected in my post and in the local press. I took care to respond to every letter of complaint or support. And I tried – so far as possible – to attend every divisional or sectional or local committee meeting that was called. These occasions were always long, sometimes stormy, but never ended on a note of hostility. 'At least,' wrote my women's chairman, Ros Rawling, after one such marathon, 'they can't complain that you don't listen.' Through it all my constituency president Pam Goodale, chairman Gordon Keymer and agent Ruth Wheelhouse – together with other officers and our office staff – remained committed to the organization. Together they sustained for me the network of contact and support that was needed to hold the party together through a difficult period.

Gradually, as John Major put his new team together, the tides of passion began to ebb. There had been, noted the *Daily Telegraph*'s political editor, 'a distinct change in atmosphere on the Conservative benches and in the Cabinet room'. Most Conservative MPs feel, he wrote, 'as if a large cloud has lifted'. For months many had felt that the Thatcher era was ending, 'but no one knew quite when or how it would happen'.[2] Now, the recovery had been equally speedy. So too in our domestic affairs. Within days of leaving office, our goods and chattels had been moved – yet again – away from our official residences. Elspeth and I were generously granted 'safe haven' for some weeks, as lodgers in the London home of Christopher and Joanna Staughton. But by Christmas we were installed in our long-term home in Warwickshire.

Elspeth and I followed a short holiday in Nassau with our first visit to Stanford. I had accepted George Shultz's invitation to serve on the university's International Advisory Council. At the moment when 'Operation Desert Storm' was reaching its climax in Kuwait, I was conferring in California – like them, free of responsibility – with Valéry Giscard d'Estaing, Helmut Schmidt, Lee Kuan Yew and others whom George Shultz had gathered round him. My transition from politician to 'elder statesman' had begun. Elspeth was able to start learning some of the lessons of 'retirement' from O'bie Shultz. Arabella too was able to escape for her long-delayed holiday in Massachusetts. At last there was relief for us all from the remorseless tension that had filled my Commons office for the past two months.

I was due to attend a regular meeting of my constituency executive very shortly after my return, on 30 January 1991. I decided that, after more than a quarter of a century on the front bench of the House of Commons, the time had come for me to yield the task of fighting the next general election to a younger man or woman. John Major, I explained, 'was leading a fresh generation of ministers in building upon all that we achieved under Margaret Thatcher's leadership'. So it would now be right, I concluded, 'for East Surrey to add its weight to the Tory wave of the future'. Nobody was disposed to disagree. John Major penned a most generous valedictory note. So too – in a characteristic scoop, two days before the event – did the leader-writer of the *Daily Mail*.[3]

Most gratifying of all – and far from untypical – was the letter which arrived ten days later from the Chairman of a constituency association who had written in very different terms less than two months before:

Dear Sir Geoffrey,
It was good of you to reply to my letter dated 27 November 1991, expressing the feelings of myself and my colleagues at the time. All that is now past.

I have to agree with the last paragraph of your letter about John Major whose selection was highly approved of here. There has certainly been a dramatic change in the reception I have received during door-to-door canvassing which has without doubt transformed our prospects of winning the next election.

With good grace, I have to admit the end result of what you did has served our best interests after all, and I wish to withdraw my harsh comments resulting from my fervent admiration of Margaret Thatcher.

I wish you well in your retirement.

Just over two years later, on 9 April 1992, John Major returned to Number 10 Downing Street, having received the re-election of his Conservative government with an overall majority of seventeen seats.

ENVOI

Within a year of Margaret Thatcher's resignation, Granada Television presented on 11 September 1991 a documentary-drama version, *Thatcher: The Final Years*, of the events leading to her fall. It is a bizarre experience to watch one's own real-life role being acted out by others. It offers an intriguing insight into the way in which history is made. At almost every moment when *my* actions, *my* words, were being depicted, I was conscious of serious, no doubt unintentional, inaccuracies. Literally nothing was quite right. Yet for all those sequences where I was not on screen, disbelief was largely suspended. The talking, moving picture is a compelling witness. 'So that's why George' – or Peter or whoever – 'did that', I found myself thinking, time and again. Beguilingly, the cameras appeared to be telling the truth, except where I positively knew them to be inventive and false.

How quickly the detail fades, becomes steadily less important. But the big questions live on. The scope for reinterpretation, for second thoughts, remains immense. Would I ever have embarked on a political career had I foreseen the agonizing acrimony that was to mark its climax? Would I have been better advised, even happier, if I had stuck to the gentler pastures of the law? Would I later have found a second chance to turn away from mainstream politics by heading instead for the pinnacles of my own profession? Certainly I enjoyed immensely my twenty years of practice at the Bar. I relished the intellectual challenges. I liked working for and with real people on real issues. I loved winning cases. And I found the camaraderie of Circuit and the Temple most agreeable. But I shrank from the idea of ending up on the bench as a judge, however exalted. I did not, as I often said, want to spend the rest of my life 'sorting out other people's messes'. I wanted to set my own agenda. That meant politics.

There was (and is) plenty of politics, of course, in law reform, reform of the courts, the legal system and the legal profession. I could easily have narrowed my sights and made it clear, either from the Treasury or from the Foreign Office, that the Woolsack, rather than an outside hope of the premiership, was my ultimate ambition. Then on the departure of Michael Havers, if not of Quintin Hailsham, Margaret could well have been eager, on subsequent form, to divert me from the political frontline. And the admirable James Mackay might never have been called upon to enlarge his role from that of a Lord of Appeal.

But even as Ted Heath's Solicitor General it had been in the wider politics of the job that I had best served the Prime Minister's purpose. That suited too my own long-term interests and ambition. So I came gladly into mainstream domestic politics when Ted Heath appointed me to his Cabinet in 1972. From that there developed the adventure of fifteen years in joint harness with Margaret Thatcher. Margaret and I did not approach that partnership from the same starting point. At least in retrospect, we took a strikingly different view of Ted Heath's 'Quiet Revolution'* in which we had both been engaged, albeit in different roles. Ironically, on Margaret's educational front there had indeed been little sign of revolution. Most of my Heathian experience, on the other hand, had been truly radical. Accession to the European Community and transformation of trade union law had both been part of my responsibility. I had myself been directly involved – and Margaret not at all – in the ambitious but fruitless deadlock over pay, prices and economic policy that had spelt the end of the Heath government. From this there sprang our essential differences of perception. For Margaret – though less clearly than for our intellectual trail-blazer, Keith Joseph – the Heath government was seen almost as part of the problem. For me it was a government that had started bravely in the right direction, and had won at least some of the battles.

Few people now doubt that our attempt to control prices and incomes by law was a mistake. Yet while I was engaged in this I applied myself to its 'enforcement' with vigour and conviction. It was not the first time Britain had seen such a policy. The Wilson–Callaghan governments were destined to repeat it once more, before our political system was purged of the idea, hopefully for good. Should the Industrial Relations Act, for the shape of which I had had principal responsibility, be similarly condemned? I still have no hesitation in rejecting that charge. Had we

---

* 'We are laying the foundations for a generation,' said Ted Heath to the Conservative Party Conference on 10 October 1970, as he commended 'A revolution so quiet and yet so total that it will go far beyond . . . this decade'.

won the first 1974 election we should certainly have needed, as I was starting to argue at the time, to amend our way step by step out of the pay-and-prices policy. The Industrial Relations Act, by contrast, we should have wished, and needed, to amend only so far as might have been necessary to secure its acceptance. Electoral success would have endorsed our strategy; we had good reason to believe that only modest practical changes would then have been needed. By this route we should have been able – ten years earlier than we did – to arrive at something like the post-Tebbit (1987) position. Britain would have been spared another decade of decline. The 1979 winter of discontent need never have happened.

What of the other, more serious charge sometimes brought against the Heath administration? Did we 'take Britain into Europe' upon the basis of a false prospectus, quite literally by politically false pretences? I have already explained just how I had myself readdressed that question in 1971, in course of preparing the European Communities Bill itself.* It may certainly be said in retrospect that we never spelt out the more complex constitutional implications in populist terms. Even the few of us who were close to the process could not have foreseen let alone have explained them all. At the expert level we had done our best to do so. The central purpose of the exercise – a political coming together for the entrenchment of peace, the advancement of prosperity, to give Europe a stronger voice in the world – had been expounded many times. The case was put very clearly, for example, by Sir Alec Douglas-Home as Foreign Secretary in 1971. 'Our application', he said, 'is a step of the utmost political significance,' which was in danger of being overlooked. We must tell the public that 'the future prospect ahead of us is uncertain unless we can . . . become part of a bigger organization . . . for political reasons'.[1]

This is indeed the objective that was effectively endorsed not just by both Houses of Parliament in 1971 but by the electorate as a whole in the referendum of 1975. It was not, I believe, in the original presentation of the European case that electors may have been misled. Only subsequently perhaps have we been less forthcoming with each other (no more so in Britain I suspect than in other countries) in exploring and spelling out the implications of this unique and developing venture in international partnership. I think we have explained less than we should have done what we are trying to achieve. We should have done and should do more, to be sure of carrying the people with us.

* See pp. 65–9 above.

None of this was troubling either Margaret Thatcher or myself as we looked together at our inheritance in the spring of 1979. At that stage we were both of one mind. The problems that Ted Heath had tried to tackle had been gravely aggravated during the Wilson–Callaghan era. It was now for us to make a second attempt to redress the balance. For that we were determined and in the end able to implement a programme of radical action – fully prepared and vigorously pre-sold.

And so came the years of triumph that ended in tragedy. Margaret Thatcher's eleven years as Prime Minister still stand as a period of remarkable achievement, albeit marred by decisive and fatal errors in her final term in office. It is all too easy to allow the conflict of later years to eclipse the scale of earlier successes. Most difficult and most lasting has been the dismantling of the malign, if unspoken, compact between state ownership and monopoly trade unionism in Britain's bloated public sector. The culmination came with the divisive but essential victory over Arthur Scargill.

Almost as fundamental were the three key economic changes we effected: the central switch of our tax structure away from demotivating burdens on enterprise and investment, the recovery of control over the public finances and the remarkable success that – for a time – we achieved against inflation. Margaret Thatcher is entitled to much of the credit for the renewed economic vitality with which we entered (and won) the 1987 election, still more so for the broader revival of self-confidence which sprang from the Falklands victory.

It was for me an exciting privilege to serve as Chancellor in a government that first arrested and then began to reverse Britain's economic decline. My policies during that period could not have been sustained without the (sometimes near solitary) support of the Prime Minister. Nor, as I believe, could they have been so decisively formulated or so calmly presented without the input that I was able to make. It had been part of my task to persuade Margaret first of the necessary and acceptable scale of the 1979 tax switch; and then of the wisdom of adopting a Medium-Term Financial Strategy. Without that we should have had no framework of discipline for the crucial 1981 Budget.

What then do I have to say to the charge that those policies, that Budget in particular, made the recession of the early 1980s worse than it had to be and inflicted avoidable damage on manufacturing industry? Clearly it might have been possible to steer a course through those tumultuous years that avoided at least a part of the intermittently stressful combination of high interest rates and high exchange rates that actually prevailed. I say 'might': even in that case any possible difference could only have been one of degree. When we were struggling against high inflation as well as a soaring borrowing requirement, interest rates were bound to be high. And with oil prices high and production coming on stream, the pound sterling was bound to be high as well. Hence the need, unquestioned in retrospect, to abolish exchange control. Hence too the need to use the 1981 Budget as a lever to crank interest rates down in the longer term – even if within six months they had perversely to rise, for a spell by twice as much, in order to save the pound from something like free fall. Life at Number 11 never was, never will be, easy.

What I can say, as the layman who has never flinched from accepting responsibility for economic management during that period, is that my experts and I studied earnestly all the advice that we could lay our hands on. From month to month and week to week we reached in good faith the best conclusions that we could. And for the eight years that followed the controversial 1981 Budget Britain enjoyed record economic growth, low inflation, rising productivity and falling public sector debt. If I am expected to accept (as I do) my share of collective responsibility for the way in which success was allowed, at the end of the 1980s, to overshoot into inflation and recession, then I must be allowed to claim credit for having sown the seeds of the very success that turned into such exuberance.

One thing from this period which I do regret is our reluctance to acknowledge sufficiently the problems of manufacturing industry. We were sometimes less ready than we should have been to heed, even if we could not mitigate, the difficulties that they faced in times of such economic turbulence. Many sectors, as I often pointed out, had been writing their own death warrants, as a result of over-manning, under-management and industrial strife. For those very reasons they were ill equipped to cope with change at the pace that had become inescapable. Often there was little we could do to help. But sometimes we seemed almost to relish the intellectual certainty of telling people that their fate was unavoidable and that their activity was replaceable, if not expendable. In my later Budgets I did lean towards helping the industrial and business sector ahead of the personal. And, as the years went by, I made some headway in correcting my own rhetoric on this topic.

So I came to serve as Foreign Secretary during a period when a prospering economy and a respected leader together generated Britain's growing influence abroad. Our Foreign Service, widely recognized (at least outside this country) as the best in the world, responded with an impressive determination to transform this challenge into an opportunity. Britain, I said on one of 324 visits to eighty countries during six years, had rediscovered the will to look outwards. Our renewed confidence abroad was based upon our rediscovery of enterprise at home. The dynamic of an increasingly successful woman Prime Minister opened many doors. Her transatlantic partnership with Ronald Reagan was especially productive. The Thatcher relationship with Mikhail Gorbachev became curiously similar and almost as fruitful.

Margaret Thatcher is reluctant to accept that her Foreign Secretary or the Foreign Office played any part in the international achievements of her second and third terms. Indeed, she argues the contrary. The Office, she says, 'magnified [Geoffrey's] faults and smothered his virtues'. I am said to have developed 'habits which the Foreign Office seems to cultivate – a reluctance to subordinate diplomatic tactics to the national interest and an insatiable appetite for nuances' and 'for compromise'.[2] It is hard indeed to understand how the Prime Minister came to leave me, with such grave inadequacies, in this important office for so long. And it is harder still to imagine that I played any part in the resolution or management of so many long-standing problems, on terms that were generally perceived as consistent with Britain's national interests: Hong Kong, Gibraltar, the Iran–Iraq War, the Anglo-Irish Agreement, the East–West agenda from Afghanistan to arms control, the establishment of strongly constructive relations with India after years of scratchy tension, the recognition of Britain as 'the keystone in the arch of Japan's relations with the European Community',[3] and, last but far from least, the achievement of many of our key objectives in that Community. Margaret is kind enough to acknowledge (writing of July 1985) that 'Geoffrey Howe seemed a competent Foreign Secretary' and then adds, revealingly, 'I had not yet taken the full measure of our disagreements.'[4] My real wickedness may thus have lain not so much in a tendency too often to agree with foreigners (although that was serious enough) as in a growing disposition not often enough to agree with the Prime Minister.

All this seems a far cry from the impressive world role that Britain was able to play during the closing years of my increasingly uneasy partnership with Margaret Thatcher. In the end, however, the economic successes that underpinned Britain's foreign policy went first too far – and then sadly awry. In the eighth successive year of apparent economic triumph we all of us began to speak, sometimes even to act, as though we believed that we really could walk upon the water. And so inevitably came the day of reckoning – of retrenchment, recession and worse. 'What cannot be denied', wrote John Biffen a little later, 'is that the state of the economy in 1990/91 hardly bore testimony to good economic management, and the political consequences have been severe.'[5]

At the heart of that economic story was the sequence of decisions about Britain's membership of the Exchange Rate Mechanism of the European Monetary System. That relationship, to which Margaret Thatcher's government had been in principle committed as early as our European election manifesto of 1979, had become increasingly important, as monetary policy became less and less predictable and more and more difficult to manage. No one now disputes that when we did finally decide to place the pound sterling within the System – still under Margaret Thatcher's premiership on 5 October 1990 – we did so at the wrong time, at the wrong rate and in the wrong way, though it was still an achievement to do it at all. For five years before that the Bank of England, the Treasury and almost every key minister had been consistently agreed on the case for early entry into the ERM. Properly managed, it would have been the right move, as Margaret Thatcher belatedly conceded, to buttress our counter-inflation policy. The Prime Minister, almost alone, had resisted that case.

I am convinced that it was that sustained refusal to contemplate, let alone accept, a collective decision on this crucial question that was at the end the cause of both economic and political downfall for Margaret Thatcher's government. Had we taken advantage of one of the recurrent opportunities to join the ERM which presented themselves from 1985 onwards, the United Kingdom would have helped to build a secure bulwark against the excesses of the boom-bust cycle of the late 1980s. We should probably have avoided too the misjudgments that marked our belated and short-lived membership from 1990 to 1992. Much of the tension which arose in that last summer as a result of German unification might well have been unavoidable. But, given a British government that had been in the System for some years, those pressures would not have been so sharply focused upon the pound sterling. By then too our Treasury and the Bank of England could have acquired experience, authority and credulity in the markets. Chancellor and Governor alike would have been much better equipped to help manage the System through the crisis conditions of September 1992. Of course, it would not have been easy. It would have been necessary to rescue the 'fixed-but-adjustable' quality of the original Exchange Rate Mechanism. The Delors Plan had pre-emptively displaced this with a premature presumption that any country which devalued was ruling itself out of Economic and Monetary Union. Long-run successful ERM membership would have made it possible, if necessary, to set aside this damaging linkage without the humiliating isolation of the pound sterling. Black Wednesday need never have happened. Britain's relations with the European Community, indeed the Community itself, could have avoided a severe setback.

Here is the real measure of the tragedy that flowed from the closing phase of Margaret Thatcher's remarkable premiership. For it was not only her government but even more that of her successor, John Major, which has had to grapple with the problems that flowed from her reluctance to address those questions collectively, and at a much earlier date. By grave misfortune, two of her most fiercely held prejudices came together to influence British policy in a damaging direction over the closing years of her time in office. The first of these was her ideological hostility to the very idea of an exchange-rate policy – even though her government had been in principle committed to that notion throughout our eleven years in office together. And the second was her mounting hostility, particularly from the date of her Bruges speech (September 1988), to any institution or idea which might strengthen the role of the European Community.

Had it not been for this double wall of unreason, we should have been able to avoid the clashes over ERM entry in 1989, which ruptured so irretrievably the solid troika which Nigel Lawson and I had once formed with Margaret Thatcher. I cannot resist the conclusion that her own reputation might well have been far greater today if she had not tested that relationship to destruction in pursuit of her own ideological obsessions.

Here is the question which I ask myself most often: was there nothing that I could have done differently, either alone or with my colleagues, that might have persuaded Margaret to approach these matters differently? Was I too craven, too reluctant to respond in kind, to shout back?

It must be said that nobody else who held a significantly different point of view from Britain's first woman Prime Minister seemed to fare better, at least in her closing years – whether alone or in concert with others. I have posed earlier the question whether Margaret Thatcher's way of obliging colleagues to choose between submission and defection was a necessary weakness of 'real leadership'. If so, then there is an inescapable tension between real leadership and the need for collective decision-making that is at the heart of good government. No participant in such a partnership that fails to work can escape a share of the responsibility for the breakdown.

For all the tears that were later to flow, we had between us succeeded in redefining, in shifting, the common ground of political debate. The mainstream of Britain's politics in the 1990s would be dominated – well beyond the Conservative Party – by three defining factors. Our politics were destined to be economically conservative, with continuing emphasis on sound finance and market liberalization; socially libertarian, with growing emphasis upon opportunity, choice and responsibility; and internationally outward-looking, with growing recognition of the need to work imaginatively in and through Europe if we were to maximize our influence in world affairs. All the signs continue to suggest that any party which moves significantly out of line with any of these principles will come under strong political pressure to return to a more mainstream position, for fear of looking isolated or outdated. Failure to do so will carry a heavy political price.

Yet strangely I had failed to drive home – failed to establish beyond challenge – the last of these 'commonsense' principles. One of the policy objectives I had defined, when launching *Crossbow* more than thirty years before, was 'a realistic appreciation of Britain's position in the world'. Yet just as we had come to over-appreciate our own economic success, so too some people had been led – not least perhaps by Margaret's personal standing – to overrate our own international weight. Even the perception of my own role as Britain's last Cold War Foreign Secretary – still with a whiff of Yalta-esque authority – may have blurred perception of the core argument that it was only from a position at the heart of Europe that we could effectively influence our own destiny. This was the essential understanding that our Prime Minister, increasingly cocooned by her own coterie and apart from her political colleagues, had determined to reject.

Margaret Thatcher was beyond argument a great Prime Minister. Her tragedy is that she may be remembered less for the brilliance of her many achievements than for the recklessness with which she later sought to impose her own increasingly uncompromising views. For Margaret Thatcher in her final years, there was no distinction to be drawn between person, government, party and nation. They merged in her mind as one seamless whole. Her interests were axiomatically those of Britain. Any criticism of her was an unpatriotic act. The insistence on the undivided sovereignty of her own opinion dressed up as the nation's sovereignty was her own undoing.

To see the tragedy for what it was and to react accordingly was not to engage in treachery but to do what I believed to be right for my party and my country. And clearly I was very far from alone. Margaret Thatcher was making a decisive break with the thirty-year-old Macmillan concept of Britain's role in Europe. She was breaking with Europe – the logic of Bruges taken to extremes – and I had to break with her. I could not know the exact consequences. I wanted to change the policies, not the leader. But if that meant the leader had to go, then so it had to be. I have no regrets whatsoever about resolving that conflict of loyalty in that way, however deeply I regretted the necessity for having to do so.

And so to the my last question to ponder. Given that I had not been able to achieve the right balance of argument within Cabinet, should I have challenged more directly for the top job? By resigning in 1989? And then building up my position? Or did I never have what it takes? Would Michael Heseltine still have been the better challenger? And better able to succeed if I had cleared the way by earlier resignation, particularly if Nigel Lawson was still destined to follow us out of government? Would a new troika on the back-benches have succeeded, where we had failed to do so in government? Those of us who get drawn into the Sisyphean process of history seem destined to leave more questions than answers in our wake. It is something to be able to believe that the stone is a little higher up the hill than when we started: some hopes fulfilled, some not, but sadness far outstripped by happiness along the way.

MEMORIAL ADDRESS FOR IAN GOW MP

ST MARGARET'S CHURCH, WESTMINSTER

22 OCTOBER 1990

The signet ring, that Jane Gow held high before a multitude of friends at Bournemouth ten days ago, inspiring us all with her resolution and composure, and her love for Ian, took my memory back to a day that Elspeth and I had spent with him some thirty years before. He was with us on holiday in France, bathing in the pounding breakers of the Atlantic coast, near Arcachon. His zest and enjoyment of the waves was immense. And so too his dismay, when he found that his signet ring – it had been his father's ring – had been wrenched from his finger by the Atlantic swell, lost beyond recall.

So soon as he was back in Britain, Ian procured a new ring, an exact replica of the old. And he cherished it dearly. Several years later, Ian, once again with characteristically bursting enthusiasm – oh! what fun he was! – was introducing our own young twins to the pleasures of a British winter, with a tremendous snowball fight in our garden. And suddenly, unbelievably for a second time, his ring was lost – deep in the snow, and undiscoverable. But this time the ring *was* found again – weeks later, when the long snows had melted. Ian's joy knew no bounds. He could teach us all how to rejoice. He was doing so almost every day of his life.

I first met him at some Bow Group gathering, when he was still at law school, fresh from service with the 15th/19th Royal Hussars. Ian never sought to describe himself as a 'natural' soldier. But how staunchly devoted he was to that fine regiment. No less than ten of his brother officers had asked him, over the years, to act as godfather to one of their children. In each case, Ian had accepted and, of course, discharged his duties with diligence.

He'd been head of the house at Winchester that I had left just ten years before him. Only a few months ago, when he was helping me compose a speech for a Wykehamist audience, Ian recalled the prayer that 'there never may be wanting a due supply of persons well qualified to serve God, both in Church and State'. No one was ever better qualified for that dual service than Ian Gow.

Deep Christian conviction was at the very centre of his life – his life with Jane, Charles and James, and his wider family. How proud he would be of Jane and the boys, in the courage and dignity they have shown since his death. In the parish of St John Kingston Vale, his earlier home, Ian served as a church warden and went on to qualify as a lay reader. And most recently, in the lively, all-embracing Eastbourne parish of St Luke, Stone Cross, he had thrown himself – with Jane and Father Jonathan and the rest of the flock – into a pattern of resurgent Christian endeavour that is profoundly moving. He was indeed a faithful servant of Church as well as State.

Ian's political apprenticeship must have started about as close to the grass-roots as it's possible to get – as my election campaign assistant in 1959, in Aberavon. Aberavon is scarcely part of the Tory heartland. And Ian had never been to Wales before. But his personal impact there was as engaging and direct as it always was in his own later campaigning years.

In his beloved Eastbourne, the town whose name will for ever be linked with his, when I was there with him earlier this year, I saw again the way in which his delightful self-mockery, his conscientious response to the smallest needs of Eastbourne people, his truly magnetic sincerity had won the affection of an entire community.

So too in the House of Commons. He made his maiden speech in Denis Healey's first Budget debate. He did not neglect to criticize the Chancellor of the Exchequer. Nor any subsequent holder of that office, I may say. Scarcely had we ever, in Ian's view, done enough to reduce the public sector borrowing requirement. Almost every time Ian took a drink, he delighted – as many of us can recall – in pointing out that he was thereby making his own modest contribution towards its further reduction.

Douglas Jay, the veteran Wykehamist who spoke immediately following Ian's maiden speech, observed, with some prescience, that he had 'shown a capacity to disagree with his own party which would endear him to both sides of the House'. And so indeed it proved. Sometimes with marvellous flashes of teasing wit. Often with speeches that were deeply serious, always carefully prepared, lucidly articulate and above all sincere. Frequently they reflected his experience as a solicitor of great wisdom, with a powerful sense of justice.

Ian was totally incapable of any kind of deceit. And the House knew that. So too did people, as time went by, in every corner of the nation. And, perhaps above all, in Ulster – the province that had enlisted his devotion ever since he had soldiered there. Amid all the strong causes for which he cared as few people could, Northern Ireland became Ian's predominant political passion. He developed a deep personal commitment to its people, which in the end came between him and the government – whose Prime Minister he had served as parliamentary private secretary, with tenacious loyalty and affection, for four years. History will regard Ian as having set standards for that office, by which others will be judged for years and years to come.

Margaret Thatcher and I had worked together in the evolution of the Anglo-Irish Agreement, deeply conscious of the historic emotions and ties we were tending. And profoundly aware too of the scale of Ian's misgivings. And, alas, the time did come when he felt obliged to end his all-too-short ministerial career, by tendering his resignation. We both sought strenuously, in friendship and with respect, but in vain, to dissuade him. It was a parting of the ways. But only on that score.

And it was the manner in which Ian handled that reluctant separation that is for me the real hallmark of his greatness. Ian closed his resignation speech with a restatement of his conviction that we were embarking upon the wrong course. And he concluded: 'With all my heart – it is quite a big heart – I pray that I am wrong.'

It was that massive openness of heart, that truly granite integrity, which were at the very core of his bubbling personality. Is it then any wonder that two of his heroes were Winston Churchill and Charles de Gaulle? He knew many of their speeches by heart and needed little prompting, not least late at night, to declaim them with romantic, almost poetic, gusto.

Ian's fearless independence, his unshakable loyalty, driven as they were by deep emotions, stand as a model to all those who grieve his tragic death. One of the most respected, warm-hearted and courageous politicians of his generation has been struck down by the brutal extremism which he so forthrightly and consistently deplored.

In this place and on this day we may be sure – he may be sure – that

Ian's oh-so-full life was not in vain. Our resolve in face of evil will never weaken. Like his own signet ring, when the snows had melted away, like his own signet ring on Jane's brave hand, Ian's witness will endure for ever, in the faith of Christ.

RESIGNATION SPEECH

13 NOVEMBER 1990

———

Mr Speaker: I remind the House that a resignation statement is heard in silence and without interruption.

4.19 p.m.

Sir Geoffrey Howe (Surrey, East): I find to my astonishment that a quarter of a century has passed since I last spoke from one of the back benches. Fortunately, however, it has been my privilege to serve for the past twelve months of that time as Leader of the House of Commons, so I have been reminded quite recently of the traditional generosity and tolerance of this place. I hope that I may count on that today as I offer to the House a statement about my resignation from the government.

It has been suggested – even, indeed, by some of my Right Hon. and Hon. friends – that I decided to resign solely because of questions of style and not on matters of substance at all. Indeed, if some of my former colleagues are to be believed, I must be the first Minister in history who has resigned because he was in full agreement with government policy. The truth is that, in many aspects of politics, style and substance complement each other. Very often, they are two sides of the same coin.

The Prime Minister and I have shared something like 700 meetings of Cabinet or Shadow Cabinet during the past eighteen years, and some 400 hours alongside each other, at more than thirty international summit meetings. For both of us, I suspect, it is a pretty daunting record. The House might well feel that something more than simple matters of style would be necessary to rupture such a well-tried relationship.

It was a privilege to serve as my Right Hon. friend's first Chancellor of the Exchequer; to share in the transformation of our industrial relations scene; to help launch our free-market programme, commencing with the abolition of exchange control; and, above all, to achieve such substantial success against inflation, getting it down within four years from 22 per cent to 4 per cent upon the basis of the strict monetary discipline involved in the Medium-Term Financial Strategy. Not one of our economic achievements would have been possible without the courage and leadership of my Right Hon. friend – and, if I may say so, they possibly derived some little benefit from the presence of a Chancellor who was not exactly a wet himself.

It was a great honour to serve for six years as Foreign and Commonwealth Secretary and to share with my Right Hon. friend in some notable achievements in the European Community – from Fontainebleau to the Single European Act. But it was as we moved on to consider the crucial monetary issues in the European context that I came to feel increasing concern. Some of the reasons for that anxiety were made very clear by my Right Hon. friend the Member for Blaby (Mr Lawson) in his resignation speech just over twelve months ago. Like him, I concluded at least five years ago that the conduct of our policy against inflation could no longer rest solely on attempts to measure and control the domestic money supply. We had no doubt that we should be helped in that battle, and, indeed, in other respects, by joining the Exchange Rate Mechanism of the European Monetary System.

There was, or should have been, nothing novel about joining the ERM; it has been a long-standing commitment. For a quarter of a century after the Second World War, we found that the very similar Bretton Woods regime did serve as a useful discipline. Now, as my Right Hon. friend the Prime Minister acknowledged two weeks ago, our entry into the ERM can be seen as an 'extra discipline for keeping down inflation'. However, it must be said that the practical conclusion has been achieved only at the cost of substantial damage to her administration and, more serious still, to its inflation achievements.

As my Right Hon. friend the Member for Blaby explained: 'The real tragedy is that we did not join the Exchange Rate Mechanism ... at least five years ago.' As he also made clear, 'That was not for want of trying.' Indeed, the so-called Madrid conditions came into existence only after the then Chancellor and I, as Foreign Secretary, made it clear that we could not continue in office unless a specific commitment to join the ERM was made.

As the House will no doubt have observed, neither member of that particular partnership now remains in office. Our successor as Chancellor of the Exchequer has, during the past year, had to devote a great deal of his considerable talents to demonstrating exactly how those Madrid conditions have been attained, so as to make it possible to fulfil a commitment whose achievement has long been in the national interest.

It is now, alas, impossible to resist the conclusion that today's higher rates of inflation could well have been avoided had the question of ERM membership been properly considered and resolved at a much earlier stage. There are, I fear, developing grounds for similar anxiety over the handling – not just at and after the Rome summit – of the wider, much more open question of economic and monetary union.

Let me first make clear certain important points on which I have no disagreement with my Right Hon. friend, the Prime Minister. I do not regard the Delors Report as some kind of sacred text that has to be accepted, or even rejected, on the nod. But it is an important working document. As I have often made plain, it is seriously deficient in significant respects.

I do not regard the Italian Presidency's management of the Rome Summit as a model of its kind – far from it. It was much the same, as my Right Hon. friend the Prime Minister will recall, in Milan some five years ago.

I do not regard it as in any sense wrong for Britain to make criticisms of that kind plainly and courteously, nor in any sense wrong for us to do so, if necessary, alone. As I have already made clear, I have, like the Prime Minister and other Right Hon. friends, fought too many European battles in a minority of one to have any illusions on that score.

But it is crucially important that we should conduct those arguments upon the basis of a clear understanding of the true relationship between this country, the Community and our Community partners. And it is here, I fear, that my Right Hon. friend the Prime Minister increasingly risks leading herself and others astray in matters of substance as well as of style.

It was the late Lord Stockton, formerly Harold Macmillan, who first put the central point clearly. As long ago as 1962, he argued that we had to place and keep ourselves within the EC. He saw it as essential then, as it is today, not to cut ourselves off from the realities of power; not to retreat into a ghetto of sentimentality about our past and so diminish our own control over our own destiny in the future.

The pity is that the Macmillan view had not been perceived more clearly a decade before in the 1950s. It would have spared us so many of the struggles of the last twenty years had we been in the Community from the outset; had we been ready, in the much too simple phrase, to 'surrender some sovereignty' at a much earlier stage.

If we had been in from the start, as almost everybody now acknowledges, we should have had more, not less, influence over the Europe in which we live today. We should never forget the lesson of that isolation, of being on the outside looking in, for the conduct of today's affairs.

We have done best when we have seen the Community not as a static entity to be resisted and contained, but as an active process which we can shape, often decisively, provided that we allow ourselves to be fully engaged in it, with confidence, with enthusiasm and in good faith.

We must at all costs avoid presenting ourselves yet again with an over-simplified choice, a false antithesis, a bogus dilemma, between one alternative, starkly labelled 'co-operation between independent sovereign states', and a second, equally crudely labelled alternative, 'centralized, federal super-state', as if there were no middle way in between.

We commit a serious error if we think always in terms of 'surrendering' sovereignty and seek to stand pat for all time on a given deal – by proclaiming, as my Right Hon. friend the Prime Minister did two weeks ago, that we have 'surrendered enough'.

The European enterprise is not and should not be seen like that – as some kind of zero-sum game. Sir Winston Churchill put it much more positively forty years ago, when he said: 'It is also possible and not less agreeable to regard' this sacrifice or merger of national sovereignty 'as the gradual assumption by all the nations concerned of that larger sovereignty which can alone protect their diverse and distinctive customs and characteristics and their national traditions.'

I have to say that I find Winston Churchill's perception a good deal more convincing, and more encouraging for the interests of our nation, than the nightmare image sometimes conjured up by my Right Hon. friend, who seems sometimes to look out upon a continent that is positively teeming with ill-intentioned people, scheming, in her words, to 'extinguish democracy', to 'dissolve our national identities' and to lead us 'through the back-door into a federal Europe'. What kind of vision is that for our business people, who trade there each day, for our financiers, who seek to make London the money capital of Europe, or for all the young people of today?

These concerns are especially important as we approach the crucial topic of economic and monetary union. We must be positively and centrally involved in this debate and not fearfully and negatively detached. The costs of disengagement here could be very serious indeed.

There is talk, of course, of a single currency for Europe. I agree that there are many difficulties about the concept – both economic and political. Of course, as I said in my letter of resignation, none of us wants the imposition of a single currency. But that is not the real risk. The eleven others cannot impose their solution on the twelfth country against its will, but they can go ahead without us. The risk is not imposition but isolation. The real threat is that of leaving ourselves with no say in the monetary arrangements that the rest of Europe chooses for itself, with Britain once again scrambling to join the club later, after the rules have been set and after the power has been distributed by others to our disadvantage. That would be the worst possible outcome.

It is to avoid just that outcome and to find a compromise both acceptable in the government and sellable in Europe that my Right Hon. friend the Chancellor has put forward his 'hard ECU' proposal. This lays careful emphasis on the possibility that the 'hard ECU' as a common currency could, given time, evolve into a single currency. I have of course supported the 'hard ECU' plan. But after Rome, and after the comments of my Right Hon. friend the Prime Minister two weeks ago, there is grave danger that the 'hard ECU' proposal is becoming untenable, because two things have happened.

The first is that my Right Hon. friend the Prime Minister has appeared to rule out from the start any compromise at any stage on any of the basic components that all the eleven other countries believe to be a part of EMU – a single currency or a permanently fixed exchange rate, a central bank or common monetary policy. Asked whether we would veto any arrangement that jeopardized the pound sterling, my Right Hon. friend replied simply, 'Yes.' That statement means not that we can block EMU but that they can go ahead without us. Is that a position that is likely to ensure, as I put it in my resignation letter, that 'we hold, and retain, a position of influence in this vital debate'? I fear not. Rather, to do so, we must, as I said, take care not to rule in or rule out any one solution absolutely. We must be seen to be part of the same negotiation.

The second thing that happened was, I fear, even more disturbing. Reporting to this House, my Right Hon. friend almost casually remarked that she did not think that many people would want to use the 'hard ECU' anyway – even as a common currency, let alone as a single one. It was remarkable – indeed, it was tragic – to hear my Right Hon. friend dismissing, with such personalized incredulity, the very idea that the 'hard ECU' proposal might find growing favour among the peoples of Europe, just as it was extraordinary to hear her assert that the whole idea of EMU might be open for consideration only by future generations. Those future generations are with us today.

How on earth are the Chancellor and the Governor of the Bank of England, commending the 'hard ECU' as they strive to, to be taken as serious participants in the debate against that kind of background noise? I believe that both the Chancellor and the Governor are cricketing enthusiasts, so I hope that there is no monopoly of cricketing metaphors. It is rather like sending your opening batsmen to the crease only for them to find, the moment the first balls are bowled, that their bats have been broken before the game by the team captain.

The point was perhaps more sharply put by a British businessman, trading in Brussels and elsewhere, who wrote to me last week, stating: 'People throughout Europe see our Prime Minister's finger-wagging and hear her passionate, "No", much more clearly than the content of the carefully worded formal texts.' He went on: 'It is too easy for them to believe that we all share her attitudes; for why else has she been our Prime Minister for so long?' My correspondent concluded: 'This is a desperately serious situation for our country.' And, sadly, I have to agree.

The tragedy is – and it is for me personally, for my party, for our whole people and for my Right Hon. friend herself, a very real tragedy – that the Prime Minister's perceived attitude towards Europe is running increasingly serious risks for the future of our nation. It risks minimizing our influence and maximizing our chances of being once again shut out. We have paid heavily in the past for late starts and squandered opportunities in Europe. We dare not let that happen again. If we detach ourselves completely, as a party or a nation, from the middle ground of Europe, the effects will be incalculable and very hard ever to correct.

In my letter of resignation, which I tendered with the utmost sadness and dismay, I said: 'Cabinet government is all about trying to persuade one another from within.' That was my commitment to government by persuasion – persuading colleagues and the nation. I have tried to do that as Foreign Secretary and since, but I realize now that the task has become futile: trying to stretch the meaning of words beyond what was credible, and trying to pretend that there was a common policy when every step forward risked being subverted by some casual comment or impulsive answer.

The conflict of loyalty, of loyalty to my Right Hon. friend the Prime Minister – and, after all, in two decades together that instinct of loyalty is still very real – and of loyalty to what I perceive to be the true interests of the nation, has become all too great. I no longer believe it possible to resolve that conflict from within this government. That is why I have resigned. In doing so, I have done what I believe to be right for my party and my country. The time has come for others to consider their own response to the tragic conflict of loyalties with which I have myself wrestled for perhaps too long.

TREASURY AND FOREIGN OFFICE MINISTERS,

PARLIAMENTARY PRIVATE SECRETARIES

AND PERMANENT SECRETARIES

HM Treasury, May 1979–June 1983

Chancellor of the Exchequer

May 1979–June 1983   Sir Geoffrey Howe

Chief Secretary

May 1979–January 1981   John Biffen
January 1981–June 1983   Leon Brittan

Minister of State

May 1979–September 1981   Peter Rees
May 1979–April 1982   Lord Cockfield
September 1981–November 1981   Jock Bruce-Gardyne
November 1981–September 1985   Barney Hayhoe
April 1982–June 1983   John Wakeham

Financial Secretary

May 1979–September 1981   Nigel Lawson
September 1981–October 1983   Nicholas Ridley

Economic Secretary

November 1981–June 1983   Jock Bruce-Gardyne

Parliamentary Private Secretary

May 1979–January 1983	Ian Stewart
February 1983–June 1983	Tim Renton

Permanent Secretary

July 1974–March 1983	Sir Douglas Wass
April 1983–May 1991	Sir Peter Middleton

Foreign and Commonwealth Office, June 1983–July 1989

Secretary of State

June 1983–July 1989	Sir Geoffrey Howe

Minister of State for Overseas Development

January 1983–September 1986	Tim Raison
September 1986–July 1989	Christopher Patten

Minister of State

June 1983–June 1987	Lady Young
June 1983–September 1985	Richard Luce
June 1983–January 1986	Malcolm Rifkind
September 1985–June 1987	Tim Renton
January 1986–July 1989	Lynda Chalker
June 1987–July 1988	David Mellor
June 1987–July 1990	Lord Glenarthur
July 1988–November 1990	William Waldegrave

Parliamentary Under Secretary

June 1983–September 1984	Ray Whitney
September 1984–September 1985	Tim Renton
September 1984–July 1989	Tim Eggar

Parliamentary Private Secretary

June 1983–September 1984 Tim Renton
June 1984–September 1986 Richard Ryder
October 1986–June 1987 Michael Forsyth
June 1987–June 1988 Virginia Bottomley
June 1988–July 1989 David Harris

Permanent Under Secretary

April 1982–June 1986 Sir Antony Acland
June 1986–June 1991 Sir Patrick Wright

(*Note*: My parliamentary private secretaries when I was Solicitor General were Kenneth Clarke, 1971–1972, and Peter Rees, 1972–November 1973; when I was Minister for Trade and Consumer Affairs, Richard Luce, November 1973–March 1974; and when I was Deputy Prime Minister and Lord President of the Council, David Harris, July 1989–November 1990.)

ABBREVIATIONS

ABM Anti-Ballistic Missile
AEU Amalgamated Engineering Union
ANC African National Congress
ASEAN Association of South-East Asian Nations
ASTMS Association of Scientific, Technical and Managerial Staffs
AUEW Amalgamated Union of Engineering Workers
CARICOM
CBI Confederation of British Industry
CFE Conventional Forces in Europe
CGT Capital gains tax
COGM Commonwealth Heads of Government Meeting
CIA Central Intelligence Agency
CND Campaign for Nuclear Disarmament
CPC Conservative Political Centre
CPRS Central Policy Review Staff
CPS Centre for Policy Studies
CSCE Conference on Security and Co-operation in Europe
CTT Capital transfer tax
DTI Department of Trade and Industry
DOP Defence and Overseas Committee of the Cabinet
E Economic Committee of the Cabinet
E(A) Economic Sub-Committee of the Cabinet
EC European Community
ECOCAB Economic Strategy Committee of the Cabinet
ECOFIN EC Council of Finance Ministers
ECU European Currency Unit
E(DL) Economic (Disposal) Sub-Committee of the Cabinet
EMS European Monetary System
EMU Economic Monetary Union
E(NI) Economic (Nationalized Industries) Sub-Committee of the Cabinet

EOC　Equal Opportunities Commission
EPG　Eminent Persons Group
ERM　Exchange Rate Mechanism
EXCO　Executive Council of Hong Kong
FCO　Foreign and Commonwealth Office
G5　Group of Five
G7　Group of Seven
G10　Group of Ten
GAB　General Arrangements to Borrow
GATT　General Agreement on Tariffs and Trade
GCHQ　Government Communications Headquarters
GDP　Gross domestic product
GNP　Gross national product
HMG　Her Majesty's Government
ICJ　International Court of Justice
IEA　Institute of Economic Affairs
IGC　Inter-Governmental Conference
IMF　International Monetary Fund
INF　Intermediate-range Nuclear Forces
IRA　Irish Republican Army
ISTC　Iron and Steel Trades Confederation
JLG　Joint Liaison Group
KGB　Soviet Committee of State Security
M0　Monetary base
M1, M3, sterling M3　Monetary aggregates
MBC　Monetary base control
MI5　Security Service
MI6　Secret Intelligence Service
MLR　Minimum Lending Rate
MNF　Multi-National Force
MOD　Ministry of Defence
MTFS　Medium-Term Financial Strategy
NAD　National Armaments Director
NATO　North Atlantic Treaty Organization
NCB　National Coal Board
NEDC　National Economic Development Council
NIRC　National Industrial Relations Court
NUT　National Union of Teachers
OD　Overseas and Defence Committee of the Cabinet
ODA　Overseas Development Administration

OD(E) Overseas and Defence (Europe) Committee of the Cabinet
OD(K) Overseas and Defence (Hong Kong) Committee of the Cabinet
ODP Overseas and Defence Committee of the Cabinet
OECD Organization for Economic Co-operation and Development
OECS Organization of Eastern Caribbean States
PAYE Pay As You Earn
PPS Parliamentary (or principal) private secretary
PSBR Public Sector Borrowing Requirement
PSL2 Monetary aggregate
RPI Retail Price index
RUSI Royal United Services Institute
SAS Special Air Service
SDI Strategic Defence Initiative
SDP Social Democratic Party
SERPS State earnings-related pension scheme
SNF Short-range Nuclear Forces
SPD Supplementary petroleum duty
START Strategic Arms Reduction Talks
SWAPO South-West African People's Organization
TCSC House of Commons Select Committee on Treasury and Civil Service
    Affairs
TGWU Transport and General Workers Union
TUC Trades Union Congress
UKOOA UK Oil Operators Association
UMELCO Unofficial Members of the Executive and Legislative Councils
VAT Value added tax
WEU Western European Union

REFERENCES

Chapter Three: Barrister Bowman

1. Jim Prior, *A Balance of Power* (Hamish Hamilton, 1986), p. 41.
2. Judy Hillman and Peter Clarke, *Geoffrey Howe: A Quiet Revolutionary* (Weidenfeld & Nicolson, 1988).

Chapter Four: In and Out of Parliament

1. *Daily Telegraph*, 23 September 1968: review of T. E. Utley, *Enoch Powell* (Kimber, 1968).
2. Geoffrey Howe, *In Place of Beveridge* (CPC, 1965).
3. Anthony Howard, *Selections from the Diaries of a Cabinet Minister* (Jonathan Cape, 1979), pp. 11 and 527–9.
4. Bradbury and others V. Enfield B. C. (1967) 3 All E.R. 434, 441.
5. *Rookes* v. *Barnard* [1964] AC 1129.
6. Prior, *Balance of Power*, p. 48.
7. Michael Moran, *The Politics of Industrial Relations* (Macmillan, 1977), p. 75.

Chapter Five: Solicitor General

1. Peter Jenkins, *The Battle of Downing Street* (C. Knight, 1970), p. 140.
2. John Campbell, *Edward Heath* (Jonathan Cape, 1993), p. 367.
3. Ibid., p. 466.
4. *Britain, the Commonwealth and Europe* (CPC, 1962).
5. J. D. B. Mitchell, 'Constitutional Aspects of British Membership of the EC (etc)', *Common Market Law Review* (1972) Vol. 9, p. 149.

Chapter Six: Into the Cabinet

1. Michael Baynes, *Advertising on Trial* (Bow Group, 1957).

Chapter Seven: Thatcher Coup

1. Campbell, *Heath*, p. 628.

Chapter Eight: The Right Approach
1. David Rose, *Liverpool Daily Post*, 14 April 1978.
2. Campbell, *Heath*, p. 711.

Chapter Nine: Last Lap
1. Margaret Thatcher, *The Downing Street Years* (HarperCollins, 1993), p. 695.
2. Bernard Donoughue, *Prime Minister* (Jonathan Cape, 1987) p. 191.

Chapter Ten: My First Budget
1. Ibid., p. 82.
2. *British Tax Review* [1977], p. 97.
3. Peter Jenkins, *Mrs Thatcher's Revolution* (Jonathan Cape, 1987), p. 48.
4. Prior, *Balance of Power*, p. 119.

Chapter Eleven: Menacing and Menaced
1. Roy Jenkins, *A Life at the Centre* (Macmillan, 1992), p. 491.
2. *Financial Weekly*, 20 April 1979.
3. *Guardian*, 24 October 1979.
4. *Observer*, 26 October 1979.
5. Prior, *Balance of Power*, p. 133.
6. Ibid., p. 121.
7. Annual Lecture, Institute of Fiscal Studies, 20 May 1991, published in *Fiscal Studies* (November 1991), vol. 12, p. 92.

Chapter Twelve: The Apex of Monetarism
1. *The Times*, 14 September 1978.
2. Geoffrey Howe, *Conservatism in the Eighties* (CPC, 1982).
3. Prior, *Balance of Power*, p. 159.
4. Ibid., p. 162.
5. Ian Gilmour, *Dancing with Dogma* (Simon & Schuster, 1992), p. 25.
6. E.g. Hugo Young, *One of Us* (final edn, Macmillan, 1991), p. 203.
7. Gilmour, *Dancing with Dogma*, p. 21.
8. Prior, *Balance of Power*, p. 140.

Chapter Thirteen: Post-Corset Distortions
1. Roy Jenkins, *Life at the Centre*, p. 501.
2. Nigel Lawson, *The View from No. 11: Memoirs of a Tory Radical* (Bantam Press, 1992), p. 85.

3. *Financial Times*, 25 November 1980.
4. *Economist*, 4 December 1980.

Chapter Fourteen: 'The Most Unpopular Budget'
1. *Financial Times*, 19 February 1981.
2. *Fiscal Studies* (November 1991), vol. 12, p. 98.
3. Thatcher, *Downing Street Years*, p. 136.
4. Alan Walters, as reported by Christopher Monckton, *Evening Standard Magazine*, September 1988, p. 22.
5. Prior, *Balance of Power*, p. 140.
6. Ibid.
7. Ibid., p. 124.
8. Francis Cripps and Wynne Godley, Guardian, 16 March 1981.

Chapter Fifteen: Summer Reshuffle
1. Prior, *Balance of Power*, p. 110.
2. Speech to Huddersfield Chamber of Commerce, 10 January 1975, written with considerable assistance from Professor Brian Griffiths.

Chapter Sixteen: Turning of the Tide
1. Norman Tebbit, *Upwardly Mobile* (Weidenfeld & Nicolson, 1988), p. 185.

Chapter Seventeen: Economic and Military Success
1. Thatcher, *Downing Street Years*, p. 188.

Chapter Eighteen: Last Autumn at the Treasury
1. Christopher Johnson, *The Economy under Mrs Thatcher* (Penguin, 1991), p. 144.
2. Michael Edwardes, *Back from the Brink* (Collins, 1983), p. 227.
3. Geoffrey Howe, *Privatization: The Way Ahead* (CPC, 1981).
4. Johnson, *Economy under Mrs Thatcher*, p. 158.
5. Howe, *Conservatism in the Eighties*.

Chapter Nineteen: Taking the World Stage
1. Thatcher, *Downing Street Years*, p. 695; Lawson, *View from No. 11*, p. 486.

Chapter Twenty: Election Call
1. Thatcher, *Downing Street Years*, p. 284.
2. Ibid., pp. 309–10; Cecil Parkinson, *Right at the Centre* (Weidenfeld & Nicolson, 1992), pp. 234–6.

Chapter Twenty-Two: Humiliation in Grenada
1. George Shultz, *Turmoil and Triumph* (Scribner's, 1993), ch. 20.
2. House of Commons Select Committee on Foreign Affairs, *Grenada*, Second Report 1983–4 (HMSO, 1984), para. 42.
3. Shultz, *Turmoil and Triumph*, p. 331.
4. Ibid., p. 239.
5. Ibid., p. 340.
6. Select Committee, *Grenada*, paras 36, 41, 45.
7. Ibid., para. 42.
8. Shultz, *Turmoil and Triumph*, p. 330.
9. Ibid., p. 331.
10. Ibid., p. 332.
11. Select Committee, *Grenada*, para. 37.
12. Shultz, *Turmoil and Triumph*, p. 334.
13. Ibid., p. 336.
14. Ibid., p. 341.
15. Ibid., p. 340.

Chapter Twenty-Three: GCHQ and the Union Ban
1. *Sunday Times*, 29 January 1984.
2. *Sunday Telegraph*, 12 February 1984.
3. *Sunday Times*, 4 March 1984.

Chapter Twenty-Five: Mao-tai for Hong Kong
1. Robert Cottrell, *The End of Hong Kong* (John Muray, 1993), p. 4.

Chapter Twenty-Six: West–West Debate
1. Shultz, *Turmoil and Triumph*, p. 231.
2. Ibid., p. 251.
3. Thatcher, *Downing Street Years*, p. 468.
4. Shultz, *Turmoil and Triumph*, p. 509.
5. Thatcher, *Downing Street Years*, p. 469.
6. Ibid.
7. Harold Macmillan, *The Past Masters* (Macmillan, 1975), p. 136.

8. Robert Rhodes James, *Anthony Eden* (Weidenfeld & Nicolson, 1986), p. 176.
9. Nicholas Henderson, *The Private Office* (Weidenfeld & Nicolson, 1984), p. 114.
10. Thatcher, *Downing Street Years*, p. 463.

Chapter Twenty-Eight: Anglo-Irish Agreement
1. Garret FitzGerald, *All in a Life* (Macmillan, 1991), p. 520.
2. Ibid., p. 524.
3. Ibid., p. 522.
4. Ibid., p. 547.
5. Ibid., p. 415.

Chapter Thirty: The Single European Act
1. Geoffrey Howe, *The Choices Facing Britain* (CPC, 1985).
2. Michael Butler, *More than a Continent* (William Heinemann, 1986), p. 116.
3. See Nigel Lawson's minute of 15 June 1981, cited in his *View from No. 11*, p. 111.
4. Ibid., pp. 488, 494.
5. *Crossbow* (April 1985), pp. 16–17.
6. Ibid.
7. Lawson, *View from No. 11*, pp. 502–4.

Chapter Thirty-One: Westland Turning Point
1. House of Commons Select Committee on Defence Affairs, *Westland plc: The Government's Decision-making*, Fourth Report 1985–6 (HMSO, 1986), para. 127.
2. Thatcher, *Downing Street Years*, p. 430.
3. Select Committee, *Westland*, para. 156.
4. Ibid., paras 154–5.
5. Prior, *Balance of Power*, p. 140.

Chapter Thirty-Two: Arguing about South Africa
1. Thatcher, *Downing Street Years*, e.g., pp. 463, 469, 519.
2. Ibid., p. 520.
3. Ibid., p. 521.

Chapter Thirty-Three: Terror and Diplomacy
1. *New York Times*, 11 January 1986.
2. Thatcher, *Downing Street Years*, p. 445.

3. Ibid., p. 443.

4. Young, *One of Us*, p. 478.

5. Geoffrey Smith, *Reagan and Thatcher* (Bodley Head, 1990), p. 197.

6. See, for example, Schultz, *Turmoil and Triumph*, pp. 793–807.

7. See, for example, Smith, *Reagan and Thatcher*, pp. 204–11.

8. Thatcher, *Downing Street Years*, p. 498.

9. Shultz, *Turmoil and Triumph*, pp. 687–8.

10. Ibid., p. 806.

Chapter Thirty-Four: My Last Election Campaign

1. Thatcher, *Downing Street Years*, p. 566.

2. Ibid., p. 558.

3. Published in pamphlet form by CPC (1987).

4. Schultz, *Turmoil and Triumph*, p. 776.

5. Thatcher, *Downing Street Years*, pp. 474–85.

6. *The Times*, 24 March 1987.

Chapter Thirty-Five: Bruges Reversal

1. Quentin Peel, *Financial Times*, 2 July 1987.

2. Thatcher, *Downing Street Years*, p. 309.

Chapter Thirty-Six: From WEU to IRA . . .

1. Quoting *Halsbury's Laws of England*, vol. 11, para. 1179.

2. Report of Salmon Committee on the Laws of Contempt, (HMSO Cmnd 4078, June 1969).

3. Robin Day, *Grand Inquisitor* (Weidenfeld & Nicolson, 1989), p. 267.

4. Ibid., p. 264.

Chapter Thirty-Seven: . . . From Nato to KGB

1. Thatcher, *Downing Street Years*, p. 584.

2. Geoffrey Howe, *The World Today* (RIIA, 1989), p. 40.

Chapter Thirty-Eight: Road to Madrid

1. Geoffrey Howe, *The Conservative Revival of Britain* (CPC, 1988).

2. Lawson, *View from No. 11*, p. 881.

3. Geoffrey Howe, 'The Waiting List Society', in *Conservative Opportunity*: Fifteen Bow Group Essays (Batsford and CPC, 1965), pp. 13–27.

4. Presented to a conference at the London School of Economics, 16–17 March 1989.

5. *Mail on Sunday*, 29 January 1989.

6. *The Times*, 3 April 1986.
7. *The Times*, 19 January 1989.
8. Letter to author from Sir Jeremy Thomas, 7 May 1989.
9. Thatcher, *Downing Street Years*, p. 656.
10. *Mail on Sunday*, 19 March 1989.
11. *Daily Telegraph*, 5 April 1989.
12. *Guardian*, 4 May 1989.
13. Thatcher, *Downing Street Years*, p. 749.
14. *Financial Times*, 19 May 1989.
15. Lawson, *View from No. 11*, p. 918.
16. *Guardian*, 30 May 1989.
17. See Thatcher, *Downing Street Years*, pp. 702ff; Lawson, *View from No. 11*, pp. 794ff.
18. *The Times*, 7 June 1986.
19. Thatcher, *Downing Street Years*, p. 704.
20. Ibid.
21. Ibid., p. 336.
22. Ibid., pp. 710, 711.
23. Ibid., p. 709.
24. Ibid., p. 712.

Chapter Thirty-Nine: Dismissed from the Foreign Office
1. *Guardian*, 29 June 1989.
2. *Independent*, 28 June 1989.
3. Thatcher, *Downing Street Years*, p. 713.
4. *Daily Mail*, 26 July 1989.
5. Thatcher, *Downing Street Years*, p. 756.
6. Ibid., p. 712.
7. *Observer*, 17 September 1989.
8. *Mail on Sunday*, 30 July 1989.
9. *Observer*, 30 July 1989.
10. *Independent*, 29 July 1989.

Chapter Forty: Stalking-Horse
1. *The Times*, 1 August 1989.
2. *The Walden Interview*, 3 September 1989.
3. *Evening Standard*, 11 October 1989.
4. Thatcher, *Downing Street Years*, p. 718.
5. *Sunday Times*, 29 October 1989.
6. *The Walden Interview*, 29 October 1989.

7. *The Times*, 31 October 1989.
8. *Financial Times*, 3 November 1989.
9. Letter to author from Will Hopper, 27 November 1989.
10. Kenneth Baker, *The Turbulent Years* (Faber & Faber, 1993), p. 320.

Chapter Forty-One: House Leader
1. Willie Whitelaw, *The Whitelaw Memoirs* (Aurum Press, 1989), p. 167; John Biffen, *Inside the House of Commons* (Graphic Books, 1989), p. 187; Prior, *Balance of Power*, p. 80.
2. Select Committee on the Infant Life (Preservation) Bill, HL Paper 50 (1987).

Chapter Forty-Two: The Rift Widens
1. Thatcher, *Downing Street Years*, p. 834.
2. Geoffrey Howe, *Too Much Law?* (CPC, 1977), p. 11.
3. *Guardian*, 28 May 1990.
4. *Daily Mail*, 13 June 1990.
5. *Daily Express*, 27 June 1990.
6. *Sunday Times*, 1 July 1990.
7. *Economist*, 17 March 1990.
8. *Observer*, 17 June 1990.
9. Various newspapers, 13 June 1990.
10. Thatcher, *Downing Street Years*, p. 792.
11. Various newspapers, 21 June 1990.
12. Geoffrey Howe, 'Sovereignty and Interdependence: Britain's Place in the World', *International Affairs* (1990), pp. 675–95.
13. *Daily Express*, 13 June 1990.
14. *Spectator*, 14 July 1990.
15. *Independent*, 17 July 1990.

Chapter Forty-Three: Resignation
1. Speech at Northampton, 27 October 1989.
2. Thatcher, *Downing Street Years*, p. 722.
3. Ibid., p. 726.
4. See ibid., p. 723.

Chapter Forty-Four: Speech
1. *Guardian*, 3 November 1990.
2. Letter to author from Vernon Bogdanor, 5 November 1990.
3. Letter to author from Alan Bristow, 4 November 1990.
4. *Mail on Sunday*, 4 November 1990.

5. *Financial Times*, 2 November 1990.
6. *Daily Mirror*, 2 November 1990.
7. *Daily Express*, 2 November 1990.
8. *Sun*, 2 November 1990.
9. *Independent*, 2 November 1990.
10. *Mail on Sunday*, 4 November 1990.
11. *Financial Times*, 2 November 1990.

Chapter Forty-Five: The Prime Minister Falls
1. *Daily Telegraph*, 8 December 1990.

Chapter Forty-Six: Aftermath
1. *Sunday Telegraph*, 25 November 1990.
2. George Jones, *Daily Telegraph*, 8 December 1990.
3. *Daily Mail*, 28 January 1991.

Envoi
1. Sir Alec Douglas-Home, *Our European Destiny* (Conservative Group for Europe, 1971).
2. Thatcher, *The Downing Street Years*, pp. 309 and 712.
3. Prime Minister Kaifu, in conversation with the author, June 1991.
4. Thatcher, *The Downing Street Years*, p. 418.
5. John Biffen, *Times Literary Supplement*, 19 July 1991.

INDEX

Bevin, Ernest 567
Biffen, John 31n, 35, 126, 198, 278, 283, 615,
  656
  and the 1980 Budget 175
  and the 1983 election 289
  and the Chancellor's 1980 Autumn Statement
    193–4
  as Chief Secretary to the Treasury 124, 130,
    141–2, 145, 150–1, 160
  and the Economic Reconstruction Group 99
  and the ERM 449, 450
  and the European Community 68
  and the Falklands conflict 245–6
  and the Heath government 74, 75
  and the Medium-Term Financial Strategy 163
  and public spending controls 189, 223
  and the Thursday Breakfast Group 147
  and the US bombing of Libya 506
Bindman, Geoffrey 43
Birch, John 432
Birch, Nigel 609
Bishop, Maurice 325–6
Bogdanor, Vernon 661
Bolivar, Simon 307
Bonner, Elena 352
Borrie, Gordon 71
Botha, Pik 478–9, 489, 490–1, 500
Botha, P.W. 485, 487, 488, 490, 491, 492, 498
Bottomley, Virginia 616
Bow Group 20, 24–5, 28, 87, 100, 110, 461,
  518, 602, 610
  publications 29–30, 31–3, 71
    Coloured People in Britain 25, 476
    Houses to Let 30
    National Wages Policy 76
    The Lifeblood of Liberty 29–30
    Work for Wales 32–3, 38, 286
Bowe, Colette 466, 470
Boyson, Rhodes 31n
Braithwaite, Rodric 564
Bramall, Edwin 315
Bray, Jeremy 156
Brezhnev, Leonid 354, 439
Brighton bombing 418–19
Bristow, Alan 462, 661
British Aerospace 517
British Leyland 188, 191, 254–5
British Steel 191
Brittan, Diana (formerly Petersen) 197, 470
Brittan, Leon 31, 91, 96, 181, 209, 223, 231,
  243, 369
  and the 1983 Budget 281
  and the 1983 election 287, 289
  as Chief Secretary at the Treasury 198–9
  and the ERM 449
  as European Commissioner 535, 640
  friendship with G.H. 461
  and G.H.'s dismissal as Foreign Secretary 587
  John Major compared with 675
  marriage 197
  moved to Department of Trade and Industry
    424, 460–1
  and public spending 219, 222, 258
  and the Westland affair 462, 464–6, 468–71,
    472, 473

  and Zola Budd 480
Brittan, Samuel 113, 197, 209
Britton, Regimental Sergeant Major 15
Brock, Angela 25
Brock, Mary 25, 26
Brock, Russell 25
Broek, Hans van den 385, 531, 577, 583
Brooke, Henry, Lord Brooke of Cumnor 34,
  284
Brooke, Peter 284, 592
Brooke-Turner, Alan 438
Brooks, Edwin 36
Broomfield, Nigel 310, 311, 354
Brown, George (later Lord George-Brown)
  678
Bruce-Gardyne, Jock 74, 75, 124, 225, 239
Brunner, Karl 185
Buck, Anthony 20, 91, 93
Budd, Alan 163
Budd, Zola 480
Budget (dog) 170, 418, 446–7
Bulgaria, G.H. visits (1985) 428–9
Bullard, Sir Julian 303, 310
Burgess, Tyrell 45
Burgh, John 59
Burns, Andrew 597
Burns, Arthur 111
Burns, Duncan 597
Burns, Sir Terence 155–6, 163, 209, 239, 241,
  282n
  and the 1981 Budget 200, 201, 202
  and the 1981 interest rate rises 226
  and the ERM 449
Burton, Richard 7
Burton, Sheila 91
Bush, George 312, 323, 354, 390, 559, 560,
  565, 629
Butcher, John 231
Buthelezi, Chief 21
Butler, R.A. 36, 194n, 242
Butler, Sir Michael 307, 400, 402, 406, 408,
  447–8, 630
Butler, Sir Robin 315, 396, 474, 475
Butt, Ronald 210
Button, Ruth and John 176
by-elections
  (1982) 248
  (1985) 444, 460
  (1986) 460
  Brecon and Radnor (1985) 444, 460
  Crosby 230, 231, 641
  Croydon North-West (1981) 229, 230
  Eastbourne (1990) 641
  Hillhead (1982) 244–5
  Mid-Staffordshire (1990) 623–4
  Orpington (1962) 34
  Richmond, Yorks (1989) 569
  Ryedale (1987) 641
  Vale of Glamorgan (1989) 571
  Warrington (1981) 181
Byers, Lord 95

Cadman, Radclyffe 21
Callaghan, James 47, 65, 67, 153, 170, 171, 194
  and the European Community 533
  government of 95–6, 107, 116–17